Also by S. A. M. Adshead

THE MODERNIZATION OF THE CHINESE SALT ADMINISTRATION
PROVINCE AND POLITICS IN LATE IMPERIAL CHINA
*CHINA IN WORLD HISTORY

Also published by Macmillan

Salt and Civilization

S. A. M. Adshead

Reader in History
University of Canterbury, Christchurch, New Zealand

MACMILLAN

First published 1992

Published by
MACMILLAN ACADEMIC AND PROFESSIONAL LTD
Houndmills, Basingstoke, Hampshire RG21 2XS
and London
Companies and representatives
throughout the world

Printed in Hong Kong

British Library Cataloguing in Publication Data
Adshead, S. A. M. (Samuel Adrian Miles) 1932–
Salt.
1. Salt, history
I. Title
553.63209
ISBN 0–333–53759–9

For Mouse
The salt has not lost its savour

Contents

List of Tables

Preface

This book hopes to provide a commodity history of salt from prehistory to the present. In Part I, the development of the production, distribution and consumption of salt is traced chronologically: a commodity history of salt in society. In Part II, six examples of government salt administrations are examined: a commodity history of salt in the state. In both parts, the scope, as far as possible, is comparative and global. In the first part, salt works in Africa, America and Australasia figure as well as those in Europe and Asia. In the second part, three examples are taken from Europe, three from Asia. The aim is a commodity history of salt as a theme in world history.

But, it may be asked, what is commodity history? As with 'what is' questions generally, instant definitions, such as, say, in this case 'the human history of immediate things', are unsatisfactory as oracular, lexicographic, or an invitation to logomachy. More helpful than such direct confrontation is an indirect approach through encirclement: delimitation of an unknown by reference to a known, either by addition or subtraction, in this case, by relating commodity history to other kinds of history. For just as has been said, a person who is lost should not ask, 'where am I'? but rather, 'where are the other places?', so an enquirer about significance should not ask, 'what is meant?' but 'where are the other meanings?'

Commodity history is not arcane. It is simply the application to a relatively new field of concepts long enunciated and utilized by the best historians, in particular the concept of a dichotomy between nature and culture. Thus Croce in his history of Naples contrasted the inert, reluctant mass with the active intellectual minority, while Trevor-Roper, in the introduction to the first collection of his essays wrote of 'the interplay between heavy social forces or intractable geographical facts and the creative or disruptive forces which wrestle with them'. One form of this dichotomy is the polarity of things and people. Within the category of things with which people interact, commodities may be regarded as a subcategory. Economists distinguish between goods produced for intermediate demand, i.e. for further processing, and goods produced for final demand, i.e. for consumption. Commodities belong to the second group: they are immediate rather than mediate things. For most of its history, salt was a commodity in this sense. Most of it was used directly in food and its role in preservation and industry was secondary. Salt first becomes significant as an industrial mineral in the *patio* process for the recovery of silver used in the Spanish mines of Mexico and Peru, as has been shown by Ursula Ewald in her book *The*

Mexican Salt Industry 1560–1980. It was not, however, until the Industrial Revolution, that salt became primarily an industrial mineral rather than a commodity. Till then, as a commodity close to its consumers, salt was subject to their changing preferences, choices and priorities. For the same reason, salt was widely used as an alimentary coding for thought structures, as has been shown for the Judaeo-Christian thought world by James E. Latham in his book *The Religious Symbolism of Salt*. Indeed, by uniting nature and culture, commodity history simply expresses that fundamental feature of the human epistemological condition which Karl Rahner termed *Geist im Welt*.

Moreover, commodity history is not new. Historians have never neglected the opportunities provided by commodities. In the interwar period, Marjorie and C. H. B. Quennell's *History of Everyday Things* emphasized the then neglected truth that history was more than kings and battles. At the same time, Pirenne's association of the end of the Ancient World with the disappearance from Western Europe of gold, silk, spices and papyrus, focused attention on the history of these commodities. In 1949 there appeared Redcliffe N. Salaman's *The History and Social Influence of the Potato*, which to many people opened a new perspective on the possibilities of history. The same year saw the publication of Fernand Braudel's *La Méditerranée et Le Monde Méditerranéen a l'époque de Philippe II*, whose middle section on precious metals, spices and grain was a powerful stimulus to commodity history in the full sense. Post-1949 only major landmarks can be mentioned. In 1964, Louis Dermigny published *La Chine et L'Occident: Le Commerce à Canton au XVIIIe siècle 1719–1833*, which was in effect a commodity history of Chinese tea in Europe. In 1978, Robert Delort brought out his *Le Commerce des Fourrures en Occident à la Fin du Moyen Age* and his subsequent *Les Animaux ont une Histoire* in 1984 heightened awareness of commodities such as honey – important both as food and as symbol – which arose from human/fauna relations. In 1987, under the editorship of Michel Mollat, there appeared the collection of essays entitled *Histoire des Pêches Maritimes en France* of which those by Jean-Claude Hocquet and Laurier Turgeon were particularly notable from the point of view of commodity history.

Although commodity history is not new, it has developed and is developing. This development may be described by saying that, while commodity history has always involved both subjective and objective poles, the human user and the natural thing, there is today greater appreciation of the subjective factor. Commodities have ceased to be mere subjects of economic laws and now take citizenship in the realms of sociology, psychology and values. Thus Dermigny, to explain the Canton conjuncture, introduces the social context of tea drinking in eighteenth-century England: the feminization of time and space in afternoon tea, their remasculinization in the high tea of the Industrial North. Similarly Delort, to explain the conjunctures of the fur trade, discusses not only climate and thermoregulation, but livery and maintenance, sumptuary laws, and the psychology of fashion. Turgeon too, to explain fluctuations in fish consumption, has recourse to changes in alimentary sensibility, the association of fish with Lent in a climate of Dechristianization, and the oscillations of medical opinion. Commodities are never mere objects produced under ineluctable technological constraints for timeless human needs. They must be not only produced, but packaged, promoted and purchased. There is constant interpenetration of the objective and the subjective. Nature is incomplete without man: a truth now acknowledged not only by historians, but also by geographers in the current shift from determinism or possibilism to systemicism, and even, in the form of the anthropic cosmological principle, by physicists. Commodity history is thus in line with other intellectual developments.

Among commodities, salt is, for the historian, doubly privileged. On the one hand, in relation to society, salt has been an object of almost universal consumption since neolithic times, entering into horizontal linkages with goods as varied as soya beans, fur, grain, timber, cotton, jute, opium, tea, as well as innumerable manufactured products. On the other hand, in relation to the state as an object of taxation and monopoly, salt has assembled a unique documentation about itself, doing half the historian's work for him.

It is not surprising, therefore, that salt has already received the attention of works of high quality. Its modern study began with the 'Questionnaire pour une enquête sur le sel dans l'histoire au moyen âge et aux temps modernes', drawn up by P. Jeannin and J. Le Goff, published first in the *Revue du Nord* for 1956, and reprinted in 1968 in the collection of essays edited by Michel Mollat, *Le Rôle du Sel dans L'Histoire*. Since then, in addition to monographs, three books in particular have been landmarks in the development of the field. In 1978, there appeared *Neptune's Gift: A History of Common Salt* by Robert P. Multhauf of the Smithsonian Institution. In 1982, Jean-Francois Bergier published *Une Histoire du Sel*. In 1985, there appeared *Le Sel et le Pouvoir de l'an mil à la Révolution française* by Jean-Claude Hocquet, who was already the author of the major study of the Venetian salt administration, as well as many articles of extraordinary richness and insight. Nevertheless, despite the excellence of what has already been done, it may be hoped that there is still room for a synopsis in English which synthesizes monographs in a perspective of commodity history and complements general studies by adding material from Asia, and, in particular, from China. For China is central to the history of salt. It provides the earliest instances, and possibly the point of diffusion, of two of its leading elements: in society, the technique of production by successive basin solar evaporation; in the state, the institution of a specialized monopoly administration or *gabelle*.

A book of this kind is more than usually dependent on the works of others and most debts can only be left to notes and bibliography. Three acknowledgements, however, must be made. First, to Thomas P. Metzger, who guided my first steps in the study of the Chinese salt administration; second, to Michel Mollat, who sent me a copy of the famous questionnaire; third, to Jean-Claude Hocquet, whose depth and breadth of scholarship have been an inspiration and an aspiration. I would like too to thank my colleagues of 1990 at Louvain in C. Section 12 'Salt and Capitalism' and at Hall in Tyrol in the international congress on the History of Salt. Finally, I must thank Dr Mary Whitehouse of the University of Canterbury for her work on the word processor and Mr Desmond Brice of the National Library of New Zealand for his compilation of the index.

S. A. M. Adshead

Part I
Salt and Society

1 Primitivity

Commodities, even the humblest, are more than simple, material objects. In their production they are rooted in technology: its raw materials, processes and sources of energy. In their distribution, they are involved with transport and trade: the mobile world of ports, routes and traffic. In their consumption, they form part of a kingdom of choice where public values and private tastes rearrange a hierarchy of necessities and luxuries. Commodities, from furs to forage, are the stuff of civilization.[1] If, like salt, they are in short supply, controllable distribution and wide demand, they will attract the fiscal interest of the state and become part of its biography too. In premodernity the revenue of the state was the state, determining its possibilities of action. Certain commodities therefore, most notable besides salt, precious minerals, liquor and tobacco, became the stuff of government during a particular phase of its development.

It is on such assumptions that this study approaches the history of salt as a theme in world history. The first part, salt and society, examines the production, distribution and consumption of salt in the major epochs of civilization from primitivity to industrialism. The second part, salt and the state, narrows the focus and examines six major salt administrations as instances of the contribution of salt to government. In both halves, however, what is sought is a human reality, an expression of *mentalité*, an object of culture rather than nature. If the human spirit is always *Geist im Welt*, then salt in its ramifications will be found to be a significant part of the *Welt*.

We begin with primitivity: salt in pre-Roman Europe, pre-Columbian America, and pre-colonial Africa. Primitive here is relative: relative to what was to come later, relative to our information. As human origins are pushed ever further into the past, as archaeological and anthropological interpretation becomes more refined, we have come to see that all our primitivities are really sophistications, the product, like ourselves, of long development and complex mental structure. The theme of this chapter, indeed, is that, as far back, or as far away, as we can go from later centres of higher civilization, the world of salt is characterized by sophistication in production, distribution and consumption. In primitivity as in modernity, salt was a citizen of culture.

SALT IN PRE-ROMAN EUROPE

As an object of archaeology, salt leaves evidence fairly abundant for its production, and scarce for its consumption. Nevertheless, the work of scholars such as Jacques Nenquin, Bernard Edeine and Jean-Paul Bertaux allow us to form a picture of salt as a commodity in the Celtic world of 500 BC to 100 AD, that unknown Far West of which Caesar's *Gallic War* gives us our first literary glimpse.[2]

Production

Three points stand out. First, salt was produced at a considerable number of sites. Nenquin estimates 350 as likely places of salt production: 100 in Gaul, 33 in Germany, 200 in Britain; and others no doubt have been or will be discovered. Second, while at most of these sites production was small and only of local significance, at some, notably in the eastern Alps, it was large and supplied more than local markets. Third, though a variety of techniques were used, the most frequent, giving rise to the characteristic *briquetage*, or shards and ashes of salt sites, was artificial evaporation of brine, sometimes reinforced by the addition of saline earth, sand or ash, in pottery vessels over wood fires. The salt industry of the Celtic world thus fell into three sections: a few major evaporation centres, many minor evaporation sites, and a few localities, generally minor, employing other techniques of production.

The three major evaporation centres were Hallstatt, Hallein and Halle, the precursors of the salines of the Salzkammergut, Salzburg and Prussian Saxony. All three names were variants of the word *hel* or *gal* meaning a brine spring and they suggest that either the settlements were founded for the production of salt or that such activity soon became their chief function. Hallstatt was the oldest. It began as a salt mine as early as 1000 BC when dry climate facilitated mining. With the onset of wetter, 'sub-Atlantic', weather from the ninth century BC, Hallstatt turned to brine as its raw material and this was how the Romans found it. Peter Wells suggests that between 150 and 300 people worked in the saline at any one time.[3] Since food had to be imported to feed the workers, Hallstatt may be regarded as a specialized industrial village. The early history of Hallein was similar: first a mine, then a source of brine. It began not long after Hallstatt and overtook it in production by the end of the pre-Christian era. Nenquin writes:

In Late-Celtic times, the Durrnberg [the producing area of Hallein] must have looked like a small town, for the area covered by the habitation-sites, the salt pans and all the secondary buildings, is estimated at about one square kilometre. The development of the salt-industry rises continuously during the whole of the La Tène period, so that even Hallstatt itself is overshadowed by Hallein-Durrnberg.[4]

Halle developed later, from 500 BC onwards, as a result of the introduction of evaporation techniques from Hallstatt and Hallein. Its production, however, soon became considerable, as 126 localities in the area have yielded *briquetage*, the standard evidence of brine evaporation.

The minor artificial evaporation sites included localities in Brittany (Morbihan), the Channel islands (Guernsey) and Lorraine (Moselle, notably Vic in the Seille valley); Nauheim north of Frankfurt, Schwäbisch Hall in Württemberg, and Hall in the Tyrol; the Fenlands around the Wash and the Essex coast from Walton to the Thames; and La Panne on the France–Belgian frontier. Unlike the major centres which were the precursors of later places of production, most of the minor sites failed to develop and probably always only supplied their own localities. Thus the Fenland sites on average only used the labour of two or three farms and production was domestic and occasional, like baking or weaving. Nevertheless, the aggregate of such production could be considerable. A site in Morbihan may have been able to produce 8000 cwt of salt a year, enough for 600 000 people, the *briquetage* works of the Seille produced for more than a local market. The Essex coast with 23 evaporation sites using reinforced brine, was another sizeable production area. Parts of Britain imported salt in pre-Roman times, but Nenquin suggests that importers will have been warned against 'carrying salt to Essex' and the home counties. Salt no doubt will have been one element in the predominance of Colchester in Caesar's Britain.

A few sites employed techniques other than the evaporation of brine over wood fires. At the Cardona salt mountain in Catalonia, salt was quarried. Carston in Norfolk may have already used the solar evaporation method it used in the seventeenth century. Gaulter Gap in Kimmeridge in Dorset used oil shale instead of wood as a fuel. Sites in Zealand obtained brine not directly from the sea or brine springs, but indirectly through filtering ashes of salt impregnated plants or turfs, a technique for concentrating salinity and economizing on fuel, which we will meet again in America and Africa. None of these methods, echoes of the past or anticipations of the future, was of sufficient importance to effect the overall picture of industry based on natural brine and wood fuel.

Distribution

Like beer, and most textiles, much of the salt in Celtic Europe was both produced and consumed domestically. Nevertheless the scale of production at the three major centres, plus Seille, Essex and Morbihan, given their eccentricity to areas of heavy population, suggest production for the market and involvement in networks of distribution. Distribution is not synonymous with trade. In premodern societies much distribution took place by gift in various forms rather than by exchange. The rich grave goods at Hallstatt may not have been acquired through an apparatus of merchants and markets, but through a palace system of prestation and redistribution. Trade, however, certainly existed as Caesar tells us that Mercury was the commonest divinity in Gaul, and to Romans at least, Mercury was a god of trade. At any rate, whether by gift or exchange, substantial quantities of salt were distributed within the Celtic economic community.

Distribution followed two main articulations. First, there was a major, east–west articulation with Halle, Hallstatt, Hallein, and Schwäbisch Hall at one end and Morbihan at the other, which served the main areas of Gallic population centring on the Auvergne, Second, there was a minor, north–south articulation with Colchester at one end and Vic, Moyenvic and Marsal at the other, which served the populations of the downlands of southeast Britain and northeast Gaul, what might be called Greater Belgica. The importance of the major articulation was increased by its partial coincidence with the routes of two other far-travelling commodities: fur from the forests of eastern Europe and amber from the Baltic littoral. Hallstatt was an entrepôt. It imported not only food for its own use, but copper and tin, weapons, and especially from 600 BC onwards, Mediterranean luxuries including African ivory, for redistribution. These imports, it may be presumed, were paid for by exports of salt, fur and amber. Grave goods in Hallstatt show it to have been in touch with Bavaria, northeast Italy and Slovenia, as well as North Africa in one direction and the Baltic in another. On the minor articulation, salt coming from both north and south, contributed to the establishment of Amiens as a centre of river and road traffic.

Another early salt route was the triangle Saint Malo, Hampshire, Cornwall, which between the eighth and sixth centuries BC was perhaps the major sea link between Britain and the Continent. Strabo tells us that the Phoenicians imported salt into Britain to buy tin. Guernsey produced salt certainly in the La Tène and possibly in the Hallstatt period. Excavations at Hengistbury Head on Christchurch harbour in Hampshire have revealed copper, ironstone and salt working, as well as the import of Gallic wine and Breton coins from the Saint Malo region. It looks as if Saint Malo was the command point in a network in which Guernsey and Hengistbury salt figured both as an export to Cornwall and an import to Brittany. Saint Malo itself was the head of a line which via Toulouse and Massilia linked the Celtic narrow seas to the Mediterranean.

These were the major routes. Beyond were the *viae salariae*, such as the Fosse which carried Fenland salt into the hinterland of Britain. Beyond again were the tracks, such as the sunken path, ultimately from the Seaford salt pans, from Ditchling beacon down into the Weald, which linked the coastal salt workings to the consumer on the hillsides of the interior.

Consumption

In the history of commodities, as in economic history generally, consumption is too often taken for granted. It is regarded as unproblematic, demand being created either by supply or by human necessity. In particular, it is often assumed that consumption of salt can be fully explained in terms of physiological need. The human body does indeed need salt. Human beings, it has been said, are miniature oceans encased in skin and salt solution is essential to blood, nerve impulses and heart action. Medical estimates of what that need is have been varied, but a current and conservative opinion places it at three grams a day or three pounds a year. Such an intake is exceeded greatly not only in all modern societies, but also in most traditional ones, where annual *per capita* consumption figures of between 5 and 10 pounds are normal. Indeed, so long as his or her diet contains sufficient meat, fish or even insects, there is no physiological necessity for a human being to ingest any additional salt. Much of the salt taken into the body is expelled via the urine as unneeded. The consumption of salt therefore is problematic. It is a fact of culture rather than nature. Pliny described salt as *necessarium elementum*, but necessary not for life, but for *vita humanior*.

The Celtic civilization which consumed the salt produced and distributed in the ways we have described is known to us from Caesar and from archaeology. It was a more pastoral world than that of the Mediterranean, possessing cattle in particular abundance, though the pig was the most common domestic animal. Lacking the heavy plough with which to attack clay soils, its agriculture was centred on the downlands and its principal food grain was barley, the most saline of the domesticated cereals. The Celtic world therefore had little natural need for salt. Culturally, however, things were different. It was a conquest society based on superior bronze and iron weapons, a Celtic or German military elite ruling over a basically Basque subject population. It was a populous, well-fed society, whose human resources not only attracted Caesar from the standpoint of the depopulated Mediterranean, but also provided abundant labour services to the elite. It was an aristocratic society, the *Cymry* or Good Companions, weak in higher level political superstructure, but well organized through a system of patrons and clients, hill-forts and villages. One of the chief institutions of this system was

the hall and the banquet where the *regulus* entertained his berserkers
and beefeaters, the *fianna*: the institution still found in *Beowulf* and
Hrothgar's hall, Heorot the hart. The hall demanded high cooking,
party cuisine out of the ordinary, and high cooking demanded salt both
to enhance flavour and to preserve. What the lord offered must be
neither insipid nor rotten. Added to food, salt prevented decay, acti-
vated latent differences in taste and created them by its uneven distribution. It thereby destroyed monotony and set up a gamut of possibilities
for cooks and gourmets. Plutarch called salt the *noblest* of foodstuffs:
what noble was to commoner, so condiment was to aliment. Gastronomy, however primitive, went hand in hand with social distance, and
may be regarded as its expression.

Salt, therefore, was a luxury in the Celtic world. It is significant that
what we hear about its use is in connection with relatively high cooking.
Thus Flemish salt was used in curing the hams for which the region was
famous. Other uses for salt were fish preservation and the preparation
of leather. Salt was a luxury but a relatively abundant one. Probably
most of it went into the preparation of cereal dishes, in the Celtic world,
porridge especially. So long as man was a hunter-gatherer, his taste for
salt remained limited. It was the coming of cereals which created the
possibility of a modest luxury based on salt. Another subject for salt and
itself a quasi-luxury was butter, which Romans of the first century AD
regarded as a peculiarly British dish. A thousand years later, Giraldus
Cambrensis wishing to illustrate Welsh wit gives as an example the
remark of a discontented guest: 'I only find fault with our hostess for
putting too little butter to her salt': a neat inversion of the two commodities – the one ordinary, the other special.[5] No doubt it was little different
on the day Caesar landed.

Salt, it is clear, by its relative abundance and its role in social differen-
tiation, was an important commodity in pre-Roman Europe. It may even
have given it its characteristic name of Gallia, which in various forms
(Galicia, Galatia, Gaul, Gwallia, Walloon, Wallachia, Vlach, Moldo-
Vlach) is found scattered from northwest Spain to central Anatolia.
Miroslav Labunka of La Salle University has argued that Ukrainian
Galicia, a Latinized version of Halich, derives its name from the local salt
mines and springs, another *hel*, *gal* or *hals* in the Greek. If this explanation is true for Ukrainian Galicia, it may also hold for at least some of the
other Galicias. Hallstatt would have been impressive to a visitor from
the Mediterranean, Anatolian Galatia contained the salt source of the
Tuz Golu, while the Wallachias embrace the salt mines of the Carpathians, certainly worked in antiquity. Spanish Galicia is more puzzling,
as neither then nor now was it associated with salt workings. Here the
explanation is probably that of the similarly placed Welsh and Walloons.
A term originally supplied to those associated with salt, later came to

refer to Romanized natives, particularly those left to shift for themselves when the legions were withdrawn. In the case of the Vlachs of Dacia, of course there was both association with salt and abandonment by the Romans, When St Paul told the Christians at Colossae near the borders of Galatia to 'let your speech be always with grace, seasoned with salt', or when Joanot Martorell in *Tirant lo blanc* makes his Breton hero to be of salt rock lineage, they may have been alluding to a then better recognized connection between salt and the Gauls. From the viewpoint of the Mediterranean, pre-Roman Europe was the land of salt, its people, salt folk.

SALT IN PRE-COLUMBIAN AMERICA

In moving from pre-Roman Europe to pre-Columbian America, one must be aware of changes in scale. Not so much in number, since Celtic Europe perhaps had a population of over 20 million and pre-Columbian America maybe no more than 50 million, as in size and consequently in our knowledge. While in Celtic Europe we can feel confident that most of the major producing sites, the distribution routes, and the centres of consumption have been identified, we can feel no such confidence in pre-Columbian America. Salt like much else remains undetailed.

Undetailed but not unknown, for reasons of both geography and history. First, the population of pre-Columbian America was very unevenly distributed. Two thirds of it was concentrated on the high plateaus of Mexico and Peru-Bolivia, where the first Europeans had good opportunities for observing the admittedly not altogether typical civilizations of the Aztecs and the Incas. When cold and wet made the plateaus less habitable, population and civilization descended to the coastal plains of the Gulf of Mexico and the inland plains of the upper Amazon and its tributaries. Like the Aztecs and the Incas, the Mayas have always attracted many investigators, while the mound culture of the plains of Beni is beginning to attract some. The highlands and lowlands of the middle Cordillera are therefore relatively well researched. Second, with regard to the dispersed population of the extremities of the Cordillera, its adjunct pampas and prairies, the associated continental islands of Laurentia, Appalachia, Venezuela and Mato Grosso, much of its life survived into the historic time of missionary, frontiersman and anthropologist. It too therefore does not lack observers. While our acquaintance with salt in pre-Columbian America is yet far from comprehensive, it is sufficient to grasp its salient feature of marginality, in a civilization itself marginal to the mainstream of human development in terms of position, numbers, techniques and ideas.

Production

The chief characteristic of salt production in pre-Columbian America were the rarity of the sites given a population equivalent to that of the Roman or Han empires, and the variety of techniques as compared with Celtic Europe. Both characteristics were shaped by the extreme compartmentalization of America: its linguistic diversity, lack of cultural uniformity, the mutual ignorance of Aztecs and Incas; all three the result of the north–south elongation of the continent and the primacy of east–west communication. A survey of salt production first in the Middle Cordillera and second in its extremities, adjuncts and associated territories, will illustrate these points.

Whether salt was produced in the mound culture of the plains of Eastern Bolivia is not known, but is likely, since its basis was arable farming and some additional salt intake in the diet would be probable. In the case of the Maya civilization of lowland Guatemala and Yucatan, the production of salt has been thoroughly investigated by Anthony P. Andrews.[6]

His investigations show three areas of production, which we may take in rising order of importance. First, there was the Pacific coast of Chiapas, Guatemala and Salvador where *sal cocida* was made by the artificial evaporation of sea brine strengthened by filtration through saline sand. Second, there were interior salines such as La Concordia in Mexico, Sacapulas and Lake Amatitlan in Guatemala, where salt was produced from spring or lake brine by either artificial or natural solar evaporation. Third, there was the north Yucatan Coast where salt was produced by planned solar evaporation in artificially constructed, gridiron shaped, basins, The Pacific and interior salines were too far from the main centres of Maya population to be of more than local importance. Today La Concordia is credited with an annual production of 5000 cwt, Sacapulas with 2000 cwt, though they may have been of greater importance earlier. Thomas Gage, the renegade English Dominican, who visited the interior salines in the early seventeenth century, wrote of Sacapulas 'the principal merchandise of this place is salt', and of Amatitlan 'this town also getteth much by the salt which here is made, or rather gathered by the lake side'.[7] Yucatan, however, was a more sizeable important producer. A Spanish source for 1603 gives the production at 346 000 cwt, half of which would have been sufficient for the estimated 3 million population of the Maya lowlands. If Yucatan practised planned solar evaporation, on this scale in the tenth century, then its salines will have been among the largest in the world.

On the Mexican plateau, there were brine springs within a short distance of Tenochtitlan. Thomas Gage commented on Mexico City that 'great quantity of salt is daily made and is part of the great trading of that city into other parts of the country: nay, part of it is sent to the Philippine Islands'.[8] Going south from the lake, the Spanish Carmelite Vazquez de Espinosa noted *c.* 1620 that 'Next comes the village of Orotlan, whose chief income is derived from salt, which they make from a brine spring'.[9] In addition there was an important group of brine springs northwest of Mexico City on the line Colima-Guadalajara. Miguel de Mendizabal has shown that there was a close correlation on the Mexican plateau between ancient salt workings and indigenous population.[10] Most of the production was by artificial evaporation either of natural brine or water poured through saline earth.

A similar pattern of small scale producing centres also prevailed on the Andes plateau. A Spanish report of 1609 described the *audiencia* of Lima as being provided with an abundance of salt, 'de diferentes generos de salinas'. There was 'a mysterious hill of rock salt' at Gramanga on the road to Cuzco, brine salt at Cuzco, earth or brine salt in many other places. The Jesuit José de Acosta refers to Cuzco:

> On a farm near to Cuzco springs a fountain of salt, which as it runs turns into salt, very white and exceeding good, the which, if it were in another country, were no small riches, yet they make very small account thereof for the store they have there.[11]

Vazquez de Espinosa describes one of the other localities: 'four leagues from Aucare, in the midst of the cold puna, lies a little Indian village of salters, called La Sal, because they make fine white salt from salt springs, boiling it in jars'.[12]

Best known of the Andes salines, however, is Santa Catalina de las Salinas in Otavalo tribal country north of Quito which had been studied by Chantal Caillavet.[13] Here in a valley at 1600 metres, a typical dry *yunga* halfway between the *altiplano* and the coastal plain, a considerable quantity of salt was made by filtering water through saline soil and then evaporating the brine over thorn-fed fires. Served by both resident and immigrant workers, Santa Catalina was regarded as the richest village in the *repartimiento* of Otavalo, itself one of the riches in the *audiencia* of Quito, and as such it was awarded to the leading conquistador of the area, Rodrigo de Salazar. Vazquez de Espinosa describes a rather similar location further north near Antioquia in Columbia: 'In early days there was lively trade and commerce on the part of the Indians with these springs; they boiled the water and made quantities of salt; and sold it all over the country'. Another important source of salt in Colombia was the salt dome of Zipaquira whose ancient workings have been studied by Marianne Cardale-Schrimpff.[14]

Beyond the Middle Cordillera, in the extremes, adjuncts and associates, salines were fewer and more diverse. In Oregon, the Yana, 'the salt people', sold their neighbours dried mud extracted from a local brine marsh.[15] In Chile, south of San Marco de Arica, Vazquez de Espinosa tells us, 'wherever you may be on these uninhabitable deserts, if you clear off four fingers of sand, or somewhat more . . . you find salt mines and slabs of salt, very white and good, and enough to supply the whole world'.[16] South again, beyond Concepcion, 'The sea runs up the river on the rising tide . . . they get quantities of fish, and also of salt, which they make by damming the seawater coming in with the tide, and caking it under the hot sun.'[17] In Nevada there was an Indian salt mine at St Thomas and in Arizona one at Camp Verde developed in the thirteenth century to a depth of 20 metres. In Louisiana, *briquetage*, on Petite Anse, the first of its famous salt domes, suggests that its brine springs were utilized in pre-Columbian times. In eastern North America, two of the brine centres later used by the Europeans, Onondaga near Syracuse, New York and Shawneetown, Illinois, had been exploited by the Indians earlier, as evidenced by Father Jerome Lallement's report on Onondaga in 1646 and by the presence of pre-European *briquetage* at Shawneetown. In eastern South America, the Araya lagoon in Venezuela, later systematically developed by the Dutch, was first exploited by the Indians, as were the natural salines of Lake Maracaibo. On his route from the Orinoco to the Rio Negro via the Cassiquiare canal, Alexander von Humboldt tells us that, 'At Jativa a salt is fabricated by the incineration of the spadix and fruit of the palm-tree *seje* or *chima* . . . the Indians of Jativa lixiviate also the ashes of the famous liana called *cupona*.[18] In Paraguay, there were river deposits at Fort Olympo near the Pantanal and at Lambare near Ascuncion. In the Argentine, there were the vast salt marshes of the Salinas Grandes, Lake Bebedero in San Luis and others in the province of Chubut. Mud salt, sand salt, solar sea salt, rock salt, brine salt, lagoon salt, ash salt, river salt, swamp salt: the picture is one of low quality, relative scarcity and diversity.

Distribution

In line with its tendency to extremes, two contrasting patterns of distribution identify themselves in pre-Columbian America: sophisticated planned economy and primitive free markets.

On the one hand, Chantal Caillavet had suggested that Santa Catalina must be seen in the context of the Inca planned economy. It functioned as an element in one of the 'vertical archipelagos', the American variant of the system of non-commercial interchange which Karl Polanyi called redistribution. The ecology of the Middle Andes was differentiated by altitude and longitude. The desert coast offered fish and guano, the dry *yungas* of the west, pimento and salt; the *altiplano* with its cold *punas* and less cold *paramos*, pastoralism, potatoes and maize; the wet *yungas* of the

east, coca, gold, manioc and wild honey. The Inca empire co-ordinated
these commodities not through markets, but by a system of tributes and
services, gifts and counter gifts, which linked the two sides of the Andes
in a series of centres on the *altiplano*. These centres were then joined
north–south by the royal Inca road to Cuzco. Santa Catalina formed part
of the northern vertical archipelago of Quito. Some of its workers were
permanent residents who were issued with clothes, coca and cereals in
return for their salt. More were temporary immigrants brought in by the
Quito authorities from their pool of labour services. With the salt so
received, the Quito authorities obtained from the eastern *yungas* the
gold they owed to the Roi Soleil at Cuzco. Gold, the product of sun and
earth, was the symbol of their loyalty to the Tawantinsuyu, the empire
of the four quarters, the sun on earth.

On the other hand, Lévi-Strauss has suggested that in Oregon, Yana
salt was exchanged in a primitive system of markets, not only for other
commodities such as fish, fur and tobacco, but also for quasi money
such as pearls and shells, and even for marriage partners. In Arkansas,
the de Soto expedition, having discovered the production of salt, noted
that the Indians carried it into other parts, to exchange for skins and
shawls. Onate, in his letter from New Mexico in 1599, spoke of 'the
wealth of the abundant salines . . . salt is the universal article of commerce of all these barbarians and their regular food, for they even eat or
suck it alone as we do sugar'.[19] Here we reach the threshold of consumption.

Consumption

Again the impression is one of extremes. In Oregon, Lévi-Strauss tells
us, the Klamath and Modoc did not use salt, while their neighbours to
the south the Achomawi, the Atsugewi and the Wintu bought much
from the Yana. It was the same in Amazonia. Lévi-Strauss writes:
'Numerous tribes, for instance the *Nambicuara* cannot bear the taste of
salt, but tribes which do enjoy it use native salt, bitter as it is, in large
quantities. There is, in fact, a strong contrast in the like and dislike of
various tribes for "hot" foods'.[20] Similarly, against Acosta's statement of
the abundance of salt at Cuzco and Onate's remark above, can be set
von Humboldt's assertion that 'of all the people on the globe the natives
of South America consume the least salt, because they scarcely eat
anything but vegetables'.[21]

These contrasts cannot plausibly be explained in terms of ecology. In
both the Rocky mountains and the Mato Grosso ecology was too uniform
and uniformly primitive: civilizations of hunting, maize or manioc. A better
explanation is in terms of social structures and the availability of alternative
food differentiators to salt, notably honey, pimento and tobacco.

The Nambikwara Indians of the Southwest Mato Grosso were a remarkably undifferentiated community. The married couple was the only stable unit in a social structure otherwise ephemeral and fluid, where the authority of the chief was highly personal and consensual. Here Nambikwara society contrasted with that of other Indians: the Caduveo of the Pantanal lowlands with their strong sense of hierarchy and aristocracy; the Bororo of the central Mato Grosso with their complex system of village moieties, clans and classes; or the similarly organized Tupi of the Amazonian edge inspired by their dynamic and polygamous chiefs. Since there was no social distance to be expressed, the Nambikwara used neither salt nor pimento, while tobacco and honey, when available, were objects of universal use. Among the Tupi, on the other hand, salt and pimento were in use as luxuries, while tobacco was completely rejected.

These food accessories formed a system. In the course of his investigations into American myth Lévi-Strauss refers frequently to the culinary code. For him the code was chiefly of interest because in combination with other codes – faunal, acoustic, meteorological, astronomical, sexual, etc. – it afforded a clue of the underlying *mythologiques*. The culinary code, however, can be taken in its own right as the cultural infrastructure, the gastronomy, behind actual food habits. The code may be represented as consisting of two axes. First, there was a horizontal axis of nature defined by salt and honey, similar because both produced spontaneously by nature, but different because bitter and sweet. Second, there was a vertical axis of culture defined by tobacco and pimento, similar because both required cultivation and processing, yet were transformable into nature as smoke and ash, but different because pungent and hot in opposite ways, Social groups usually combined elements of nature and culture, so the grid provided four possible combinations: tobacco and honey, honey and pimento, pimento and

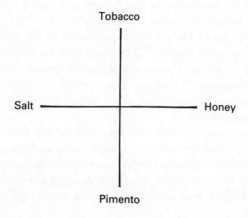

salt, salt and tobacco. The first possibility was actualized by the Nambik-wara who used neither salt nor pimento but had a sweet tooth and were inveterate smokers. The second was actualized by the Caduveo and the Bororo and South American peoples generally, for whom 'le miel sauv-age offre pour les Indiens un attrait que n'égale celui d'aucune autre nourriture' and who 'fassent du piment, qui est leur condiment princi-pal, un disjoncteur de la nature et de la culture'.[22] The third was actualized by the Tupi who used salt and pimento but not tobacco; the fourth by the Indians of Oregon who used salt and tobacco but not honey. Salt therefore in pre-Columbian America was one option in a spectrum of flavourings, a pole in a system of polarities. It could be universal in one community, disregarded or unknown in another not necessarily dissimilar. Von Humboldt may have been right in thinking South American *per capita* consumption of salt the lowest in the world, but this was as much a fact of culture as of nature.

SALT IN PRE-COLONIAL AFRICA

Pre-colonial Africa survived longer into modern times than pre-Columbian America. Its places of salt production, distribution routes and patterns of consumption are therefore better known. Indeed, more generally, pre-Columbian America and pre-colonial Africa contrast, except in the matter of population which in both cases may have been as much as 50 million. Thus the hypertrophy of the state in the Maya, Aztec and Inca empires contrasts with its more limited, local, develop-ment in Africa, except relatively late or where touched by Indonesia, Islam or the European slave trade. Contrariwise, the Amerindian *pueblo*, though strong in defence and survival, lacked the expansionary power of the African communities which produced the Bantu *Drang nach Suden* or the dynamism of modern Iboland. Similarly, the underdevelopment of metallurgy by American Indian society contrasts with the precocious iron and brass technology of Niger-Congo society. America and Africa were each strong where the other was weak and vice versa. It was the same in the field of salt. If salt was a luxury in the Celtic world and a semi-luxury in America, in Africa it was a semi-necessity: intensively produced, extensively traded and widely consumed, though in low *per capita* quantities. For in all three areas, *per capita* consumption probably hardly attained the 5 lb level which may be taken as the upper limit of primitivity.

The African salt world is best understood as falling into three sub-worlds, of which in pre-colonial times, the first two were more import-ant than the third. The first was latitudinal, stretching across the sahel of North Africa from the Atlantic to the Red Sea. The second was longitudinal, following the Great Rift valley from Eritrea to Malawi. The third was latitudinal again, stretching across the much shorter and less well defined sahel of southern Africa from the waters of the Benguela current to those of the Mozambique channel.

These three subworlds should be set against a background of African historical geography.[23] The ecology of Africa is organized according to a double stratification. First, east–west, there are successive strata which stretch uniformly and horizontally across the continent: coast, mountain, desert, sahel, savannah, forest, savannah, sahel, desert, mountain, coast. Second, north–south, there is a single, switchback stratum of mountain, rift and lake superimposed vertically up and down the horizontal stratification. Historically, until *c.* 1500, the main centres of African population fell into three groups. First, in the savannah, there were subdesert communities based on cereals, notably millet. Second, again in the savannah, there were subforest communities based on tubers, notably yams. Third, in the vertical supradesert, supraforest zone, there were interlacustrine communities based on sorghum, cattle and bananas. In general, the subdesert communities were well organized politically, the subforest communities less well organized though with a considerable equipment of social institutions especially in religion, while the interlacustrine communities were again well organized politically. In this schema, subdesert states are represented in the north by the principalities of Jenne, Mali, Songhay, Sokoto, Kano, Bornu, Kanem and Darfur, and in the south by the kingdoms of the Monomatapa in Zimbabwe, the Khamas in Botswana and Queen Jinga of Malamba in Angola. Subforest societies are represented in the north by the Mossi of the Upper Volta and the Yoruba and Ibo communities of Nigeria, and in the south by the considerable populations of Katanga and the Portuguese Congo. The interlacustrine states are represented by the empire of the Negus, the kingdom of the Kabaka, the Tusi aristocracies of Rwanda-Burundi, the Bantu chieftaincies of Swaziland and Lesotho.

The three subworlds of pre-colonial African salt corresponded with this stratification. The northern, latitudinal subworld, based on desert salt mines or pits was associated with the subdesert states of the north African savannah. The north–south longitudinal subworld, based on lake, earth or ash salt, was associated with the interlacustral states of the Rift valley. The southern, latitudinal subworld, based again on mines and pits, was associated with the subdesert states of the southern African savannah.

Production

The northern subworld of pre-colonial African salt produced its salt in a line of salines from Senegal to Darfur: Awlil, Idjil, Taghaza, Taoudenni,

Amadro, Teguidda, Manga, Fachi, Bilma and Darfur itself. The first five were salt mines. Idjil in Mauretania is still a major opencast centre today. It may have been in operation in the eighth century since it is possibly mentioned by the Anonymous of Ravenna; it was visited by Cadamosto in 1455; and described by Fernandes and Pacheco early in the sixteenth century. Teguidda, Fachi and Bilma possessed springs or pits which produced salt by natural solar evaporation. Manga and Darfur produced by the filtering of saline earths or ash and the artificial evaporation of the subsequent brine by boiling. P. Gouletquer and D. Kleinmann in their study of salt and Tuareg society have suggested that these distinctions represent an evolution: an expansion of production to meet increased demand.[24] Rock salt, easiest to exploit, came first: first from Idjil, then from Taghaza where the mines were described by Ibn Battuta in 1352, finally from Taoudenni north of Timbuktu, especially when Taghaza was pre-empted by Morocco. Solar salt came second: at Teguidda, Fachi and Bilma, with the resurgence of the *mais* of Bornu at the end of the sixteenth century. Earth and ash salt at Manga and Darfur came last, because they required fuel, scarce and expensive in this part of the world, and delivered an inferior product where sodium chloride was extensively adulterated with other salts. Indeed at Darfur, production of salt in the eighteenth century developed as a by-product of the soda which figured in the great annual caravan to Cairo.

In the nineteenth century the largest producing centre of the northern subworld was the sultanate of Bornu.[25] Paul E. Lovejoy, in his study of the Bornu salt industry, writes, 'The production and distribution of salt had a unique position in the economy of Borno before 1900. Probably more salt was traded within its borders than anywhere else in precolonial Africa.'[26] He argues that 'the prosperity of the state was closely related to salt production',[27] and estimated that, 'the annual output of all types of Borno salt was probably of the order of six thousand to nine thousand five hundred metric tons'.[28] A maximum of 200 000 cwt, this is the largest production figure we hear of in pre-colonial Africa. Half came from the desert salines, of Fachi and Bilma where the sultan's government used the labour of 25 000 slaves; half from the *sahel* to the southwest of Lake Chad, where 25 000 free immigrant labourers from the south worked in temporary camps under the supervision of aristocratic owner-managers at boiling the filtered brine, or in collecting the ersatz salt of sodium carbonate, which some consumers preferred for their millet porridge.

Another major producer of the African northern subworld was Taoudenni,[29] whose annual production can be estimated at 100 000 cwt. Taoudenni first came into prominence in the sixteenth century when Taghaza, the former supplier of the Upper Niger basin, was occupied by the sultan of Morocco, part of its production being diverted north. Taoudenni itself came under Moroccan rule in 1591 when the sultan's expeditionary force occupied Timbuktu, the headquarters of the south-bound trade. In the course of time, however, the *caid* became independent, elected by the local 'Moroccan' soldiers, while economic control reverted to the Timbuktu mercantile ring, of which Taoudenni was in effect an antenna. Timbuktu supplied both the slaves who did the mining and the credit with which the Taoudenni community purchased its supplies. It was not a large community: 50 residents and 200 floating population, so productivity was much higher than at Bornu. The purity of the sodium chloride was also higher.

The north–south subworld of the pre-colonial African salt produced its salt in a line of salines from Uganda to Malawi: Kibero near Lake Albert, Kasenyi near Lake George, Katwe near Lake Edward, Kaksingiri on Lake Victoria, Uvinza near the northern end of Lake Tanganyika, Ivuna near Lake Rukwa, Kazembe near Lake Mweru, sites in central Malawi, near Lake Chilwa and just north of the Zambezi, with offshoots on the upper Lualaba and Katanga. The most widespread method of production was the filtration of saline earth or ashes followed by boiling. This was practised at Kibero, the upper Lualaba, Kaksingiri, Ivuna and central Malawi. It was probably the oldest method too and in this part of Africa there was no shortage of fuel. Production by these means, however, was generally small: a few hundred to a few thousand cwt.

The two largest producers in this subworld were Uvinza, 20 000 cwt. a year, and Katwe, 50 000 cwt. At Uvinza where salt had perhaps been made in the fifth century AD in the days of Indonesian influences, production was by the boiling in earthenware vessels of rich brine drawn from salt springs and allowed to concentrate first by solar evaporation in artificial pits.[30] The springs were owned by the three Vinza sultans, originally from Rwanda who each, in successive years, took a tithe collected by their agents on the spot. The actual workers, however, were immigrants, some from as far away as Burundi. Twenty thousand came annually to the site, many of them staying only the ten days sufficient to make a load of 50 lb to carry away. Other immigrants brought food and other supplies to exchange for salt made by more permanent workers. Some of these latter had acquired customary rights to particular springs and for most of the time Uvinza was a community of 200 huts and a population of two to three thousand. Stanley described the scene in 1878: 'A square mile of ground is strewn with broken pots, embers of fire, the refuse of the salt, lumps of burnt clay, and ruined huts'.[31]

At Katwe production, which had possibly been exploited since the fourteenth century, was by solar evaporation from a lake.[32] Duke Adolphus Frederick of Mecklenburg described it in 1910:

'the place offers an extraordinary aspect. The wonderful wine-red colouring of the water spread out at our feet like a sea of blood, the blue canopy of the heavens, separated by the yellow sand-dunes from the ruddy water, presented a curious contrast such as we were hardly likely to meet with again.'[33]

Two if not three methods were in use. First, under the action of the sun, sodium chloride deposited itself naturally at the bottom of the lake and 'the salt is simply gathered up by a number of men, who enter the water absolutely naked and wade about collecting it'.[34] Second, solar evaporation could be artificially promoted after the manner of the Mayas in Yucatan.

The following method is also adopted: on the two sides of a small ditch, flat basins or troughs, of three to five metres square are fashioned by heaping up sand and clay. These are filled with about a foot of water taken from the ditch by means of a scoop or by hand. The power of the sun causes the water in the various divisions to evaporate so rapidly, that after the expiration of six days only a salt residue remains at the bottom.[35]

The Duke concluded that 'the salt thus obtained is finer and whiter than that which is broken away from the bed of the lake.'[36] Though it seems that the best salt of all – no doubt because least mixed with other minerals – was gathered from the lake while it was still in suspension just below the surface of the water. The lake was owned by the Sultan of Toro, a not always dependent vassal of the greater rulers of Uganda. It was the object of considerable political rivalry in pre-colonial times as later between Belgium and England.

The southern subworld of pre-colonial African salt produced its salt in an irregular line of salines from the Atlantic to the Indian ocean: Loango in the Portuguese Congo, Ndemba near the mouth of the Cuanza in the Ndongo kingdom of Angola, the Makarikari salt pans in Botswana, the Zoutpansberg in the northern Transvaal, and the island of Pemba off the coast of Tanzania. Loango and Pemba produced by boiling seawater; Makarikari was a *sebkha* or natural saline, as were probably the early Zoutpansberg workings; while Ndemba, the best developed source in pre-colonial times, was, like Idjil in the north, a mine. All these salines, it may be supposed, were only developed gradually as the Bantu population expanded into southern Africa, bringing agriculture with them.

Distribution

In pre-colonial Africa salt was distributed by two kinds of network which may be termed Islamic and Bantu, though it must be remembered that the Islam in question was a purely Black one, the result of conversion not conquest. Both networks therefore were African.

The Islamic networks operated in the African northern subworld. In general they ran in a single direction, north to south, from the desert saline via a caravan city of the sahel or the savannah to the land of yams and forests beyond, though some salt went north from Taghaza, Taoudenni and perhaps Darfur to the coast. The chief means of transport was the camel. At Taoudenni 40 000 camels were in use in the salt trade: 23 000 on the route to Timbuktu, 16 500 to Gao to the east, 500 to Goundam to the west. The camels belonged to local desert nomads and transport costs were high: 75 per cent of ex-mine value, three barrels of salt out of four. At Bilma too, whose salt was served by 70 000 camels, the trade passed increasingly under the control of the Tuareg of Air once they came to realize its value. Nevertheless, the nomad needed to market his royalties among the sedentarists and so could never dispense with the sedentary merchant with whom the trade had started.

These merchants were often outsiders: in Timbuktu they claimed to be of Moroccan origin; but in the usual Islamic fashion, they were members of the *sadr*, the notables, the local oligarchy of religious and civil leaders. The religious leaders in turn participated in the trade. The marabouts, holy men who were the Maghrebin variant of dervish Islam and dominated its religious life from the sixteenth century on, lent money to both merchants (Jewish as well as Muslim) and nomads, operated insurance and acted as arbitrators in commercial disputes.[37] Trade and religion thus went hand in hand. Merchants and nomads needed to be in good standing with the marabout, who in turn needed them as disciples and clients. Trade in salt was thus inscribed in a wider circle of relationships whose *raison d'être* transcended the economic. The Maghreb was provincial: it needed to import from the Mediterranean. The sahel and savannah caravan cities, the bridgeheads of the Islamic cultural revolution south of the Sahara, were more provincial still. They too needed to import, and to import must export products from further south: gold, slaves, ivory, gum, ambergris, ostrich feathers. The sale of salt, if it could be popularized, was one means of commanding these commodities for export to the north, whence the gold might pass on to the Mediterranean. Alternatively salt might be exported to the north. Again, northern interests might seek to cut out the middle-man by taking over the salt mines themselves as the Moroccans did in 1591. In the African northern subworld, salt became part of the adventure of Islam: its slow beginnings, internal divisions and long-term success.

The Bantu networks operated in the African north, south and southern subworlds. Most frequently they ran in two directions: east and west from the raised backbone of Africa to the savannah and forest on either side. The chief means of transport was head loading and the human porter: part of the constant movement on foot so characteristic of Black Africa. On the lakes themselves, however, canoes were used: from Katwe across Lake Edward to Rwanda or from Uvinza up Lake Tanganyika to Burundi. At Uvinza, the average load of the porters was 25 kg, more than twice a generous estimate for the annual consumption of themselves and their families. Clearly they were traders in a small way as well as consumers, who sold to other traders.

Thanks to this network, Uvinza salt was widely diffused: 'In the second half of the nineteenth century Vinza salt was sold as far north as Lake Victoria and Burundi; as far east as Ugogo; as far south as the Ruaha valley; and over much of the eastern Congo'.[38] Uvinza salt furthermore played some part in the movement of ivory and slaves to Zanzibar, just as Ndemba salt played some part in the movement of ivory and slaves to Luanda. Yet compared to those of Taoudenni, the horizons of Uvinza salt were circumscribed in a localized exchange of foodstuffs, cloth and goats between villagers, the royalties from which were useful sidelines for the sultans but nothing more. On Lake Victoria too, 'A preparation of dried bananas was one of the main trade items used in exchange for the salt, and it seems likely that iron and iron tools were also used for this purpose'.[39] One is dealing with a *cabotage*.

It was the same at Katwe. Here salt was sold through four agents appointed by the sultan. Some went 'westward into the eastern Congo for fifty miles or more beyond the present Uganda–Congo border',[40] some south to Rwanda, and others east to Lake Victoria and the frontier of Uvinza salt. Charles Good estimates that 'around 1890 Katwe's hinterland covered as much as 35 000 square miles of territory within and on both sides of the western rift valley'.[41] Yet compared to that of Bornu, the air of Katwe salt was relatively restricted: a group of counties rather than a country. The fact that the Arabs from the east coast never took control of the Katwe salt trade is further evidence of its isolation, small scale and lack of dynamism. Yet Katwe was the biggest centre in the Bantu networks.

Consumption

Both the Islamic and the Bantu networks led to the sedentary Middle African population of some 35 million people. Consumption therefore was dominated by its dietary structures. Besides contemporary observation, these are known from two sources: first, medieval Muslim literature which has been studied by Tadeusz Lewicki;[42] second, archaeology, notably Jenne Jeno in the Niger interior delta and the West Lake site at Lake Victoria, both of which go back to the first centuries BC. Human alimentary demand dominated, but there was demand for salt for animals, for example at Katwe where a subsidiary lake was known as the 'buffalo clinic', and for industrial salt, as at Bornu for tanning and tobacco processing.

African diet was not static in the pre-colonial era. Although millet and yams were its basis, the Indonesians added bananas and rice, the Arabs coconuts, the Europeans from America in the sixteenth century maize and sweet potatoes, in the seventeenth manioc and pineapples, in the eighteenth guava and groundnuts. By the end of the eighteenth century the ecology of Senegal was based on maize, manioc and sweet potatoes, all transplants from America. Yet no alimentary stratum made salt of major significance. Basic physiological needs for salt were met by fish which was prominent in the diet at both Jenne-Jeno and round Lake Victoria, and probably had been still more prominent in the days of Mega-Chad before the great dessication, while cultural demand only developed to a limited extent before the colonial era, mainly as a result of conversion to Islam.

Tadeusz Lewicki sets out the case. First, 'by comparison with food of vegetable origin, meat played only a minor part in the nourishment of the West African peoples during the Middle Ages'.[43] Consequently, 'salt, so indispensable for a number of dishes in Europe and in Muslim countries, was only consumed in small quantities by the medieval peoples of West Africa. Salt was quite a rarity and very expensive, as attested by nearly all the Arabic authors'.[44] A major authority here is Al Hasan ibn Mohammed al Wesaz al Fasi, better known as Leo Africanus, who wrote a *Descrizione dell' Africa* for Leo X.

> In the greater part of Africa, there is no other salt but that obtained from the mines by digging underground galleries. . . . There is grey salt, white salt and red salt. In Barbary, it is found in large quantities; in Numidia [the northern Sahara] it is rather rare, but sufficient, while it is altogether absent in Negroland, particularly in inner Ethiopia [the southern part of West Africa and Central Africa] where a pound of salt costs half a ducat. That is why the people of that country do not put it into salt cellars set on the table, but when eating bread they hold a piece of salt in the hand and lick it so as not to use too much.[45]

Lewicki concludes, 'As we can see, salt in the Middle Ages was a great rarity in West Africa, and the price was exceedingly high. Everything seems to point to the fact that salt was used only in very small quantities in the food of the local population'.[46]

Nor did things change after 1500.

> Even at the present day, rock salt is used very sparingly in the fare of many West African peoples. Thus, for example, the Yoruba of Southern Nigeria add salt to yam porridge only when the yam is of poor

quality . . . and the Fulani, though they flavour their millet porridge with strongly-flavoured sauces, do not add salt, which continues to be a luxury.[47]

There is no reason to suppose that the position was different south of the equator. Africa, comparatively undifferentiated in its society, had little need of the Celtic and American salt coding of social differences. The adoption by the African northern subworld of Islam, a religion of modest affluence accustomed to salt, no doubt raised consumption by its new patterns of diet, but, because of its social egalitarianism, it did not alter the basic pattern. *Per capita* consumption of salt remained low in Africa.

Conclusion

In this first chapter we have endeavoured to carry the history of human salt as far back as possible. Three general conclusions emerge from the salt worlds of pre-Roman Europe, pre-Columbian America and pre-colonial Africa.

First, with regard to production, primitive methods of making salt were not simple. The most widespread method of salt production was boiled, earth or ash, salt, a process of considerable complexity dependent on the availability of cheap pottery and fuel. Most likely this complexity was borrowed from the complexity of domestic cooking of which, even when natural brine was substituted for filtered water, salt making remained an extension. Cooking, Lévi-Strauss tells us, is along with speech, a distinctive human characteristic, and uninsipid food, one may suppose, was always allied with spiced talk. Salt, however, was only one of a number of condiments and its supply was limited by the level of technology. In particular, except in the Maya empire with its remarkable evaporation basins, one is struck with the relatively little use of the sea, which in traditional times was to become the chief source of salt. Africa especially turned its back on the sea.[48]

Second, with regard to distribution, the argument sometimes advanced that salt was a major item of early circulation whether by gift or exchange, is dubious. Except in minimal quantities which most diets provided without deliberation, salt was an inessential, a relative luxury. No doubt relative luxuries have never been absent from human societies: but salt was in addition a bulky luxury. So long as transportation was confined to head loading or to domestic animals such as the llama or the camel, its diffusion could not be large. Before salt could become a major item of circulation, water transport, the only economic form of movement for bulky goods in premodern times, had to become more developed. Just as the sea had to emerge as a source of supply, so it, and still more rivers linking it to continental interiors, had to become a means of communication.

Finally, as regards consumption, one must not underestimate the complexity of the reasons which lay behind the use of salt from earliest times. Lévi-Strauss's analogy between eating and speaking should be taken seriously. A complex gastronomy lies behind food habits in the same way as language lies behind speech. Both, no doubt, in turn rest again on deeper structures of the human morphogenetic field. Gastronomy is important because it is part of the universal human tendency to make distinctions. This is Lévi-Strauss's principle that if nature abhors a vacuum, culture abhors a plenum.[49] The basic function of salt in food would seem to be that of differentiation, the culinary equivalent of modification in speech. Salt differentiates in two ways: by variation of its own presence and by enhancement of other flavours. By both means, it mobilizes, so to speak, perceptibles for the sense of taste. As the Chinese usurper emperor Wang Mang put it in a decree of AD 17, 'salt is the general of foods' (*fu yen, shih-yao chih chiang*).[50] It marshals other comestibles in order of battle and sends them into the fray as required. As speech expresses thought, so salt impresses sense. Hardly edible in itself and without odour, salt was a cause of edibility and savour in other things. Salt like speech was essentially semiotic. As such it could convey a variety of meanings, of which the clearest in early times was social distance: high cooking, low cooking, above or below the salt.

Yet social distance alone is insufficient to account for the fact that almost all known human societies, even the most primitive, consume *per capita* more salt than they physiologically require. Salt, it has been said, is the primordial addiction.[51] Physiology not only does not explain, but adds a new dimension to the problem, since animals, having achieved the appropriate physiological level, quickly manifest salt satiety.[52] Some other factor, primordial yet cultural, must be involved. A factor which would fulfil these criteria would be one in the field of health: salt as a medicine, especially as a supposed remedy against intestinal parasites and their associated diseases.

Not much is known about medicine in the late palaeolithic and early neolithic when, it may be supposed, salt addiction began. This, however, is no reason for thinking that it did not exist or that it was not, according to its lights, rational and even scientific. The development of the basic cereals required considerable observation, discussion and experimentation and there is every reason to suppose that the same powers would have been deployed in the field of health, though, no doubt, with less success. Primitive medicine would not have been simply folk medicine. Most likely, it would have been the property of an elite of shamans, witch-doctors and medicine men with pretensions to professionalism. Some clues to the pharmacology of such an elite is provided by the medicine of antiquity which incorporated part of it.

Mineral drugs, salt especially, played a considerable part in all the pharmacopoeias. Thus the Syrian *Book of Medicines*, a Nestorian work, basically Hippocratic, but incorporating Near Eastern elements, recommends the salt of Cappadocia as good for the stomach and good for those who faint from loss of blood.[53] Similarly, the *Charaka-Samhita*, a *summa* of traditional Indian medicine, supposedly going back to the tenth century BC, has a long list of uses for salt: emollient, emetic, 'in enemata (with or without oils)', eyesalve, 'for application to wounds after operation, for injection into the urethra', etc.[54] Interestingly, it also warns against the excessive use of salt: 'These men who are habituated to excessive measures of salt, suffer from absence of hair, baldness (partial or entire) of head, whiteness of hair, and relaxation of the flesh. All these occur long before maturity of years comes in'.[55] Again, the *Huang-ti nei-ching Su-wen*, the foundation of traditional Chinese medicine, is similarly ambivalent about salt. On the one hand, 'salt nourishes the kidneys, and the kidneys strengthen the bones and the marrow, and the marrow strengthens the liver'; on the other hand 'salt is injurious to the blood' and excess of salty flavor hardens the pulse'.[56]

In particular, all three medical traditions regard salt as positively indicated in the treatment of internal parasites. *The Book of Medicines* in recommending certain herbs as vermifuges says 'they will also kill worms if the water in which they have been boiled with salt and natron be injected through the anus into the belly'.[57] The *Charaka-Samhita*, in its discussion of 'worms that are born of external impurities', recommends 'administering errhines, emetics, purgatives and enemata', most of which contain salt: 'then throwing some *sarjjika* [sodium carbonate] and salt over it, the preparation should be applied to the anal canal as enemata'.[58] More generally re worms we are told: 'The destruction of their origin is accomplished by the use of such articles (as food and drink) as are pungent, bitter, astringent, alkaline and hot'.[59] The Chinese tradition being more holistic is less explicit, but two of the five viscera, the liver and the kidneys, are benefited by salt: 'the kidneys crave the salty flavor'.[60] Finally, in his examination of the religious symbolism of salt in the Bible and Church fathers, James E. Latham finds that the theme of preservation or incorruption, which includes the counteraction of worms, 'is by far the most universal throughout the history of salt symbolism'.[61] Later, he argues, 'salt that does away with corruption both material and spiritual, is equally effective against worms' and cites a statement from Hastings to the effect that salt is 'a preventative to the development of intestinal worms'.[62] Whether salt is in fact effective against worms is beside the point. It is a widespread belief and probably an ancient one. Even in the 1976 edition of an Indian handbook on the salt industry it is roundly declared: 'Too much deficiency of salt in the human body would give rise to worms in the stomach'.[63] It is not unreasonable therefore to suppose that salt formed part of early medicine: a primitive Paracelsism of the neolithic.

So long as man was a hunter-gatherer, whether nomadic, or from a fixed point on a lake or coast, or some mixture of the two, he would have had no physiological need for salt, though he would certainly have been acquainted with it from the salt licks of natural salines used by his prey. With the shift to cereals, however, some of the population may have fallen below the 3 lb *per capita* minimum, if they did not continue to eat sufficient animal protein. At the same time, the neolithic revolution to agriculture and pastoralism was accompanied by a temporary worsening of human health conditions. By settling down, man exposed himself to more infection and acquired tuberculosis from animals, malaria from insects, and a battery of diseases (schistosomiasis, kala-azar and uta, elephantiasis, hookworm, river blindness etc.) from protozoan and metazoan intestinal parasites.[64] Grmek has argued that it was these endemics, rather than the epidemics more typical of later periods, which defined the characteristic pathology of pre-antiquity and antiquity.[65] In these circumstances, it would not be surprising that salt, known as a means of preventing corruption in dead bodies, was recommended by medical opinion as a remedy for the living, nor that what was begun in sickness was continued in health. In China, opium addiction started in this way. Its use began as a prophylaxis against malaria and tuberculosis: it continued as social accomplishment, entertainment and minimum luxury. The story of salt, one may suppose, was similar. Part of the struggle of culture against nature, a weapon of culture supplied by nature,[66] salt became part of culture itself. Salt addiction thus had two origins, both cultural: one bodily and therapeutic, the other intellectual and semiotic. Already in primitivity salt was essential to *vita humanior*.

2 Antiquity

Between primitivity and antiquity – the classical empires of the Mediterranean, the ancient Middle East, pre-Muslim India and Han China – there was a great gulf fixed. It was a gulf not of technology, for here antiquity was conservative rather than innovative, but of management: politics in the west, bureaucracy in the east. Both politics and bureaucracy required the new higher literacy of classical languages embodied in canonical texts: Homer, the Zend Avesta, the Vedas and Upanishads, and the five Confucian classics. Pre-classical language, mainly unwritten, was confined to the spatial, the specific, the objective, the human and the concrete. Classical language, essentially written, provided concepts for the temporal, the generic, the subjective, the divine and the abstract. The new classical languages everywhere widened horizons, but they created a deep social division between those who possessed the new literacy, the aristocracy and urban males with a minimum degree of leisure, and those who did not, women and country people – farmers, fishermen and miners. Antiquity was elitist, sexist and also generalist. If it refused technical professionalism, this was not due to slavery or to disdain of the banausic, but to a well-founded conviction that this was not then the best line of advance. Antiquity enjoyed a higher standard of living than primitivity not through new technology but through better management of old. The wisdom of Athena promised more than the skill of Metis and the sage was uncrowned king.

The new classical world modified the role of salt in society. With higher living standards, salt was more widely produced, distributed and consumed. In production, technology continued with little change. The only major development was the increased exploitation of the sea, which by 500 AD provided the larger part of the salt consumed by civilized men. In distribution, water began to take the lead from the land, though the economy it served was still 'embedded' in its sociology and was only occasionally and anomalously capitalist. In consumption, though salt ceased to be a luxury, indeed now formed part of a minimum definition of civilized living, civilized living itself was a privilege and salt was associated chiefly with its culinary centrepiece: fish. These themes in their variations will now be pursued across the four major civilizations of antiquity between about 500 BC and 500 AD.

SALT IN ATHENS, ALEXANDRIA AND ROME

Production

The writers of classical Athens were not much interested in salt as a
commodity. Herodotus has a remarkably scientific account of the salt
domes of North Africa, but his references to human exploitation of salt
are minimal: Xerxes passing the Phrygian salt lake, sturgeon being
pickled at the mouth of the Dnieper, Greek exiles working at a salt
source in Khuzistan. Salt was most significant as an obstacle to agriculture. Thucydides does not mention salt at all, though we learn from
Aristophanes' *Acharnians* that the blockade of Megara interrupted the
export of salt and garlic to Athens. The salt in question 'was collected
from salt flats along the south coast',[1] i.e. it was the result of a simple
process of natural solar evaporation. Athens also had similar sources
closer. One of her coastal *demes*, or local communities, was called Halai
Aixomedes, the salines of Aixone, after a coastal lagoon, and another,
Anaphlystos, contained a salt lake. The picture is of supply by many
small, local, marine salines. Distant sources do not figure, though some
salt may have been obtained from the island of Melos. Aristotle was
interested in salt as a natural phenomenon, but in his *Meteorologica*, he
mentions only three places of production: Chaonia in Epirus where
brine from a spring was boiled, Umbria where brine was made by the
filtration of the ash of salt plants, and Sicania in Sicily where salt was
made by an unspecified process.

Alexandria was Athens writ large. Primarily a place of civic association, it was less of a polis and more of an emporium on account of its
greater size and need to buy from abroad. Egypt lacked many of the
requirements of a Hellenistic kingdom: wood, iron, tin, precious metals
and horses. Salt, however, was not one of the absentees. It was obtain-
able locally from four sources using three methods: rock salt mined in
the desert, notably at the temple of Zeus Ammon in the oasis of Siwa;
lake salt, artificially evaporated from brine obtained in the Fayum; sea
salt, naturally evaporated in the lagoons near Lake Mareotis; and rock
salt again, mined at Pelusium on the Damietta arm of the Nile. A similar
pattern of local sources, limited supply prevailed in other Hellenistic
cities. Antioch probably obtained its salt from Cyprus: either the two salt
lakes of Larnaca, or the salt marshes of Salamis. Lysimachus, one of
Alexander's successors, tried unsuccessfully to tax the wind evaporated
sea salt of Tragasae which supplied the cities of northern Ionia and
eastern Thrace. At Ephesus salines were owned by the famous temple of
Artemis and at Priene by the temple of Athena Polias. We know of a
source of salt near Thessalonika because Livy tells us that the Romans,
in the treaty following the battle of Pydna in 168 BC, forbad import into

Macedonia, probably to deprive the local regime of a fiscal resource.

Rome was Alexandria writ even larger. Under both the republic and the empire, her principal supply of salt lay close at hand in the artificial solar salines constructed at the mouth of the Tiber. Those on the north bank were the older and remained for a long time the property of the southernmost Etruscan city of Veii, which only fell to the Romans in 396 BC. Livy tells us that the city of Ostia was founded and the first salines established on the south bank by King Ancus Martius (640–616) to avoid dependence on the Etruscans. The north bank salines, however, remained the more important and after 396 were annexed to the Roman state as the *Salinae Romanae*. With the advent of *pax Romana* and the expanding urban population, both Ostia and the *Salinae Romanae* increased their supply. Archaeology has identified the salines. The method of production was single basin rather than successive basin solar evaporation, a technique more sophisticated than the lagoon salt of Athens and Alexandria, but less sophisticated than the successive basin method which was to be used in the Middle Ages. The scale of production, however, must have been considerable. If Rome at its height had a population of two million, it will have required at least 100 000 cwt of salt a year. To this one must add the requirements of the Campagna and of the back country supplied by the Via Salaria, so that total output will have reached 200 000 cwt. This figure, comparable to the production of Bornu in nineteenth-century North Africa, highlights both the achievements and limitations of the ancient economy.

The mouth of the Tiber, of course, was not the only place in the Roman world where salt was produced. Rome, by its expansion northwest and southeast, became the heir to the salt systems of the Celtic and Hellenistic worlds. The Hallstatt and Hallein complexes were incorporated into the *limes*. Gregory of Tours tells us that the great frontier city of Trier was supplied with salt from Lorraine via the Moselle. The Essex salines were stimulated by the Roman development of London. We learn from Strabo that salt from the brine springs of Salins in Franche Comté sometimes found its way to Rome via the import of choice salt pork. These springs, little used in Celtic times, had probably been developed in connection with the needs of the Roman army. In the east, Dio Chrysostom refers to the same Black Sea lagoons mentioned by Herodotus. He visited Olbia at the confluence of the Bug and the Dnieper and, *à propos* of the marshes, writes: 'it is here also that we find the vast number of salt-works from which most of the barbarians buy their salt, as do also those Greeks and Scythians who occupy the Tauric Chersonese';[2] another typically short-range source of supply. In addition, Rome acquired the salines pioneered by Carthage in Portugal, Spain and the Balearic islands and those developed by the Greeks in Magna Graecia, in particular the salt lakes of Tarentum and Sicily.

Strabo and Pliny between them mention over fifty sites where salt was produced in the Roman world, to which a further 25 can be added from other literary sources: an inscription in Dacia, a passage in Rutilius Namatianus, references to *salinae* in the Ravenna cosmography; and from archaeology.

These sites used a wide variety of techniques. Pliny, the most systematic of ancient writers on salt, divides them into two categories, artificial and natural, *sal omnis aut fit aut gignitur*, subdivided by the process involved, condensation or evaporation, *utrumque pluribus modis, sed causa gemina coacto umore vel siccato.*[3] He ends therefore with four basic types: artificial condensation, natural condensation, artificial evaporation, natural evaporation.

Pliny takes the last first because he regards it as the most important. He divides it into three subtypes. First, there are bodies of water which evaporate completely in summer. He instances the Tarentine lagoon and the Sicilian lakes of Cocanicus and Gela. Next, there are bodies of water which evaporate only on the edges. Here he gives the example of the Phrygian and Cappadocian salt lakes, of which the most important was Lake Tatta, the modern Tuz Golu, between Caesarea and Iconium. In modern times the annual yield of salt from the lake has been estimated at 380 000 cwt, sufficient by itself for the 8 million inhabitants of classical Anatolia.[4] Anatolia, however, also received salt, as we know from Strabo, from mines, springs and wells in the valley of the Halys, which gave the river its name. Finally, there are bodies of water which evaporate only partially but right to the centre. He instances Aspendus in Pamphylia on the southern coast of Asia Minor where there was a notable inland salt lake, possibly, along with Cyprus, a source of supply for Antioch.

Second, Pliny discusses salt from natural condensation, which for him means salt mountains and salt mines. Of the first he gives as an example the Salt Range in northwest India, to which we will return below. Of the second he instances Gerrha in northeast Arabia, Pelusium, the oasis of Siwa, inland Cyrenaica and a site in Andulusia. Gerrha, one of the terminals of the incense trade, had already attracted the attention of Strabo:

> After sailing along the coast of Arabia for a distance of two thousand four hundred stadia, one comes to Gerrha, a city situated on a deep gulf; it is inhabited by Chaldaeans, exiles from Babylon; the soil contains salt and the people live in houses made of salt; and since flakes of salt continually scale off owing to the scorching heat of the rays of the sun and fall away, the people frequently sprinkle the houses with water and thus keep the walls firm.[5]

Next, Pliny turns to salt from artificial evaporation, essentially solar evaporation of marine brine. He gives as examples the African coast round Utica, Crete and the Egyptian coast, but not, surprisingly, Ostia. He writes: 'Of artificial salt there are various kinds. The usual one, and the most plentiful, is made in salt pools by running into them seawater, not without streams of fresh water, but rain helps very much, and above all much warm sunshine, without which it does not dry out'.[6] Pliny's insistence on the indispensability of fresh water and rain is puzzling, because these are generally regarded as the enemy of the solar salt maker. The most likely explanation is that where marine brine is completely evaporated in a single basin, magnesium salts remain mixed with the sodium chloride and give it a bitter taste. These salts must then be removed by washing with fresh water. If this explanation is correct, it would confirm that the method of evaporation was by single basin only, since one of the advantages of the medieval successive basin method was to separate the sodium chloride before the sedimentation of magnesium salts.

Finally, Pliny discusses salt from artificial condensation which for him meant manufacture either from inland brine springs and wells, or from the ashes of salt plants. Of the first, he gives as example the Cappadocian springs and wells and the springs of Epirus referred to by Aristotle, but not, again surprisingly, the Halles, Vics or Witches of the Celtic world. Of the second, he instances its widespread practice in Gaul and Germany.

Three points are striking about the salt world presented by Pliny. First, its technological conservatism. More than an adaptation to local conditions, the variety of techniques used indicated that none of them was sufficiently superior to compete effectively with the others and so establish a real dominance. Second, a partial consequence, there was no long-distance trade in salt, since no technique could carry competitively the costs even of sea transport. Third, a further corollary, there is little continuity between the salt sources of the Roman world and those of the Middle Ages. There is no Venice, no Dalmatia, no Trapani, no Raz al Makhbaz, hardly an Ibiza or La Mata. Only the salt lakes of Larnaca continued to produce from the late Bronze Age to modern times. The Roman geography of salt was natural rather than cultural, tied still to flats, lagoons, lakes which dried up, and outcrops.

Distribution

Thanks to Strabo and Pliny we are reasonably well informed about how salt was produced in the Roman empire. We are much less well informed about how it was distributed. This is not accidental. Only exceptionally clear-sighted contemporaries like Aristotle perceived the economic as a distinct department of social life in antiquity and for the most part economics was in fact deeply embedded in other relationships of mutuality, dominance or dependence. The principal form of such relationships was what Paul Veyne calls euergetism: the provision to their fellow citizens by Greek civic notabilities, Hellenistic kings, Roman grandees and imperial Caesars, of buildings, services, entertainment and welfare generally.[7] Salt does not figure prominently in the inscriptions which are the chief evidence for the euergetist system, no doubt because being a short-range transaction it did not require much capital and so its supply was not socially prestigious. But there are indications that salt formed part of the system at least intermittently.

Livy tells us that King Ancus Martius gave the people six measures of salt as largesse. This was not a historical statement, but approbation of Augustus via attribution to an idealized patriarchal past. For in 33 BC, not long before Livy commenced writing, Augustus had appointed his friend and henchman Agrippa to the office of aedilis or commissioner of public works. Dio Cassius tells us that Agrippa

> without taking anything from the public treasury, repaired all the public buildings and all the streets, cleaned out the sewers and sailed through them into the Tiber. . . . Furthermore he distributed olive oil and salt to all, and furnished the baths free of charge throughout the year for the use of both men and women.[8]

Agrippa's spell as aedilis was exceptional. It was a move to win the plebs on the eve of the campaign of Actium and convince it that the Caesarian cosa nostra would bring back the golden age. But there are signs that salt, along with grain, regularly formed part of the *annona* or government distribution. When Lars Porsena was at the gates in 508 BC, Livy tells us, 'The question of subsistence received special attention and some were sent to the Volsci and others to Cumae to buy up corn. Again, the monopoly of salt, the price of which was very high, was taken out of the hands of individuals and wholly assumed by the government'.[9] This sounds like an aetiological myth justifying later practice, a suspicion confirmed by what Livy has to say about a more historical episode in 204 BC when Hannibal was at the gates. In that year, the censors Marcus Livius and Claudius Nero, recent victors over Hasdrubal at the Metaurus, established a new tax out of the salt *annona*, *vectigal etiam novum ex salaria annona*.[10] Under the old system, salt had been sold at Rome and throughout Italy at the low, indeed probably subsidized, price of 6 pounds for 1 *as*.[11] Under the new, the low price was maintained at Rome, while other places had to pay tax in proportion to their distance from the salines. In other words, what remained *annona* at Rome became *vectigal* elsewhere. For this piece of legerdemain, Marcus Livius received the cognomen of *Salinator*. Under the later republic, according to a text of Cato, the distribution of salt was in the hands of persons known as *salinatores aerarii*, treasury salt operators, who sold salt at below market prices. Agrippa's innovation therefore consisted in buying salt out of his own pocket, or more likely with funds supplied by Augustus out of the patrimonium Caesaris, the imperial dynastic estate, and distributing it at no price as a piece of euergetism.

For the early empire less information is available. From the reign of Septimius Severus, however, there is an inscription in which Restitutianus Cornelianus, member of the treasury committee of sixteen and treasurer, *aerarius*, of the Roman salines, together with his daughter Ingenua, make a dedication, for the health of the imperial family, to the genius of the salt carriers of the whole city and zone of the Roman salines, *saccarii salarii totius orbis campi salinarum Romanarum*.[12] Codedicators with them are three imperial procurators. While the institutional details are not clear, this looks like a system of what the Chinese were to call *kuan-tu shang-pan* (officials supervise, merchants manage), to supply the city with cheap salt. The procurators would supervise, the treasury committee and the salines chest would buy the salt, and the salt carriers, one of whose boats was represented on the side of the inscription, would transport it to Rome. If this was so, then an indirect government monopoly would have replaced the tax farm of the *salinatores aerarii* between the republic and the empire.

This reconstruction also makes it less surprising to be told by the *Chronography of 354* that Emperor Aurelian (270–275) introduced the free distribution of salt as part of the *annona, sal . . . populo dari jussit gratuito*.[13] Septimius Severus had already extended the *annona* from grain to oil, and Alexander Severus to pork. Aurelian, by including wine and salt, made the *annona*, a comprehensive welfare service in basic foodstuffs: a policy in line with his building of the walls of Rome and his image as *restitutor orbis*. How long this service lasted is not clear. An inscription shortly after the death of Constantine has a dedication to that emperor by the *corpus salariorum*, which suggests that the salt *annona* may have ended with the transfer of the capital to Constantinople, and the indirect monopoly of privileged merchants been restored. A decree of Honorius and Arcadius confirms the exclusive trading privileges of the *mancipes* or *conductores salinarum*: a decree which was still in force under Justinian. Earlier, a decree of Valentinian and Valens in 365, shows that for some time (decrees of former emperors are referred to) the *mancipes salinarum* were also *mancipes thermarum*, concessionaries of the imperial baths. Possibly the profits on salt financed the losses on the baths, but more likely both activities had a welfare aspect, since a decree of Honorius and Arcadius of 400 exempts such salines from tax.[14]

Thus from Ancus Martius to Honorius and beyond, the picture of the Roman salt administration, if that is the right term, was not that of an exploitive gabelle, but of a public service. Its aim, like that of euergetistic institutions generally, was not to make money but to lose it. It is possible that similar salt administrations existed at other cities where there was an *annona*: Alexandria, Constantinople and perhaps Antioch.

Consumption

Though Pliny describes medicinal uses for salt, most salt in Western antiquity was alimentary salt, and most alimentary salt was used in cooking or on table in the preparation of cereal based dishes: barley porridge in the case of the early Romans, baker baked wheat bread in the case of later antiquity. So much is clear, but for the alimentary use of salt beyond daily bread we are much more in the dark. Meals, we know, were of more than alimentary significance to ancient Mediterranean society, because they were seen as generative of the strong non-kinship ties which were its distinguishing characteristic, but exactly how salt figured in them we do not know.[15] Two considerations, however, about the evolution of Mediterranean diet casts some light on the matter.

In the first place, a structural point. Throughout classical antiquity one is struck with the importance of fish and fish products, especially fish sauce, the famous *garum*; the gentleman's relish of antiquity.[16] Fish was the obvious main course as meat is with us: not a luxury, but the dish whose absence signified deprivation. When Libanius wishes to puff the affluence of fourth-century Antioch, it is the abundance of fish that he emphasizes. Even the poor, he says, are not deprived of this food. The sea supplies the rich, the lake supplies the poor and the river supplies both equally. Bread, Libanius finds no need to mention: it can be taken for granted, at least in a city like Antioch with good water communications. The use of *garum* too was widespread to make cereals palatable and to supply dietary deficiencies. The Romans, it has been said, believed in *garum* with everything, but, though widely produced in the Mediterranean, certain places such as Clazomenae in Asia Minor, Carthagena, Pompeii and Leptis were famous for their product either in quantity or quality. *Garum* was both an extension of the dominance of fish and a substitute for it in secondary meals or when the budget was tight. Fish in its various forms, like salt, was a necessity, not for life as was bread, but for the good life, the life of man in civil association. A considerable quantity of salt, therefore, in the classical west will have been used in the preservation of fish and the preparation of fish foods. The preparation of *garum*, for example, required one or two parts salt to every eight parts fish.

In the second place, a conjunctional point. Classical Mediterranean diet was not static. In the first half of antiquity, it received from the east a mainly vegetable reinforcement, notably fruit: lemons from the Levant, cherries from Asia Minor, apricots and peaches proximately from Armenia and Persia ultimately from China. None of these of course affected the consumption of salt. In the second half of antiquity, however, the influence of the north became dominant, particularly that of the imperial *limes* with its distinctive style in food, clothes, hair fashions and general deportment. Here again Aurelian was significant. His confirmation of the *annona* in pork suggests that what had been a luxury or an exotic had now become something to which the common man could and did aspire. The pig, of course, was not unknown in the Mediterranean but was much more abundant on the edges of the oak forests of the north. Under the early empire even the best hams had come from Belgium and Franche Comté, rear areas of the Roman armies. Pork, therefore, was part of the *limes* lifestyle which the military emperors of the third century brought into the heartland of the Mediterranean, along with slang and battle dress, Mithraism and extravagant loyalty to the empire. The *limes* was privileged. The excavations at Vindolanda on Hadrian's wall, for example, show a higher standard of living in housing, clothes and food, particularly in meat consumption, than in the empire generally. Rostovtzev was wrong. The revolution of the third century was not of a military proletariat, but of a military elite whose way of life was in part adopted by the society it tried, but failed to conquer. More meat, more pork especially, more salt was part of that way of life. Hence the need for new sources of supply on the Welsh border, Lorraine, Franche Comté and Dacia, new quantities for Rome itself. For it was not only the Orontes which flowed into the Tiber, but also the salt-bearing rivers of the north: the Thames, the Loire and the Moselle.

SALT IN THE ANCIENT MIDDLE EAST

Production

As will be seen more clearly when we come to the early Islamic world in the next chapter, the supply of salt in the Middle East was abundant but of low quality. A region of desert and high evaporation, it was well provided with natural salt lakes, salt domes, rock salt, salt basins and salt steppe. The *Cambridge History of Iran* notes 300 salt domes in central Persia alone and comments: 'Most of these occur in districts with low rainfall, so that the soluble salt enjoys an unusual permanence at the surface. Consequently salt domes make an imposing contribution to the geomorphology'.[17] Salt domes, associated with the petroleum deposits, were similarly frequent in the southwest along the Persian gulf, especially in the Bandar Abbas region. Herodotus's salt source in Khuzistan, at which Greek expatriates were working, produced bitumen and oil as well as salt. In the northeast, rock salt was exploited, especially in the neighbourhood of Nishapur, the Sassanian military headquarters in Khorasan on the Turanian *limes*: 'One locally unfortunate feature is the outcropping of gypsum and rock-salt, especially north of the Juvain river, which greatly increases the salinity of ground water in those districts'.[18] In Iran salt was a natural phenomenon, and an unwelcome one, rather than a human product. It was the same in the Aramaic world. Iraq was served by a large number of small salt producing sources, most of them producing by primitive methods.[19] Most of the references to salt in the Old Testament are to geographical features or to the destructive effects of salt: the kings joined together 'in the vale of Siddim, which is the salt sea' (Gen. 14.3); Abimelech strewing Shechem with salt (Jud. 9.45); David defeating the Syrians 'in the valley of salt' (II Sam. 8.13); Zephaniah prophesying for Moab, 'the breeding of nettles, and saltpits, and a perpetual desolation' (Zeph. 2.9); Jeremiah condemning the ungodly to 'inhabit the parched places in the wilderness, in a salt land and not inhabited' (Jer. 17.6). Salt has to be produced, or at least gathered: Strabo mentions Lake Urmia, Pliny possibly the Aral Sea and Karabogaz bay; but its production was not problematical.

Distribution

Because production was not problematical, distribution was not big business. Salt formed part of the entrepôt trade of the caravan city of Palmyra: an inscription of 37 AD shows a tax farmer levying both import and export duties on local salt; but not, it would seem, a very significant part. Another reason for the relative absence of trade in salt was transportation costs which inhibited competition between salts of different qualities. In the ancient Middle East, the camel had not yet conquered the cart.[20] The Achaemenid empire with its royal road to Susa was *par excellence* a highway state, Trajan paved roads in Syria, and the Roman army on the eastern *limes* used carts in its baggage train as late as the fourth century AD. Carts and camels were already competing at Palmyra in 137 and Diocletian's price edict of 301 shows the advantage lay with camels, but probably there were not yet enough of them, especially one-humped Arabian dromedaries, to defeat the cart decisively. With transport costs high, there was little incentive to move a bulky commodity like salt long distance, when local, if inferior, supplies were nearly everywhere available.

Consumption

Because salt was readily available, its use was normal. Jesus ben Sirach writes: 'The principal things for the whole use of man's life are water, fire, iron and salt, flour of wheat, honey, milk and the blood of the grape, and oil and clothing' (*Ecclesiasticus* 39.26). Meat and fish, one notices, are absent from this list. It was a cereal civilization as compared to the Mediterranean or the *limes*, so the consumption of salt, while universal, may not have been large. If salt was normal, it was also natural. Where the Greeks excluded salt from their animal sacrifices, the Hebrews included it with theirs: 'And every oblation of thy meat offering shalt thou season with salt; neither shall thou suffer the salt of the covenant of thy God to be lacking from thy meat; with all thine offerings thou shalt offer salt' (Lev. 2.13). Salt became a symbol of grace: 'Have salt in yourselves, and have peace one with another' (Mark 9.50); 'Let your speech be always with grace, seasoned with salt' (Col. 4.6). The Christian community itself was compared with salt: 'Ye are the salt of the earth' (Matthew 5.13); both ordinary yet extraordinary, a perfect image of the *plebs sancta Dei*.

SALT IN PRE-MUSLIM INDIA

Ancient India was one of the wonders of the pre-modern world. The society over which ruled successively the Mauryas, the Bactrian Greeks, the Kushans, the Guptas, Harsha, and the Rajput Pratiharas, held perhaps half the human population of antiquity. It had in rice the best cereal, in cotton the best textile, in the elephant the best animal, and in sugar the best condiment. In Sanskrit, it had an incomparable classical language, in the Buddha, the first world saviour, and in its number system the future basis of world numeracy. Unfortunately little is known about salt in this society and that little mostly from foreigners like Megasthenes and Hsüan-tsang.

Production

Under this heading salt by natural condensation, Pliny says, 'There are also mountains of natural salt, such as Oromenus in India, where it is cut out like blocks of stone from a quarry, and ever replaces itself, bringing greater revenues to the rajahs than those from gold and pearls'.[21] By Oromenus, Pliny meant the Punjab Salt Range on the right bank of the Jelum south of Rawalpindi, whose mines of Khewra, Warcha and Kalabagh under the *raj* produced 4 000 000 cwt of salt a year. Strabo even says that the Salt Range contained 'mineral salt sufficient for the whole of India'.[22] How much of India it in fact supplied is not clear, but it is the only source mentioned by Western authors despite their considerable knowledge of India. The Chinese pilgrim Hsuan-tsang, however, in the seventh century, mentions another source. *A propos* of Sind, he writes: 'They find here a great quantity of salt, which is red like cinnabar; also white salt, black salt and rock salt. In different places, both far and near, this salt is used for medicine'.[23] Here perhaps is a reference to the spontaneous salt of the Rann of Kutch. Another reference to this part of India as producing abundant salt is in the *Charaka-Samhita*, probably compiled in the first or second centuries AD. Speaking of excess consumption of salt, it mentions the Valhikas, the Saurashtrakas, the Saindhavas and the Sauvirakas, all of whom may be located in this area. A third probably active source of salt was the solar evaporation basins of Didwana in Jodhpur where an inscription testifies to the existence of the town in 195 AD and where an ancient salt well was excavated in 1878.[24] Punjab, Sind, Gujerat and Rajasthan were thus all producing salt in ancient India.

Distribution

Some of this salt will most likely have travelled by river to the main centres of Indian population and state power in Gandhara and Magadha. Some kind of euergetism is also to be presumed.

A consistent feature of premodern India was the high proportion of its products redistributed by the state, whether central or local, by means of donation. Indian imperial states especially were vast travelling shows, perambulating *durbars*, which redistributed the goods they acquired by gift or levy. Hsüan-tsang describes one of the great quinquennial gift giving and receiving sessions, the *Pancavarsha*, conducted by Emperor Harsha. Here the emperor first gave away everything he acquired over the past five years to various groups – religious, social, economic etc. – and then received new gifts from his 18 vassal kings, so that he ended as rich, or richer, than he began. Salt is not specifically mentioned among the gifts and counter-gifts, but no doubt it figured among the foodstuffs in so far as it was a significant item of Indian diet at this time.

Consumption

India, one must remember, was at this time a Buddhist country. Hsüan-tsang tells us that Harsha 'caused the use of animal food to cease throughout the Five Indias and he prohibited the taking of life under severe penalties'.[25] Moreover, the rising Hindu reformation with its cult of the cow was a vegetarian religion too. Though a meatless, cereal diet, particularly of rice the least saline of the food grains, might seem to require a large intake of salt, in fact high *per capita* salt consumption has always been associated with meat eating. India's vegetarianism, therefore, limited the consumption of salt. Another limiting factor was the availability of other food flavourings. Even more than pre-Columbian America, India was the classic land of hot foods and it was the pioneer of honey's substitute and supplanter, sugar. It is probable, therefore, that the level of salt consumption in ancient India was lower than in the Middle East or the Mediterranean. When the *Charaka-Samhita* speaks of excess consumption of salt, it may be referring to levels no more than normal elsewhere. Forward in so many things, ancient India was backward in this.

SALT IN HAN CHINA

Production

The two Han empires, 206 BC to 220 AD, separated by the brief Hsin dynasty of the reforming minister Wang Mang 8 to 23 AD, were the rough equivalent of the Roman empire. At the height of the Han period, say between 100 BC and 100 AD, salt was produced in four areas: on the coast of the Po-hai in modern Shantung and Hopei, the former kingdom of Ch'i; on the seacoast south of the Yangtze in modern Kiangsu, the former kingdom of Wu; from the salt lakes of the northwest, particularly the An-i *hsien* salt lake in modern Shansi; and from salt wells in western Szechwan, the former kingdom of Shu. Of these four areas, the Po-hai was the most important. Four techniques were in use. On the seacoast, marine brine was artificially evaporated either in pottery containers or iron pans. At the lakes, salt either formed by natural evaporation or was produced by one or other of the above two techniques of artificial evaporation. With the wells, they had first to be drilled. Their brine was then artificially evaporated in iron pans, natural gas sometimes being the fuel. The Chinese salt industry was technologically more innovative than those of the West, where neither iron pans, nor deep wells, nor natural gas were employed. This technical sophistication of the Han may be seen as the culmination of five stages of development.

Ancient China's first source of salt was probably the natural evaporation of the salt lakes of the northwest. Its centre of gravity lay in the interior, in the modern provinces of Shansi, Honan, Shensi and Kansu. For a long time the coastal provinces, active earlier in prehistory, remained underdeveloped. A number of early sites in Kansu, notably Chung-wei and T'ien-shui, are close to sources of salt, and it may be that China's ambivalent relationship to the steppe, so crucial for its history, began in the need to import salt from the transborder lakes. Natural evaporation was soon followed by artificial evaporation at the numerous brine springs and saline earth deposits of the northwest. The Chinese character for salt, *yen* is a pictograph which consists of three sub-pictographs of a servant, a brine pool and a pottery cooking vessel. Here was a *briquetage* industry like that of Celtic Europe.

Next came sea salt. As the modern provinces of Shantung and Hopei became fully part of China as the kingdom of Ch'i, there developed the artificial evaporation of marine brine in pottery containers. The earliest written testimony to the production of salt in China is in the *Yü-kung* or Tribute of Yü section of the *shu-ching* or classic of history. The *Yü-kung* purports to be an account of the hydraulic activities of Emperor Yü, founder of the Hsia dynasty 2205–1766 BC. Archaeology has yet to confirm the existence of the Hsia and Yü sounds like a heroized demi-urge, so the *Yü-kung* is best taken as referring to the time of its own composition, which was probably around 800 BC. It describes the territory of Ch'ing-chou between the sea and Mount T'ai: 'The soil of this province was whitish and rich; near the sea were wide tracts of salt land. . . . Its articles of tribute were salt, fine grass-cloth, and the productions of the sea of various kinds; with silk, hemp, lead, pinetrees, and strange stones, from the valleys of the T'ai'.[26] All these products were typical of Ch'i and one may suppose that sea salt was presented to the Chou high king because it was superior to the lake, spring and earth salt of the interior.

The development of the Ch'i salt industry is also referred to by Ssu-ma Ch'ien, the Herodotus of China, in his *Shih-chi* or historical records. He attributes its origins, more plausibly but still prematurely, to the founder of the state of Ch'i, the *t'ai-kung* Lu Shang, former minister to the first high king of the Chou dynasty in the twelfth century BC. The *t'ai-kung*, he tells, 'favoured the profitable trade in fish and salt'; so that 'Ch'i became a great kingdom'.[27] In another passage he says that when Lu Shang was enfeofed with Ch'i, 'the land was barren and brackish, and the population scarce', so he encouraged the arts and crafts, among them, 'the circulation at home and abroad of fish and salt'.[28] A more probable figure for the first patron of the salt industry in Ch'i was another man also mentioned by Ssu-ma Ch'ien and, in one passage, in connection with a salt tax. This was Kuan-tzu, or Kuan Chung, minister to Duke Huan of Ch'i 685–643, the first *pa* or non-imperial hegemon over the till then autonomous princes of the Chou confederation. Kuan-tzu existed, and was credited later with the invention of the *yen-cheng* or salt administration, and it is quite plausible that Ch'i's greatness was founded on his mobilization of this resource, as Ssu-ma Ch'ien implies.

Ssu-ma Ch'ien is also a key witness for the third major development: the introduction of iron technology to the salt industry. In *Shih-chi* 129, there is a passage *I Tun yung ku yen ch'i*, which is usually translated, 'I

Tun rose to prominence by producing salt in ponds'. It might be concluded from this that I Tun introduced artificial solar evaporation in small basins, the technique used at Yucatan and Ostia and described by Pliny and Rutilius Namatianus. But this is unlikely. All the other references to salt making in ancient Chinese texts are to artificial evaporation of brine by boiling. The character *ku* used to describe how I Tun made his salt is an uncommon one, but like the character for salt itself *yen*, its base is the cooking vessel radical. It is related to two other characters, also pronounced *ku* and based on the same radical, which mean 'a pot for boiling meat and vegetables' and 'the ditch through which salt water is led to the pans where it is evaporated'. In another Han period text, roughly contemporary with Ssu-ma Ch'ien, the *Chou-li*, which also deals with salt administration, *ku* is used in conjunction with a character *chu*, 'to warm water or cook', in a passage on boiling brine to produce salt. *Ku* therefore says nothing about ponds or solar evaporation.

What then was I Tun's innovation? The clue is supplied by the passage in the *Shih-chi* which immediately follows and describes another monied man: 'Kuo Tsung of Han Tan made a business by smelting iron'. I Tun, it may be supposed, was the first industrialist to use iron instead of pottery vessels in the manufacture of salt, an innovation which permitted a vast increase in scale of operations. Both I Tun and Kuo Tsung were associated with another monied man, Fan Li or Chu Kung, an ex-minister of King Kou-chien of Yüeh, 496–465, who came to Ch'i around the middle of the fifth century and developed long-distance trading networks. These networks were served by the salt produced by the introduction of the iron pan to the Ch'i seacoast.

The fourth major development in salt production under the Han was the opening of salt wells in the southwest: the kingdom of Shu, the western half of modern Szechwan. Here the chief source is the *Hua-yang kuo-chih* (Record of the Country South of Mount Hua), a gazetteer, the first in fact of this class of Chinese literature, composed in 347 by Ch'ang Ch'u, extracts from which about salt are usefully collected in the *Ssu-ch'uan yen-fa-chih* (Treatise on the salt laws of Szechwan) compiled by Governor-General Ting Pao-chen in 1882.[29]

Salt was produced in western Szechwan, probably from brine springs, by the pre-Chinese inhabitants before the conquest of the area by the kingdom of Ch'in which began in the reign of its king Hui-wen, 337–311 BC. Chinese predominance, however, was not fully established till the advent in the reign of Hsiao-wen in the middle of the third century BC of Governor Li Ping. He dug the first salt wells, at Chengtu, and erected the Kuan-hsien barrage to operate the amazing artificial inland delta which is still functioning today. He also sank salt wells in Chia-ting to the south, the precursors of the future Lo-shan and Chien-wei salines,

salines, and other salt wells appeared at Kuang-han to the northeast of Chengtu. What the Ch'in state began, the Han aristocracy continued. Salt wells, along with fishponds, tea gardens, copper and iron mines, regularly formed part of their colonial latifundia in Szechwan. Thus in Nan-tu, it was the Feng clan who owned the fishponds and salt wells, in Shih-fang near the head of the T'o, the Yang clan. Under the eastern Han, Chinese colonization began to move into the kingdom of Pa, eastern Szechwan. By 64 AD salt was being produced in the Yangtze gorges and production had probably commenced at Fu-shun, the site of the future great centre of Tzu-liu-ching. In the reign of Emperor Ho-ti, 89–106 AD, salt wells were sunk at Nan-pu on the upper Chia-ling, another later well-known producing area.

The development of Szechwan was of more than local significance. There can be little doubt that the mobilization of its resources played a part in the victory of Ch'in over Ch'i, which until then thanks to its salt revenue, had seemed the most likely contender for the empire of all under heaven. The same resources also played a part in the victory of the aristocracy over the state which is a leading theme of the two Han dynasties. Pan Ku, the successor of Ssu-ma Ch'ien tells us about the millionaire Lo P'ou of Chengtu who 'monopolized profits from salt wells', multiplied his capital tenfold, and used his wealth to establish an advantageous partnership at Ch'ang-an with the relatives of the future usurper Wang Mang.[30] Technologically Szechwan was advanced. The techniques for sinking and operating wells were sophisticated. In some areas, natural gas, earliest of modern energy sources, was already being used to evaporate well brine. We first hear of the so-called firewells at Lin-ch'iung, the future of Ch'iung-chou, to the west of Chengtu in the third year of Emperor Hsüan, 70 BC. Both deep drilling and natural gas had a big future before them and not only in the salt industry.

The fifth major development in the salt industry under the Han was the beginning of large-scale production in the southeast: the kingdom of Wu just south of the Yangtze in the modern province of Kiangsu. This development is associated by Ssu-ma Ch'ien with Liu P'i, the vassal king of Wu who led the revolt of 154 BC against Emperor Ching: 'Liu P'i set about inviting fugitives from all over the empire to come to his kingdom, minted cash from the copper ore in ever-increasing quantities, and boiled the sea water to extract salt, so that he was able to dispense with the poll tax, and his kingdom enjoyed great wealth and prosperity'.[31] Pan Ku adds the information that the wealth of the king of Wu equalled that of the Son of Heaven i.e. the emperor. In later times, the area immediately south of the Yangtze imported rather than produced salt, but Sung-kiang south of Shanghai was a salt-boiling centre and this may have been where Liu P'i founded his industry.

Distribution

In ancient China, even more than in the Mediterranean because society was less mobile, the economic was deeply embedded in the social. However, precocious in the physical technology of salt, China was no less so in its social technology, with the earliest development of an effective state salt administration (*yen-cheng*). The administration caused controversy. As a step towards the isolation of the economic, it was opposed by the cultured elite, the exponents of generalist, unprofessional social leadership. Controversy gave rise to literature. The *Yen-tieh lun* (Discourses on salt and iron) is wholly concerned with the salt administration, the *Kuan-tzu* partly so, and there are further passages in Ssu-ma Ch'ien and Pan Ku. Thanks to this literature a picture can be obtained of the distribution of salt in ancient China.

The earliest text on the salt administration is the *Kuan-tzu*.[32] It purports to give the economic advice of Kuan Chung, minister to Duke Huan of Ch'i, 685–643. In fact it must be dated to around 300 BC and ascribed to the ministers of King Hsüan of Ch'i, 319–301 who were struggling to maintain the predominance of their eastern state against the rise of Ch'in in the west. Through the person of Kuan-tzu the ministers advocated a state monopoly covering both domestically produced and imported salt:

> If salt is sold to our state at fifteen coins per *fu*, we can buy the salt at fifteen and sell it for one hundred. Even though we do not actually produce the commodity, all we need do is to import the commodity, and then set the resale price. We can thus take revenues from what other states produce.[33]

The ministers also envisaged an export trade:

> Your Highness may spend his excess revenue in dredging the rivers. The salt should be transported southward upstream to Liang, Chao, Sung, Wei and Pu Yang. Crude food without salt makes people suffer from swellings, so inhabitants of localities where salt is not produced will buy salt even at high prices.[34]

The ministers ended: 'Salt thus has the singularly important power to maintain the basic economy of our state. Your Highness, in felling trees and cutting straw to boil sea water into salt, will actually be taking advantage of the wealth of the whole empire'.[35] The proposal was adopted, though it was not enough to save Ch'i from Ch'in.

It was sufficiently successful, however, to be copied by Ch'in. After

the unification of China in 221 BC, the first emperor, Ch'in Shih-
huang-ti, we are told on the authority of the Confucian philosopher-
statesman Tung Chung-shu, 'made the profits on salt and iron twenty
times those of old'.[36] Relief from the monopoly was one of the boons
conferred on the empire by the early Han, but in 120 BC, on the advice of
the imperial secretary Chang T'ang, imperial secretary in the government of emperor Han Wu-ti, a salt boiler from Ch'i, Tung-kuo Hsien-
yang and an ironmaster from Nan-yang'. K'ung Chin, were appointed
to investigate the possibility of reactivating the monopoly. In 117 they
reported and recommended a system based on government control of
iron-casting: 'We propose that manufacturing of salt be leased to those
people who would furnish their own capital and undertake salt evaporation through the use of tools belonging to the government. To them the
government shall furnish evaporating pans on a rental basis'.[37] There
was to be stringent enforcement: 'Those who should dare clandestinely
to cast iron vessels or utensils, and to produce salt by evaporation,
should be fettered on the left foot, their utensils and things being
confiscated'.[38] In 116 the monopoly was put into effect, K'ung Chin
becoming minister of agriculture. In 110 this position was taken by the
rising statesman Sang Hung-yang who, as virtual prime minister, remained in charge of the salt administration for the next thirty years.

    In 81 BC, not long after the death of Han Wu-ti in 87, the salt
administration came under concerted attack from the Confucian officials. The case was argued before Emperor Chao-ti between the Confucians and Sang Hung-yang and is preserved in the *Yen-t'ieh lun*.
Superficially the argument appears to be between private enterprise and
etatism, but really it is about something prior: embedded against disem-
bedded economy, generalists against specialists, ritual against reason.
This is why the *Yen-t'ieh lun*, which represents the rapportage of the
Confucian side, provides little economic or technical information, because the Confucians rejected the professionalism such details would
imply. The debate was a stalemate. Sang Hung-yang, the Confucians'
arch-enemy fell from power the following year, but the monopoly
continued. In 44 BC in the reign of Emperor Yüan-ti, following first flood
and then famine, the throne, again under Confucian pressure, con-
sented to abolish the monopoly. But it was restored in 41 because of
budgetary exigencies, notably an expedition to Sogdia, perhaps in
attenuated form. Wang Mang reactivated the monopoly to such an
extent that it became identified with his style of government and was
abolished by the eastern Han on their restoration in 23 AD. It was briefly
restored during the reign of Emperor Chang-ti, 75–88 AD, another
period of military expansion into Central Asia. The Confucians, however, continued to oppose. Their leader, imperial secretary Chu Hui
argued: 'The Son of Heaven does not discuss possessions or non-

possessions, a lord does not discuss quantities. . . . Government sale of salt means to compete with subjects for profit. These are not measures fit for wise rulers'.[39] Thereafter the salt administration went into abeyance for 600 years.

The *yen-cheng*, unlike the *annona salaria*, was in opposition to the mores of a non-economic society, so where Emperor Aurelian strengthened the one, Emperor Chang-ti abolished the other. Control of the distribution of salt reverted to the great estates which produced it and a few great merchants like Tiao Hsien as described by Ssu-ma Ch'ien:

> The people of Ch'i generally despise slaves, but Tiao Hsien alone valued them and appreciated their worth. Most men worry in particular about slaves who are too cunning and clever, but Tiao Hsien gladly acquired all he could of this kind and put them to work for him, sending them out to make a profit peddling fish and salt . . . and in the end managed by their labour to acquire a fortune of twenty or thirty million cash. Hence the saying 'Is it better to have a title in the government or to work for Tiao Hsien?'[40]

Consumption

Our texts tell us comparatively little about how salt was consumed in ancient China. As in the Mediterranean we have to deduce it from what we know of the general food context.[41] Thus again we can be sure that most salt was used for alimentary purposes and that most alimentary salt was used in the preparation of cereal based dishes. But whereas in the west the general movement of diet in antiquity was from *puls* to *panis*, barley or emmer porridge to wheaten bread, in China the movement was from millet chupattis to wheat noodles in the north and to boiled rice in the south. In both areas, however, the Mediterranean and China, the probable mechanism behind the movements was the change from the simple pestle and mortar of Mesolithic times to its inverted form the rotary milor quern. The rotary mill could be operated by hand, animal power or by water, and by the end of antiquity the water mill was a major instrument of cereal processing in both west and east. But whereas in the west this development took place within the context of non-kinship institutions – the *polis*, the Roman super-*polis* and especially the imperial *limes*, in the east it took place within the context of a kinship institution, the great estate which could 'close its gates and become a market in itself'.[42]

Another similarity in difference between the Mediterranean and China was the importance of fish in the diet. But whereas in the Mediterranean this meant chiefly naturally-bred sea fish, in China it meant chiefly artificially-bred pond fish. The invention of this kind of

pisciculture in China is ascribed to the millionaire ex-bureaucrat Fan Li
or Chu Kung, the friend of the salt boiler I Tun and the ironmaster Kuo
Tsung, around 450 BC. Fish ponds in the interior and iron salt pans on
the coast went conveniently together, just as at a later date the aristocratic estates of Szechwan combined fishponds and salt wells.

Salt was from early antiquity a normal part of Chinese diet. The
Shu-ching of *c*. 800 BC names salt as the first of the five primary flavours
along with bitter, sour, acrid and sweet, which in turn derived from the
five elements – water, fire, wood, metal and earth. Mencius, 372–289,
wishing to describe the lowly origins of a minister, says that he came
from a background of selling fish and salt. The *Kuan-tzu*, *c*. 300 BC,
ventures the first estimate for *per capita* salt consumption: 'A man
consumes four and a half *sheng* of salt per month; a woman two and a
half; a child one and a half'.[43] A family of husband, wife and two
children would thus consume 10 *sheng* a month, 120 *sheng* a year, a *per
capita* annual average of 30 *sheng*. The *sheng* was a unit of capacity, a
hundredth part of a *shih* which in pre-Han times was the equivalent of 10
litres. Thirty *sheng* would thus be the equivalent of 3 litres of salt which
would weigh approximately 6 lb. This is a rather high figure for a
premodern society: Cato only allowed 2 lb a head for his slaves. But it is
a possible figure, and of course if one assumes four children instead of
two, it falls to just over 5 lb. No doubt too the authors of the *Kuan-tzu*
were rounding out and perhaps exaggerating the fiscal benefits they
hoped to attain. Yet it may well be that consumption of salt in China,
thanks to superior methods of production and more aggressive marketing, was higher than anywhere else in the ancient world. China had
reached the critical 5 lb *per capita* ceiling: the other classical civilizations
had not. A disequilibrium had opened up between east and west in
production, distribution and consumption. A flow of technology, institutions and lifestyle from China to the non-Chinese world was thus to
be expected.

3 The Dark and Light Ages

The term 'dark ages' is familiar enough in connection with the period 500 to 1000. However, as applied to world history, it suffers from Europocentrism, even West-Europocentrism. For in China, Islam and Eastern Europe, these, far from being dark ages, were ages of maximum light. In China, Emperor Hsüan-tsung, 712–756, under whom T'ang institutions and culture reached their height and the Chinese empire its greatest extent, was actually known as *ming-huang*, the emperor of light. In Islam, the reign of Caliph Haroun al-Rashid, 789–809, is generally regarded as the apogee of early Islamdom. In Eastern Europe, Emperor Basil II Bulgaroctonus, 963–1023, recovered not only Bulgaria but also Antioch and Armenia, besides strengthening control in southern Italy and effecting the conversion of Rus in 988. Against these achievements, it is the darkness of Western Europe, the successive failures of the Goths, the Merovingians and the Carolingians, which seems anomalous. Yet there was one common feature of the history of Eurasia between 500 and 1000. If antiquity had been the age of classics, what followed it was the age of scripture and exegesis. To the languages of the classics and the words of the philosophers was now added the Word of revelation: Bible and Tradition, Koran and *hadith*, *sutra* and *sastra*, *t'ung* and *fu*, Gita and Vedanta. Everywhere the Word created new institutions for its hearers, notably military and monastic institutions strangely linked, but also a new climate of opinion which cut through the elitism, sexism and generalism of antiquity to produce solidarity, feminism and expertise.[1] Where Western Europe differed was that with the collapse of empire and the failure of attempts to restore it, those institutions and that climate came to lodge not, as elsewhere, in an imperial state, but in a non-imperial society, whose early political failures produced darkness rather than light.

Salt therefore functioned in a new institutional milieu in the dark and light ages. This milieu brought both advantages and disadvantages. On the one hand, salt benefited from the democratization of foodstuffs, from the lavishness of armies, from the wider diffusion of the tastes of pastoral people, from Lent and Friday fasting which encouraged meat eating at other times and raised the level of protein consumption. On the other hand, salt was injured by Hindu and Buddhist vegetarianism, by Taoist dietary techniques, and by Ramadan and by the Muslim prohibition of pork. On balance, however, salt benefited. In production, the period saw the beginnings of the new process of successive basin solar evaporation which was to dominate world supply until the nineteenth century. In distribution, it saw an increase in the mobility of salt

47

by both river and sea, a widening of market horizons, and the first major government involvement in long-distance trade. In consumption, demand for salt was expanded by the needs of barbarian armies, consumerist capitals and religious foundations. Yet the dark and light ages were a seed time rather than a harvest. By 1000 change had not gone far. Moreover, it was not yet clear that the richest harvest of the coming of the Word was not to be in light Byzantium, Islam or China, but in dark Western Europe.

SALT IN T'ANG CHINA

Under the T'ang dynasty, 618–907, China, politically reunited after four centuries of division, was the largest and most highly organized state in the world, its society the most populous and affluent, its ideology, Buddhist and Taoist, the fullest articulated in social institutions and critical thought. These facts reflected themselves in striking advances in the production, distribution and consumption of salt.

Production

Here the most significant development was the beginning of successive basin solar evaporation at the An-i *hsien* salt lake of Ho-tung salt division in present day Shansi province. Before examining the evidence and establishing the chronology, let us be clear as to what this development involved.

The Chinese term for solar evaporation was *shai* and it was contrasted with artificial boiling *chien*. But just as there is more than one kind of *chien*, so there was more than one kind of *shai*. First, there was *natural* solar evaporation, occurring spontaneously and without human intervention, on the edge of the sea, marine lagoons and salt lakes, in desert salt basins, and beside salt springs. Such natural evaporation by the sun, sometimes aided by the wind, was man's earliest source of salt, as it had been for the animals from whom he learnt it. It required no investment beside the labour of collection and no scientific knowledge. Widely diffused and exploited in the Near and Middle East, such sources of supply were known in medieval Europe by the Arabic-derived name of *sebkha*. The Chinese were familiar with *sebkas* from the salt lakes of the Sino-Mongolian borderlands and used the term *lao-ts'ai* (lit., 'dragging and gathering') for the process. Second, there was *simple* solar evaporation in a single artificially constructed basin: sometimes two basins if the brine was first reinforced by saline earth, sand, plants or ash. This technique required some capital investment and some scientific knowledge, but essentially the sun and wind were left to do their

work. Single basin evaporation was used by Africans at Katwe; by the
Romans at the mouth of the Tiber and on the Tuscan coast;[2] by Indians
on the Rann of Kutch and at Didwana in Rajasthan, perhaps also in the
south of their peninsula, in Travancore and the Tamil Nadu; by Chinese
in Fukien and Kwangtung before the time of the Ming dynasty; and by
the Mayas in Yucatan. Single basin solar evaporation was a widespread
and often invented technique.

Third, there was *complex* or successive basin solar evaporation, which
used a series of artificially constructed basins for catchment or storage,
concentration, condensation and crystallization. The number and length
of the series (its terms and their subdivision) varied according to local
circumstances of terrain, the original salinity of the brine used, weather
and the degree of purity desired, but was always more than two. In the
nineteenth century, the total number of basins at Ho-tung was 8, in
Ch'ang-lu 7 or 9, in Manchuria 19 or 21, in Shantung 5, in Huai-pei 9.
The basins were usually divided into three groups: catchment or concen-
trators, condensers and crystallizers. Moreover, there was often a fixed
ratio of five to one of the combined catchment and condensers to the
crystallizers. In the first, brine reached the degree of salinity at which its
component minerals began to deposit, in the second, unwanted calcium
compounds deposited; in the third, sodium chloride deposited and
could be removed without contamination from the equally unwanted
magnesium compounds. This technique demanded much capital investment and considerable scientific knowledge: the chemical composition
of the brine, the order of sedimentation of its various compounds, the
rate of evaporation in different meteorological conditions. It was
capable, however, of producing salt of a high degree of purity. Furthermore, sometimes more important to the premodern consumer, it was
capable of producing different kinds of salt: fine, small grained, castor
salt if the process was used quickly; coarse, large grained, granulated
salt if the process was used slowly; fast or slow often depending more
on the weather than the salt-maker. Successive basin solar evaporation
was at first a restricted and probably once invented technique: invented
in China, at the An-i *hsien* salt lake of Ho-tung.

In modern times, the form of solar evaporation practised at the An-i
hsien lake was known as *chih-hsi chiao-shai* (lit., 'establish fields, pour and
solar evaporate')[3] or *hsi-shai* (lit., 'field solar evaporation') for short. In
the final edition of the *Yen-cheng shih-lu* (veritable records of the salt
administration),[4] the *hsi* are described as 100 feet long and 70 feet broad
and divided into eight sections (*tuan*). Brine was assembled in the first
section, concentrated in section 2 where it began to turn red, and
evaporated in sections 3 to 7 to allow the calcium to deposit. In section 8,
salt crystals began to form on the surface and could be collected, leaving
behind the bitterns – the bitter magnesium salts. This process, which

could supply salt of up to 95 per cent purity, had been in continuous use at An-i *hsien* since the late Ming or early Ch'ing.

The earliest reference to *hsi* in connection with salt making at An-i *hsien* is in Tu Yu's *t'ung-tien* or institutional encyclopaedia of around 800 AD, which refers to three grades of salt-making *hsi*, upper, middle and lower – *shang*, *chung*, *hsia*. A little later, the T'ang *literatus* Ts'ui Ao mentions not only the *hsi* but specifically *hsi-shai* as a process. Did *hsi-shai* mean in the ninth century what it meant in the seventeenth: i.e. a *succession* of basins? There are a number of indications to suggest that it did. Ts'ui Ao's description is not easy to follow, but it portrays a complex system of dykes, gutters, wells, watercourses and *hsi*, which sounds more than a battery of single evaporation basins. Another T'ang author, the poet Liu Tsung-yuan, writing in 808, says, again rather vaguely, that watercourses, dykes, *hsi* and lesser fields 'communicate alternately in a spiral' (*chiao-ts'o lun-chun*)[5] which is further suggestive of successive basins. The term *hsi* reappears in the Sung, and though the lake reverted to being a *sebkha* using the *lao-ts'ai* method in the Yüan and early Ming, the compilers in the early Ch'ing of the *Ho-tung yen-fa-chih* (treatise on the Ho-tung salt laws) clearly regarded the *chih-hsi chiao-shai* method then in use as the same as that used under the T'ang.

Indeed, the *hsi-shai* method probably goes back before the T'ang. In the reign of the second T'ang emperor T'ai-tsung, 627–650, there was already a temple to the weather god at An-i *hsien*, significant because the behaviour of the wind was the crucial factor in the *hsi-shai* method. A Ming writer refers to *hsi* as a Liang term, the Liang being the legitimate dynasty between 502 and 557, while the Toba Wei ruler Hsüan Wu-ti, 499–515, who had actual control of the An-i *hsien* area, set up some kind of government office to control the salt lake. Before this, the trail gives out, but it would be reasonable to associate the beginning of the *hsi-shai* method with the founding in 493 of the new Toba Wei capital at Loyang, just across the Yellow River from An-i *hsien*. The new capital was a luxury city designed to fuse the aristocracies of the invading Toba and the indigenous Chinese[6] and it will have demanded quality salt, which could not be supplied by the natural *lao-ts'ai shai* of the northwest lakes or the primitive earth salt already boiled in Shansi, but which could be supplied by the more capital intensive and scientific procedure of *chih-hsi chiao-shai*. The annual production in the high T'ang period has been estimated at 200 000 cwt, more than enough for a city which, in the days of Empress Wu when it was again an imperial capital, was credited with a population of a million.

The long-term significance of the beginning of successive basin solar evaporation at An-i *hsien* should not obscure the importance of other developments in China in the same period.

First, artificial boiling (*chien*) of sea water, which had been the mainstay of salt production in China since the time of Kuan-tzu, was further expanded. It expanded from its two home territories of Ch'i and Wu, Shantung and Kiangsu south of the Yangtze, to meet in the region south of the Huai, the future Huai-nan in Kiangsu north of the Yangtze. The appearance of these new salines, which were eventually to become the most important in China, may be associated with the development of Nanking as an imperial city of one million people during the *Nan-pei ch'ao*, the period of the northern and southern dynasties, in particular under the Liang dynasty.[7] In the T'ang period, marine *chien* salt still provided about two thirds of the salt consumed in China or around 2 400 000 cwt.

Next, the period 500 to 1000 saw considerable development in another *chien* salt, the Szechwan well brine-boiling industry, particularly in the eighth and early ninth centuries, when the number of wells rose from 90 to 640. Most of this development took place in the centre of the province between the Min and the T'o, the T'ang circuit of Chien-nan. Here there were 460 wells as compared to 136 in the north and west and 41 in the southeast. The foundations of this expansion had been laid earlier. The opening of the Ling-chou well in Jen-shou, supposedly 300 feet broad and 800 feet deep, was associated with the names of the Taoist patriarch Chang Tao-ling and his grandson Chang Lu in the closing years of the Han. Technology and Taoism were frequently linked at this time and the theocracy the Changs founded in Szechwan was probably based in part on the well owning gentry of the province. Under the Chin, 265 to 420, we hear of development in the Yangtze gorges: 100 wells at Yun-yang, 20 in Wan-hsien; and Ling-chou received further attention in the reign of Hsiao-wu between 376 and 396. Yen-t'ing saline was founded in 535 under the Liang, while the salines of P'eng-shui in the southeast triangle are first mentioned under the Sui. The real take-off, however, was in the golden eighth century. By the end of it, Fu-shun had seven wells, its neighbours Jung-hsien and Wei-yuan 15 and 16 apiece, Tzu-chou at least 11, Nei-chiang 26, all these places being in the favoured Min T'o region. Drilling had improved. Fu-shun is credibly reported at 250 feet under the T'ang, Ling-chou by the tenth century at 500 feet, while the deepest we hear of under the Han is the 30 feet fire well at Ch'iung-chou. Only two production figures are given by the *Ssu-ch'uan yen-fa-chih*: Fu-shun 3600 cwt and Ling-chou 8000 cwt. If 640 wells are averaged at 500 cwt each, it would give a provincial production of 320 000 cwt, about a tenth of China's total. Even so some salt had to be imported into the northern part of the province from the An-i *hsien* lake. Szechwan was already a rich province, under Emperor Hsüan-tsung, the fief of the Yang family, court nobility and relatives of his famous consort Yang Kuei-fei.

Finally, with the shift of imperial power westward and the rise in importance in the eighth century of the frontier armies or *chün*, salt produced by natural evaporation in the lakes of the Sino-Mongolian borderland was increasingly called into contribution. The borderland lakes provided the coarse salt for the northwest armies, as the An-i *hsien hsi-shai* process provided the fine for the imperial capitals. The *Hsin T'ang-shu* mentions 13 lakes in use. Four were in Yen-chou prefecture in northern Shensi and corresponded with the modern Hua-ma chih, a long-term rival of An-i *hsien*,[8] and the Otogh lakes of the Ordos. Seven were in Ling-chou and corresponded to the lakes of Ninghsia: Abalai, Alabruka, Ho-tun and Chilantai. One was in western Kansu and another, Hu-lo, in An-pei military protectorate, may be identified with one or other of the salt lakes of Chahar. No doubt the borderland salt lakes had supplied China occasionally since antiquity or before, but it is in the T-ang period that they are first specified as regular suppliers. Given that armies are large consumers, they may have provided as much as 70 000 cwt a year. The lakes themselves are generally under military control.

T'ang China thus obtained its salt by four distinct methods: natural *shai* in the borderlands; well *chien* in Szechwan with wood, natural gas or coal as the fuel; marine *chien* on the coast with wood as the fuel; and the new process, complex *shai* at the An-i *hsien* lake.

Distribution

Despite the building of the Grand Canal, the T'ang empire, like its predecessor was a road state. Indeed, thanks to the development of the inland salines of Shansi, Szechwan, and the northwest borderlands, it is likely that a higher percentage of salt travelled by land than under the Han. Shansi and borderland salt certainly travelled by land. Liu Tsung-yuan describes the transport from An-i *hsien* as by donkey, mule, ox and horse: west to Shansi and Kansu, south to Hupei, north to Hopei and east to Honan.[9] Borderland salt used the same animals and camels as well, Szechwan had a good river network, but the considerable number of production sites suggests a pattern of mainly localized trade by pack animal: what later would be called the *p'iao-an*. Only in those regions supplied by maritime salt was transport mainly by water.

We know something of the pattern of this waterborne trade through the biggest change in distribution in the T'ang period: the reintroduction of the salt administration, suspended since the beginning of the Eastern Han, in 763 by Liu Yen, minister to Emperor Tai-tsung, 762–779, one of the greatest of Chinese administrators. The background to this was the rebellion of the frontier marshal An Lu-shan against Emperor Hsüan-tsung in 755; the bare survival of the empire under his son Su-tsung as many provinces seceded, and the pressing need under his grandson Tai-tsung for a new source of revenue, requiring only selective territorial control, but available in the southeast, whence came the grain supplies for the imperial capitals.

Liu Yen met this need by having himself appointed special commissioner for salt and grain transport, and by using the revenue of the Chiang-huai salt administration, the future salt divisions of Huai-nan and Liang-che, to finance the dispatch of grain from the Yangtze delta along the Grand Canal to Ch'ang-an. Liu established his headquarters at Yang-chou on the north bank of the Yangtze where the Grand Canal crossed the river on its way northwest. The Chiang-huai administration functioned at three levels. First, near the coast were the *chien*, directorates, which bought the salt from the producers and sold it to the transport merchants who moved it to the consuming areas. The principal *chien* were Chia-hsing, Hsin-t'ing, Lin-p'ing and Lan-t'ing in the old kingdom of Wu south of the Yangtze and Yen-ch'eng and Hai-ling in the new Huai salines north of it. The official sale price included the tax which could amount to ten times the cost price. Second, at some but no great distance from the salines, there were four *ch'ang*, markets: Hu-chou, Hang-chou and Yueh-chou in the south, Lien-shui in the north; to which the officials transported salt and from which the merchants purchased it. A mixture of sales promotion and desire to curb the smuggling which was prevalent on the coast was probably the reason for this alternative sales outlet. Third, there were 13 *hsün-yuan*, branch establishments on transport routes and in consuming areas. One function was surveillance: to make sure that all salt passing through or being disembarked had paid tax and had not been smuggled from the boiling pans. Another may have been tax collection. Although the rule was taxation at source, at the *chien* or *ch'ang* (*chiu-ch'ang cheng-shui*) on the principle first tax then salt (*hsien-k'o hou-yen*), in practice it may have suited both officials and merchants to take only a token at source and to collect the bulk of what was due on the resale of the salt at the *hsün-yuan* to the provincial distributor, on the principle first salt then tax (*hsien-yen hou-k'o*). In this way the officials would receive their taxes where they needed them, on the Grand Canal, while the transport merchants would require less capital for their business since the tax, the greater part of the outlay, would be paid in effect by the local distributors. This was certainly the system after the T'ang period and it may have been in operation from near the beginning.

At any rate the locations of the *hsün-yuan* provide us with a map of the distribution of Chiang-huai salt, the largest network in China. The principal consuming area was the canal zone of eastern Honan and northern Anhwei. Thus in Honan, the *hsün-yuan* of Cheng-hua, Pien-chou (Kaifeng), Cheng-hu and Sung-chou (Kuei-te) were on the Grand Canal, while that of Huai-hsi (Ju-kuang) was connected with it by the Huai river. In Anhwei, Yung-ch'iao and Ssu-chou were on the Grand

Canal, as was Yang-chou *hsün-yuan* in Kiangsu. A secondary consuming area lay southwest along the Yangtze in western Kiangsu and central and southern Anhwei. Here were the *hsün-yuan* of Che-hsi (Chinkiang), Pai-sha (I-cheng) and Lu-shou (Ho-fei). The remaining two *hsün-yuan* supplied outlying regions in eastern Shantung and western Honan.

On all these routes trade was conducted by privileged merchants working closely with the officials. Chinese salt administrators evolved a convenient shorthand for describing the various ways of organizing the distribution of salt. The terms *kuan*, official, *shang*, privileged merchant, and *min*, the people, i.e. anyone, were used to qualify various functions or phases in the business: *tu* (supervision), *pan* (management), *chih* (manufacture), *shou* (initial acquisition), *yün* (transportation), *hsiao* (distribution), *mai* (sales). In terms of this analysis, the system established by Liu Yen was *min-chih kuan-shou shang-yün shang-hsiao* (people manufacture, officials acquire, merchants transport, merchants distribute). Because tax and transport increased the capital required in the business, the merchants were men of substance, a *de facto* monopoly before being a *de jure* one. A late T'ang poem describes a merchant putting his two sons into the salt and timber trades, which together with tea, formed the triple basis for the rise of the merchant class. From time to time, Chinese officials considered taking a greater share of the business, *kuan-yün kuan-hsiao* (officials transport, officials distribute), but the idea was always rejected on the score of bureaucratic over-extension, the consequent danger of corruption and the difficulty of procuring capital on the scale required. Against one such proposal in 822 the famous Neo-Confucian moralist and stylist Han Yü wrote a celebrated memorial.[10]

Chiang-huai was the most sophisticated of the new distribution agencies and the largest in terms of salt handled, but from 763, the monopoly was applied, though less effectively, at other salines. Because of the virtual independence of their governors, the marine *chien* salines of Hopei and Shantung, perhaps a third of the total, never really formed part of the imperial monopoly. In 819, at the height of Emperor Hsien-tsung's reassertion of power, Chiang-huai established two offices in Shantung and one in Hopei, but they had to be abandoned in 822. The inland salines required less control than those of the coast. The An-i *hsien* salt was controlled by the *tu-chih*, department of public revenue, a branch of the *hu-pu*, the board of revenue in Ch'ang-an, itself then a section of the *shang-shu sheng* or department of state. Most likely there were officials at the lake performing the same functions as the *chien* in Chiang-huai. A considerable revenue was collected. The *tu-chih* also came to control the salt wells of Szechwan, but here the localized nature of the trade prevented much government interference. In theory too, the *tu-chih* was in charge of the salt lakes of the borderlands, but in practice they were at the disposal of their military commanders.

Consumption

No estimates for *per capita* consumption of salt, like those of the *Kuan-tzu*, have survived from the T'ang. Moreover, although the T'ang give us our earliest production figures for individual centres, they were complied by literati not overly interested in such details and are not entirely satisfactory. Nevertheless, since the size of population had not much changed while the number of producing centres had increased, and in general T'ang China was more urbanized and affluent than Han China, it would be reasonable to suppose that consumption of salt expanded from, say 5 lb per head in 250 to 7 lb in 750. This rise in consumption was shaped by three factors.

First, between Han and T'ang there was a revolution in Chinese agriculture. The average size of family farm roughly doubled through the expansion of the women's section of agriculture: pigs, chickens and ducks, and silk worms. Meat was still a luxury, but one more widely available, and the early eighth-century pharmacologist Meng Shen felt it worthwhile to warn against beef and too much pork. Concomitant with the rise of meat was an increase in the intake of pepper, both the native fagara (*chiao*) and black pepper (*hu-chiao*, barbarian pepper) from Southeast Asia. In literature, pepper and salt were frequently linked and contrasted as fancy and plain. But in truth where pepper was, salt was likely to be too.

Second, T'ang China, like the later Roman empire and early dark age Europe, was influenced by the life-style of the *limes*, in China's case by the world of the steppe where both meat and salt were abundant. The T'ang histories emphasize the supply of the frontier armies as a component of the salt trade. The *Old T'ang History* tells us that in 727 Hsiao Sung, president of the board of war, was appointed commissioner for the salt lakes of Kuan-nei, that is those of Hua-ma-ch'ih and Ning-hsia, and that hereafter this position was regularly conjoined to that of Shuo-fang *chieh-tu-shih* or military governor of this part of the frontier. One of the later holders of the Shuo-fang post was An Ssu-shun, cousin of the rebel An Lu-shan, and another was the Nestorian general Kuo Tzu-i who was in charge of the suppression of the rebellion. The *New T'ang History* tells us that the T'ien-ti and Chen-wu armies of the An-pei protectorate – general in modern Suiyuan were supplied from Hu-lo salt lake: probably Er-lien, a white salt lake in West Sunit in modern Chahar; while the Yu-chou, Ta-t'ung and Heng-ye armies of the An-tung protectorate general in northern Shansi and Chihli operated *yen-t'un*, military agricultural colonies for salt, which probably worked the earth salt deposits of what was later known as Chin-pei. As in Europe, the *limes* life-style involved more meat, and more meat involved more salt. We hear of a son of the great Emperor T'ai-tsung at the beginning of the seventh century, who could even bring himself to eat the unchinese foodstuff of mutton.

Finally, there was the impact of Buddhism. In some ways, as an ascetic, vegetarian religion, Buddhism inhibited the consumption of salt. Moreover, Indian cooking which invaded China in the T'ang period and began to convert it from something more like Japanese cuisine to 'Chinese' cuisine, emphasized hot and sweet rather than salt and bitter. Yet on balance Buddhism encouraged the consumption of salt, for in China it was a religion of the rich laity, a spirituality of luxury and expenditure. In the diary of the Japanese monk Ennin who visited China toward the middle of the ninth century, we hear so much of the *chai* or vegetarian banquets that such laity gave to monks, that one infers that banquets where religious were absent were *not* vegetarian. Moreover, sophisticated vegetarianism encouraged the use of pickles and under the T'ang salt and vinegar were prime modes of pickling. Again, Buddhism increased sensibility. In particular it heightened the sense of smell, and one of the peculiarities of salt is that while it has so pronounced a taste, in pure forms it has virtually no smell, certainly not an unpleasant smell.

T'ang China was the most civilized society of its day. A new method of salt production, a new partnership between government and business in distribution, and new levels of consumption, were significant ingredients in that civilization.

SALT IN EARLY ISLAM

If T'ang China was the most civilized place in the Dark Ages, early Islamdom ran it a close second. Moreover, the world of the Abbasids was in touch with China and drew on Chinese achievements, diffusing them as Needham has shown, elsewhere.[11] Yet where T'ang China was the product of a restoration, conservative in form but radical in substance because of new elements implanted in its nucleus, early Islamdom was the product of a counter-cultural revolution, radical in form but conservative in substance because the elements of antiquity were reshuffled rather than renewed. Early Islamdom, in the universe of salt as in other fields, was more significant as relay – from antiquity, from India, from China – than as point of origin. As Newman saw, in the age of revelations, Islam had no new doctrine except its own divine origin.[12] In this case it is best to take the categories of production, distribution and consumption in reverse order.

Consumption

The coming of Islam everywhere increased the consumption of salt. When statistics first became available, they reveal a *per capita* consumption of salt in Islamdom closer to that of early modern Europe than to those of premodern India or China. Thus in the nineteenth century, the Ottoman empire, the richest of the Islamic lands, had an annual consumption of 16 lb per head, while Chinese Turkestan, one of the poorest, had a consumption of 15 lb per head, as compared to China, generally 9–10 lb and India 8 lb. Prestatistical evidence suggests that these high levels were not new. In Abbasid times, there was a saying 'salt in cooking is as necessary as grammar in speech' (*al-milh fil ta-am kal nahw fil kalam*).[13] Maimonides, doctor as well as philosopher, recommended the use of much salt in bread making. Another doctor warned against too much salt, and in the tenth century, *halum*, a salted cheese, was regarded as the characteristic food of Egypt,[14] while in Iraq salt fish was the principal source of protein for the poor. In Iraq too, much salt was used in preservation, notably in the fried meat product known as *namaksud*. In the Nejd, Doughty found in every Bedouin tent a store which contained 'certain lumps of rock salt, for they will eat nothing insipid'.[15]

The coming of Islam raised the consumption of salt because it raised all consumption. Contrary to what is often supposed, early Islam, or more accurately the Islamdom it created,[16] was not an austere religion. The desert, whose isolated communities of camel-drivers and itinerant merchants, hitherto dependent on alien caravan cities, had been united by Islam and mobilized against the sedentary world, gave it familiarity with animals as food. But early Islamic diet was not that of the Bedouin, who lived off the milk products of his animals and ate meat sparingly. Evolved not in the desert, but in subdesert palaces and in camp cities on the edge of the conquered territories, early Islamic diet mixed the occasional meat banquet of the Bedouin with the best non-meat dishes the sedentary world had to offer. The result was what must have seemed to nomad and sedentarist alike a kind of party *en permanence*: meat, wheat bread instead of barley, fruit, and sugar – Turkish delights. In comparison with this alimentary luxury in which the convert to Islam might hope to participate, the prohibitions against pork and alcohol were only details, shibboleths of the community.

For the high consumptivity of early Islam was underpinned by its unique sociology. From the reign of the Caliph al-Mutasim, 833–842, the leading institution in the Islamic community was the professional army of privileged slaves, *mamluks*, for whom the caliph built the city of Samarra and who, under his successors, became first overmighty subjects and then ruling servants. Peacetime soldiers are notoriously extravagant, especially in matters of food. Samarra was built on a lavish scale. The mosque was the biggest in the world, its minaret a replica of the tower of Babel; marble was brought from Latakia and from the shrine of St Menas outside Alexandria; while the city gates came from Amorium in Phrygia newly conquered from the Byzantines. Regulation houses in the city had up to 50 rooms apiece, with special quarters arranged around courtyards for men and women, summer and winter. Against such a background food consumption was high. Not everyone in Islamdom lived like a *mamluk*, but it is the apex of society which sets the standard and whose conspicuous consumption in the long run becomes the norm. At the beginning of the sixteenth century, Leo Africanus tells us that at Fez, a typical Islamic capital, 'The common sort did set on the pot with fresh meat every week, but the gentleman and richer sort every day, and as often as they list' – generally twice a day.[17] In seventeenth-century Constantinople, a city of 7–800 000, the citizens consumed 7 million sheep and goats a year as well as 200 000 cattle.[18] By its origin and in its development Islam encouraged the consumption of meat and hence of salt.

Distribution

Since sources of salt were widely available in early Islamdom, long-distance distribution was not a major problem. Islam, however, raised standards of salt as of other things, and some sources came to be preferred over others. In Abbasid Baghdad, we are told, 'two kinds of salt were used: the ordinary common salt and the Andarani salt, the latter variety being the more prized. *Milh Andarani* was brought from the rocks of Andaran, a place near Nishapur. . . . 'The cooking manuals preferred Andarane salt for all varieties of cooking'.[19] Nishapur, in Khorasan, was some distance from Baghdad or Samarra, so that here, and no doubt in the case of other Islamic capital, new consumption did produce a new demand for distribution. It was a demand which early Islam readily met.

First, Islam was founded on local camel networks, like the butter caravan of 170 camels which Doughty accompanied from Aneyza to Mecca.[20] Like all successful societies, early Islamdom invested in itself and became a cause as well as an effect of the predominance of the camel over the cart in the Middle East. Any estimate of world camel population at successive dates must be conjectural, but the following hypothesis may be advanced. In 1981 world camel population was 15 million, of which 5 million were in Somalia, 2.5 million in Arabia, and the remaining 7.5 million scattered in Syria, Iraq, Turkey, North Africa, Persia and the Turkestans, subsidiarily also in India, China and Australia. The

Islamic explosion, it may be supposed, increased the percentage of camels outside the Somalo-Arabian nucleus from one sixth to one half. At the same time, the number of camels inside the nucleus probably increased by a factor of three. On these assumptions, in 600 AD, there will have been a total of 3 million camels: 2.5 million in the nucleus, 500 000 outside. For those outside the nucleus, an even arithmetical progression would give 2.5 million camels by 1000 AD, 5 million by 1500 and 7.5 million by 1900. Hence between 600 and 1000 Islam quintupled the number of camels outside the nucleus. In the fourth century Synesius of Cyrene regarded 5000 camels as a probable figure for the herds of a whole tribe; while in the eleventh century the geographer al-Bakri spoke of 1000 camels a day entering the market of Badja in the hinterland of Tunis to transport grain long distance, which would imply a pool of some tens of thousands.[21] In the nineteenth century Tuareg tribes could mobilize 10 000 camels and in the twentieth nearly 30 000.[22]

Second, Islam gave the merchant an honoured place in the *umma*, the community of the faithful. In view of theories of 'capitalist religions', Weber's Calvinism, Gernet's Mahayana, this remark needs amplification. It does not mean that Islamic institutions objectively and in the long run were favourable to the growth of a capitalist economy. Indeed, the Dark Age Christian attitude of *mercator vix Christianus* may have done more in this direction, by putting business into a secular sphere of the economic, than the partial Muslim sacralization of the merchant. It does not mean either that early Islam appealed especially to merchants or that many early Muslims were merchants. Hitti notes that, 'The early merchants were Christians, Jews and Zoroastrians'[23] and it was not until the Abbasids that a Muslim merchant class developed. What the statement does mean is that the early caliphate and *sharia* (religious law) placed no obstacles in the way of a calling which had been followed by the Prophet himself.

Finally, early Islam was a religion of mobility. It deracinated individuals, giving them a new identity, often a new name, in the religious community. It redefined social obligations, providing new neighbours and new enemies. It deterritorialized allegiances, taking people from one end of Islamdom to another. Soldiers recruited in Khorasan might end their service in Morocco. All this fostered distribution in the common market of Islamdom.

Production

Supply too was not at first a major problem. Arabia contained numerous natural solar salines, the word *sebkha* itself, as mentioned above, being of Arab origin. Doughty is witness for the northwest Nejd. There were three major producing areas: the sea at Wejh; 'the mountain Misma, for the provision of Hayil',[24] the local capital; and most important of all, Teyma. Here,

> 'In the grounds below the last cultivated soil, are salt beds, the famous *memlahat Teyma*. Thither resort the poorer Beduins, to dig it freely: and this is much, they say, sweeter to their taste than the sea-salt from Wejh. Teyma rock-salt is the daily source of the thousand nomad kettles in all these parts of Arabia'.[25]

Apart from these major producing areas much salt was there for the picking up. On the route to Medina between Hayil and Kheybar, 'there is many times seen upon the lava fields a glistering under the sun as of distant water; it is but dry clay glazed over with salt'.[26] Near Aneyza, 'all the nigh valley grounds were white with *subbakha* . . . there is a salt bed, where salt is digged for Aneyza'.[27] On the route between Aneyza and Mecca, 'near the sunsetting we rode over a wide ground crusted with salt'.[28] St John Philby is witness for the southeast Nejd. Between Aneyza and Riyadh, there is frequent mention of 'the salty sabkha surface', as well as a description of a major deposit which 'forms a self-contained basin having the appearance of a vast frozen lake covered with snow'. 'From this salt-pan', Philby continues, 'the people of Sirr, Mudhnib and Aushaziya draw their supplies, having a prescriptive right to carry away as much as they please without payment'.[29] In the Nejd, therefore, the original sword arm of Islam, supply was not a problem.

It was not a problem either in the nearer Islamic lands. In Syria, there were salt deposits near Aleppo and in the Lebanon. Outside Iraq, there were the natural solar salines of the Persian Gulf, as well as the more distant mines of Nishapur and Ormuz. Inside Iraq, there were the widespread salines we noted in Chapter 1. Egypt still had the sources of supply it had in antiquity and in addition new natural marine salines at Damietta. In the further Islamic lands too, in so far as these belonged to the desert belt, supply was no problem. In north Africa, Islam took over and developed the northern latitudinal subworld of salines from Senegal to Darfur. In Central Asia, Chinese sources reveal a similar pattern of a few major and many minor sources of supply.

Thus in twentieth-century Sinkiang, 32 out of the 77 *hsien* produced salt and probably others could have if it had been economic. In Zungharia, the northern half of the province, there were eight sources, four major, four minor. The major sources were the lakes of Ching-ho near Ebi-nor which supplied Ili; the Ta-pan lakes southeast of Urumehi which supplied the capital; the T'ang-ch'ao-ch'u lakes out in the steppe near Airan Kol which supplied Manas and Chuguchak; and the Ch'i-chuech-ching lakes northeast of Turfan which supplied Barkol and Hami. All these lakes produced by natural evaporation and salt only needed collection by human labour. In addition there were four minor sources: the Hu-t'u-pi basin in Chang-ch'i *hsien* west of Urumchi; Barkol lake; Wu-su basin between Manas and Ili; and two small lakes at Chuguchak. In the Tarim basin, in the south of the province, 24 places produced salt and most of the major oases had a source close at hand. Thus Turfan had soda and stone salt; Karashahr had basin and soda salt; Kucha had rock salt, earth salt, soda salt and basin salt; Aksu and Osh Turfan had rock salt; Kashgar had soda brine; Yarkand had rock salt and soda salt; and Khotan had soda salt, stone salt and earth salt. All these sources would have been available to the first Muslim rulers of the country, the Karakhanids, in the tenth century.

But beyond the desert belt, Islamdom with its high consumption, ran short and had to capture, stimulate or create new sources of supply. Syria in later times imported from Egypt or Turkey and maybe already needed to do so. It is significant that the first maritime expedition ever made by Muslim forces was that of the Emir Muawiya to Cyprus in 653, which resulted in the occupation of the two salt lakes of Larnaca. Since the Larnacan lakes were one of the few sources of supply to continue uninterruptedly from antiquity to the Middle Ages, it is difficult not to see this expedition as in part designed to secure salt for Muslim Damascus. Similarly, on the opposite frontier of Islam, the opening of single basin solar evaporation works at Sultanpur in the Punjab and of successive basin solar evaporation works at the Sambhar and Bharatpur salt lakes in Rajasthan, are associated with the earliest days of Islam in India. These works were probably stimulated by Muslim demand from the invasions of Mahmud of Ghazni and from the Delhi sultanate with its slave armies. Again, in North Africa, the marine *sebkhas* of Djerba, Zarzis, Ras al-Makhbaz and Tripoli do not appear to have been exploited in Antiquity and were probably developed by the Muslim rulers of Tunisia, the Aghlabids, the Fatimids, the Kalbids and the Zirids.

The most interesting of the new Muslim sources of salt are the six salines in western Europe which employed the new technique of successive basin solar evaporation pioneered at An-i *hsien* from around 500 AD. Here we must face the problem of independent discovery or diffusion. In favour of independent discovery is the argument that the step from simple, single basin evaporation, which certainly existed in classical antiquity, to complex, successive basin evaporation, is not large, and might have been taken by anyone under appropriate circumstances. Moreover, while the Chinese applied the technique to a lake, the Muslims in Europe applied it to the sea. In favour of diffusion, is the closeness of the similarity between the developed form of the technique in east and west, in particular as regards non-necessary, even dysfunctional, details. For while a triple division of catchment, condensers and crystallizers may be inherent in a technique which separates sodium chloride from water, calcium and magnesium, as may the peculiar spatial layout in which the technique expresses itself, the particular five to one ratio of combined catchment and condensers to crystallizers, so widely used, is not technologically necessary. Indeed, modern improvements to the technique have largely consisted in dropping this particular ratio.[30] The existence of this unnecessary detail in so many salines is therefore an argument for diffusion from a single source. Such diffusion from China via Central Asia to Muslim Sicily and Spain is already accepted in this period in the case of paper making. The Abbasids were in contact with China from the time of the rebellion of An Lu-shan, so were the Samanids of Bokhara, and Mahmud of Ghazni received an embassy from the Liao dynasty. Perhaps the most reasonable compromise would be a stimulus diffusion: someone from Ho-tung giving someone from Khorasan the bare idea of successive basin solar evaporation, possibly with the ratio of catchment–condensers to crystallizers. This idea was then taken up in the Islamic cultural common market, first in the Muslim far west in the Mediterranean, then in the Muslim far east in the salt lakes of Rajasthan.

The six Muslim Mediterranean salines were Manfredonia in Apulia, the modern Margherita di Savoia, the earliest of the Adriatic fields to use the successive basin technique, and today again Italy's largest supplier; Tortosa at the mouth of the Ebro; Ibiza; La Mata south of Alicante; San Lucar de Barraneda north of Cadiz; and Setubal south of Lisbon. Manfredonia itself was only founded in 1263, but it replaced the Roman colony of Siponto, which was given a Romanesque cathedral by the Normans as late as 1117 but subsequently became malarial. The Peutinger Tables show salines at Siponto in antiquity, but they were probably of the single basin solar evaporation variety and of only local significance. The first mention of large-scale salines, hence probably of the successive basin variety, is in 1015 when a grant of a *casale* Santa Maria de Salinis was made to a local bishop. This was at a time when Apulia was again under Byzantine control, but the big, new salines most likely went back to the Muslim Aghlabid emirate of Bari between 841 and 871. Tortosa del Ebro was in Muslim hands from *c.* 820 to 1148. It was raided, possibly partly for its salt supplies, by a Pisano–Genoese expedition in 1093. Ibiza, Muslim from the eighth century to 1235, is reported by a Muslim geographer of the eleventh century as providing salt for the greater part of Africa, that is, Tunisia and Algeria. Ibiza may have produced salt in antiquity: legend attributed the first exploitation to the Carthaginians, but it was the Muslims who, by the successive basin technique, first made it a major centre. La Mata in the kingdom of Valencia, also known as Cap Cervera, was based on one of two saline lagoons of which the other, Torrevieja, has been the more productive in modern times. Although nearby Cartagena was an important Roman mining centre, it is not clear that the lagoons were exploited. The foundation, less than 20 miles away, of Murcia in the eighth century by Abd er Rahman II would have supplied the necessary demand stimulus, though the direction was later assumed by Valencia. San Lucar de Barrameda, likewise, probably owed its development to the expansion of Seville as the second capital of Moorish Shain in the tenth century. Setubal, too, dominated by the Alcazar do Sal, was also a Muslim foundation, presumably for the supply of Moorish Lisbon before its capture by the Crusaders in 1147.

In these six salines, all of which had fallen to Christendom by the end of the thirteenth century, early Islam had provided her rival with technological tools of almost unlimited potentiality. Not for the first or last time what had begun in China was to come to perfection in Christendom through the amplifying mediation of the Moors.

SALT IN EARLY BYZANTIUM

If in China and Islam the period 500 to 1000 were ages of light, in Byzantium it was an age of twilight. Like Gibbon, we tend to assume that it was the twilight of evening, but until the disasters of Manzikert, Myriokephalon and the Fourth Crusade, this was far from evident. One can imagine a new imperial *renovatio mundi* which would have converted the preceding uncertainties into the twilight of morning. In fact, early Byzantium from Heraclius to Basil Bulgaroctonus contained both kinds of twilight and it was perhaps only events which decided which of the two was to prevail. This duality of archaism and modernity was reflected in the early Byzantine world of salt.

Production

The empire received its salt from three main sources: in the south from the Aegean, in the east from the Black Sea, and in the west from the Adriatic. These sources show varying degrees of continuity and discontinuity with antiquity, depending largely on the evolution of Byzantine urban and military institutions.

In the south, the Byzantines were heirs to the local classical salines of Thessalonica and Athens. In the Cyclades, Tinos, Paros and Naxos appear alongside Melos. It may be that it was now that Melos changed to successive basin evaporation, though a more likely date would be following the fourth crusade under the Venetian duchy of Naxos. Beyond the Aegean, Nicephorus Phocas recovered Crete, which had been in Muslim hands since 827, in 960. Here he inherited the new post-antique saline of Candia which, since the Muslims had come from

Spain, may have been of the successive basin variety. In 965 he re-covered Cyprus and the natural salines of San Lazzaro at Larnaca. All these southern salines lay under the aegis of the three maritime themes, or naval districts, of Pamphylia, the Dodecanese and Samos. The conti-nuities with antiquity are more striking than the discontinuities.

In the Black Sea, continuities and discontinuities were more evenly balanced. The principal salines lay in the coastal strip from the mouths of the Bug and Dnieper, through the southern Crimea, to the straits of Kerch, which in 833 the Emperor Theophilus constituted the theme, or military district, of Cherson: Cherson being south of Sebastopol and not to be confused with the modern Kherson on the Dnieper. In this strip, some of the salines were old: those mentioned by Herodotus and Dio Chrysostom near Kinburn at the mouth of the Bug and the Dnieper. Others, Perekop, Cherson itself and Caffa, the former Theodosia, were new. All were natural salines, *sebkhas* or *limans* as they are frequently called in the Black Sea. Yet the scale of production and the range of diffusion was a discontinuity. Subsequently the khanate of Krim Tartary was to obtain 60 per cent of its revenue from these salines.

In the west, discontinuity prevailed over continuity. Here one finds a line of salines, none of them certainly existing in antiquity, associated with the four themes established between 800 and 878 to defend the empire from the new Muslim maritime thrust from the west and to provide the base for the recovery of Southern Italy and hopefully Sicily. In the theme of Dalmatia were the islands of Arbe and Pago north of Zara; Sebenico, Trau, Salona and Spoleto south; Stagno near Ragusa; and Cattaro. In the theme of Dyrrachium were Durazzo itself and Valona; in the theme of Cephalonia the salines of the Ionian islands; and in the theme of Nicopolis, those of the bay of Lepanto. Beyond their direct jurisdiction the Byzantines could draw on the salt resources of their satellite Venice at Torcello and points north. In addition, from 876 the Byzantines acquired the Manfredonia/Siponto salines in Apulia from the Muslims.

Of these sources of supply the most interesting is Pago. It was under the control of Diadora or Zara, the capital of Byzantine Dalmatia, which already in the time of Constantine Porphyrogenitus (948–952) is de-scribed as 'a big city'.[31] When the emperor wrote, the island was uninhabited, but not long afterwards it became a major producer of salt and one of the first in Christian territory to use the successive basin method. For Cassiodorus's remark in his letter to the Venetians in 523, 'All your emulation centres on the salt-works: instead of ploughs and scythes, you turn cylinders',[32] suggests that the earliest method of salt production at Venice was by artificial boiling in the briquetage cylinders so familiar from Celtic Europe. Before the foundation of Venice, *sebkhas* probably existed in the Adriatic because Bishop Chromatius of Aquileia, the patron of St Jerome, in his commentary on the Gospel of St Matthew, speaks of the production of salt from the sea under the influence of sun and wind.[33] Successive basin evaporation as later practised at Chioggia was probably borrowed from Pago in the tenth century and was the reason for the eclipse of Torcello, to Constantine Porphyrogenitus still a great emporium, by the southern centre.

Distribution

The considerable number of salines used in the early Byzantine empire indicates that distribution continued to follow the classical pattern of relatively short distances by sea or river. Most major centres of population and many minor ones had their own sources of supply close at hand. Nevertheless there were two areas where there are signs of something new: long-distance maritime transport. First, it is difficult not to believe that the Russians sometimes brought Crimean salt to Constantinople in addition to the fur, slaves, honey and wax which are usually ascribed to them, especially if, as Omeljan Pritsak has suggested, they really formed a kind of international trading consortium. Their route down the Dnieper, as described by Constantine Porphyrogenitus, would have taken them past the Kinburn *limans*. Moreover, Cherson supplied salt from Perekop to the capital. In Ottoman times, Caffa too was numbered among the sources of supply for Constantinople. So it may be that the Russian connection goes back to the days when 'the silver trumpets of the Basileus still called across the Bosphorus'.[34] Second, it has been supposed that Venice supplied Constantinople with salt. This is improbable. Constantinople had adequate supplies nearer at hand and Venice's chief export to the imperial city was timber, a bulky commodity which left little space for salt even as ballast. Indeed the only official reference to Venice in this respect, a decree of the end of the tenth century in the *Synopsis Basilicorum* which prohibits Venetian *export* of salt from Constantinople, makes sense in this context. The Venetians, having deposited their timber, would be looking for another bulky commodity to take at least part of the way home and were thus seeking to break into the redistributive trade of the capital. But the existence of this trade points to the fact that some salt was being carried sufficient distance by sea to justify the use of relatively large vessels. Again, the Venetians may have brought back salt from Muslim North Africa, and traded it within the Byzantine empire nominally from Constantinople, in return for the supply of timber and arms against which Emperor John Tzimisces vainly protested in 971. It is likely that in some shape or form marine transport of salt was already part of Venice's complex economic relationship with *Romania*.

Consumption

Besides the imperial city itself, the leading institutions of the early
Byzantine empire were the themes and the monasteries. Both encouraged the consumption of salt: the themes by the luxury of armed forces,
especially in meat; the monasteries by the asceticism which imposed fish
eating in rules of abstinence, fast days and the two Lents of Advent and
Easter. For the rest, early Byzantine diet followed the pattern of late
antiquity: classical frugality in protein and animal fats, overlaid by *limes*
affluence. In this case it was not the porcine *limes* of northern Europe,
but the ovine *limes* of Anatolia whence the new military dynasties – the
Isaurians, the Phrygians, the 'Macedonians' – came. Byzantine civilization was lavish in building, ornament, furnishing and clothes. Even the
Iconoclasts were not against art but only devotional art. Constantinople
was self-consciously a city of marvels, and this, in combination with the
long monetary stability which reduced the abstention of uncertainty,
increased the propensity to consume. Christianity, furthermore, did
away with the sumptuarism which lay at the root of ancient hostility to
consumerism. Even in the twelfth century when its prosperity had
already been undermined, Constantinople was regarded by the Spanish
Jew Benjamin of Tudela, who had seen Baghdad, Alexandria and
Samarkand, as the richest city in the world: 'Wealth like that of Constantinople is not to be found in the whole world'.[35] Some of this affluence
rubbed off to raise the consumption of salt.

SALT IN WESTERN EUROPE

Here, after Oriental light and Byzantine twilight, we reach darkness: no
splendid imperial cities, no lavish frontier armies, abstract social order
dissolved into concrete intersubjectivities. Yet the darkness was relative:
a matter of the state rather than society or even culture. Beneath political
division, lesser institutions – royal households, monasteries, *castra*,
manors – directed not unsuccessfully a Latin Christendom deprived of
Sicily, Spain and much of the western Mediterranean, but expanded to
include Ireland and western Germany. In the history of salt this has
been called the domanial age[36] and it was not without its constructive
achievements. Foundations are seldom impressive but they are the basis
of future building.

Production

During the Dark Ages, the pattern of the salt industry of the Celtic
world, little changed by the Romans, was considerably modified. In

Rome itself and in Languedoc there was also major innovation.

In the weak brine sector, the coastal salt industry of the north and west, there were two changes. Both involved a retreat of the old *briquetage* technique, so that henceforward it was confined to Normandy, the *pays de quart bouillon* of the traditional *gabelle*.[37] First, in England, coastal brine was replaced in importance by stronger inland brine from pits and wells. Domesday Book still shows coastal salines: 34 in Lincolnshire, 21 in Essex; but their significance seems purely local.[38] The inland salines, on the other hand, evidence of whose exploitation in Roman times is hard to come by, were now of regional, possibly national significance. In Worcestershire, there were at least 300 salt pans.[39] Pans varied in productivity, but 20 *mettae*, 160 bushels, 80 cwt was the average: a total of 24 000 cwt, enough for between a quarter and half a million people. Droitwich was worth 76 pounds a year to the Conqueror. The Cheshire wiches – Nantwich, Middlewich, and Northwich – were together worth 37 pounds, so their production may be reckoned at another 10 000 cwt.[40] In both Worcestershire and Cheshire the brine was evaporated, probably in lead vessels, another innovation, over wood fires. The first mention of the Worcestershire salt industry is in the charter of King Aethelbald of Mercia of 716–717 which grants to the church of Worcester, 'a portion of land on which salt is wont to be produced, at the south side of the river which is called Salwarp . . . for the construction of three salt-houses and six furnaces'.[41] Worcestershire, it is noteworthy, was a particularly strong monastic county in the Dark Ages: the home of St Oswald in the tenth century, St Wulfstan in the eleventh, and the base for the post-1066 revival at Whitby, Durham and St Mary's, York.

Second, in France, coastal brine was increasingly treated not by artificial boiling, but first by simple and later by complex solar evaporation. Consequently the industry moved south towards the sun: from Morbihan to the Guérande just north of the Loire[42] and to Noirmoutier and Bourgneuf south of it, and eventually to the Ile de Ré and Brouage north of the Gironde estuary. The beginning of presumably simple solar evaporation at Noirmoutier is credited to St Philibert who died there in 684[43] on the model of salines he had seen at Bordeaux, but if the Guérande was already in operation, it would seem the more obvious model. The island was already 'a centre of the salt trade for the whole of western Europe'[44] when the Vikings occupied it on a permanent basis in 842. Possibly it was Vikings, who took part in the abortive expedition to Seville in 844, who introduced the technique of successive basin evaporation to the Bay of Biscay, though it is difficult to be certain that the technique existed there before 1000.

In the strong brine sector, the inland salt industry of the south and east, there was extension rather than substitution. In Moselle, the core of Lotharingia, the salines of the Seille were redeveloped in the tenth century under the leadership of the bishop of Metz. To the south, Salins in Franche Comté, possibly exploited in Roman times, was further developed by monasteries in the sixth and again in the eighth century. Also in Franche Comté, Lons Le Saunier was the site of salines exploited in the tenth century by the abbey of Cluny.[45] Like Worcestershire, Lorraine too in the Dark Ages was a major focus of monastic revival around the abbey of Gorze. In Germany, Hallstatt, Hallein and Halle received a northern extension in Luneburg which was the subject of a grant by Emperor Otto I to the monastery of St Michael in 955. Another German saline which was developed at this time was Sooden in Hesse northeast of Kassel.

Meanwhile, in the south, at Rome, in the days of the *Adelspapsttum*, and the Holy Roman Republic, there was a more considerable innovation. In the first half of the tenth century, the cartularies of a number of monasteries in Latium such as Farfa and Subiaco contain notarial contracts relating to renewed activity at salines at the mouth of the Tiber: Bordunaria to the south, Porto to the north. What is most significant about this activity is that reference in these contracts to compartments (*areae, petiolae*), circuits (*fila*) and linkages (*pedicae*) strongly suggests that production was now by successive basin solar evaporation. Rome would seem to be the earliest example of this technique in Latin Christendom, since it is not clear that Venice had adopted it at this date. Not only was there a discontinuity with antiquity in matter of technique, but also in location, since the mouth of the Tiber was further to the west than it had been in the days of the Caesars. Except for John X's defeat of the Saracens at the Garigliano in 915, the early tenth-century papacy has not received a good press, but the introduction of a new method of salt production in a new place, should stand to its credit, or to that of its aristocratic patrons. Production, it is true, was only for local supply. Salt going up the river or the *Via salaria*, to the Sabine country, corresponded to grain, oil and wine coming down. But in the course of time the trade gave rise to a producer's guild, the *schola salinariorum* and gave support to a transport guild, the *schola sandalariorum*, which operated a fleet of flat-bottomed barges on the Tiber.[46]

In Languedoc too, successive basin solar evaporation was introduced before the end of the first millennium. The first production of salt in Languedoc, presumably in *sebkha* or single basin form, was traditionally ascribed to Sejanus. In 822 Louis the Pious made a grant of salines at Narbonne to the abbey of St Benedict of Aniane: salines, again, presumably on this basis. But in 990, a grant by Viscountess Adelaide of Narbonne to the canons of Saint Just at a place called *in scalas* suggests successive basin evaporation. This impression is confirmed by a sale in 1054 by the Count of Toulouse to a religious house in Beziers of lands *cum salinis cum coctoriis et matricibus et planiciis*, i.e. a triple set of basins for concentration, condensation and crystallization.[47] The new technique will have been brought to Languedoc either from Rome or perhaps more likely from Muslim Spain.

Distribution

In the Dark Ages salt began to travel greater distances. H. C. Darby writes: 'Many places in adjoining counties possessed either salt-pans in Droitwich or rights to salt there'.[48] In Herefordshire there were eleven such places, in Gloucestershire seven, in Warwickshire six, Shropshire three, Oxfordshire two, Buckinghamshire one. Via the Thames, Worcestershire salt reached London when it came under Mercian rule, Westminster Abbey in particular having the right to be supplied.[49] Droitwich also used the rivers of the Severn Valley to supply places such as Gloucester and Evesham. Noirmoutier was a market for wine as well as salt, and it may be that the Vikings initiated the links between the Bay and the Baltic which their successors the Hanseatics were to develop into one of the great trade routes of medieval Europe. Everywhere the Vikings revealed the importance of rivers: as lines of attack first, as trade routes second. They were the first people to exploit Europe's circumterranean seas which the Mediterranean empires had neglected. Marine salt was one of the earliest commodities these seas would carry.

Consumption

As in the Byzantine east, the outstanding consumers were military men and monasteries, but the military were not metropolitan marshals but marcher lords and manorial chiefs, and monasteries created cities rather than vice versa. The consumption of salt reflected this pattern. In Brittany, the rise of the Guérande salines may be associated with the emergence of Nantes as the headquarters of the duke. In England, Droitwich, under the protection of the kings of Mercia, supplied the religious communities of the Severn valley. In Lotharingia, Vic belonged to the bishop of Metz, Dieuze to the abbey of St Maxime at Trier, Moyenvic to the canons of St Gengoult of Toul. In Normandy the old-fashioned *briquetage* salines of Bouteilles found outlets in the abbeys of Rouen, the ducal capital, Fécamp and Jumièges.

What was consumed was still principally cereals in the form of bread. But the Dark Ages also saw an increase in the consumption of meat and fish. It was in the Dark Ages that the peculiar European form of mixed farming, the symbiosis of *ager* and *saltus*, field and forest, was established. In the forest, the dominant domestic animal was the pig fed on acorns and beechmast. In Domesday Book, forests are reckoned according to the number of pigs they can support: 120 000 in south Essex and east Hertfordshire, for example. *Piscaria* were perhaps an even more important source of protein, since the Rule of St Benedict forbade meat to all but sick monks, and Lent and fast days forbade it to the laity for nearly a quarter of the year. Domesday Book indicates that river fisheries were more important than maritime. Wherever there was a mill race, and this was a time when water-wheels were spreading, there were weirs, stews and meres for fish. *Piscaria* were particularly abundant on the lower Severn, the Worcestershire Avon and the upper Thames, all areas served by Droitwich salt. Cambridgeshire, the isle of Ely, served by salt from the Wash, specialized in eels: four areas produced over 100 000 of them a year. Cheese was another source of protein on the increase in the Dark Ages. The coastal hundreds of Essex were already significant producers and this no doubt was part of the reason for the survival of that county's *briquetage* salt industry. In Cheshire too, salt and cheese were linked from the beginning with Chester, the seat of both a marcher fortress and a minster, being founded in 907 by Ethelfleda, Lady of the Mercians.

Western Europe was far from static in its Dark Ages. Consumption and distribution were on the move, but above all production, at Rome, Languedoc and at the mouth of the Loire had discovered for itself or received from outside, the gift of successive basin solar evaporation. For it was on the basis of this gift that new heights in production, distribution and consumption were to be reached in the Middle Ages, 1000–1500.

4 The Middle Ages

The Middle Ages were of great importance in the history of salt. Between 1000 and 1500, the major characteristics of the salt trade as it was to remain until the coming of industrialism, were defined in a pattern of a double global bifurcation.

First, there was a manifest bifurcation between the extremities and the middle: between, on the one hand, China and Western Europe, and on the other, India, Islam and Byzantium. In the Middle Ages China and Western Europe took the lead. It is there that one finds the principal development of techniques in production, institutions in distribution, outlets in consumption. In India, Islam and Byzantium, by contrast, there was relative stagnation. This impression of stagnation may be due to inadequate evidence, but it corresponds with the overall histories of the area. India, divided between a Muslim north and a Hindu south, was crushed by an excessive state apparatus, imperial and local. The only significant developments were the rise of the Bengal and Orissa *panga* or boiling salt industry to supply the new Muslim rulers of northeast India and of the Madras and Travancore successive basin solar evaporation salt industry to supply the Chola empire and the new Hindu society of the Tamil Nadu. Bengal chose *chien* rather than *shai* because of the rainfall and in Madras *shai* will have been introduced either from Sambhar and Bharatpur or possibly direct from China with which the Cholas were in touch. Islam, limited in energy by shortage of timber and crippled in demography by both the Mongol invasions and the Black Death, lost many of the salines it had earlier established to Christians or Hindus, and failed to replace them. Byzantium, a once active empire on the way to becoming a passive city state, did not need to look beyond the Black Sea and the Aegean for its sources of supply nor beyond cabotage for its suppliers. Dynamism, in production, distribution and consumption, passed to China which escaped the Black Death and to Western Europe which escaped the Mongol invasions.

Second, there was a latent bifurcation between the unified, bureaucratic empire of China and the pluralistic, clerico-commercial republic of Western Europe. Both were dynamic: in scale, technology, institutions and consumer demand. But the dynamism was displayed to dissimilar degrees and in differing fields. In China, the dynamism was primarily institutional: the elaboration of a regionalized system of joint state/private distribution, which was to last with only permutations of detail down to the twentieth century. In technology, however, dynamism was less evident, surprisingly so in view of the record of the Han and the

71

T'ang. China, having pioneered successive basin solar evaporation, made little use of her invention and discarded it in the area of its invention. Similarly, the Szechwan deep well and natural gas industry, the most advanced technologically anywhere in the world, was engulfed, after a period of rapid growth, in the disaster of its province in the Mongol invasions. In Western Europe, on the other hand, dynamism was both institutional and technological: the elaboration of a set of powerful urban distributive networks and the consequent deployment of successive basin solar evaporation in what amounted to a medieval energy revolution. In turn, the wholehearted adoption of solar energy oriented Western Europe toward regional specialization, unlimited growth and further dynamism. In Western Europe, institutions and technology went hand in hand, whereas in China they pulled in different directions. Behind this contrast lay a more basic one of milieu. In Europe, salt, for all the concern of princes and city governments, was part of society, with a thrust toward the technical and the economic. In China, salt, for all the involvement of technicians and businessmen, was part of the state, with a thrust toward the cultural and the political. In salt, as in so much else, the Middle Ages formed a watershed in the histories of China and Europe.

SALT IN MEDIEVAL CHINA

In the Middle Ages, China with a larger and more widely diffused population of 150 million, became a subcontinent, a veritable United States. The history of its salt business thus needs to be studied in terms of its parts. But besides being a diverse subcontinent, medieval China, under the Sung, Yüan and early Ming, was also a unified empire whose institutions at least shaped and in some cases created the parts in question. The history of salt in medieval China must therefore commence with the effect of the whole on the parts, the role of the imperial *yen-cheng* in particular.

In the last chapter, we noted the reestablishment of the imperial salt administration, in abeyance since the early years of Eastern Han, by Liu Yen, minister to T'ang emperor Tai-tsung, 762–779. The T'ang system was continued by the Five Dynasties, 907–960, and by the early Sung. It was not until the early twelfth century that major restructuring was undertaken by Ts'ai Ching, minister to Sung emperor Hui-tsung, 1101–1126, the second great Chinese salt administrator. Unlike Liu Yen, Ts'ai Ching has not had a good press. Traditional historiography, unfairly associating his ministry with the great disaster which befell the Sung in 1127, the fall of K'ai-feng to the Jurched, regarded him as a typical 'bad last minister', while for the salt reformers of the twentieth century, Ts'ai Ching's name was synonymous with what they regarded as the evils of the notorious *yin* system'. In fact, the *yin* system, in essence if not in all its accidents, was not evil. It was a remarkable piece of administrative ingenuity which stood the test of time by being adopted, sooner or later, by every regime in China down from the Sung to the Republic.

Ts'ai Ching faced a more complex task than Liu Yen. The population had tripled from 50 million to 150 million. More salt, around 10 million cwt, was being produced at a greater number of places for a bigger and more diversified market. If the state was to achieve its fiscal and social goals in salt administration as defined by the catch phrase *kuo-chi min-sheng* (state's finances, people's livelihood), it must allow regional diversity, limit its responsibilities, and take a partner. Ts'ai Ching thus became the founder of three interlocking institutions: *yin-ti* or territorial salt divisions, each with their own officials and procedures as established by the various *yen-fa chih* (treatises on the salt laws); *chien-chieh chuan-mai*, indirect monopoly, by which the state was not involved directly in manufacture, transport or marketing; and *kuan-tu shang-pan* (officials supervise, merchants manage), partnership between officials and privileged merchants in which the officials laid down guidelines and received taxes and the merchants supplied capital and took profit. These three elements remained characteristic of Chinese salt administration down to the reforms of Sir Richard Dane, the third great Chinese salt administrator.

Ts'ai Ching's system was never without critics. Orthodox Confucians, using the arguments of the literati in the *Yen-t'ieh lun*, feared official corruption by contact with business. Less orthodox Confucians like Ts'ai Ching's predecessor Wang An-shih objected to the creation by the government of an oligarchy of monopolists. Salt reformers variously wanted the government to go further or less far; towards complete, direct monopoly operated by officials, or towards simply levying tax at source and allowing the salt business to organize itself. These debates lasted as long as the salt administration and gave rise to fashions in bureaucratic philosophy and regional variations in bureaucratic practice.

The most serious attempt to recast Ts'ai Ching's system was made under the early Ming in the so called *k'ai-chung fa* (the law of opening the centre) promulgated by Emperor Hung-wu as part of his overall design for a more corporatist society. Under the *k'ai-chung fa*, which was based on precedents in the early Sung under Emperor T'ai-tsung, 976–998, merchants desiring to participate in the salt trade had to win entitlement by supplying grain to the imperial armies on the frontier: so many bushels for so many hundredweight. In this way, by monitoring all transactions through the capital ('opening to the centre'), privilege would be made dependent on antecedent service. Yet the *k'ai-chung fa* never worked satisfactorily. Its social contract philosophy contaminated business with non-economic purposes which businessmen sought not unnaturally and not unsuccessfully to circumvent. Frontier grain and domestic salt did not naturally go together and the attempt to force a marriage was tantamount to a crippling social surcharge on the trade which forced capital out of it. Suspended in the late fifteenth century through the efforts of the reforming minister of revenue Yen Ch'i, the *k'ai-chung fa* was restored in the early sixteenth century more in form than in fact, and was finally abolished in Huai-nan, the largest of the salt divisions, in 1617.

The salt administration affected principally production and distribution. Consumption, however, was more influenced by changes in Chinese diet in the Sung period. Thanks to contemporary accounts of the *wa-tzu* or pleasure quarters of the imperial capitals, K'ai-feng for the Northern Sung, Hang-chou for the Southern, we know a good deal about this. Three meals a day was now taken for granted in the cities and the intensification of urbanization placed a higher percentage of Chinese population in cities than ever before or since. With the introduction to China by Emperor Chen-tsung, 998–1023, of quick growing and drought resistant strains from Champa, rice, the least saline of the cereals, definitely replaced wheat as the number one food grain. Protein consumption increased: soybean everywhere; lamb, kid and mutton in the north; pork, fish and poultry in the south. In the Middle Ages, pepper was a good index of protein and Marco Polo was amazed at the quantity of pepper absorbed by China: 'I assure you that for one spice ship that goes to Alexandria or elsewhere to pick up pepper for export to Christendom, Zaiton [the port for Hang-chou] is visited by a hundred'.[2] Again, 'According to the figures ascertained by Messer Marco from an official of the Great Khan's customs, the pepper consumed daily in the city of Kinsai [Hang-chou] for its own use amounts to 43 cart-loads, each cart-load consisting of 223 lbs'[3]: an amount equal on an annual basis to more than what the whole of Europe imported in 1500.[4] Moreover tastes were becoming more sophisticated and the Southern Sung in particular created what has been called the world's first cuisine.[5] These changes were reflected in *per capita* consumption of salt, at least in certain areas. The *Yüan-shih* estimates that the nearly 20 million inhabitants of the metropolitan provinces of Liang-che and Chiang-tung, i.e. northern Chekiang and southern Kiangsu, consumed 10 lb of salt per head per year: the highest consumption figures suggested anywhere up to that time, and indeed until much later.[6]

Against this background of imperial administration and social affluence, the particular histories of the principal salt divisions may now be set.

Ho-tung

Between 1000 and 1500 the salt industry at the An-i *hsien* lake underwent vicissitudes which well illustrate the technological hesitation of medieval China. In 996, production, all of it by successive basin solar evaporation, *chih-hsi chiao-shai*, was estimated at 400 000 cwt, double the figure for the high T'ang period. The intervening years when An-i *hsien* had been the principal supplier to the ephemeral regimes of North China, had been kind to Ho-tung. Indeed, it could almost be said that Ho-tung financed the reunification of China by the Sung, who rewarded it by assigning to its sales area both Lo-yang the former T'ang capital and K'ai-feng the new Sung capital. Ho-tung flourished under the Northern Sung. Production rose to 763 215 cwt in 1023, to 825 000 cwt in 1048 when new markets were opened in Szechwan, and to a million cwt by the end of the century. In 1105, 2400 new *hsi*, or sets of salt basins, were opened. During Ts'ai Ching's ministry productive capacity may have reached 1.5 million cwt as a result of an expanding market extending over four provinces. Under the Northern Sung, it was the premier salt division.

Like the Northern Sung, Ho-tung was engulfed by the disaster of 1127. An-i *hsien* lay on the route of one of the two Jurched armies which invaded China in 1126 and it is probable that its elaborate works suffered considerable damage. K'ai-feng ceased to be an imperial capital; Honan became debatable ground between the Chin and the Southern Sung, Shensi was partitioned between the Chin and the Hsi Hsia, the masters of the Ninghsia lakes whose rival red salt could be supplied to Shansi by the Yellow River. Under these blows, production at An-i *hsien* suffered a calamitous decline. The Mongols established a tax bureau in 1230 but by 1252 the annual production quota was only 60 000 cwt. Under the early Yüan, there was some recovery: 256 000 cwt in 1273, 328 000 in 1307, but it was not until later Yüan that it became considerable – 408 000 cwt in 1309, 738 000 in 1319.[7] Even so the best levels of the Northern Sung were not attained.

The recovery, moreover, was on a different and technologically less sophisticated basis. During the Yüan period, as a result of competition from the *sebkhas* of the northwest whose salt was cheaper and doubtless protected by powerful Mongol interests, the producers at An-i *hsien* abandoned the *hsi-shai* method of successive basin evaporation in favour of what was called *lao-ts'ai* (lit., 'dragging and gathering'), i.e. harvesting the natural crystallization of the lake. To survive against the Mongol-backed *sebkhas*, Ho-tung had to become a *sebkha* itself, despite the technological regression involved. *Lao-ts'ai* continued in the early Ming.[8] The original production quota was 608 000 cwt, but by the end of the fifteenth century this had risen to 840 000 cwt, and by the later sixteenth to 1 240 000 cwt. By this time, however, *hsi-shai* had been revived though it was not to triumph definitely until the seventeenth century under the Ch'ing, and Ho-tung was always to have trouble from Ninghsia red salt from the Chilantai lake in Alashan. Ho-tung was an energetic but precarious saline. Its instability attached itself to the *hsi-shai* method whose marginal advantages were not always sufficient to overcome comparative production and transport costs. Further, Ho-tung lacked political clout. After the Northern Sung, it did not enjoy the favour of the salt administration. For example, the Wan-li emperor deprived it of its markets in eastern Honan which immediately reduced its production quota to 840 000 cwt again.

Ch'ang-lu

Successive basin solar evaporation found its second home and won its greatest successes in China in Ch'ang-lu, the line of salines from the eastern end of the Great Wall to the frontiers of Shantung, from which were supplied Chihli and eastern Honan. Its success was unofficial in its beginnings, slow in its progress, and much influenced by political vicissitudes. Ch'ang-lu first became a significant supplier under the Yüan when the capital was at Peking, but on the basis of earth filtration and boiling rather than solar evaporation, which only became important under the Ming, and only dominant by the early seventeenth century.

Part of what became Ch'ang-lu had been included in the ancient state of Ch'i where flourished one of the oldest branches of the Chinese salt industry: the boiling of marine brine in iron vessels. Its significance, however, was eclipsed from the Han by the successive rise of Wu, Ho-tung, Szechwan, the northwest and Huai-nan. Under the Northern Wei, 386–535, there were 2252 registered furnaces, but they only produced 3000 cwt of salt, a mere domestic industry. In the silver T'ang period, after a certain degree of development, the salines fell out of the salt administration because the area was controlled by the northeast governors who were virtually independent of the court. Similarly the Northern Sung had to relinquish the northern half of Chihli to the Khitan kingdom of Liao. There is reference to a boiling (*chien*) salt industry there in the negotiations between the Sung and Jurched for a partition of the area which led eventually to the disaster of 1127. In discussion the Jurched supplied a document which stated that the salines in the Liao half of Chihli manufactured 110 000 cwt of salt a year.[9] For the Chinese half, the *Sung-shih* provides some figures, all for *chien* salt: 50 000 cwt in 968, 200 000 cwt in 1045, 120 000 cwt in 1083, 175 700 in 1084. The joint production of Ch'ang-lu probably reached 300 000 cwt by the beginning of the twelfth century. Progress continued under the Jurched Chin whose capital was at Yen-ching, the modern Peking. A document of 1191 in the reign of Emperor Chang-tsung refers to private boiling, a sign that the official quotas were under pressure.

The earliest Yüan quota, in 1240, was only 138 000 cwt. By 1243, however, the quota had been increased to 360 000, perhaps the old Chin figure, and thereafter it increased steadily: 427 500 cwt in 1265, 800 000 cwt in 1275, 1 162 400 cwt in 1285. That all this was *chien* is confirmed by Marco Polo:

> Leaving Ho-kien-fu, we travel southwards for three days and reach another city called Changlu. . . . You must know that a great quantity of salt is produced here by the following process. Men take a sort of earth, which is very saline, and of this they make great mounds. Over these they pour a lot of water, so that it trickles down through it and becomes briny owing to the property of the earth. Then they collect this water by means of pipes and put it in big vats and big iron cauldrons not more than four fingers deep and boil it thoroughly. The salt thus produced is very pure and white and fine-grained. And I assure you that it is exported into many countries round about and is a great source of wealth to the inhabitants and of revenue to the Great Khan.[10]

Except in the matter of fuel, Polo's account is exemplary in its detail and the final sentence evokes the basic salt administration principle of *kuo-chi min-sheng*, significantly in an inverted European form.

In the later Yüan, under the growing demand of the Mongol court and military establishment, the Ch'ang-lu quotas were further increased: 1 400 000 cwt in 1290, 1 800 000 cwt in 1308, 1 600 000 cwt in 1329. Now the earliest Ming documents on Ch'ang-lu speak not only of cauldrons (*hu*) and pans (*kuo*) and grasslands (*ts'ao-tang*) to provide them with fuel, but also of *t'an-ti* (lit., 'foreshore land'). *T'an* was the name given on the coast to the series of basins which at An-i *hsien* were called *hsi* (lit., 'fields'). The inference must be that the final spurt of salt production at Ch'ang-lu under the Yüan was based on successive basin solar evaporation, probably as a result of unofficial initiative, perhaps by refugees from An-i *hsien*. With the fall of the Yüan, however, production in Ch'ang-lu declined dramatically. The earliest Ming quota was for only 252 610 cwt, and though this was raised to 315 765 cwt in 1443 as a result of the restoration of the capital to Peking, and to 452 000 cwt in 1500, most of the early references are to *chien* rather than *shai*. It was only in the sixteenth century, when production was boosted to 1 319 052 cwt in 1590, that *t'an-shai* definitely reappeared, the first clear reference in the Ming *hui-tien* being to 1522. Successive basin solar evaporation then was introduced to Ch'ang-lu in the fourteenth century, but with the collapse of demand following the expulsion of the Mongols, it went, as in Ho-tung, into temporary abeyance, only to revive with the high Ming prosperity of the Chia-ching and Wan-li reigns.

Shantung and Huai-pei

The *Ming-shih* reports two other salt divisions as producing by the *shai* method: Shantung in part, Huai-pei wholly. In both areas successive basin solar evaporation was probably introduced from Ch'ang-lu only in the course of the Ming period. The principal salines in Shantung were always in the northwest close to the border with Chihli and the northern course of the Yellow River. Indeed, from 1446 the Ch'ang-lu salt censor doubled as Shantung salt intendant, so closely were the two areas associated. Under the Yüan, Shantung, like Ch'ang-lu, became a considerable producer. Its quota rose from 287 992 cwt in 1269 to 589 948 cwt in 1275, 1 000 000 cwt in 1269 and 1 240 000 cwt in 1329. Under the early Ming, the Shantung quota was reduced to 573 550 cwt, but this was a lesser cut than in Ch'ang-lu. That production survived better in Shantung than in Ch'ang-lu was probably due to the fact that its chief market, the canal zone of western Shantung, lost population less than did the Mongol headquarters area of northern Chihli. The early Ming references to Shantung down to the mid-sixteenth century are to *chien* or boiled salt, though there is a mention of *t'an* in 1450. In the late sixteenth century, however, a local *littérateur* Kan I-chi refers to *shai* salt and at the end of the dynasty another, Kuo Wu-ch'ang, in a poem *Pity the Salt Worker (min yen-ting)*, puts *shai* and *chien* on a level of equality.

The early history of Huai-pei, in later times one of the major centres of successive basin solar evaporation in China, is obscure. The *Sung-shih* speaks only of Huai-nan, but it includes in that division the three yards (*ch'ang*, a territorial subdivision of the salt administration) of Hai-chou and the salines of Hai-k'ou which later made up Huai-pei. The *Yüan-shih*, on the other hand, speaks of Liang-huai, the two Huai, but it does not separately mention the Hai-chou and Hai-k'ou salines. Under the Northern Sung, the Huai-pei salines supplied a quota of 313 500 cwt of boiled salt. From 1127, however, the area became a battleground between the Southern Sung and first the Jurched Chin and then the Mongols. Moreover, from 1194 the shift of the Yellow River to the south of the Shantung peninsula made Huai-pei effectively part of north China. The Ming assigned Huai-pei a quota of 324 368 cwt, distinct for the first time from Huai-nan. That, as in Shantung, production survived better in Huai-pei than in Ch'ang-lu was due again to association with the canal zone, and to the fact that its principal outlet, northern Anhwei, was the cradle of the Ming dynasty. Emperor Hung-wu even considered making Feng-yang, its major centre, an imperial capital. As regards

technology, the first definite reference to successive basin solar evaporation in Huai-pei is in the Chia-ching edition of the local *yen-fa-chih* in the
mid-sixteenth century.

Thus by 1500 China's great invention of successive basin solar evaporation only survived precariously at favoured points on the eastern
seaboard, thanks in effect to political patronage in those areas. Despite
its cheapness and economy of energy, it was not well regarded by the
salt administration which considered coarse-grained *shai* as inferior to
fine-grained *chien*.

Szechwan

Meanwhile, China's other great invention, deep-drilled wells and evaporation by natural gas, coal or wood, fared little better. In mid T'ang,
when in the days of the Yang family, it was almost a second metropolitan province, the output of the 640 wells of Szechwan can be reckoned at
320 000 cwt. In the silver T'ang period, Szechwan suffered from invasions from both Tibet and the Lolo kingdom of Nan-chao. During the
Five Dynasties and early Sung, Szechwan had mixed fortunes: prosperous independence as the kingdom of Shu under the ex-salt smuggler
Wang Chien, invasion from the north and unsuccessful resistance to
Sung unification. It is not surprising then that the first Sung figures
show only 98 wells in operation with a total production of 161 691 cwt.
Recovery, however, was rapid. Old centres, like Ling-chou and Ta-ning,
reopened and expanded production: new centres, like Yun-yang and
Jung-ch'ang, commenced operations. By the end of the tenth century,
Szechwan was producing 362 000 cwt of salt itself, and soon needed to
import 177 700 cwt from Ho-tung and the northwest lakes. In the course
of the eleventh century, Szechwan increased the number of its wells to
822 and its production to 640 000 cwt. By 1100 it was again one of the
major producers of the empire.

Ts'ai Ching exempted Szechwan from his *yin-fa* both because it was
still a developing area and because he doubted the applicability of his
system to so many widely scattered wells. This privilege could not
outlast the disaster of 1127. With the loss of the Ho-tung salt lake to the
Jurched, the empire was desperately short of revenue. In 1132 an able
governor of Szechwan Chao K'ai introduced the *yin-fa*. The rate of tax
was doubled, but either the rate was more comprehensively applied
than the old or production had increased or both, because the yield
quintupled from 800 000 strings of cash to 4 million. In the early years of
the Southern Sung, Szechwan regularly supplied nearly a fifth of the salt
revenue, and that was most of the revenue there was. For a brief period,
1134 to 1137, Chao K'ai tried to push the revenue to 20 million strings of
cash, but economic hardship forced him to retreat: it was said that the

sale of Szechwan salt exhausted the empire's monetary stock. Even so, Chao K'ai's revenue, new and unassigned, was crucial in the war. It is not too much to suggest that Chao K'ai financed the famous campaign of Yueh Fei which ensured the survival of the Sung empire. After the war, taxes fell first to 3 million, then to 1 600 000, but there was considerable backlog, and further remissions were made in 1179 and 1192. In general, however, Szechwan was prosperous in these years. Like the rest of the Southern Sung empire, population was increasing, and it is likely that the production of salt reached a million cwt by the beginning of the thirteenth century. Chao K'ai's system had left room for the industry to grow.

In the second half of the thirteenth century, however, Szechwan became a battlefield between the Mongols and the Sung. War and disease, possibly the Black Death, reduced the population which did not recover till the eighteenth century. Though Chengtu remained an impressive city and the capital of a Mongol subkingdom, Marco Polo describes much of the rest of the province as a wilderness: 'infested with lions, bears and other wild beasts . . . many towns and villages and hamlets lying ruined and desolate. . . . This desolate country, infested by dangerous wildbeasts, extends for twenty days' journey, without shelter or food except perhaps every third or fourth day'. The Mongols did not assign a quota to Szechwan until 1285 when a figure of only 41 804 cwt was allocated. In 1289 they increased the quota to 68 608 cwt and in 1331, as the province recovered to 115 640 cwt. Under the early Ming recovery continued to be slow: a quota of 181 315 cwt in the middle years of Hung-wu, 1368–1398, 206 666 cwt in the middle years of Hung-chih, 1488–1506. The *Ssu-ch'uan yen-fa-chih* contains a localized breakdown of production in the two periods (see Table 4.1).

Except in the two districts of Jen-shou and Chien-wei which supplied Chengtu the picture is one of steady, unspectacular growth on existing bases. In the sixteenth century the pace quickened but in 1558 the quota was only 357 057 cwt, less than it had been at the end of the tenth century. The Ming corporate state did little to promote distant Szechwan, one of the last areas of China to be subjected to its rule, and preferred to leave it as a source of raw materials, particularly timber. Political disfavour, added to the earlier effects of war, ensured that deep wells and high energy did no better in medieval China than successive basin solar evaporation.

The southeast

In the southeast lay the two major salines of Huai-nan and Liang-che, the heart of the medieval salt administration, dynamic in output but conservative in technology. Both produced by the *chien* method of the

Table 4.1 Salt production in Szechwan in the early Ming

District	Quota, 1368–98 (cwt)	Quota 1458–1506 (cwt)
Chien-chou	19 196	27 940
Chien-wei	8 448	26 188
P'eng-shui	2 268	7 322
Chung-chou	1 642	2 878
Yun-yang	21 246	24 985
Chung-chiang	2 443	9 213
Chin-t'ang	4 908	4 908
Sui-ning	2 245	5 563
T'ung-ch'uan	2 242	6 345
Jung-hsien	7 255	9 959
Fu-shun	18 880	36 792
Tzu-chou	3 213	12 441
Nei-chiang	6 940	10 756
Jen-shou	389	12 376
Total	101 315	206 666

artificial boiling of reinforced brine which had been practised in China since at least 500 BC. They differed, however, as to the source of brine and the technique of reinforcement. In Huai-nan the source of brine was the marshes left behind by East China's advancing shoreline. Here the water was more saline than that of the adjacent sea which was constantly diluted by the two influents, the Huang-ho and the Yangtze. Before being boiled, this subsoil brine was reinforced by filtration through the ashes of wetland plants, which had absorbed the marsh sodium chloride, burnt in the previous boiling. In this way a rich brine was obtained and fuel costs were minimized. Another variant of the process is described in the Customs report of 1906:

> Salt is produced in Huai-nan by the curious process of spreading reed ashes over ground rich in salt. The ashes absorb the salt when the two are collected and cleaned with water – that is, the salt is dissolved and the ashes rejected – then the water is evaporated, leaving behind the salt in crystals.[12]

In Liang-che the source of brine was the sea. Before boiling, it was treated in one of two ways of which the first resembled part of the Huai-nan process, while the second was different. In northern Chekiang or Liang-che West, essentially the coast between Hang-chou and Shang-hai, the *shai-hui* (evaporation of ash) or *t'an-hui* (spreading of ash) process was followed. Marine brine was run into basins which had been strewn with saline ash. The resulting liquid was then transferred directly to generally an iron boiling-pan at another site. In southern Chekiang, Liang-che East, essentially the coast between Hang-chou and the Fukien border, the *kua-ni* (scraping of mud) process was followed. Marine brine was run into basins and allowed to evaporate completely. This was done several times. The resulting saline earth was then used to filter sea water to produce the final brine for usually a bamboo boiling-pan. As Edmund H. Worthy, the expert on Liang-che in the Sung period, says: 'These differences in production techniques were not apparently fundamental'.[13] Over time *kua-ni* tended to win out over *t'an-hui* because it reduced transport costs by combining preparation and boiling at a single site, where *t'an-hui* operated at two. Lixivation of ash was only resorted to where brine was unusually weak or plants unusually saline. It is the *t'an-hui* technique, however, which is described beautifully illustrated in the *Ao-po-t'u* of the salt official Ch'en Ch'un published around 1334.

All the *chien* techniques practised in Huai-nan and Liang-che were complicated and costly. Why were they not replaced by *shai*, as had happened on the Biscayan coast of France, was happening in Ch'ang-lu, Shantung and Huai-pei and would eventually, much later, happen in Chekiang? A mixture of technical and institutional factors suggest themselves.

First, in the Lower Yangtze region, *shai* faced problems of weak marine brine, insufficient summer sunshine because of the monsoon, and pollution during the long exposure in the basins. These problems could, in part at least, be overcome, but they had not been overcome in the medieval period. Since *chien* was already in possession, *shai* needed more than a minimal advantage in cost or quality to compete successfully, and this, despite its lower fuel bills, it did not yet enjoy. Objectively it was less pure, clean and white. Subjectively the Chinese consumer, except for some fishing interests, preferred small crystals to large. Second, it is likely that *shai* received no official encouragement. The cauldrons, pans and trays of the *chien* process were convenient control points for the salt administration, while the extended basins and heaps of the *shai* process, apparently unpoliceable, were an open invitation to smuggling. Government regulation of boiling implements was not always enforceable, but at least they were somewhere to begin. Third, while *shai* had no fuel costs so long as the sun shone, the capital cost of establishing and maintaining a set of evaporation basins was greater than that of acquiring marsh, grassland and cauldrons. Amortisement, in other words, was more significant in the decision to invest than unit cost. For all the simplicity of its techniques, successive basin evaporation stood closer economically to the capital intensive brine and fire well industry of Szechwan than it did to the traditional *chien* industry. But for a variety of reasons: high interest rates, an unsatisfactory legal system, guild restrictions; Chinese business preferred short-term amortisement. It sought to minimize risk rather than manage it. Business, therefore, did not pursue what technology offered.

Similar in their technology, Huai-nan and Liang-che differed in their degree of dynamism. Huai-nan, starting higher, rose less fast, but retained its position at the top. The earliest Sung quota was 781 000 cwt. This figure was not improved upon before 1127 and Huai-nan was temporarily surpassed by Ho-tung. With the move to the south, however, expansion began: 1 340 500 cwt in 1170, 1 950 000 cwt in 1245. The earliest Yüan quota, in 1279, was for 2 350 492 cwt. This was increased to 2 600 000 cwt in 1289 and to 3 800 800 cwt in 1329, though this last figure may contain up to 500 000 cwt attributable to Huai-pei. Under the Ming, the Huai-nan quota was initially reduced to 1 085 987 cwt, but by the sixteenth century the combined Liang-huai quotas had risen again to 2 820 730 cwt. The impetus for growth came from the up-river markets of Anhwei, Kiangsi, Hupei and Hunan, in contradistinction to the T'ang when the canal zone had been primary. It was this Yangtze trade which so impressed Marco Polo at Shih-erh-wei or Sinju, the port of Yang-chou:

> The chief article of commerce on the river is salt, which traders load at this city and carry throughout all the regions lying on the river and also up-country away from the main stream along the tributaries, supplying all the regions through which they flow. For this reason salt is brought from a long stretch of the sea-coast into Sinju and there it is put on board ship and transported into all these regions. The same ships also carry iron. On their return journey downstream they bring into this city wood, charcoal, hemp, and many other articles on which the coastal regions are dependent.[14]

Liang-che, on the other hand, from a lower starting point rose faster but less far. Its impetus for growth came from the booming market in its own vicinity: the nearly 20 million inhabitants of southern Kiangsu and northern Chekiang, in particular the great city of Hang-chou which may have had a population of 6 million and the scarcely less great city of Soochow, the showpieces of Marco Polo's China. The earliest Sung quota for Liang-che was for only 287 500 cwt. By 1031 it had been raised to 395 000 cwt, and by the end of the eleventh century to 500 000 cwt. It was the arrival of the imperial capital after 1127, however, which really produced a take-off: 985 000 cwt in 1170, over 1 million in the early thirteenth century. The Mongol invasion initially resulted in a check: 368 592 cwt in 1277, 874 248 cwt in 1281. But the advance was soon resumed: 1 400 000 cwt in 1289, 1 600 000 cwt in 1299, 2 million in 1329. The Ming who disliked Hang-chou and Soochow because they had opposed their revolution, reduced the quota to 881 880 cwt, but by the sixteenth century it had risen to 1 434 302 cwt again. Marco Polo is again a witness to the volume:

> I will till you next of the immense revenue that the Great Khan draws from this city of Kinsai [Hang-chou]. . . . First I will tell you of the salt, since this makes the biggest contribution to the total. . . . The reason for it is that, since the city stands on the edge of the sea, there are many lagoons or marshes nearby in which the seawater condenses in summer, and such quantities of salt are dug out that they supply the needs of five other kingdoms of the province of Manzi [South China].[15]

Marco Polo was right to be impressed by Huai-nan and Liang-che. By a mixture of favourable market opportunities, government support and considerably technical ingenuity at least, they recovered a lead for *chien* over *shai* in China which was not lost until the nineteenth century.

Fukien and Kwangtung

Finally, beyond the southeast lay the minor divisions of Fukien and Kwangtung. Both started with low Northern Sung quotas: 50 000 cwt for Fukien, 12 000 cwt for Kwangtung. Both developed under the Southern Sung, Fukien in particular because it contained the great port of Ch'uan-chou, Marco Polo's Zaiton. Under the Yüan, Fukien reached a quota of 520 000 cwt, Kwangtung of 204 000 cwt, which were reduced by the early Ming to 418 290 cwt and 187 421 cwt, the least reduction Emperor Hung-wu made anywhere. Both the *Yüan-shih* and the *Ming-shih* regard the principal method of production in Fukien and Kwangtung as *chien*, but there are also indications of the presence of *shai*. Thus a Mongol legal work, the *Ta Yüan Huang-cheng kuo-ch'ao tien-chang ts'ung-chi*, probably of the early fourteenth century, mentions *shai* in the two Yüan provinces of Chiang-che and Chiang-hsi which covered Fukien and Kwangtung, while the Yung-cheng edition of the Kwangtung *t'ung-chih* or provincial gazetteer has a reference to *shai* under the date 1461. Most likely, however, the *shai* in question was not successive basin evaporation, but simple evaporation, which was later characteristic of a number of sites in Fukien where brine was evaporated in jars (*ch'eng*), pits (*k'an*) and mound-pools (*ch'iu*). Successive basin solar evaporation was only brought to the far south at a later date.

Medieval China astonished Marco Polo by the manifest affluence of its high consumerism and the first European travellers of the period of the Great Discoveries were only slightly less astonished. But in many ways medieval China was less creative and dynamic than had been China in the days of the T'ang when it had been sustained both by secular cosmopolitanism and by religious triumphalism. Medieval China had contracted its horizons both within and without. Fundamentally, it was a cut flower civilization.[16]

SALT IN MEDIEVAL WESTERN EUROPE

Like medieval China, medieval Western Europe was a subcontinent. The history of its salt business too thus needs to be studied in terms of its parts. True, it was a smaller subcontinent, 750 000 square miles to China's 1.5 million square miles, but with the same average density of population. Sung China had a population of 150 million before the Mongol invasions: Latin Christendom had a population of 70 million before the Black Death. Indeed, Latin Christendom was fuller and more crowded than Sung China. Chinese horticultural farming was puncti-form, a scatter, however heavy, of discontinuous oases in a wilderness. European mixed arable and pastoral farming was areal and by the thirteenth century colonization had created landscapes where cultiva-tion was continuous from steeple to steeple and which supported the highest density of agricultural population in European history. This full world of medieval Latin Christendom, as Pierre Chaunu has called it,[17] was not made any less full by the Black Death. For the survivors of that holocaust raised their living standards, particularly in terms of animal protein – meat, cheese, butter and fish – and hence their requirements for space. Shortage of space, the temporary closing of the European frontier, produced a Teilhardian involution: a development at points of maximum pressure, of organization to compensate for the absence of mass. One expression of this proliferation of new institutional forms in medieval Europe, which went back to the eleventh century,[18] was the rise of regional salt networks, *ordines salis*, comparable to, but different from, the *yin-ti* of medieval China. It was the *ordines salis* which supplied the increased demands of European diet by telecommanding a techno-logical revolution: the victory of successive basin solar evaporation. Whereas in medieval China it was only consumption and distribution which changed, in medieval Europe it was consumption, distribution and production. But the reason for the contrast lay in the difference between the bureaucratic *yin-ti* and the business *ordo salis*.[19]

Genoa

As with so many innovations: marine insurance, gold coinage, circum-terranean voyaging, oceanic exploration, African reconnaissance; it was Genoa which pioneered the *ordo salis* – a regional salt network as opposed to simple trading in salt. Spreadeagled against the Apennines, without an agricultural hinterland, and militarily unfortifiable, Genoa was a typical pressure point for whom attack was the best defence. An Algiers in reverse, the Genoese plutocracy began as a lootocracy plundering the Muslim south. Unlike Algiers, however, Genoa passed from raid to trade: from the auction of stolen goods to the entrepôt of commodities, prominent among them salt. At its height in the mid-fifteenth century, the Genoese salt office handled nearly 500 000 cwt of salt a year. As Jacques Heers has shown, salt became a *primum mobile* in the Genoese commercial empire.[20] With salt Genoa obtained the metal goods of Milan which she redistributed throughout the Mediterranean. With salt Genoa seasoned the salami she exported along the Italian coast and bought raw silk in Naples and Sicily to supply the weavers of Lucca whose velvet she sold in Lyon to buyers from Paris. With salt Genoa mobilized wheat for herself in Tuscany and alum for the world of textiles in Tolfa. Genoa also used salt to open markets for its re-exports in France, Aragon and Castile, as well as in many points of the Muslim world. Import, export and entrepôt, Genoa used salt to generate trade for herself.

Genoese salt evolved through three stages. First, between 1150 and 1250, Genoa bought locally: from Hyères between Toulon and Nice, from Cagliari in Sardinia, and from Tortosa at the mouth of the Ebro. Hyères had probably produced salt in Roman times. Its names, Areae, 'the flats', may refer to salt fields: a *sebkha* or a group of single basins such as those described by Rutilius Namatianus on the coast of Tuscany. Production at Hyères is mentioned in a document of Leo VIII in 963. But it was Genoese demand, consolidated in treaties in 1138 and 1174 and eventually a monopoly agreement in 1229 which led to the introduction of successive basin evaporation and made Hyères more than a local supplier, the concern, not only of the abbey of St Victor and the seigneur of Fos, but of the count of Provence. By the fourteenth century production of Hyères had reached 200 000 cwt a year and until the fifteenth century it was Genoa's number one supplier. Cagliari was another producing centre whose development through the introduction of successive basin evaporation was due to Genoa in partnership or rivalry with Pisa in the eleventh and twelfth century. Soon, Cagliari produced 100 000 cwt a year, of which Genoa took half for the supply, chiefly, of Naples. Since at a later period, Cagliari became the largest single supplier to the Italian salt monopoly, its early development by Genoa was a matter of some importance in the Mediterranean.[21] Tortosa, on the other hand, was a former Muslim producing centre. Its salt was consumed principally by Barcelona and, via the Ebro, inland Aragon, in both places competing with Cardona rock salt. Possibly 25 000 cwt a year entered the Genoese network.

Second, from 1250 to 1400, especially from the restoration of the Palaeologi in 1261 to the war of Chioggia in 1380, years when her seapower was at its height, Genoa bought from distant suppliers: the Crimea, Cyprus, Alexandria. Ras al-Makhbaz, Ibiza, La Mata, Torrevieja. Once again Genoa was the pioneer in a move which others copied and for which there were two main reasons. First, as her commercial horizons expanded, Genoa needed more salt for her complex system of exchanges, from more places, since diplomatic difficulties, with Aragon over Ibiza or with the papacy over trade with the infidel might temporarily close down a particular source of supply. Second, Genoa also pioneered the use of large northern type ships in the Mediterranean, whether her own or hired from Ragusa or the Basque ports. Since bulky goods predominated on outward journeys from Genoa, there was cargo space for an equally bulky commodity like salt on the return journey. It might be cheaper to ship Crimean salt on a ship coming home from Tana, or Ibiza salt on a ship coming from London, than direct from Hyères, Cagliari or Tortosa. In this period, Genoa made use of a wide range of suppliers, without forcing the development of any particular one, of which Cyprus under the Lusignans with its *sebkha* at Larnaca was one of the largest.

Third, from 1400 to 1500, Genoa, following her defeat by Venice, the closure of the steppe route to the Black Sea, and the rise of the Ottomans, once more concentrated on the western Mediterranean: Hyères and Tortosa, La Mata and Torrevieja, and above all Ibiza.[22] By origin Balearic successive basin solar evaporation was Muslim and was directed to the Islamic cities of the Maghreb and even after the islands became Christian in 1235 we still hear of consignments of salt taking this route. At Ibiza the salines belonged first to the three seigneurs who organized the conquest, then to the archbishop of Tarragona, and finally to the crown of Aragon. The first record of the Genoese there is in 1258 and by 1284 they were already the principal buyers. However, the scale remained limited. In 1361 70 000 cwt was considered a large export to Genoa; and the trade was often interrupted by bad relations between the republic and the crown. In the fifteenth century trade in the red salt of Ibiza really took off. In the year May 1450 to May 1451 the Genoese bought 400 000 cwt, and as other buyers such as Venice and Barcelona were also making substantial purchases, total production will have reached 600 000 cwt. A fifteenth-century Catalan described Ibiza as 'el salero de todo el mundo',[23] but Genoese demand was dominant. The same was also true at the Valencian salines of La Mata and Torrevieja, with a joint production of 200 000 cwt, which were useful to the Genoese as an alternative to the Catalan sources. The Genoese also traded at the major Castilian saline, San Lucar de Barrameda, from which they transported salt to the Muslim kingdom of Grenada. Thus throughout the western Mediterranean Genoese demand led the acceleration of the production of salt by successive basin solar evaporation. It was only appropriate that the super Genoese, Columbus, should obtain part of the finance for his first voyage from Luis de Santangel, royal superintendent of the salines of La Mata. Mediterranean Spain financed Atlantic via the cosmopolitan relay of Valencia.

Venice

What Genoa began, Venice continued. Venice was more institutionalized than Genoa: it was a huge regulated company rather than a congerie of competing millionaires. The Venetian *ordo salis* was likewise more highly formalized than the Genoese. The Venetians referred to salt as *'il vero fondamento del nostro stato'*.[24] It was, indeed, even more important to them than to the Genoese because its function and the system were different. To Genoa salt was ignition, to Venice it was fuel. Like the Dutch later, the Genoese were 'wagoners of all seas': *'Genovesi faciunt facta sua cum navibus'*, it was said.[25] They operated a multilateral Baltic exchange, with other people's shipping as well as their own, which often by-passed Genoa altogether. The Venetians, on the other hand, were principals, not just providers of business services. They operated a bilateral commodity supply in which ideally all transactions should pass through Venice as head office. The provision of salt to the Po valley was an early and profitable part of Venice's commodity business, useful too for ensuring a countervailing supply of grain. But over time that function came second to the role of salt in subsidizing Venetian shipping and indirectly the whole business community of the republic.

From 1281 the Venetian state paid a subsidy on all salt brought to the city from the more distant suppliers in the outer Mediterranean. These subsidies enabled Venetian shippers to transport other commodities, notably spices, at lower freight rates than their competitors, either in the same ships or in other vessels, such as galleys, chartered by them. In this way the Venetians were able to dominate the international commodity markets. The subsidies were paid ultimately by Venice's customers for salt, but by raising the price of a relatively inelastic everyday commodity, the Venetians were able to lower the cost of relatively elastic luxury commodities. Moreover, the subsidies, paid in the form of bank credits, increased the money supply and eased the *strettezza* which was so often a bottleneck in traditional economies, especially in the later Middle Ages. Salt credits formed part of a complex system of fiduciary money, assignment and clearance which lubricated not only the commodity business, but the entire turnover of state and society. By increasing business activity, they may even have created new wealth for Venice's trading partners out of which the subsidies could be paid. For the Venetians, salt was not a commodity among commodities: more than a *primum mobile*, it greased the wheels of all the working parts and fuelled its motor.

Like Genoese, Venetian salt evolved through three stages. First, between 1000 and 1250, Venice sought to enforce a sales monopoly in the Po valley for her own local sources of supply. Unlike Genoa, Venice had salt on her doorstep: at Chioggia where new successive basin solar evaporation salines commenced operations early in the eleventh century and in her Istrian dependencies of Muggia, Capodistria and especially Piran. Equally, Venice faced local competition: from Comacchio owned by the Benedictine abbeys of the delta, notably Pomposa; from Cervia under the archbishop of Ravenna; and, more distantly, from Pago, controlled now by the commune of Zara. Against Comacchio, Venice's Chioggia and Piran (where the technique may have arrived from Siponto earlier than at Chioggia) pitted large scale successive basin evaporation against small scale single basin evaporation, but Cervia and Pago also practised the successive basin method. The Venetian salt administration therefore resorted to a variety of expedients: forcible closure at Comacchio, and alternation of destruction and partnership at Cervia, the imposition of quotas at Pago. One way or another the dominance of Venetian controlled salt was assured, with Piran gradually taking the lead from Chioggia which was crippled by storm damage at the beginning of the thirteenth century.

Next, with an expanding clientele for her salt in northern and central Italy, Venice from 1250 to 1400 bought from the further Mediterranean: the Muslim *sebkhas* of Alexandria, Tripoli, Ras al-Makhbaz and Zarzis; the Christian successive basin salines of Cagliari, Ibiza and La Mata; the Christian *sebkhas* of the Crimea and Cyprus. While no one supplier was preeminent, Ibiza, conveniently placed on the route back from Bruges and the north, was one of the largest. Begun for commercial reasons, the appeal to Mediterranean salt was continued for economic and political. The Venetian authorities saw in the subsidization of long-distance salt imports a means of achieving competitive advantage for other commodities through lower freight rates. Between 1250 and 1400 Venice and Genoa competed for salt throughout the Mediterranean as part of their general rivalry for trade, their particular rivalry for spices. That competition Venice won largely because of her use of the salt subsidy as an investment incentive. Moreover, Venice, unlike Genoa, was concerned to maintain the number of large ships in her service as a naval reserve and the salt subsidy acted to good effect here too. In the four naval wars of the fourteenth century, it was Venice's political cohesion and stamina, as exemplified in the war of Chioggia, which brought her victory over Genoa's disunity and lack of direction.

Finally, from 1400 to 1500, Venice, despite her successes at sea and in trade, increasingly concentrated on the eastern Mediterranean. Just as Genoa, only half defeated, focused on the red salt of Ibiza, Venice, only half victorious, focused on the white salt of Cyprus. Cyprus became a Venetian protectorate in 1473, a territorial possession in 1489. Even before that, the Corner family, active in the island since the middle of the fourteenth century, had so improved the two salt lakes at Larnaca with protective works, evaporation areas and water-raising devices that the ancient *sebkha* became in effect a successive basin artificial saltern. By the beginning of the fifteenth century, Cyprus was the number two producer in the Mediterranean after Ibiza with an annual productive capacity of 400 000 cwt. Some of this went to eastern Turkey and northern Syria, but most to Venice. In 1463 Venice came into possession of Cervia again which was taken into partnership and in 1473 produced over 160 000 cwt of salt for the Venetian network. Pago, with a productive capacity of 200 000 cwt, was compelled to offer three-quarters of its salt to Venice, and Piran, with the same capacity, the whole of it, any surpluses being exported to Croatia and not Italy. In 1493, 320 000 cwt of salt were landed at Venice for distribution to the Po valley. The total amount of salt handled directly by the Venetian monopoly was around 400 000 cwt, little less than the quantity operated by the Genoese salt empire, while its indirect sway was greater. It was loans raised by the salt office which allowed Venice to survive the terrible crisis of the League of Cambrai and to advance into a new period of differently structured prosperity in the sixteenth century. If salt paid for the new diffusion of Genoa, it also paid for the new concentration of Venice.

Rhône

Passing over a number of lesser urban maritime salt networks such as Barcelona and the Balearics, Pisa and Sardinia, we turn to the major Mediterranean river network: that along the Rhône from the salines of Peccais near Aigues-Mortes and those of the Camargue south of Arles to eastern Languedoc, Avignon, northern Provence, Lyon, Dauphiné, and southern Burgundy. This network is known to us in particular from the account books of the Florentine Francesco di Marco Datini who traded at Peccais, 1376–1379. From the days of the Avignon papacy, it was an Italian, specifically Tuscan, trade route. Datini's consortium was a subsidiary of his Avignon company which in turn was part of the world-wide Datini group. This route became the basis for the *petite gabelle*, the oldest stratum of the French salt monopoly.[26] Italian in operation, it was French in direction.

Languedoc passed to the French crown in the early thirteenth century as a result of the Albigensian crusade. In 1246 St Louis established the fortified town of Aigues-Mortes, the first French Mediterranean port. Salines already existed to the east at Peccais, owned by the abbey of Psalmodi and the seigneurs of Uzès and Aimargues. In 1290 they were acquired by the French crown and developed with the assistance of Italian entrepreneurs, and doubtless, technicians. By 1300 there were 16 salines in operation, covering 1000 hectares, and with a production of 300 000 cwt. Peccais was the number three producer in the Mediterranean after Ibiza and Cyprus. The method was successive basin. One of the salines called 'The Terraces' (*della Terraza*) was divided into two parts, while another, 'The Curve' (*della Churba*) was divided into three or four: names and divisions indicative of the familiar lay-out of catchment, condensers and crystallizers.

In 1301 the King of France agreed with his relative the Count of Provence, who was also King of Naples, that Peccais should supply 'two-thirds of the needs of the Kingdom and half the needs of the Empire' (that is their combined territories in the southeast). The remaining one third and one half were to be supplied by the salines of Provence, notably those of the Camargue. Provence, where a salt administration had been established by Count Charles I in 1259, was already a considerable producer, also by the successive basin method.[27] Around 200 000 cwt each were produced by three sets of salines: in the Camargue south of Arles; along the coast east of the Rhône, notably at the lagoon of Berre west of Marseille which supplied the muleteers with salt for Aix and the valley of the Durance; and at Hyères where, as we have seen, Genoa was dominant. Under the agreement, Peccais dominated the river ports of Beaucaire, Avignon, Orange, Pont-Saint-Esprit, Valence and Lyon, while the other salines took other routes. No doubt there were hidden advantages to the Count of Provence, as the agreement formed part of the wider alliance of the Count as King of Naples, France, the Avignon papacy and the Florentine bankers. Datini himself did not long stay in it: profit margins were too small because of excessive taxation in the kingdom as opposed to the provinces of the Empire. The French monarchy was in the middle of the Hundred Years War and drove a hard bargain. But if Datini got out, the network continued under Tuscan direction as one of the major articulations of Mediterranean salt. It was not unrepresentative of other lesser articulations which followed water routes from the coast to the interior: the Neretva to Bosnia, the Ebro to Aragon, the Aude to inner Languedoc, the Arno to Tuscany, the Drin to Albania. Always, where possible, salt followed water routes to reduce transportation costs. Only where there were no navigable rivers, as from the *sebkhas* of Roussillon to the eastern Pyrenees, was there recourse to cart tracks and mule trails.[28] To use rivers merchants must accept partnership with princes.

The Hanse

In northern Europe, with its weaker marine brine and cloudier skies, successive basin solar evaporation, though attempted as far north as Lymington in Hampshire, could not flourish. The increased demand generated by more meat and fish had initially to be met by other techniques: mines, wells, brine reinforcement. In the long run, however, the solution was to link the cold, fishy seas of the north with the warm, brine rich seas of the south. This connection was made by the Hanse, the first regional salt network in northern Europe.[29]

The Hanse was the civilized successor to the Viking international. Although delegates from 70 to 170 towns attended its diets, it was less a league of cities than an interurban community: an association of families united by business, marriage and a common pidgin. Lübeck was only the focus of the community. Founded in 1158 and recognized as a free imperial city in 1227, in 1356 she organized the Hanse diets, in 1370 imposed peace on Denmark, in 1388 capitulations on Bruges. Yet Lübeck was no Genoa or Venice. The reality of the Hanse lay not in its central institutions, but in its eastern colonies, such as Königsberg, Riga, Dorpat or Reval and in its Kontors, its overseas offices: the Sankt Peterhof at Novgorod, the Deutsche Brucke at Bergen, the steelyard in London, the agencies in Bruges and Bourgneuf. Here, as in the European concessions of the China coast, the Hansards conducted their business triumphantly or modestly as circumstances dictated. The essence of that business was liaison: between the now semi-mature economy of the west and the new colonial Christendom of the Baltic – the conquered lands of Prussia, the converted lands of Lithuania. Concretely this meant the exchange of western textiles, wines, spices and manufactured goods against the raw materials of the east – timber, fur, honey, wax, tar, cereals and fish. In this exchange, salt figured both as a western manufactured product and as a constituent in the eastern fisheries, then centred off the coast of Skane. Salt was a major element in the Baltic trade. Of 1700 ships entering Reval between 1426 and 1496, 1216 carried salt and the annual volume of import amounted to 120 000 cwt. Reval, moreover, was not the greatest Hanseatic salt port. That title fell to Königsberg, which in the fifteenth century imported around 400 000 cwt, chiefly for Lithuania, the Hanse's biggest customer for salt.

As with Genoa and Venice, the Hanseatic salt trade evolved through three stages. First, in the twelfth and thirteenth centuries, to supply the growing needs of the Skane fisheries, Lübeck obtained salt from the mines and wells of Lüneburg across the Elbe to the southwest. Lüneburg is first mentioned as producing salt in a charter of Otto I in 935. In the eleventh century its salt resources were developed by the dukes of Saxony, notably Henry the Lion. In the twelfth century control passed to the local bourgeoisie, the *Sulfmeister*, under the auspices of Lübeck. By 1205 production is said to have reached 100 000 cwt. In the thirteenth century production expanded again and by 1300 reached 300 000 cwt. Lüneburg was the largest producing centre in northern Europe.

The rise of Lüneburg was part of a wider revival in the Middle Ages of the German inland rich brine salines.[30] In this revival a considerable part was played by monasteries of the Cistercian order, especially the subsidiaries of the French house of Morimond. The Cistercians avoided feudal revenues, they were pastoralists rather than arable farmers, and hence needed salt for their animals and dairy products. From this, since the Cistercians were intelligent and recruited from among the enterprising rural classes, it was a short step into salt production, though the fruits of their enterprise often passed rapidly from the monks to prelates or princes. In the Salzkammergut, new brine shafts and boiling plant were opened at Aussee around 1147 by the Cistercian monastery of Rein and by 1392–3 the works were selling 200 000 cwt a year. Hallstatt was revived at the end of the twelfth century. Here the Cistercian houses of Neuburg and Engelszell were involved. In 1336 the works sold 120 000 cwt. In Salzburg production was developed at Reichenhall and Berchtesgaden by both the archbishop and the duke of Bavaria. By 1500, Reichenhall, in whose development the Cistercian monastery of Raitenhaslach had played a part, was producing 170 000 cwt a year. Hallein-Durrenberg, however, remained the chief producer with an output in 1498 of 460 000 cwt. Here again, a Cistercian house, Salem on Lake Constance, assisted the archbishop in the early days. He continued to share control, or lack of it, with neighbouring religious houses, gentry and local bourgeosie or 'boiling lords', *Siedherren*. Another saline which was assisted by the Cistercians was Hall in the Tirol whose production was stimulated by the pastoral monastery of Stams further up the Inntal.

Not all the revivals were monastic in origin. In Saxony, Halle was redeveloped by the archbishop of Magdeburg, first in collaboration with, then in competition against, the local aristocracy, the *Pfannerschaft*, or salt *Junkers* who controlled both pans and fuel supply. By the end of the fifteenth century, Halle and its newly developed subsidiary Stassfurt were producing 200 000 cwt a year, a considerable proportion of which was exported to Bohemia. In other cases, the development of salines was due to free cities: for example, Schwäbisch Hall in Württemberg. Medieval Germany was a big producer of salt with already considerable technical expertise in mining, piping and boiling. The rise, or rerise, of local salines as a source of wealth to independent prelates, local magnates and free cities, was a considerable factor in the genesis of political particularism in late medieval Germany. Lübeck itself is an example of this.

Second, in the fourteenth century, as even Lüneburg became insufficient for the growing demands of Scandinavia and the Baltic, especially
with the development of the fur trade to Bruges, Lübeck obtained sea
salt from the west. In the so-called *Baienfahrt*, the Hansards resumed the
route of the Vikings and turned to the successive basin, solar evaporation salines of the Bay of Biscay. The 'Bay' originally referred specifically
to the bay of Bourgneuf just south of the Loire and to the east of
Noirmoutier. Here 20 miles of coast shared between the dukes of
Brittany, the county of Poitou and the marches common to both,
produced low quality but abundant and cheap salt. Particularly under
the Montfort dukes of Brittany, who enjoyed the benefit of neutrality in
the Hundred Years War, gave easy leases and kept taxes low, the Breton
and Poitevin gentry and the local abbeys eagerly invested in salt production. The dukes gave privileges to the Hansards and established a court
of the bay to administer mercantile law. By the fifteenth century Bourgneuf had become the principal source of salt for the Baltic as well as
exporting to the Low Countries and England. Between 1427 and 1433, of
314 ships entering Reval, 105 came from Bourgneuf as against 103 from
Lübeck, but of the salt landed, 100 000 cwt was Bay salt as against
20 000 cwt from Lüneburg. Gradually, however, especially after 1450 as
the ravages of the Hundred Years War were repaired, the focus of the
trade shifted south from Bourgneuf to Brouage in Saintonge, part of the
commercial empire of La Rochelle. These southern salines enjoyed the
advantages of greater sun and closer proximity to the source of the other
major French export to the north, claret. By the beginning of the
sixteenth century, the total amount of salt passing through the Sound
from the west was of the order of 1 600 000 cwt, of which at least
three-quarters came from the Biscayan salines: say 400 000 cwt from
Bourgneuf and 800 000 cwt from Brouage. These salines also supplied
considerable quantities of salt to France itself via the Seine, the Loire and
the Garonne, which, like the Rhône, were rivers of salt.

Finally, in the fifteenth century, in the so-called *Spanienfahrt*, the
Hanse reached out to the Iberian successive basin solar evaporation
salines of Setubal in Portugal, San Lucar de Barrameda, and Ibiza. As
early as 1404, a Venetian source reports six Hanseatic ships at Ibiza
loading salt.[31] From 1410 Setubal salt, *Lissaboner salz*, was regularly
quoted at Dantzig alongside Biscay salt, *Baiensalz*. The Hansards may
have obtained 300 000 cwt a year from Setubal by the end of the
fourteenth century and 100 000 cwt from the Castilian and Aragonese
salines. Altogether, combining the figures from Lüneburg, Bourgneuf,
Brouage and Iberian salines, the Hanse handled nearly 2 million cwt of
salt a year, not far short of that handled by Liang-che in its palmiest days
under the Yüan. It was an impressive achievement for what remained,

compared to Mediterranean sophistications, a rather primitive form of business organization.

England

A second regional salt network in the north of Europe was that conducted by the London city companies, in particular the Salters.[32] With 120 parishes and a population of at least 40 000 by the end of the twelfth century, medieval London was not only the primate city of England but also, through its link to the Low Countries and to Aquitaine, a major centre of international commerce. Of this commerce the city companies were the focus. The first guild appears in 1180 in association with the maintenance of London bridge. The Pepperers, the precursor of the Grocers, were active in the thirteenth century. As regards the Salters, in 1345 an Alderman John Gloucester founded two chantries in St Mary Mounthaunt on the basis of receipts from the Salt Wharf. In 1454 the Salters acquired a hall in Bread street. Salters were lords mayor in 1475, 1487, 1494, 1530, and 1542. Though, like all the city companies, the Salters were generalists rather than specialists, trade in salt, in particular its supply to the bakers, fishmongers and cheesemongers closely associated with them, was one of their main activities, though they had to share it with the Mercers and Grocers.

Medieval England both imported and exported salt. At the Conquest the largest single source was the brine pits of Droitwich in Worcestershire. These provided 24 000 cwt of good quality salt for the Midlands and via the river port of Lechlade for London. Droitwich received a royal charter in 1215 and, under the leadership of its burgesses, production was expanded to 32 000 cwt by 1500. A similar production may be credited to the Cheshire wiches which exported to Wales and Ireland as well as supplying the north of England. But with a population of 3 million before the Black Death and again in 1500, England, with a high standard of living and a protein rich diet, needed between 150 000 and 225 000 cwt a year. Some of this came from Lincolnshire, whose earth and brine boiling industry experienced a modest revival between 1100 and 1300, because there was also an export trade via Boston to the Low Countries where the rise of the fisheries was increasing demand beyond the capacity of the Zeeland peat salt industry of the island of Tolen. But neither in quality nor quantity was Lincolnshire adequate for London. As with the Hanse, the solution was the route west to the Bay of Biscay. Thanks to the early connection with Aquitaine, Brouage was possibly the first point of supply, but with the Hundred Years War, neutral Bourgneuf came to provide London with between 70 and 90 per cent of its imports between 1350 and 1450. In addition, there was an indepen-

dent route from the West Country, in particular Bristol and Exeter, to
the Breton salines.[33] Bristol merchants also went further afield, to
Setubal, and to Spain, probably San Lucar de Barrameda. Between them
London, Bristol and Exeter imported around 100 000 cwt of salt a year,
and possibly more, since it has been reckoned that England absorbed
15–20 per cent of the total volume of Bay salt brought to northern
Europe.[34] English, Dutch, Hansard and Breton ships were all involved
in the traffic, but what most impresses is the sophistication and flexi-
bility of London institutions in the later medieval period. The Hanse
handled more, but the city companies were already its superior in
organization.

Franche Comté and Poland-Lithuania

Sophisticated organization in Franche Comté and Poland-Lithuania, in
production rather than distribution, marked the two regional networks
operated by the Grande Saunerie at Salins and by the royal mines at
Wieliczka-Bochnia.[35] Salins and Wieliczka had much in common. Both
were brine mines digging deep into the earth to tap subterranean
springs whose brine was then brought to the surface and evaporated
over wood fires. Both served captive markets which, because they were
far from the sea, were prepared to pay high prices for their salt. Both
were developed under princely patronage and to princely advantage
though both faced private competition which in the medieval period
was not entirely overcome.

   Although the Franche Comté had produced salt in Roman times and
in the Dark Ages, it was not until the thirteenth century that its
production, based on 11–12 per cent salinity brine and abundant local
timber, became considerable and by 1500 reached 150 000 cwt. The
principal centre of production was Salins on the Furieuse in the present
day department of the Jura. Here three saltworks developed in the
thirteenth century.[36] First, in the upper town, Bourg Dessus, there was
the Grande Saunerie, a large complex of buildings containing two
groups of salt wells, in which half the shares were held by the count
palatine, one third by the house of Orange and one sixth by local
notables. Second, again in the upper town, there was the Chauderette, a
small boiling establishment also owned by local notables, which was
almost a subsidiary of the Grande Saunerie, since it was supplied with
brine from the Saunerie wells. Third, in the lower town, the Bourg
Dessous, there was the Puits à Muire, another sizeable salt boiling
complex with its own wells, owned one third by ecclesiastics, among
whom the Cistercians were prominent, and two thirds by laymen,
chiefly members of the local lesser nobility who supplied the timber so
crucial in production. All the Salins works were sophisticated techno-

logically, especially in their devices for pumping brine from the wells to the boiling pans.

Institutionally, the history of Salins consisted of the attempts of the counts palatine, who subsequently became first dukes of Burgundy, then rulers of the Low Countries under that title and finally kings of Spain, to become dominant within the Grande Saunerie and to make the Bourg Dessus pre-eminent over the Bourg Dessous. In these attempts the counts eventually succeeded, but only at the end of the sixteenth century when the brine was losing salinity, wood was becoming scarce and competition from hitherto underdeveloped Lorraine was increasing. Nevertheless, even short of complete success, the duke-counts took an active and constructive role in the industry. The Grande Saunerie was developed particularly during the reign of Charles the Bold, 1467–1477, when production was about 100 000 cwt a year. The Grande Saunerie sought to establish a monopoly sales area throughout both the Burgundies and western Switzerland in the face of French sea salt coming variously by the Seine, the Loire and the Rhône. It also had to face the competition of the Lorraine wells and to accommodate the ambitions of the Bourg Dessous and the Chauderette, which had the support of local interests. Charles the Bold planned to make the Grande Saunerie a key economic element in his reconstruction of the middle kingdom of Lotharingia as the grand duchy of the west. In this, as in much else, he overplayed his hand and failed, but the Grande Saunerie survived his fall, and by 1500 was reviving under his son-in-law, Emperor Maximilian.

Wieliczka was on a bigger scale and was more successful as a princely institution. The first works, developed between the tenth and thirteenth centuries, used saline springs or shallow wells. Then from 1290 deep mining for rock salt was undertaken. Finally, especially with the introduction of vast wooden wheels for pumping, the underground brine springs discovered in the great galleries hollowed out by the earlier mining, were called into contribution. Wieliczka was particularly developed during the reign of Casimir the Great, 1333–1370, the refounder of the Polish state on a new eastern orientation. He brought in foreign capital, expertise and superintendence and in 1368 codified the laws relating to the mines. In the fourteenth century the mines provided one third of the royal revenue and met many new expenses. For example, when the university at nearby Cracow was founded in 1364, the salaries of the professors were charged to the salt account. In the fifteenth century, when the Polish state was reinforced by the union with Lithuania, the grand duchy of the east, Wieliczka continued both to support royal finance and to attract foreign investment. Under the Jagellons, lessees of the mine included Frenchmen, Italians, Germans and Jews as well as Poles. By 1500 production amounted to 160 000 cwt a year.[37] Wieliczka supplied not only southern Poland – the north was supplied by Hanseatic salt from Dantzig – but also White Russia, northern Hungary and the eastern part of the lands of the crown of St Wenceslas: Silesia and Moravia. Like the Grande Saunerie, however, Wieliczka faced private competition: not only from Hanseatic salt in Lithuania proper, but also from the ancient salt mines and wells in Galicia, which had been developed in the thirteenth century by the Volhynian princes of the Romanovichi dynasty. In theory these mines and wells had fallen to the Polish crown as part of its share in the Galician–Volhynian succession, but in practice, since they were numerous and scattered, they escaped its control and came under that of the Ukrainian nobility. Galician salt, like German, fostered particularism, first in the Romanovichi state and then in the double commonwealth of Poland-Lithuania.

Both China and Europe saw considerable development of salt and salt administrations in the Middle Ages, but it was under different managements and in different directions. In China, it was the work of regional imperial salt administrations and its effect was technologically conservative, despite China's earlier advance. In Europe, though some princes were already active, it was the work of urban consortia building on monastic enterprise and its effect, despite Europe's earlier backwardness, was technologically innovative. In Europe the sap was still rising. In China, on the other hand, it had risen so far and had then fallen back. In 1500 production was substantially lower than it had been in 1300: 7 million cwt compared to 10 million.[38]

5 Late Tradition, Early Modernity

In salt, as in other things, the period 1500 to 1800 looked both ways: back to tradition and forward to modernity. On the one hand, a whole premodern ecology, elaborated, developed and refined from antiquity, reached maturity and won its last triumphs. On the other hand, there appeared the shoots of a new ecology which were already providing the firstfruits of a different harvest. In production, controlled solar evaporation extended its by now ancient empire, but coal and natural gas also expanded their newer kingdoms. In distribution, the sailing ship remained dominant and reached new technical perfections, but it now sailed regularly on the ocean as well as seas, rivers and canals. In consumption, alimentary demand retained its primacy, but diet patterns were changing and a fresh market opened with the first stirrings of industrial chemistry.

Across this spectrum of tradition and modernity, the major civilized societies were unevenly distributed. Europe, surcharging medieval urbanism with renaissance mercantilism and enlightenment liberalism, was most modern. Islam, master now of Constantinople and Mughal India but slave of its own dervishism, was most traditional. China, in its silver age under the Ming and the Ch'ing, lay in between, though closer to Europe than to Islam. The contrast between early modern Europe and late traditional China is really too strong. Under the enlightened rule of the late Ming ministers, the high Ch'ing emperors and the early nineteenth-century viceroys, Chinese society, set free from over-regulation, regained some of the momentum it had lost under the late Sung and early Ming. Yet by 1800, even before the Industrial Revolution which was a result as much as a cause of its supremacy, Europe, and specifically England, was beginning to draw ahead in the world of salt in terms of modernity of production, scope of distribution and size of *per capita* consumption. Thus European distribution was beginning to spill over into other parts of the world and to lay the foundations of a European, again specifically English, world order in salt. By 1875 Cheshire was exporting to five continents: 150 000 tons to Europe (here, significantly we move from hundredweights to tons), 250 000 tons to North America, 25 000 tons each to Africa and Australia, 300 000 tons to India, as well as supplying 700 000 tons to the domestic market.[1] Only China, from which the import of salt was specifically excluded by the treaty of Tientsin in 1858, escaped the empire of Cheshire.

SALT IN EARLY MODERN EUROPE

Europe in the early modern period may be divided into four interrelated subregions. First, there was the old Mediterranean endocentre, now relativized and relegated to junior partnership by its former colonies in the north. Second, there was the new Circumterranean exocentre, decolonized since the sixteenth century and thenceforward dominant through its mastery of the Baltic and the Ocean. Third, there were the continental heartlands from the Bay of Biscay to the Carpathians, despite the efforts of Colbert and Cameralism as much subject to the new masters as to the old. Finally, there were the new lands of America and Muscovy, both in Europe's orbit culturally, but the first a European colony economically, the second an *economie monde* of its own.

Some factors relevant to the history of salt affected all four subregions. Of these the most important between 1500 and 1800 were changes in diet. The history of European diet down to the twentieth century may be understood schematically in terms of successive emphasis on carbohydrates, protein and fats. In the early neolithic, the primacy of carbohydrates in the form of cereals, *panem quotidianum*, was established for the mass of the population. Then, from late antiquity, the *limes* lifestyle, multiplied by the 'full world' of the thirteenth century and extended by the new pastoralism of Le Roy Ladurie's post-Black Death century of rare man,[2] brought a new emphasis on protein: pork, fish, mutton and beef. Finally, as indicated by Jean-Louis Flandrin,[3] from the fifteenth century, as a result of the decolonization, spread and eventual Europeanization of Northern taste, emphasis is shifted to fats: butter, lard, cheese and cream. First, there was a move from a spicy low fat diet to a richer, high fat diet. Butter and lard replaced olive oil in the fry-pan. Onions, garlic, shalots, mushrooms and truffles replaced vinegar, almonds, cumin, saffron and cinnamon as flavourings. At the same time, consumption of cheese increased: the patrician cheeses (most of the famous brands – Brie, Stilton, Double Gloucester, Edam, Gouda, Gruyère, Emmental – seem to go back to the sixteenth or seventeenth centuries) as part of the mutation of taste from spicy to rich; the plebeian cheeses as part of the ongoing popularization of protein in centuries when man was no longer rare and meat had temporarily priced itself out of the market. Finally, cream came into wider use with the progress of patisserie, the advent of chocolate and coffee, and the invention of the new feminine meal of afternoon tea.

Cheese, butter and lard all required more salt for their preservation and preparation. The shift from spicy to rich meant more salt in cooking and more table salt, lest blandness turn to insipidity. The flavour creating function of salt was even more necessary in weakly flavoured non-spicy 'cold' foods than in strongly flavoured spicy 'hot' foods. The cattle which produced the milk required more salt than pigs and sheep. Alimentary demand for salt in Europe consequently increased sharply in the early modern period. Of this revolution in fats, the Low Countries were the epicentre, Rubens the painter and the vogue for still life the artistic expression. The Low Countries were the first centre of the dairy industry. From the fourteenth century, landowners in Hainaut began converting arable into pasture, in particular for cattle, both beef and dairy. Brabant followed suit in the fifteenth century, Flanders and Holland in the sixteenth, Frisia and Groningen in the seventeenth.[4] It is not surprising, therefore, that this area, already preeminent in fisheries, became a major focus of the salt trade in the early modern period. Equally, the parallel decline of the spice trade weighed heavily on the older focus of the European marine salt trade, the Mediterranean.

The Mediterranean

The early modern period, at least from the seventeenth century, is usually regarded as one of decline for the Mediterranean. In salt matters, however, Hocquet has shown that mutation is a better characterization than decline.[5] True, the *ordines salis* of the greater city states contracted or disappeared, but they were replaced by smaller local networks which may, in the aggregate, have carried as much or more salt. This regionalization of the Mediterranean salt trade was effected by three developments: the rise of Trapani, the shift of major entrepôts to local sources of supply, and the rise of minor entrepôts.

Until the middle of the sixteenth century, Trapani had been at most a source of local salt supply. Thereafter, until about 1600, it became a major contributor to the salt empires of Genoa and Venice. Trapani partially eclipsed Ibiza and Cyprus, both of which went into decline at this time, by no means exclusively because of the Barbary raids on the one and Ottoman occupation in the other. It is not easy to explain the sudden rise of Trapani, based on advanced successive basin solar evaporation. Sicily was best known in the epoque of Philip II as a source of grain, but this cannot be the explanation because grain and salt contraindicated each other since both were/bulk goods which competed for the same cargo space. More likely, the explanation was urban and military. The two Sicilies under Philip II were prosperous.[6] Palermo in particular grew rapidly as a centre of conspicuous consumption and culture. Moreover, Sicily was a naval frontier against the Ottomans into which the Spanish empire found it necessary to inject capital. Ships bringing consumer goods and military supplies to Sicilian waters were therefore glad of salt as ballast on their return journeys to Genoa and Venice. Genoa and Venice, for their part, were glad to contribute such ships because both the Atlantic alum trade of the one via Ibiza and the

Levantine pepper trade of the other via Cyprus were falling into decay as northern Europe discovered its own sources of alum and the Dutch dominated the spice islands.

The dominance of Trapani did not much outlast 1600. The seventeenth century was less prosperous for the two Sicilies than the sixteenth. Naples, Palermo and Messina all saw revolts against Spanish authority. Consequently, the consumer trade declined, while the naval frontier was run down, as the Ottomans, like the Spanish, turned their face from the Mediterranean. Genoa still took salt from Trapani, but an increasing percentage of its supply came from mainland Spain, with which its trade was particularly active: Seville, La Mata and Torrevieja, Tortosa and Cardona. Venice abandoned Trapani even more dramatically. It did not exploit the salines it had established in Crete to replace those of Cyprus, but increasingly sought its supplies close at hand in the Terra da Mar: Muggia, Capodistria, Piran, Pago, Sebenico, Corfu and Santa Maura. By the middle of the seventeenth century the *ordines salis* were things of the past, part of the wreck of empire in a period of portfolio readjustment.

With salt no longer of more than incidental interest to the major business cities of the Mediterranean, minor cities moved into the trade to operate less pretentious networks on shorter distance routes. Thus Messina became the distributor for Trapani salt in southern Italy. Ancona, under papal protection, relayed a variety of salts to the mouth of the Po, whence it invaded the markets of Lombardy long disputed between Venice and Genoa. Ragusa, decolonized from both Genoa and Venice, took control of the salt of Apulia (Manfredonia and Barletta) and diffused it more widely in the Balkans via the Neretva and the Drin. Cyprus, deposed from its international role, returned to being a local supplier to southern Turkey and northern Syria, under the lead of Jewish merchants from Smyrna and Greek shipping. In the western Mediterranean, Ibiza continued to produce its red salt, but in the seventeenth century, overtaxed, underprotected from Barbary pirates, and badly hit by malaria, its international status declined and nearby Algiers became its principal outlet when trade expanded again in the eighteenth century. Ibiza operated on a different basis: as an occasional source of exports to South America, particularly the Plate, and as subsidiary to Setubal in the Circumterranean trade to the north. Salt had ceased to be a prime mover of Mediterranean trade, just as the Mediterranean had ceased to be a prime mover of world trade.

The Circumterranean

Between 1500 and 1800 leadership in the European economy passed from the Mediterranean to the Circumterranean. That maritime space of successive narrow seas from Gibraltar to St Petersburg also became the dominant sector of the European salt trade. Its epicentre was the Low Countries, 'premier consommateur du monde' as Chaunu calls them,[7] and leadership was exerted successively by Antwerp, Amsterdam and Liverpool.

First, Antwerp.[8] Already in the Middle Ages, the Low Countries, with their precocious industrial urbanization, high living standards, and increasing involvement in fisheries as herrings moved from Skane to the Dogger bank, were a major consumer of salt. They met their demand from two sources: the peat salt boiling industry of the island of Tolen and the mainland Zeeland town of Zevenbergen or the earth salt boiling industry of Lincolnshire exporting through the town of Boston. By the beginning of the fifteenth century these old-fashioned sources of supply were becoming inadequate. Flemish shipmasters began to take the Viking/Hanseatic Circumterranean route to Bourgneuf, Brouage and points south. In 1421 the St Elizabeth's day flood submerged the island of Tolen and inflicted heavy damage on the saltworks around Zeven-bergen. Moreover peat was in short supply and polder and dyke interests increasingly hostile to digging. The Low Countries, therefore, steadily expanded their imports of Atlantic solar salt. Consumers, how-ever, felt that its quality – purity, shape and colour – left something to be desired, especially for high grade foodstuffs, so there developed, for the first time in history a refining industry to process coarse salt to the required quality. The Atlantic salt was reduced to brine and then recrystallized by boiling to produce a smaller grained, more saline product. The location of this refining industry was first the outer islands of Zeeland, notably Schouwen, and later Ostend. By the middle of the sixteenth century, there were 400 salt refining establishments with a total output of 800 000 cwt, perhaps half the total salt supply of the Low Countries.

Initially, Malines, the staple of imported salt since 1358, was the headquarters of the trade, but in the sixteenth century, its functions, like those of so many other towns, were increasingly taken over by Ant-werp. Antwerp, 'capitale mondiale crée du dehors', was a *novum* in European economic history.[9] Neither a city state nor a royal capital it was the precursor of New York rather than Amsterdam or London. It was a city of immigrants, magnetic rather than minatory in its imperial-ism, without ships or colonies, yet precocious in its financial techniques. In the salt trade, the lead was taken by groups of expatriate Italians and Spaniards: Benevento, Schiappalaria, Salamanca, Baroncelli, who were natural intermediaries to Setubal and Seville.[10] These groups sought unsuccessfully to persuade Philip II, his regents in the Low Countries and the local estates to give them formal monopolies of import and distribution. Philip, too prudent here as too rash elsewhere, felt that a gabelle might be the last straw to his northern subjects and so passed up the opportunity of acquiring a large revenue with less friction than some of his other expedients. The trade, however, continued till Antwerp's prosperity was rent apart by Protestant terrorism and Catholic counter-terrorism.

Second, Amsterdam.[11] With the partial destruction of the Flemish Wall Street, business migrated to Amsterdam, first the junior partner of Antwerp, then its successor. Amsterdam became the Venice of the north, a half London, and as Descartes called it, the inventory of everything possible, a kind of European Harrods. Unlike Antwerp, Amsterdam was both a city state and a territorial capital, both magnetic and minatory in its imperialism. It had the largest merchant fleet in Europe, it scattered its colonists round the world and invested in everything, speculations as well as blue chips. In this last respect, the Dutch, the wagoners of all seas, were the successors of the Genoese. Inevitably salt formed part of their portfolio. Though more conservative in its financial techniques than Antwerp (in many respects it was the last medieval *emporium* rather than the first modern business capital) Amsterdam made two major innovations in the European salt trade.

First, it was Amsterdam rather than Antwerp which unified the import to the Low Countries and the export to the Baltic to create a single maritime space from Ibiza to the Neva. It was Dutch enterprise which cut the ground from under the Hanseatic liaison, though the decline of the Hanse towns is often predated and exaggerated. The Hanse had lived on an interface and had existed to bridge a gap. The Dutch, by creating a permanent entrepôt at Amsterdam with its own system of agents, filled that gap and eliminated the interface. It was under their leadership that the Circumterranean first became a real unity. Second, when temporarily excluded from Setubal by Philip II, Amsterdam, already 'la capitale mondiale du sel',[12] replied by appropriating the natural lagoon salt of Araya on the Venezuelan coast. The Dutch occupation of Araya was triply significant. It was the first serious encroachment on Spanish claimed territory; its salt was the first bulk commodity to become a regular item of commerce from the New World; and its arrival represented a unification of Atlantic as well as Circumterranean space. Araya did not long retain its importance. Exclusion from Setubal, frequently circumvented by Hanseatic flags of convenience, did not last, and if Spanish sources were closed, the French salt ports of Guérande, Bourgneuf and Brouage were generally open. Nevertheless, Araya was the herald of the unified salt world of Liverpool. Amsterdam produced a new extensification in salt trade just as Antwerp had produced a new intensification.

Finally, Liverpool.[13] Between 1500 and 1800 England passed from being a largely salt importing country to being a largely salt exporting one. From a position of relative passivity in the international salt trade she passed to one of relative dominance. From colony she became empire. Of these developments, Liverpool, a village in 1600, the second port of the United Kingdom in 1850, was the prime agent and beneficiary.

In 1500 England was already a large consumer of salt because of its high meat consumption and dairy industries. It obtained its requirements of approximately 250 000 cwt a year from three sources: the French Biscayan coast, especially Brouage and points south; Droitwich and the three Cheshire wiches, and the ancient Lincolnshire earth salt industry. In the sixteenth century, Lincolnshire followed Zeeland into irremediable decline. Brouage, though ideologically sympathetic to England because of its Huguenot masters, lost much of its trade through too frequent interruptions of trade on account of the wars of religion. Worcestershire and Cheshire, however, made good progress with Nantwich taking the lead from Droitwich because of richer brine (25 per cent to 12 per cent), better fuel resources (coal as well as timber) and a bigger dairy market (Cheshire cheese). But Cheshire too was held back by the high cost of land transport for the finished product.

The real innovation of the sixteenth century was the rise of the Durham salt industry at South Shields and Sunderland.[14] Based on weak marine brine but abundant cheap coal, it was the first salt industry anywhere outside Szechwan to be based systematically on a modern fuel. The rise of Tyneside was a by-product of the growth of the London market and in particular of the supply of its fuel requirements by Newcastle coal. Though Tyneside required six to eight tons of coal to make a ton of salt compared to Cheshire's 1 ton (and in the case of Northwich 12 cwt), at the beginning of the eighteenth century, South Shields had to pay only 2s a ton for its coal where Northwich had to pay 16s 8d. The reason was transport costs: in Cheshire coal had to come overland where in Durham it simply came down the Tyne. Furthermore, the Durham industry used smallcoal, an otherwise unmarketable by-product of the largecoal produced for the London market, which the coalmasters were glad to dispose of to the salt makers at a knockdown price, where the Cheshire producers had to pay full price. In Durham, indeed, the coal interests were dependent on salt interests rather than vice versa. Moreover, the coal industry, plus the glass, brick, brewing and saltpetre industries it had attracted, generated abundant freight between the Tyne and the Thames, whereas if Cheshire salt ever got to Liverpool, it would not find shipping to take it anywhere except to Ireland. So despite its weak brine, by 1700, thanks to cheap fuel and cheap transport, the 170 iron pans of Tyneside were producing around 325 000 cwt of salt a year. This was a considerable proportion of the 500 000 cwt now required by England's 5 million inhabitants. In fact, the output of Durham was divided about equally between London, the east coast fisheries and the Baltic. The remainder of England's needs was supplied by the wiches, Brouage (*c.* 150 000 cwt) and Setubal, though at this last, Ireland seems to have been a bigger purchaser than England.

Yet in the long run, Tyneside was not going to be able to hold out against Cheshire with its richer brine. The turning point came with the River Weaver Navigation Act in 1721. Over the next thirty years (there had to be a new act in 1759–60), the combined, if sometimes conflicting, river efforts of Liverpool merchants and Cheshire county families such as the Flemings, Booths, Egertons, and Warburtons, turned a once insignificant stream into 'one of the finest navigations in England'[15] which linked the brine of mid-Cheshire to the coal of south Lancashire and the sea. In 1732, 100 000 cwt of salt were shipped down the Weaver, in 1764 360 000 cwt, in 1796 2 million, in 1820 3 600 000, in 1830 6 million. Coal from St Helens and Wigan went up the Weaver, salt came down it to Liverpool and beyond. Northwich, the special bailiwick of the Cheshire families, the Fleming Lords de Tabley in particular, closer to St Helens and Liverpool and with the better brine, now took the lead from Nantwich, though by 1800 it was being eclipsed by Winsford which was even better served by the Weaver and received more investment from Liverpool. Liverpool itself, no longer an Irish packet port but by now, in succession to Bristol, England's leading centre for the American planta-tions, was surcharged by salt to expand into new fields: salt for cotton in the American south, salt for grain and wood in the Baltic, salt for wool in Australia, salt for jute in Bengal. By 1800 Liverpool was becoming England's Genoa and Venice combined, using salt to open markets for manufactured goods and subsidize freight rates for imported raw ma-terials. At the same time English domestic consumption had risen to 2 000 000 cwt: 20 lb *per capita* for 10 million people, as a single market second only to that of France. By 1817 there were 16 500 salt workers in Cheshire, plus 5000 boatmen, plus another 5000 ancillary personnel: ironmongers, shipwrights, carpenters, bricklayers, ropemakers and sail-makers. With a total production in the early nineteenth century of around 4 million cwt, it was the most dynamic salt industry in Europe and already played a world role.

The Continental Heartlands

In the continental heartlands between the maritime networks of the Mediterranean and the Circumterranean lay the river and land networks of Continental Europe. These networks may most conveniently be analysed under four headings derived ultimately from the foundations of Europe in the partition of the Carolingian empire: France, Lothar-ingia, Germany and Ultra-Germany.

Ancien régime France was the largest salt market in Europe because of its premature overpopulation and relatively high standard of living. On the eve of the revolution, the official gabelle statistics credited its 25 million population with a *per capita* consumption of 13 lb and an aggregate consumption of 3 400 000 cwt a year.[16] These figures were probably understated for they left out of account much Breton salt produced in Guérande and Bourgneuf. Brittany both consumed much salt itself and was notorious for smuggling across the internal customs barriers into the rest of France. Probably the total amount of salt consumed in France was around 4 million cwt.

The number one source of supply, in 1800 as in 1500, was the successive basin solar evaporation fields at Brouage on the Atlantic coast south of La Rochelle in the province of Saintonge.[17] Until the rise of Cheshire at the end of the eighteenth century, it was the most productive saline in Europe. Owned largely by retired naval officers and handled by ex-Huguenot merchants from La Rochelle, the Brouage salines supplied via the sea and the Seine a million cwt to the territories of the *grande gabelle* in northern France; via the Charente and the Garonne 600 000 cwt to the *provinces redimées* where the salt tax had been commuted to a surcharge on the *taille* (*kai kuei ti-ting* as Chinese administrators would have put it); and via the Channel ports 400 000 cwt to the *pays francs* of Artois and Flanders/Hainaut where there was no salt tax. It was an impressive network. Yet Brouage was on the decline. Its export trade, 1 million cwt at the mid-century had fallen to 200 000 cwt on the eve of the revolution mainly as result of England's capture of the Baltic trade from the Dutch who were no longer buying at either Brouage or Setubal.

The second source of supply was Guérande and Bourgneuf, on either side of the mouth of the Loire, with a production of 1 million cwt. It supplied the *pays franc* of Brittany, the French cod fisheries, some export to the West of England and Ireland, and, generally illegally, part of the Loire valley. Yet Breton salt too was not dynamic. Once aristocratic in ownership, the salines were becoming increasingly artisanal and limited in their horizons. The great days of the Bay, it was felt, were over. Nantes, the commercial capital of the region, never saw itself as a salt port. Next in importance came Languedoc and Provence: the royal saline of Peccais, the private salines of the Camargue and Berre, which straddled the mouth of the Rhône as Guérande and Bourgneuf straddled the Loire. They supplied 540 000 cwt to the territories of the *petite gabelle*, mostly via the Rhône, and also some exports to Savoy and Switzerland. Finally, leaving aside the ancient earth salt boiling industry of the Quart Bouillon which supplied 115 000 cwt of salt to local markets in western Normandy and the Cherbourg peninsula, there were the inland boiling salines of Franche Comté and Lorraine. These supplied 275 000 cwt to their own region of the *pays de salines*, but were really more significant as exporters to Lotharingia.

Lotharingia may be defined as the Rhineland beyond the reach of Dutch salt. Dutch salt seldom passed Trier. It was one of the failures of Amsterdam, perhaps of the Dutch republic more generally, not to make the Rhine a major salt route and the chief source of supply for Lotharingia. For, with inadequate supplies of its own, Lotharingia was a large and attractive market, which was competed for between Venice, Genoa, Peccais, Salins, Lorraine and a number of German *halls*. With so many potential suppliers, customers could be selective and made their choices as much for diplomatic as economic reasons.[18] Over time, the prime beneficiary was France. Colbert had great hopes of Salins in Franche Comté when it was acquired by the French crown under the treaty of Nymegen in 1678. In the sixteenth century Salins had formed part of the patronage empire of Philip II's minister Cardinal Granvelle, archbishop of Malines, and in the seventeenth century it figured in the financial empire of Philip IV's merchant banker Francois Grenus. But, by the time France acquired it, as a result of weakening brine and shortage of timber, the Grande Saunerie was past its best and proved a disappointment, at least as regards the export trade.

Much better results were achieved by the salines of Lorraine: Dieuze, Moyenvic and Chateau Salins; almost a little Cheshire, where the brine reached a salinity of 15 per cent and where coal fuel was introduced in 1753.[19] In the early modern period, the Lorraine salines underwent three periods of intensive development and export promotion: under Duke Charles III (1545–1608), Duke Leopold (1697–1729) and under the restored French rule after 1738. For example, under Duke Leopold, production at Chateau Salins and Dieuze increased from 100 000 cwt to over 300 000 cwt. By 1787 the three Lorraine salines produced 535 275 cwt against a Franche Comté production of 180 269 cwt. Of the grand total of 715 000 cwt for the French inland salines, 440 000 cwt was exported eastward. In addition there was a continued import into Savoy from Peccais of perhaps 100 000 cwt. Another beneficiary of the Lotharingian market was the Lutheran free city of Schwäbisch Hall on the eastern side of the Rhine.[20] A local producer already in Celtic times, in the period after the Thirty Years War, Schwäbisch Hall under an energetic mayor, Georg Friedrich Seifferheld, developed a considerable trade to Heidelberg, Speyer and Strasbourg which by the beginning of the nineteenth century may have amounted to 100 000 cwt a year. Finally, in the period under review, two Lotharingian powers, the duchy of Savoy at Moutiers and the canton of Berne at Bex in the southeast Vaud, endeavoured to lessen their dependence on outside supplies, by developing weak brine springs through the new German technique of 'graduation' (*Gradierung*).

In both cases, however, only a few thousand cwt a year were produced.

The introduction of graduation is the main interest of the German salt industry between 1500 and 1800. Graduation, the last major innovation in the traditional, premodern salt industry, was a technique of preconcentrating brine in order to save subsequent fuel costs. It was a technique to combat the falling salinity, rising timber prices, and perhaps damper weather, which afflicted many traditional sources of salt in early modern Germany. A graduation house was essentially a wind tunnel, subdivided by filters of straw, brushwood or thorn to increase exposure to the air, through which brine was passed to reduce its water content. By this means, brine of 3 per cent salinity could be enriched to 12, 14 or even 18 per cent salinity, thus reducing fuel costs by 66 per cent or more.[21] Graduation houses were immense structures. At Bex, the graduation house was 220 m long, at Moutiers four graduation houses designed as a single unit totalled a kilometre in length; and Claude-Nicholas Ledoux designed one of 496 m at Chaux to which he planned to pipe brine from Salins 21 km away. Graduation used what the cold seventeenth and eighteenth centuries had, i.e. wind, to substitute for what they never had or had less – sun and timber.

Graduation went back to the sixteenth century. Graduation houses (*Leckwerk*) are reported at the minor salines of Sulz (Württemberg) and Sulza (Thuringia) between 1568 and 1571 and at Nauheim (Hesse) in 1579. Multhauf has an illustration of a design for a graduation house in 1595 smaller but recognizably the same as that designed by Ledoux. A seventeenth-century map of Weissbach/Niedernhall on the estates of Prince Hohenlohe near Stuttgart suggests that there was a graduation house there from 1607. In 1615, we are told, Reichenhall (Bavaria) followed Sooden (Hesse) in installing a *Leckwerk*. A woodcut of Sulz dated to 1643 clearly shows graduation houses, though very short ones compared to what were to come later. Graduation therefore was an invention of Lutheran West Germany, the world of Agricola's *De re metallica*. But it was in the eighteenth century that graduation was most fully developed. Jacob Leupold, a famous engineer, introduced a graduation device into the royal Prussian salines of Grossensalza/Schönebeck near Halle in 1715, which Waitz von Eschen, a Hessian *Salinist*, later transformed into 'the longest series of graduation houses in Europe'.[22] Schwäbisch Hall acquired a first graduation house in 1739, a second in 1745, a third in 1748, a fourth and fifth in 1749, a sixth around 1756, each several hundred metres long. In 1787, Sooden had 22 graduation houses and in 1796 Wimpfen in Württemberg two particularly impressive ones. The effect of these developments is hard to assess. Schwäbisch Hall was certainly prosperous in the eighteenth century and by 1800 Grossensalza/Schönebeck at 600 000 cwt a year had become the second largest saline in Germany. But in most cases it is hard to resist the impression that graduation only served to keep inefficient local salt-works alive and thus contributed to maintain the political particularism of the Reich.

Two other technical innovations were more forward looking: the piping of brine to places where fuel was cheaper or wind stronger, and the use of coal as fuel. In the early seventeenth century, Hans Reiffen-stuhl constructed a 33-km brine conduit for the duke of Bavaria between the brine springs at Reichenhall and evaporation plant at Traunstein. This conduit operated successfully throughout the eighteenth century. From 1805 it was renewed with new pumps by the engineer Georg von Reichenbach and extended at either end: 1810 Reichenhall to Rosenmein and 1817 Berchtesgaden, a revived brine source, to Reichenhall, now reinvigorated as a boiling centre; the total distance from Berchtesgaden to Rosenheim being 108 km. Thanks to these developments, the elector of Bavaria's share of the Salzburg group of salines took the lead over those of the archbishop. In the early nineteenth century production at Reichenhall and its associates reached 460 000 cwt a year. The arch-bishop's saline at Hallein, however, was not far behind, and the Salz-kammergut group of salines (Hallstatt, Ischl, Ebensee also linked by conduit and Aussee), which had been extensively developed by the Habsburgs in the eighteenth century as supplier to Bohemia, was currently the largest producer in Germany with a production of 1 million cwt a year. The other innovation, coal fuel, was found from 1714 in the salines opened by the king of Prussia at Königsborn in his Rhineland territories and from 1738 in the salines developed for the elector of Saxony by J. G. Borlach at Artern, Kosen, Kotschau and Teuditz in his section of the Halle group. In neither case had much progress been made by 1800 in terms of production. Despite much useful experimenta-tion the German salt industry remained unmodernized. With a popula-tion about the same as that of France, 25 million, Germany consumed two and a half million cwt of salt – high for a traditional economy, low for a modern.

Beyond Germany lay a region predominantly of rock salt. Wieliczka, the most famous of the mines, had gone over to underground brine in the fifteenth century.[23] Production was developed in the sixteenth century by the Jagellon and Vasa kings and by 1600 had reached 640 000 cwt. In the seventeenth century Wieliczka ran into difficulties: flooding, due in part to the climatic fluctuation; a fire in 1644, caused no doubt by gas, which lasted 8 months; and the Swedish-Cossack occupa-tion of 1655 during the so-called Deluge. By 1675 production had fallen to 260 000 cwt. Under the Saxon kings, however, who brought in German experts such as J. G. Borlach, royal administrator 1743–1750, Wieliczka revived, but on the basis of mining once again rather than brine. It was at this time that the greater chambers still to be seen today were hewn under the direction of the Polish geologist Stanislaw Staszic. Good use too was made of Poland's abundant horse-power both above and below ground. By 1750 production had reached 840 000 cwt. Between 1763 and 1772 there was a further period of political disorder leading up to the First Partition. With the establishment of Habsburg rule in 1772 progress resumed and by 1800 Wieliczka and its associate Bochnia produced 1 120 000 cwt a year, more than any single German saline. The Partitions of Poland – Lithuania also gave the Habsburgs control of the Galician salines of right bank Ukraine, of which the two most important were Drohobycz south of Lvov and Kolomiyya northwest of Czernowitz.

South of Poland the most important rock salt workings were in Greater Hungary, a land of cattle and *Ochsenbaronen* as Poland-Lithuania was a land of horses and Uhlans. Soovar in Slovakia, exploited as a mine from the seventeenth century, as a brine well after 1752, produced about 100 000 cwt in 1800. Ronaszek in northeastern Transylvania produced 680 000 cwt in 1800, Torda in the Maros valley produced 500 000 cwt in 1815. Both these large mines had been developed after the recovery of the area by the Habsburgs from the Ottomans at the end of the seventeenth century. Unlike divided, particularist Germany, the pattern in the Habsburg lands was one of a few, large-scale salines, a reflection of and a support for imperial unity. A similar pattern, though in different and contrasting contexts, also prevailed in the two new lands on Europe's periphery: the Muscovite empire of the Russias and the European colonies in the Americas.

The New Lands

Russia and America were similar yet different in their salt networks at the end of the eighteenth century. They were similar in their total population, 20 to 25 million apiece, and in a high *per capita* consumption of 15 to 20 lb by their European population. They were different in the reasons for that high demand and that while Russia was largely self-sufficient, both Americas imported most of their supply. *Economie monde* and colony therefore confronted each other.

The production, distribution and consumption of salt in the Muscovite lands had three unusual features.[24] First, in production, in the early stratum of the native boiling industry, which lay in the northeast, there was a precocious development of deep drilling. Brine was first obtained, chiefly by monasteries, from the White Sea, but latterly from brine wells in the valley of the Northern Dvina and its western and eastern tributaries, the Sukhoma and the Vychegda. Here, as early as the sixteenth century, wells were drilled as deep as 500 feet. It is difficult not to wonder whether Muscovy, so long subordinate to the Golden Horde,

had not imported Chinese techniques of deep drilling for brine, ultimately from Szechwan. Second, in distribution, Russian salt, thanks to
the size of the country and the availability of river communication (the
great artery of the Volga preeminently) travelled immense distances.
Already in the fifteenth century, according to the Venetian travellers
Barbaro and Contarini, Moscow drew part of its supplies from the
coastal *sebkhas* of Astrakhan. Third, in consumption, one is struck by the
at least 20 lb *per capita* figure for early modern Russia. Three factors
probably were at work here. First, the relative failure of serfdom in
Russia to increase productivity and extract a surplus, with the consequent survival of the *mir* or village commune, led to the retention of
resources at the grass roots. Second, it led to the expenditure of those
resources in accordance with *mujik* preferences: children and food rather
than housing, and food much salted, such as fish, pickled cabbage,
borshch, *shchii* and *zakuski*, to make the huge carbohydrate intake necessary for thermoregulation in the Russian climate, palatable. Again,
medieval Russia was an exporter of honey, but with the retreat of the
forests and bee keeping, salt was substituted rather than sugar. Finally,
vodka and salt each stimulated the consumption of the other. Though
traditional Russia was not badly fed, its high consumption of salt was a
sign of tradition rather than modernity.

In 1800 the Russian empire had a population of 20 million which
consumed over 4 million cwt of salt a year. With regard to supply, it was
highly self-contained. Only the Baltic provinces, under a privilege
confirmed by Catherine the Great, imported salt: a few 100 000 cwt,
mainly via Riga from Setubal in non-Russian ships. The rest of the
country, except for the old Novgorodian Russia of the northeast where a
number of minor sources (Staraya Russa, Balachna, Archangel, Vol-
ogda, Soligalic) boiled brine for local consumption, was supplied by a
few massive salines on the eastern rim of the empire.

The oldest, and in 1800, still the premier in terms of both quantity and
quality, was Solikamsk high up on the Kama. Solikamsk, the descend-
ant and successor of the northeastern salines, had been developed at the
end of the sixteenth century by the Stroganovs, the Conquistadors of
Siberia. In 1800, 1 700 000 cwt of salt was produced here from brine
wells, drilled to a depth of over 200 feet, by boiling with wood fuel. It
was distributed by river to the provinces of northern Russia as far west
as St Petersburg. Second in importance was Lake Elton in the steppe
east of the Volga beyond the future Stalingrad. This was a vast natural,
solar and wind evaporated, saline, from which, beginning in 1748,
1 500 000 cwt of salt was extracted annually for supply to central Russia
by a mixture of land and water routes. Next, in between, in the latitude
of Saratov, but further east, open cast mining commenced in 1754 at the
salt dome and quarry of Ilek, 40 miles south of Orenburg. Ilek supplied

up to 250 000 cwt a year, by cart mainly to Ufa, Kazan and Nijni Novgorod. To the south, the Astrakhan coastal *sebkhas* continued to send salt and sturgeon up the Volga, being credited in 1775 with an output of 220 000 cwt. Further east again, Tobolsk and western Siberia obtained supplies from the Zunghar salt lake of Yamysh up the Irtysh in Kazakhstan, whose annual salt fair beginning on Assumption Day was an occasion for international commerce in Inner Asia. Beyond that still, Irkutsk and eastern Siberia, obtained salt from lakes near the Chinese border. Finally in 1783, the Tsardom acquired the natural salines of the Krim Tartar khanate: Kinburn, Perekop and the Crimea itself, which eventually provided a million cwt of salt for the left bank Ukraine.

In 1800 the two Americas had a population of 25 million; 5 million in Nordic America, 20 million in Iberian America. Each consumed about one and a half million cwt a year. Consumption was differentiated by colour. While America, 10 million, had the high consumption of Europeans, higher in the case of Nordics than Iberians; Red and Black America, 15 million, had the low consumption of relative primitivity.

Like Russia, early modern America took over and developed existing salines. In 1788 New York State acquired Onondaga near Syracuse. In 1797 it was leased to an entrepreneur who by 1801 was producing 36 000 cwt a year. Shawneetown in Illinois was likewise developed and by 1829 was producing 60 000 cwt a year. Similarly in Ecuador the Spaniards took over the salt of Otavalo and turned it into Santa Catalina de las Salinas to provide supplies for their Indian tributaries. In his survey in the early seventeenth century, Vazquez de Espinosa describes a multitude of small salines half creole, half native. In Yucatan, the old Mayan solar evaporation sites were updated by a full series of basins. Campeche became the salt port for Vera Cruz and Mexico, adding this plebeian commodity to its dyewoods and the supposed wonder drug gaiac. Santo Domingo was another area where, following the Amerindians, the Spaniards combined salt and gaiac. Here the principal marine salines were at Monte Christo and Yaguana on the north coast and Puerto Hermoso close to the capital. Less like Russia, however, the Americans developed new local salines: Barnstaple on the north shore of Cape Cod for Massachusetts (in 1829 200 000 cwt); Kanawha in West Virginia for Trans-Appalachia (in 1810 280 000 cwt); Saltville in southwest Virginia for Tennessee; Guayaquil for Ecuador; San Luiz and Recife for Bahia; Yocalla, Coipasa and Uyuni for Potosi.

Yet the production of all these places, especially before 1800, was small. Unlike the Russians, the Americans were supplied essentially from overseas by their metropolises: Liverpool in the case of Nordic America, the cotton/salt connection at New Orleans being particularly important; Seville, Cadiz and Ibiza in the case of Spanish America; Lisbon, Setubal, the Cape Verde islands and Angola in the case of Brazil.

Table 5.1 Production of salt in Europe around 1800

Place	Quantity (cwt)
Mediterranean	2 500 000
England	4 000 000
France	4 500 000
Lotharingia	500 000
Germany	2 500 000
Ultra Germany	2 000 000
Russia	4 000 000
The Americas	1 000 000
Total	21 000 000

By the end of the eighteenth century the Americas had emerged as providers of relatively bulky commodities: timber, tobacco, cotton, sugar, coffee, cocoa etc. Cheap freight therefore was available for a bulk commodity to cross the Atlantic in the opposite direction. Local producers with high colonial costs stood little chance against metropolitan competition. When, during the war of independence, the United States was cut off from Liverpool, it switched, not to its own domestic supplies, but to Setubal where in 1796 117 American vessels were to be found shipping 600 000 cwt of salt. Ibiza was another international market where United States buyers were to be found. Unlike Russia, the Americas were part of the world economy for salt.

In 1500, 100 million Europeans had consumed 7 million cwt of salt. Between 1500 and 1800 absolute consumption tripled, *per capita* consumption rose by 50 per cent. By 1800, Europe's various salt networks were providing more than 20 million cwt of salt for the 200 million odd inhabitants of the European world. As we shall see this was more both absolutely and *per capita* than what was being provided in China. Even before the Industrial Revolution came to multiply demand and supply, European society had, on average, well passed the critical 15 lb *per capita* point which may be regarded as the ceiling of salt consumption for an advanced traditional society. Three factors in particular had led to this result: a richer diet, especially in terms of proteins and fats; a greater use of maritime transportation leading to specialization in salt supply; and more experimentation in different methods of production than anywhere else in the world. Furthermore, not only did Europe use a wider variety of techniques than anywhere else, but also, except in the case of natural gas in Szechwan, she applied them with greater efficiency. By 1800 Europe was already well advanced in the transition from late tradition to early modernity.

SALT IN OTTOMAN ISLAM AND MUGHAL INDIA

In both the Muslim world and the Indian subcontinent late tradition was more evident than early modernity between 1500 and 1800. Politically Islam and India were dominated in this period by their latest, post-Mongol imperial constructs, the Ottoman and Mughal empires. Both states expressed themselves in their capitals: the Ottoman empire, its power rooted in Constantinople and under the necessity of return there at the end of each compaigning season; the Mughal empire, a Central Asian transplant, like early Irano-Indian empires constantly on the move as a mixture of army and entertainment, and only returning to Agra or Delhi to regroup.

Ottoman Constantinople

In the late seventeenth century when imperial Constantinople reached its final autumnal splendours, contemporary sources mention ten places as supplying the depots of the *tuz emin*, the intendant of salt.[25] These were Egypt, probably Damietta; Ahyolu or Anchialos on the Black Sea south of Varna; Wallachia, i.e. part of Romania; Caffa in the Crimea; Silivri and Cekmese, both on the Marmora; Aynos at the mouth of the Maritsa north of the Gallipoli peninsula; Saruhan, the Ottoman province of Smyrna and the locale of the major salt producing centre of Phocaea; the islands of the Archipelago, among which Mytilene will probably already have been prominent; and Kilas, a salt mine whose identity remains uncertain. The picture is traditional, even archaic: many, small local salines combining to supply the huge capital by sea. With a population of 800 000 which consumed 4 million sheep, 3 million lambs and goats, 200 000 cattle a year and 500 000 kilos of bread a day, Constantinople required 100 000 cwt of salt a year, maybe 150 000 cwt. If Islam generally was a party *en permanence*, Ottoman Stamboul was a super party, *capitale ventre*, as Mantran calls it. Of the various sources of supply for salt, two were of special significance: the Crimea where the khans added the new salines of Or (Perekop) to those of Kinburn, Kherson and Caffa; and Wallachia, the Ottoman side of the Carpathian rock salt area, in particular the salt mountain of Slanic north of Bucharest where mining commenced in 1689. The increased importance of the Wallachian provinces, their hospodars and their Phanariot merchants, and the general Balkanization of Constantinople from the later seventeenth century, was in part due to the capital's greater dependence on Romanian salt as well as grain and meat. Thanks to its increased wealth and printing presses, Burcharest, the headquarters for Slanic, became almost as much a capital for eastern orthodoxy as the Phanar or Jerusalem.

Mughal Agra

If Constantinople continued the pattern of European antiquity of many
small suppliers by sea, Agra continued the pattern of Indian antiquity of
a few, large suppliers by land.[26] Under the Mughals, Agra was a city of a
million people in the heart of what was essentially a land state. There is
no indication of marine salt from the salines of Bombay, Madras and
Bengal entering the upper Ganges valley. Indeed, Agra is reported as
exporting salt to Bengal and Assam in return for rice, wheat and butter.
The ancient mines of the Salt Range no doubt made some contribution to
the capital, but their principal market was in the Punjab. Babur in his
memoirs regarded them as being in tribal territory and not fully under
government control. Agra's chief source of salt, both for itself and for
export, was almost certainly the salt lakes of the Rajputana, modern
Rajasthan, of which the most important were Bharatpur, close to the
capital, and Sambhar, further away. To judge from mid nineteenth-
century figures compiled under the *raj*, the total amount of salt supplied
to the 50 million people of the Mughal central provinces was around 3
million cwt, of which a million came from Bharatpur and half a million
from Sambhar. Under the *raj*, however, Sambhar became the principal
supplier to northern India, so more is known of its history.

The origins of Sambhar as a major producer went back to the earliest
days of Islam in India. Under the Mughals, Sambhar was worked by the
government of Akbar and his successors down to the reign of Ahmad
Shah (1748–54), after which time it became the property of the Rajput
rulers of Jaipur and Jodhpur. Production was in the main by successive
basin solar evaporation, though some spontaneously occurring salt was
also collected. The basins were grouped either in permanent structures
(*kyars*) of between 28 and 184 acres with 20 to 60 basins apiece, or in
temporary enclosures of about 5000 square feet erected annually. Each
of these groupings contained inside its own catchment, condensers and
crystallizers and they produced the coarse, large-grained salt known in
India as Baragra, with a slight discoloration of grey, green or pink owing
to microorganisms. Distribution was effected by pack camel to Delhi,
Agra and Oudh, and thence by water to Bihar, Bengal and Assam, and
by 10 000 pack bullocks owned by the hereditary group known as
Banjaras to Central India. According to Ashton, 'these Banjaras were
traders, carriers and distributors combined; they purchased salt, con-
veyed it to areas of consumption on their bullocks, and retailed it from
town to town and from village to village'.[27] Though not technically a
caste, as the French seventeenth-century traveller Tavernier believed,
the Banjaras were typical of the hereditary occupation units which
operated so much of Indian society below the level of whatever kind of

government presided over it. It was such Hindu units which served and survived the huge camps and capitals of the Mughals.

SALT IN EARLY MODERN CHINA

China contrasted with both western Europe and Islam and India. Thanks to a massive increase in population, considerable changes in diet, and the need to adapt to an energy crisis, China was less traditional than Islam and India. Thanks to the distribution of power in its society, the predominance of non-maritime forms of transportation, and the *vis inertiae* of the salt administration, China was less modernizing than Europe. Like Greater Europe, however, China was regionalized and is best considered as four interrelated subregions. First, there was the south and the old medieval social heartland of the Yangtze delta. Second, there was the north and the new political and military head-quarters centring on Peking and the metropolitan province of Chihli. Third, there was the centre, the great trade route of the Yangtze and its associated lakes the Tung-t'ing and P'o-yang. Finally, there was the west, the new lands in Szechwan and beyond the wall.

A number of factors affected all four subregions. Of these the most important for salt between 1500–1800 were interrelated changes in demography, diet and energy sources.

First, early modern China was demographically dynamic. Between 1500 and 1800 the population increased from 100 million to 300 million. This was the era of the conquest of China by the Chinese, an increase and diffusion of population which turned a federation of intensely cultivated oases into an approximation to Chaunu's 'full world' of northern medieval Europe on a vaster scale. Population increase began simply as a rebound to the losses of the thirteenth and fourteenth century through war, disease and revolution. The tide continued – the word explosion is not appropriate since the growth was only 1 per cent a year, not the modern 2 per cent – principally through the introduction of the American food plants, the green gold of Columbus, which altered China more than his yellow or white bullion changed Europe. Maize, sweet potatoes, peanuts, Irish potatoes, chilli and tomatoes gave a new world to the Chinese farmer. Land hitherto uncultivable: on hillsides, between seasons, in the interstices, above the mist line, below the riverbank; could now be put to productive use, and with comparatively little labour. More time was available for terracing rice paddies and providing for their irrigation. More irrigated land meant earlier and more universal marriage. This in turn meant more children, the first luxury of the poor: more mouths, but also more security, and more hands for sowing, weeding and terracing. By 1800 an accelerating cycle of land, people, land had been established, which was only checked after 1850 by war, revolution and urbanization. For the early modern demographic tide was basically rural. By causing villages, hamlets and farmsteads to proliferate, it reduced the non-rural percentage of the population. It multiplied small towns at the base of the urban pyramid and divided the megapoleis at the apex.[28] Early modern China was ruled therefore by a powerful undertow, radical in strength, yet conservative in technology and limited horizons. It was the dynamism of innumerable calculating farmers, their wives and children.

Next, these changes in crops, topography and family structure affected diet.[29] As megapoleis contracted, as small towns multiplied, and small holdings proliferated, the cuisine of the rich gave way to the cuisine of the moderately affluent poor. While *per capita* calories were maintained, even were increased between 1500–1800, the protein percentage probably fell and carbohydrates increased. Within the category of proteins, beef was replaced by pork, animal protein by fish, fish by vegetables, in particular by the soybean, that amazing combination of protein and fat. Chinese diet, like European, showed a shift in the direction of more fats, but more modestly, from vegetables (soy, rape, sesame, groundnuts, poppy) more than animals, and as substitute for protein rather than supplement. There was an increase in the popularity of light frying (*ch'ao*) the vegetable dishes (*ts'ao*) which accompanied the basic noodles or rice (*fan*), and deep-frying (*cha*) was also widespread. Unlike Europe, however, the advance of fats was not accompanied by a retreat of spices. On the contrary, the rise in carbohydrates led to greater demand for flavouring. Thus the introduction of chilli, particularly to Szechwan and Hunan, led to the development of one of the most distinctive of Chinese regional cuisines.[30] Fagara, ginger and mustard also remained in extensive demand. The import of pepper from Indonesia declined in the seventeenth and early eighteenth centuries, as meat consumption declined in South China, but a new import from Siam developed in the early nineteenth century in response to the new demand for flavour.[31]

As a result of these developments, demand for salt, the most plebeian and versatile of flavour enhancers, increased. In the north, it was said, people liked to eat salt, in the south sweet, but this broad dichotomy only reflected the two areas' relative poverty and wealth. In fact all areas were increasing their consumption of salt in food preparation. From Newchwang in southern Manchuria a customs official wrote: 'Salted vegetables are eaten in enormous quantities; salted fish, shrimps, crabs, beef and pork, and the favourite pickled beancurd all form articles of diet in universal use.'[32] At Ta-t'ung in Anhwei a salt official commented on local fluctuations in demand:

In the 7th moon, it then being the season for manufacturing soy, the chief ingredient of which is salt, the demand again becomes brisk, while in the 9th and 10th moons the sale reaches its highest point, the salt being much in demand at the end of autumn for the preparation of winter food, i.e., for pickling vegetables, salting fish, etc.[33]

From Chengtu in Szechwan, a consular official having stated that: 'Probably no province in China has a greater variety of vegetables than Ssuch'uan, whose inhabitants indulge fearlessly in almost everything green' goes on to say, 'Several of the above vegetables are pickled by being steeped in brine for from fifteen days to a month. Twenty pounds of salt are allowed to every 133.3 lbs of vegetables.'[34] North, south and west were alike in their enhanced demand for salt.

Finally, the supply of salt was affected by changes in the availability of energy. These changes were rooted in the same situation which was changing demography and diet. The expanding agricultural frontier of more land, more people, more land was steadily denuding China of trees: the more Chinese, the fewer forests. As a result, from the mid-sixteenth century, there were signs in many parts of the empire and in many sectors of its economy of a growing shortage of timber: for fuel, house construction, shipbuilding and handicraft. These shortages amounted to an energy crisis in early modern China.[35] The evidence for this is particularly striking from Szechwan, whose forests had until then been the supplier of last resort for as far away as Peking. The records of *mu-cheng*, or imperial timber administration, in Szechwan show increasing difficulty in supplying masts for the imperial dockyard in Nanking or beams for the imperial palaces in Peking.[36] If even the court went short, less privileged consumers went even shorter. Like other energy users, therefore, salt producers in China between 1500 and 1800 were under compulsion to switch to cheaper or more abundant sources of fuel than wood. It was this combination of higher costs and bigger demand which produced the dominant trend of the early modern Chinese salt industry: a switch from wood to solar evaporation, coal or natural gas. Under the imperatives of the energy crisis, China reactivated its own invention: successive basin solar evaporation. It was this trend which the conservatism of the salt administration tried, not unsuccessfully, to delay in its own interests and in those of the traditional wood-fired boiling industry. The result of trend and counter-trend was a mixture of modernity and tradition.

The South

With its summer monsoon rain, humidity, occasional typhoons, rocky coast and massive inflow of fresh water from the Yangtze, the Min and the West river, south China was not well suited to solar evaporation. Before modern times, it only found a home in Fukien south of the Min and then, apparently, in a single rather than successive basin form. Nevertheless, in response to the demographic, dietary and energy factors outlined above, two new forms of successive basin solar evaporation were introduced into the region in the early modern period, while the methods used in Fukien were also modified in this direction.

The most important, and probably the earliest of the developments took place in Liang-kuang.[37] By the end of the Ch'ing period it had become the fourth salt division in the empire. In terms of environment and climate, Liang-kuang, with its headquarters at Canton, held an intermediate position in south China: less fresh water entered the seas from its rivers than from the Yangtze in Liang-che; more rain and humidity came from its skies than in Fukien. Until early modern times, most salt in Liang-kuang had been made by boiling, but with rising population and falling fuel supplies, resort had to be had to solar evaporation to meet demand. The method of successive basin evaporation evolved to suit the circumstances of Liang-kuang was known as *lou-shai*, 'filter' or more accurately 'filtery' *shai*, since the technique did not always involve the use of an actual filter, and the term *lou* by the twentieth century had come to mean simply a salt works.

Lou-shai existed in three forms. In the first, known as *shai-sha*, marine brine held in a small reservoir, was reinforced by filtration through a leaching vat (*lou*) lined with specially prepared saline sand, before evaporation in a final basin lined with stone to increase radiant heat, which could be filled and emptied quickly (to and from storage wells) as weather dictated. Reservoir, preparation fields plus vat, and evaporation basins were the familiar catchment, condensers and crystallizers of the successive basin solar evaporation process. In the second form, known as *shai-shui*, the small reservoir was retained, but the leaching vat was eliminated. Its preparation fields were converted into four pebble-lined condensers which, used successively, increased the salinity of the marine brine until it was ready to be run into the fifth basin, the crystallizer. Here the successive phases of catchment, condensation and crystallization were clearer than in the *shai-sha* method, as was the traditional 5:1 ratio of the first two to the third. In the third form, characteristic of the western saltworks of Liang-kuang, this ratio was abandoned. The reservoir was enlarged and one or two more condensing basins were added, so that the catchment-condensers : crystallizers area ratio was closer to the 10:1 figure of the French Mediterranean salines or the 15:1 practised in California. This change in ratio would have increased considerably the productivity of the saline as well as improving the quality of the product.

We have not yet determined the exact chronology of these developments, partly because in any given text, the word *lou* may mean an actual filter or simply a filtery. To judge from the distribution of different methods in the twentieth century, the *shai-sha* (or *lou-shai* in a narrow sense) method begin in Ch'ao-chou prefecture in the east of Kwangtung in the sixteenth century and gradually drove the existing boiling method westward until it survived to any extent only at Pakhoi and on Hainan. A reference in the Hui-chou prefectural gazetteer to a tax imposed in 1683 on increased *lou* suggests that the seventeenth century, a time when the shortage of timber was beginning to bite, was the chief period of expansion. As regards the *shai-shui*, the non-*lou* form of *lou-shai*, its introduction to the Hong Kong area is associated with immigrants from Hui-chou, in particular the double county of Hai-lu-feng, which contained the major salt producing area of Kan-pai. Kan-pai, which supplied salt for Liang-kuang's expanding markets in southern Hunan, is certainly a plausible place for the origin of *shai-shui* as a substitute for *shai-sha*. In time this origin may go back to the eighteenth century. In 1756 a memorial of Liang-kuang governor-general Yang Ying-chu, which described the opening of new salines at the two works of Mou-hui and Tien-mou in Kao-chou in western Kwangtung used the phrase *chiu-t'ien kuan-shai*, 'at the fields pour and solar evaporate', which is more suggestive of *shai-shui* than *shai-sha*.[38] Against this interpretation is the fact that the 1884 edition of the *yen-fa-chih* contains illustrations and diagrams only of *shai-sha*, not of *shai-shui*. But such handbooks were often conservative and their illustrations and diagrams conventionalized, so this argument need not be compelling. As regards the third development, the western variant of *shai-shui* with its new internal ratios, this is still more difficult to date. Most likely, it did not appear until the late nineteenth or early twentieth century, the opening of new salines in the Lei-chou peninsula, its principal locale, when the western saltworks of Kwangtung began to overtake those of the east in their supply both of Canton and of Kwangsi to their north. What can be said is that thanks to these developments, Liang-kuang expanded its production from 187 421 cwt under the early Ming to 1 629 020 cwt in 1800 and to 4 million by 1900.

North of Liang-kuang lay the salt division of Fukien.[39] Here, away from the outflow of the Yangtze and with a climate less wet than Kwangtung or Chekiang, solar evaporation, probably of a rather primitive single basin kind, had been practised, alongside boiling, since at least Yüan times. In the early modern period, three developments took place. First, the Liang-kuang *lou-shai shai-sha*, i.e. the use of an actual filter, was introduced from Ch'ao-chou to southern Fukien, which supplied that area and via its Han river the Fukien prefecture of Ting-chou, with some of its salt. Second, the traditional single basins, the jars (*ch'eng*), pits (*k'an*) and mound-pools (*ch'iu*) were rearranged to form a successive basin series which eliminated the need for filtration. Third, especially in the reigns of Yung-cheng (1722–1735) and Ch'ien-lung (1735–1796), boiling was increasingly eliminated by the various kinds of *shai*, so that by the end of the nineteenth century Fukien was a completely solar evaporating division. Its production increased from 418 290 cwt under the early Ming to 1 000 000 in 1800 and 1 300 000 in 1900.

Significant developments also took place further north again, in the salt division of Liang-che which included not only Chekiang and parts of Anhwei and Kiangsi to the west, but also, to the north, the so-called Su Wu-shu, the five areas associated with Soochou: i.e. Kiangsu south of the Yangtze, one of the most highly cultivated, thickly urbanized and densely populated areas in the world. In the Middle Ages, Lian-che had been the most dynamic salt division in China in terms of output, at least under the Sung and Yüan. But its technology remained static, a *chien* industry which boiled marine brine reinforced either by the *t'an-hui* (spreading of ash) or the *kua-ni* (scraping of mud) techniques. In the reigns of Chia-ch'ing (1796–1820) and Tao-kuang (1820–1850), as the timber position worsened, a new solar evaporation technique was introduced which over the nineteenth century became predominant. This was *pan-shai* (board solar evaporation): solar evaporation of marine brine reinforced by *kua-ni* in movable wooden boxes or trays. The boxes were relatively small: 'about two and a half meters long, one meter wide and three to six centimeters deep'.[40] Their advantage was two-fold: movability to avoid bad weather and rapid evaporation in good weather. In combination with a reservoir and *kua-ni*, their use constituted a new version of successive basin solar evaporation, one which, like the western version of *shai-shui* in Liang-kuang, had a higher catchment-condensers : crystallizers ratio than 5:1. The *pan* or tray was in effect a mobile crystallizer.

Pan-shai was developed first at Tai-shan in the Chusan archipelago in eastern Chekiang and thence spread to Yü-yao, Shao-hsing and Ningpo on the mainland, Ting-hai in the archipelago, and eventually Sungkiang in southern Kiangsu and even Lu-ssu in T'ung-chou north of the Yangtze.[41] From the fact that in the early days, *pan shai* salt from Tai-shan was called *ssu-yen* (private, illicit or smuggled salt) whereas only boiled salt was *kuan-yen* (official or regulation salt), it may be inferred that *pan-shai* was developed by private enterprise, the Chusan archipelago being a notoriously lawless area, and was only subsequently accepted as legitimate by the authorities. Much of the output of Chusan and Yü-yao was shipped across Hangchow bay to the Su Wu-shu urban market. Short water routes were always difficult for the traditional salt administration to control, so, since *pan-shai* was both basically cheaper and initially less taxed than boiled salt, its diffusion could not be prevented and the *yen-cheng* had to accept the *fait accompli*. By the end of the dynasty, the success of *pan-shai* was evident and half a million boxes were being used.[42] In the mid-twentieth century, *pan-shai* produced two-thirds of the 6 million cwt output of Liang-che, 1 300 000 cwt in the Chusan archipelago and 2 500 000 cwt at Yü-yao. Long before that, Che salt had begun to figure prominently in complaints of smuggling into the Huai areas of Kiangsi. Through *pan-shai* Liang-che had re-acquired dynamism. Its production rose from 1 434 000 cwt in the sixteenth century to 2 416 191 cwt in 1800 and to 3 500 000 in 1900. Moreover, with the rise of *pan-shai*, the dominance of successive basin solar evaporation was secured along the whole coast of south China from Shanghai to Hainan.

The North

In the treeless terrain in the north where the energy crisis was at its worst, successive basin solar evaporation won further successes in the early modern period: restoration in Ho-tung, extension in Ch'ang-lu and Shantung, and introduction in Manchuria. Yet, except in Manchuria, these successes were not unclouded.

At Ho-tung's An-i *hsien* salt lake, successive basin solar evaporation (*hsi-shai*) had been abandoned in favour of harvesting the natural crystallization (*lao-ts'ai*) in the Yüan period. It was revived tentatively in the late Ming as demand increased, regulations were relaxed and possibly weather conditions changed, but it was not until the early Ch'ing that, in a memorial of Li Shih-ch'ien who became salt censor in 1685, there was official recognition of the combination of *hsi* (paddocks) and *chiao-shai* (pour and evaporate). However by 1730, according to salt censor Shih-se, all salt at Ho-tung, a total of 853 894 cwt, was being produced by this method. In the eighteenth century, there were technical improvements: 'A merchant of the eastern works *tung-ch'ang* Liu Fou-ho invented the method of boring wells and evaporating the water *chueh-ching chiao-shai*'.[43] The purity of the salt was thereby increased from 89 per cent to 96 per cent and the western works where wells could not be sunk gradually went out of business. Production expanded. Two additions to the quota, one of 100 000 *yin* and the other of 140 000 *yin* (a *yin* in Ho-tung at that time equalled 2 cwt) are noted in the *shih-lu*. In 1792 the governor of Shansi Feng Kuang-hsiung remarked on the extent of the trade and the prosperity of output. By 1800 Ho-tung was at a peak of premodern efficiency. Its productive capacity may already have reached the 2 million cwt with which Baron von Richthofen credited it in 1870.[44]

Two factors lay behind this success.[45] First, privatization. Under the Ming, in accordance with that dynasty's preference for planned economy, production at Ho-tung was virtually a nationalized industry.

Corvée labour was used for *lao-ts'ai* and all salt was delivered to the officials. The Ch'ing, however, gave greater freedom to the energetic merchants of the three small towns of Yun-ch'eng, An-i and Chiao-chou close to the lake. In 1649 the saltfields (*hsi*) were returned to private ownership and corvée labour was discontinued. In 1725 it was discontinued for the conduits and dykes necessary to the maintenance of the lake, which were henceforward a charge on the exchequer – in effect a tax rebate. In 1791, at the suggestion of governor Feng Kuang-hsiung, the salt administration in Ho-tung was dismantled and the salt tax was converted into a surcharge on the land tax (*kuei ti-ting*) – another subsidy to the trade. This experiment was not persisted in, but the concomitant period of free trade (*min-yün min-hsiao*) permanently enlarged the sales of lake salt even when tax and monopoly were restored. Second, the growth of the Honan market. Throughout the Ch'ing period, Ho-tung supplied designated districts in each province did not vary very much, but the amount of salt supplied did. In 1730 Honan was supplied only 158 280 cwt; in 1912 565 876 cwt. Honan, noted especially for its cotton and sesame, was a typical province of the expanding agricultural frontier with a growing population and demand for salt.

Yet in spite of these factors, the prosperity of the An-i *hsien* salt lake remained precarious. It had to face competition from the cheaper salt of the Mongolian lake *sebkhas* in the Ordos, Alashan and at Hua-ma chih within the wall; from the better, successive basin solar salt of Ch'ang-lu on the coast; and from the inferior, but closer at hand, boiled earth salt of northern Shansi. The wet eighteenth century caused interruptions to production, notably in 1757; the dry nineteenth century caused interruptions to distribution and consumption, notably during the great drought famine of 1877–8. Without a governor-general to back it, Ho-tung, in the immediate province of Shansi, lacked political clout. Above all, like Sambhar in India, it remained landlocked, its salt imprisoned by the high cost of land transport in a traditional economy. Average sales therefore at around 1 500 000 cwt a year, remained below productive capacity. Except in favourable circumstances Ho-tung always had to fight for its markets.

In Ch'ang-lu, successive basin solar evaporation, locally known as *t'an-shai*, had probably been introduced during the late Yüan. It went into abeyance in the early Ming, but was reintroduced in the course of the prosperous sixteenth century. In 1726, eight out of sixteen *ch'ang* used *t'an-shai*; in 1873 seven out of ten and those the most important. It was on the basis of *t'an-shai* that Ch'ang-lu had expanded in the late Ming and continued to do so under the early and middle Ch'ing. Table 5.2 below lists the number of *yin*, or certificates to handle salt, issued, their quantification, the amounts of salt traded and tax collected.

Again, as with Ho-tung, two factors lay behind these results. First,

Table 5.2 Ch'ang-lu salt division, 1500–1848

Date	Yin (no.)	Value (lb)	Quantity (cwt)	Tax (taels)
1500	180 800	250	452 000	
1590	219 842	600	1 319 052	
1643	239 350	650	1 559 025	
1644	719 550	225	1 638 988	181 200
1722	921 546	250	2 303 865	426 852
1726	966 046	300	2 898 138	
1771	966 046	300	2 898 138	560 000
1820	966 046	300	2 898 138	1 025 800
1835	966 046	378	3 602 674	2 000 000
1840	866 046	418	3 620 072	2 000 000
1848	682 446	568	3 867 154	1 369 416

demography. Ch'ang-lu supplied the whole of the metropolitan province of Chihli and the eastern half of Honan. The population of Chihli rose from 14 million in 1749 to 23 million in 1850; that of Honan from 13 million to 24 million. In both provinces demographic growth was primarily in the rural sector on the nitrogen rich plain of the lower Yellow River, but in the case of Chihli the urbanization of the two megapoleis Peking and Tientsin and of the cities in the Grand Canal zone has also to be taken into consideration. Second, administration. Unlike Ho-tung, the salt administration in Ch'ang-lu was closely associated with the imperial government. Indeed, one might speak of a kind of bureaucratic capitalism in Ch'ang-lu. This association had first positive and then negative effects.[46]

Under the early Ch'ing control of Ch'ang-lu was in the hands of an informal consortium of senior Bannermen (*ch'i-jen*, the political and military nation of the Manchu state), headed successively by Ming-ju, leader of one of the two major court factions, and by Prince Yin-t'ang, his relative by marriage and heir of his wealth, the K'ang-hsi emperor's ninth son. Despite its monopolistic character, the consortium was neither restrictionist nor exclusive. For successful operation it needed expansion of sales and used a Chinese clientele to get it. In 1644, the government of Dorgon opened up the existing oligarchy by dividing the Ming 239 350 *yin* by three to make 719 550 *yin* and by slightly increasing the *yin*, formerly 650 lb now 225 lb. Over the reign of K'ang-hsi, the number of *yin* was increased to 921 546 and its value to 250 lb, so that by 1722, Ch'ang-lu was distributing 2 303 865 cwt as compared to 1 638 988 cwt in 1644. Rates of tax per *yin* increased concomitantly as did business profit, official and, especially, unofficial.

On his accession in 1722 the Yung-cheng emperor embarked in a

clean-up of Ch'ang-lu. This was part of general bureaucratic rationalization characteristic of his reign, but also an attack on the Yin-t'ang clique
which had opposed his succession. Yung-cheng's agent was a new salt
censor Mang-ku-li, who, under the supervision of Prince I, the emperor's brother and intimate adviser, was given an extended term and a
conjoint appointment in the *ta-li ssu*, the court of appeal, to show the
government meant business. The emperor's expressed intention was to
love and nurture both merchants and people. Private profit was to be
returned to public channels. The salt merchant An Ch'i, the son of
Ming-ju's factor, was compelled to disgorge by rebuilding the walls of
Tientsin at his own expense. The number of *yin* was advanced to
966 046, the *yin* was increased to 300 lb, and taxes were not significantly
increased. Profit became less conspicuous and more official.

In the long run, however, the beneficiary of Mang-ku-li's reforms
were neither the merchants nor the taxpayer nor even the board of
revenue, but the *Nei-wu fu*, the imperial household department. The
Nei-wu fu was the *éminence grise* of the second half of the Ch'ing period.
It functioned as an imperial privy purse outside regular bureaucratic
channels and benevolences from businessmen became a major source of
its funds. Its control of the Ch'ang-lu salt censorate was an instrument
for this purpose. Ch'ang-lu merchants subscribed 100 000 taels in 1732
to the war against the Zunghars; 200 000 in 1748 to the suppression of
the first Chin-ch'uan rebellion in the Tibetan borderlands; with Shantung, 200 000 in 1759 to the Ili agricultural military colony; 600 000 in
1772 to the suppression of the second Chin-ch'uan rebellion; 500 000 in
1788 to the pacification of Taiwan; 500 000 in 1792 to Fu-k'ang-an's
campaign in Tibet; a million in 1796 for use against the White Lotus
rebellion in central China. So long as trade boomed, benevolences were
not unreasonable as substitutes for additional taxation. But toward the
end of the eighteenth century, the telltale memorials on obstructed *yin*,
stagnant sales and incompleted quotas, showed that the boom was over.
Moreover China was running into a hydraulic crisis.[47] Work became
necessary on the waterways of the northeast: ten thousands for the
recurrent expenses of the Chihli waterways, millions for major works on
the Grand Canal in 1809 and on the Yellow River high dyke at Jung-yang
in Honan in 1825. This time the Ch'ang-lu merchants could not pay. The
Nei-wu fu lent them treasury funds, but at sustantial rates of interest and
with a quadrupling of the tax levy: 500 000 taels in mid Ch'ien-lung to 2
million taels in mid Tao-kuang. The cure was worse than the disease.
Saddled with rising prices, falling sales, mounting evasion and a debt of
23 million taels, the once dynamic division slid into depression.

By 1848, Ch'ang-lu was in effect bankrupt. In that year, the *Nei-wu fu*
endeavoured to put its house in order. A commission headed by an
imperial prince, Ts'ai Ch'uan, the Ting chün-wang, controller of the

imperial clan court and commandant of the Peking gendarmerie, carried out a comprehensive reform.[48] The number of *yin*, already scaled down from 966 046 to 866 046 in 1840, was further reduced to 682 446. The size of the *yin*, already increased from 378 lb in 1840, was further increased to 568 lb. The tax levy was reduced from around 2 million taels to 1 369 416 taels. A slow amortization of the debt was arranged and unofficial fees to local officials, which had destroyed much of the profitability, were more strictly prohibited. It was a bold scheme, but before its merits could be tested, China was plunged into internal rebellion and foreign war which changed the whole situation for salt and salt administration.

To the south, Shantung figured as Ch'ang-lu's junior partner. Until 1837 when jurisdiction was transferred to the governor, Shantung salt was under the control of the Ch'ang-lu salt censor and hence indirectly of first the Banner consortium and then of the *Nei-wu fu*. The earliest Ming quota had been 573 550 cwt. In 1826 the quantity handled by the salt administration was 1 250 000 cwt and additional salt was produced in the promontory and either consumed locally or exported to Korea by sea. Production was by both *chien* and *shai*, but solar evaporation was the growth area. At the outset of the dynasty, there had been 19 small producing areas (*ch'ang*), but by the middle of the nineteenth century, eight large ones. Essentially, in the course of the eighteenth century, a number of minor sites had been eliminated by the advance of four *shai* areas near the mouth of the Hsiao-ch'ing ho, a river running south of and parallel to the present (but not till 1853) bed of the Yellow River. These areas: Yung-li, Yung-fou, Kuan-t'ai and Wang-kang; supplied via the Hsiao-ch'ing ho over two-thirds of the salt distributed in the division. In particular they supplied the growing agricultural and commercial market of the Grand Canal zone in western Shantung. As in Ch'ang-lu, the Shantung salt merchants were forced to make benevolences to the *Nei-wu fu*, and by the early nineteenth century, there was the same mixture of accumulated *yin*, unpaid back taxes, massive smuggling and a huge debt of between 5 and 8 million taels. Like Ch'ang-lu, Shantung rose by demography and was bankrupted by bureaucracy.

To the north, Manchuria, though it had no formal salt administration until the twentieth century, was also an area where Banner interests and the *Nei-wu fu* were influential in the salt trade. Here, however, in their own bailiwick, their influence was more beneficial. Salt had been produced by boiling in what was to become Manchuria as far back as the preimperial kingdom of Yen. The Han appointed salt officials to Liao-hsi; the Liao and the Chin in the early Middle Ages established definite *Ch'ang*; and under the Ming, there were 12 such *ch'ang* in operation. The Ch'ing increased the number to 20 and placed them under the Mukden prefect who acted as Fengtien salt controller. In 1679 the K'ang-hsi emperor ordered the *tsao-hu* (the furnace households) to make cauldrons (*kuo*) and he established a quota of 13 700 *yin* preparatory to levying a tax. In 1681 he thought better of it and granted freedom of boiling and selling salt. It was not until 1867 that imperial taxes were levied on Manchurian salt. Under these conditions, and with the growing Chinese population of Manchuria, production expanded from no more than 50 000 cwt in 1644 to more than 300 000 in 1800. Successive basin solar evaporation was introduced from 1691 and steadily replaced boiling which was non-existent by the nineteenth century.[49] Private enterprises was left in control: 'In Fengtien salt is not manufactured by the provincial Government; anyone may lease land and establish salt pans'.[50] The pans established were of advanced type: five large concentrating basins, eight smaller condensing basins, six to eight crystallizing basins smaller still. It was a sophisticated circuit of 20-odd basins compared with eight in Ho-tung, nine in Ch'ang-lu and five in Shantung. In some works experiments were being made with an improved catchment-condensers : crystallizers ratio. In Fengtien the Manchu authorities allowed Chinese ingenuity and enterprise its head.

The Centre

In the south and north solar evaporation in various forms made substantial progress. In the centre, on the other hand, in the key Liang-huai salt division, the traditional boiling industry, despite considerable challenge both from without and from within, proved remarkably resilient.

Liang-huai was the premier salt division in terms both of salt distributed and revenue collected.[51] At the end of the Ming period, Liang-huai distributed 705 180 *yin* of salt. Each *yin* covered 400 lb and 542 968 *yin* (2 171 874 cwt) were assigned to Huai-nan and 162 145 *yin* (648 736 cwt) to Huai-pei. Huai-nan salt was *chien*. Huai-pei salt was *shai*. Huai-nan consisted of those parts of Kiangsu, Anhwei, Kiangsi, Hupei and Hunan readily accessible by the Yangtze: Huai-pei, of northern Kiangsu, northern and central Anhwei, and eastern Honan accessible by a chain of lesser water routes. The Ch'ing did not change the system fundamentally. They multiplied the *yin* by two and divided its value by the same, probably in order to enlarge the charmed circle of the salt merchants. By 1700 the number of *yin* had only increased to 1 425 949 but each *yin* now covered 267 lb. There was no change in the proportions of *chien* and *shai*. By 1750 there was a further increase in the size of the *yin* to approximately 350 lb, but again no change in the ratio of Huai-nan to Huai-pei. By 1800 there had been more considerable change. The number of *yin* had been increased to 1 680 000 and the size of the *yin* to 400 lb, but while the allocation to Huai-nan had increased to

Table 5.3 Liang-huai salt division, 1600–1850

Date	Yin (no.)	Value (lb)	Quantity (cwt)	Huai-pei (cwt)
1643	705 180	400	2 820 720	648 736
1644	1 410 360	200	2 820 720	648 736
1700	1 425 949	267	3 802 530	864 982
1750	1 425 949	350	4 990 826	1 135 288
1800	1 680 000	400	6 720 000	1 160 000
1830	1 680 000	500/400	8 140 000	2 040 000
1850	1 350 000	600/400	7 670 000	2 240 000

1 390 000 *yin* (5 460 000 cwt), that to Huai-pei had decreased to 290 000 *yin* (1 160 000 cwt), only marginally more than its 1750 allocation in terms of weight. This overall increase, but relative decline, of Huai-pei reflected the demographic dynamism of the upriver provinces as compared to the relative stagnation of the northern strip away from the river. As the censor Wang Ch'eng put it in 1795 'Liang-huai is the core of the salt tax and the core of Liang-huai is the Ch'u-kang', i.e., the sales areas in Hupei and Hunan.[52]

In 1830 the Nanking governor-general T'ao Chu made even more radical changes. As part of a package to meet the complex crisis from which Liang-huai, like other salt divisions, was then suffering, he increased the size of the *yin* in Huai-nan to 500 lb and reduced the Huai-pei quota to 260 000 *Yin* of 400 lb (1 040 000 cwt). At the same time, to mop up excess production in Huai-pei and to reduce the average price of salt in Huai-nan, he assigned 200 000 *yin* (1 million cwt) of Huai-pei *shai* for sale in the Huai-nan sales area. Because of this export, production in Huai-pei nearly doubled. It increased again under a further adjustment just before the Taiping rebellion in 1850. The number of Huai-nan *yin* was reduced from 1 390 000 to 1 090 000, but the *yin* was increased to 600 lb. Of these *yin*, 200 000 came from Huai-pei, but quantified now at 600 lb instead of 500 lb. In spite of this increase in the volume of *shai*, however, what impresses about the record of Liang-huai between 1600 and 1850 is the ability of the traditional *chien* industry to supply the needs of the expanding Yangtze market and to remain competitive against less taxed and lower cost rivals.

Liang-huai was an area of both high taxation and high cost. It provided a third of the salt consumed in China, but two thirds of the salt tax. Moreover, since the advent of the Ch'ing, taxation had increased faster than production: 950 000 taels in 1641, 2 500 000 in 1700, 5 million in 1800. Costwise too Liang-huai's position had worsened. In 1500 it had been surrounded by other *chien* salts with no competitive advantage. In

1800, there was *t'an-shai* in Ch'ang-lu, *pan-shai* in Liang-che, *lou-shai* in
Liang-kuang, as well as the internal threat to Huai-nan *chien* from
Huai-pei *shai*. Only Szechwan produced *chien* and there taxation was
particularly low. Liang-huai was in effect under siege. In 1734 an edict of
the Yung-cheng emperor complained of Szechwan and Kwangtung salt
in Hupei and Hunan, Chang-lu salt in Honan, Chekiang salt in Kiangsi.
In 1786 a first suggestion was made that Huai-pei *shai* make up deficiencies in Huai-nan *chien*. In 1795, Ho-tung salt, temporarily relieved
of taxation by the reforms of governor Feng Kuang-hsiung, joined the
besiegers and Shantung as well as Ch'ang-lu salt was reported in
Honan. In 1820 a comprehensive report described five kinds of encroachment on Huai-nan: Szechwan in Hupei and Hunan; Ho-tung and
Ch'ang-lu in Hupei; Kwangtung in Hunan; Fukien, Chekiang and
Kwangtung in Kiangsi. Most serious of all was smuggling to Kiangsu
from Ch'ang-lu via the Grand Canal by the grain tribute fleet returning
from Tientsin. This was an old problem, but it reached new heights in
the early nineteenth century when T'ao Chu estimated it at a million cwt
a year.[53] Under these attacks Liang-huai in the early nineteenth century
showed signs of collapse. In 1822 264 000 *yin* were sold in Hupei and
Hunan where the quota was 779 900 *yin*, smugglers daily multiplied,
and in 1828 the accumulated deficit amounted to over 60 million taels.[54]

That Liang-huai survived the siege was due to three factors. First, *vis
inertiae*, official and mercantile. The Ch'ing state obtained a large revenue from Liang-huai. The Liang-huai merchants formed the largest
single accumulation of capital in the empire. Neither would be eager to
abandon established positions for new uncertainties. Second, whatever
its disadvantages, Huai-nan had the great advantage of the Yangtze:
convenient for official control, inexpensive for merchant distribution.
All other salts, except Szechwan, faced at least transshipment, probably
overland transportation. *Shai* might be cheaper in production: *chien* still
had an edge in distribution. Moreover, besides being a route, the
Yangtze was a set of relationships: export brokers, junk guilds, insurance agencies, warehouse facilities, import brokers, provincial distributors, retail networks. All this Huai-nan had long manipulated and
dominated and could deny access to competitors. Finally, and more
importantly, administrative skill. The Liang-huai authorities, notably
T'ao Chu, Kiangsu governor 1825–1830 and Nanking governor-general
1830–1839, confronted their besiegers with consummate counter-
siegecreft worthy of China's best military traditions.[55] T'ao Chu blended
conciliation, coercion and competition. By channelling Huai-pei *shai* into
Huai-nan, he conciliated the producers of *shai*, made possible effective
coercion against Ch'ang-lu salt coming down the Grand Canal, and by
reducing the price of salt sold in Huai-nan improved its competitiveness

vis-à-vis its rivals. T'ao Chu achieved the seemingly impossible feat of making *shai* reinforce *chien*, radicalism subserve conservatism.

The West

In the early modern period, population was increasing in the west both by immigration and natural increase: principally in the red basin of Szechwan, but also in the surrounding highlands – the Yunnan-Kweichow plateau to the south, the Wei basin of Shensi-Kansu and other selected parts of the Hsi-pei to the north. Three salt producing areas took advantage of this expansion of China's western rim: Szechwan with a slow, steady advance which foreshadowed its preeminence in the late empire and early republic; Yunnan with the speed and initiative characteristic of a developing mining area; Mongolia with a sudden, temporary eruption which projected its hothouse rise in the early Communist period.

In Szechwan production of salt had increased from 101 315 cwt in 1368 to 206 666 cwt around 1500. The sixteenth century was prosperous in Szechwan as elsewhere in China and production rose to 357 052 cwt in 1558. It may have reached half a million cwt in the early seventeenth century when the Portuguese Jesuit Gabriel Magellan was so impressed with the province. Then came the rebellion of the murderous religious enthusiast Chang Hsien-chung and the Manchu conquest under Haoge which together reduced the population by several million. The earliest Ch'ing quotas provided only 170 976 cwt for distribution, two thirds of it by local, short distance land routes. Under Shun-chih production recovered to 361 076 cwt, but considerable quantities had to be imported from Ho-tung because the wells were not yet fully repaired. By 1730, however, the province had fully recovered and was poised for take-off. The Yung-cheng provincial gazetteer of that year provided 798 416 cwt for distribution: 240 116 cwt in *lu-yin* for short-distance land routes in the north and centre and 558 300 cwt in *shui-yin* for long-distance water routes in the south and on the circumference. For the remainder of the eighteenth century expansion continued steadily. The *shih-lu* are full of announcements of the sinking of new wells and of requests for additional *yin* both by land and water. By the time of the Chia-ch'ing edition of the provincial gazetteer in 1815, the quotas provided 2 026 262 cwt for distribution: 550 312 cwt by *lu-yin*, 11 475 950 by *shui-yin*.

A major reason for this expansion was the fact that Szechwan supplied not only itself (the import from Ho-tung had long ceased), but also most of Kweichow, part of Yunnan and increasingly, if illegally, western Hupei. So intractable had the problem of Szechwan smuggling down the Yangtze become, that in 1788 the eight most western districts of Hupei were formally reassigned to Szechwan. The quota for Hupei, however, was only 78 810 cwt and that for the Yunnan trade which had begun in 1726 only 100 608 cwt. The heart of Szechwan's 'foreign' trade was the export to Kweichow, the *Ch'ien pien-an*. This had grown from 339 450 cwt in 1730 to 534 306 cwt in 1815.

The growth in exports, together with the growing shortage of timber, was responsible for production of Szechwan shifting from the wood-burning wells of the upper Chia-ling: She-hung and P'eng-ch'i in T'ung-chuan prefecture; to the coal and gas-burning wells of the lower Min and T'o – Chien-wei in Chia-ting prefecture and Fu-shun in Hsü-chou prefecture. In 1815 Chien-wei which supplied Yunnan and much of Kweichow was the premier producing area. With its combination of shallow wells and coal fuel, it was a lesser Lorraine or little Cheshire. In 1662 it had a quota of 84 *shui-yin* and 1491 *lu-yin*, a total of 10 164 cwt of salt. In 1815 it had a quota of 4998 *shui-yin* and 27 734 *lu-yin*, a total of 350 836 cwt of salt. 25 154 of its *lu-yin* went to Yunnan, 3996 of its *shui-yin* went to Kweichow. Chien-wei was one of the frontier boom towns of the empire. Not far behind and also exporting to Kweichow were the gas-burning wells of Fu-shun with a quota of 3986 *shui-yin* and 2182 *lu-yin*, a total of 208 028 cwt. Fu-shun had been the leading producer in the early Ming and was to be again under the late Ch'ing, but temporarily it had been eclipsed by Chien-wei's capture of the export market. This advantage Chien-wei enjoyed less through its intrinsic merits than through closer proximity to the provincial capital at Chengtu and hence political influence. Chien-wei was an up-to-date saline: it was also the governor-general's saline.

Although Yunnan imported salt – 100 000 cwt from Szechwan, maybe 25 000 from Kwangtung – to supply its eastern districts on the escarpment, on the plateau itself it had salines of its own, which in 1800 produced possibly as much as 375 000 cwt. These salines formed three groups: Hei-ching in the east near the provincial capital Kunming; Pei-ching in the west near Tali the old indigenous capital; and Mo-hei-ching or Shih-kao ching in the south near Szemao close to the Laotian and Burmese borders. Although known as *ching* or wells, many of the Yunnan salines, particularly those in the Mo-hei-ching group, were in the nature of shafts or mines, though the low grade rock salt was generally turned into brine and evaporated over wood fires. The growth of the Yunnan salines in the Ch'ing period was the product of two forces. First, Chinese mining enterprise, often Chinese Muslim enterprise, which in the eighteenth century was turning Yunnan into China's major source of base metals – copper, tin and zinc. Second, the extension of direct Chinese rule into the area, the so-called *kai-t'u kuei-liu*, initiated particularly by the Manchu governor-general O-er-t'ai between

Table 5.4 Production of salt in China, 1500 and 1800 (cwt)

Place	1500	1800
Liang-kuang	187 421	1 629 020
Fukien	418 290	1 000 000
Liang-che	1 434 000	2 416 191
Ho-tung	500 000	1 500 000
Ch'ang-lu	452 000	2 898 138
Shantung	573 550	1 250 000
Manchuria	100 000	300 000
Liang-huai	2 820 720	6 720 000
Szechwan	206 666	2 026 262
Yunnan	–	375 000
Mongolia	–	200 000
Total	6 692 647	20 314 611

1725 and 1732. At first the officials kept strict control over production, distribution and retail so that salt amounted to a nationalized industry, but, in the reign of Chia-ch'ing, *kuan-yün kuan-hsiao* was converted into *min-yün min-hsiao*. In theory production distribution and retail were returned to private enterprise and the state confined itself to levying a tax at source (*chiu-ch'ang cheng-shui*), though in practice considerable control was retained through advances to the producers. Nevertheless Yunnan is an example of business and bureaucracy cooperating in relative harmony.

If Chinese mining enterprise lay behind the growth of the Yunnan salines, Chinese commercial enterprise lay behind the growth of Mongolian salt.[56] The *sebkha* lakes of the Sino-Mongolian borderlands, the equivalent of Lake Elton in the Russian steppe, produced salt by natural solar crystallization. They only needed incentive for exploitation and in the early modern period such incentive was provided by the growth of Chinese population in the border areas and by the need of the Mongol aristocracy and their mercantile agents to find some export commodity to pay for their increasing imports of Chinese consumer goods – grain, tea, textiles, metal products and opium – to which Chinese commercial enterprise had introduced them.

In the early modern period, two of the borderland lakes made brief but significant appearances in the record. First, Hua-ma-ch'ih in Kansu just south of the wall competed effectively with Ho-tung salt in the western Shensi prefecture of Feng-hsiang. Its salt also sometimes reached Sian in the heart of the Wei basin. Its competition was sufficiently serious to be the subject of an appendix to Chapter One of the Yung-cheng edition of the *yen-fa chih*. Natural *shai* enjoyed a cost advantage over successive basin *shai* and Hua-ma-ch'ih was less taxed than

Ho-tung , so the Ho-tung authorities were worried. *Per contra*, Hua-ma-ch'ih had to face long land transportation routes to the main centres of Chinese population and had less political backing than Ho-tung, so that their fears did not then eventuate.

Chilantai, on the other hand, in Alashan west of the Yellow River, had the support of the Mongol princes of Alashan, highly sinified and sometimes husbands of imperial princesses, and of the powerful Chinese Muslim merchant community of Ninghsia. Thanks to their support, the Ming and early Ch'ing prohibitions against the import of red salt from Chilantai were gradually relaxed and it began to take the river route down the Huang-ho to northern Shansi and points south. This invasion of red salt – noted in 1758, developed by 1782, legitimated in 1788 – affected Ho-tung. Governor Feng Kuang-hsiung's temporary abolition in 1791 of the salt administration there and the conversion of the salt duty into a surcharge on the land tax (*kuei ti-ting*) was designed to improve the competitive position of Ho-tung. In fact, the reform encouraged the inflow of Mongolian salt by disbanding the preventive services along with the rest of the salt administration. Ho-tung salt therefore sought markets further south where, freed from taxation, it could compete with Ch'ang-lu and Huai-pei salt which still paid tax. In consequence of pressure from these salt divisions, in 1807 the Ho-tung salt administration was restored, the import of red salt by river was again prohibited and Shansi preventive authority was extended to Chilantai, Hua-ma-ch'ih and the river ports. An attempt in 1822 to reopen the river route from Chilantai was negated. One of the principal opponents was the elder statesman Na-yen-ch'eng, governor-general of Shensi-Kansu 1822–1825, who distrusted both the Alashan prince and the Chinese Muslim merchants. Whatever the economic considerations, political exigencies prevailed in the Chinese salt administration. China was not to feel a pressing political need for transborder salt until the age of industrialization.

A comparison between China and Europe in the early modern period may conclude this chapter. In 1500, in China as in Europe, 100 million people consumed 7 million cwt of salt. Between 1500 and 1800, in China as in Europe, absolute production and consumption tripled to 20 million cwt. But whereas in Europe, population had only risen to 200 million so that *per capita* consumption had risen by 50 per cent, in China, population had risen to 300 million so that *per capita* consumption had remained the same. Moreover, the means used to boost production in the Chinese and European worlds were different. In China, despite the rediscovery of successive basin solar evaporation, its extension into new areas and diversification into new forms, despite the progress of the semi-industrial Szechwan salines based on deep drilling and neotechnic fuels, the centrepiece of Chinese salt, consciously maintained as such by the imperial administration, remained Liang-huai, and specifically Huai-nan based on the ancient subsoil brine plus boiling method. In Europe, on the other hand, subsoil brine plus boiling had virtually disappeared, successive basin solar evaporation was already being overtaken by salt based on deep brine and new fuels. In distribution, the absence of imperial regulation in Europe permitted the beginning of a world market in salt and in consumption the percentage of salt used for non-alimentary purposes (fisheries, silver production, tanning, glass-making, fur processing etc.) was almost certainly higher in Europe than in China. In the early modern period, the sap was beginning to rise again in China, but it was not enough to overtake a Europe which was about to turn over to steam.

6 Modernity

Between 1800 and the present the salt industry throughout the world underwent a process which may be called modernization. But, while the process was universal, its degree varied and its expression differed, largely in accordance with positions established in the previous age of late tradition and early modernity. Thus modernization went furthest in Europe where it had begun, least far in Islam and India to which it was diffused, with China, relatively independent, in an intermediate position. Everywhere modernization meant diversification of demand, and innovation in transport, but while in Europe and its offshoots this led to a turning away from solar evaporated salt toward rock salt and brine salt, in Africa, Islam, India and China, it led to increasing reliance on such salt whether from the sea or from lakes. In Europe, modernization meant the eclipse of *shai*; in China, its hypertrophy and, with the successful conclusion of its siege of Huai-nan, an eclipse of *chien*. Everywhere, there were shifts in location – but not the same shifts. In the European world leadership in production passed from England to the United States and within the United States from New York and Michigan to Louisiana and Texas. In China, following a concentration in the northeast, there was a shift from the coast to the interior, as there was too in Russia. On the other hand, in Africa, Islam and India, the coast took the lead from the interior. Everywhere, there were increases in scale, but the rates of increase were very uneven between regions. The picture is one of limited diversity in overriding unity.

Table 6.1 World production of salt, 1800, 1950, 1985 (tons)

Region	1800	1950	1985
Greater Europe	1 050 000	40 000 000	150 000 000
China	1 000 000	3 500 000	33 000 000
Islam	100 000	1 500 000	3 000 000
India	300 000	3 000 000	10 000 000
Africa	50 000	2 000 000	4 000 000
Total	2 500 000	50 000 000	200 000 000

Modernization wears two faces. On the one hand, it may be viewed abstractly as that process of sophistication which an institution or technology undergoes when the number of units in the institution or stages in the technology increases. Modernization is complexification based on number. Thus between 1800 and the present, more salt was produced through increasingly complex means, distributed by higher energy using devices, and consumed in an ever greater variety of ends. On the other hand, modernization may be viewed concretely in terms of particular changes, identified in the components of the institutional structure or technological operation under consideration. In the case of salt, this means an examination of general changes in the production, distribution and consumption of salt in the modern period preliminary to focusing on the variations in different parts of the world.

Production

In fundamentals, the production of salt changed less than its distribution. Though new mining technology and better access through modern transport made rock salt of greater significance, the two historic processes of *shai* and *chien*, solar and non-solar evaporation of brine, marine or non-marine, continued to predominate. That *chien* predominated in Europe, while *shai* predominated in non-Europe was due not only to local comparative costs but also to attitudes to energy which had deep roots in their respective societies. Ever since readily accessible local supplies of timber ceased to be abundant, in Islam in the early Middle Ages,[1] in Europe and China in the sixteenth and seventeenth centuries, Europe had maintained a high energy solution to its problems in seeking new sources, while non-Europe had adopted a low energy solution. Thus Europe became predisposed to *chien* and man-made energy, non-Europe to *shai* and natural energy. From this dichotomy flowed others. The European salt industry through its supersession of *shai* increasingly escaped the constraints of weather and the seasonal rhythms these imposed, while the non-European salt industry remained, indeed became more, subject to the variations of sunshine, rain and wind. For non-Europe, the year was still made by nature; for Europe increasingly by culture.

Where change took place was in the supply of brine and the sources of energy for evaporation used in the *chien* process. The two major changes were deep drilling for brine and non-traditional sources of energy – coal, natural gas and electricity – for evaporation. Both had their precedents in Szechwan, in the brine and fire wells developed in the Han period at Lin-ch'iung and Ling-chou and locally associated with the name of Chang Tao-ling, the founder of Five Pecks of Rice Taoism. Indeed, the predominant technology of the modern European salt industry may be regarded as the generalization and improvement of what had been begun by Szechwan. Szechwan itself, of course, had not stood still since the Han. The deepest well then recorded was 800 feet, but by the nineteenth century, depths of 4000 feet were being achieved by drilling which might last 20 years. Similarly, techniques for handling the dangerous natural gas had been considerably improved. Nevertheless, Europe was soon to do better than Szechwan.

The advent of deep drilling in Europe is usually associated with the appearance of the first Artesian wells at Lillers in the Pas-de-Calais, the heart of Chaunu's 'full world', around 1126. However, the technique, whether derived from China as Needham believes or independently evolved, was not applied, except in Russia, to obtaining brine until the early nineteenth century. Then it began to be used by a number of German salt experts, or 'salinists', prospecting in the lower Neckar valley on behalf of the governments of the princely states of Württemberg and Baden and the *Reichstadt* of Wimpfen. Of these experts the most notable was Carl Christian Glenk (1779–1845) from Schwäbisch Hall. In 1818 he found rock salt at 142 metres at what became the Ludwigshalle near Wimpfen. In 1835 he found salt at 135 metres at Schweizerhalle near Basle, the basis of the modern Swiss industry of the Aargau which has ended the republic's ancient dependence on imports. At both these places, and at other deep drilling sites, the discovery was exploited, not by mining, but by introducing water to form a concentrated brine, which was then brought to the surface and evaporated in the usual way. This technique, which does not appear to have been in earlier use in Szechwan or elsewhere in China, has since become standard European practice.

What had been in earlier use in Szechwan was the specialized, rotary drillhead known as 'jars'. Jars came into the technology of drilling both on the Continent and in the United States in the 1830s and 1840s. Since an account of what went on in Szechwan had been published by the French missionary priest Father Imbert in 1829, it is possible that China influenced Europe. However in 1841 a patent for jars was given to one William Morris of Kanawha in West Virginia, so the American discovery at least may have been independent. Certainly it was in the United States that deep drilling had its greatest impact. Salt and petroleum spurred each other on to fresh discoveries. By 1985 artificial brine from deep wells was the principal raw material of the four leading salt producing states: Louisiana, Texas, Michigan and New York, though in Michigan mining ran it a close second. On the Continent, deep drilling created new salt industries at Dombasle, southeast of Nancy where France found compensation for the Lorraine salines lost to Germany in 1871; Borth, north of Duisburg where West Germany found compensation for the Stassfurt deposits lost to the East in 1945; Winterswijk in Guelderland and Hengelo in Overijssel, where Holland, so long the great importer, found compensation for its age old deficiencies. In England, deep drilling by the firm of Bolckow and Vaughan, which in 1857 led to the discovery of salt at 400 metres on Teesside, laid the foundations for ICI's salt industries at Billingham and Wilton in Cleveland. More generally, deep drilling revealed the hitherto unsuspected extent of non-marine salt deposits. Their exploitation was part of the new conquest of inner space first called for by the Jesuit magus Athanasius Kircher in his *Mundus subterraneus* of 1665.

Brine, whether marine or non-marine, natural or artificial, needed to be evaporated, or at least treated, since some of the new demand from the chemical industry was for brine rather than salt. The *chien* salt industry therefore, particularly in its new form of vacuum-pan evaporation, participated fully in the development or diffusion of new sources of energy: coal, steam, petroleum, natural gas, nuclear power, electricity on its various bases.

Once again Szechwan was the prototype for a major salt industry using non-traditional fuels in the coal of Chien-wei and the natural gas of Tzu-liu-ching. In sixteenth-century England, salt in Tyneside along with glass, bricks and brewing, pioneered the regular use of coal in European industry. Staffordshire coal began to be used at Nantwich in the mid-seventeenth century and in the eighteenth century demand for South Lancashire coal by Northwich and Winsford helped lay the energy foundation for England's industrial northwest. On the Continent, coal was experimented with in the seventeenth century in Franche Comté and applied in the eighteenth century, notably in Lorraine and at the Prussian salines of Königsborn and Werl in the Ruhr and in the Saxon salines of Artern, Kosen, Durrenberg and Teuditz near Halle,[2] but it was not until the nineteenth century that the industry as a whole shifted from a wood to a coal basis, as for example at Stassfurt which then became the leading German saline. In the United States, the association of petroleum and salt led to the development of the first natural gas based salt industry. In Holland too, the new natural gas finds in Groningen could be supplied to the new salt industries at Winterwijk and Hengelo in the land provinces. Siberian natural gas also, whether used in the Soviet Union or Western Europe or Japan, will sooner or later be harnessed to salt using chemical industries. In Switzerland the thermocompression evaporation technique used by the Rhine salines consortium in the Aargau could be powered by the electricity generated by the river itself at its falls.[3] In Japan, where lack of sun and shortage of timber had long limited production and produced dependence on external supplies, electrodialysis of sea water to concentrate brine, developed originally for desalinization purposes, opened a new chapter not only in the production of sea salt, but also in the exploitation of marine minerals generally. For many other minerals as well as salt, the ocean is the ultimate reserve, a fact which must foreshadow a new economy of coastal shelves, maritime development and sea power.

Distribution

For distribution modernization may be defined in terms of the use of
canals, steamships, railways, trucks and pipelines for the distribution of
salt and brine. Except for aeroplanes for which its bulky products were
not suited, the salt industry made extensive use of modern methods of
transport as they became available. The salt industry also contributed to
the canalization of the Weaver in Cheshire and of the Ruhr in the
Rhineland. Salt provided freight for steamships and railways as it had
provided ballast for galleons and junks. Salt's greatest contribution
perhaps was in the area of pipelines. In the piping of brine to a
convenient source of fuel, in this case natural gas wells, Szechwan had
again been the pioneer, but only in hollowed bamboo and up to a
distance of seven miles. This distance was surpassed in Bavaria at
Reichenhall in the work both of Reiffenstuhl in the early seventeenth
century and of Reichenbach at the beginning of the nineteenth. Moreover, Reiffenstuhl's pipes were of lead and Reichenbach's of cast iron.[4]
Another place where pipes became important was Salins in Franche-
Comté. Here, between 1775 and 1779, Claude-Nicholas Ledoux, as part
of his reconstruction of the saltworks, built a double conduit of 21.25 km
from the old salt springs of the Grande Saunerie to a new evaporating
centre lower down between the villages of Arc and Senans, equipped
with a mile long graduation house in a suitably exposed position, and
close to the royal forest of Chaux which would be able to supply fuel for
an indefinite period. The original pipes were of wood, but over the
nineteenth century and down to the closing of the saline in 1962, they
were successively replaced by lead, iron and plastic.[5]

   The salt industry was profoundly affected by the introduction of
modern transportation. This was particularly true in the *shai* branch of
the industry where geographical factors were paramount. Thus in India,
the spatial organization of the salt trade was reshaped by the steamship,
while in China it was reshaped by the railway and the truck. In the *chien*
branch of the industry, however, the ability of the deep drill and new
energy sources to create a saltworks almost anywhere greatly reduced
the significance of the long and even medium distance salt trade. Salt
has become less of an international commodity than it once was. Nevertheless, despite the achievements of deep drills and energy sources and
the promise of electrodialysis from the sea and the piping of brine, a
number of major salt routes, mainly in *shai* salt, were still to be found in
the twentieth century: Ibiza to Scotland, Iceland and Scandinavia; Taiwan, Siam and Australia to Japan; Siam to Malaysia and Indonesia;
Canada, Mexico and the Bahamas to the United States. All these routes,
of course, used modern methods of transportation. *Shai* salt was not yet

played out and so long as it lasted so too would long-distance distribution.

Consumption

It was in consumption that the greatest change took place. Indeed, the changes in production and distribution were dependent upon those in consumption. These changes were twofold: first, another increase in the alimentary market, quite significant on a traditional scale of quantities, but quite dwarfed by, secondly, a massive increase in the non-alimentary market.

In 1982 the adult consumption of alimentary salt in the United States was around 16 lb a year, 50 per cent higher than a century earlier, when North America, particularly the southern states, was already among the highest alimentary consumers.[6] Other Western countries and Japan reached similar if lesser levels. The basic cause of this increase was what may be called the Crosse and Blackwell revolution, from the English firm, members of the Salters company in London, whose products played a leading role in developments in the British Isles. Essentially, the revolution consisted in the rise of the large scale prepared foods industry: tinned soups, frozen dinners, canned preparations, take-aways, junkfoods; tins of sardines, potato chips, burgers, tomato sauce, pickles, pretzels and pizzas; and, in the east, all the applications of monosodium glutamate.[7] All these contained considerable quantities of salt, more than their equivalents prepared domestically from fresh ingredients. Unlike the earlier revolutions in carbohydrates, protein and fats: the successive ages of wheat, millet and rice, fish and pork, butter, cheese and lard; this latest revolution in diet concerned processing rather than materials. Cooking, from being the conversion of the raw to the cooked, became the conversion of the precooked to the overcooked. As such it was primarily a social change, associated with urbanization, increased employment of women outside the home, and a shift in taste from sweet to savoury, a reaction against the Victorian fashion for sugar when puddings, cakes and confectionery represented affluence and indulgence. A social change, it was also a mass change, opposed by the elites of orthodox and alternative medicine, the various kinds of *nouvelle cuisine*, and the cults of the natural and organic. A mass change, and a phenomenon of culture, it probably on balance improved the overall level of diet. Even the increase in hypertension, with which its critics associated it, may have been due less to the quantity of sodium as such than to the absence of countervailing potassium. At any rate the latest revolution in diet increased the consumption alimentary salt and hence the production of salt.

Much more important quantitatively, however, in increasing the production and consumption of salt was the growth of the non-alimentary market. In 1800 at least 90 per cent of all salt was directed to human alimentary consumption: table salt, of course, but more importantly salt used in the food preparation industries – sardines and anchovies, pig products, cheese and butter, pickled vegetables, soy sauce, corned beef. Indeed, almost the only salt which did not end up in the human body was that fed to animals, that used in fish packing (as opposed to fish salting), and the small quantities used as fertilizer, in medicine and in dust laying. In industry the only considerable consumer was the amalgam salt/mercury process for silver, as used for example at the great mining camp of Potosi. In 1985 at least 90 per cent of all salt was directed to non-alimentary consumption. Of the new consumers, by far the most important, taking 70 per cent of all salt produced, was the chemical industry. Indeed, the extent to which a salt industry is integrated with the chemical industry is the best ostensive measure of its degree of modernization. Potosi and its successors, once marginal, have now conquered the heart of the salt market. Another new consumer, far behind chemicals but ahead now of alimentation and taking 10–15 per cent of all salt produced, was the roads in winter: salt for the removal of snow and ice, one of the properties of sodium chloride being to lower the freezing point of water. If it be true, as was argued by the 'Eurasian' school of geographers,[8] that the future march of civilization will be toward the Poles, or if some new ice age overtakes our current interglaciality, this is an outlet destined for great expansion – the new frontier of salt. For the moment, however, the chemical industry stands dominant in the consumption of salt and this is the essence of its modern transformation.

Between 1800 and 1985, the salt industry was involved in three successive chemical revolutions, each divided into stages according to the process involved or the product being manufactured.[9]

First, there was the alkali revolution: the production of soda (sodium carbonate) from salt or brine by the Leblanc, Solvay or Castner/Kellner processes. Soda was an essential raw material for the glass, soap and textile industries, both traditional and modern. Natural soda was not so much rare – the United States today obtains most of its supply from natural sources – as difficult of access in premodern conditions. In the eighteenth century, therefore, natural soda from Egypt or Syria had to be supplemented by soda processed from Spanish *barilla* or Scottish kelp, but, as demand increased, the supply of these obscure raw materials (semi-natural sodium carbonate) became inadequate. Experiments were undertaken to synthesize soda and in 1791 Nicolas Leblanc, physician to the Duke of Orleans, produced a workable process of which the essential was the application of sulphuric acid to common salt. The

Leblanc process was taken up, however, not in France, but in Britain: first in Glasgow, already a centre of the kelping industry; then on Tyneside, where coal was available; and finally at Widnes, close to sources of coal and salt and outlets in glass, soap and textiles.

The Leblanc industry was an essential element of the early industrial revolution, but the process was inefficient and blighting. Despite its development of chlorine bleach as a by-product, it could not absorb its sulphurous fumes or hydrochloric waste. For these reasons, it was replaced in the last third of the nineteenth century, first on the Continent, then in England and finally everywhere, by the ammonia/salt process pioneered in 1861 by the Belgian industrialist Ernest Solvay. The Solvay process required more limestone, more salt or brine, but less coal and no sulphuric acid. It was more capital intensive, but it produced less unusable waste. Though not tied to its brine sources, the Solvay industry showed more tendency than the Leblanc to settle in salt towns and produce its own raw material. Thus Brunner Mond, the English representative of the Solvay international, settled at Winnington near Northwich, which they turned into a company town and the parent of ICI's Salt Division. Solvay at once made Leblanc seem antiquated, though in England especially, the older industry organized in the United Alkali company was a long time dying. In 1895, a third competitor appeared in the electrolytic separation of brine into sodium, chlorine and hydrogen compounds developed by the American H. Y. Castner and the Austrian C. Kellner. Castner/Kellner was expensive when it first appeared because of its electricity requirements. It was a greater threat to Leblanc than to Solvay and was in fact soon integrated into the techniques used by the Solvay group of companies. Its real importance, once cheaper electricity became available, was as a producer not of ordinary but of caustic soda (sodium hydroxide), which came into increased demand in the next phase of chemical development.

Second, there was the synthetics revolution: the synthesis of aniline dyes, rayon, phenolic plastics and (not strictly a synthetic) aluminium. In none of these industries was salt the primary raw material, but in all salt products, in particular sodium hydroxide, were important secondary raw materials. The first of the synthetics to be economically significant was aniline dyes because of their high value and because down to 1914 they were virtually a German monopoly. The leading company was the Ludwigshafen firm of BASF (Badische Anilin und Soda Fabrik) which was founded in 1865 and became the centrepiece of I. G. Farben which so terrified its foreign competitors between the wars. Sodium hydroxide, i.e. caustic soda, and hence salt, was required in the processing of aniline and Ludwigshafen was well placed to mobilize the resources of German Lorraine to the west and Stassfurt to the east. It was the same with the first synthetic textile, rayon, or artificial silk as it was called by its patentee, Count Hilaire Bernigaud de Chardonnet (1839–1924), a pupil of Pasteur's, who developed it at his Besançon works from 1891. The primary raw material of rayon was cellulose, from leaves, wood or cotton; but the process required considerable quantities of sodium hydroxide in the treatment. Besançon was conveniently situated between the old French salines at Salins and the new French salines south of Nancy. Similarly, phenol, the raw material for the first plastic, Bakelite, developed in the United States in 1909 by the Belgian chemical engineer Leo Hendrik Bakeland (1863–1944) contained no sodium or chlorine, but its preparation from coal tar or its derivative benzene, required caustic soda. Aluminium of course was an element, but its lengthy preparation from bauxite, developed from 1886 by Charles Martin Hall (1863–1914) in the United States and by Paul L. T. Héroult (1863–1914) in France made it a quasi-synthetic, the first artificial metal. In the preparation of the bauxite for electrolysis, sodium carbonate or sodium hydroxide played an essential part. Synthetics increased the demand for salt significantly.

Third, there was the revolution of chlorinated hydrocarbons, synthetics for synthetics in the form of organic compounds such as ethylene chloride, vinyl chloride, chlorobenzene, carbontetrachloride, tri and tetra chloroethylene. Unlike the two earlier chemical revolutions, this one is a good illustration of the thesis that industrialization is not the same thing as scientific or technological discovery, for most of these substances were identified in laboratories and described in scientific papers in the first flush of organic chemistry in the first half of the nineteenth century. There, however, they remained until the twentieth century, as much for social as technological reasons, found uses for them as raw materials for such things as refrigerants and aerosol propellants (carbon tetrachloride), cleaning fluids (tri and tetra chloroethylene), anti-freeze, anti-knock and 'scavenge' (ethylene chloride), pesticides (chlorobenzene), non-phenolic plastics (vinyl chloride), and the solvents necessary to their production (ethylene chloride again). The significance of these ubiquitous and polygamous compounds for the salt industry was that they all required chlorine to substitute for one or more of the hydrogen atoms of the original hydrocarbons. Just as the alkali and synthetics revolutions had required sodium or its compounds, so the new revolution required chlorine and its compounds. Chlorine, from being noxious waste only partially used in bleach, now became the primary object of manufacture. By the last third of the twentieth century nearly half of all salt produced was being turned into chlorine. The chief function of salt in the world economy was as raw material for chlorine.

It was a crucial function, but an inconspicuous one except to *cognoscenti* and a limited one. Because of the new methods of production, a lower proportion of supply needed to be distributed long distance and most salt was now distributed for intermediate rather than final demand, so that ultimate consumers might be unaware of their dependence for, say anti-freeze, on salt. Moreover, salt was only relevant to part of the total chemical revolution and that in turn was only part of the whole industrial revolution. In the case of ICI, for example, the Salt Division was always a Cinderella. Salt played no part in the history of Nobel Industries, one of the four firms which merged in 1926 to form ICI, and little part in the history of the Billingham fertilizer plant which was the first initiative of that merger. Similarly, in the new technology of the 1980s, nuclear fuels, the computer revolution, genetic engineering, new materials and integrated flexible manufacturing systems; salt only played a role through its contribution to chlorinated hydrocarbons. In itself this pattern of cruciality and inconspicuousness is not remarkable. For, if, at its most abstract, modernization is characterized by increase of scale and complexity, then it is only likely that the particular components subject to the process will be characterized by greater versatility but less preeminence, more power but less dominance. So at least it was with salt.

THE EUROPEAN WORLD

Europe's modernization took place in fundamental continuity with its past. As Chaunu has shown,[10] the industrial map of 1900 reflects the literacy map of 1600, though perhaps less exactly than he believes. Consequently it is possible to use the same regional categories as in the previous chapter, but because of the developments which had taken place, it is necessary to take them in a different order: the Circumterranean, the Continental heartlands, the Mediterranean, the new lands; and to add Africa which, through the operation of the slave trade and colonialism, became an associate member of the European world in the modern period.

The Circumterranean

In the Circumterranean the dominating force was England and the Cheshire salt industry. Down to the First World War, during which it was overtaken by the United States, England was the largest producer of salt in the European world. The Continent, though producing increasing quantities as it industrialized and decreasingly dependent on outside supplies, did not challenge England's dominance. In the history of the English salt industry between 1800 and 1950, two themes intertwine: overall expansion and the rise and fall of exports. Both were related to the rise of the chemical industry, which increasingly absorbed England's production and led other countries to develop their own sources of supply. In the case of salt, modernization meant deinternationalization. England, from being the workshop of the world, had to learn to be her own workshop.

By the beginning of the nineteenth century, Cheshire was already the major factor in the international trade in salt. It had captured the traditional Baltic markets from the Hansards and Dutch, and hence from their Latin suppliers, and it was developing an extensive exchange against cotton with the southern United States. Salt was a weapon against Napoleon's continental system and a pillar of the first industrial revolution. In 1844 the ports of the British East Indies were opened to Cheshire salt and in 1863, at the height of the American Civil War and the cotton famine, Bengal was opened at the instance of Hermann Eugen Falk, a leading manufacturer and founder in 1858 of the Salt Chamber of Commerce. Thanks to this access Cheshire soon over-powered the native Indian *chien* industry and Bengal became its number one foreign market. In 1880 when the old Cheshire industry, with its centre now at Winsford, reached its height, over half its 2 million tons production was exported, to mainly alimentary markets. Of the other half which was consumed domestically, half was decomposed by the Leblanc industry at Glasgow, on Tyneside and at Runcorn, St Helens and above all Widnes, leaving the rest for the British alimentary market, the fisheries and lesser industries. Since 1800 the industry had expanded enormously both internationally and domestically but essentially on the same basis. Internally too the industry had not much changed its structure: aristocratic ground landlords and proprietors, many small operators among a few large ones, a largely familial or artisanal work-force. It was an industry before the bourgeoisie or the proletariat. Ludwig Mond's mother-in-law wrote of Winnington in 1873: 'The salt manufacturers are not like us. They are not educated or sociable people. Like most people in England, they are artisans who have worked their way up.'[11]

From 1880 the industry began to change. On the one hand, exports ran into increasing difficulty. There was the loss of the American market to native producers, Russian tariffs in the Baltic, competition in Bengal from cheaper Spanish and Red Sea solar evaporated salt, local pro-duction in South Australia, industrial disputes on the docks and in the coal mines. The Salt Union, a cartel formed in 1888, fought back with quotas and restrictionism, but the cure was worse than the disease. By 1912 the export of salt from Cheshire was down to 0.5 million tons in a context in which world consumption of salt was increasing rapidly. On the other hand, in the domestic market, the chemical revolutions were continuing, new sources of salt were being developed, and new kinds of business structure organized. In 1874 John Brunner and Ludwig Mond opened the first English Solvay works at Winnington outside Northwich. Both men significantly had Continental background – Brunner, Swiss and Mond, German Jewish; and operated with the blessing of Solvay himself. In 1882, the deep sources of salt discovered on Teesside in 1857 were brought into production for the Tyneside Leblanc industry. Just as Brunner Mond operated an integrated structure of salt and Solvay, so Teesside deep drilling could only be operated by large firms such as Bolckow and Vaughan or Tenants. Winsford and Widnes declined together. In 1887 Widnes and its Leblanc associates decomposed 380 000 tons of salt, in 1892 275 000, in 1914 less again. The Solvay process, by comparison, decomposed 10 000 tons in 1878, 400 000 tons in 1894. By 1950 England produced 4 million tons of salt, double her production in 1914, and by 1985 10 million tons. Most of this was consumed at home by the chemical industry, in particular by the synthetics and chlorinated hydrocarbons industries established by ICI at Wilton on Teesside after the Second World War. If Winnington shifted the centre of the Cheshire industry from Winsford to Northwich, Wilton made the fortune of Middlesborough as a producer of salt. Wilton marked the rebirth of the English chemical industry. After pioneering the Leblanc industry, England for a long time lagged behind in the chemical race. Solvay was pioneered on the Continent. Aniline dyes were left to Germany, rayon to France, bakelite and aluminium to the United States and France. It was only with Wilton that England returned to its heritage of industrial chemicals.

The Continental Heartlands

The economic development of the Continent in modern times has been dominated by the emergence of the major industrial axis of the Rhineland,[12] which has tended to associate all other centres, for example in Britain and northern Italy, with itself. This axis was the original basis of the European Economic Community. Since the chemical industry was an important component of the axis, not so much in its origins when coal, steel and engineering were preeminent as in its middle development, it has drawn the salt industry to itself to create a new Lotharingian salt zone. Essentially supranational in its thrust, the new Rhenania had Dutch, Belgian, Swiss, French, even Italian components, as well as German. Till after the Second World War, however, this thrust was masked by the prevailing political structures, so that the Continental heartlands are best analysed with regard to the three political divisions of France, imperial Germany and the Habsburg empire, notwithstanding their economic superficiality.

In 1800, French salt production was 225 000 tons: 160 000 tons by solar evaporation from the Atlantic salines of Guérande, Bourgneuf and

Brouage; 27 500 tons by solar evaporation from the Mediterranean salines of Peccais, the Camargue, Berre and Hyères; and 37 500 tons by coal and wood evaporation from the inland salines of Lorraine and Franche Comté at Dieuze, Moyenvic, Chateau-Salins, Salins and Mont-morot. In 1950, French salt production was over 2 million tons: 50 000 tons from the Atlantic, chiefly Guérande; 500 000 tons from the Mediterranean, chiefly the Camargue; and 1 500 000 tons from the inland salines, chiefly Lorraine. In 1985, French salt production was over 7 million tons: 10 000 tons from the Atlantic, a million tons from the Mediterranean, 6 million tons from the inland salines. The three themes were overall expansion, shift in location, and concentration within locations, adding up to the predominance of Lorraine.

These changes in production were the result of changes in distribution and consumption: the rise of the railways and the chemical industries. Until the middle of the nineteenth century Atlantic salt held up well in a France whose economic dynamic had been partly choked off by the revolution. In 1850 Atlantic production reached a high point of 220 000 tons. It still had the advantage of cost over inland salt and the increase in sunshine from the midcentury benefited it as much as the Mediterranean. Under Napoleon III France began to change. The grey colour of Atlantic salt gave offence to consumers, it no longer commanded regular ballast space in shipping; it was poorly served by the railways and it was far from the new chemical markets of the northeast. The Lorraine salines, on the other hand, were well served by the railway network centring on Paris. They were strategically situated between Solvay's headquarters at Charleroi and Lille and Lyon, the hands of France as Paris was its head. In 1879 and 1886 Solvay sank new salt wells at Dombasle in the valley of the Meurthe southeast of Nancy to compensate France for those she had lost to the Germans along the Seille at Dieuze, Moyenvic and Chateau-Salins and was soon producing two thirds of France's caustic soda as well as most of her sodium carbonate.[13] By 1875 the French inland salines were producing more than they had before the war. The Mediterranean salines, where during the nineteenth century considerable improvements were made in the catchment-condensers: crystallizers ratio thereby increasing productivity, were well placed not only for Lyon, but also for the newer industries of northern Italy and the newest industry of Toulouse, aluminium in particular. By its oil pipeline, Marseille was in touch with Strasbourg and the Rhineland and counted salt as one of its assets in its competition with Genoa and Trieste to be the Europort of the south. The attractive influence of the Rhineland industrial whirlpool thus shifted the French salt industry eastward. In the west, the saline which survived best was the Guérande, the most local in its clientele, the least tied into the European market.

In 1800 the territories which were to comprise the German empire produced 130 000 tons of salt, witness to Germany's relative economic

Table 6.2 Salt production in the Habsburg Empire, 1800 and 1912 (tons)

Place	1800	1912
Hallein	15 000	24 059
Salzkammergut	50 000	128 160
Wieliczka/Bochnia	56 000	144 380
Soovar	5 000	10 000
Ronaszek	34 000	100 000
Torda and Maros Ujvar	25 000	160 000
Hall in Tyrol	15 000	17 448
Istria	—	16 303
Dalmatia	—	4 523
Galicia	10 000	67 583
Total	210 000	662 456

backwardness compared with France. Production was scattered round twenty-odd salines, the result of political particularism, none of them on a large scale. The two largest groups were those of Prussia at Grossensalza/Schönebeck, Halle and Stassfurt (60 000 tons) and of Bavaria at Reichenhall, Berchtesgaden, Traunstein and Rosenheim (25 000 tons). Next came those of Saxony at Artern, Kosen, Kotschau, Teuditz and Saxon Durrenberg (20 000 tons), Hanover at Lüneburg (11 000 tons) and Württemberg at Sulz, Niedernhall and Wilhelmshall (5000 tons). Production roughly followed political importance.

In 1900, however, Germany produced 1 000 000 tons, in 1950 5 million tons, in 1985 10 million tons. In addition in 1900 Germany obtained around 75 000 tons of salt from the former French salines in Lorraine. This expansion was accompanied by concentration. Many of the smaller salines, such as Schwäbisch Hall which in 1802 became part of Württemberg, went into decline, after a period of growth in the first half of the nineteenth century. Thus Schwäbisch Hall produced 1500 tons in 1800, 25 000 tons in 1850, 500 tons in 1900, though other sites in the areas were being developed. On the eve of the First World War, one third of Germany's salt came from the Stassfurt area, another from Württemberg. Stassfurt supplied the domestic needs of north Germany and the chemical industry at Cologne (Bayer). It was also associated with the chemical industry via potassium products for agricultural fertilizer of which it had a virtual world monopoly down to 1914. Similarly, Württemberg supplied the chemical industry at Frankfurt (Hoechst) and Ludwigshafen (BASF). Lorraine too was significant for Ludwigshafen, while Bavaria, which continued to produce 40 000 tons of salt a year, was mainly concerned with the domestic needs of south Germany. As in France, the Rhineland was the dominant economic influence, though it did not itself became a producer till after the Second World War and the secession of the east. The German chemical industry

Table 6.3 Salt production in Italy, 1910, 1939, 1955 (tons)

Type of salt	1910	1939	1955
Tuscan rock	16 600	584 286	806 532
Calabrian rock	5 011	11 374	10 375
Sicilian rock	34 186	86 926	184 782
Sea salt	447 440	680 519	841 677
Total	503 237	1 363 108	1 843 538

was precocious and progressive. Nevertheless, until after 1919 and the loss of Lorraine, perhaps until after 1945 and the loss of Stassfurt, its development of salt resources was far from adequate. Here, as elsewhere, imperial Germany had a modern façade but a traditional substructure.

It was the other way round with the other German state, the Habsburg empire. Since 1772 the Habsburgs had been masters of the major Polish and minor Galician salines; since 1802 of those of the archbishop of Salzburg at Hallein; and since 1815 of the former Venetian salines of Istria and Dalmatia. In 1800 production of salt in the Habsburg empire had been relatively large and concentrated, larger and more concentrated than that of northern Germany. By 1912, production had increased, but by a lesser factor than in the north, and was more widely diffused, particularly to the outer rim of the empire in Poland and Hungary. These patterns were a reflection of the relative absence of industrial, specifically chemical, revolution in the Habsburg lands. Unlike France, the Danubian empire stood largely outside the influence of the Rhineland. The Danube itself, despite the projects of Baron Bruck and the later theorists of Mitteleuropa, was never an industrial cyclotron like the Rhine. The Habsburg economy, however traditional it may have been, provided a good substructure on which its successor states could build. Thus independent Poland pushed production at Wieliczka and in Galicia to 488 662 tons in 1932, of which 104 672 tons were brine for industry. In 1953 after the loss of Galicia production was over a million tons and by 1985 Poland produced 5 million tons. What was sown on the Danube was harvested on the Vistula. Similarly independent Romania, which after 1919 added the Hungarian salines of Ronaszek, Torda and Maros-Ujvar (Ocna-Mures) to its own impressive mine at Slanic in Wallachia and brine sources at Cacica and Tirgu-Ocna in Moldavia, by 1985 produced 5 million tons and was a considerable exporter to the rest of the Communist world.

The Mediterranean

Here the most significant modern development, more pronounced in Italy than Spain, was the rise of inland rock salt at the expense of successive basin solar evaporated marine salt. It was a development of the twentieth century concomitant with the rise of the chemical industry in Barcelona and Milan and the chief beneficiaries were Cardona in Catalonia and Volterra in Tuscany. Until then the rising requirements of the nineteenth century were met by traditional successive basin solar evaporation sources. Thus in Spain in 1905, San Lucar de Barrameda provided 24 000 tons, Torrevieja and La Mata provided 149 000 tons, and Ibiza, 20 000 tons in 1800, provided 81 000 tons in 1905. In Italy in 1905, out of a total production of 437 699 tons, 170 000 tons was provided by Trapani and associated Sicilian salines, 151 824 tons by Cagliari, and around 50 000 tons by Margherita di Savoia, the former Barletta and one of Europe's oldest successive basin evaporation works. Another sign of Spanish and Italian traditionalism was the continued importance of exports. In 1875 Italy exported 26 000 tons of salt to India and down to 1914 had markets in Greece, Turkey and the Balkans. In 1886, an Italian from Trapani, Agostino Burgarella, founded the Red Sea salt industry at Aden, whose significance we shall see in the next section. Spain also exported small quantities to India in 1875, but it was not until the twentieth century that it found there a considerable if volatile outlet: 100 000 tons in 1909, 50 000-odd in the 1920s, 84 000 tons in 1930.

In 1900 Spain and Italy both produced around 500 000 tons a year, mostly by solar evaporation. By 1965, however, 40 per cent of Spain's production of nearly 2 million tons came from non-marine sources of which Cardona was the principal, while 66 per cent of Italy's production of 3 million came from rock salt, chiefly from Volterra.[14] Salt had been mined at Volterra as far back as the twelfth century when control was disputed between the bishop and the local commune. Later, control passed to Florence and by 1825 production had reached 500 tons. After steady but unspectacular growth in the nineteenth century, production was taken over in the 1920s by the Solvay company. Solvay was always international in its approach to both chemicals and salt, so much so that during the Second World War, the firm had to split into Allied and Axis moieties. It was as a result of Solvay colonization that rock salt took the lead from sea salt in Italy. Volterra was in a sense the southernmost prolongation of the Rhineland, the fulcrum of the new Europe.

The New Lands

In addition to the centripetal acceleration imparted by the Rhineland, the European world was also, and increasingly, subject to the centrifugal acceleration imparted by the new lands: the major new lands of Russia and the United States, the minor new lands of Brazil and Japan. In all these places there was remarkable increase in the scale of salt production, though the trajectories followed were no means the same.

Russia was already in 1800 a major producer of salt, while the United States, Brazil and Japan were not. The United States, however, was a major consumer, and rapidly became an ever bigger one, while Brazil and Japan were not and did not. These factors shaped the curves of progress. In Russia production of salt rose from 235 000 tons in 1800, to over 1 500 000 in 1900, 5 million in 1950, 20 million in 1985. In the United States, production of salt rose from 10 000 tons or less in 1800, to 3 million in 1914, 17 million in 1950, 50 million in 1985. In Brazil, while alimentary independence was attained in the nineteenth century under the empire, serious development only began in the 1930s under Vargas. Production rose from 390 000 tons in 1936 to 740 000 tons on the eve of the Second World War, a million tons in 1950, 2 million in 1975 and was planned to reach 10 million tons in the course of the 1980s. In Japan, production rose from 200 000 tons in 1800, to half a million in 1914, 1 million in 1950, 2 million in 1975 and 5 million in 1985. In addition both the United States and Japan continued to import salt: the United States particularly from Canada (Ontario), Mexico and the Bahamas (Turks and Caicos islands); Japan particularly from Taiwan, Siam and Australia.

In Russia the increase of production in the nineteenth century was based on the development of three sources. First, it was based on the Bakhmut (Artemovsk) mines northeast of the modern Dnepropetrovsk in the Donets industrial area. These mines were only opened from 1876, but production rose rapidly to reach a figure of nearly 400 000 tons by 1900: a good example of Russia's industrial dynamism in the late Tsarist era. Second, there were the Crimean salines (Kinburn, Perekop, Eupatoria (Kherson), Theodosia (Caffa) and Genichesk), only recently acquired and not fully utilized in 1800, but which in 1900 produced over 500 000 tons. Third, there was Lake Baskuncak north of Astrakhan, which produced over 300 000 tons in 1900 and increasingly took the place of Lake Elton to the north. The second and third of these sources were *sebkhas*, natural solar evaporation salines (though successive basin methods were being introduced at Genichesk) and required little capital investment. Their problem was access and distribution, but the development of railways to south Russia (to Sebastopol, for example) and steam navigation on the Volga allowed them to expand and to compete effectively against boiled salt from Solikamsk. Solikamsk still produced over 300 000 tons in 1900, but it was beginning to experience serious fuel problems.

Transport factors continued to dominate in the twentieth century. In 1970, Artemovsk still produced 43 per cent of Soviet output of 12 million tons. Lake Baskuncak, which was then supplying 4 million tons a year, was the next largest single source of salt in the Soviet Union thanks to its access to the Volga.[15] On the Caspian, solar evaporated salt was also produced at Baku and Krasnovodsk. With the further development of the railways and the shift of industry to the east during the Second World War, new expansion was based on the brine of western Siberia: Barabinsk west of Novosibirsk, Lake Abakanskoe south of Krasnoyaisk, and Usole Sibirskoye northwest of Irkutsk; points on the Trans-Siberian railway where there was considerable development of the chemical industry. The Soviet Union also benefited from its acquisitions in the west: the brine salt of Galicia from Poland and the rock salt of sub-Carpathian Ukraine from Czechoslovakia and Hungary, in particular the mines of Uzhgorod. Finally, coming on to the horizon in the 1980s, were the rock salt deposits of the Vilui in eastern Siberia, the Soviet republic of Yakutia, Halford Mackinder's Lenaland. They had been known since 1789 but were not exploited because of lack of both communications and market. Here in the far north, the kingdom of the KGB, road deglaciation was likely to be as important a source of demand as the chemical industry. Siberia, Russia's land of the future as predicted by Muraviev-Amursky and Bakunin in the 1880s, would have to be also a land of salt.

In the United States too there was accumulation of sources and shifts in the leading areas. Down to the Civil War, Onondaga in New York and Kanawha in West Virginia remained the principal domestic sources of supply. Ohio was beginning to catch up on New York and Pennsylvania was a considerable producer, but except for Saltville in Virginia, the South produced nothing and was dependent on English imports for its large requirements. The South's situation was highly inconvenient during the Union blockade. A Confederate officer went so far as to attribute the defeat of the South to the shortage of salt for men, animals and food processing, in particular bacon curing.[16·] In the expansion of production between the Civil War and 1914, New York led the way, closely followed by Michigan and at some distance by Kansas and Ohio. Within New York, however, the centre of production shifted from Onondaga near Syracuse to Warsaw near Buffalo, where in 1878 oil drillers found salt at a depth of 300 metres. The presence of salt had long been suspected. Indeed, it is possible that Buffalo was named after animals attracted to a salt lick. But it was the 'Chinese' technology of the oil industry, pioneered by Edwin L. Drake in Pennsylvania, which discovered it. By 1950 New York had been pushed into second place by Michigan, where salt was mined and evaporated from brine in about equal quantities. By the 1980s, however, Michigan in turn had been overtaken by Louisiana and Texas, first equal, New York now being in fourth place and Ohio in fifth. In Louisiana and Texas the source was the famous salt domes of the coastal plain and points inland. Here, salt was first mined or quarried, but with the development of the petroleum industry and the improvement of drilling effected by A. F. Lucas (of Croat origin, first called Lucic and a graduate of Graz Polytech) in the 1890s, they were exploited by deep wells. In its combination of deep drilling, petroleum, natural gas and brine, the Gulf of Mexico was the American Szechwan.

In Brazil,[17] European salt production, by successive basin solar evaporation, was developed first by the Jesuits at San Luis in Maranhao and then by the Dutch in Pernambuco. Production was for local consumption on the sugar plantations, especially at Recife, and also for export by sea to Bahia, Rio de Janeiro and Sao Paulo. The Portuguese authorities, however, wished to keep Brazil as a tied market for Setubal and in the colonial period these initiatives were not allowed to develop. Under the empire, domestic production was encouraged, but Maranhao and Pernambuco were superseded by Rio Grande do Norte, especially the town of Macau which by 1939 produced two thirds of Brazil's salt. Macau exported internally north to Para and thence to Amazonas, south to Rio de Janeiro, Sao Paulo and then to Parana, and externally to Uruguay where the beef industry provided a large market. Production, however, remained traditional and small scale until the 1970s when the government invested heavily in protective dykes and port facilities. In 1975 three quarters of the 2 million ton national production still came from Rio Grande do Norte. But the plans to expand production to 10 million tons during 1980s were based on the extraction as brine of the huge rock salt deposits at Maceio in Alagoas and Aratu in Bahia and its subsequent separation into sodium, chlorine and hydrogen by the Castner/Kellner electrolytic process for caustic soda and chlorine products. Though the traditional northeast remained the centre of the Brazilian salt industry, there was, as in Latin Europe, a shift away from solar evaporated marine salt for alimentary purposes toward artificially evaporated inland salt for chemical purposes.

In Japan,[18] conditions were not well suited to the two chief methods of salt production in early modernity. There were no brine wells for inland *chien* and the summer was too wet for marine *shai*, whether natural or artificial. Premodern Japan was too far distant from the Asian mainland for regular imports, so salt was produced by a method akin to that of Celtic Europe, the Quart Bouillon of *ancien régime* France or the *kua-ni* technique of Liang-che under the Sung. Marine brine was enriched by successive leaching through saline sand and then boiled in special pans. The boiling pans were of stone which was expensive to heat, the product was not of good quality, and the only modern feature was the use of coal as fuel, notably in the south because in the north fir and bamboos were more common. The process was small scale (salt gardens were spoken of), old-fashioned and inefficient. Until the eighteenth century, Japan was probably not a large consumer of salt. It had not experienced the successive consumer revolutions of medieval and early modern China and its diet was still essentially that of the early T'ang. The earliest European missionaries all stressed the frugality of the

Japanese and the best informed of them, the Jesuit Father Luis Frois specifically says 'Our ordinary food is white bread; that of the Japanese is unsalted, boiled rice'.[19] In the eighteenth century, however, the stabilization of the population, the increase of circulation in the Inland sea and beyond, the growth of supercities like Edo, Osaka and Kyoto, raised standards of living dramatically. By 1800 when population was around 25 million, production of salt reached 200 000 tons, 16 lb *per capita*, higher than *ancien régime* France. The salt industry was a typical late Tokugawa combination of archaism in production and modernity in consumption, which provided a good basis for later development.

In the nineteenth century, as population grew and modern industry was introduced, production expanded and in 1885 reached nearly 1 million tons, but on the old basis except that iron pans replaced stone and graduation was experimented with. Though salt could be produced along most of the coast of Japan south of Hokkaido, the leading area, where three quarters of the output came from, was southwest Honshu beyond Osaka and northern Shikoku. The most dynamic, though not initially the largest producer, was Eastern Sanuki near Takamatsu in Shikoku, the champion of competition in the salt industry which became law in 1888. In the long run, however, competition injured the Japanese *kua-ni* industry. Its costs were high, its product unsatisfactory, so it could be undersold by solar evaporated salt from Japan's colonial empire in Liao-tung, Kiaochow and Taiwan and from Japan's satellites in Manchuria and North China.

In the twentieth century Japan became a major importer of salt stimulating the growth of production in her neighbours. Contrariwise, by 1914 the domestic production of salt had fallen to 500 000 tons. Even after the loss of her colonies and satellites, Japan remained dependent on the import of salt for her chemicals to a degree unusual in an industrial great power. In 1967 Japan produced 985 000 tons of salt and imported 4 486 000 tons to meet alimentary demand of 1 174 000 tons and chemical demand of 4 180 000 tons.[20] It was only in the 1970s with the development of marine brine concentration by electrodialysis that Japan became a major producer of salt: 2 million tons in 1975, 5 million tons in 1985. Even so Japan continued to import as much salt as she produced. A byproduct of this was the development in the 1970s of a major solar evaporation industry in Western Australia. Australia had hitherto produced only for her own needs chiefly by successive basin solar evaporation at a site near Adelaide in South Australia. Now, in response to Japanese demand, new successive basin plants were developed at Port Hedland, Dampier, Exmouth Gulf and Shark Bay and a natural evaporation site at Lake McLeod, all in Western Australia. Here productive capacity rose to 5 million tons. None the less, despite the continuation of imports, the electrodialysis process marked an important development in the Japanese salt industry and in the supply of the most dynamic of the new lands of the European world. Western Australia was already on the lookout for other markets.

Africa

In the course of the nineteenth century, Africa became, for the time being, an associate member of the European world. At the same time, and on a more permanent basis, it was also further associated with the Islamic world, by such movements as the Fulani *jihad* from the west and the Senussi reformation from the east. Mecca became an African capital as well as London and Paris. Africa acquired more dimensions and had to adapt to a more diversified environment. Though Islam had long made the desert a frontier and the slave trade, Christian and Muslim, had turned Africa inside out by forcing it to face the sea, it was not until the nineteenth and twentieth centuries that the pattern of the salt trade described in Chapter 1 began to be affected and then only to a limited extent.

The principal change was an increase in the role of sea salt. Primitive Africa had turned its back on the sea. Small quantities of salt had been produced on the coast, notably in Dahomey, Iboland, near the mouth of the Congo and in Eritrea, generally by natural solar evaporation, but trade in it was small and short distance except from Eritrea to Ethiopia. With the slave trade, salt became an item of commerce from the coast to the interior and with modern transport, a significant item. In West Africa, the Senegal, the Gambia, the Volta[21] and the Niger became salt routes on the European and Chinese model. In East Africa, the Italians exploited the connection in salt between Eritrea and Ethiopia, and salt from Pemba was an element in the dominance of Zanzibar over the hinterland. 'When the flute is heard in Zanzibar' it was said, 'all Africa east of the Lakes must dance'.[22] Nevertheless these new currents from the sea did not subvert the older ones coming from the desert and the lakes. In Niger, Bilma was still a major salt producing centre in the 1970s and Tuareg camels were holding their own against Libyan lorries.[23] In Tanganyika the German Saline-Gottorp company, supported by the district officer W. Goering brother of the future Reichsmarshal, took over the Uvinza brine springs in 1902 and by 1914 had increased productive capacity from 20 000 cwt to 80 000 cwt. The advent of the railway in 1914 increased the sales area for Uvinza salt to include Rhodesia and Kenya as well as eastern Congo. Production was expanded by the introduction of successive basin solar evaporation and by 1968 reached 600 000 cwt.[24] In Mauretania the anciently worked deposit of Idjil was reactivated by decolonization and credited in 1982 with a greatly increased production.[25] Africa, only an associate member of the

European world, perhaps a dissociating member, built anew on the foundations it had inherited from primitivity.

OTTOMAN ISLAM AND BRITISH INDIA

Here modernization went less far than in the European world and took different forms. Alimentary consumption rose through European influence, but consumption as a whole was not surcharged by the chemical revolutions. Modern methods of distribution were introduced, but these benefited not inland brine wells or rock deposits, but a few, large scale, successive basin solar evaporation, marine salines. Ottoman Islam and British India present a profile of protomodernization not unlike that of medieval or early modern Europe.

Ottoman Islam

Until 1800 the pattern of the salt trade in the Ottoman empire was still basically that of classical antiquity. Numerous small salines, mostly marine, mainly *sebkhas*, supplied adjacent cities via short-distance routes. Thus Salonika had its own salines at the mouth of the Vardar; Smyrna was adjacent to that of Phocea; Cairo had Rosetta and Damietta; Cyprus supplied Adana and Beirut; Trebizond, Sivas and Tokat were supplied from the mines, springs and wells of the Halys; Konia, Erzerum and Aleppo each had their own local sources of salt. As in most of the Islamic world, supply was not really a problem. Constantinople, it is true, because of its vast size and superconsumption, required some ten centres to supply it, but the principle of supply remained the same. In salt as in much else, Islam eviscerated but embalmed antiquity and so preserved it.

For much of the nineteenth century this pattern continued. In 1881, however, as a result of the so-called decree of Muharrem of 20 December of that year, control of salt passed to the European administered Ottoman Public Debt administration[26] which pursued an active policy of trade promotion to increase revenue. At the same time railway construction began from Constantinople, Smyrna and Salonika into the hinterlands of Anatolia and Rumelia and consumption, always high in an Islamic land, was raised by partial Europeanization of diet. The result was an increase in the production, distribution and consumption of salt and the emergence of a more modern pattern of supply by a few major centres.

In 1882–3, the first year of operations by the Ottoman Public Debt Administration, the amount of salt handled was around 200 000 tons, of which 150 000 tons were consumed within the empire and 50 000 tons exported. In 1911–12, on the eve of Turkey's loss of most of Rumelia which makes subsequent comparison difficult, the amount of salt handled was around 350 000 tons, of which 250 000 tons were consumed within the empire and 100 000 tons exported. Of this 350 000 tons, 100 000 tons came from the single centre of Phocea near Smyrna. Phocea, which as a small producer dated back to the Genoese, had benefited from railway communication with Afion Karahissar and the interior of Anatolia and steamboat communication with Constantinople. Constantinople in turn was a secondary distribution centre. It had steamer links to depots on the Marmara and the Black Sea and rail links to Adrianople in one direction and, via Uskudar, to Eskisehir, Ankara and Konia in the other. With the loss of the Crimean salines in 1774, Constantinople had became increasingly dependent on Phocea. Production there increased from 8500 tons in 1848 to 58 000 in 1867 and to 76 000 in 1890. At Phocea production was in the hands of a guild of hereditary smallholders, but in 1909–10 it was expropriated in the interest of fewer but larger units of organization with more evaporation basins per unit. Mytilene on Lesbos, Turkish till 1912, was the number two European producer. Here the administration operated through salaried labourers rather than subcontractors. Mytilene supplied Salonika as well as Constantinople and via them Rumelia and an export trade to Serbia and Bulgaria. The European provinces required 50 000 tons a year and the Balkan export some 20 000 tons. In Asia, the major producer was Salif in the Yemen, most of whose annual total of 80 000 tons of rock salt was exported to India, Singapore and East Africa, in that order. In the interior, Konia and Central Anatolia were mainly supplied from the Tuz Golu, Strabo's Lake Tatta, while Erzerum and eastern Anatolia, with inadequate supplies from the Halys, imported from Lake Urmia via Khoi. Lake Urmia also supplied Mosul and Baghdad, while southern Iraq was supplied from the Persian Gulf, the salt dome of Ormuz in particular and the marshes of Basra. Thus the Ottoman empire had become both an importer and an exporter of salt as well as a long-distance distributor within its own borders. The pattern of its salt trade had been at least partially modernized.

British India

Under the *raj*, India was divided for salt administration purposes into four areas comparable with the *yin-ti* or salt divisions of China: Bengal, Bombay, Madras and Northern India. In 1930 when the Indian Tariff Board was collecting evidence for its enquiry into the salt trade,[27] each of these areas consumed around 500 000 tons a year. Bengal, however, was the most important from the point of view of modernization.

Bengal covered not only itself but also Assam, Orissa, Burma and part of Bihar. In 1763 the East India company received the *diwan*, or financial administration of Bengal, from the government of the Mughal. The *diwan* included a salt monopoly. The authorities advanced funds to subcontractors who produced salt by boiling marine brine in a technique, known as panga, similar to that of Huai-nan and the authorities then marketed the product. The system was never satisfactory.[28] The advances squeezed the producer, the salt was neither cheap nor abundant nor good quality, and the company received inadequate return. In 1863, with the ending of company rule, the monopoly was abolished in favour of an excise. Moreover, under pressure from Cheshire, imports were allowed to compete with the local product. Within ten years the Bengal *chien* industry had almost ceased to exist. It was a classic case of economic imperialism, for the beneficiary of free trade was not Indian *shai*, but, for the most part, English *chien*. In 1875–6, 306 385 tons of salt were imported from England, mostly from Cheshire. The next biggest suppliers were Italy (probably Trapani) 26 390 tons and Arabia (probably Salif in the Ottoman Yemen) 19 261 tons. Cheshire, however, did not long hold its predominance. In 1891 the Salt Union complained of competition from Aden, in 1897 from Arabia and the Red Sea, and in 1909 from Spanish solar salt. In 1926 Bengal and its dependencies imported around 600 000 tons of salt. Of this Cheshire provided 60 000 tons against Aden 200 000 tons, Egypt 150 000, Italian East Africa 60 000 tons.

The rise of the Red Sea salines was a major event in Indian salt history. By 1930, Aden, Port Said, Massawa, Djibouti, Cape Gardafui and Salif had built up a productive capacity of 750 000 tons a year and new salines were being opened. Except for Salif, all these saltworks were of successive basin solar evaporation type and they constituted one of the largest groups using this technique. All were relatively new and they owed their existence to the Indian market. As G. L. Saron, managing director of the Port Said Salt Association, told the Tariff Board in 1930: 'all the salt works from Port Said southwards are entirely dependent on the Indian market'.[29] The first of the new India oriented salt works was that founded in 1886 at Aden by Agostino Burgarella from Trapani. Indeed, the whole Red Sea enterprise might be regarded as a migration of Mediterranean *shai* towards more promising circumstances. In 1930 the Aden Salt Works was still owned by the Burgarellas who employed 400 labourers and produced 150 000 tons of salt a year. They had been joined, however, by three Indian owned firms: the Indo-Aden salt works from Bombay, the Little Aden Salt Industrial company, and Hajeebhoy Aden salt works; which between them produced another 150 000 tons of salt a year. Port Said commenced operations under an English joint stock company in 1899, Massawa and Djibouti after the

First World War, and Cape Gardafui in the 1930s. A new salt industry was created with India in mind.

What made the Red Sea salines competitive in Bengal not only against Cheshire *chien* but against *shai* from other parts of India? Against Cheshire *chien*, it was production, specifically fuel, costs, but against Indian *shai*, it was, all the witnesses to the Tariff Board enquiry agreed, distribution costs, specifically freight rates. Port Said and Aden were coaling ports. Colliers from India or Europe could, by taking on salt, avoid returning empty or going on to India in ballast. The Indo-Aden salt works put the matter clearly in its submission: 'Aden being a distributing and coaling port it has been that at times it is in a fair position so far as freight facilities are concerned and therefore her salt cost is lower in price in India.'[30] It was the old ability to juxtapose bulky cargoes on which the Mediterranean *ordines salis* had been built: the salt law of ballast, that port will be most favoured which most enjoys ballast transport.

The Indian producers recognized what they were up against and hoped for subsidies or protection. Thus the southern India chamber of commerce at Madras stated: 'The chief obstacle to marketing Indian salt is the high freight both by rail and by sea as against the low ballast rates prevailing for imported salt'.[31] The representatives of Dhrangadhra state, north of Bombay on the Rann of Kutch, argued: 'We consider that the Indian salt industry should be further assisted by lower freight on long distances',[32] particularly on the railways. Mr Dinshaw of the Eduljee Dinshaw salt works of Karachi was more concerned with shipping: 'It is well known that the freight from Europe to any port in the Indian Empire is much less than the freight from Karachi or Dwarka to Rangoon and Calcutta'.[33] Jodhpur state, which had an interest in the Sambhar lake, balanced both rail and ships: 'The whole question then seems to turn on the issue of freight. Is it possible to see adjust freight rates from the Rajputana salt resources to any portion of the Bengal market as to make the total inclusive rate for salt at certain centres equal to the rates at which imported salt can be sold at these centres?'[34] The answer was, it was not, so long as the Calcutta importers of salt, the taxpayer, and Bengal exporters of other goods, had any say in the matter. For as the Port Said representatives were quick to point out: 'The more ships come with salt, the more ships there are which are free to take back cargo from Calcutta and allow reduced freight'.[35] Bengal did not oppose the supersession of its own salt industry because other industries were thereby encouraged, notably jute.

The three other Indian salt divisions, Bombay, Madras and Northern India were alike in being able to retain command of their traditional markets. Bombay and Madras were alike in that distribution, at least in its initial stages, was by sea, whereas in Northern India it was by rail.

Otherwise the three divisions differed considerably.

In Bombay, which covered most of the west coast of India, the units of production were large, relatively concentrated, new and partly foreign owned. Thus at Karachi, the English-owned Grax Ltd had only commenced operations in 1927, but produced 25 000 tons in 1930. The Luxmi salt works, also at Karachi, had only begun in 1928, while the Moon salt company, established in 1878, was considered old. Further south, on the Gulf of Kutch, the Okha salt works, with some foreign investment, had been started in 1926, yet in 1930 had a productive capacity of 130 000 tons, which the management assured the Tariff Board could easily be increased to 450 000 tons, if only quotas were imposed on Aden and freight rates adjusted. In Madras, on the other hand, the units of production were small, relatively dispersed, old and owned by the government, though farmed out on a long-term basis. Madras was divided into twelve circles and 60 factories all the way from Madras itself to Tuticorin. Because the units of production were small and scattered, freight rates were even worse in Madras than Bombay and Madras did not even aspire to the Bengal market seeing no advantage to itself in protection. That Madras was inward looking where Bombay was outward looking was also owing to the fact that salt consumption *per capita* in Madras was nearly double that of the rest of India:[36] a reflection no doubt of the long-standing commercialization and higher living standards of the Tamil Nadu. Bombay was the real enemy of Aden.

In Northern India, standing somewhat apart, supply came from the two massive sources of the Punjab salt range and the Sambhar salt lake, the ancient creation of India's Greek and Muslim invaders. The mines of Khewra, Warcha and Kalabagh in the salt range supplied the Punjab. The salt lakes of Sambhar, Didwana and Pachbadra supplied the United Provinces, part of Bihar, Central India and Rajputana. Distribution was by rail. In 1902 Ashton described the changes which the railway had brought to Sambhar and its trade:

> 'salt can be cheaply and expeditiously transported in all directions by railway, and the great droves of Banjara bullocks escorted by armed men are no longer to be seen anywhere. . . . Traders resident in areas of consumption many hundreds of miles distant, pay the price and the small fee for clearance into the nearest Government treasury or post office and send the necessary empty bags to the lake, whence their salt is sent to them expeditiously by railway'.[37]

Since 'transport by sea is very much cheaper than transport by rail',[38] Northern India did not expand at the expense of Bombay and Madras. Equally it could make no headway in Bengal. Red Sea salt paid 8 rupees a ton from Aden to Calcutta and 12 from Calcutta to the railhead at

Buxar, while Sambhar paid 22 rupees a ton to Buxar.[39] Distribution costs were the dominant factor in the Indian salt trade down to Independence.

In India modernization took the form, as in the Ottoman empire, of the progress of large scale *shai*, using modern methods of transport, but with little change in consumption. In China this pattern was to be repeated with the railway substituted for the steamer, but modified by features of supply and demand more reminiscent of Europe.

CHINA – LATE IMPERIAL, REPUBLICAN AND EARLY COMMUNIST

China in the modern period held a position intermediate between the European world and the worlds of Islam and India. As in Europe, though not to the same extent, more sophisticated alimentation and the chemical revolutions made an impact on consumption. As in Islam and India, *shai* extended its advantage over *chien*, but not without considerable competition from an advanced form of *chien*. As everywhere, modern means of distribution made their appearance and affected the salt trade profoundly. Yet China's intermediate position was neither a stage in transition nor a *juste milieu*. It reflected contemporary China's deep ambiguity to both tradition and modernity, so that the course of events under the late empire, the republic and the early Communist state led eventually to a double rejection of both.

The Late Empire

In the deep brine and gas wells of Tzu-liu-ching in Fu-shun district, Szechwan province, nineteenth-century China already possessed a salt industry which was in principle modern in production.[40] The principal modernizing developments under the late empire were the growing importance, first, of Szechwan salt in China, and second, of Tzu-liu-ching salt in Szechwan. Under the late empire and into the republic, Tzu-liu-ching, or Tzu-kung as it was called through association with its twin in next door Jung-hsien district, Kung-ching, became China's leading salt producing centre. Foreigners were deeply impressed by Tzu-liu-ching. In 1871 Baron von Richthofen described it as 'the most populous and lively region of Szechwan'.[41] In 1916 H. K. Richardson declared that 'The people of this town have a bustle and an energy that is more characteristic of an American oil well district than a Chinese city'.[42] In 1941 G. R. G. Worcester said that, 'The salt wells of Tzeliutsing deserve to be associated with the Great Wall and the Grand Canal as monuments to the industry and foresight of the ancient Chinese'.[43] At the height of its prosperity as capital of the salt industry and one of the world's first industrial cities, Tzu-liu-ching had a population of between 800 000 and a million, the largest workforce ever assembled by a salt industry.

These developments, as much else in modern China, began with the Taiping rebellion, the millennarian kingdom of Hung Hsiu-ch'uan who proclaimed himself the new Melchizedek, the second messiah of the Apocalypse and the younger brother of Jesus Christ. Installed in Nanking from 1853 to 1864, the Taipings deeply affected the salt administration. First, they temporarily overran the defences of Huai-nan. With the rebels in Nanking and Kiangsu east, west and north a battlefield, Huai-nan *chien* salt from the coast was no longer able to reach the upriver provinces of Anhwei, Kiangsi, Hupei and Hunan, the so-called four *an*. Huai-nan's besiegers were quick to seize their opportunity. Kwangtung *lou-shai* flooded into southern Hunan and Kiangsi, Liang-che *pan-shai* into eastern Kiangsi, Ho-tung *hsi-shai* into northern Hupei and Anhwei, but, above all, Szechwan *chien* flooded into Hupei and northern Hunan. As the veteran salt administrator Wang Shao-chi put it in 1872, 'the dealers in Szechwan took advantage of the situation and formed troops by hundreds and thousands, armed with rifles and big guns, and sailed down to the east. The officials were not in a position to intervene'.[44] The imperial viceroys were not in a position to intervene, he might have added, because they were busy fighting the Taipings and needed a new source of revenue just as their subjects needed a new source of salt. Of the producing centres in Szechwan, it was Tzu-liu-ching, disprivileged in the existing system of quotas and hence with a surplus, which took the lead in the new traffic and virtually monopolized it. The new traffic was known as the *chi-Ch'u* or assistance to Ch'u, i.e. Hupei and Hunan. After the suppression of the rebellion in 1854, Huai-nan, backed by the powerful Liang-kiang governor-general, Tseng Kuo-fan made a determined effort to recover its sales monopoly. By this time, however, the vested interests of both the Szechwan and the Hu-kuang authorities in the *chi-Ch'u* were too strong and Liang-kiang had to be content with some of the tax and a monopoly in eastern Hupei and Hunan. In western Hupei the sale of Szechwan salt was legitimated. Tzu-liu-ching had added 540 000 cwt a year to its trade.

A second outcome of the Taiping rebellion was the establishment throughout China of what amounted to a dual system of leading and support viceroyalties. One region would conduct operations against enemies or organize modernization schemes, while another region, less encumbered, supplied the necessary funds. Regional roles were not immutable and could be interchanged, but in fact, until just before the revolution of 1911, Szechwan was always a support viceroyalty. Until the Taiping rebellion, its levels of taxation had been low, but its increasing wealth on the agricultural frontier gave it great potential, and in particular its expanding salt trade was an obvious target. To provide funds for the reconquest of Sinkiang from Yakub Beg by Shen-kan Governor-general Tso Tsung-t'ang, Ting Pao-chen, Szechwan governor-general between 1876 and 1886, carried out a famous reform of the local salt administration, which was at first criticized, then widely acclaimed.

The centrepiece of the reform and the most productive part fiscally was the *Tien-Ch'ien pien-an kuan-yün*, 'official transport to the frontier ports of Yunnan and Kweichow'. In effect Ting Pao-chen nationalized a key sector of the province's salt trade: the traffic to Yunnan, Kweichow and 33 districts of Szechwan which adjoined them along the Yangtze. At the time it was an ambitious and unprecedented scheme designed to increase trade as well as taxes, though later it was copied in Manchuria for the trade from Fengtien to Kirin and Heilungkiang. Initially, Ting gave the lion's share of the *pien-an* to Chien-wei rather than to Tzu-liu-ching, but he left the arrangements flexible and between 1885 and 1910, Tzu-liu-ching because of its lower costs, better product and greater initiative came to dominate the *pien-an* as it did the *chi-Ch'u*. Both trades virtually doubled between those years. Meanwhile inside Szechwan, the interdistrict, largely waterborne trade, the *chi-an* and the local purely landborne trade, the *p'iao-an* were also expanding. Here too Tzu-liu-ching came to hold a dominant position, though not until the republic when the foreign salt *gabelle*, introduced by the reorganization loan agreement of 1913 and under the energetic leadership of the ex-Indian salt administrator Sir Richard Dane, liberalized the old system of quotas and tied markets and allowed Tzu-liu-ching's competitive advantages full scope. Dominant in exports, Tzu-liu-ching now became dominant at home.

Before 1911, however, the trend had been toward greater state control, but this too opened new horizons to Szechwan and Tzu-liu-ching. In 1903 Governor-general Ts'en Ch'un-hsuan extended *kuan-yün* (official transport) from the *pien-an* of Yunnan, Kweichow and adjacent Szechwan to the waterborne trade of 38 districts of the *chi-an* in central Szechwan. In 1909 Governor-general Chao Erh-hsün attempted to go further and to create what was in effect a complete state monopoly of distribution within Szechwan. He proposed to extend *kuan-yün* not only to the *p'iao*, or landborne trade of the 38 districts of the domestic state monopoly (*chi-an kuan-yün*), but also to that of the 68 districts of the *p'iao-an* in northern Szechwan which consumed only landborne salt.[45] At the same time, to compensate private enterprise for these further instalments of state control and to reassure producers, particularly at Tzu-liu-ching, against restriction by the state monopoly, Chao Erh-hsün also supported an earlier proposal by a Szechwan official in Peking, Kan Ta-chang, to extend the *chi-Ch'u*, which was still partly operated by

Table 6.4 Tzu-liu-ching salt distributions, 1882–1948 (cwt)

Area	1882	1910	1919	1933	1948
P'iao-an	17 732	45 530	621 385	680 000	c.700 000
Chi-an	9 650	175 488	1 288 460	802 440	c.1 500 000
Pien-an	449 170	1 016 382	879 240	671 850	c.1 000 000
Chi-Ch'u	540 000	972 000	631 800	990 000	c.1 200 000
Total	1 016 552	2 208 200	3 415 885	3 144 290	c.4 400 000

private enterprise, to cover the whole of Hupei and Hunan.[46] Szechwan salt, Kan argued, would have no difficulty in disposing of Huai salt, since Szechwan *hua* or crystalline salt, was as good as foreign refined salt, while Huai-nan *chien* was frequently adulterated, a significant suggestion of rising consumer expectations. Chao Erh-hsün was offering Tzu-liu-ching a new market of around 3 million cwt.

In fact nothing came of these imaginative proposals which were aborted by the revolution of 1911. The foreign inspectorate had no objection to an extension of the *chi-Ch'u*, indeed attempted to facilitate it by an auditorate at Chungking, but the disorders of the warlord period prevented any increase in, indeed often interrupted, trade in Szechwan salt down the Yangtze until the Second World War when a new increase began. Early Communist policies did not favour the capital intensity of the Szechwan *chien* industry and population of Tzu-kung declined to 300 000 in 1958. Tzu-liu-ching never fulfilled the potential output of 6 million cwt with which G. R. G. Worcester credited it. Moreover, though steam engines replaced the buffaloes, steel hausers the bamboos and a railway was projected to replace the crooked-bow junks on the river between the town and the T'o, Tzu-liu-ching did not move beyond its own proto-modernity. Like so much of the modern potential of traditional China, Tzu-liu-ching was allowed to run to waste by the Communists for political reasons.

The Republic

Besides the deep wells of Szechwan, successive basin solar evaporation had been China's gift to the technology of salt. The principal modernizing developments under the republic 1912 to 1949 were the growing importance first of the northeast arc of *t'an-shai* salines, and second of Ch'ang-lu within that arc. These developments were based on modern transportation and the non-enforcement of divisional frontiers by the reformed salt administration as led by the foreign inspectorate. Also associated with Ch'ang-lu were two more marginal modernizing

Table 6.5 Regional percentages of salt production in China, 1900–1957

Region	1900	1919	1931–5	1948	1957
Northeast	35	58	57	56	85
Southeast	41	21	23	22	7
Interior	24	21	20	22	8

developments: the growth of a refined salt industry, evidence of greater consumer sophistication, and the establishment of a Solvay soda industry for the beginnings of a chemical market. Production, distribution and consumption all saw considerable change of a modernizing kind under the republic. Of this change, Tientsin, the capital of Ch'ang-lu, was the epicentre.

Table 6.5 shows the contributions of the different regions to China's total salt production. The northeast covers the salt divisions of Manchuria, Ch'ang-lu, Shantung and Huai-pei. The southeast covers the salt divisions of Huai-nan, Sung-kiang (the Su Wu-shu areas of Kiangsu belonging to Liang-che which the foreign inspectorate made into a separate division), Liang-che, Fukien and Kwangtung. The interior covers Ho-tung, the northwest salines (K'ou-pei, Chin-pei and Hua-ting), Szechwan and Yunnan. It will be seen that the shift from the dominance of the southeast, which had been characteristic of China since the T'ang, to that of the northeast, began in the first two decades of this century and was completed in the early days of the Communists. The shift was the result first of railway building – 5000 miles opened between 1900 and 1912 – second of the liberalism of the foreign inspectorate, and third of the willingness of the early Communists to build on these assets.

Ch'ang-lu was most advantaged by the railways. A Chinese writer described the situation in 1915: 'upon the completion of the Peking–Mukden, Peking–Hankow, Peking–Kalgan and Tientsin–Pukow lines, salt was increasingly transported by rail, and for convenience of rail transportation, Ch'ang-lu had the edge over all other salines'.[47] Strategically situated close to the centre of the railway network at Peking, Ch'ang-lu salt invaded Mongolia via the Peking to Kalgan line, Shantung via the Tientsin–Pukow line, and Chin-pei via the Cheng-ting to Taiyuan branch line from the Peking–Hankow main line. Ho-tung was reached by both the Peking–Hankow and Lunghai lines, while the Peking–Hankow also carried Ch'ang-lu salt into Huai-pei and even into the Szechwan half Hupei. Again, Ch'ang-lu sent its bittern block (magnesium chloride), a valuable residue of salt making used in beancurd and tobacco manufacture, along the Peking–Mukden line to compete with that of Fengtien in Manchuria. Increasingly Ch'ang-lu salt went by rail rather than by water. At Han-ku, which became the principal Ch'ang-lu saline, salt transported by rail increased from next to nothing in 1913 to nearly 60 per cent in 1917.

The results of Ch'ang-lu's use of the railway were seen most clearly in Honan. In 1911 that province was divided between four salt divisions: Ch'ang-lu (62 districts), Ho-tung (34), Huai-pei (14) and Shantung (9). By 1920 Ch'ang-lu had entirely captured the fourteen Huai-pei districts in the Ju-kuang prefectures 'by its advantage of railway transportation' and was making serious inroads into those of Ho-tung. In 1919, the Ho-tung inspectors noted that 'the encroachment by Changlu salt sellers into the Hotung eastern area, made possible by the cheaper railway haulage' was 'a very serious matter and it is affecting all trade in the south-western part of this Province', that is, Honan.[48] Thanks to the railways Honan was attached more completely than before to Ch'ang-lu: all its districts were now within range of Ch'ang-lu salt.

The railway contributed as well to significant internal developments in Ch'ang-lu. First, it contributed to the final victory of *t'an-shai*, successive basin solar evaporation. By 1933, seven out of seven salines areas produced by this means. The ascent of *shai* over *chien* which had begun in the Ming was now complete. Second, it contributed to the concentration of production in the vicinity of Tientsin. Before 1685 Ch'ang-lu had consisted of 24 *ch'ang* or salt administrative areas scattered all the way along the coast of Chihli and at some points inland from the Great Wall to the borders of Shantung. By 1912 administrative reforms had reduced these to eight, but between 1913 and 1925 they were reduced effectively to two: Feng-ts'ai to north and south of the Hai-ho, Tientsin's exit to the sea, and Lu-t'ai or Han-ku, a little to the north again; both within convenient access to the railway yards. Third, it contributed to the opening of new salines. Under the Japanese satellite regime of Hua-pei-kuo, the number of *t'an* or successive basin solar evaporation units increased from 317 to 728, most of whose output went by rail, though some, to the Yangtze, Korea and Japan went by steamer. Finally, the railway contributed to increased production on both old and new *t'an*. Between 1850 and 1900 production in Ch'ang-lu fluctuated below a ceiling of 4 million cwt. By 1920, it was regularly 6 million cwt, in the 1930s 7 million cwt and in 1948, thanks to the opening of the new *t'an*, 14 million cwt. At the end of the republic, Ch'ang-lu was the premier salt division, ahead now of Szechwan, producing a quarter of China's total supply. Most of this came from within a few miles of Tientsin and was processed through the city. What Tzu-liu-ching had been to the late empire, Tientsin, thanks to the railways and free trade, was to the republic.

Manchuria and Shantung also had good access to railways. Thanks to the Russians and Japanese, Manchuria had the best railway network of any region in China, based on the T of the west–east Chinese Eastern railway from Manchuli to Vladivostok and the north–south South Manchurian railway from Harbin to Dairen. These lines were particularly used by the government transportation service to move salt from the coast in Fengtien to the two northern provinces of Kirin and Heilungkiang. In 1915, 'Salt destined for Kirin was, for the most part, transported by the South Manchurian Railway', while 'Salt destined for Heilungkiang was shipped by sea to Vladivostok and then by the Chinese Eastern Railway to the Central Depot at Harbin', a procedure changed in 1917 to direct rail shipment to Harbin by the South Manchuria Railway.[49] Ch'ang-ch'un in particular, the future capital of Manchukuo, became important as an interior railway market, the auditors for the two northern provinces noting in 1919 that 'This large salt trade materially added to the prosperity of the city of Changchun'.[50] When the state of Manchukuo was established in 1932, the emperor took up residence in the headquarters of the salt administration.[51]

Shantung had the east–west Tsingtao to Tsinan line as well as a section of the north–south Tientsin to Pukow line. The Tsingtao to Tsinan was of particular advantage after the retrocession to China under the Washington treaty of 1922 of the former German and then Japanese concession of Kiaochow. Under German rule, Kiaochow had become an important centre of salt production, part of the overall plan to make the port the Hong Kong of the north. The unit of production at Kiaochow was the *fu*, literally 'pair' – a *fu* consisted of four *t'ung* or circuits each composed of 10 to 20 basins, for which the term *hsi* or paddock was used – the original word used for a basin in Ho-tung under the T'ang. The *hsi* were arranged in three groups for concentration, condensation and crystallization in the usual way. The *fu* were small, 30 *mou* or five acres. Before the railway there were no more than 26 of them and they found it difficult to compete against local boiling works. With the railway, there came to be over 2000 *fu* and Kiaochow became the premier salt area of Shantung. In 1948 of the 7 million cwt assigned to Shantung, nearly 4 million came from Kiaochow. Of this some was exported by sea to Japan, Korea or Hong Kong, or to the former Yangtze *an* of Huai-nan, but what went inland went by rail. Kiaochow, like Tientsin, was one of the boom towns of republican China.

Huai-pei, the southernmost salt division of the four in the northeast arc, was the beneficiary of modern liberalism rather than modern transportation, though it had access to the Lunghai line going west and used steamers going south. In 1830, as part of his plan to revive Liang-huai, Liang-kiang Governo-general T'ao Chu assigned 200 000 *yin* of Huai-pei salt for dispatch to Yangchow and subsequent sale in Huai-nan: a move intended to reduce the average, and hence market, price to the consumer. Transportation was by canal: 'A semi-official establishment,

Table 6.6 Huai-pei shipments to Huai-nan (cwt)

Year	Huai-pei shipments	Huai-nan production
1910	1 119 000	3 628 053
1913	c.2 000 000	2 882 617
1914	3 164 590	2 093 370
1915	2 685 000	2 236 085
1916	2 602 094	1 978 580
1917	1 349 060	3 198 687
1918	3 245 281	2 994 559
1919	4 548 075	2 863 536
1920	2 391 525	1 404 157
1921	4 007 611	1 057 185
1922	4 256 218	554 196
1933	3 815 000	992 000
1948	c.4 000 000	481 502

called the Kiangyunchu or River Transportation Company, held the monopoly of transporting salt by canal from the Huaipei works to Shiherhwei:[52] Governor-general Tseng Kuo-fan, who re-established Liang-huai once more after the Taiping rebellion, thought T'ao's remedy was the disease rather than inoculation and reduced the amount to 36 982 *yin*. By the end of the empire, however, the quota for Huai-pei supplies to Huai-nan had been increased again to 149 200 *yin* of 750 lb each, i.e. 1 119 000 cwt, a large injection of *shai* into the world of *chien*.

In addition, in 1910 three companies began to open successive basin solar evaporation salines in southeast Huai-pei, specifically to produce salt to be sent by sea to Shiherhwei, the port of Yangchow. These salines were known collectively as Chi-nan, 'assistance to the south', and paralleled the *chi-Ch'u* in Szechwan, 'assistance to Ch'u'. They represented a further installment of what had been instituted by T'ao Chu. Chi-nan developed rapidly. 'Many of the shareholders in these Companies are influential, and the tendency of the administration is to favour Chinan as compared with Panchungling salt from the other works' in Huai-pei.[53] In 1915 before the foreign inspectorate was fully in the saddle, a quota of 100 000 *yin* of 800 lb, i.e. 800 000 cwt, was assigned to this Chi-nan trade. As early as 1913 the inspectors had reported that 'the total supply from Huai-pei to Huainan districts constituted about half of the quantity consumed in the four Yangtze provinces',[54] i.e. about 2 million cwt. Although the foreign inspectorate had not initiated the Chi-nan trade, it approved of it as a piece of liberalization and did not hold it to the quota of 100 000 *yin*. Moreover, it permitted Huai-pei salt to be shipped direct to the Yangtze ports of Huai-nan bypassing Shiherhwei and Yangchow altogether. So there were now three ways for Huai-pei salt to enter Huai-nan: the Kiang-

yunchu, Chi-nan, and direct shipment. In 1919 Huai-pei supplied
4 548 075 cwt of salt to Huai-nan, almost the whole estimated consumption. Of this amount, the Kiangyunchu handled 954 780 cwt, the Chi-
nan works 2 693 812 cwt and direct shipment 899 483 cwt. A total
2 554 196 cwt were transported by steamers, 1 292 551 by sea-going
junks and 701 328 by canal junks.[55]

By the early 1920s then the writing was on the wall for Huai-nan.
Under the Kuomintang its vested interests managed to achieve a modest
recovery, but at the end of the Pacific War the decline in its production
was resumed. Since the late Ch'ing, attempts had been made to introduce the Liang-che method of *pan-shai* production, but this never spread
beyond Lu-ssu *ch'ang* of T'ung-chou and presumably was found ineffective in checking the progress of Huai-pei *t'an-shai*. Only a residue of
Huai-nan *chien* survived in 1948: the last bastion of what had been the
predominant form of salt manufacture in China. The victory of *shai* over
chien was a kind of modernization.

Another kind of modernization which emerged in China under the
republic was the growth of a refined salt industry. In Europe, refined
salt, 'salt upon salt' as it was called in England since the process
involved the dissolution of crude salt in water and its re-evaporation,
had been produced since the fifteenth century. The first major production centre was the Low Countries where high grade fine salt was in
demand first from the fishing industry and then from the increasingly
sophisticated palates of the Burgundian age. In China, though the
technology was known and occasionally applied (for example, to
Kwangtung salt for the Hunan market), refined salt did not appear in
any quantity until the nineteenth century, when small quantities were
imported into the treaty ports for European consumption. Chinese
gradually acquired European tastes. As Ching Pen-po (Ching Hsueh-
ling), salt reformer and pioneer of the refined salt industry in China, put
it: 'It is human nature "to love the good and hate the evil" . . . people
saw that foreign salt was reasonably priced and excellent in quality'.[56]

In July 1914 Ching Pen-po established the Chiu-ta salt refining company at Tientsin. Difficulties with capital and technology prevented
production until December 1915 and in 1916 it only reached 452 cwt.
Thereafter progress was steady: 12 895 cwt in 1917, 83 129 cwt in 1918,
155 292 cwt in 1919, 320 821 cwt in 1920. In 1921 Chiu-ta was joined at
Tientsin by a competitor, T'ung-ta founded by Wang Yen-ch'uan, but its
production only commenced in 1926 and remained small. In 1926, the
Fu-hai refinery at Newchwang opened, as did the T'ung-yi works at
Chefoo, and a number of refineries were attempted at Kiaochow though
without permanent success. Chiu-ta was unaffected and retained its
lead in the industry. In 1923 its production reached a high point of

459 560 cwt, and if it fell to around 300 000 cwt for the next few years, this was more the result of political disturbance than competition. In 1933 Chiu-ta, with a capitalization of $12 100 000, was back producing 600 000 cwt a year, while T'ung-ta only produced 30 000 cwt. Refined salt found its principal outlets in Tientsin itself, Shanghai and the four Yangtze *an* of Huai-nan, especially Wuhan. In 1922, Hupei took 206 522 cwt, Hunan 45 360, Kiangsi 202 430 and Anhwei 32 079. Here in the new urban China of the treaty ports, there were more modern patterns of consumption and a definite mutation in alimentary taste. One of Ching Pen-po's successful byproducts at Tientsin was toothpaste and the first monosodium glutamate factory was opened in Shanghai in 1923.[57]

Finally, in 1921, also at Tientsin, there was an even more modernizing innovation. Fan Hsü-tung, a chemical engineer from Hunan who had graduated from MIT in 1917 and become managing director of Chiu-ta, founded the Yung-li Soda Company, also known as the Pacific Alkali Company, to pioneer in China the manufacture of soda by the Solvay ammonia salt process. The background to this initiative, the beginning of the modern chemical industry in China, was Brunner Mond's success between 1900 and 1914 in finding a market for modern alkali in China. Henry Glendinning, the company's representative in Shanghai, enlisted as sales manager a former Episcopal Methodist missionary, Edward S. Little, who proved adept at marketing alkali products. In 1902 Brunner Mond sold 3500 tons, in 1905 13 000 tons and in 1914, 32 000 tons. In 1913 China was actually the company's second major export market.[58] It was this market that Fan Hsü-tung set out to capture for the Chinese producer.

Fan served as chief engineer of Yung-li from 1921 to 1949. His service included a move to Chien-wei in Szechwan during the Japanese War and he remained on the mainland when the Communists came to power. The Yung-li factory was adjacent to the Chiu-ta works, the company was originally capitalized at $400 000 and output was planned at 15 tons a day, a target which was doubled by 1929. In 1926, Yung-li was already sufficiently successful to be joined at Tientsin by a competitor, the Pohai Chemical Industries Company, founded by Nieh T'ang-ku, also from Hunan, with a capitalization of $200 000. By 1933 Yung-li's capitalization had been increased to $2 million and Pohai's to $1 300 000. Progress continued so that 'by 1937, domestic production of soda-ash had reached between 180 and 200 tons a day and the volume of sales inside China was higher than the total of imports from Britain for that year'.[59] China in 1937 will therefore have been consuming over 100 000 tons of alkali a year, the equivalent of 250 000 tons of salt: only the amount Britain had been consuming in the 1850s, it is true, but a big

step for a traditional economy. Republican China therefore saw significant modernization in the production, distribution and consumption of
salt.

Early Communist China[60]

Under Chairman Mao, the institutions and policies of the People's
Republic were marked by a high degree of volatility. Though the
political conquest of society by the party remained a constant, a variety
of means was employed to this end. Indeed, *révolution en permanence* was
regarded as the optimum environment for its furtherance even to the
extent, in the Cultural Revolution, of directing revolution against the
party itself. In the periods of the Soviet model 1949 to 1956 and the Great
Leap Forward 1957 to 1961, another constant emerged, associated with
the first: a rejection of both tradition and modernity as normally understood. This constant found its expression in the institutions and policies
established and pursued for the production, distribution and consumption of salt.

In salt production, the Communists wished for a sharp increase which
would mark a dramatic break with the past. Thus the first five year
plan[61] proposed to raise the production of salt 52.8 per cent from nearly
5 million tons in 1952 to over 7.5 million tons in 1957, notwithstanding
that the 5 million tons itself was nearly double the best year of the
Kuomintang. Overproduction had been the traditional preoccupation,
now it was underproduction. Yet, because of Communist reluctance to
invest in light industry, because of an increasing preference in all
industry for labour intensivity rather than capital intensivity, the means
adopted to this non-traditional end were non-modern. The four major
salines of Manchuria, Ch'ang-lu, Shantung and Huai-pei continued to
expand and by 1957 provided 85 per cent of China's salt. But for its big
increases, the party looked not to the sophisticated *shai* of the northeast,
nor to further deep drilling in Szechwan, but to the primitive *sebkhas* of
the northwest, especially Abalai and Chilantai in Alashan and Ch'a-k'a
in Koko-nor. In 1948 the Alashan lakes produced under 50 000 tons; by
1957 over 300 000 tons. At Lake Ch'a-k'a progress was slower:
60 000 cwt in 1948, 90 000 cwt in 1954; but hopes were even higher. In
1955 a Communist source estimated its reserves at '260 million tons – a
quantity sufficient to feed 600 million at a per capita consumption rate of
8 kilograms per annum for over a hundred years'.[62] A production target
of 230 000 tons was set for that year.

Another area where hopes were reposed was Sinkiang, particularly
Ching-ho near Ebi-nor in Zungharia whose four salt lakes had supplied
108 000 cwt to Ili in 1943. In 1955 the same source noted: 'Threatened by
a sustained shortage of supply, the Sinkiang Salt Administration saw to

it that the working force at Ts'ing-ho be organized for exploratory purposes. Penetrating deeper and deeper into the Gobi Desert, they discovered in 1954 at Sha-chuan-tse near Ts'ing-ho a salt basin containing 80 000 tons of high grade salt of 96.20 per cent sodium chloride strength'.[63] The Communist programme for production was based on a mixture of gigantism and reprimitivization.

Distribution likewise mixed modernity and tradition or rejected both. Early Communist railway priorities were strategic rather than commercial. Thus the Lanchow–Sinkiang line linked up with the Turksib; the Chining–Erhlien line crossed outer Mongolia to meet the Trans-Siberian; the Paotow–Lanchow line joined inner Mongolia and the Chinese northwest; the Lanchow–Tsaidam–Lhasa combined rail and highway extended Chinese power in Tibet; all basically under political imperatives. These lines, it is true, brought rail transport closer to the new saltfields of Alashan, Koko-nor and Zungharia, but obliquely so that traditional transport was still required. Thus in Alashan in 1957, 80–90 lorries took salt to the railheads, but also 90 000 camels, more than had been employed in the days of the foreign inspectorate under the republic. Unlike Sambhar, no railway was constructed with a saltfield in mind, unless it was the Litang to Chanchiang line which served the new saltfields of the Leichow peninsula and Hainan. Hainan itself was a mixture of strategic outpost, devil's island and new frontier.

Finally, consumption emerged neither wholly traditional nor fully modern. Communist sources were proud to indicate an increased consumption of salt by industry: 540 000 tons in 1953, 950 000 tons in 1955, 1 320 000 tons in 1957. But alimentary demand remained crushingly predominant as the Communists signally failed to control the growth of population. Lanchow was designated as the centre of a new chemical industry, partly because of its proximity to the new salt supplies of the northwest and its position at the hub of the new transborder railways. But the chemical targets for 1957 remained modest: 476 000 tons of ordinary soda and 154 000 tons of caustic soda; raw materials for the two earlier stages of the chemical revolution. Chlorine and chlorinated hydrocarbons, the raw materials of the third stage of the chemical revolution, did not figure in the first five year plan because they were too consumerist. The party was anachronistically obsessed with heavy industry and the supposedly demiurgic role of coal and steel. It looked not to tomorrow, but to an imaginary yesterday it felt China had missed, and aimed at a perpetual purgatory – investment without output, production without consumption, a Long March to nowhere.

Yet an increasing proportion of China's salt was being absorbed in industry as in other parts of the world. The world of salt in the modern age, though varied, was basically undivided. As salt had once served to variegate taste, express distinctions and avoid the plenum which culture

abhors, so now, under its components of sodium and chlorine, it serves
to create the multiplicity of consumables which pursue the same end of
vita humanior. So long as this end is held in view no salt need lose its
savour. Trade in salt may diminish, since high technology had made its
production possible almost anywhere, but its industrial consumption is
unlikely to decline. There is no substitute for salt.

Part II
Salt and the State

7 The Venetian Salt Administration

The second part of this study is devoted to salt and the state, specifically to six salt administrations which have played a significant role in the lives of major states. From production, distribution and consumption, the analysis turns to monopolies, limited or extended, direct or indirect; to fiscality, welfare and diplomacy; to what the state did in the salt administration and what the salt administration did in the state. We begin with some delineation of what is meant by a salt administration and an account of the categories we propose to use in the analysis of examples which follows.

A salt administration is more than laws about salt. On the one hand, it is more than state property in salt. Thus while Pliny says that the rulers of Northern India owned the mines of the Punjab Salt Range and obtained a large income from them, there was properly no Saka or Kushan salt administration. Similarly, both Charlemagne and Otto II claimed regalian rights over the salt wells of Lorraine, as no doubt had the Merovingians and the authorities of the *limes* before them, but there was no Carolingian or Ottonian salt administration. Again, in 959, Marozia, *senatrix omnium Romanorum* and sister of Pope John XIII, presented a saltworks, probably at the mouth of the Tiber to the Benedictine abbey of Subiaco, but this is no ground for attributing a salt administration to the Holy Roman republic.[1] Bela III of Hungary, 1172–1196, obtained a substantial proportion of his income from the salt mines of Transylvania, but there was no Arpad salt administration.[2] Equally a toll levied on salt along with other commodities, like that placed by the Lombard king, Liutprand (712–744) on salt from Commachio moving up the Po, does not constitute a salt administration. Salt administrations must be specialized, more than fiscal and have reached a certain degree of bureaucratic articulation. On the other hand, one hesitates to call the Roman imperial *annona* in salt instituted by Emperor Aurelian a salt administration because, although bureaucratically specialized and articulated, it lacked the fiscal element altogether. It was a pure welfare agency, a euergetism designed to lose rather than make money for the state. This was the case too with the activities of the *tuz emin* or intendant of salt in sixteenth-century Constantinople. In a true salt administration, there must be both fiscal and welfare elements: *kuo-chi min-sheng* (state's taxes and people's livelihood), as the Chinese put it; though welfare might be variously defined.

In terms of this definition, salt administrations have not always existed. Indeed, with the possible exception of the Ptolemaic planned economy, they existed nowhere outside China until the thirteenth century. Moreover salt administrations in this sense, have largely ceased to exist today everywhere, despite the continued importance of salt as a commodity and a raw material. Some general considerations may be put forward to explain these facts.

Salt administration involves taxation, bureaucracy and specialization and the existence of these elements rests on other institutional presuppositions. Thus taxation presupposes a distinction between the property of the state and the property of society and an orderly means of transforming part of the second into the first. Bureaucracy presupposes a more than household, patrimonial or city state articulation of central power and a supply of literate, trained, disciplined personnel to staff it. This in turn presupposes writing, literary languages and paper or paper substitutes. Specialization presupposes the possibility of treating salt differently from other commodities. *De facto* this implies a conspicuous, substantial and long-distance trade in salt, identifiable and controllable by bureaucracy for taxation, and, as we shall see, other purposes. Clearly these presuppositions were not everywhere or always completely fulfilled. Salt administrations were creatures of circumstance. In particular, they belonged to a specific condition of the state when it was strong enough to operate a specialized bureaucratic institution, weak enough to need one because unable to operate a more general bureaucracy. Salt administrations belong to the adolescence or senescence of central power. Conversely, in the infancy, maturity or dotage of the state, salt administrations are non-existent: either because the state is too weak to operate them or because the state is too strong to find them useful. These were the conditions of states outside China before the thirteenth century and after the twentieth.

Of all the salt administrations, that of China had the longest and most continuous history. Even if we consign the salt administration of Kuan-tzu, minister to Duke Huan of Ch'i, 685–643, to the realm of invented genealogy, there certainly was a salt administration in Ch'i in the reign of King Hsüan, 319–301, which was continued into the empire after 221 by Ch'in Shih Huang-ti. The salt administration was abolished by the Western Han from 202, but it was reintroduced by Han Wu-ti in 116, and continued, with a brief intermission between 44 and 41, until 23 AD when it was again abolished, this time by the newly restored Eastern Han, as part of the reaction against the etatisme of the usurper Emperor Wang Mang. From 23 AD, with the exception of a short restoration in the reign of Chang-ti 75–88, the abolition held until 763 when a new salt administration was established by Liu Yen minister to the T'ang emperor Tai-tsung. From Silver T'ang to People's Republic, the salt administration remained in continuous existence as a major institution of the state. One of a number of specialized agencies, for copper procurement, river administration, grain transport, horse administration, tea administration, the salt administration had its own laws, records, vocabulary and traditions of procedure. In this complex and sophisticated documentation, it possessed a higher degree of self-conscious awareness of its own operations than the salt administrations in any other part of the world. It is therefore from China that we can best draw conceptual tools for analysing salt administrations anywhere, in particular from the Ch'ing period when the traditional Chinese system reached its maturity. It is one of the benefits of recent advances in Chinese history to have given us the elements of a philosophy of salt administration.

Traditional Chinese thinking about salt was dichotomistic. First, it distinguished, implicitly, between what the state did in the salt administration from what the salt administration did in the state. Next, within the first category, it distinguished between the presence of the state and its operations: the *t'i* and the *yung*, substance and function, in the Neo-Confucian terminology which came naturally to Chinese administrators. Third, with regard to the presence of the state, the *t'i*, another pair of dichotomies appeared. The salt reformer Ching Pen-po suggested, in the first number of his journal *Yen-cheng tsa-chih* (Salt Administration Miscellany) in 1912, that all salt administrations could be divided into taxation systems (*fu-shui hsi*) in which the state confined its activities to levying tax, and business systems (*ying-yeh hsi*) where its activities embraced commercial operations as well. In other words administration could be either limited or extended. Finally, both kinds of administration could be either direct (*chih-chieh chuan-mai*), i.e. conducted at each stage by officials, or indirect (*chien-chieh chuan-mai*), i.e. conducted through privileged merchants or left to private enterprise, under official supervision only.

To describe the various forms of state presence, limited or extended, direct or indirect, Chinese salt administrators made use of the convenient shorthand referred to in Chapter 3. Group terms, *kuan* (official), *shang* (privileged merchants), *min* (the people), were applied to function terms, *tu* (supervision), *pan* (management), *chih* (manufacture), *shou* (acquisition), *yün* (transportation), *hsiao* (distribution), *mai* (sales) to make a composite description. Thus in 1912 Ching Pen-po and his friends of the *Yen-cheng tsa-chih* described the system they wanted as *kuan-shou*, *kuan-yün*, *kuan mai*, official acquisition, official transport, official sales. Only production would be left to private enterprise, *min-chih*, and perhaps eventually not even that. At most times and in most of the salt divisions and their parts, however, the Chinese salt administration was less etatiste than this. It was extended, more than fiscal, but its operation was indirect, through privileged merchants rather than officials. The commonest general description of the Chinese salt administration therefore was *kuan-tu shang-pan*, official supervision and merchant management. It was a shorthand formula for a state monopoly, extended but indirect.

With regard to the operations of the state monopoly, the *yung*, Chinese salt administrators made another dichotomy: *kuo-chi* (the state's taxes) and *min-sheng* (the people's livelihood). The primary function of the salt administration was fiscal: the assessment, collection and receipt of tax. Here again there were divergent possibilities. Assessment might be comprehensive or partial, progressive or regressive, equitable or inequitable, under one head or many. Collection, too, might be single or multiple, at one place or several. It might be made in advance of commercial transaction (*hsien-k'o hou-yen*, 'first tax, then salt'), perhaps at source (*chiu-ch'ang cheng-shui*, 'at the yard levy tax'), or in arrear (*hsien-yen hou-li*, 'first salt then toll'), perhaps at the outlet (*an*, 'port'), where it passed from the previleged merchant to the provincial distributor. Receipt might be consolidated in a single treasury, or divided among several, earmarked for particular expenses, or paid into general account. Each of these fiscal options had their advantages and disadvantages which were warmly debated among Chinese salt administrators in the successive editions of the *Huang-ch'ao ching-shih wen-pien* (Collected Essays on state craft under the Reigning Dynasty) between 1826 and 1902. Out of these debates emerged a departmental philosophy which held that comprehensive taxation at source was impossible, that transport merchants could not be expected to pay tax in advance before they received cash from the local distributors, that collection should take two bites at the cherry, that both producing and consuming provinces had a right to the proceeds, that emergencies justified extra taxes for particular purposes paid into special treasuries. But even in conservative China, conventional wisdom in salt administration seldom went unchallenged for long. The salt reformer was nearly as familiar a figure as the salt administrator, especially with regard to the non-fiscal aspects of the *yen-cheng*.

For the salt administration was not simply a fiscal agency. It was also a primitive social service. Besides *kuo-chi*, there was also *min-sheng*, the people's livelihood. Under the rubric *min-sheng*, the salt administration sought to ensure the consumer, especially in outlying areas, a supply of salt at prices he could afford to pay, something market forces, it was believed, were not always capable of ensuring. *Min-chieh tan-shih*,[3] 'the people are eating insipid food', was a recognized symptom of social breakdown and a danger signal for an upsurge of banditry. Chinese history was full of rebels who had started as *hsiao*, 'owls', i.e. salt smugglers: Wang Chien who founded the state of Shu in Szechwan at the end of the T'ang; Chang Shih-ch'eng, the rival of Chu Yuan-chang at the beginning of the Ming; Chang Lo-hsing, the leader of the Nien

rebellion, toward the end of the Ch'ing. In general Chinese salt administrators gave *min-sheng* a welfare denotation, but since 'the people'
included not only farmers but also others, like fishermen, who required
salt in their businesses, it could have an economic aspect as well. Thus
Ching Pen-po first became interested in salt reform when he championed the interests of the fishing industry of eastern Chekiang against
the restrictionist policies of the salt division of Liang-che. In Szechwan,
the salt administration was well aware that exports of salt to Hu-kuang
paid for the province's imports from downriver. More significant, however, to Chinese administrators was the cultural dimension of the salt
administration. In Ho-tung the salt administration was associated with a
Confucian college of higher education and a noted local *feng-shui* temple.
The *Liang-huai yen-fa-chih* of 1870 has sections on colleges, orphanages,
lifeboats, fire agency, free ferry, pharmacy and a public graveyard, with
all of which the salt administration was in some way involved. Again,
the *Ssu-ch'uan yen-fa-chih*, complied by Governor-General Ting Pao-chen
in 1882, in addition to current administrative practice, contains maps,
pictures of processes, historical material, as well as a chapter on local
temples and a bibliography of salt extending back to the Han. In
Ch'ang-lu too the salt administration was associated with a number of
temples, colleges and schools. It was part of the living landscape.

Chinese officials were also aware of the role of the salt administration
in the state, not only in regular finance, but in other ways and in civil
and military emergencies. In 1901 an edict to the Grand Council declared
that 'salt affairs are the staple of the state's annual income'. Till the
mid-nineteenth century, the imperial household department (*nei-wu fu*),
the emperor's privy purse, drew a substantial portion of its revenue,
directly or indirectly, from its connections with the salt trade. Emperors
stayed in salt merchants' villas on their southern progresses (*nan-hsün*).
Salt merchants, for a price of course, received honorary degrees and
their sons preferred entry in the examination system. In the Ch'ing
period at least, the old slogan *chung-nung ping-shang* ('strengthen agriculture, weaken commerce') gave way to another, *yü-kuo hsü-shang* ('To
enrich the state, be kind to merchants'). By 1800 salt receipts, because
they were relatively unearmarked and readily expandable, had become
the reserve revenue of the empire. In the nineteenth century both the
traditional reconquest of Inner Asia in the interior and the military
modernization on the coast drew heavily on revenue provided by Ting
Pao-chen's reform of the Szechwan salt administration. By the end of
the dynasty, 'my solution is an increase in the price of salt' had become a
refrain in the memorials of harassed governors-general and overuse
precipitated the revolution of 1911.

On occasion the salt administration served diplomatic purposes,
especially in the Sino-Mongolian borderlands. Thus the Oirat prince of

Alashan, west of the Yellow River in the future province of Ninghsia, who was the owner of four productive salt lakes, was given privileged terms of import to China, because he was the primary Ch'ing ally among the Mongol princes of the northwest. More frequent was the mobilization of salt money for civil and military emergencies. In the eighteenth century, the Liang-huai monopolists maintained a number of well-stocked famine relief granaries at Yang-chou and elsewhere.[4] Ch'ang-lu provided by special taxes for emergency works on the Huang-ho in 1809, 1925 and 1927. Above all salt merchants advanced funds for war. An article in the *Yen-cheng tsa-chih* on the history of Ch'ang-lu describes how the merchants of that division, together with those of Shantung, Huai-nan and Liang-che subscribed a total of 30 million taels for the great campaigns of the empire.[5] They subscribed to the suppression of the first Chin-ch'uan rebellion in 1748; to the conquest of Zungharia in 1755; to the establishment of the Ili military agricultural colony in 1759; to the suppression of the second Chin-ch'uan rebellion in 1773 and of the Taiwan rebellion in 1788; to the Gurkha campaign of 1792; and to the campaign against the White Lotus in 1796. The glories of the Ch'ien-lung period were partly financed by salt. Salt served the state just as the state shaped the world of salt. Thus it continued in China down to the advent of the Communists.

The long history of the Chinese salt administration, its experimentation with most of the combinations and permutations of such specialized bureaucracy, and its articulation of a sophisticated vocabulary for the discussion of its problems provide convenient analytical tools for looking at salt administrations in other parts of the world. Our theme is salt and the state, for the purpose of comparative analysis we have chosen six which are both significant in themselves and reasonably well documented: Venice, *ancien régime* France, the Habsburg and Ottoman empires, India under the *raj*, China itself under the late empire and early republic. Our aim is to see what is the same and what is singular. We begin with Venice, the unique but still characteristic, medieval European mercantile city state.

THE STATE IN THE VENETIAN SALT ADMINISTRATION

The Venetian salt administration had a long history too.[6] The Venetian destruction of the monastic salines of Comacchio in 932 was probably designed to achieve a sales monopoly in the Po valley, though in fact it seems to have benefited the archbishop of Ravenna's salines at Cervia, which commenced successive basin solar evaporation between 965–975, rather than any of the *Serenissima*'s.[7] Chioggia, however, got into its stride in the course of the eleventh century. A treaty with Capodistria in

1182 and legislation in 1184 and 1187 show the Venetian state already concerned to monopolize production, expand sales and hypothecate revenue from Chioggia: all signs of incipient salt administration, coincident with Venice's greater power at sea and on the mainland, following the half mythical but certainly successful mediation of Doge Sebastiano Ziani in 1177 between Frederick Barbarossa and Alexander III. It was not, however, until the beginning of difficulties at Chioggia, the abandonment of local protectionism and the advent of imports from beyond the Adriatic that the Venetian salt administration was fully fledged.[8] From the middle of the thirteenth century to the middle of the seventeenth century it was a major institution of the state, and it was of particular importance from the war of Chioggia in 1378, which finally ruined the old salines, to the war of the Holy League in 1570. We shall focus on it in the second half of the sixteenth century, à l'epoque de *Philippe II*, where evidence is particularly abundant, but because the institution did not change its essential character, though in ceaseless motion as regards detail, we shall not deny ourselves backward and forward glances when apposite. Primarily, however, we are concerned with the salt administration in Mannerist and early Baroque Venice: the Venice of the *Redentore* and the *Salute*.

Sun Yat-sen once called for capitalism to create socialism. The Venetian salt administration, like Venetian institutions generally, presents the opposite case: socialism creating capitalism, a *polis* secreting an *emporium*, the public underpinning the private. Like the Chinese, the Venetian salt administration was extended and indirect. It too could be characterized as *kuan-tu shang-pan*, official supervision and merchant management. Unlike the Chinese, however, the relationship between the two was not merely symbiotic but monolithic. In China, officials and merchants had different principles of legitimation and formed two parallel hierarchies, however much they interconnected to their mutual benefit. In Venice, officials and merchants had the same principle of legitimation and formed part of a single hierarchy, however much public and private interests might appear to conflict. In China, *shang-pan* existed for *kuan-tu* and the people it represented. In Venice, the state existed for the merchant oligarchy because it was the people. China was a bureaucratic empire, Venice was a *polis/emporium* and this difference coloured all the state's activities in the salt administration.

Overall official supervision was exercised by three institutions: the *Collegio del Sal*, the *Ufficio del Sal* headed by the *Provveditori al Sal*, and the *Camera Salis*. The *Collegio* made policy decisions. It was a top level body, a cabinet committee in effect, on which sat senior political figures such as the *savi grandi*, the ducal councillors and the heads of the *Quarantia*. Besides formulating policy, it drafted bills for submission to the Grand Council, Senate or Ten, whichever was the effective legislative or ordinative body of the republic. In Chinese terms, the *Collegio* may be compared to a governor-general or governor in his capacity as head of a salt division. The *Ufficio* made administrative decisions and implemented them. It was a department of salt affairs with the three, later six, *Provveditori* its permanent under-secretaries. From the middle of the fifteenth century, two out of three were constantly absent from Venice, inspecting salt works and auditing the accounts of subordinate offices in Venice's mainland or overseas possessions. The *Provveditori* were the heart of the official component in the Venetian salt administration. They may be compared in China to the salt commissioners (*yen-yün shih, yen-fa tao*), the administrative heads of the regional salt divisions. The *Camera* handled money, or, as we shall see, more frequently promissory notes: outpayments to transport merchants, in payments from tax farmers. It also handled the considerable superstructure of cash and credit which was built on these foundations. The role of the *Camera*, as in effect a bank, was one of the most original features of the Venetian salt administration. For this there was no real equivalent in China, unless it be the complicated transactions between the *nei-wu fu* (imperial household department) and the merchant monopolists of Ch'ang-lu at the turn of the eighteenth and nineteenth centuries. But where Peking and Tientsin, metropolis and market, were two, Venice, *polis/emporium*, was one.

These three institutions operated in four distinct areas: Venice itself, the *Stato da Terra*, the *Stato da Mar*, and the Venetian co-prosperity sphere beyond her own borders to which the *Serenissima* supplied salt. In each of these areas the salt administration functioned in a different way.

Venice itself was privileged both positively and negatively. As a consumer, Venice paid less tax than other parts of Venetian territory and received its salt at cost price from the administration's warehouses at the Dogana da Mar to the east of the *Salute* and at the eastern end of the Giudecca. Here Venice might be compared to Tientsin or Peking in Ch'ang-lu or to the *shih-an* districts of Kiangsu in Liang-huai. On the other hand, as a producer, Venice's salines, both the older ones near Torcello and the newer ones at Chioggia, were discriminated against in favour of more distant suppliers either in the Adriatic or beyond. Here China affords no parallel to Venice's systematic preference for long-distance commerce, though the salt administration did occasionally suppress salines close to urban centres which were unusually difficult to police.

The *Stato da Terra* was the Venetian territories on the Italian mainland, *Terre Ferme*: the Veneto, Friuli and Venetian Lombardy. For the purposes of salt administration, it was divided in 13 tax farms (*dazio, daze*) each conferred for two years to a farmer (*daziero*) following an auction as to the quantity to be sold at a price fixed by the salt administration. In addition, 10 communes, of which Grado and Rovigo were the most significant, had partially bought themselves out of the salt administration, and were privileged, like Venice itself, to pay tax at lower rates and to farm the taxes themselves. The *Stato da Terra* was the core of the Venetian salt administration from the strictly fiscal point of view. Producing no salt of its own, it paid tax at the heaviest rates, increasing roughly in proportion to distance from Venice and provided at least four fifths of the receipts. A rich, urbanized interior market, in China it may be compared to Chihli and Honan in Ch'ang-lu or to the four upriver Yangtze *an* in Liang-huai. It was also significant as the route to some of Venice's best export markets for salt.

The *Stato da Mar* was Venice's overseas possession: the satellite cities of Istria and Dalmatia such as Piran, Pola, Zara and Sebenico and the colonial territories of Corfu and the other Ionian islands, Crete and Cyprus. It produced, consumed and exported salt both to Venice and to the Balkans. Though tax was levied on salt leaving the fields, the rates were light and *Stato da Mar* was much less important revenue-wise than the *Stato da Terra*. Production-wise, however, the *Stato da Mar* supplied the greater part of the salt handled by the administration. In China, there was no real equivalent to the *Stato da Mar*, the nearest comparables being the Chusan archipelago in relation to Shanghai, Taiwan in relation to Fukien and Hainan in relation to Canton.

The Venetian co-prosperity sphere was the place to which the *Serenissima* sold salt, generally through government to government arrangements. These places included at various times, Ducal Lombardy, the Romagna, Emilia, the March of Ancona, southern Switzerland, Carinthia, Carniola, Croatia and parts of Bosnia and Albania. They were not, of course, under any formal jurisdiction of the Venetian salt administration. But they were part of its concern, for economic and diplomatic rather than fiscal reasons. Fiscally, they could not be charged high prices inflated by tax for fear of their turning to Venice's competitors: Genoa, Ancona and Ragusa. Economically, however, the salt administration sometimes permitted the sale of Venetian salt at less than cost price in order to obtain entry for other Venetian goods which paid better.[9] Once again, Venice's export markets had no analogue in China, except marginally where Ch'ang-lu exported to Mongolia or on the borders of Yunnan with Vietnam and Burma.

Let us now focus on the *Stato da Terra*. Here the system in operation might be described in Chinese terms as *min-chih, shang-yün, kuan-shou, shang-hsiao*: people manufacture, merchant transport, official acquisition, merchant distribution. At no stage did the state actually own the salt.[10] At every stage, from producer to retailer, the trade was subject to government regulation. The state was in effect a broker,[11] or commission agent with a huge fee: a situation similar to that of Liang-huai,

Liang-che and Kwangtung. Nor did the state provide capital. Again one is reminded of Liang-huai where the standard argument for the privileges of the transport merchants was the impossibility of the state's finding sufficient capital of its own to buy the salt on the coast and transport it upriver. What the Venetian salt administration did provide, however, from 1281, was a substantial freight bounty (*noli*) on salt brought long distance from beyond the Adriatic: Ras al-Makhbaz, Cyprus, Ibiza and Trapani. The *noli* became part of the highly original banking function of the Venetian salt administration which had no real equivalence in China. Prices and bounties fluctuated, but in rough terms, the cost price of salt was a ducat or less a ton and transport charges to Venice were 3 ducats a ton. At Venice the importer received a bounty of 8 ducats a ton. Since salt was finally sold to the retailer or the public at around 33 ducats a ton, the bounty amounted to nearly a quarter of the capital involved. In China, the state might be as, or even more, deeply involved in the salt business as in Venice, but it would be on its own account via *kuan-yün* (official transport) not in the form of subsidies to merchants.

The first stage of the trade was production. The Venetian salt administration obtained a considerable part of its salt from outside the territories of the *Serenissima*: from Ras al-Makhbaz, Cagliari, Alexandria, the Crimea, Ibiza, Trapani and Apulia. Here management of production took various forms, from nationalized industry at Cagliari to private enterprise at Trapani, but none of them, of course, was the result of prescription by the Venetian salt administration. Within the territories of the *Serenissima*, ownership and management took two forms. In the satellite cities: Muggia, Capodistria, Piran, Pago (Zara) and Sebenico; the salt administration was content to leave private enterprise in charge, *min-chih*, subject to regulation about quantity, disposal and price. In the case of the colonial territories, the Ionian islands and Cyprus, Venice inherited crown rights from the Angevins and the Lusignans. These rights were generally leased to private *conductores*, though in the case of the Larnaca salt lakes, San Lazzaro, the government paid wages and effected improvements which turned a *sebkha* into a man-made successive basin evaporation plant: a partnership reminiscent of the works at the An-i *hsien* salt lake.[12] Basically, the Venetian state was not very concerned with production as such. What concerned it was price, freight and possible competition. Thus at Pago, the premier Adriatic saline, the *Collegio* insisted that three-quarters of the salt be sold to Venetian merchants, leaving only one quarter for sale by local merchants over the mountains into Croatia. At Piran, the salt administration demanded the whole production, but it took the precaution of fixing the price slightly higher than that paid by the muleteers, the *Mussolati* from Ljubljana. At Capodistria and Muggia, the salt administration took only one tenth, but the remainder could only be exported by land to Carniola/Slovenia and the valley of the Sava, so that there was no danger of competition anywhere with Venetian waterborne salt.[13] As in China, what the salt administration in Venice aimed at primarily was a monopoly of salt travelling long distance by water.

The second stage of the trade was the transport of salt to Venice. In theory it was open to anyone, even to non-nationals, some of whom did in fact participate. In practice, however, because the basis of the *noli* shifted from merchandise to ships, it was increasingly confined to a ring of privileged merchants, *shang-yün*: owners of galleons, conglomerate traders and members of the patriciate.[14] This was so particularly in the long-distance trade from the islands or semi-islands of the Mediterranean where the use of galleons was essential. Indeed, as we shall see, the freight bounty paid by the administration on such salt alone was intended by the oligarchy as a subsidy to itself, its trade and its shipping. With the decline of Mediterranean salt at Venice and the rise of Adriatic salt from Muggia, Capodistria, Piran, Pago and Sebenico, both phenomena of the seventeenth century essentially, the salt oligarchy widened to a democracy, since on these runs ships of lighter tonnage, *marciliani* and *trabachi*, were used, and no freight bounty was paid.[15] At the same time, the governing class of the Venetian state was turning in on itself from trade to agriculture and industry and was losing interest in the salt monopoly.

The third stage of the trade was the receipt and storage of salt at Venice. This was at all times under strict official control, *kuan-shou*, because here was the greatest danger of tax evasion. Although the salt administration never acquired the ownership, all salt imported had to be deposited in its magazines at the Dogana and on the Giudecca which were in effect bonded warehouses. On entry the transport merchant paid a 20 per cent import duty on his salt, but in the case of long-distance salt, this got swallowed up in the much larger freight bounty the state paid or at least acknowledged it owed. On leaving the warehouse, however, salt became liable, except in Venice itself, to the main duty of 200–300 percent.[16] Hence the danger of smuggling unless all salt was canalized through warehouses under official control.

The fourth stage of the trade was distribution from Venice to the *Stato da Terra*. Here there was another set of privileged merchants, *shang-hsiao*. From its warehouses, the administration arranged for the sale of the transport merchant's salt to the *daziero* or tax farmer. The sale took place through an auction, but what was at issue was not the price, which was fixed, but the quantity to be sold in each area or *dazio*.[17] Unlike the transport merchants, the *dazieri* belonged characteristically not to the metropolitan Venetian patriciate itself, but to its junior partner, the provincial oligarchies of the mainland cities. In 1493 the Council of Ten specifically forbad any Venetian noble to acquire a *dazio*, whether as principal, partner or guarantor,[18] though given the complexity of Venetian business with its interlocking syndicates, it must have been difficult to enforce this disinvestment provision. Having acquired title to his salt, though not actually paying for it or the massive tax included in the price, the *daziero* arranged for its transport to his district by barge[19] and subsequent resale, again at prices fixed by the *Ufficio*, to either retailers or the public. Only when the consumer had paid was there a general settlement of debt and credit between the various levels of the salt administration.

To Chinese eyes, the Venetian version of *kuan-tu shang-pan* would have seemed familiar enough, if unduly favourable to the merchants. It was more like South China, Kwangtung especially, where the *dazie* were paralleled by the *kuei* or farms, than North China, because official power was spread thinner the further it got from the imperial capital. What would have puzzled a traditional Chinese official about the Venetian salt administration would have been neither the structure nor the operations for levying the state's taxes, *kuo-chi*, but the conception of people's livelihood, *min-sheng*, and the role the salt administration played in the life of the state.

THE STATE'S TAXES IN THE VENETIAN SALT ADMINISTRATION

The three basic fiscal operations of any salt administration are the assessment, collection and receipt of tax. These operations took place in Venice as in China but in a different geographical milieu and institutional context, which gave the whole a distinctive colouring.

Assessment

For any tax there is an object of assessment. 'Income Tax, if I may be allowed to say so', an English judge is reported to have said, 'is a tax on income'. It sounds simple, but what is income for tax purposes is a matter of considerable complexity. It is the same with many abstract objects of assessment: capital gains, value added, expenditure, estate. It is one of the advantages of more concrete objects of assessment, such as salt, liquor, tea, tobacco, automobiles or windows, that they suffer relatively less from problems of definition. Relatively, because, as we saw in Chapter 1, other compounds besides sodium chloride may serve the same functions as salt. Moreover, with low quality earth salt, there is the problem of deciding what percentage of sodium chloride suffices to constitute salt for tax purposes. In general, however, salt is salt, and this is a great administrative help to a premodern bureaucracy with limited resources and expertise. *Per contra*, the difficulty with salt as with all concrete objects of assessment is that there is no physical mean as of distinguishing salt which has not paid tax from salt which has. The real problem of salt administration is to make assessment as comprehensive as possible in the face of legal avoidance and illegal evasion. For the two enemies of the salt tax assessor are the exempt and the smuggler, the two categories often overlapping.

In China until the twentieth century no real attempt was made to make assessment comprehensive in the sense of all salt paying tax. Conventional wisdom held that the state lacked the administrative resources and that any attempt to achieve more than a certain degree of control would prove counterproductive.[20] Salt officialdom recognized that it must tax in accordance with inability to avoid rather than with ability to pay. In practice this meant concentrating assessment on salt travelling long distance by water, preferably by river or canal. This alone could be identified and controlled, especially if it was conducted by the officials themselves (*kuan-yün*), or by privileged merchants (*shang-yün*) for whom tax was an acceptable part of the cost of a profitable monopoly. Such salt was heavily assessed. By contrast, salt travelling short distance by water: up a creek or across an estuary; or either short or long distance by land on trails radiating from a well or *sebkha*; was lightly assessed. Such salt paid nothing, or at reduced rates, or a lump sum bearing no relation to the quantity involved, which was collected as a surcharge to the land tax (*kuei-ting*). This lack of comprehensiveness of assessment was related both to the superficiality of imperial government and the contiguity in a continental state of producing and consuming districts. Chinese administrators had to reconcile themselves – or thought they had to reconcile themselves, for in the twentieth century Sir Richard Dane was to teach them differently – to not being able to tax all salt.

In Venice the geographical milieu was different or could be made different. One reason for the favour shown by the *ordo salis* to Mediterranean as opposed to local or Adriatic salt in the system of freight bounties was to make, as far as possible, all salt at Venice long-distance water-borne salt. Salt arriving by galleons owned by well known public figures was easier to get into the warehouses of *Ufficio* than salt creeping through the marshes in barges from Chioggia or carried across the sea in petty craft from the Slav coast. The bounty system also expressed a different institutional context in which the transport merchants were given an incentive for making a full declaration of the salt they had imported, whereas in China transport merchants were notorious for using such devices as wastage allowances to carry salt in excess of their assessment – a quasi-legal form of smuggling. In Venice we hear much less of avoidance and evasion than in China. A Chinese salt official would have been surprised by the relative absence of 'owls' in Venice and the ease with which Venetian salt officials assumed that all salt could and should be brought under assessment, at least in the *Stato da Terra*.

Collection

If, from a Chinese point of view, over-optimism characterized the Venetian attitude to assessment, the Venetian attitude to collection was characterized by undue pessimism. In any salt tax, the consumer always pays ultimately. What varies is the point or points of collection: one, two or many; at source, in advance, in arrear, how far in arrear. Chinese salt administrators rejected collection at source (*chiu-ch'ang cheng-shui*) for the same reasons as they rejected comprehensive assessment and because it imposed too great a burden on the transport merchant who would have to find cash for salt, freight and tax months before he could hope to recoup from the local distributor, *an-shang*, or the consumer. Nevertheless, collection at source was operated in some salt divisions, notably at the Ho-tung salt lake and at the Yunnan salt wells, and in most, Chinese salt officials preferred to collect early rather than late, once rather than more than once. Thus in Ch'ang-lu, tax was collected at Tientsin upriver from the salines; in Shantung, at Tsinan, not so far from the northern mouth of the Huang-ho where the works were; in Kwang-tung, at Canton, some distance from most of the salines, but before salt entered the distribution networks. Liang-huai, often typical of Chinese salt divisions, was here rather exceptional. In the Huai-nan section, the transport merchant paid first a small levy in advance at Yang-chou in accordance with the principle of first tax then salt (*hsien-k'o hou-yen*) and then a much larger levy in arrear at Wuhan in accordance with the principle of first salt then toll (*hsien-yen hou-li*).[21] This regime of relatively late collection in Huai-nan was justified by the exceptional scale of its trade and by the heavy burdens which the transport merchants already bore in conducting it. In Liang-huai, but in Liang-huai alone, most tax was collected not at Yang-chou when the salt passed from the producer to the transport merchant, the *tsao-hu* or *ch'ang-shang* to the *yün-shang*, but at Wuhan when the salt passed from the transport merchant to the provincial distributor, the *yün-shang* to the *an-shang*.

In Venetian terms, the equivalent of Wuhan was Venice itself where salt passed from the importer via the *Ufficio* (here the equivalent of the Hankow *tu-hsiao* or provincial sales officer) to the *daziero*. But in the Venetian salt administration, tax was not collected at this point. It was collected when the salt passed from the *daziero* to the retailer and the consumer: in Chinese terms from the *an-shang* to the shopkeeper, peddler and public. Indeed, it was not always collected even then. For the *daziero* might delay payment, so as to retain salt funds in his own hands for a period of profitable private use. There were penalties for delay, but the salt administration was prepared to waive these, extend the deadlines and in effect make the *daziero* a loan of tax receipts, in return for an immediate cash payment, subsequent interest and help with its own debts to the transport merchants for freight bounties.[22] From a Chinese point of view, tax in Venice was collected very far down the line from producer to consumer and after too much delay. The underlying reason was a difference in institutional context: in China the assumption was cash, whereas in Venice the assumption was credit; in China the official came first, in Venice the merchant.

Receipt

The same difference also coloured the fate of tax after collection. From a Chinese point of view, the Venetian system of receipt was both simple and complex. It was simple in that there was only one salt tax and it was all paid ultimately into the *Camera Salis*. In China, on the other hand, there were frequently multiple heads of assessment at a single point and several treasuries into which receipts were paid. Thus in 1900, Liang-huai salt arriving at Wuhan paid tax under ten heads of assessment, the proceeds of which were shared between nine treasuries under the control of five sets of mutually independent authorities. In China, receipts were not consolidated and individual heads of assessment were assigned to particular items of expenditure. In Venice, receipts were consolidated, if not in a central treasury for all state revenue, at least into the *Camera Salis*, whose funds could be assigned to any purpose by the *Collegio*.

The Venetian system was complex in that the transactions of the *Camera* were as much in credit as in cash and functioned within an interlocking system of public and private money markets which had no real equivalent in traditional China. For instance, the *Camera* paid the transport merchant his freight bounty or *noli* not in cash but in credits, *fedi*, in effect undated promissory notes whose payment depended on the state of the *Camera*'s resources and other commitments.[23] *Fedi* were transferable and marketable, so merchants who wanted cash quickly sold them at a discount to richer members of the patriciate who could afford to wait, to brokers, *sensari*, who specialized in government bills, or to *dazieri* who used them to settle their obligations to the *Camera*, by setting a credit from the salt administration against a debt to it.[24] Overall, debts to the salt administration, i.e. salt tax, exceeded credit from it, i.e. freight bounties, but this procedure of *sconto*, 'compensation', unless controlled, threatened to increase its cash-flow problems. From 1493 *sconto* was brought under increasing regulation.[25] To *dazieri* beyond the Mincio, i.e. in Venetian Lombardy, *sconto* was forbidden altogether and payment in cash was insisted on. To *dazieri* within the Mincio, i.e. in the Veneto and Friuli, *sconto* was permitted up to a certain proportion of debt; the *scontadori*,[26] i.e. the *dazieri* so privileged, had to pay 10 per cent of the sum in cash to the *Camera* to maintain its cash-flow; and in return received an extension of their deadlines, and hence a further use of their cash in hand, from 12 to 18 months. *Sconto*, even thus regulated, was not entirely satisfactory to the *Camera* since it postposed ultimate payment in cash, but it enabled the salt adminis-tration to pay off the backlog of unpaid *fedi* which had accumulated during the wars at the turn of the fifteenth and sixteenth centuries.

In the sixteenth century, the *Collegio* tried to avoid backlog, and in general was successful in doing so, but in the early 1560s, a conjuncture of excellent salt harvests in Cyprus with the end of bad wheat harvests in Italy which had tied up shipping, brought massive importations and a new crisis.[27]. This time the *Camera* had recourse, not to its own debtors, the *dazieri*, but to the Mint, the *Zecca*, where Venetians went to make deposits of money and valuables. The *Zecca* advanced a loan, whose interest and repayment were assigned to the *dazieri* and to the proceeds of exports of salt to Milan. Here was another compex credit operation which would have seemed strange, indeed reprehensible, to Chinese salt administrators. Strange, because the result of tardy collection of cash receipts: reprehensible, because it caused the sovereign power to borrow from its own subjects. This was something the Chinese state before the twentieth century felt to be beneath its dignity, a sign of weakness rather than of strength. In Venice, on the other hand, it was the glory of the state that it could call on its people for financial assistance, even if it had to pay them well for having it.[28] The state's taxes, similar in their procedures in China and Venice, functioned in different environments.

THE PEOPLE'S LIVELIHOOD IN THE VENETIAN SALT ADMINISTRATION

Traditional salt administrations were seldom purely fiscal in function. Besides *kuo-chi*, the state's taxes, there was *min-sheng*, the people's livelihood. In China, *min-sheng* embraced considerations of welfare, economics and culture, but of these, welfare, the desire to avoid the social breakdown of 'the people are eating insipid food' was the most pressing. In Venice too, there was a non-fiscal aspect of salt adminis-tration, but it was conceived in economic rather than welfare terms. For in Europe, and perhaps Europe alone, the economic was no longer embedded in the sociological, and, differentiated out, could become the object of special promotion.[29] In Venice, the salt administration was used to promote entrepôt trade, money supply and certain kinds of shipping: all, if not people's livelihood, at least patricians' business.

Entrepôt Trade

When the *noli*, or freight bounty on imported salt, was first introduced in 1281, it was calculated on the tonnage of goods exported from Venice.[30] Moreover the measure was obligatory not facultative. All merchants who exported were obliged to import salt, even though they received a handsome bounty for doing so. In this way, all Venetian merchants who exported or reexported, and that meant virtually the whole mercantile community, were compelled to become salt merchants. Unlike China, salt was not a specialism. Later, at a date which Hocquet is not able to establish definitely,[31] the obligation and the bounty came to rest on the ship as such and its captain or supercargo. But ship and captain were simply instruments of the shipowner and his associates, who, as a typical Venetian *fraterna*, or partnership for a limited term, generally held cargo space on both the outward and homeward journeys. So the system was not radically changed except that the circle of merchants who received bounties was now narrower than before, since it was necessary to be both a shipowner and an exporter/importer. The principle remained the same: businessmen who were not specialized salt merchants received a subsidy for importing salt long distance. The subsidy came in the first instance from public funds, mediately at the expense of local producers in the Adriatic, but in the last resort from the consumers of salt, especially in the *Stato da Terra*.

The aim of these measures was not simply to produce a stream of salt which could be taxed to the state's advantage. Another aim, of even greater importance to the Venetian patriciate, was the promotion of the city's entrepôt trade, the lifeblood of its existence as an emporium. Venice's problem may be stated as follows. For all goods freight was a major consideration in competitiveness and profitability. What Venice imported was relatively light: pepper, fine spices, sugar, leather, wax; though bulky goods figured secondarily – wheat, wool, cotton, alum, soda. What Venice exported was relatively heavy: timber, glass, equipment for the Crusades, textiles, metals, manufactured goods; though light goods figured secondarily as reexports – pepper, fine spices etc. Light goods could be handled profitably by galleys because they carried cargoes on both their outward and inward journeys. Heavy goods were much less profitable, because they had to be carried in galleons, and galleons often had to return in ballast or with cargoes whose freight did not cover the cost of operation. In accordance with their principle of maximum profit by diversification – trade anything anywhere – most

Venetians engaged in both galley and galleon trade, but they could not indefinitely use galley profits to subsidize galleon losses. What was needed to prevent disinvestment, maintain diversification and to expand business activity, was for the state to give a freight bounty to a bulky, long distance, galleon carried import commodity.

Salt from the outer Mediterranean fitted these requirements admirably. Unlike the alternatives of wheat, cotton, alum or soda, it was both an object of mass consumption and in fairly regular, predictable demand. If the import of salt long distance became profitable, as the *ordo salis* made it profitable, average freight rates to the merchant on his various commodities would fall. Then the Venetian entrepôt trader could lower his prices and so beat his Genoese, Catalan or Ragusan competitors. Already in the prosperous thirteenth century competition between entrepôt *emporia* was fierce, but it became fiercer in the depressed fourteenth and fifteenth centuries. It is not too much to say that it was the *ordo salis* which allowed Venice to remain competitive in those years and to defeat its rivals economically as well as politically. In the sixteenth century, when prosperity returned, Venice turned away from entrepôt to agriculture and industry and the importance of the *ordo salis* gradually declined. Thanks to the freight bounties, Venice kept her prices down, except of course the price of salt to her own subjects. A mass commodity at home subsidized luxury commodities abroad: the domestic poor were taxed for the benefit of the foreign rich. But even the consumer may have been better off overall as a result of the general economic acceleration effected by the system. Salt may have cost more in Padua, Verona, Bergamo and Brescia, but the consumer may have had a bigger income with which to buy it, so that to him salt indeed may have been relatively cheaper. As Hocquet says, in Venice salt mobilized a whole society in the interests of merchant capitalism[32] – to the advantage of everyone.

Money Supply

Another kind of acceleration was imparted by the salt administration to the Venetian economy by its expansion of the money supply.

This expansion took several forms, all of them variants of the principle that all increases in debt or credit are increases in money supply. First, the obligation to import salt in return, not for cash, but for undated promissory notes or cash futures, was tantamount not only to a forced loan from the transport merchants, but also to an increase in money in the shape of transferable and discountable government debt. Second, when *sconto*, the transfer to and discount of *fedi* by the *daziero*, became a regular practice arranged by the *Ufficio* itself, it was frequently accompanied by a postponement of the *daziero*'s date of payment. This was tantamount to a loan to him by the government, an equivalence recognized by the fact that he paid 10 per cent for the privilege,[33] and hence an increase in money supply. Third, from the fact that the *daziero* was willing to borrow back his own debt to the government, it must be inferred that he himself was conducting either capital or money operations which brought in more than 10 per cent. That such money operations were possible is shown by the fact that, in the fifteenth century, only interest rates which exceeded 15–18 per cent were considered usurious by the Church or in any way unusual.[34] Finally, the *Serenissima* itself used what it was owed by the *dazieri* as security for loans to itself. It both paid interest on them and repaid their capital by means of *fedi* on the *Camera Salis* which then entered once more into the cycle of *sconto*.[35] Thus in 1509, when Venice was in the middle of one of the worst crises in its history, the *Monte Novissimo*, the war loan, was placed under the direction of the *Ufficio*. Credits in the *Ufficio* became in effect a form of money which could be used to pay taxes, subscribe to government loans, or even to speculate in *fedi*.

In a traditional economy, in which bullion was still the principal form of money, insufficiency of supply was a greater danger than inflation. This was particularly so in the bullion-poor fourteenth and fifteenth centuries. The operations of the Venetian salt administration, which not only added to money supply but also multiplied it by increasing its velocity, could not fail to have an accelerating effect on the Venetian economy. Though salt might take a larger slice of the cake through state tax and monopoly price, the cake itself was bigger, because its growth was not inhibited, as elsewhere, by monetary insufficiency. Before the advent of the American mines, which in a sense threw the European monetary system back to a lower level of development, growth was lubricated more by fiduciary paper than actual bullion. The *ordo salis* contributed to that fiduciary paper.

Shipping

In addition to its subsidization of the entrepôt trade and its expansion of the money supply, the salt administration also promoted the acceleration of the Venetian economy by its contribution to business overheads in the form of shipping.

As a maritime public, the *Serenissima* was accustomed from an early date to contributing to shipping by building galleys at the Arsenal and auctioning their use to private investors in the *muda* system of convoy. This system was designed particularly to foster and protect the import and reexport of pepper and fine spices. It was not until the fifteenth century that the state began to take measures to increase the number of galleons in Venetian service, using salt funds for the purpose. First, the state commenced the construction of galleons on its own account. Two were ordered in 1453, the salt administration being one of the two agencies to which costs were assigned, and four more in 1490. Next, from 1469, the salt administration made loans to private shipowners to build galleons, repayable in salt brought from Cryprus and Ibiza over the four years after the first voyage. In 1534/5 freight bounties were increased to help in the repayment of loans and the time was extended to eight, later ten, years. Finally, foreign ships were allowed to naturalize themselves at Venice and Venetians were encouraged to buy vessels from abroad. Thanks to these measures, largely supported by salt funds because of the association between shipping, freight bounties, salt credits and revenue, Venice succeeded in maintaining, indeed improving her position as a shipowning community, where Genoa came increasingly to rely on foreign shipping – Basque, Ragusan and Nordic. It was only in the seventeenth century when salt once more came from the Adriatic, when freight bounties were no longer paid, when patricians preferred to invest in villas or silk factories,[36] that the Venetian galleon fleet declined along with the salt administration itself.

Societies, it has been said, tend to invest in themselves.[37] The economic activities of the Venetian salt administration in entrepôt trade, money supply and shipping are an example of that principle. They consolidated that alliance of big ships, big palaces on the Grand Canal, big estates on Terre Ferme, big family seats in the Grand Council, which was the social basis of the Venetian republic during its classic age.[38] The policy of the Venetian state in investing in its own infrastructure involved taxing the poor to subsidize the rich, but on a more profound calculation of profit and loss, it probably benefited the generality as much as Chinese welfare policy. It was not that the Chinese salt administration was philanthropic while the Venetian was not, but that public interest was conceived less simply in Venice and that in Venice there was a greater degree of osmosis between officials and merchants. The Chinese slogans *ping-shang yin-er ping-min* (To weaken commerce is to weaken the people) and *yü-kuo hsü-shang* (To enrich the state, be kind to merchants) were in the first case negative and in the second basically state centred. Certainly they were less forthright than the Venetian affirmation that salt was *il vero fundamento del nostro stato*, where *stato* meant not just the state, but society as well, the whole body politic.

Finally, beyond economics and sociology, the salt administration was also indirectly a patron of Venetian culture, another aspect of *min-sheng*. In addition to their position at the head of the *Ufficio*, the *Provveditori* held conjoint appointment as *Officiali sopra Rialto*.[39] In this capacity they acted as a ministry of works in charge of the maintenance of public buildings, the embellishment of churches, the upkeep of the Lido and the city's other hydraulic defences. Some of these items of expenditure had special sources of income assigned to them, but others were met out of salt surplus. Thus architects, painters, sculptors and other artists, engaged in the creation of the splendours of sixteenth-century Venice might have their salaries provided for by the *Provveditori*. The light of the world, one might say, was paid for by the salt of the earth.

THE SALT ADMINISTRATION IN THE VENETIAN STATE

Throughout the Middle Ages and early modernity, Venice was always at least a second class power, often something more, and between the dogeship of Francesco Foscari and the war of the League of Cambrai, an incipient superpower. As in China, the salt administration contributed to the greatness of the state in various ways: a proportion of regular finance obviously, but also to diplomacy and emergencies civil and military.

Regular Finance

It is not easy to establish the net receipts of the *Camera Salis*, total revenue of the *Serenissima*, and consequently the proportion of the one to the other. Table 7.1, however, is not likely to be very far out. Proportion of the total is not the only criterion for the importance of a tax. Factors such as relative regularity, certainty and availability for appropriation also need to be taken into consideration. Nevertheless, Table 7.1 suggests that the salt tax was of most significance at the beginning and at the end of the period under review: that is, the adolescence and senescence of the *Serenissima* as a great power.

Such a conjuncture is typical of salt taxes. One of their advantages in that they can be operated successfully with less than complete territorial control by the state. A state in the noonday of its power will be able to levy direct taxes on land, income or capital, but in the twilight of its growth, indirect taxes such as tolls, customs, excise or a salt tax may be all that is within its grasp until full power is achieved or recovered. Salt is the tax of the state builder: in China, of Sang Hung-yang of the Han or Liu Yen of the T'ang; in Venice, of the doges of the thirteenth century after Enrico Dandolo. Once the state is built, salt is relativized. Thus Venice, from the dogeship of Francesco Foscari to the war of the League of Cambrai, drew the greatest part of its revenue from the tribute of its subject cities and from direct taxes on its own citizens. In his discussion of the Venetian budget for 1500, F. C. Lane comments: 'Two of the largest items of receipts had been absent a century or two earlier: the payments from the mainland cities and the direct taxes collected in Venice'.[40] Another point to be noted about Table 7.1 is that while salt tax receipts rose between 1550 and 1650: in an exceptional year, 1582,

Table 7.1 Venetian salt and total revenues, 1400–1500 (ducats)

Year	Salt revenue	%	Total revenue
1400	150 000	30	500 000
1450	150 000	15	1 000 000
1500	100 000	10	1 000 000
1550	200 000	13	1 500 000
1600	300 000	15	2 000 000
1650	350 000	12	3 000 000

reaching a figure of over 600 000 ducats;[41] salt was losing its blue chip status. It came increasingly from the Adriatic salines, so ceased to carry a freight bounty and was less invested in by the patrician oligarchy. So in the last years of the republic, the dotage of the state, salt again became, as it had been in the state's infancy before the twelfth century, just a commodity subject to a sales tax.

Diplomacy

Two themes in the history of the Venetian salt administration are salt and diplomacy and diplomacy and salt. Between them they divide the territories of Venice's coprosperity sphere.

In the Mediterranean, thanks to abundant sources of supply, there was a buyer's market for salt. Sales of salt depended on diplomacy and trade followed the flag. The extent of Venice's salt empire depended on her political power and not vice versa. Thus when the *Serenissima* was at the height of its power, it sold salt not only in Milan, Mantua and Ferrara, but also in the Romagna, the March of Ancona, Emilia, even Perugia and Spoleto. Visconti and Sforza, Borgia pope and Este thought it worthwhile to eat the salt of Venice. Following the decline of Venetian power after 1509, things changed. With the need to conciliate the Papacy to break up the hostile coalition and the definite cession of Cervia and access to the Po in 1532, Venice progressively lost her market south of the river and in Emilia to Papal salt, mainly from Trapani and Ibiza, imported via the new transit emporium of Ancona. In Milan too, as the *Serenissima*'s diplomatic horizons contracted after the war of Cyprus, Venetian salt lost ground to landborne salt from Genoa and riverborne salt from Ancona. Spanish governors of Milan had nothing to hope or fear from Venice: much from Genoa and the Papacy.

Beyond the Mediterranean, in the pastoral highlands of southern Switzerland, Inner Austria, Croatia and Bosnia, where supply was weak and demand was strong, there was a seller's market for salt. Salt could be an instrument of diplomacy and the flag followed trade. This was particularly true in two areas: the Grisons and Inner Austria. In the period leading up to the Thirty Years' War, Venice was a member of the anti-Spanish bloc headed by France. Her chief contribution to that bloc was her potential influence in Switzerland: the Grisons in particular, which controlled the Spanish communications from Milan to the Rhine via the Valtelline. A means of actualizing that influence, at least of gaining goodwill, was the provision of Venetian salt to compete with Spanish salt from Franche Comté and Austrian salt from Tyrol. The expansion of sales of Venetian salt to southern Switzerland in general, the Protestant Grisons in particular, at the end of the sixteenth century, was thus a matter of significance in international diplomacy. Similarly, the provision of salt from Muggia, Capodistria, Piran and Pago to Inner Austria and the Croatian *militärgrenze* was a means of appeasing the Habsburgs of Graz and Vienna with whom Venice's relations were ambivalent. On the one hand, the eastern Habsburgs were allies of their Spanish cousins. Venice was virtually at war with the first between 1615 and 1617 in the campaign of Gradisca against the Uskoks and with the second between 1618 and 1619 when the Duke of Ossuna was Spanish viceroy in Naples. On the other hand, the eastern Habsburgs were potential allies for Venice against the Ottomans. Salt exports therefore were a means to secure local peace on the Isonzo while remaining globally anti-Spain, and to edge Vienna towards the stance which led eventually to the Holy League of 1684 between Austria, Poland and Venice against the Sultan. In the meanwhile, the Sultan might be appeased by the export of salt from Pago to Bosnia and from Sebenico and Corfu via Cattaro to Montenegro and Albania. With both the Habsburgs and the Ottomans, salt was a means of establishing minimum links, staving off hostilities, paving the way for alliances: an element in senescent Venice's highly successful *Ostpolitik*.

Civil Emergencies

The two commonest civil emergencies of premodern Europe were plague and famine. With both the Venetian salt administration was involved by its shipping: in the first case passively, in the second actively.

Venice was one of the first states in Europe to establish an effective quarantine service against the inroads of *yersinia pestis* from Central Asia and the new plague reservoir of Kurdistan.[42] *Provveditori di Sanita* were appointed in 1348. Further isolation laws were adopted in 1403 and a hospital established on San Lazzaro from which all lazarets were named. The board of health obtained additional powers in 1483. Its growing success was commemorated by the building of the *Redentore* in 1576 and

of the *Salute* in 1631, which celebrated at once divine power and bureaucratic effectiveness. To the *Provveditori di Sanita*, ships bringing in salt
were subject like any other. Their regulations added to the delays and
hence costs of the trade. Galleons coming from Cyprus so close to
known plague ports will have been particularly suspect. Salt ships
indeed may on occasion have been responsible for bringing plague to
Venice, since cotton, which often filled the upper decks of ships carrying
salt in the hold, was notoriously able to carry parasites.[43] Thus the
contraction of Venice's salt import to the Adriatic may have been a factor
in the growing success of the health administration.

With famine, salt was involved in two ways both concerning wheat.
In times of plenty, salt and wheat were partners. Wheat coming down
the rivers of northern Italy was balanced by salt going up. Barges could
take salt one way, wheat the other. Times of famine, salt and wheat
were rivals. When northern Italy could no longer supply Venice and
wheat had to be brought from the grain surplus ports of the Mediterranean – Palermo for Sicily, Volo for Thessaly – salt and wheat competed
for galleon hold space. As a rival, salt could easily be overriden by the
higher priorities of the *Officium Frumenti*. Indeed, it was a welcome rival,
since it kept shipping in being during out-of-emergency periods and
provided funds which could be mobilized to buy wheat. Though the
wheat office, like the Mint, received deposits, i.e. could borrow from the
public, it was generally in deficit, while the salt office, having more
income than outgoings, was generally in surplus, at least for credit
purposes. Salt and wheat therefore complemented each other. Again,
low wheat prices allowed large imports of salt, high wheat prices
compelled small imports of salt. Good times for salt paid for bad times
for wheat. Without the regular activity of the salt office, the irregular
activity of the wheat office would not have had the funds to buy grain or
the ships to transport it.[44] The salt administration therefore can claim
some credit for Venice's relative immunity from killing famine in the
sixteenth century.

Military Emergency

War was another emergency with which the Venetian salt administration was involved. As noted above, one of the advantages of a salt tax
is that it can still be collected in times of political weakness. In 1284, the
Grand Council armed a squadron for the coasts of Istria against the
growing disorder in the lands of the Crown of St Stephen during the
reign of Ladislas the Cuman, through the application of salt revenues. In
the early fifteenth century when Francesco Sforza was still a Venetian
condottiere, he received his pay through the salt office. During the critical
phase of the first Turkish war between 1470 and 1479, the war of

Negroponte, the salt office was often called upon to contribute funds or lend its credit. Finally, during the dark days after the battle of Agnadello during the war of the League of Cambrai, it was the salt office which assumed responsibility for the *Monte Novissimo* which tided the *Serenissima* over the emergency until its diplomacy could dissolve the coalition.[45] On this occasion, the salt administration might really claim to have saved the state.

Thus viewed from a Chinese perspective, the Venetian *ordo salis* appears as a true *yen-cheng*: fiscal, more than fiscal, bureaucratic and specialized. Structurally the Venetian salt administration was comparable to one of the major salt divisions of China, though it existed in a different geographical milieu and expressed different social values. Is it possible China actually influenced Venice? Most historians of Europe would reject the suggestion and Hocquet argues a fundamental continuity between earlier ecclesiastical and seigneurial salt institutions on the one hand and later communal and royal salt institutions on the other.[46] Yet there are some arguments in favour of a limited kind of diffusionism.

First, as we have argued, there is a discontinuity between state income from salt and a fully-fledged salt administration. It is striking that salt administrations appear rather suddenly in Europe in the century which experienced what Donald Lach calls 'the revelation of Cathay'.[47] True, this argument is not decisive because the more sophisticated anti-diffusionist theories can accommodate discontinuous as well as continuous change,[48] but it is suggestive.

Second, Chinese influence at this time is not impossible. In physical technology Joseph Needham makes a strong if traditional case for the transmission of the stern-post rudder, the magnetic compass and gunpowder in the twelfth and thirteenth centuries.[49] His information that the *trabaca* or *trabaccolo*, the salt lugger of Chioggia, not only uses a Chinese type sail, but also has the two Chinese features of absence of keel and huge rudders, is even more suggestive.[50] In the realm of ideas, there are indications of the influence of religious Taoism and Chinese alchemy in the writings of Albertus Magnus, Roger Bacon, the author of the *Aurora Consurgens*, Arnold of Villanova, John of Rupescissa the French Franciscan, and Petrus Bonus of Ferrara, probably transmitted through Arab sources: Rhazes, we know, had a Chinese pupil.[51] In particular, the conjuncture in the sixth part of Bacon's *Opus maius* of longevity theory, explosives and the transmutation of metals, seems too close to Chinese alchemy to be explained without influence from the east. If physical technology and iatrochemical theory could travel, why not administrative institutions?

Third, there is some reason to suppose Chinese influence was actual. The best evidence for diffusion is the presence in a process of some characteristic, but functionally unnecessary, even dysfunctional, detail. In the case of the parallel question of the diffusion from China of the technique of successive basin solar evaporation, that detail is the ratio of catchment and of condensers to crystallizers. In the case of salt adminis- tration structure, it is the rejection of deduction at source, *chiu-ch'ang cheng-shui* as the method of collection. In neither China nor Europe was deduction at source unknown. It was practised by Liu Yen of the T'ang and at the Polish saline of Wieliczka. But it was avoided both in Sung China and *Trecento* Venice, more for ideological than genuine adminis- trative reasons: an aesthetic preference almost, which could share a common origin. It is difficult not to think that the architects of the Venetian *ordo salis* knew something about the arrangements in Huai-nan or Ch'ang-lu.

Fourth, there is the evidence and possible influence of Marco Polo. Certainly Marco Polo regarded the salt administration as one of the *mirabilia* of China and claimed to have been governor of Yang-chou, the headquarters of Huai-nan, for three years.[52] In Ch'ang-lu, he notes that salt 'is a great source of wealth to the inhabitants and of revenue to the Great Khan'.[53] In Huai-an, the entrepôt for Huai-pei, he comments: 'The salt made here is exported to meet the needs of forty cities and more. So the Great Khan derives a huge revenue from this city, both from the salt and from the imposts on its trade'.[54] Going on into Huai-nan, he says: 'And at every place between here and the Ocean are produced great quantities of salt. . . . And you may take my word for it that the revenue accruing to the Great Khan from this source is so stupendous that, unless it were seen, it could scarcely be credited'.[55] Finally on arrival at Hangchow or Hsing-tsai, the 'temporary' capital of the Southern Sung, in Liang-che he writes:

> I will tell you next of the immense revenue that the Great Khan draws from this city of Kinsai. . . . First I will tell you of the salt, since this makes the biggest contribution to the total. You may take it for a fact that the salt of this city yields an average yearly income of 80 *tomauns* of gold: as a *tomaun* is equivalent to 70 000 *saggi* of gold, this brings the total to 5 600 000 *saggi* of which every *saggio* is worth more than a gold florin or ducat. This is indeed a thing to marvel at and an inordinate sum of money.[56]

When Marco Polo returned to Venice in 1295 and when his book was published around 1300, parts of the Venetian salt administration were already in existence. It could be argued then that Polo, or his ghost- writer Rustichello da Pisa, included so much about salt precisely because his Venetian public at least was already interested in it. But it must be remembered that Marco's uncles had returned from Peking in 1270 and would have been in a position to report on Ch'ang-lu. Moreover it is not certain that even the elder Polos were the first Venetians to go to China. The question of a Chinese influence, if not on the origins, then on the development and ultimate shape of the Venetian salt administration must therefore remain open. Certainly China and Venice, and perhaps at that time China and Venice alone, shared the conviction, basic to salt administrations, that salt was special: *'cum sal sit res diversa plurimum ab aliis mercacionibus'.*[57]

8 The French Salt Administration

From the greatest of the medieval European mercantile city states, we pass to the greatest of the early modern European bureaucratic monarchies. The *Gabelle*, as it existed from Colbert's ordinance of May 1680 to the revolution of 1789, was more like the Chinese salt administration than the Venetian. Like China, France was continental rather than maritime. As in China, so in France, rivers or canals were until the nineteenth century, the principal means of communication, rather than the sea or roads. As with successive Chinese dynasties, the French state was sacred and authoritarian, territorial and bureaucratic. In both China and France, the educated classes prized a semi-secular classicism in thought and action. A traditional Chinese salt administrator would have found himself more at home in the *Gabelle* than in the *Ufficio*. Colbert was blood brother to Sang Hung-yang, Liu Yen, Ts'ai Ching and a host of Chinese politician administrators, where the magnificoes of Venice were, in both cases, only distant relatives.

Yet *ancien régime* France was not imperial China. It was a state among states in a European world increasingly dominated by the sea and its trade. Much salt even in France took maritime routes. Colbert was a mandarin, but he had also to be a merchant. Here problems began. The French state might be bureaucratic: French society was not, but nor was it capitalistic either. The need to mobilize a non-capitalist economy in the interests of a bureaucratic state in an increasingly capitalist world, gave rise to the peculiar French institution of *finance*, of which Colbert was a leading exponent.[1] *Finance*, in the sense of a special kind of bureaucratic capitalism, had no true analogy in imperial China, unless it be the *ortaq* in the brief Yüan period. Something like it, however, did exist in republican China in the days of the Kuomintang.[2] Colbert was closer in type to T. V. Soong than to the famous mandarins named above. He was *par excellence* a reformist representative of *finance*. The *Gabelle*, which he did more than anyone else to shape, reflected the influence of *finance* at every level: the state in the salt administration, the state's taxes, the people's livelihood, and the salt administration in the state. The *Gabelle* under the *ancien régime* is often regarded as typical of salt administrations. Indeed, it has given its name to them all. Yet in fact it was highly untypical and idiosyncratic and most of its singularity derived from its association with the Colbertian phenomenon of *finance*.

204

THE STATE IN THE FRENCH SALT ADMINISTRATION

In France, as in China and Venice, salt administration had a long history. The first *Gabelle*, as opposed to simple taxation of or profit from salt by the state, was established by Count Charles of Provence, brother of St Louis, in 1259 for the salines of Berre west of Marseille. In 1290 the French crown acquired the salines at Peccais near Aigues Mortes. In 1301 an agreement, renewed in 1358, between the King of France and the Count of Provence to share the markets supplied by the Rhône between the salines of Aigues Mortes and the Camargue, laid the basis for the future *Pays de Petite Gabelle*. In 1341 Philip VI established the *Pays de Grande Gabelle* in northern France, his successor John consolidated it, and in 1369 it was intensified by his successor Charles V, to become a permanent financial support for the monarchy during its subsequent vicissitudes in the late Middle Ages and early modernity. In 1541, Francis I 'attempted a radical reform of the salt tax'[3] though without success. In June 1660, Louis XIV, recapitulating the experience of the two cardinals, referred to the *Gabelle* as 'un des principeaux soutiens de la dépense de notre Etat'.[4] It was, however, only with Colbert's ordinance of May 1680 which rationalized the institutions which had evolved over the preceding three centuries that the *Gabelle* reached its final and fullest form.

Like the Chinese and Venetian salt administrations, the *Gabelle* was both extended and indirect. It involved more than the taxation of salt and it did not operate exclusively through officials. As in China and Venice, it too could be characterized as *kuan-tu shang-pan*, official supervision and merchant management. But the importance of *finance* from the fall of Foucquet to the onset of the Revolution gave that formula a specifically French sense. Functions divided in China, united in Venice, in France were confused. Bureaucratic capitalism in France, as later under the Kuomintang, was more bureaucratic than capitalist, but it had feet in several camps. Thus Colbert was a mandarin acting as a merchant and becoming a marquis.

As an institution, *finance* grows at the interface of two weaknesses. On the one hand, there is a weakness of the state which cannot pay its way through taxes and lacks the credit to borrow from a public bank or formalized gilt-edged market. On the other hand, there is a weakness of business which cannot pay its way through profits and lacks the prospectus rating to raise capital from public subscription or a formalized new equity market. Bureaucratic capitalism meets these deficiencies by supplying the state with short-term loans and business with long-term capital, while first taking for itself turnover commissions, loan interest and business profit as well as 'invisibles' in the shape of political influence and social honour. In this way bureaucratic capitalism performs a service for the body politic which could be performed in no other way, at a cost which may not in fact be high. The public, however, sees the cost but not the service, so bureaucratic capitalism is seldom popular or esteemed, though at the end of the *ancien régime* Necker managed to be both a financier and a demagogue. In China, salt officials and salt merchants were two. In Venice they were one. In *ancien régime* France, they were a third party: a *tertius gaudens* between real officials, civil and military above, and real merchants, or rather the national bourgeoisie of rentiers and urban landowners, below. *Finance* was powerful but vulnerable and this produced the mixture of harshness and laxity which characterized the *Gabelle*. Both *kuan-tu* and *shang-pan* existed not for themselves but for a third thing. As Mollien, Napoleon's treasury minister said, 'La finance se croyait en possession d'état, comme la noblesse et la magistrature'.[5]

Overall official supervision was exercised by Colbert's successor the *controlleur-générale des finances*, by the *conseil des finances* which dated back to September 1661, and by the *comité contentieux des finances* which was established in June 1777. Within the government, the controller-general was more than a chancellor of the exchequer, less than a first lord of the treasury. He was the single most important minister, but in a ministry more like the American than the British cabinet, which did not bear collective responsibility and to which he could not appoint. Moreover, his office, the *contrôle général*, only gradually and imperfectly built up anything like treasury control over the expenditure of other departments. The *conseil des finances* was a top level committee of ministers and senior civil servants. Designed to provide leadership and to act as a clearing house, the *conseil* lacked the expertise and time to fulfil either function effectively and ended as a rubber stamp or occasional sounding board, which met only seven to eight times a year. More effective administratively was the *comité contentieux*. This was a working party of senior civil servants, mostly bureau chiefs from the controller-general's office, which handled routine and technicalities and left him free for policy. It became in effect the directorate of his department.

The *Gabelle* was only one tax under the purview of the controller-general and, as we shall see, one of diminishing importance as the state progressed. In the day-to-day administration of the *Gabelle*, the chief role was played, not by any group of civil servants, but by the *fermiers-généraux*, who contracted, six years at a time, for the customs, Paris *octroi*, salt and tobacco taxes which they then recovered, with profit from the consumers.[6] Unlike the *dazieri* in the *Stato da Terra*, each of whom administered his own farm, the farmers-general were a collectivity, in effect a joint stock company. Their nearest equivalent in China were the *kuei-shang* or farm merchants in Kwangtung who in the last years of the empire farmed the Weising lottery and the salt taxes. Like the *kuei-shang*, the farmers-general were a private body conducting public business for profit. In the eighteenth century they evolved into a remarkably efficient organization with a rational division of functions according to operations and areas, salaries rather than fees, promotion by merit, holidays with pay, and a superannuation fund.[7] The value of the farm steadily increased over the eighteenth century both to the government and to the shareholders. Technically, the farmers-general were a model piece of privatization: *finance* at its best and most rational. It is not without significance that Lavoisier was a working and effective member of its management.

The *Gabelle* was more centrally organized than the salt administration in China, but less centrally organized than that in Venice. Within France, it was arranged in six zones, roughly the equivalent of salt divisions or *yin-ti* in China, to which one should add a seventh, France's export market for salt, roughly the equivalent of Venice's coprosperity sphere. The six domestic zones were the *Pays de Grande Gabelle*, the *Pays de Petite Gabelle*, the *Pays de Salines*, the *Pays redimées*, the *Pays exempts* and the *Quart Bouillon*.

Table 8.1 The *Gabelle* in 1789

Zone	Population	Salt (cwt)	Per capita (livres)	Price (sous per livres)
Grande Gabelle	8 300 000	760 000	9	12–13
Petite Gabelle	4 600 000	540 000	12	6–8
Pays de Salines	1 960 000	275 000	14	2–6
Pays redimées	4 625 000	830 000	18	2
Pays exempts	4 730 000	830 000	18	1
Quart Bouillon	585 000	115 000	19	4
Export	—	650 000	—	—
Total	24 800 000	4 000 000	—	—

The Grand Gabelle

The salt administration was most highly organized in the *Pays de Grande Gabelle*, which produced two thirds of the revenue from one third of the population and one quarter of the salt distributed domestically. The *Grande Gabelle* covered most of northern France, the heartland of royal authority, and was what most people thought of in connection with salt administration. In its structure, it epitomized the fiscal inequalities, the incompleteness of the state, and the disregard of public opinion prevalent in the *ancien régime*. Yet in its way the *Grande Gabelle* was a remarkable fiscal contrivance. In Chinese terms its organization could be described as *min-chih, shang-shou, shang-yün, kuan-hsiao* (people produce, merchants receive, merchants transport, officials distribute), though this combination is never in fact found in China.

Salt for the *Grande Gabelle* was supplied by sea from the successive basin solar evaporation works at Brouage in Saintonge, the largest in Europe. These works were owned privately, could be bought and sold freely, and formed a normal avenue of investment. Among the investors, ecclesiastical corporations had at one time been prominent, but by the eighteenth century, as a result of the wars of religion in general and the revolt of La Rochelle in particular, they had become less conspicuous. The only outstanding elements among the heterogeneous owners were merchants from La Rochelle, magistrates from Bordeaux and retired naval officers from Rochefort. As a rule owners did not manage their own salines. These were leased to saltmasters (*sauniers*) on a *métayage* basis of two thirds of the harvest plus right of prior sale to the owner, one third plus right of cultivation of unused margins to the tenant. Both ownership and tenancy were small scale. Ten sets of evaporating basins was the average for ownership: about 12.5 acres *in toto*. Tenants generally confined their activity to four or five sets. Salt making in Saintonge was artisanal and familial, except for the large holdings of a few merchants and magistrates, and thus could safely be left to private enterprise.

Once it left the salines, salt entered a world dominated by the privileged merchants who were the key element in the *Grande Gabelle*. As in China, the salt trade was much divided. First, local merchants bought from the owners and tenants. Next, the local merchants sold to provincial merchants, generally from La Rochelle. Finally, export brokers, for much of the eighteenth century the Vallet families of Salignac and La Touche, bought from the provincial merchants and sold to the commissary-general of the *Gabelle*, i.e., the buying agent of the farmers-general. Reminiscent of export brokers in China, the *ch'ang-shang* in Huai-nan or the *ao-sheng* in Liang-che, the Vallet were powerful figures, frequently complained of by the producers. They owned 300 saltfields which gave them a sizeable stake in the supply. They engaged in trade on their own account to the *Pays redimées*. They imported salt from Portugal to keep down local prices. They exported salt to the Baltic as well as supplying it to the *Gabelle*. Moreover they acquired the commissary-general himself as a son in law, purchased offices in the local judiciary, acquired seigneuries and *noblesse*, and eventually through a fortunate marriage inherited Diane de Poitiers' chateaux of Chenonceaux. Though in the end they lost the position of monopoly export brokers at Brouage through the opposition of local interests supported by court protectors, they remained part of the successful world of *finance*. Furthermore they were succeeded by another *finance* ring and the producers were never able to deal direct with the commissary-general as they wished.

From the personal empires of the export brokers, salt passed into the impersonal hands of the farmers-general. The commissary-general had his headquarters successively at Brouage itself, Marennes and Ars, with suboffices at La Rochelle, Angoullins, Saint-Laurent-de-la Brée and Marans. Marennes was the chief port. Monopoly fleets, *flottes du Parti*, of up to 50 ships, sailed thence irregularly to the ports of northern France: Honfleur, Caen, St Valéry-sur-Somme, St Valéry-en-Caux, Dieppe, Le Tréport. The *Gabelle* did not itself own the ships. Transport was subcontracted, mainly to shipmasters from those ports, or to Dutch or Hanseatic vessels; but also secondarily to smaller Breton ships or local shipping from Saintonge and Aunis. Transport was to the warehouses of the *Gabelle* at the Channel ports, that at Honfleur at the mouth of the Seine being particularly important because of the Paris market.

From the warehouses at the ports, salt was taken, again under subcontract, by barge as far as possible, by cart thereafter, to the 253 *greniers à sel* or salt depots which were the distributing agency of the salt administration in the *Pays de Grande Gabelle*. Along with the role of *finance* noted above and the institution of *sel de devoir* to be discussed below, the *greniers à sel* were a unique feature of the French salt administration. This will be plain from the next section where their function in relation to the state's taxes is examined. One facet of that uniqueness was that, though the salt remained the property of the farmers-general until it passed into the hands of the public, the *greniers à sel* were official bodies exercising the coercive power of the state. Whereas in China the power of officials or privileged merchants generally ran out at the level of retail, in France official control began there. The nearest analogue in China to the *greniers à sel* were the government sales offices set up after 1908 in northern Manchuria, 25 in Kirin and 18 in Heilungkiang, to supply local retailers. But these bodies operated further upstream and did not have the same fiscal functions as the French institution. Among major salt administrations, the *greniers à sel* were unique to France.

The Petite Gabelle

The salt administration was less highly organized in the *Pays de Petite Gabelle*: Languedoc, Provence, part of the Auvergne and the valley of the Rhône. However, from one fifth of the French population and one sixth of the salt it consumed, it produced one quarter of the salt revenue. The *Petite Gabelle* was the oldest stratum of the French salt administration. It went back to Charles of Anjou's nationalization of the salines of Berre in

1259 and the subsequent cartel agreements of the King of France and Count of provence to share the markets of the Midi in both the Kingdom and the Empire. In Chinese terms its organization could be described as *kuan-chih, shang-yün, shang-hsiao* (officials produce, merchants transport, merchants distribute), an inversion of the position in the *Grande Gabelle*, which again did not exist in China.

Salt for the *Petite Gabelle* was supplied by the successive basin solar evaporation salines of Languedoc and Provence: Sigean (Narbonne), Agde and Peccais in Languedoc; Camargue, Berre, Hyères in Provence. Except for Agde, all these were of considerable antiquity as producers of salt, going back to the Dark Ages and even to Roman times, though not, of course, as using the successive basin method. Agde only became a major producer after 1681 when it became the southern terminus of the Canal du Midi. Peccais, the principal source of salt for the *Petite Gabelle* was owned by the crown, though leased to subcontractors, and there was a considerable official presence always at Berre and most of the other salines. In this country of *allodia* rather than fiefs, where Roman law was less modified by custom than in the north, the notion of state property in minerals came naturally, and this was probably the background to Charles of Anjou's original nationalization of Berre.

From the salines, salt passed into the hands of privileged merchants. In the eighteenth century, they were no longer Florentine as they had been in the fourteenth, but French, part of the world of *finance* and associates of the farmers-general. Louis Dermigny, in the course of a comparison between the sociology of Liang-huai and that of the *Gabelle*, traces the history of the Vassal family of Agde and Montpellier, who were salt merchants, financial officials, farmers-general, marrying into the high robe before the Revolution and into the Napoleonic aristocracy after it.[8] The Vassal at Agde-*Vas saliens* according to their coat of arms – were similar to the Vallet at Brouage. Unlike the Vallet, however, they were not just export brokers but transport merchants as well. From the salines, they and their kind transported the salt, by water mainly – the Canal du Midi for Languedoc, the Rhône and its tributaries such as the Isère for other parts of the *Petite Gabelle* – to 135 *greniers à sel*, which sold to wholesalers, salt vendors and retailers, and direct to the public. In the *Petite Gabelle*, the *greniers à sel* were less under official direction than those in the *Grande Gabelle* and the officials were those of the local Estates rather than the crown. Except at the level of production the *Petite Gabelle* was in effect a merchant rather than an official monopoly. There were an interlocking series of merchants who acted as subsidiaries of the farmers-general. Thus in the small distributing centre of Romans on the Isère, the salt trade was in the hands of the 20–30 members of the elite guild of St Matthew: an appropriate patron for the publicans and sinners of a micro-world of *finance*.[9]

The Pays de Salines

These comprised, in order of acquisition by the crown, the Trois Évêchés, Alsace, Franche Comté and ducal Lorraine. They were distinctive in being supplied not by marine salt but by inland wells, whose brine was boiled to produce what in China would be called *chien* salt. They contained 8 per cent of the French population, consumed about 7 per cent of the salt, and produced about one twelfth of the revenue. The salt administration was quite highly organized in the *Pays de Salines*, but it was concentrated almost exclusively at the beginning of the circuit from producer to consumer. In Chinese terms, its organization could be described as *kuan-chih, shang-yün, min-hsiao* (officials produce, merchants transport, people distribute), yet again a combination not found in China.

In 1789 the *Gabelle* operated six sets of wells in the *Pays de Salines*. In order of output these were Dieuze, Moyenvic, Chateau-Salins, in Lorraine; Salins, Montmorot and Chaux (or Arc et Senans) in Franche Comté. All had come into the possession of the French crown relatively recently, but partly for this reason had not had time to suffer privatization. Moyenvic in the bishopric of Metz had been in French hands since Henry II's occupation of the Trois Évêchés in 1552, but was reoccupied by the emperor during the Thirty Years' War and was not securely French till the peace of Westphalia in 1648. Dieuze and Chateau-Salins, in ducal Lorraine, were occupied by Richelieu in 1634 and remained effectively French till the peace of Ryswick in 1697 restored the duke. It was not until the cession of the duchy in 1738 by the Treaty of Vienna to Louis XV's father-in-law Stanislas Leszcynski that France obtained definite control. Salins came into French possession in 1679 when the treaty of Nymegen transferred Franche Comté from the Habsburgs to the Bourbons. Montmorot and Chaux were new establishments of the eighteenth century, set up chiefly to supply Swiss export markets: in the case of Montmorot, notably to Neuchâtel.

In both Lorraine and Franche Comté, the French crown inherited traditions of state control of production. In Lorraine, the export of salt to Alsace and Switzerland, Strasbourg and Basle in particular, as well as to the Palatinate and Trier, had been the principal financial support of the dukes during their two periods of genuine independence at the end of the sixteenth century and at the beginning of the eighteenth. At times salt provided them with half or even two thirds of their budget and one authority has referred to 'ducal capitalism'.[10] In Franche Comté, the *Grande Saunerie* or *Grande Saline* in the upper town at Salins had been, as we have seen, a major interest of the Burgundian Duke-Counts and their Habsburg successors extended it to the *Puits à Muire* or *Petite Saline* in the lower town. By 1665 the King of Spain was the sole shareholder in both concerns, a position transferred to the King of France in 1679.[11] Montmorot, however, was the creation of private enterprise, first from Neuchâtel, later from Paris, but it was entirely dependent on supplies of wood arranged by the intendant and subdelegate.[12] Arc et Senans, on the other hand, was the work of the *Conseil du Roi* itself acting through Claude-Nicholas Ledoux as inspector-general of the salines of Franche Comté.

Although at each of the six production centres of the *Pays de Salines* there was a large element of regalian right, management and marketing were in the hands of privileged merchants, either the farmers-general themselves or financial groups associated with them. Thus at Arc et Senans, Ledoux worked with a group headed by Jean-Roux Monelor, who was also active at Montmorot. These privileged merchants arranged for the transportation of salt, mainly by land, to the consuming centres. In the *Pays de Salines*, there was no *greniers à sel* and wholesale and retail were left to private enterprise. All in all the system worked well. *Per capita* consumption of salt was 50 per cent higher in the *Pays de Salines* than in the *Grande Gabelle* and there was much less friction. In addition the *Pays de Salines* was the most technically innovative of the sections of the *Gabelle*, as is evidenced by the introduction of coal at Dieuze, graduation (wind tunnelling) at Arc et Senans, and improved stoves and hydraulic pumps at Salins. Already under the *ancien régime* the *Pays de Salines* was building its future as part of the successful Rhenanian France of the nineteenth and twentieth centuries.

The Pays Redimées

The salt administration was only lightly organized in the *Pays redimées*, but this fact was a significant aspect of the *Gabelle* as a whole which powerfully contributed to its less satisfactory features.

The *Pays redimées* lay in the southwest, essentially the old Anglo-Angevin duchy of Greater Aquitaine. They included Poitou, most of the Auvergne, the Angoumois, Limousin and Périgord, Aunis and Saintonge, Guyenne and Gascony. As English territory till the middle of the fifteenth century, Aquitaine had never formed part of either the *Grande* or *Petite Gabelle*. In 1541 Francis I undertook an ambitious reform which if successful might have altered the history of the *Gabelle*, even of the monarchy.[13] First, by the edict of Châtellerault of 1 June, he changed the existing light sales taxes on salt in the southwest into a single heavy duty to be collected on the saltfield: the system in China known as *chiu-ch'ang cheng-shui* or deduction at source. In April 1542 the rate of duty was reduced by nearly half, but the scheme still ran into strong opposition, especially from La Rochelle, and in May 1543 it was dropped. Next year, however, in ordinances of 1 July and December, the King adopted an alternative approach. He planned to extend the *Grande Gabelle* system of *greniers à sel* to all provinces except Brittany and the lands of the *Petite Gabelle*. This move produced the much more serious disturbance of the *Pitauts*.[14] This was a revolt of farmers, village notables and lower clergy which, between 1542 and 1548, spread from the backblocks of Angoulême to the vineyards of the Gironde to the mob and even magistrates of Bordeaux, with the cry 'Vive le Roi sans Gabelle', and put 40 000 men under arms.[15]

Faced with this prototype of the leagues of the second half of the sixteenth century, the new king, Henry II, who had come to the throne in 1547, retreated. In 1553, at war with the emperor in Germany and Italy and near the end of his financial resources, he agreed to abandon permanently radical salt reform and existing salt taxes in return for a guaranteed annual income. This was to be raised by tolls on salt and other commodities travelling inland, notably via the Charente and the Garonne. Other factors which no doubt influenced the King were the increasing prosperity of this part of Atlantic France and hence the potential value of its tolls, especially on wine; the lingering inclination of Bordeaux to look to a still imperial England; and the growth of Protestantism in the area. At the beginning of one's reign it was best to be prudent.

The importance of Henry II's retreat has not always been sufficiently appreciated. From a purely administrative point of view, there was something to be said for it. Geographically, the *Pays redimées* were not unlike Liang-che: a sea of straits, islands and a salt producing foreshore; a thickly populated, urbanized estuary; and a thinly populated mountain backdrop. Salt producing areas, like Aunis and Saintonge, or in China, the Chusan archipelago and nearby coast, were notoriously difficult to tax, except by measures most *ancien régimes* deemed beyond their grasp. Similarly, urbanized regions close to scattered salt works, like the Gironde, or in China the Su Wu-shu, were hard to control effectively. Finally, a mountain backdrop like the Limousin or Gascony, or in China rural, inland Chekiang, would not repay a heavy investment in salt administration. Best, it might be argued, to ride on a loose rein.

Yet there were arguments the other way. First, the failure to impose the *Gabelle* on the southwest, a failure enshrined in Colbert's ordinance of 1680, was a confession of political weakness. It was a symptom of that incompleteness of the state which was to dog the French monarchy till the Revolution and to be one cause of its downfall. Second, the *Pays redimées* were large consumers of salt: larger in fact on both counts than the *Grande Gabelle*. All salt administrations are incomplete to greater or less extent, but the existence of the *Pays redimées*, a free trade area in low priced salt with open frontiers, made the administration of the *Grande Gabelle* that much harder. All salt administrations tend to blame their own shortcomings on smuggling, but there is no doubt that there was considerable contraband from Poitou to Anjou.

The farmers-general made several attempts in the eighteenth century to assert a measure of control over the *Pays redimées*. Trade there was handled by *fournisseurs* who imported salt; *minotiers*, primary whole-salers, who distributed it from 40 depots; *marchands de sel* and *revendi-deurs*, secondary and tertiary wholesalers; and *regrattiers*, retailers. In 1722 the General Farm tried to limit the number of *minotiers* at the depots and impose on them fixed import quotas. In 1749 Machault, as part of his programme of increasing taxation of which the *vingtième* was the showpiece, gave the General Farm the right to nominate the *minotiers* and tightened up on the quotas. These measures were strongly opposed by the *Parlement* of Bordeaux. In 1773, during the period when the *parlements* were suspended, Terray gave the General Farm a monopoly of sale to the *Pays redimées*, i.e. allowed it virtually to take over the *fournisseurs* and the *minotiers*. With the return of the *parlements*, how-ever, Turgot, who had learnt his trade as intendant in the Limousin and as a physiocrat was no friend to the *Gabelle*, in 1774 restored the status quo of nominations and quotas. Thus, though the General Farm did not absorb the *Pays redimées*, it did increase its power over it significantly. Nevertheless, this advance did not recover the ground lost by Henry II to the *Pitauts*. The *Gabelle* remained radically incomplete.

The Pays exempts

The salt administration was least highly organized in the *Pays exempts* at the opposite end of the spectrum from the *Grande Gabelle*. As with the *Pays redimées*, exemption of certain areas was a fact of importance for the *Gabelle* as a whole, because the *Pays exempts* were large consumers of salt, first equal with the *Pays redimées* in absolute quantity and with them only just behind the *Quart Bouillon* in *per capita* consumption. The two most significant of the *Pays exempts* were Brittany and the new territories of the northeast: Artois, French Flanders and Hainaut. Essentially the *Pays exempts*, which also included Navarre plus a few coast areas, were territories originally not part of France and not endowed with salt administrations of their own, which on their inclusion in the kingdom, were given exemption from the *Gabelle* as a privilege, or bribe, for membership.

From an administrative point of view, the northeastern territories would not have been difficult to include within the *Gabelle*. They were supplied by sea via Boulogne, Calais and Dunkirk, whose merchants came to buy at Brouage and ship from Marennes, just as the farmers-general did. Taxation by Paris might have led to an influx of salt from the Austrian Netherlands which also supplied itself partly from Brouage via

Ostend, but this could probably have been contained. As it was, the northeastern merchants were sometimes accused by the farmers-general of offloading salt on the coasts of the *Grande Gabelle* as they passed by, though this maritime contraband does not seem to have been a major problem. Basically it was the politics of a sensitive frontier which kept the northeast out of the *Gabelle*, but fiscally it was unfortunate because these provinces were rich, urbanized and industrial.

More serious was Breton smuggling, especially on the forested border with Maine and Anjou and in the Loire Valley. Brittany of course was a major producer of salt at Bourgneuf and Guérande and it was perhaps only the export trade, the large local consumption by the fisheries, plus a certain conservatism in the organization of production which prevented the smuggling problem from being worse than it was. Colbert avoided tangling with Breton autonomy: probably because of his concern for the fisheries and the navy. Subsequently, as with the *Pays redimées*, the farmers-general tried to establish rights of policing in Brittany, but these attempts were vigorously opposed by the Estates and the *Parlement* of Rennes. In 1770 Terray annoyed Breton public opinion by prohibiting temporarily the export of salt to provide against a harvest shortfall of Brouage salt for the *Pays redimées* and the northeast, he said; to give the farmers-general a monopoly of purchase, the Estates said. So strong was the opposition that the minister had to withdraw the prohibition within a month, much to the embarrassment of the intendant who had gone out on the line for him. Later the export trade of Guérande was hit by the costly American War: another source of friction which joined the threat of higher taxation in generating the Breton *fronde*, which ushered in the Revolution.[16] Even more than the *Pays redimées*, the *Pays exempts* were an instance of the incompleteness of the French state and its salt administration, so that it weighed too heavily on a single area. The fault of the *Gabelle* was not to tax salt, but not to tax enough salt.

The Quart Bouillon

An anomaly but an interesting one, the *Quart Bouillon* comprised the modern department of Manche. With a population of 585 000, it consumed 155 000 cwt of salt a year, all of it produced locally. The *Quart Bouillon* combined modernity and primitivity. On the one hand, it had the highest *per capita* consumption of salt of any section of the *Gabelle*. On the other hand, it produced its salt by a method of boiling marine brine reinforced by filtration through the ash of saline plants or salt-impregnated sand which, except for the lead vats in which evaporation took place, went back directly to Celtic Europe.[17] On this salt which was produced by 380 privately owned establishments, the farmers-general collected a light excise from *bureaux de revente* near the salines. Their main worry was that *Quart Bouillon* salt might be smuggled into the *Grande Gabelle*, as some certainly was. Accordingly the opening of new boiling establishments was forbidden, the number of employees at each establishment was limited and no more than 80 days a year might be worked. It was a system in Chinese terms of *min-chih, shang-shou, min-hsiao* (people manufacture, merchants receive, people distribute) with no transport since the sales were purely local. Localism it was which maintained the *Quart Bouillon*. During the financial stringency of the Thirty Years' War, the extension of the *Grande Gabelle* to the *Quart Bouillon* was mooted, but Richelieu, like Henry II in the southwest, was intimidated by the *Nu-Pieds*, a revolt of farmers, local notables and lower clergy, the Norman equivalent of the *Pitauts*.[18] Normandy in the eighteenth century was a rich agricultural area, successful and literate. At the price of primitivity of production, the inhabitants of the *Quart Bouillon*, a poorer part of it, could afford modernity of consumption through exclusion from the *Grande Gabelle*.

Export

In addition to their domestic commitments, four sections of the *Gabelle* also supplied foreign markets and in three of these the salt administration was involved.

First, the *Grande Gabelle*, through its source of supply at Brouage, also supplied the northern market of the Austrian Netherlands, Holland and the Baltic. Its privileged merchants invested in this trade in their private capacities and its profit and loss offset those of their official business. Overtime losses may have outweighed profits, because the French salt trade to the north declined in the eighteenth century because of dyseconomies of scale at home, high freight and increasing competition from Cheshire. Second, the *Petite Gabelle*, through its source of supply at Peccais, also supplied the eastern market of the Catholic cantons of southern Switzerland opened by the Franco-Swiss treaties of 1658, 1663 and 1674. This export was known as the *sel d'alliance*. Third, the *Pays de Salines*, Franche Comté, acquired in 1679 and Lorraine fully controlled from 1738, through their sources of supply at Salins, Montmorot, Arc et Senans, Dieuze, Chateau-Salins and Moyenvic, also supplied another eastern market: the Protestant cantons of western Switzerland, opened by a series of treaties between 1677 and 1782, together with parts of the Palatinate, Trier and Luxemburg. This export was known as the *sel de commerce*, but both it and the *sel d'alliance* were the concern of the French government in Paris because of their diplomatic aspects and neither were simple commercial operations.

Finally, the *Pays exempt* of Brittany also exported salt: mainly to the Austrian Netherlands, Holland and the Baltic, but in addition to Ireland,

Wales and the English West Country, especially Exeter. In this trade, the *Gabelle* was not directly involved. Indeed, it disapproved of it as a possible source of smuggling and would have preferred to keep Breton salt as a reserve supply for the domestic market. But the export continued and Parisian *finance* became involved to some extent via the smuggling of tea and alcohol to England which accompanied it, especially from the boom salt and smuggling port of Roscoff on the north coast of Brittany.[19] With export, as with other matters, the *Gabelle* occupied a middle position between Venice and China, less concerned than Venice, more concerned than China. In 1789, though fallen from the best days of Bourgneuf and Brouage, the export of salt from France was still a considerable quantity.

THE STATE'S TAXES IN THE FRENCH SALT ADMINISTRATION

In the assessment, collection and receipt of tax, the *Gabelle* showed many similarities to the salt administration under the Ch'ing, but also notable differences: in what was assessed, where collection was made, and whither tax was sent. These differences stemmed from the dominance of *finance*, the fact that what was being operated was a tax farming system, and the basic weaknesses of both the state and business on which that dominance rested.

Assessment

In both China and France, much salt went unassessed and assessment was consequently inequitable, but underassessment and inequity went much further in France than in China. In 1541, as we have seen, the ministers of Francis I proposed to make the salt tax comprehensive by deducting tax at source near the salines, what in China would have been called *chiu-ch'ang cheng-shui*. Similar schemes were mooted by Richelieu in 1628 and by Calonne in 1787, but in all three cases the government retreated in the face of opposition.[20] These retreats both shaped the character of the *Gabelle* and had serious repercussions in the finances of the *ancien régime*. In 1789 the *Gabelle* raised nearly 60 m livres from the 4 million cwt of salt produced in France, an average of 15 livres a cwt. But nearly 40 m livres of this was raised from the less than 1 million cwt of salt consumed in the *Grande Gabelle*, an average of 40 livre a cwt. If Francis I, Richelieu or Calonne had succeeded in taxing all salt in France, then the rate could have been reduced to 20 livres a cwt and the state would have obtained 80 m livres instead of 60 m livres. Such an increase of 20 m livres would have been sufficient to finance a loan of 200 m livres, very useful in sudden deficit or wartime finance. The failure to tax all salt, much more glaring in France than in Venice, made the *Gabelle* at once inadequate to the state and, where it did operate, oppressive to society.

Such inequities existed in China, but they were less extreme and more was done about them. Thus in 1800, as we have seen, Liang-huai, like the *Grande Gabelle*, provided two thirds of the tax, though from a third, not a quarter, of the salt. By 1900, however, these figures had changed to 28 per cent and 19 per cent. In Szechwan, a province about the size of France, in 1900, the *pien-an* or border ports along the Yangtze and in Kweichow and Yunnan produced 40 per cent of the tax from 24 per cent of the salt, while the *chi-an* or reckoned ports in Central Szechwan produced 14 per cent of the tax from 33 per cent of the salt. From 1903, however, measures were taken to rectify this imbalance, so that by 1918 the *pien-an* paid 19 per cent of the tax, the *chi-an* 33 per cent. In France, the inequity of the *Grande Gabelle* was more extreme and less was done about it long term.

The inequity was compounded by the object of assessment. This was the *sel de devoir*: the obligatory purchase of 7 lb of salt by those liable to the tax, which, as Pasquier notes, gave it the character of a direct, rather than an indirect impost; in effect, a poll tax.[21] The *sel de devoir* was not absolutely unique to France. It was also to be found in the monopoly administered by Piacenza over salt from Salsomaggiore from the period 1270–1280 and there are indications that the principle of a certain *per capita* consumption was at one time used at least for calculating the potential yield of each *Dazio* in the *Stato da Terra*.[22] The *Gabelle*, however, alone among major salt administrations, made *sel de devoir* a major and permanent feature of its assessment in the key sector, the *Grande Gabelle*.

The *sel de devoir* was introduced into the *Grande Gabelle* in 1369 by Charles V.[23] Was it borrowed from Italy where Charles of Anjou, the founder of the *Petite Gabelle*, had been lord of Piacenza? This is unlikely both because of the long time lag and because the *sel de devoir* never formed part of the *Petite Gabelle*. Nor does Marco Polo's account of the salt administration under the Yüan contain any hint of obligatory purchase by the consumer, a practice which in fact never existed in China. More likely, the *sel de devoir*, with its implicit assumption that taxation is of people rather than things, was a product of the circumstances of the mid-fourteenth century when the monarchy, barely standing after the disasters of the reign of John II, was trying to operate a kind of *levée en masse* against its enemies internal and external. The *sel de devoir* was a counterpart to the *taille personelle* which, originally seigneurial, was 'lent' to the crown to pay the ransom of John II in 1356 and became exclusively royal in 1439 under Charles VII. It expressed the limited power of a monarchy which had made itself immediate in the feudal sense, but not fully territorial.

Collection

Salt tax was collected in the *Grande Gabelle*, the *Petite Gabelle*, the *Pays de Salines*, and the *Quart Bouillon*. As has been noted, the collections in the *Grande Gabelle* were the most important. The collecting agency was the *grenier à sel*, a state rather than mercantile body, which collected tax at a single point and at the latest possible moment: when salt passed to the consumer. Two factors lay behind this late point of collection. First, the object of assessment was the individual taxpayer's *sel de devoir* rather than trade in salt in general. Second, collection in accordance with what the Chinese would have called *hsien-yen hou-li* (first salt then toll), minimized the need for capital on the part of the farmers-general. If tax had been deducted at source in accordance with *hsien-k'o hou-yen* (first tax then salt), far more capital would have been required and it is doubtful if French business could have provided it. Collection by *grenier à sel* direct from the public reflected the weakness of French business, just as assessment only in the *Gabelle* of *sel de devoir* reflected the incompleteness of the French state.

In the *Grande Gabelle* there were three kinds of *grenier à sel*. First there were 181 *greniers de vente volontaire*. This did not mean, as some have supposed, that the taxpayer was free to buy his salt or not. Except in privileged Burgundy, this kind of freedom did not exist in the *Grande Gabelle*. What was free in the territories of the *greniers de vente volontaire*, which were mainly in the middle of the *Grande Gabelle* where evasion by buying salt smuggled in from other sections of the *Gabelle* was difficult, was the time of purchase. The taxpayer could choose the moment of paying his salt/poll tax to suit his own convenience. Second, there were 35 *greniers de sel d'impôt*, which were mainly on the borders of the *Grande Gabelle*. Here the taxpayer had no freedom of time. In each parish, village collectors were appointed by the officials of the *grenier à sel* to collect half of what was due by the middle of February each year and thereafter one eighth at the end of each quarter. It was the business of the collectors to hustle payment along and to distrain on goods for non-payment, the village as a whole being liable if even distraint failed to produce the requisite. Finally, there were 37 *greniers mixtes*, between the border and the middle, where some parishes had *vente volontaire*, others *sel d'impôt*. In the territories of all three kinds of *grenier*, the *sel de devoir* was only for the table: 'à l'usage du pot et salière seulement'. Further salt could be purchased, for things like bacon or ham curing, *grosses salaisons* and for feeding to animals, but only under strict safeguard and declaration of purpose by the buyer. Since the *sel de devoir* was 7 lb and the official *per capita* consumption of salt in the *Grande Gabelle* was 9 lb, *grosses salaisons* and animal foodstuffs amounted to 2 lb a head per year.

In the *Petite Gabelle* too there were *greniers à sel*, but there, since there was no *sel de devoir*, they were only depots like the sales offices in Kirin and Heilungkiang, from which wholesalers, retailers and consumers bought, paying the tax in the price of salt. Purchasers were, however, under the obligation to buy salt from the particular *grenier à sel* in whose territory they lived. In earlier times multiple collections of tax were made by tolls along the Rhone and its tributaries, but in the course of the eighteenth century most of these seem to have been suppressed. In the *Pays de Salines*, there were no *greniers à sel*. Tax was therefore paid at source by the merchants as it left the factory in accordance with the principle *hsien-k'o hou-yen*. That this was possible argues greater capital resources in the merchants of the progressive east. The same system was also operated in the *Quart Bouillon*. In the *Pays redimées*, there was no salt tax as such, though salt did fall under local transit taxes especially on rivers like the Charente and Garonne. In the *Pays exempts* salt was not taxed at all. Salt exported was generally untaxed in the case of Brouage and Breton salt; taxed in the case of salt from Peccais, Franche Comté and Lorraine. None of these collections, of course, compared with that of the *Grande Gabelle*.

Receipt

One of the major achievements of French financial administration during the last century of the *ancien régime* was centralization of tax receipts. This was something never attempted in China before the last decade of the empire and never accomplished before the revolution of 1911. In France particular progress was made during the ministry of Archbishop Loménie de Brienne 1787–8, an inept politician and unedifying pastor, but an excellent administrator. He brought back and extended the centralizing work of the first Necker ministry 1776–81 after the previous plurality of treasuries had been allowed to revive by Calonne. Necker's famous *compte rendu* of 1781, much less defective when its principles and purpose are understood than his contemporary critics or subsequent historians have allowed, was a firstfruit of this centralization.[24] This document may be compared to the imperial Chinese budgets of 1910, 1911 and 1912 drawn up under the direction of the energetic minister of finance Duke Tsai-tse.

Centralization of receipt left fewer balances in local or private hands for less lengthy periods. It therefore deprived *finance* of opportunities for profit, but in itself centralization was not against *finance*. It simply forced it to adopt more modern methods of borrowing from and lending to the state and to maximize profits by expanding the scale of operations rather than by maintaining a high rate of costs. Such modernization was particularly striking in the case of the *Gabelle* where the farmers-general centralized the receipts of their own organization several decades before this was done in state finances as a whole. Balances were no longer left for long periods in the *greniers à sel*, but were transferred to the farmers-general consolidated account through their private banking networks. The growth of these networks was really a precondition for centraliz-ation as was the replacement of fees by salaries and expense accounts within the salt administration. In its system of receipt, the *Gabelle* in 1789 was more modern than the Venetian salt administration in 1600 or the Ch'ing salt administration in 1900. What was much less modern was the assessment and collection from which the receipt was drawn. Here the *Gabelle* compares less favourably with Venice or China. It was an effi-cient organization operating an inefficient system: inefficient in the last resort because of the weakness of the state and the underdevelopment of society.

THE PEOPLE'S LIVELIHOOD IN THE FRENCH SALT ADMINISTRATION

At first sight no two things seem less associated than the *Gabelle* and people's livelihood. Unbalanced in its structure and uneven in its operation, the *Gabelle* was either disliked as a fact or feared as a threat. Both as fact and threat the *Gabelle* was a common ingredient in popular unrest. Salt smugglers were popular figures and it is significant that the boastful Parisian glazier Jacques-Louis Ménétra claimed in his semi-fictional autobiography to have known the famous *faux-saunier* Louis Mandrin.[25] The attitude of public opinion was well expressed by the slogan of the Pitauts: *Vive le roi sans gabelle*. Objectively too, the *Gabelle* did not promote the use of salt. In the *Grande Gabelle* where the salt administration was strongest, there consumption of salt was lowest. People's livelihood, one might say, was entirely subordinate to the taxes of the state. Nevertheless, such a view would be superficial. It makes implicitly too materialistic a definition of livelihood and fails to localize the *Gabelle* within the spectrum of the state's activities. When thus localized, the *Gabelle* can be seen as making a major contribution to the old political culture of the French monarchy and a minor contribution to the economic promotion by which Colbert sought to produce a new political culture. In this orientation to culture rather than to economy, the French salt administration was more like the Chinese than the Venetian, with the difference that in France the spirit of the state was, so to speak, Legalist rather than Confucian: an empire of punishments rather than rites.

Political Culture

Georges Pagès in a passage of deep insight wrote of the monarchy of the *ancien régime*: 'Elle a commis l'erreur irréparable de croire qu'il suffit à un gouvernement d'être fort'.[26] Isolated by its administrative strength, when it needed public support to finance itself at the end of the eighteenth century, it could not mobilize it. Such alienation from society was not a detail of seventeenth-century development. It had deep roots in the character of the French monarchy and the ideology of *ancien régime* monarchy generally. The French state, more than the English, was an artificial creation by the monarchy from above. Province was added to province by force as much as by inheritance. France came from outside: it was not secreted from within. Moreover, monarchy was not primarily philanthropic but majestic. In Chinese terms its *wei* aspect outweighed its *wen* aspect. As Erasmus said, the eagle was a fitting symbol of monarchy because it was 'neither beautiful, nor musical, nor fit for food . . . able and eager to do more harm than all'.[27] Made in the image of God – did not Bossuet say that the royal throne is not the throne of a man but the throne of God himself? – the king must exercise justice as well as mercy. In this justice, severity had a proper, indeed primary, place. If God was a divinity of reprobation as well as grace, a *Deus absconditus*, so the king was a source of severity as well as clemency, a *rex absconditus*. The king might be loved, but must be feared. The state of the *ancien régime* was Giant the Jack killer and de Maistre was right to see the executioner as the epitome of legitimacy.

The *Gabelle* formed part of this universe of fear.[28] Arthur Young was speaking of French fiscality generally when he wrote: 'The penal code of finance makes one shudder at the horrors of punishment inadequate to the crime', but the twelve examples he proceeds to give are all from the salt laws, by which 3400 people a year – men, women and children – were sent to prison or the galleys.[29] No doubt the French state did not seek deliberately to make the *Gabelle* oppressive and terrifying. Because of its unbalanced character and heavy incidence on the *Grande Gabelle*, it came to form part of the royal liturgy of criminal justice: arrests, preliminary torture, condemnation, breakings on the wheel. The *gabellous*, the salt police attached to each *grenier à sel*, had the right to search houses and persons on suspicion, stop people in the street or in transit between localities, and to make arrests without a warrant. Each *grenier à sel* had its own court to judge offences against the salt laws and, on paper at least, penalties were severe. Salt law was never fully 'civilized' even though increasingly in the eighteenth century practice did not live up to, or down to, theory. Thus at the *grenier à sel* of Sainte Menhould in the Argonne, where much salt was needed for its famous pork products, a *grenier sel d'impôt* between the *Grande Gabelle* and the *Pays de Salines*, no one was sent to the galleys between 1779 and 1790. Most of the 800 odd cases judged ended in acquittal, no penalty or light fines, which could not always be collected because of the poverty of those concerned. Only 15 cases were awarded the full statutory penalty. The *gabellous*, often illiterate, without horses and aware of their unpopularity with public and judges alike, concentrated on minor offenders or a few parishes or individuals with whom they were in feud, leaving the large scale organized smuggling from the *Pays de Salines* mostly alone.[30] By 1789 the bark of the *Gabelle* was worse than its bite, but this did not mean a better image for it. What it did mean was that the whole universe of fear was breaking up and this was one reason why the *Gabelle*, which could not disengage itself from it, was abolished in 1790.

Economic Promotion

In fact, as Voltaire saw, the universe of fear had begun to melt as early as the reign of Louis XIV. One indication was the economic promotion which Colbert, among other mercantilists, borrowed from the medieval emporia to give bureaucratic monarchy both a sounder financial basis and a better public face. Monarchy must be not only majestic but useful. In this programme, the *Gabelle* played a part in two of Colbert's projects: the expansion of foreign trade by privileged companies and the increase of domestic circulation by improved communication.[31]

The last century of the *ancien régime* was the golden age of Maritime France. All three of its major ports – Nantes, Bordeaux, Marseille – were in close proximity to salt fields and trade in salt was an ingredient in their prosperity. Although in the eighteenth century that prosperity was developed mainly by private enterprise, Colbert's privileged companies played some part in its genesis. Particularly was this so in the case of Bordeaux and the *Compagnie du Nord*. This *kuan-tu shang-pan* company was established by Colbert in 1669 with a double aim: to expand exports, to the Baltic essentially, in wine, brandy, salt and textiles, in return for imports of grain, wood, iron and copper; and to capture the freight for French rather than Dutch shipping. Like most of Colbert's ventures, the company was by no means a total success. French merchants were reluctant to invest and exporters continued to prefer Dutch or English freight rates. Nevertheless some expansion of export in salt was achieved, particularly in the direction of Denmark which also wanted to escape from the Dutch monopoly. Denmark then included Norway, developing fast because of the timber trade, with which trade became particularly active.

Colbert was actively interested in the salt trade. He believed French salt was the best in the world, but he admitted that its grey colour placed it at a disadvantage with the whiter Portuguese and Spanish salt in the markets of the north. In 1669 and 1671 we find him writing to the directors of the *Compagnie du Nord* asking what they could do about this. In 1669 he urges the directors to establish salt warehouses in Göteborg and Gotland. In 1670 he tells them that the French ambassador in Copenhagen is arranging to supply Norway with salt from Brouage. In 1671 he congratulates them on their treaty with the Elector of Brandenburg to supply salt and hopes for a similar treaty with the Tsar of Muscovy to supply via Archangel. If Colbert failed to break the Dutch hold on the mainline to the Baltic, he does seem to have had some success in opening byelines by side doors. These markets were then handed on to the private enterprise of the eighteenth century.[32]

Colbert was also keen to promote internal commerce. Here the most important project with which the *Gabelle* was associated was the *Canal du Midi*. Basically an improvement of the Garonne and the Aude plus the construction of an interconnection and terminals, the *Canal des Deux Mers* as it was otherwise known, thus linked the Atlantic and the Mediterranean. Long projected, the canal was completed between 1661 and 1681 by Paul Riquet of Beziers, director of the farm of the salines of Languedoc in the *Petite Gabelle*. He was a correspondent of Colbert's. Colbert allowed him to charge some of the expenses to the *Gabelle* and rewarded him with further rights to farm the salt of Peccais, for whose export to Switzerland he was arranging.[33] The *Canal du Midi* was very much a salt administration achievement. While its general effect as an economic stimulant was somewhat disappointing: Arthur Young found what he felt was the usual French combination of communication without circulation, magnificence without trade;[34] it helped to make the fortune of the salt of Agde at its Mediterranean terminus.

Fisheries were another aspect of the French economy Colbert wished to promote. In the seventeenth century, there were two French fishing industries: the long-distance cod fishery on the Grand Banks in Newfoundland waters based on the port of Sables-d'Olonne south of the Loire; and the short-distance sardine fishery in inshore waters based on the island of Belle-Isle at its mouth. Both fisheries used French Atlantic salt, especially Breton salt from Bourgneuf, which at the height of the industry in the early eighteenth century was virtually monopolized by it, though some operators preferred the whiter, larger grained salt of Setubal. Colbert assisted the fisheries by virtually exempting them from the *Gabelle* and by not attempting to extend its administration to their salines in the Guérande and Bourgneuf in the *Pays exempt* of Brittany. One estimate puts the consumption of salt by the French fisheries as high as 800 000 cwt a year.

Economic promotion by the *Gabelle* did not cease with Colbert. It tended, however, to shift from the coast to the continent, from marine salt to the salt wells of the *Pays de Salines*. In Lorraine there was the introduction of coal instead of wood at Dieuze. In Franche Comté, there was improvement to the pans and the introduction of hydraulic pumps at Salins, while at Arc et Senans, Ledoux used the German techniques of piping and graduation to bring brine from Salins and to optimize the use of timber from state forests, all within a social context of planned urbanization. Ledoux was the last great figure of the traditional *Gabelle*[35] and characteristic of it in his insistence on the government of men as much as the management of things. In the plan of Ledoux for the ideal salt city of Chaux, *Gabelle* and people's livelihood were to be finally fully associated. The scheme, however, aroused much hostility from other potential users of timber and was cut short by the Revolution.

THE SALT ADMINISTRATION IN THE FRENCH STATE

As in China and Venice, so in France, the salt administration served the state, not only by providing regular finance, but as a diplomatic lever and as a standby in military and civil emergency.

Regular Finance

The evolution of the *gabelle* in relation to other revenues of the French crown follows the rule that salt revenues are generally of greatest importance in periods of the weakness of the state, in this case in the adolescence of the monarchy.

Francis I tried to make salt a major fiscal foundation of the state, but he, or rather Henry II, failed, defeated by the rebellion of the *Pitauts*, that protoleague. Sully, in the wake of the defeat of the Great League, was more successful and the revived monarchy of Henry IV owed much to his measures. Richelieu, to fight the life and death struggle of the

Table 8.2 French salt and total revenues, 1515–1789 (livres)

Year	Salt revenue	%	Total revenue
1515	284 000	6	5 000 000
1547	700 000	8	9 000 000
1576	1 000 000	6	16 000 000
1607	5 000 000	17	30 000 000
1641	20 000 000	25	80 000 000
1681	24 000 000	20	120 000 000
1715	18 000 000	15	120 000 000
1726	27 000 000	14	200 000 000
1762	35 000 000	9	375 000 000
1774	45 000 000	14	400 000 000
1789	60 000 000	12	500 000 000

Thirty Years' War, carried the process to its greatest lengths, undeterred by the anti-*Gabelle* rebellion of the *Nu-Pieds*. He began by wishing to universalize the *Gabelle* like Francis I, but ended by intensifying it like Henry II. Colbert rationalized what Richelieu had done by reducing rates but increasing yields. His achievement was not essentially bettered till the middle of the eighteenth century, when yields began to increase again, due as much to mild inflation and moderate population increase as to any change in the system. The *Gabelle*'s proportion of total taxes, however, began to fall as new sources of revenue like the *traites* and the *vingtièmes* came to the fore. By 1789 the French state, aware of the ongoing opposition to the *Gabelle*, had the choice of universalizing it at a lower rate (Calonne) or abolishing it altogether (Necker). It is not surprising that the National Assembly opted for abolition. Necker would have substituted some other object of taxation, possibly an income tax. It is a sign of the fiscal incapacity of the National Assembly that it substituted nothing, but via the *assignats* relied on inflation, the tax which nobody votes.

It is commonly believed that the fiscal system of the *ancien régime* was a major cause of the revolution. It would be fairer to blame public misunderstanding and the failure of Turgot, Necker, Calonne and Brienne, like the four wise men and the elephant, to see and tackle more than one aspect of the problem at a time. In itself, the French fiscal system was not bad. It contained a good mix of direct and indirect taxes which together tapped a wide base. Its incidence was not heavy, France being less heavily taxed than England; its collection costs were not unduly high and were being reduced by the farmers-general; and its effects were not economically inhibitory, as shown by the fact that growth rates were faster in France than in England in the eighteenth century.[36] Moreover, the French national debt was not large given the wealth of the country and the state. Nevertheless, three reforms were highly desirable, in all of which the *Gabelle* might have played a constructive part.

First, with the rise in government expenditure almost everywhere in Europe during the second half of the eighteenth century, it was desirable that the French state raise more revenue. It was vain to suppose that this could be obtained by abolishing the exemptions of the so-called privileged classes. The agitation against the privileged was like modern pressure against expense accounts: it could only achieve trivial results. Budget deficits cannot be filled by taxing the rich but only by taxing everyone. Calonne's return to the programme of Francis I and Richelieu of universalizing the salt tax would have been a good way of doing this, almost certainly cheaper and more administratively convenient than the Physiocrat programme of a universal land tax advocated by Turgot and taken up by the National Assembly.

Second, since no modern state can finance war out of ordinary revenue, it was desirable that the French state possess better borrowing facilities, for longer term and at lower rates of interest. Again, a universal salt tax would have been excellent security for such loans organized through a national bank, since a tax on alimentary salt is relatively inelastic except with regard to long-term demographic movements. A series of salt loans would have carried the French monarchy through the American, Revolutionary and Napoleonic wars, if these had still taken place. Moreover, the loans would have increased the money supply, perhaps desirable in itself at a time of depression, in a less harmful way than the *assignats*.

Third, as Turgot saw, a national bank was not really practicable without a constitution: a new sense of community between state and society. The state must become, not merely powerful, but popular. What better way of acquiring public support where it was most needed, in heartland France, than by championing the interests of the taxpayers of the *Grande Gabelle* against the non-payers of the other sections of the *Gabelle*? What French finance required was not social revolution, but topographical revolution: a shift from the poorer interior to the richer coast, with the coast being compensated by economic policies which encouraged Maritime France. A modernized salt administration would have been an effective expression of such a shift. The Revolution did almost the opposite of what was needed. It abolished the *Gabelle*, shifted the burden of taxation to the land, and ruined the prosperity of Maritime France by foreign war and the Continental System. Consequently in France, unlike England, nineteenth-century industrialization was in discontinuity with eighteenth-century commercialization. The salt administration was never given its chance of playing a part in the rejuvenation of French finance.

Diplomacy

If Colbert made use of French diplomacy in northern Europe to promote the sale of Brouage salt via the *Compagnie du Nord*, he and successive French governments also made use of salt to promote French diplomacy. Especially was this so on the land frontier to the east, in particular the region between Trier, the furthest point of penetration of Dutch borne sea salt, and the Valais, the furthest point of penetration of Mediterranean salt from Genoa or Venice.[37] This was a zone both of maximum opportunity for well salt from Lorraine and Franche Comté and of maximum military sensitivity for France. Out of this conjuncture was born the salt diplomacy of the *ancien régime*.[38] This diplomacy aimed to obtain, by means of export of salt, at the lowest dialogue, at best *entente*, with the lesser but significant states which lay between France and the Germans. Diplomacy indeed sometimes outran the capacities of the salt industry on which it was based. Hence in part the economic promotion noted above at Dieuze, Salins and Arc et Senans.

The zone divided itself into two halves, Switzerland and the Middle Rhineland, with Basle, the hinge, belonging to both.

In Switzerland French salt diplomacy operated in two tiers. First and earlier, France needed an alliance with the Catholic cantons: to recruit mercenaries, to establish credibility as a protector of Catholics outside France, mostly non-French speaking, but above all to remove these pawns from the Spanish side of the chessboard and to deny Spain uninterrupted communication between Milan, Franche Comté till 1679, and the Low countries. Contact with the Valais had been established in the sixteenth century by the salt trade of the *Petite Gabelle*, through Geneva.[39] More extended relations were promoted by the *sel d'alliance* provided first from Peccais, then from Salins, later from Lorraine to the cantons of Solothurn, Fribourg, Lucerne, Zug, Schwyz, Unterwald, and Uri. Second and later, France needed an alliance with the dominant Protestant cantons of Berne, Zurich and Neuchâtel, together with the city of Basle, in order to preserve access to the Protestant bank and to secure Switzerland as a whole for France's system of client states. These relations were promoted by the *sel de commerce* provided by the salines of Lorraine and Franche Comté, whose sales France sought to expand at the expense of Bavarian salt from Reichenhall and Habsburg salt from Hall in Tyrol and Hallein. Except in the eastern cantons such as St Gallen, Schaffhausen, Grisons and Thurgau, French salt enjoyed considerable success. Further, within both groups of allies, Catholic and Protestant, the French government was able to support pro-French oligarchies by establishing them as salt monopolitans.

In the Middle Rhineland until 1738 there was rivalry between salt from Dieuze and Chateau-Salins in ducal Lorraine and salt from Moyenvic in the French-owned bishopric of Metz. In this rivalry, the duke was remarkably successful because he had better supplies of timber and a greater economic interest at stake than the French government. After 1738 France could treat the Lorraine salines as a whole and turned ducal promotion to more diplomatic ends. Thus via Lorraine salt, Paris sought to extend its influence in Luxemburg, Trier, the Saarland, Zweibrucken, Spire and Baden. Since, from the treaty of Ryswick in 1697, France had had to abandon her policy of securing her eastern frontier by force and *réunion*, salt formed a useful part of the new policy of obtaining security by mainly diplomatic means. Napoleon's reconstruction of Switzerland, the basis of the modern Confederation and arguably the most successful part of his foreign policy, followed in paths first opened by the diplomatic use of the *Gabelle* by the *ancien régime*.

Emergency

The *Gabelle* was born in the emergency following the battle of Sluys in 1340 when Philip VI, faced with the invasion of Edward III, established the first *grenier à sel*. The *sel de devoir* too was introduced by Charles V in a period of crisis for the French monarchy. Sully and Richelieu, the two greatest intensifiers of the *Gabelle*, both faced major internal and external problems. Yet all these were military emergencies. Compared with China or Venice, one misses in France the element of civil emergency and philanthropy as associated with salt administration. Salt is conspicuously absent from famine relief or the fight against plague, though this latter was something Colbert cared for deeply. Moreover, it was not until the late nineteenth century and the Solvay company's commissions to the Nancy school of ceramics and glassware that salt merchants in France played much part in artistic patronage.[40] The image of the *Gabelle*, like that of the state, remained severe, one might say Jansenist, even Puritan. The root cause was the dominance of *finance*, the factor which most distinguishes the *Gabelle* from the mandarin salt administration of China and the mercantile salt administration of Venice. *Finance* did for the state and society what they could not do for themselves. It mobilized resources in an inert, continental context. But, bastard child of inadequate parents and a defective relationship, *finance* enjoyed no status and displayed no magnanimity. If the fault of the monarchy was to believe it sufficient to be strong, the fault of *finance* was to act as if it was sufficient to be rich. Consequently the *Gabelle* appeared to most Frenchmen as purely exploitive. Its real services to state finance, royal diplomacy and economic development were ignored. Its real potential for development was thrown aside. It took a person of unusual insight, like Richelieu, to appreciate the *Gabelle*.

Together with *finance* as an explanation of the special features of the *Gabelle*, one must set the character of the French monarchy and in particular its peculiar combination of seigneurial elements and elements derived from Roman law. This combination gave the French state what a Chinese would regard as a non-Confucian, Legalist colouring. Thus in China officials seldom managed directly the beginning and end of the circuit from producer to consumer, i.e. manufacture and retail. This would have been considered Legalism. In France, however, officials did both: manufacture in the south and east ultimately because of Roman law: retail in the north ultimately because of a misappropriated seigneurialism. In the middle, on the other hand, in acquisition, transport and distribution, where mandarins exercised their maximum influence, the French monarchy was content in calling in the services of *finance*. *Gabelle*, monarchy and *finance* lived and died together.

9 The Habsburg Salt Administration

From the greatest of the European bureaucratic monarchies we pass to the greatest of the European aristocratic monarchies. From the relatively national *Gabelle* in France we move to the more dynastic Habsburg salt administration. Under this title we shall be concerned only with the Habsburgs of the east, the Habsburgs of Vienna. We shall be concerned for them throughout the long period from the battle of the Marchfield in 1278, which gave this dynasty of Suabian origin the duchies of Upper and Lower Austria and Styria, until the dissolution of the Habsburg state in 1918, though our primary focus will be on the making of the Habsburg state between 1500 and 1700 when salt administration was of the greatest significance.[1] We shall not concern ourselves with the Habsburgs of the west, the Habsburgs of Brussels, Valladolid and Madrid, though during their briefer span from the battle of Nancy in 1477 to the death of Charles the Sufferer in 1700, they too conducted salt administration in Salins, Ibiza, Setubal etc. For them, masters of new worlds, salt was of relatively less significance than for their poorer cousins on the Danube or the Moldau.

The Habsburg Salt Administration was more like that of China or France than that of Venice, as is only to be expected from another continental, territorial state. But it was like part of the *yen-cheng*, part of the *Gabelle* rather than the whole, just as the Habsburg empire was only like aspects of China, aspects of France. Specifically, the Habsburg salt administration was like the salt division of Szechwan or the *Pays de Salines*, a monopoly based on rural points of industrial production and serving upland surrounds: just as the Habsburg state, with its marriages, militarism and monasteries, reminds us of one of the aristocratic dynasties of the *Nan-pei ch'ao*; Leopold I a latter day Liang Wu-ti. For despite increasing officialdom, what Karl Kraus was to call *Burokretinismus*,[2] the Habsburg state was never fully bureaucratic in the Chinese or louisquatorzien sense. It operated more through the Church, diplomacy and the aristocracy of the *Gutsherrschaften*, the peculiar East European form of the landed estate, half colonial plantation, half industrial enterprise. The Habsburg emperor was a super-landlord. It is significant that the root of the Habsburg salt administration was the *Salzkammergut*, the salt chamber estates, which formed an imperial domain extraterritorial to the three *Lände* of Salzburg, Upper Austria and Styria in which it was situated. Characteristic too, its headquarters at

Ischl became from 1822 the preferred summer residence of the imperial family in its private capacity. Where the *yen-cheng* was fully bureaucratic, the *Ufficio* a business and the *Gabelle* a branch of *finance*, the Habsburg salt administration was basically a form of estate management. Its control of production was based on regalian right or *Landeshoheit*, and its monopoly of sale was a variant of *banalité* or what in Eastern Europe was known as *Anfeilszwang* or *educillatio*.[3] Management was pursued according to the prevalent philosophy of the age: Christian occultism in the seventeenth century; the international enlightenment in the eighteenth century; British economics, French chemistry and German technology in the nineteenth century; but estate management it remained. This feature may be seen at each level of our analysis: the state in the salt administration, the state's taxes, the people's livelihood, and the salt administration in the state.

THE STATE IN THE HABSBURG SALT ADMINISTRATION

The Habsburg state was a somewhat Protean entity. Over its long history it altered its territorial structure on many occasions by expansion, contraction, or internal subdivision through the practice, so long persisted in and so revelatory of the estate management outlook, of dynastic secundogeniture. Even the term Danubian, which seems best to describe the dynasty's scope, has to be qualified in the light of its possession, at one time or another of northeast Switzerland, Alsace, Belgium, Milan, Venice, Silesia, Little Poland and Galicia. It is best therefore to begin an examination of the Habsburg salt administration at a single late date in its existence, the early twentieth century, and then work back over the history of its various components[4] Of the territories mentioned above as once Habsburg which do not figure in Table 9.1 below, only Venice had ever produced salt in significant quantities, and by 1797 when the Habsburgs absorbed the *Serenissima*, production at Chioggia had fallen to a low ebb.

In all its territories, the policy of the Habsburg state in relation to salt was essentially the same: the establishment of regalian rights by means of Roman law and their exploitation by a sales monopoly conducted as far as possible by officials at least to the level of wholesale. It was in Chinese terms a system of *kuan-chih, kuan-yün, kuan-mai* (official manufacture, official transport, official sales). When the salt reformer Chang Chien in 1913 wanted to advocate such a system for China, Austria-Hungary was the first European country he cited in its support.[5] Within Europe too, the Habsburg salt administration became the prototype for similar state monopolies such as those of Italy, Switzerland, Greece, Romania, Serbia and the Ottoman empire. Unlike the *Gabelle*, the

Table 9.1 The Habsburg salt administration, 1912

Area	Quantity (cwt)
Salzkammergut	2 563 198
Hall in Tyrol	348 952
Hallein	481 174
Wieliczka-Bochnia	2 287 600
East Galicia	1 951 600
Istria	326 060
Dalmatia	90 472
Total Austria	8 049 116
Royal Hungary	2 200 000
Transylvania	3 200 000
Total Hungary	5 400 000
Imperial total	13 499 116

Salzmonopol was highly diffusive of itself. It was systematic rather than idiosyncratic.

Except in Royal Hungary and Transylvania which had their own institutions, and even to some extent there, all Habsburg regalian salt rights were under the supervision of the *Hofkammer*, established from 1525, reorganized at the end of the seventeenth century and transformed into a ministry of finance in 1816. Though the *Hofkammer* contained jurists and officials, the so-called cameralists, it was until the nineteenth century a court rather than a bureaucratic body. In the seventeenth century, when Habsburg institutions were being put in place, its presidents included members of the high aristocracy such as Ulrich Franz Kolovrat and Georg Ludwig von Sinzendorf (1656–1680), senior ecclesiastics like the abbots of Kremsmunster and Lilienfeld or the Croat Cardinal Kollonich (1692–1694) later archbishop of Esztergom and would be Richelieu of Hungary, as well as Christoph Ignaz Abele (1680–1685), one of the few commoners to rise into the upper levels of government. Though the *Hofkammer* does not enjoy a good reputation for efficiency: an earlier historiography regarded Sinzendorf in particular as one of the worst and most corrupt financiers in seventeenth-century Europe; like its military parallel the *Hofkriegsrat*, it was probably as efficient as it could be and needed to be in Danubian circumstances.[6] At all events, as regards salt, it pursued consistent and relatively successful policies over a long period of time in its various territories.

The Salzkammergut

This was the earliest, and until the development of the Transylvanian mines in the second half of the nineteenth century, the largest producer of salt under Habsburg control. In 1912 the Salzkammergut, which took its name both from the *Hofkammer* and from the *Salzkammer* or salt treasuries it supplied in Bohemia, comprised four centres which produced as follows: Ebensee 1 612 550 cwt, Ischl 327 376 cwt, Hallstatt 170 564 cwt, and Aussee 481 174 cwt. Ebensee, Ischl and Hallstatt were in Upper Austria, Aussee in Styria. All four salines produced salt by boiling brine, the fuel being wood until the late nineteenth century, but Ebensee had no brine source of its own, drawing its supplies from Ischl and Hallstatt higher up the valley of the Traun. Ischl, Hallstatt and Aussee all possessed salt mines from which brine was obtained by the technique of controlled flooding of underground chambers known as *Sinkwerk*. The brine was then piped to evaporation houses in the four centres. This technique, incidentally, is still essential to the modern salt industry, for example in Michigan.

Hallstatt, of course, was a saline of great antiquity, going back to pre-Roman, Celtic times, as first a mine and then a source of brine for evaporation. Used by the Romans, Hallstatt was abandoned by them around 350 AD, probably as a result of Valentinian I's reorganization of the *limes*. It is next heard of in a document of 1305 from the small religious house of Traunkirchen which indicates that production had resumed in the twelfth century. Hallstatt, therefore, was probably not a large producer of salt when it was taken over by the Habsburgs as part of the spoils of 1278. By 1336 it was producing 124 000 cwt a year and by the end of the fourteenth century 186 000 cwt, much less than Lüneburg for example. Frederick III took an interest in the saline, as did Maximilian I, but its production never much exceeded 200 000 cwt, probably as a result of its inaccessibility to timber supplies for fuel. It was the problem of fuel at Hallstatt which led to the development of the salines lower down the Traun.

The other saline the Habsburgs inherited in the Salzkammergut was Aussee in the duchy of Styria. Possibly used by the Romans, Aussee is first reported definitely as a saline in 1147 in a grant by Ottakar III of two pans to the Cistercian monastery of Rein, founded in 1129, which was already working them. A pioneer in the technique of *Sinkwerk*, Aussee in 1336 produced 144 000 cwt and by the end of the fourteenth century 200 000 cwt. Further development took place in the first half of the sixteenth century under Ferdinand I, perhaps in response to the establishment of the *Militärgrenze* against the Turk. A peak production of 432 000 cwt was reached in 1559, which was not bettered till the nineteenth century, as with Hallstatt, probably because of fuel problems. Nevertheless between 1350 and 1550 the Habsburgs had at least doubled salt production in the Salzkammergut which they had inherited.

Between 1550 and the outbreak of the Thirty Years' War, the Habsburgs established two new centres in the Salzkammergut. First, in 1571,

Table 9.2 Production in the Salzkammergut, 1278–1912

Date	Quantity (cwt)
1278	100 000
1350	267 000
1550	632 000
1628	800 000
1800	1 100 000
1892	1 500 000
1912	2 543 198

under the auspices of Maximilian II, a new saline was opened at Ischl at the confluence of its own river and the Traun. Ischl possessed its own mine with a series of eventually 12 horizontal *Sinkwerk* at the head of another local stream the Salzbach, but from 1595 it was also supplied with brine by Hallstatt. Ischl did not become a big producer quickly. Before the middle of the eighteenth century it is never credited with more than 74 000 cwt, but it opened the way to further developments. By 1778 it had made a leap to reach a peak of 374 000 cwt, which was not surpassed by 1912. Second, in 1607, under the auspices of Rudolf II, a new boiling establishment supplied with brine from Ischl and Hallstatt was opened at Ebensee where the Traun enters the Traunsee. Ebensee too made a slow start: 54 000 cwt in 1618, 96 000 cwt in 1701, 132 000 cwt in 1746; but, like Ischl, it moved forward at the end of the eighteenth century to 530 000 cwt in 1804, becoming the leading producer of the Salzkammergut group. Even by 1650 the new salines of the Lower Traun had probably raised salt production in the Salzkammergut by nearly one third. If the whole span of production from 1278 to 1912 is considered, Habsburg stewardship is impressive, especially in the later sixteenth century.[7]

This was the period in which the philosophy of Christian occultism, natural magic and alchemy reached a first peak of influence, particularly at the court of Rudolf II whose doctor was the alchemist physician Michael Maier and who was the patron of the Polish alchemist Sendivogius. It is difficult not to see this philosophy as an inspiration behind the development of the Salzkammergut. Salt was one of the three super elements (really processes, the *hsing* of Chinese *wu-hsing* theory) of Paracelsian medicine: the one added by him to the older alchemical duality of mercury and sulphur. The *De Sulphure*, attributed to Sendivogius in the *Musaeum Hermeticum* published in Frankfurt in 1678, analysed the emergence of sulphur, mercury and salt in terms of the interaction of the traditional earth, air fire and water. The late seventeenth-century magus Johann Friedrich von Rain, who defined alchemy as 'the occult part of natural philosophy, and therefore a most necessary part of physics',[8] regarded salt, the product of mercury and sulphur, as the core of the philosopher's stone and the earthly counterpart of the third person of the Trinity. Finally, Athanasius Kircher, The Aquinas of Christian occultism, stressed 'salt, the basis of all natural productions, and the admirable variety of salts'. In his *Mundus Subterraneus* of 1665, Book VI deals with 'the vertue of salt and its Auxiliaries, the differences whereof are largely discoursed of, together with the way of extracting the same'; Book VIII examines salt as a mineral and mineralizer; Book X contains 'a Discourse of salt pits, and the way of making salt'.[9] Common salt, Kircher affirms, is the semen of the earth: *Dico salem communem esse terrae semen*. Salt in its various forms as principle, element and class of element was therefore the key to what Kircher called *centrosophia*, the wisdom of the underground world, as he wrote *de elemento terrae vero et genuino, id est salis*.[10]

Ideas such as these were not without influence at the highest levels. Ferdinand III appointed Johann Konrad Richthausen, a well known mine owner and alchemist as tutor to his son the King of Hungary. He subsequently became superintendent of the royal mines in Hungary and was ennobled under the splendidly Taoist title of Baron von Chaos.[11] The emperor corresponded on alchemical topics with his brother the Archduke Leopold William who conducted experiments along with his chamberlain during his various appointments at Vienna, Brussels and Laibach. At the *Hofkammer* itself was Johann Joachim Becher, an early cameralist and adviser on metallurgy, but also an alchemist who used the pseudonym of Solinus Salzthal. The president, Sinzendorf, was a patron of alchemists as were many other members of the Baroque elite.[12]

Philosophy therefore encouraged mineral development. Like any other great landlord, the Habsburgs, in their management of the Salzkammergut, were concerned with maximizing the profits of their *Herrschaft*. They were also concerned with the supply of salt to their subjects in their hereditary lands, the *Erblände*, particularly Upper and Lower Austria and Styria, since Carinthia and Carniola could draw part of their salt from the Venetian salines of Muggia, Capo d'Istria, Piran and Pago.

Beyond that, however, the Salzkammergut was important in maintaining Habsburg control in Bohemia and Moravia. The lands of the crown of St Wenceslas were the jewel in the Habsburg crown, what made the Danubian monarchy a great power. In the second half of the seventeenth century they provided over half the revenue of the Habsburg state. One of the best means of extracting resources from an area where, because of the novel imposition of the system of great estates, it was difficult and undesirable to levy a land tax, was a salt monopoly. Greater Bohemia was one of the largest and richest saltless regions of Europe and therefore potentially one of the most lucrative markets. In its northern section, Silesia, the natural sources of supply were Wie-liczka, Halle, or sea salt coming up the Oder, and between 1657 and 1683 the Habsburgs held a lien on Wieliczka to the advantage of the branch *Hofkammer* at Breslau. In Bohemia proper and Moravia, the Salzkammer-gut was the natural source of supply, but it faced competition from Halle in the north and Bavarian Reichenhall and Salzburg Hallein in the south. Of these competitors, Reichenhall was the most serious both because of its technical proficiency and because, down to 1700, Bavaria was the most valued Habsburg ally in Germany. It became an object of Habsburg policy to exclude Bavarian salt from Bohemia, even at the price of allowing Reichenhall, as a compensation, to capture markets in the west from Hall in Tyrol. In 1706, when Bavaria was taking the anti-Habsburg side in the war of the Spanish succession, its salt was finally legally excluded from Bohemia and thereafter the Habsburgs were able to enforce the Salzkammergut monopoly.[13] Its salt was both a source of revenue and a means of building up a pro-Habsburg clientele through the privilege of distribution. What the White Mountain won, the Salz-kammergut consolidated.

Hall in Tyrol

The Habsburgs acquired the Tyrol, which then included its southern extension into Italy, in 1363 as the heirs of the last countess, the famous Margaret Maultasch. However, it was peculiarly subject to periods of secundogeniture, 1379–1490, 1564–1595, 1602–1618, 1619–1655, so that it only became permanently attached to the main body of the empire under Leopold I. The exploitation of the saline at Hall, fifteen miles below Innsbruck on the Inn, preceded the coming of the dynasty, and was for a long time under the control of the Cistercian house of Stams founded in 1273. Duke Rudolf the Founder, the first Habsburg count, reasserted regalian rights and introduced the technique of the *Sinkwerk* from Aussee to increase production. In the fifteenth century production still only reached 50–60 000 cwt a year, but it was useful to the dynasty for the supply of the saltless *Vorlände*, its original nucleus in southern Alsace, Baden, Suabia and northern Switzerland. In 1477 Archduke Sigismund of the Tyrol established his mint in Hall, as witness the *Münzturm*, financed no doubt in part by sales of salt for bullion. At the beginning of the sixteenth century production advanced to 100 000 cwt during the reign of Maximilian I who made Innsbruck his capital and extended the frontiers of the Tyrol. Montaigne visited Hall in 1580 or 1581 in the days of Archduke Ferdinand of Schloss Ambras fame and was impressed by the scale of operations and the extent of the market. The saline, he commented with some exaggeration, 'provides all Ger-many'.[14] By the beginning of the seventeenth century, thanks to promotion by the secundogeniture archdukes, production had risen to 300 000 cwt. Thereafter production fell to around 200 000 cwt as a result, first of increased competition from Reichenhall which was reformed by Hans Reiffenstuhl in 1617–1618, and second of the loss of Habsburg Alsace and the Breisgau in 1648. There was another advance at the end of the eighteenth century associated with increased exports to Switzerland, more pans, the use of coal as fuel and the opening of a chemical factory for sal ammoniac in 1787–1788.[15] However, in the nineteenth century, Hall did little more than maintain itself, declining slightly to its 1912 figure of 328 952 cwt.

The activities of the Habsburg salt administration at Hall were marked by a tendency to intellectual innovation in the ages both of alchemy and chemistry. First, at the beginning of the seventeenth century, Archduke Maximilian made a determined effort to improve the productivity of the saline which was threatened by shortage of fuel. A mission was sent to Parma to study the methods in use at Salsomaggiore. As a result, a bronze pan instead of the usual iron ones was tried, and various schemes for fuel-less salt, probably early forms of graduation, were discussed and perhaps experimented with. Some of these schemes have an alchemical ring to them and Archduke Maximilian, like his brother Rudolf II, was a patron of Christian magic, as witness the dedication to him by Philip Müller of his *Miracula et Mysteria Chymico-medica* which went through four editions between 1610 and 1623.[16] Next, at the end of the eighteenth century, Hall came under the influence of the Tübingen physician, J. A. Weber, a pioneer in the analysis and use of mother liquors, i.e. the residue of brine after the sodium chloride has been extracted, and hence of the modern chemical industry. This intellectuality of Hall in Tyrol was due fundamentally to the position of Innsbruck: at the crossroads of routes going north/south and east/west, belonging more to the open world of the Rhine than to the closed world of the Danube.

Hallein

The ancient saltworks of the archbishop of Salzburg, supplied with brine by a *Sinkwerk* on the adjoining Dürrenberg, only came into the possession of the Habsburgs in 1803 as part of Napoleon's mediatization of the ecclesiastical principalities in the *Reichsdeputations-hauptschlusz* of that year. Hallein, however, had long been of concern to the Habsburg salt administration as a potential rival to the Salzkammergut as a source of supply for Bohemia. The archbishops in the early modern period, of whom probably the most notable was the princely Wolf Dietrich von Raittenau 1587–1611, liked to take stances independent of the Habsburgs: for example, letting their university be run by the Benedictines where most of the Habsburg universities were run by the Jesuits. The competition of Salzburg salt had therefore to be taken seriously, especially as it enjoyed better water communications to the east than the Salzkammergut. Hallein had been redeveloped in the thirteenth century with assistance from the Cistercians of Salem by Archbishop Eberhard II after he had lost control of Reichenhall to the duke of Bavaria in 1198. Already at the beginning of the sixteenth century, there was achieved a production of over 400 000 cwt. By the middle of it, promoted by the archbishop who progressively bought out the private interests of the *Siedherren* or boiler lords with whom he had formerly shared control, it reached over 600 000 cwt, nearly as much as the Salzkammergut. This growth was mainly the result of an expansion of trade to Bohemia. In the second half of the sixteenth century, Maximilian II and Rudolf II took steps to exclude Salzburg salt from the lands of the crown of St Wenceslas, so that by 1628 when Habsburg control of Bohemia was becoming effective, production at Hallein had fallen back to 400 000 cwt.

Between 1594 and 1611 Archbishop Raittenau, seeing what was happening, entered into a series of agreements with the duke of Bavaria to sell him 300 000 cwt of Hallein salt for distribution via the Bavarian marketing system. Even after the Reiffenstuhl reforms, the production of salt at Reichenhall and Traunstein, though of superior quality, only reached 268 000 cwt, so the duke was glad to have his quality reinforced by the Archbishop's quantity. Together Bavaria and Salzburg were able to present a formidable competition, not so much to the Salzkammergut in the east, where they recognized the battle as lost, as to Hall in Tyrol in the west. South Germany, particularly Württemberg, was supplied via the Danube by the Bavarian depot at Donauworth. There was also export to Franconia, and northern Switzerland. To please their ally and protect their monopoly in Bohemia, the Habsburgs gave partial consent to the new arrangements in the so-called Rosenheimer Salt Trade agreement of 1649 which remained in force until the 1690s when Habsburg–Bavarian relations deteriorated.[17]

The Bavaria–Salzburg cartel was remarkably successful until near the end of the eighteenth century in keeping Hall in Tyrol in a subordinate position. Hallein was able to maintain a production of 400 000 cwt to Hall's 200 000 cwt, despite the low reputation of its salt. In 1753 Württemberg gave Bavaria a monopoly of its salt supply in return for duty-free entry of its wine. This agreement was renewed in 1802, formed part of the bilateral customs union of 1828, and acted as a prototype for the North German *Zollverein* of 1833–1834. By this time Bavaria and Salzburg had parted company. Initially, the cartel had maximized advantages: Hallein quantity, Reichenhall quality, Bavarian access to Germany and Switzerland, French diplomatic support. Subsequently it worked less well. At the end of the eighteenth century production at Reichenhall rose to over 400 000 cwt and it was to rise further to 600 000 cwt in 1822 with Reichenbach's modernization of Reichenhall and Traunstein and the opening of the new boiling plant at Rosenheim from 1810. Bavaria increasingly no longer needed Salzburg. At the same time, Hall in Tyrol was reviving and expanding its markets in Switzerland. Hallein therefore was probably not too sorry to see the cartel dissolved and to be absorbed into the Habsburg empire. In the nineteenth century its production expanded gently to 481 174 cwt in 1912, a satisfactory result in that its markets were now mainly domestic. Reichenhall, having added quantity to quality and producing 800 000 cwt in 1895, now dominated south Germany while the opening of Schweizerhalle and the salines of Basle and the Aargau from 1835 meant that Switzerland was no longer dependent on imports. Württemberg too was now more than self-supporting; Hallein, like Salzburg, could fade into prosperous provinciality.

Wieliczka-Bochnia and East Galicia

The Habsburgs acquired possession of the ancient salines of Wieliczka-Bochnia and East Galicia in 1772 as part of their share of the first partition of Poland, though earlier, between 1657 and 1683 they had held a lien on Wieliczka-Bochnia as a result of their support of Poland during the invasion of Charles X of Sweden. Salt had provided 40 per cent of the revenue of the Saxon kings,[18] so the acquisition constituted a valuable asset for Maria Theresa's government. In 1772 the two salt mines of Wieliczka and Bochnia near Cracow produced 840 000 cwt of rock salt, while the dispersed salt springs of East Galicia from Przemysl to the Bukovina (acquired in 1775), ten in number in 1912 and probably more in the eighteenth century, produced 280 000 cwt of boiled salt: a total for Austrian Poland of 1 120 000 cwt. This was already more than was being produced by the Salzkammergut. The Polish crown had asserted its regalian rights as early as 1278, Casimir the Great issued his famous salt statute in 1368, to structure production at Wieliczka, and the Jagellon, Vasa and Saxon dynasties had extended royal control, so that by 1772 there was in effect a system of *kuan-chih, kuan-yün, kuan-hsiao*. The crown controlled production, supervised transport via the Vistula, the northern Bug and the Narew, and established depots to sell to wholesalers, retailers and the public. In the interests of internal equity and external protection, the Polish state assigned sales areas to rock and boiled salt. East Galician boiled salt, being whiter in colour and smaller grained and to that extent of superior quality, was assigned areas in the west in the lower Vistula and Posen, where it could compete with imported Baltic salt from Brouage, Setubal and Cheshire. Wieliczka-Bochnia rock salt, being grey-black in colour, and larger grained, and to that extent of inferior quality, was assigned sales areas in the centre, the middle Vistula, Warsaw itself, and in the east, Mazowia, Podlachia and southern Lithuania where foreign salt would find it harder to penetrate.

The Habsburgs continued the basic structure of the Polish salt administration, which was really the same as that of the *Hofkammer* with regard to the Salzkammergut, but the context had been changed radically by the partition of Poland. As a result of the partition, both sets of salines had lost their traditional markets in northern Poland: the west to Prussian salt from Halle and the new German salines, the east to Russian salt from the Crimea acquired by the Tsarina in 1774. Nevertheless, between 1772 and 1912 production in Austrian Poland quadrupled, doubling at Wieliczka-Bochnia and increasing nearly sevenfold in East Galicia. Three factors lay behind this expansion: first, a new export of Wieliczka-Bochnia salt to Bohemia, Moravia and Slovakia, with the completion of the *Kaiser Ferdinand Nordbahn* at the mid-century[19] and as Salzkammergut salt was absorbed by Austria proper; second, an increased preference, with modest affluence, within Austrian Poland for the whiter East Galician salt at the expense of Wieliczka-Bochnia; and third, at the end of the nineteenth century and the beginning of the twentieth century, the absorption of any Wieliczka-Bochnia surplus by the embryonic chemical industry at Cracow which by 1932 was using 2 million cwt a year. Austrian Poland, therefore, was the counterpart to Salzburg in the west. Both, formerly turned away from the Danube, were redirected towards it by inclusion in the Habsburg empire. In the field of salt, Bruck's notion of the *Siebzigmillionenreich* a common market of Central Europe unified by the railways, had some reality.

Istria and Dalmatia

The Habsburgs acquired the county of Istria centring on Pazin in 1374, the city of Trieste in 1382, and Gorizia with eastern Friuli in 1500. However, they did not acquire the area of the saltfields, the margraviate of Istria and the duchy of Dalmatia, which together with the forementioned territories became known after 1815 as the Küstenland, until the peace of Campo Formio in 1797 extinguished the Venetian republic. For the saltfields of Istria and Dalmatia were those with which we are already familiar as the Adriatic salines of the *Serenissima*. By 1912 these had been reduced to six: Capodistria, Pirano, Strugnano in Istria; Arbe, Pago and Stagno in Dalmatia. In that year, Pirano was the largest producer in Istria at 174 266 cwt, Pago the largest producer in Dalmatia at 69 472 cwt. These figures are well below those of the best years of the sixteenth century when both Piran and Pago may each have produced 400 000 cwt.[20] At the end of the eighteenth century, Pago and Piran, along with Capodistria, were still Venice's largest suppliers,[21] though demand had fallen with the decline of Venetian entrepôt trade, and may have produced 200 000 cwt apiece. Why did the Habsburgs fail to conserve this level of production, as they had in Salzburg, or even increase it, as they had in Austrian Poland? One might have expected the Adriatic salines to have benefited from the *Sudbahn* between Vienna and Trieste, just as the Polish salines benefited from the *Nordbahn* between Vienna and Cracow. Trieste after all was the shop window of Bruck's *Mitteleuropa* and his own base.

Two explanations suggest themselves. First, while the Adriatic salines, like those in Poland, were cut off from major traditional markets by their union with the Habsburg state (at least eventually: Venetia was Austrian till 1866), the loss in the west was more radical than in the east. The salines of Piran and Pago had been to a considerable extent a Venetian creation, while those of Wieliczka-Bochnia and East Galicia were not creations of Poland-Lithuania, rather vice versa. Second, in the *Erblände*, especially Inner Austria, where Adriatic salt might have hoped for new markets, it was confronted with the competition of Salzkammergut salt which, although more expensive, was of superior quality. All over Europe in the nineteenth century, solar evaporated sea salt was losing ground to artificially evaporated brine well salt. The Adriatic's real parallel was not Poland, but the French Atlantic whose *shai* salt steadily lost ground to the *chien* salt of Lorraine. Only in a minority of cases of which the French Mediterranean, remarkable also for its technical innovations, is the prime example, did marine *shai* draw any benefit from the railways. Moreover, the Adriatic salines were disadvantaged by being in Austria rather than Hungary, for, despite nominal free trade agreements, this cut them off from another potential new market (or rather an expanded old one): Croatia and Trans-Danubian Hungary which were secured by the more dynamic production of eastern Hungary. Finally, production at Piran and Pago, like that on the French Atlantic coast, remained too artisanal in its structures and outlook to achieve the competitiveness necessary to defeat its rivals and exploit its opportunities. Pago in particular, one of the earliest of European successive basin solar evaporation salines, suffered under Habsburg rule and it is not surprising to find Dalmatia a focus of Yugoslav neo-nationalism.

Royal Hungary and Transylvania

The lands of the crown of St Stephen, Greater Hungary, formally entered the title of the Habsburgs as a result of the battle of Mohacs in 1526. But between 1526 and 1683, the defeat of the Turks below the walls of Vienna by John Sobieski, Hungary was actually divided into three parts: Royal Hungary, itself divided three ways, upper, lower and

Croatia, under the Habsburgs; Turkish Hungary under the Ottoman Pasha at Budapest; and Transylvania, a deutero Hungary under its own elected princes, with its capital generally at Alba Julia (Gyulafehervar). The three Hungarys were not reunited under the Habsburgs until the reconquest following the siege of Vienna. The reconquest was legalized by the peace of Karlowitz with the Ottomans in 1699, but Habsburg rule was not finally accepted till the peace of Szatmar with the Magyar and in particular Transylvanian nobility in 1711.[22]

The Hungarian salines, mostly mines, less spectacular Wieliczkas, were situated on the inside rim of the Carpathians in Upper Hungary (Felvidek) and in the inner parts of Transylvania. In Upper Hungary, the two main sites were Soovar near Kassa (Kosice) in Slovakia and Ronaszek in Maramaros county in northeast Romania. Another significant site was Ujvar Sugatag not far from Ronaszek. In Transylvania, the two main sites were Torda and Ujvar Maros, respectively in the contiguous upper valleys of the Szamos (Somes) and Maros (Mures), the inner districts of the Principality. By 1912 all four were considerable producers of salt with an output of over a million cwt apiece. Most of this productive capacity was built up in the course of the nineteenth century, the period of Hungary's greatest social and political revival. In the middle of the eighteenth century the production of Hungary was 1 250 000 cwt; by the early nineteenth century it had only risen to at most 1 460 000 cwt. By 1900 production was reckoned at nearly 4 million cwt and by 1912 it had reached 5 400 000 cwt. Greater Hungary was not far behind Greater Austria.

As with Salzburg and Hallein, the Habsburgs had been concerned with Hungarian salt long before the peace of Karlowitz. After all, 1 250 000 cwt was a large production: more than Wieliczka in 1772 (840 000 cwt), more than the Salzkammergut in 1800 (1 100 000 cwt). Moreover, the salines were situated in areas remote from and recalcitrant to Habsburg authority where a considerable part of the population was Protestant. Central European Protestantism (Lutheran, Calvinist and Unitarian) is a phenomenon too often overlooked by historians of Western Europe overinfluenced by Weber. Like Huguenotism in western and southern France, it was in part financed by control of sources of salt. If, as Evans shows, the Habsburgs obtained limited acceptance in the lands of the crown of St Wenceslas, while they met with limited rejection in the lands of the crown of St Stephen, part of the reason was that Bohemia had no salt and could be made dependent on the Salzkammergut, while Hungary had plenty and could not.

All four major leaders of semi-Protestant Magyar autonomism financed their movements to a considerable extent through salt revenues. Istvan Bocskai, the leader of the revolt against the first Habsburg attempt at centralization at the beginning of the seventeenth century, established his headquarters at Kassa from where he was well placed to exercise control over the salt mine at Soovar. Gabor Bethlen, perhaps the most hopeful of the princes of Transylvania, drew one third of his private revenue, which was much larger than that voted to him by the Diet, from land but, 'The other two-thirds were provided by salt works and other mines, customs duties and the mint'.[23] The salt works in question were probably those of Torda and Maros Ujvar. In the revolt of Imre Thököly between 1678 and 1685, we are told that 'The keystone of his government was the *Zipser Kammer*, the financial and administrative institution of his Upper Hungarian acquisitions, which he "inherited" from the Habsburgs when he took Kassa',[24] i.e. the branch of the *Hofkammer* which managed Soovar. Finally, Ferenc II Rakoczi, the leader of the Magyar revolt during the war of the Spanish succession, was high sheriff of Saros county in which Soovar was situated and had extended possessions in the Upper Tisza valley. In 1694 when he first planned his revolt, 'he saw the possibilities of his vineyards at Tokaj, salt mines at Maramaros, and the industry of the burghers in the towns and cities that lay along the trade routes to Poland and Transylvania'.[25] At the height of his power Rakoczi will have controlled all four major Hungarian salines: Soovar, Ronaszek, Torda and Maros Ujvar.

It was essential therefore that if the Habsburgs were to control Hungary, and this was the basis of their new European status as a superpower at the end of the seventeenth century, they should assert their regalian rights over these salines. That done, however, the dynasty did not have much interest in their further development. Its aim was to deny to others rather than to exploit itself. The expansion of production in the nineteenth century, particularly at Maros Ujvar, was less its work than that of the new Hungarian state born out of the *Ausgleich* of 1867.

Bosnia-Herzegovina

The last saline to come into the possession of the Habsburg state was Tuzla (Turkish 'place of salt') on the Jala, acquired from the Turks when Bosnia-Herzegovina was first occupied in 1878 and then formally annexed to the empire during the crisis of 1908. The territory, after 1908 a *Reichland*, i.e. the joint property of Austria and Hungary, was administered from 1878 by the common ministry of finance of the two partners in the Dual Monarchy, the successor of the *Hofkammer*, which was headed from 1882 to 1903 by Benjamin von Kallay, a Magyar. Kallay believed in economic development for Bosnia and in particular in encouragement of the old Muslim, once Cathar, ruling class to participate in modern social and political life, his aim being to neutralize Serbian irredentism from across the border. On both counts Tuzla benefited. An ancient brine source used for salt manufacture by boiling since Roman times and before, Tuzla had become a supply point for the Ottoman army on its annual peregrinations north, as well as for the local population of Bosnia, and by the twentieth century its inhabitants were largely Muslim. Tuzla therefore was promoted. Its activity was one of the reasons for the decline of Dalmatian salt, and by the time of the kingdom of Yugoslavia, a Solvay soda factory had been added to the saltworks. In 1912 its production was not large, probably of the order of 200 000 cwt.

The Empire, Milan and the Low Countries

Until 1806, the Habsburg ruler was not only king, archduke, duke, count etc. of his various territories, but also Holy Roman emperor. In the past, scholarship downplayed the imperial functions of the Habsburgs, certainly at least from the peace of Westphalia onwards, but recent reinterpretation has increasingly recognized these functions as real if limited. In the field of salt administration imperial activity has not yet been fully reassessed, but there seems scope for it in at least three areas.

First, the crown imperial sometimes held shares in salines beyond the borders of its own hereditary or elective lands, particularly, it would seem, in the imperial free cities or *Reichstädte*. For example, in Schwäbisch Hall around 1300, the crown held five out of the 111 *Pfannen*, or entitlements to pans of brine, by which property rights in the saline were reckoned. By 1500 these crown rights had lapsed, perhaps as a result of a diminution of Habsburg concern for the *Vorland* of Suabia, but it would be interesting to know the process of their lapsing and whether similar saline rights existed elsewhere. Second, since the reign of Maximilian I, there had been three imperial institutions before which litigation over salt matters may from time to time have come: the *Reichskammergericht* (imperial chamber court: not to be confused with the *Hofkammer*), basically a civil court for disputes between immediate vassals, which generally sat at Speyer; the *Reichshofrat* (Aulic Council) at Vienna with civil and criminal jurisdiction over both mean and immediate vassals; and the *Reichshofkanzlei* (imperial chancery: to be distinguished from the *Österreichische Hofkanzlei*), also at Vienna, though nominally under the direction of the archbishop of Mainz, which exercised the residual justice of the emperor throughout the empire. In Germany, salt and the law were closely associated. In Schwäbisch Hall, the jurist Georg Bernhard Arnold wrote a treatise on the natural, Roman and canon law of emphyteusis with special reference to property in salt, *bona salinaria*. Law does not imply litigation, but it raises the possibility of it, and only a careful examination of the cases coming before the three imperial institutions will decide the extent to which they were involved in salt administration. Third, the eighteenth century saw the development in Germany of a kind of supranational salt consortium headed by the Saxon cameralist Beust, the ancestor of Friedrich Ferdinand von Beust the negotiator of the *Ausgleich*, which managed not only the salines of Saxony, but also those of a number of lesser states: Mainz, Speyer, the Palatinate etc.[26] Since Saxony, the base for Beust's operations, was a long-term Habsburg ally, it is difficult to believe that his activities, which extended to Poland, the Vaud, Savoy and even Norway, were not approved of, even inspired by, Vienna, particularly as they did not include Prussia or Bavaria, the Habsburgs principal rivals in Germany. The Habsburgs operated, it would seem, a definite imperial *Salzpolitik*.

Milan the eastern Habsburgs acquired as part of their share in their Spanish cousins' inheritance in the Utrecht/Rastatt settlement of 1713–14. In Milan the Habsburgs were importers of salt, and like their predecessors, they had a choice of supply: by land from Genoa, or by river from Venice or Ancona, the ultimate source being Ibiza, Trapani, Apulia or the Adriatic salines. References in French sources to the import of red salt into the Valais from Milan indicates that Ibiza was the ultimate source with the probable implication that the intermediate supplier was Genoa.[27] On the other hand, Ancona also frequently handled Ibiza salt. Another reference to Neapolitan salt in the Valais, i.e. white salt from Apulia, which was also transported by Ancona particularly when coastal shipping for salt became more important than long distance, suggest the new Adriatic entrepôt as a major supplier of Milan and its Swiss dependencies.[28] The close relations between the Habsburgs and the Holy See in the eighteenth and nineteenth centuries would confirm this, since Ancona formed part of the Papal States and was a source of profit to the Curia and indirectly of influence for Vienna. From the late eighteenth century the Habsburgs also enjoyed close relations with the Bourbons of Naples.

In the Low Countries, the modern Belgium, another acquisition by the Utrecht/Rastatt settlement, the Habsburgs were again importers of salt: from Portugal, France and England. Here the most interesting development was the revival in 1756 of plans mooted in the days of Philip II for a state monopoly of import, in the form of the imperial salt refinery at Ostend.[29]

The Low Countries, both north and south, had always shown a preference for refined salt, which was preferred not only for domestic use, but also for fishing and dairy purposes. In this case, refinement meant the conversion to brine of greyish, large grained, solar evaporated salt from the Atlantic coast or the Mediterranean and its boiling to produce a smaller grained and whiter salt. Before the middle of the eighteenth century the Austrian Netherlands was served either by its own small scale refining industry in southern Brabant, or, and to a greater extent, by the Dutch refining industry in Zealand. The Dutch exported to the south both by a legal trade, entrenched by preferential tariffs under the peace of Westphalia and the Barrier treaty of 1715, and by smuggling. This Dutch dominance of the salt supply was part of the wider ascendancy of Amsterdam over the trade of the Circumterranean in general and the trade of its former senior partners in Flanders in particular, this second enforced by the permanent closure of the Scheldt. Dutch dominance, however, cost the government in Brussels both revenue and economic opportunity, and it is not surprising that proposals for import monopolies and circumvention of the tariff provisions were mooted in 1736, 1750, 1751 and again in 1754.

It was not until 1756, with the financial pressures of the Seven Years War, that the Habsburg government, under the leadership of its minister plenipotentiary to the Netherlands, Johann-Karl Cobenzl, 'the Austrian Colbert', felt strong enough to defy both local refiners and the Dutch and establish an imperial refinery at Ostend. In the initial ten year contract with the manager, Charles Levasseur of Tournai, the refinery was not given a monopoly of import, production or distribution, but this was clearly the long-term objective. It was given from the first advantageous inland freight rates and later a privileged position in a new protective tariff aimed at inhibiting imports from abroad. The refinery operated under imperial control from 1756 to 1770. It constructed impressive buildings which are illustrated in the *Encyclopédie*; it installed six evaporation pans powered by coal, one of the first continental salt works to use this fuel successfully; and under efficient management it produced good quality salt which forced a reduction of prices in Antwerp, Brussels and Malines. A reference to 30 or 40 vessels expected at Ostend bearing grey Dalmatian salt suggests an interesting partnership with Trieste, another developing Habsburg port, but the remark may refer only to a kind of salt, i.e. coarse, coloured, unrefined.

In toto, however, Cobenzl's attempt to recreate in Belgium the monopoly conditions of Central Europe must be regarded as a failure. The refinery was undercapitalized, so that its production was never sufficient to allow it to proceed to the state of attempting a genuine monopoly, though its privileged competition antagonized existing domestic producers. Equally the protective tariffs annoyed foreign interests, notably the French authorities who were trying to promote the sale of Lorraine salt in Luxemburg.[30] Since France and Austria were by now allies, French pressure at Vienna was able to obtain the reduction of the tariffs in 1768, thereby impairing the protection. In 1770, on the death of Cobenzl, its most consistent supporter, the imperial refinery was privatized. As a private company, it was still trading in 1788, but to judge from the destinations of exports from Brouage and Setubal, Ostend never became a great salt port. No doubt, as with the Ostend East India company at the beginning of Habsburg rule in the Low Countries, there was implacable Dutch hostility to any indirect revival of Antwerp. It was probably Dutch smuggling rather than French resentment which was responsible for undermining Cobenzl's scheme. Either way Habsburg enlightenment was thwarted to the disadvantage of Belgium, of whose nineteenth-century industrial revival the precocious use of coal, probably form Liège, at Ostend may be regarded as a precursor.[31]

Thus though less formalized in its operations than Venice in the *Ufficio* or the Bourbons in the *Gabelle*, the Habsburg state was deeply concerned with salt administration from Ostend to Tuzla and from Pago to Eastern Galicia. The assertion of regalian rights to salt, if possible from producer to consumer and under direct official control, formed a consistent modality of its action from the battle of the Marchfield to the annexation of Bosnia-Herzegovina. Like any family of prudent landlords, the Habsburgs held on from one generation to another, adding acre to acre, saline to saline.

THE STATE'S TAXES IN THE HABSBURG SALT ADMINISTRATION

The Habsburg and Bourbon states were at least comparable bodies. Schönbrunn is often compared with Versailles and we have already compared Cobenzl with Colbert. Both states began in a court, expanded into nobilities of both birth and merit, allied with the Church, and established a civil and military bureaucracy which meshed more or less well with the autonomous institutions of society and culture. Yet with regard to the fiscal aspect of salt administration: the assessment, collection and receipt of tax; differences predominated over similarities. The *Salzmonopol* contrasted rather than compared with the *Gabelle* for reasons which lay deep in the different structure of production, distribution and consumption in the Danubian lands.

Assessment

Compared with the Bourbon *Gabelle*, the Habsburg *Salzmonopol* was more comprehensive in its assessment of salt to tax. The basic reason was geographical. The structure of production in the Danubian lands was not too difficult to bring under comprehensive control. Danubia was like Szechwan, in particular like southern Szechwan, what was known in the days of the foreign inspectorate as Ch'uan-nan. Indeed, European accounts of Szechwan in the nineteenth century often compared it with Greater Hungary as another land of the four rivers.[32] A similar comparison, could easily be worked out between Greater Austria and Ch'uan-pei, northern Szechwan. Chengtu might be Vienna,

Chungking might be Budapest. Both Szechwan and Danubia were supplied with salt from a limited number of wells and mines. The structure was punctiform and hence susceptible of control. From the point of view of salt administration Danubia was better than Szechwan in that while Szechwan was supplied by a few large centres but also by many small ones all of which had to be controlled, Danubia was generally supplied only by large ones. Disregarding East Galicia, Danubia was supplied essentially by only 12 salines: seven in Greater Austria (Hallein, the four Salzkammergut salines, Hall in Tyrol and Wieliczka-Bochnia) and five in Greater Hungary (Soovar, Ronaszek, Ujvar-Sugatag, Torda, Maros-Ujvar). Szechwan, on the other hand, was supplied by 40 salines, though the foreign inspectorate managed to reduce the number to 26: 15 in Ch'uan-nan, of which only seven took part in the long-distance waterborne trade; 11 in Ch'uan-pei, the equivalent of the 10 in East Galicia. The final positions therefore were not so different. Danubia and Szechwan were alike too in being comparatively immune from external smuggling. Both were too far from the sea for their artificially boiled salt to be competed against by cheaper solar evaporated marine salt except marginally: Canton salt in Kweichow, Adriatic salt in Inner Austria and Croatia.

Because of these geographical circumstances, the *Salzmonopol*, unlike the *Gabelle*, could aspire to comprehensive assessment, the taxation of all salt. No doubt, as in Szechwan, it was difficult to control movement in the immediate vicinity of the saline. Every mine or well was surrounded by a small tax-free zone. Unlike Szechwan, however, the Habsburg salines were often in sparsely inhabited areas, so that such avoidance mattered less. Salzburg might benefit from Hallein, Cracow might benefit from Wieliczka-Bochnia, but not much smuggling could take place from the Salzkammergut, Soovar or Maros Ujvar. What the Habsburg salt administration did not have, however, were whole tracts of tax-free territory like the *Pays redimées* or the *Pays exempts*, and this despite the fact that the Habsburg state was in general less powerful than the Bourbon. The Danubian situation of a small group of inland salt points plus a minority of salt coast was more controllable than the French situation of considerable lengths of maritime salt coast plus a minority of inland salt points. The Habsburgs, therefore, were relatively successful in universalizing and enforcing their assertion of regalian right over salt. Moreover in most cases they did not have to make the assertion themselves. It had already been done by the Babenberg dukes in the Salzkammergut, by the counts of the Tyrol at Hall, by the archbishops at Hallein, by the kings of Poland at Wieliczka-Bochnia, by the Romanovichi in East Galicia, by the Rakoczis at Soovar, Ronaszek and Ujvar-Sugatag, by the princes of Transylvania in Torda and Maros-Ujvar. Only in Provence and in the Franche Comté was the French crown in the happy position of succeeding to a centralizing localism. In salt too, the old maxim held: *bella gerant alii, tu, felix Austria, nube!*

Collection

As with the *Tabakregie* introduced in 1784, the Habsburg state aimed at complete control of the trade: production, transport and distribution. Ideally, salt was controlled by the state from the moment it emerged from the vat to the moment it passed across the counter in a shop. In practice, down to the reorganization of the monopolies in the nineteenth century, the ideal was not always achieved. Many operations were farmed to local agency, but the ideal ensured that the point of collection of tax followed the French rather than the Chinese pattern. Collection took place low down on the course from producer to consumer in accordance with the principle of *hsien-yen hou-li*, first salt then tax. Unlike France, however, there was no *sel de devoir*, the levy on salt was not a poll tax on individuals, and the salt trade formed part of the regular interchanges of the great estate with the outside world. The *Herrschaft*, the basic social unit of the Danubian world, was a business. It exchanged its grain, cattle, fish, beer and spirits, and mineral products (silver, iron, copper, lead, mercury) for textiles, manufactured goods, salt and consumer luxuries. It did this, not indirectly through the towns which in Eastern Europe had ceased to be business centres, but directly through independent traders, frequently non-native and often itinerant: German, Dutch or Jewish; in the case of the Wallenstein estates, Hans de Witte, the Flemish Calvinist from Antwerp.[33] For the bailiff of a great estate, salt would be in part a consumer luxury, in part an industrial necessity for carp packaging which he bought on credit from his usual non-urban supplier. The peasant, compelled by *Anfeilszwang* to buy in the lord's shop, paid tax, not so much by a high price for salt as he would in the *Grande Gabelle*, as by *robot*, compulsory service, on the lord's land. For the bailiff too, working in a partly non-monetary economy, salt might be acquired as a result of a complicated set of *troc* operations.

In this way salt was not singled out as a high priced monopoly commodity as it was by the *Gabelle*. Consequently, though there were serious peasant disturbances during the establishment of the new *Herrschaft* system, as for example in Bohemia in 1680, they did not take the form of anti-salt administration revolts like those of the *Pitauts*, the *Croquants* and the *Nu Pieds*. The Habsburg state, less bureaucratic and more aristocratic than the Valois-Bourbon, was better able to shelter behind the powers of society. Salt tax collection, therefore, was less frictionful in the Habsburg lands than in France. *Faux-saunage*, the constant guerrilla war of the smugglers against the *gabellous* with public opinion on the side of the smugglers, does not seem to have been a problem in Danubia. Instead, what was a problem, for example at Wieliczka-Bochnia, was evasion through privileged aristocratic buying and resale which in Poland could amount to 20 per cent of output.[34] In France, the state was incomplete. In the Habsburg lands, it was limited, below a certain level simply non-existent. In salt tax collection the Habsburg state attempted less than the Bourbon but achieved more of what it attempted.

Receipt

At first sight, the Habsburg system of receipt, even before the nineteenth-century reforms, appears a centralized one, equivalent to that only achieved by the Bourbons at the very end of the *ancien régime*. From 1525, the *Hofkammer* had theoretical control of all crown revenue, regalian, direct and indirect, not only in the Erblände, but also in Bohemia, Royal Hungary and eventually in the *Neo-Acquistica* of former Turkish Hungary. In fact the appearance was misleading. There were three major limitations to the effectiveness of this centralization which down to the nineteenth century kept the imperial treasury divided.

First, besides the *Hofkammer* itself at Vienna, there were the branch offices at Innsbruck and Graz as relics of secundogeniture, the *komorniei* at Prague, another *kammer* at Breslau, the *kamara* or *Camera Hungarica* at Pozsony capital of Royal Hungary, and the *Zipser Kammer* of Szepes at Kassa in the Felvidek. Despite their names these were as much rivals as subordinates. Second, the main *Hofkammer* itself was marked by a lack of rationalization, particularly in distinguishing the public and private application of credits. In 1680 Georg Ludwig von Sinzendorf, who had been president of the *Hofkammer* for the preceding 24 years, was convicted of embezzling 2 million florins of public money, some 25 per cent of a regular annual income of 8 million. The conviction may not have been fair, any more than that of Foucquet 20 years before; Sinzendorf was possibly trying to reform the system by concentrating it in his person.[35] Moreover as we have seen from Venice, private profit at public expense is not necessarily injurious to society, however unaesthetic to modern taste. But the facts point to a lack of centralization of receipt in the full sense. Third, unlike the *Gabelle*, the *Salzmonopol* could not build on a centralized banking network like that of the farmers-general and *finance*. Until the creation of a national bank in 1816 and still more the coming to Vienna of Rothschild and Hirsch after 1848, there was no proper public banking system in the Habsburg lands. Of course, like all *ancien régimes*, the Habsburg state made transfers and borrowed by anticipating and assigning revenues, but its agencies for doing so were more particular and less unified than in France.

Despite the façade of the *Hofkammer*, receipts therefore were not really centralized and at the disposal of a minister of finance until the nineteenth century, the age of Schwarzenberg, Bach and Bruck. Till then the Habsburg state in its management of its taxes remained in many ways a super *Herrschaft*, a landed proprietor ruling above, in and through other landed proprietors.

THE PEOPLE'S LIVELIHOOD IN THE HABSBURG SALT ADMINISTRATION

In the social dimension of their salt administration, the eastern Habsburgs stood closer to China than to Venice or France. The reason for this was the importance in both the Danubian monarchy and the traditional Chinese state of a higher ideological component than in western European states. In Venice the social dimension of the salt administration was economic: the subsidization of the rich by the poor for their mutual enrichment. In France, it was political: the reiteration of the severe but compelling image of the half-sacred, half-secular state of Louis XIV. In China and the Habsburg lands, it was cultural: Confucian in the first case, Latin Baroque Catholic in the second. If the state's taxes were collected by the Habsburgs through one major Danubian social institution, the great estate, they were expended by them for the benefit of another, the Church, and in particular, the religious orders: *Österreich Klösterreich*, Austria land of religious houses.

The most notable example of the subsidization of the Church by the state through the salt administration was the so called *Salzvertrag* or salt treaty of 1630.[36] This formed part of the post-White Mountain, Habsburg settlement of Bohemia as the financial-ecclesiastical counterpart to the *Verneuerte Landesordnung* of 1627. Under the *Salzvertrag*, an agreement between the pope and the emperor arranged by Archbishop Harrach of Prague and his Capuchin adviser Valerian Magni, the Church, having already recovered substantial amounts of property as a result of the Habsburg reconquest, agreed to renounce any further claims on lands alienated since Hussite times, in return for one quarter gulder on every barrel of salt imported into Bohemia. The agreement, a resealing of the alliance between Church and state, was not reached, however, without considerable misgivings on the part of the Church. Indeed, outright opposition to it was voiced by Caspar von Questenburg, head of the influential Premonstratensian house at Strahov outside Prague. This opposition was significant because the Premonstratensian white canons were the single most important religious order in Bohemia, their founder St Norbert recently elevated as the patron of the newly recatholicized kingdom.

It is not difficult to understand the grounds of Questenberg's opposition. First, the Church was being offered income in exchange for capital.
Second, while the capital it was being asked to give up was land, the
most valuable kind of asset in central European terms, the income to be
substituted was commercial in character, and hence, again in central
European terms, neither prestigious nor secure. Third, this income from
the salt monopoly was a royal gift and what could be given might be
withdrawn. The Church was being asked to become a salariat: to shift its
fiscal foundations from society to the state; the principle subsequently of
louisquatorzien Gallicanism, Josephism and Napoleon's concordat. Finally it is likely that Questenberg saw the treaty as effecting a redistribution of the resources of the Church. The lands being renounced were
the property of the older monastic orders: the Benedictines, the Augusti-
nians (of which the Premonstratensians were the reformed branch) and
Cistercians. The revenue being acquired might well go to the new
orders: the Irish Observant Franciscans, the Capuchins and, most dis-
agreeable of all from Questenberg's point of view, the Jesuits, with
whom the Premonstratensians were in particular rivalry over education.

The connection between Jesuit foundations and the salt monopoly is
not well documented, but nevertheless suggestive. The Jesuits were an
urban order, *magnas Ignatius urbes*, and were frequently financed by
commerce. In Japan the Jesuit mission was paid for by the Great Ship
from Macao. In France the Jesuits were involved in the West Indian
trade and were eventually ruined by it. In Brazil, indeed, in the seventeenth century, the salines of Maranhao were run by the Jesuits. Nevertheless in Danubia the association between the geography of Jesuit
foundations and the geography of salt; production points, routes, distribution centres; seems too close for coincidence. Thus we find the Jesuits
at Hall in Tyrol, Linz the export port for the Salzkammergut, Ingolstadt
close to the Bavarian distribution centre of Donauworth. We find them
at Nagyszombat (Tyrnau) near the branch office of the *Hofkammer* at
Poszony which controlled the mines of Hungary, at Kassa near the
saline of Soovar, at Ungvar the headquarters for the mines of subcar-
pathian Ruthenia, Koloszvar in the heart of the Szamos salt producing
area, Gyulafehervar in the Maros area. In addition the Habsburgs
supported the Jesuits beyond their own dominions. They subsidized the
works of Athanasius Kircher and supplied men and funds to the 'Portuguese' Jesuit mission in Peking, one of whose most notable members,
August von Hallerstein from Laibach, president of the tribunal of
astronomy 1746–1774 was a friend of Leopold I's daughter Maria Anna,
his brother being a leading Jesuit at Vienna and confessor to Maria
Theresa's brother-in-law Charles of Lorraine.[37]

The Jesuits were not the whole of the Counter-Reformation in Eastern
Europe. Its main body was the older monastic orders, its flanks the

various kinds of friar, notably Capuchins in Bohemia, Paulines in Hungary. Yet the Jesuits, shown the way by Canisius and Pazmany, were the vanguard, with their international perspective the whole *in* the Counter-Reformation, and as such peculiarly dependent on initial crown support and subsidization, whose readiest source was salt revenue. The early Jesuits, the age of Canisius and Pazmany, probably owed much to Habsburg possession and contemporaneous development of salt resources, beginning with the Salzkammergut, where Ischl was opened in 1571 and Ebensee in 1607. Paradoxically, the Salzkammergut itself was a strongly Protestant area, as were so many of the mining districts of Germany. As a result, the Habsburgs and the Jesuits had to tolerate heresy there, so that as late as 1879 nearly a third of the population was Protestant. Thus curiously the spiritual and the material intertwined.

Mercantilism in the sense of conscious economic promotion by the state was slow to come to the Habsburg lands. Nevertheless, some of the state's interest in salines rubbed off on to other forms of mining as works like Kircher's *Mundus Subterraneus* drew attention to the wonders of inner space contrasted with the oceanic or astronomic space of Western Europeans. Though the Habsburgs alienated many of their Styrian iron mines to the aristocracy in the 1560s, they attempted with some success to recover them after 1625 via the *Innerbergen hauptgewerk- schaft*. They retained and enveloped the mercury mines at Idria in Carniola, which were used as security for Dutch loans after 1650 and copper mines in northern Royal Hungary, the modern Slovakia. Copper was exported westward via the Danube, probably ultimately to Amsterdam, and the need for uninterrupted passage across Bavaria was one reason why until near the end of the seventeenth century, the Habsburgs tolerated the export of Reichenhall to Bohemia and accepted its competition in the *Vorlände* as a necessary evil.[38] The interests of mining as a whole thus affected the structure of the salt administration. Another area of proto-mercantilism where salt may have figured was the *Orien- talehandelscherkompagnie* founded in 1667 to promote trade down the Danube to the Ottoman empire, primarily in textiles but also in mineral products, salt being one of the commodities imported by the Turks from Transylvania. Thus although economic considerations in Colbert's sense were not central to the Habsburg conception of salt administration, they were not entirely absent from it.[39]

THE SALT ADMINISTRATION IN THE HABSBURG STATE

As China, Venice and France, so in the Habsburg empire, the salt administration served the state in regular finance, diplomacy and emergency. In general, the *Gabelle* was the closest analogue to the

Salzmonopol in the position it occupied in the state, but once again, except in diplomacy, the services received by the Habsburgs were rather different from those received by the Bourbons because of the character of their state as a partnership with the 200-odd familes of the high aristocracy.

Regular Finance

Here it is best to focus on the reign of Leopold I, 1657–1705, the adolescence of the Habsburg state as a great power, when the salt revenues were of greatest significance to it. Compared with the Bourbon kingdom, salt revenues in the Habsburg empire were simultaneously of lesser proportion but greater importance in the total revenue and expenditure. In the Habsburg empire, salt was universally but not heavily taxed: the opposite to the position in *ancien régime* France where it was heavily but not universally taxed. Toward the end of the seventeenth century, the total revenue of the Habsburg state was in a normal year (though there were not many normal years) around 10 million florins. Of this, the salt monopoly provided around 1 million florins: 10 per cent compared with the 20 per cent the *Gabelle* provided the French state in 1681. Nevertheless, a cameralist source in the seventeenth century speaks of salt as the brightest jewel in the crown of the *Hofkammer*.

The justification for this opinion lay in the peculiar profile of Habsburg finance. Unlike the Bourbons, the Habsburgs, because of their partnership with the aristocracy, could not tax land directly: there was no *taille* in Danubia. The *Hofkammer* received two kinds of revenue. First, there was the *Camerale*, or ordinary revenue, from crown lands (much alienated), tolls (not much trade), mines (iron, copper, quicksilver) and the *Salzmonopol*, which in 1700 totalled around 3 million florins. Second, there was the *Militare*, or extraordinary revenue, requested by the *Hofkriegsrat* in the light of military needs and vote by the Estates generally in the form of taxes on the beer and spirits consumed by the peasants, which in 1700, totalled around 7 million florins. The trouble was that the levies voted by the Estates came in slowly, irregularly and incompletely and in the meantime armies had to be raised, equipped and paid. Moreover, to a greater extent than the Bourbon monarchy, the Habsburg state was in chronic, structural deficit. Combined *Camerale* and *Militare* seldom provided more than half total government expenditure which by 1700 had risen to at least 20 million florins a year. Clearly the government financed itself by borrowing. Danubian society and the Habsburg state could not produce a class of *finance* as it existed in France. The Habsburg state therefore borrowed from abroad: from their allies, the English and the Dutch, and from their protégés, the Jews of Frankfurt.

Here the salt revenues were useful as security. In 1695 Samuel Oppen-
heimer of Frankfurt lent 3 200 000 to the court of Vienna. His initial
repayment of capital and interest of 800 000 florins came 100 000 from
the *Salzampt* of Lower Austria and 200 000 from its *Deputationsampt* in
Prague. Nevertheless, Habsburg credit was not good in commercial
terms. Vienna, therefore, had to borrow chiefly from its own supporters:
ministers like Sinzendorf and Kollonich, religious houses like the Schot-
tenkirche in the capital or the Cistercian abbey of Zwettl, cathedral
chapters like that of Esztergom, members of the aristocracy like Prince
Schwarzenberg or Prince Dietrichstein; often the same people who
managed the estates and were organizing the armies. In 1700 80 per cent
of the government's debt of 22 million florins was held by such people.
Here again the *Salzmonopol* helped. Aristocrats, especially in Bohemia,
needed salt for their estates and the interest on their loans could be met
by free deliveries, while the principal was met in theory out of the
eventual *Militare*, or in fact out of grants of land acquired by war,
especially in Hungary. Habsburg finance was complex, a continuous
robbing of Peter to pay Paul with Hans the peasant eventually paying
the piper. By their regularity and reliability the salt revenues, though
not a large part of *Hofkammer* receipts, were an essential lubricant in the
process. Even in periods of military confusion, and Vienna was the most
threatenable capital in Europe, the salt trade could be expected to go on
underneath. To a *Hofkammer* official salt must have seemed a jewel indeed.
Salt was essential to credit and, like any landlord, the Habsburgs lived on
credit.

Diplomacy

Salt supported not only Habsburg arms but also Habsburg diplomacy.
In particular, the Habsburgs were successful players of salt politics in
eastern Switzerland. Here where their image, as hereditary oppressors
and patrons of the Counter-Reformation, was bad and their arms, as the
defeat of the Archduke Leopold in 1624 showed, were weak, they had
need of other leverage.

Like France, the Habsburg state operated in Switzerland at two levels.
First in the southeast, the Habsburgs needed leverage with the Prot-
estant Grisons which until 1797 were the predominant power in the
Valtelline. The Valtelline was the Catholic valley of the Upper Adda
which on the north contained the Bernina and Umrail passes to the
Engadine, i.e. the Upper Inntal, on the east the Stelvio (Stilfserjoch) pass
to the upper Adige and thence to the Brenner, and on the south the
Aprica pass to the Val Camonica and Venetian territory. The role of the
Valtelline as part of the Spanish road between Milan and the Netherlands is well known and its story is usually told in terms of the Thirty

Years War and Richelieu's successful interventions in 1625 and 1635. But in fact Richelieu's interventions were only temporarily successful and by 1640 the Valtelline had been reopened to Habsburg forces. Moreover, the passes continued to be important after 1648, particularly the Stelvio which, quite apart from any wider north–south perspectives, was the only link between Milan and the Tyrol outside Venetian territory. Prince Eugene had to watch the Valtelline during his Italian campaigns in the war of the Spanish succession and from 1714 Milan itself formed part of the territory of the Viennese Habsburgs. Indeed even after the Habsburgs acquired Venice and annexed the Valtelline, the Stelvio continued to be of significance as is shown by the construction, on the present line, of the Stilfserjoch road by the Austrian engineer Karl Donegani between 1820 and 1824.[40] The Grisons therefore were an ongoing problem. Salt, therefore, always needed in pastoral Switzerland, was a useful lever. Here the Habsburgs were in a strong position. Hall in Tyrol was the closest source of supply and, though its production costs were higher than Venetian sea salt, its transport costs were lower. Moreover the progressive abandonment by Venice of its role as a salt entrepôt left it without a rival, since France never signed a salt treaty with the Grisons and Bavarian salt rarely penetrated so far.

Second, in the northeast, the Habsburgs needed, if less imperatively, leverage with the cantons, again mainly Protestant, to the south of Lake Constance and the Rhine: St Gallen, Appenzell, Schaffhausen, and above all Zurich. They needed this to preserve an alternative route to the usual one north of the lake from Bregenz in the Vorarlberg to the scattered Habsburg territories in southern Suabia and then to the Breisgau in Baden and the Sundgau of southern Alsace. Again, the history of these routes is usually analysed in terms of the Thirty Years War and north–south communications, but in fact the Habsburgs retained some of the *Vorlände* till 1815, and the Breisgau in particular, with its prestigious Erasmian, non-Jesuit university at Freiburg, was a useful point of support for Habsburg policy in Germany. Habsburg salt diplomacy, however, faced more competition in northeast Switzerland than southeast. France signed salt treaties with Zurich in 1742, 1743, and 1768 and 1780, usually for several years' import at a time.[41] Zurich also bought Reichenhall salt from Bavaria. In competition round Lake Constance, Bavaria, especially after the modernization of Reichenhall and Traunstein at the turn of the eighteenth and nineteenth centuries, at least held its own from its depot at Lindau against the Tyrol with its depot at Bregenz. Hall's greater success southwest as compared with northwest may have been a factor in the Habsburg's decision in 1815 to abandon the *Vorlände*, except for the Vorarlberg itself, but to retain Milan and the Valtelline.

Emergencies

The two greatest military emergencies faced by the Habsburgs in the seventeenth century were the Bohemian revolt of 1618 and the Ottoman siege of Vienna in 1683. In the resolution of both, the battle of the White Mountain and the battle of the Kahlenberg, salt revenues played a part, albeit in the background. Although in pose a military monarchy, on both occasions the dynasty found itself without an army and had to have recourse to the arms of others: those of Bavaria in 1620, those of Poland in 1683. Grillparzer's famous apostrophe to Radetzsky, *In deinem Lager ist Österreich*, perhaps only became true in the nineteenth century.

In the treaty with Maximilian of Bavaria, himself the master of the newly updated Reichenhall, Ferdinand II had to agree to pay the expenses of Tilly and the army of the Catholic league. Soon in debt to the Duke to the tune of 3 million gulden, nearly a year's income, the emperor was forced to mortgage to him Upper Austria and its revenues including those of the Salzkammergut, which were not recovered till the peace of Prague in 1635. So severe was the Duke's exploitation that there was a major peasant revolt in 1625–26 with the decisive battle at Gmunden and further rumblings in 1632 and 1634. Similarly, in the treaty with John Sobieski, Leopold I had to agree to pay the expenses of the King and the army of the Polish republic. The charge was laid mainly on the Silesian *Kammer* at Breslau and one of the assets which was transferred in the transaction was the lien on the revenues of Wieliczka–Bochnia, which the Habsburgs had acquired in 1657 as the price of their own assistance to Poland during the invasion of Charles X of Sweden. Ferdinand in other words paid John Sobieski by returning his own mortgaged salt revenues. As John Stoye puts it: 'He surrendered a mortgage on the great salt mine of Wieliczka, south of Cracow, which had been exploited by his own revenue-officers in Tarnowske (Silesia) for a number of years'.[42] Thus in the first emergency the emperor granted a salt mortgage, in the second he surrendered one, but in both cases salt contributed to military relief.

For civil emergencies, such as the plague visitations, of which that of 1679, which killed 12 000 people in Vienna and prompted the erection after the siege of the *Pestsaüle* in the *Graben*, was the most notable, we have little information how their costs were met. It is difficult not to believe that the *Hofkammer* and its salt revenues were not involved as the source of funds of first resort.

The Habsburg state pressed less heavily but more evenly on its society than did the Bourbon. Its salt administration likewise was less oppressive and more equitable than the *Gabelle*. Consequently it did not attract the kind of hostility which the *Gabelle* had accumulated by 1789 and so was able to survive into the nineteenth and twentieth centuries as one of a group of state monopolies. Nonetheless, the Habsburg state, like the *Serenissima*, was more deeply committed to salt administration than the French state. At the beginning, indeed, the archduke, like the king of Hungary before him, the king of Poland–Lithuania at the same time and the prince of Transylvania subsequently, had few other reliable sources of revenue. In the closed, slow moving and bucolic world of Eastern Europe, salt was a mobile element, exploitable by the state as an engine of other mobilizations. Danubia, like Szechwan in many ways, had less good river communications but better roads than the Chinese province where pack animals were the rule on land. The great carts, with their teams of four horses loaded with half dozen barrels of salt, dragging themselves over the highly imperfect but functioning roads of Danubia, were a real factor in the development of a translocal political power. The Habsburg empire was in its way as remarkable expression of European political genius as the Venetian republic or the Bourbon monarchy. Beginning with *Herrschaften* and *Landeshoheit*, it and its aristocracy turned provincial Vienna into a major capital which secreted a non-aristocratic bureaucracy, upheld the cosmopolitan culture of Latin Baroque Catholicism, and held the backdoor of Europe against the Ottomans. Like the *Serenissima*, the Habsburg state had its foundations in salt, but what was built on those foundations was different: different from either Venice or France.

10 The Ottoman Salt Administration

From Europe's greatest aristocratic monarchy we pass to its long time enemy, Islam's greatest meritocratic monarchy. In the period when the salt administration was of greatest significance to it, however, the Ottoman state was a friend of the Habsburg empire and from Islamic was becoming first dynastic and then Turkish nationalist. In this chapter we make three further transpositions. First, we leave Europe, though for much of its history the Ottoman empire was more a Balkan than an Anatolian state. Second, we enter modern times, for our focus will be the last period of Ottoman history, 1881–1923, where it was the first period of Habsburg. Third, we move into the world of imperialism, the European-centred world order, and its role in modernization. For the salt administration with which we shall be concerned functioned under the Ottoman public debt administration, a typical synarchic institution characteristic of that world order.[1] These transpositions will be maintained in the subsequent chapters on the Indian salt administration under the *raj* and the Chinese salt administration under the late empire and early republic. Salt administrations, we have argued, are characteristic of the beginning or end of states. It is not surprising therefore that in the last three chapters of this study, we move from the mature European core of the world order to its declining or renascent non-European periphery.[2] We end where all salt administrations began: in China.

The Ottoman salt administration was not a traditional Islamic institution. It was a European-inspired, nineteenth-century modernizing innovation. It reached its greatest significance under the aegis of the Ottoman public debt administration, a partly European staffed body, which was established by the decree of Muharrem of 23 November 1881. The salt administration itself, however, had been instituted by the Ottoman government itself in 1861 as part of the Tanzimat or reform movement begun by Sultan Abdulmecit I (1839–61) and continued by his brother Abdulaziz (1861–76). In its structure, the Ottoman salt administration, like much of the Tanzimat, was modelled on the Habsburg *Salzmonopol*. This is only to be expected because of proximity, frequent contact of officials, subsequent alliance, and the fact that in the nineteenth century the Habsburg and Ottoman empires shared the problem of being a state without a people and the need to establish an identity which would reinforce bureaucracy with public support. In its context, however, the Ottoman salt administration diverged from the Habsburg.

It was more Mediterranean and less continental and thereby stood closer to the Venetian salt administration, whose heir in some sites it was.

The Ottoman salt administration therefore was an original creation. It was part of that often underrated creativity which the Ottoman state, in conjunction with foreign advice, manifested in the last half century of its existence.[3] The Ottoman empire was not decadent. As in the parallel case of the Habsburgs, the fact of death as a result of the First World War does not prove moribundity before it. The Ottoman salt administration functioned in fact at the end of an old empire. It might also have been functioning at the beginning of a new one. For this was what the Turkey of Abdulhamit II (1876–1909) and the Committee of Union and Progress really was. If the empire was overthrown, it was not because it was decadent, but because some of its leaders overestimated its new-found strength and engaged precipitately in a premature war, as much against its friends as its enemies. The theme of the Ottoman salt administration, therefore, is the intelligent use of synarchy, foreign participation in a domestic institution, to reinvigorate an old state.[4] This theme is expressed at each level of analysis: the state in the salt administration, the state's taxes, the people's livelihood, and the salt administration in the state.

THE STATE IN THE OTTOMAN SALT ADMINISTRATION

Until 1861 there was properly no Ottoman salt administration. As argued in Chapter 3, salt was relatively abundant in the original Islamic lands. Its trade was short distance, by land and generally unimportant. Salt taxes therefore did not form part of classical Islamic fiscality. This consisted of *ushr* or in Turkish *öşür*, tithe, a subdivision of *zakat*, alms; *kharaj*, probably from the Greek *choregia*, land tax, inherited from the Byzantine empire; *jizyah*, capitation on non- Muslims, sometimes rationalized as scutage, compensation for exemption from military service; and, more contested because it lacked Koranic precedent, *tamgha*, tax on trade levied via the guilds. Nevertheless, although there was no generalized imperial salt administration, there were five local salt administrations grounded in particular state functions and circumstances, which form the background to the law of 1861.

First, in Constantinople, as noted above in Chapter 5, there was the *tuz emin*, the intendant of salt.[5] He saw to the supply certainly of the ruling institution, *Osmanlilar*, and probably of the city population as a whole, who were regarded, not as subjects, *rayas*, but as citizens, an extension of the palace and central government. Placed alongside the *sehir emin*, the prefect of the city, in charge of buildings and water, the *arpa emin*, the barley intendant, in charge of bread, and the *odun emin*, the wood intendant, in charge of fuel, the *tuz emin* was a welfare rather than a fiscal officer. What he operated was an *annona* rather than a *gabelle*, designed to lose money rather than make it.

Second, in the Crimea, an Ottoman satellite state from the fifteenth century until the treaty of Kuçuk Kaynarca in 1774, a number of salines belonged to the Giray khan: in particular, the *sebkhas* of Kinburn, Perekop and Caffa.[6] They provided one of his principal sources of revenue: 60 per cent at the time of Russian annexation, according to one report. This was a matter of some moment for the Ottoman Sultan because the Khan not only supplied Constantinople with some of its salt, but also, with its revenue, provided the Ottoman army with its light cavalry. In 1783 the Crimean salines passed to the Russian state and formed part of the Tsarist salt administration, systematized by Catherine the Great in 1781, which lasted down to 1818.

Third, in Egypt, salt production at Rosetta was claimed as a *muqata'a* or tax farm by the Mamluk emirs.[7] From its profit, they paid an *iltizam* or quota into the imperial treasury in Egypt, the *Hazine-i Amire*. The treasury, having met the local costs of Egypt, the expenses of the Ottoman guardianship of the Holy Places, and the needs of Constantinople for sugar, rice, lentils and coffee, sent the balance to the capital as the *Irsaliyye*, the Egyptian remittance, which formed a large item in the Ottoman budget. Two thirds of the Egyptian revenues came as *kharaj* from the land and the proportion of salt in the non-land taxes was not large. Nevertheless Egyptian salt played some part in the *Irsaliyye* which was the chief financial factor in converting the Spartan conquest-empire of Selim I into the Baroque splendours of Selim II and the age of Sinan. In the eighteenth century, the Mamluk emirs diverted most of the *Irsaliyye* to their own use, but eventually their endemic feuds enabled the Ottoman authorities to replace it by *hulvan* or payment by one emir for assuming the *muqata'a* of another: a neat substitution of an enforceable death duty for an unenforceable income tax. With the establishment of Mehmet Ali, feuds and *hulvan* ceased, but with the improvement in relations between Constantinople and Cairo after 1848, *Irsaliyye* was resumed vestigially until the final separation of the two states in 1914. Under the aegis of Lord Cromer, considerable reforms were introduced between 1892 and 1905 by Mr Hooker, director-general of the salt department. Salaried retailers were replaced by licensed retailers paid by commission, an increased number of retailers was provided, tax rates and prices were reduced, compulsory purchase (possibly a French influence) was abolished, and smuggling from the works was reduced by a British officered coastguard service. As a result, sales of tax paid salt in Egypt trebled from 33 000 tons to 100 000 tons. Lord Cromer, however, was not interested in increasing the yield which actually fell from £233 000 in 1891 to £182 000 in 1904 and on 1 January 1906 the salt

Table 10.1 Salt sales and revenue in Egypt, 1891–1906

Date	Sales (tons)	Revenue (£)
1891	30 380	233 000
1892	39 800	179 000
1893	45 300	—
1894	45 000	178 000
1895	44 000	176 000
1896	46 540	184 000
1897	48 850	198 000
1898	48 880	194 000
1899	50 140	—
1900	48 691	207 000
1901	52 221	223 000
1902	53 425	186 000
1903	57 000	189 000
1904	60 000	182 000
1906	100 000	—

monopoly was abolished altogether. The final instalments of the *Irsaliyye* therefore contained no salt component.

Fourth, salt, whether in the form of regalian rights or, more likely, tolls, formed part of the revenues of the local rulers, of Azerbaijan when this territory was taken over by the Ottomans at the end of the sixteenth century.[8] The salt in question was probably that of Lake Urmia, which has a salinity three-fifths that of the Dead Sea, though some of the bays of the Caspian are highly saline, despite the fact that the sea itself is nearly fresh. Azerbaijan did not long remain in Ottoman hands, being recovered by Shah Abbas in the early seventeenth century. The Ottomans regained control briefly at the end of the First World War, but there was no time to install a salt administration, though smuggling from Lake Urmia had previously been a problem in eastern Anatolia, Mosul and Baghdad.

Fifthly, on Crete the Ottomans inherited the salines which had been developed by the Venetian state to replace those lost on Cyprus, but never really used for this purpose.[9] The Sultan acquired possession of the island, after the almost interminable siege, in 1669, and of the salines, La Suda in the west and Spinalonga in the east, which had been reserved to the *Serenissima*, in 1715. La Suda produced low grade black salt, Spinalonga high grade white, but the salines seem to have been in a ruinous condition even before the end of Venetian occupation. The Cretan salines did not figure in the operations of the Ottoman public debt administration. Indeed, in 1911–12 just before its cession to Greece, Crete was an importer of salt from other Turkish centres.

This then was the background, or lack of it, to the law of 1861. Until then the Ottoman empire, like most Islamic states, was only locally involved in salt administration. On 24 November 1861, however, a salt works department *Memleke Müdürlügu* was set up within the ministry of finance *Nezaret-i Maliye*. 'The ownership, production and sale of all salt in the empire was now made a government monopoly. . . . District salt offices were established around the empire to supervise production and sell salt in quantity to dealers', who then sold to retailers or the public.[10] In 1909 there were over 200 of these offices and the number was constantly being increased to avoid local corners. In Chinese terms the system was one of *kuan-chih, kuan-yün, kuan-mai* (officials manufacture, officials transport, officials sell), i.e. a direct and extended monopoly. There was not much Islamic precedent for such a system. True, a 'basic Şeriat regulation allowed the state treasury to take one-fifth of the produce of all mines in the empire, whether they were on public or private land'.[11] But this provided a royalty, like the Spanish *quinto* on silver in the New World, rather than a regalian right. As we have just seen, it had not been widely invoked. It was not clear that marine salines, the principal source of salt in the Ottoman empire, were regarded as mines in this sense.

The antecedents of the Ottoman salt administration must be sought abroad. The obvious place to look is the Habsburg empire where a similar system of *kuan-chih, kuan-yün kuan-mai* was in operation. Relations between Vienna and Constantinople were close in the Tanzimat era as both states wanted to check Russia without permanently antagonizing her. Austria, the non-combatant, it has been said, was the real loser by the Crimean War. In 1856, the Habsburg government sent M. Lackenbacher as financial adviser to the Sublime Porte. In 1858 he was joined by British and French advisers who from 1860 together with him formed the *Conseil Supérieur des Finances*. In 1861, however, the Austrian would still have been its most experienced member. In addition Polish and Hungarian political exiles often took service in the Ottoman bureaucracy: for example, Michel Lattas, a Croat who, as Ömar Lufti Paşa, suppressed a revolt in Bosnia-Herzegovina and became a successful governor of Baghdad. Since neither Britain nor France at that date had a salt administration, it would seem most likely that the Ottoman salt administration was modelled on that of the Habsburg empire. It was a piece of Tanzimat modernization.

The immediate purpose of the new institution was debt service. Its revenues were devoted 'primarily to retiring paper money and bonds',[12] in particular those issued by the Ottoman bank. The bank had been set up as a private company with mainly English money in 1856 and was converted into a state reserve agency as the Imperial Ottoman bank in 1863, by which time French lending was as important as British. Because

of its various modernization programmes, the expenditure of the Ottoman state consistently exceeded its revenue. It had begun large-scale
borrowing during the Crimean War, both at home via the Armenian and
Jewish banking communities and abroad on the London money market.
The year 1861 was of particular financial stringency because of the
troubles in Bosnia-Herzegovina. Moreover, a programme of naval rearmament, which, under the leadership of Mahmut Nedim Paşa and the
English Admiral August Charles Hobart-Hampden, was to make the
Ottoman navy by 1876 the third most powerful in Europe in terms of
hardware, was already in prospect.

All these liabilities, past, present and future, lay behind the search for
new sources of revenue: stamp duty; a tobacco monopoly in 1860,
another Habsburg feature; and finally the salt monopoly in 1861. As in
the Habsburg empire, the rate of the new salt tax was not high. In 1881
on the eve of the establishment of the Ottoman public debt administration, the yield of the salt monopoly was approximately £600 000,
raised from some 150 000 tons of salt subject to tax: a rate of 0.5*d* a lb. As
a proportion of total revenue, the salt tax only amounted to 4 per cent.
But it was an unearmarked 4 per cent, one really received by the
treasury and not sticking to the fingers of the tax farmers and it was
equivalent of nearly half of what the debt service was scaled down to in
1879, £1 350 000.[13] To have created such an institution from scratch was
a notable achievement on the part of the Tanzimat regime.

Borrowing, however, continued. Between 1854 and 1875 the Ottoman
state borrowed internally and externally a total of £210 million. This was
not the reckless profligacy it is sometimes represented. Most of the
money was spent on state building, war not of the Porte's choosing, and
rearmament to avert further war. Even the much criticized palace of
Dolmabahçe on the edge of the Bosphorus in Beyoglu could be justified
as giving the monarchy a more European image than that projected by
the Seraglio. Moreover, borrowing was accompanied by increases in
revenue which rose from £2 million in 1829 to £10 million 1860 to £16
million in 1875.

What was unsatisfactory was not the debt or the purposes for which it
was borrowed, but the rate of interest and the debt service which by
1867 absorbed 80 per cent of the imperial revenue, say £12 million.[14] The
rate of interest was unsatisfactory because Ottoman credit was poor and
Ottoman credit was poor because imperial revenue was uncertain.
Imperial revenue was uncertain because the Ottoman state was too poor
to pay a salaried civil service to collect it to the full. Tax farming, the
mugata'a system, abolished in the enthusiasm of the early days of the
Tanzimat, had had to be restored in 1855 for the land taxes, *ushr* and
kharaj, the principal source of revenue. Farming is not necessarily a
wasteful or unmodern method of tax collection. We have seen this in the

case of the farmers-general in the *Gabelle*. But in the Ottoman empire, as operated by unpopular Armenians and Jews in conjunction with recalcitrant or grasping local authorities, it was systematically wasteful. The British ambassador to the Porte, Sir Henry Bulwer, described the situation to the Foreign secretary, Lord John Russell, in a letter of 12 November 1860:

> Your Lordship, however, is perfectly right in considering that the main and principal evil of the Turkish Administration – one in which I am sorry to say the Christians bear an equal share with the Turks – is the corruption which generally prevades it, and which renders the taxation at once grinding to the people and insufficient for the exigencies of the state.[15]

The Ottoman state, committed by modernization to rising expenditure, was caught in a vicious circle of inadequate revenue, inefficient tax collection, inadequate revenue, from which borrowing was the only way out. But borrowing in this situation was like drinking salt water as an answer to thirst.

The crisis came in 1878. At the end of the reign of Abdulaziz the accumulated debt stood at £140 million. The first two years of the reign of Abdulhamit II, which saw the Russo–Turkish war, added £70 million to this to produce a grand total in 1878 of £210 million. The Ottoman state emerged from the Congress of Berlin, where it lost two fifths of its territory and one fifth of its population, bankrupt in the sense of being unable both to meet current commitments, which included an indemnity of £60 million to Russia, and to raise further loans either at home or abroad. The Sultan's credit was exhausted.

The government of Abdulhamit II, under Gazi Osman Paşa and Ahmet Cerdet Paşa, a soldier and a canonist, reacted energetically to the crisis. Between 1878 and 1881 it took a series of measures which put Ottoman finance on a new footing. First, the accumulated debt was consolidated, converted and reduced to £124 million. Second, a ceiling was set on debt servicing at around 25 per cent of the budget. Third, by the decree of Muharrem of 23 November 1881, a public debt commission (*Düyun-u Umumiye Komisyonu*) was established. It was a special treasury department, separate from the ministry of finance, to administer and reform with foreign advice and assistance, certain designated revenues for the servicing of the scaled down debt. The foreign advice came from England, the Netherlands, France, Germany, Italy and Austria-Hungary who, together with the Ottoman state and the Galata bankers (i.e. the Armenian and Jewish financiers who handled the internal debt), each nominated one of the eight delegates who formed the council, with the British and French delegates acting as presidents alternate years. The staff was planned at 3000, 2 per cent foreign, 98 per cent Ottoman of whom not more than 7 per cent might be Christian. Of the designated revenues, the principal in order of importance in 1882–3 were tobacco (£878 813), salt (£618 029), spirits (£178 860) and stamps (£146 762). The yield of the designated revenues in that year was £1 873 895, about 10 per cent of a total revenue of £17–18 million.

The Ottoman public debt administration, as the commission came to call itself in English, belonged to a family of similar institutions which came into existence between the Crimean War and the First World War. In 1869 an international debt commission had been established in Tunisia. In 1876 the *Caisse de la Dette Publique* was set up in Egypt. In Persia a team of Belgians participated in the administration of the customs between 1898 and 1915.[16] Subsequently, the whole financial administration came under the control of two Americans, i.e. in terms of then political alignments, neutral financial missions: that of W. Morgan Shuster, treasurer-general of Persia, 1891–1912, followed by that of Arthur C. Millspaugh, administrator-general of the finances of Persia, 1922–1927. Between 1912 and 1914 Joseph Mornard, the Belgian head of the customs, acted as treasurer-general following Shuster's dismissal through Russian pressure. In China, the Sino-foreign imperial maritime customs had been established in 1854.[17] From 1894 it became the security for a number of foreign war and indemnity loans. The Sino-foreign salt inspectorate, which will concern us in Chapter 12, was instituted as a result of the massive reorganization loan of 1913.[18] All these institutions involved the principle of synarchy: foreign participation in the domestic administration of an independent state. All were concerned with fiscal reform, generally in the context of debt service. All were international in character, an expression of a European-centred world order which was more than the sum of Western imperialisms.

Very few of the synarchies were the product simply of Western *diktat*. As John K. Fairbank was the first to realize, non-European diplomacy in the age of imperialism was much less spineless and ineffective than a reading only of European diplomatic sources might lead one to suppose. Synarchy, which had many Asian but few Western precedents, served non-European as well as European purposes. Negatively, it served to avoid more radical forms of intervention or to neutralize a single aggressor by associating him with several. Positively, synarchy served to break out of the vicious circle of inadequate revenue, inefficient tax collection, inadequate revenue, by the introduction of cheap, skilled and incorrupt foreign administrators. Furthermore, such administrators, not deep in local politics or shackled by tacit assumptions, could investigate objectively and act radically, provided the task was not of too great complexity and support was forthcoming from the host government. Synarchy could do for states what they could not do for themselves. It was a means whereby non-European states could plug themselves into the new social technology of fiscal administration. It was a vehicle of modernization.

Sir Henry Bulwer was particularly aware of this aspect of synarchy. The Ottoman empire, he argued, must be modernized by Europeans who would train its citizens in the fields of finance, army, navy, telegraph and public works: 'Let the Sultan do as Peter the Great did, as even Mehmet Ali did: let him invite Europeans on honourable terms into his service; let him make use of them in honourable and responsible situations, and in a little time Turkey would be suffiently Europeanized to look Europe fairly in the face'.[19] Earlier, Bulwer had concluded his analysis of 'corruption': 'I am convinced that if it is to be dealt with effectually, Europeans must be employed in the Financial Adminis-tration of Turkey, and given complete control both as to the persons they should employ, the salaries they should give, and the punishments they should inflict'. Not only would an enlarged revenue result, but 'a new class of functionaries might be formed; whilst the honesty and regularity established in one branch of the Administration would intro-duce, eventually a change in the others'.[20]

Sultan Abdulhamit shared Bulwer's views. As against his more con-servative or nationalist advisers, he was positively in favour of the Ottoman public debt administration, not only for the reduction of the debt, but also for the reforms it was likely to bring. The most significant foreigners subsequently employed were Sir Vincent Caillard, a military engineer, who was alternate president 1883 to 1898 and the principal architect of the institution; Sir Adam Block, a consular officer and later chief dragoman at the British embassy, who was alternate president from 1903 to 1923, and the institution's master builder during its greatest days; and M. Leon Pissard who was general manager from 1906 to 1914 and chief foreman. Block's annual and special reports give the im-pression that he was in charge of policy. But he needed and received the support of the Ottoman government. In his special report for 1909–10, he was loud in the praise of Cavit, the minister of finance in the new government of the Committee of Union and Progress: 'It is my duty to put on record, that since the present Minister of Finance came into office, the relations between the Government and the Council of the Debt Administration have become more intimate and cordial than they have ever been hitherto'. He continued:

Djavid Bey has from the first thoroughly appreciated the work done by the Council of the Public Debt, and has realised that the interests of the Government and of the Debt Administration are identical. In the Chamber of Deputies and elsewhere, His Excellency has fearlessly and persistently supported the Debt Administration in the face of much hostile criticism on the part of the chauvinistic element of the press and of the population, which was only too ready to find fault with everything that was not purely Ottoman.[21]

With such support, however, he could accomplish much. Block was the Sir Robert Hart of the Ottoman public debt administration.

Like Hart, Caillard and Block were cautious in their approach to their hosts' finance. Of the Ottoman revenues confided to the administration's charge, the largest in 1881, the tobacco monopoly, continued to be farmed out, though the *mugata'a* was given no longer to Armenian and Jewish finance, but to Credit Anstalt of Vienna, Bleichroder of Berlin and the Imperial Ottoman bank. Similarly in the salt administration, the Turkish *eminet* system of direct and extended control was maintained though a new dynamism was imported to its policies. Here Sir Adam Block was less radical than Sir Richard Dane in the Chinese foreign salt *gabelle* who endeavoured to reduce official participation to taxation at source with freedom of production before and distribution after. Nevertheless, under the new regime the amount of taxed salt consumed domestically increased significantly and a sizeable export trade was developed for the first time. In addition, small quantities continued to be sent to Samos and Crete which, although nominally Ottoman till 1913, were in fact already lost to Greece. The rise in domestically consumed taxed salt was probably due as much to diminished evasion through administrative efficiency as to increased demand through rising living standards, though both factors were present. In 1909–10 Sir Adam Block commented:

Thanks to the control of our Inspectors, the more or less automatic extension of the depot service, the development of the railway system and certain police measures taken along the coast of Trebizond and elsewhere to prevent smuggling, the sale of salt in the salt works and depots has increased from 150 000 tons in 1882/3 to 230 000 tons in 1906/7, or an increase of about 3 300 tons a year.[22]

Table 10.2 sets out the development. It should be remembered that the Ottoman empire was at war with Italy from September 1911 to October 1912 and with the Balkan powers from October 1912 to March 1914 during which time she lost her territories in Libya, Albania, Macedonia and Western Thrace. From 1919 too the empire and with it the Ottoman public debt administration was in the throes of dissolution. Between 1881 and 1910, however, the administration had nearly doubled the quantity of salt brought to taxation. This result was achieved by ownership, or at least close control, of production and by a considerable

Table 10.2 Salt taxed in the Ottoman Empire, 1882–1923 (tons)

Year	Domestic consumption	Export	Total
1888–3	150 000	20 000	170 000
1903–4	218 199	63 993	285 015
1904–5	220 198	70 228	293 291
1905–6	228 037	71 521	302 722
1906–7	227 350	100 001	329 932
1907–8	237 657	85 742	326 920
1908–9	—	—	335 923
1909–10	239 382	116 072	358 890
1910–11	243 409	66 375	312 508
1911–12	261 947	80 612	346 625
1912–13	202 342	37 673	243 439
1913–14	218 782	71 665	293 218
1919–20	119 714	—	123 387
1921–2	61 161	5 550	66 965
1922–3	36 562	5 101	41 666

degree of supervision of distribution at the coastal depots and inland railway stations, as well as active promotion of sales.

The salt so taxed and distributed was produced in two groups of salines. First, there were coastal salines. The most important of these was Phocea or Foca in the Gulf of Smyrna which produced 100 000 tons a year. Next in importance was Mitylene, *c.* 50 000 tons a year, followed by Salonika, 15 000 tons, Trebizond, Tuzla in the Gulf of Edremit, Tripoli of Libya and the salines of Albania at Durazzo and Valona. Second, there were inland salines. These included mines of which the most important was Salif in the Yemen, 70 000 tons a year, followed by those of Hadji Bektash (Tuzkoy) near Kayseri, Sivas and Ankara, and *sebkhas* such as the Tuz Golu of Konya (Kotch Hissar), Pliny's Lake Tatta, the *sebkha* of Djebaul near Aleppo or the desert pans of Bevara and Sebaa west of Mosul. Production at most of these salines was farmed out to private enterprise, but at Phocea and Mitylene it was conducted directly by the officials. At Mitylene the work was done through salaried labourers: at Phocea through hereditary guilds of salt workers, though in 1909–10 these were expropriated and replaced by salaried staff. The mine at Salif too seems to have been a direct government enterprise.

To facilitate control and prevent smuggling the administration pursued a deliberate policy of concentration. It encouraged fewer but larger salines and discouraged the smaller centres both on the coast and in the interior. One has the impression that Sir Adam Block would really have liked Phocea to have been the sole source of supply for Rumelia and Anatolia. Such a move, however, with its wide political and social implications would have brought the administration to the limits of the possible for synarchy in salt administration. Synarchy, strong in some directions, in matters fiscal and technical, was by its semi-foreign character weak in others, in matters political and social. It simultaneously reinforced but limited the role of the state in the Ottoman salt administration.

THE STATE'S TAXES IN THE OTTOMAN SALT ADMINISTRATION

Like the Habsburg empire, which had a production in 1912 of 13 million cwt, the Ottoman empire, with a production of 6 or 7 million cwt, was comparable in *scale* to one of the major salt divisions of China. Unlike the Habsburg empire, however, which had similarities to Szechwan, the Ottoman empire, on account of its sprawling geography, diversity of ecologies and mixture of marine, rail and road communications, was not easily comparable in *structure* to any particular Chinese division. Perhaps the nearest analogue was Ch'ang-lu which in the early twentieth century had the same elements of a capital, an old waterway, new railways and camel caravans on the fringes. But the arrangement of the elements was different. Where Ch'ang-lu's waterway was the Grand Canal, the Ottoman empire's was the Dardanelles, the Marmara and the Bosphorus. Moreover, in its export trade, the Ottoman empire had a maritime, even an oceanic dimension denied to Ch'ang-lu till the Second World War. Though both the Habsburgs and the Ottomans operated a system of direct and extended monopoly, a system also found in China in Szechwan and northern Manchuria, the different structural context gave a special character in the Ottoman empire to the basic functions of assessment, collection and receipt.

Assessment

The Ottoman public debt administration was less comprehensive in its assessment of salt to tax than the *Salzmonopol*, though more comprehensive than the *Gabelle* since there were no *Pays exempt* or *Pays redimées*. Smuggling certainly existed: from Khoi and Urmia to Erzerum, Mosul and Baghdad; from Russia, presumably the Crimea, to Pontic Anatolia; from Egypt to Syria; and in the immediate vicinity of the Ottoman salines. Nevertheless it was impressive to tax 200 000 tons of salt consumed by 25 million people: 16 lb *per capita*, a high figure for a still largely premodern economy. By 1912 there cannot have been much salt that went untaxed in the Ottoman empire.

The explanation of this, in the geographical and administrative circumstances, remarkable achievement lay in the modern character and particular configuration of the transportation system. The Ottoman salt administration, unlike the *Gabelle* or the *Salzmonopol*, took shape at the same time as a centralized network of steamships and railways.

First, modern transport performed a preliminary canalization of trade which greatly facilitated assessment to tax. Salt, a bulky commodity, in whose final price transport costs always figure prominently, was quick to abandon the sailing ship, the cart and the camel for the steamer and railway as far as they would go. The area where the administration found the greatest difficulty both in providing adequate supplies and in preventing smuggling was eastern Anatolia where the railways gave out. Even there some routes were reasonably well defined. At Trebizond, for example, the camels which brought down grain from the interior took back salt for the upland farming communities. Further south, in Kurdistan and Armenia, with shortage of supply and high transport costs which encouraged evasion, things were more difficult. The report of 1905–6 specifically contrasts the good areas served by the railways: Smyrna, Konya, Salonika, Beirut, Ankara; with the bad areas not so served: Baghdad, Benghazi, Mosul, Seerdt, Trebizond and Mitylene. Fortunately the railway areas held the bulk of the population and consumed most of the salt.

Second, the configuration of the system was an unusually centralized one, which again facilitated control. Constantinople was simultaneously a Shanghai and a Peking: the headquarters of steam and commerce, the crossroads of rail and politics. The main steamer route of the empire ran from Smyrna to Samsun past the Golden Horn. The two main rail articulations were the northwest oriental line from Constantinople via Edirne to Sofia completed in 1874 with a branch line to Salonika in 1894 and the southeast Anatolian line. Starting in Constantinople, this ran in two variants: Haydarpaşa, Ankara, Konya, 1896 and Haydarpaşa, Eskişehir, Konya, 1894; which then diverged again to become the Hama–Damascus line and eventually the Hejaz–Holy places railway, and the Aleppo to Mosul line, the penultimate stage of the Berlin to Baghdad railway. All these routes and the goods they carried could be kept under the purview of the Ottoman public debt administration at the capital. Secondary routes not linked to the capital also served the salt administration well: the Smyrna to Salonika steamship route; the Salonika to Monastir railway complete in 1892: the Smyrna to Alaşehir line complete by 1894 and extended to Afyon Karahissar on the Anatolian railway in 1897; the Smyrna to Aidin line also complete by 1894. All these were very useful from the point of view of assessing Phocea salt. It was only in the outlying regions of the empire: Albania, Epirus, Libya, Kurdistan, Armenia, that the salt administration could not rely on modern transportation to canalize the trade and make it conspicuous enough to assess.

Collection

In Bourbon France and in the Habsburg empire, tax was collected from
the consumer when he obtained his salt from the *grenier à sel* or the
lord's grocery. It was collected low down the course from producer to
consumer in accordance with the principle of *hsien-yen hou-li*, 'first salt,
then toll', payment in arrear. In the Ottoman empire, on the other hand,
tax was collected at an intermediate stage in accordance with the principle of *hsien-k'o hou-yen*, 'first tax, then salt', payment in advance. If
some attempts were made to move collection lower down, this was for
commercial rather than administrative reasons, to prevent cornering of
local markets by *de facto* monopolitans, who might prefer to sell less salt
at a high price rather than more salt at a low price, to the disadvantage of
the revenue and consumers alike. Under the salt monopoly law of
24 November 1861, 'District salt offices were established around the
empire to supervise production and sell salt in quantity to dealers, who
were allowed to collect an additional fixed amount to provide a profit
and compensate for transport costs'.[23] In other words, the merchants
had to prepay the tax and the price paid by the consumer was fixed by the
administration. However, there are indications that before 1881 neither
the prepayment of tax nor the fixity of price was rigidly enforced. The
administration saw its revenue delayed and the public saw its price
enhanced. The Ottoman public debt administration after 1881 achieved
higher levels of enforcement. Tax was collected at one of three points:
the place of extraction or production, the depots or administrative
offices out in the provinces, and at particular railway stations in between. In Sir Adam Block's time particularly, the administration pursued a
policy of increasing the number of provincial depots to widen the circle of
merchants participating and so to expand sales: a policy similar to T'ao
Chu's *p'iao* system in Huai-pei and to Sir Richard Dane's *kuan-yuan* in
Szechwan. Some success was achieved in this direction. In 1904–5 over
half the salt was sold at the place of extraction, in 1913–14 less than half.

Dependence on modern transport brought disadvantages as well as
advantages. The Italian War of 1911–12 interfered with the trade in salt
in both the Aegean and the Red Sea, though anticipation of the blockade
increased sales in that year and made it one of the best in the administration's history. The effects on collection came in 1912–13 when the
Greek blockade succeeded the Italian and there was a fall of 100 000 tons
in the salt handled by the administration (Table 10.2). War, however,
could bring opportunity for Ottoman salt. During the First World War,
Smyrna displaced Egypt as the principal source of supply for Syria. Even
during the broken back conditions of 1918–1923, when much of the
Anatolian railway was out of action for normal traffic, the salt administration continued to function. In the last two years, 1921–2 and 1922–3,

Table 10.3 Sales of salt in the Ottoman Empire, 1904–23 (tons)

Year	Place of extraction	Depots	Railway	Total
1904–5	125 902	81 471	12 824	220 198
1905–6	127 491	85 964	14 582	228 037
1906–7	117 491	92 348	17 511	227 350
1907–8	119 848	97 135	20 673	237 657
1909–10	129 656	84 076	25 649	239 382
1910–11	121 930	92 357	29 121	243 409
1911–12	126 127	103 427	32 191	261 947
1912–13	92 824	87 380	22 138	202 342
1913–14	98 745	98 548	21 487	218 782
1919–20	64 961	47 162	7 591	119 714
1921–2	16 599	37 225	7 337	61 161
1922–3	12 222	19 985	4 355	36 562

depot sales exceeded sales at the place of extraction. Salt could still be brought by steamer from Smyrna to Kasimpaşa on the Beyoglu side of the Golden Horn and to depots on the Marmara and on the Black Sea coast. The advantages of Constantinople and modern transport were considerable in collection as well as assessment.

Receipt

The Ottoman public debt administration had been founded primarily as a debt collecting agency. It is not surprising, therefore, that from the beginning it aimed at centralization of receipt in the interests of the bondholders. That it was able to do so successfully was due to the presence in the Ottoman empire of an effective banking network. At the top there was the Imperial Ottoman Bank, itself one of the principal bondholders, whose organization had been developed in the 1860s by the Englishman James Lewis Farley, its accountant-general, though the institution subsequently became more French than British. The Ottoman bank had several dozen branches in all the main centres of the empire, which could be used to transfer tax funds to its main branch in Constantinople. However, the administration had more depots than the bank had branches and for transfer from these recourse had to be had to what in China would have been called native bankers, i.e. the Jewish and Armenian networks which had served the empire before the penetration of European finance. As noted above, the Galata bankers, as they were known, were entitled to nominate one of the eight delegates or board members of the Ottoman public debt administration, so their co-operation was not difficult to enlist.

Under Sir Adam Block, centralization of receipt was also assisted by the good relations which existed between him and Cavit Bey, minister of finance 1908–1915, the converted Jew from Salonika who was the representative in the government of the Committee of Union and Progress of the Galata banking interests. We have seen how in his report of 1909–10 Block commented on the suppport his organization had received from Cavit, especially in the matter of the reform of the Phocea salt industry, one of the most politically sensitive operations the administration had yet undertaken. He wrote: 'Since the advent to power of Djavid Bey, the present distinguished and enlightened Minister of Finance, all questions at issue between the council and the Government have been promptly settled without friction'.[24] By this time, the Ottoman public debt administration was much more than a debt collecting agency. Not only was its surplus now a source of revenue to the Ottoman state and if centralized a source of strength to the government in Constantinople, but it was also a basis of credit and an instrument for economic promotion. Cavit therefore had every reason to support the administration, for the people's livelihood as well as for the state's taxes.

THE PEOPLE'S LIVELIHOOD IN THE OTTOMAN SALT ADMINISTRATION

When the Ottoman public debt administration was established by the decree of Muharrem in 1881, salt was its no. 2 source of revenue after tobacco. By the eve of the First World War, salt, directly administered, had overtaken tobacco, farmed out. Furthermore, as fresh loans had been raised, new sources of revenue, approximately equal to the old had been acquired: mainly *öşür* or tithe, but also the 3 per cent customs surtax of 1907 of about £1 million supervised by Sir Richard Crawford the British adviser in the ministry of finance. Thanks to these increases of revenue from both old and new sources, the Ottoman public debt administration had near trebled its income, was running at a surplus and was able to undertake various kinds of welfare activity.

For, as Sir Adam Block put it in his special report for 1905–6: 'The council of Administration of the Debt has never adopted the *role* of mere

Table 10.4 Income of the Ottoman Public Debt Administration, 1882–1914 (£)

Year	Tobacco	Salt	Total income
1882–3	878 813	618 029	1 874 895
1883–4	—	658 554	—
1904–5	833 510	949 892	2 996 519
1907–8	899 352	1 123 886	3 919 002
1911–12	961 226	1 196 637	—
1913–14	942 600	1 103 023	5 382 472

bailiffs of the Bondholders clamouring for their pound of flesh. Over and over again we have come to the assistance of the Government, and time out of number we have given an impetus to industries in the country'.[25] The administration's extra fiscal welfare activities may be seen both within the salt industry and beyond it.

First, since salt was at all times its first or second source of revenue, the Ottoman public debt administration promoted the production and sale of salt both within the empire and in an export trade. Within the empire, it wanted to see more salt consumed, especially in eastern, or what might be called outer, Anatolia. In his special report for 1907–8 Sir Adam Block wrote:

The first step towards increasing the profits of the Salt Monopoly is to secure a sufficient supply of salt in the Eastern districts of Asia Minor at the lowest possible price. It is estimated that there is today a demand for a further amount of 20 000 tons, and once this salt is produced and placed within easy reach of the consumer, attention may be turned towards other districts which depend today upon contraband salt.

He continued:

Fewer salt pans must be worked and more salt must be extracted from the ramainder. If the Administration obtains the assistance of technical engineers, there is no reason why the salt extracted should not in two or three years be sufficient to meet the demand. If the salt pans cannot contrary to the general belief produce the salt in sufficient quantities, then recourse must be had to the salt mines, which should be opened up and worked on modern lines.[26]

In pursuit of these objectives, major reconstruction and modernization was undertaken at Phocea (possibly a realignment of the basins to produce a new catchment-condensers : crystallizers ratio similar to that used in the French Mediterranean saline) and an Austrian engineer from Wieliczka-Bochnia was employed to make a report on the eastern Anatolian mines.

Within the empire, the administration also wanted to see salt sold cheaper. In the 1907–8 special report, Block noted that, 'The existing law fixes the price of salt sold by the Administration in the salines and depots, but leaves untouched the retail price of sale by the salt merchants.' As a result, 'The dealer makes a corner in salt and demands exorbitant prices and the purchaser has either to be defrauded or to go without salt'. Action by the Administration was necessary: 'The question requires immediate examination and the Government will do well to consider the advisability of framing new regulations. It is, however, indispensable that we should constitute the necessary reserve stocks in the interior before we can hope to prevent the local cornering of the salt supply.'[27] In the special report for 1909–10, Block restated this aim:

The chief object of the Administration is not only to regulate and increase as far as possible the production of salt so as to suffice for the actual needs of the population, but at the same time to accumulate stocks in the principal centres to prevent any attempts at a corner in this commodity.[28]

The following year, 1910–11, he returned to the subject. Having discussed the reforms at Phocea, he continued:

Important as these reforms are, their achievement has, unfortunately though inevitably, retarded our initial effort to ensure a sufficiency of salt production in those regions of Asia Minor and European Turkey which still suffer from shortage of supplies, and which Phocea salt cannot reach. We hope however to be able, from 1912 onwards again to devote our special efforts to this urgent reform, the result of which ought to be not only to increase considerably our immediate profits, but also by enabling us to control completely the retail trade (to the exclusion of intermediary speculators), to lay the basis for a general readjustment of prices in the interest of fisc and consumer alike.[29]

Outside the empire, the administration promoted export. Before 1882 the export of salt from the Ottoman empire had been limited: about 20 000 tons a year mainly to the former Turkish provinces of the Balkans such as Serbia and Bulgaria. In the early part of the twentieth century, the administration opened a new trade to India and Singapore and in 1913–14 a mission was planned to the Far East to investigate further markets. For the Singapore trade, only one figure is available: 10 452 tons for 1906–7; but for the Balkans and India (which possibly includes the trade to Singapore) a series can be obtained (Table 10.5). Most of the salt exported to India was rock salt from Salif in the Yemen, but a little came from Phocea. In 1910–11 it was hoped that the reorganization would allow Phocea to compete with British and Spanish salt in India as well as with Tunisian and Italian salt which was reducing Ottoman markets in the Balkans, Bulgaria in particular. Salif, however, was the most important new source of salt developed by the administration. Its development was perhaps one reason why the Yemen remained relatively loyal to the Ottoman empire during the First World War.

Next, the Ottoman public debt administration concerned itself with railways. Blaisdell believes that 'Under the aegis of the Public Debt

Table 10.5 Exports of salt from the Ottoman Empire, 1882–1923 (tons)

Year	Balkans	India	Total
1882–3	20 000	—	20 000
1903–4	17 115	46 878	63 993
1904–5	18 855	51 373	70 228
1905–6	2 154	69 367	71 521
1906–7	13 301	86 699	100 000
1907–8	9 612	76 128	85 740
1909–10	12 465	103 606	116 606
1910–11	3 903	62 471	66 374
1911–12	4 394	76 217	80 611
1912–13	2 603	35 068	37 673
1913–14	2 124	69 541	71 665
1921–2	—	—	5 550
1922–3	—	—	5 101

Administration railroad construction in Turkey received its greatest impetus'.[30] The administration needed more railways to expand sales and facilitate assessment and collection: railway promoters needed the financial backing of the administration. Sir Vincent Caillard initiated the policy of giving such backing and secured the support of the Sultan for it. Thanks to its growing surplus, the administration was able to pay kilometre subsidies to the railway companies to ensure profitability in the early years. This policy was applied first in 1888 to the Haydarpaşa to Ankara line. It was used in the Salonika–Constantinople, Salonika–Monastir and Eskişehir–Konya lines in the 1890s. Subsequently it was applied in the extensions of the Anatolian railways to Damascus and Baghdad. Blaisdell comments: 'It is a question whether any of these enterprises would have been undertaken had it not been for the existence of the Administration of the Public Debt'.[31] Block certainly saw railway building as a means of economic promotion. In his special report for 1905–6, he stated: 'I have said that the economic conditions of the country are improving. The chief factor in the improvement is the construction of railways'. He continued: 'where railways have been built they have brought with them increased civilisation, tranquillity, better administration followed at once by increased production and prosperity . . . where there were Nomad tents there are now villages, where there were villages towns are being built'. He concluded: 'All things considered, Turkey is, I venture to affirm, in a better condition than at any time since the Crimean war'.[32] Railways were an important element in the revival of the Ottoman empire in the late nineteenth and early twentieth century and in its ability to sustain a four-front war not so unsuccessfully between 1914 and 1918.

Third, the Ottoman public debt administration promoted the salt using industries, especially fisheries, olives and tobacco, by ensuring continual supplies at reasonable prices. The whole strategy of the administration with regard to salt was based on the tactic of increasing yield by holding, or if possible by reducing, rates of tax and prices. Sir Adam Block in particular was opposed to shortsighted price increases, which might produce a short-term rise in receipts, but must result in a long-term fall in demand. It was partly this desire to keep prices down which led Block to favour concentration of production at Phocea. Solar evaporated salt generally was priced at 15 paras a kilo where rock salt was priced at 23 paras a kilo and Phocea salt was particularly abundant, good quality and cheap.

Finally, the Ottoman public debt administration was one of the factors which in the nineteenth and early twentieth centuries drew the Ottoman empire out of its island universe into the then European-centred world order. Most of those who have studied this process have stressed its economic aspect and the peripheralization of the Ottoman economy from a provider of essential transit services to a provider only of primary products.[33] In fact, the primary products provided by the Ottoman empire were not of great significance either for it or the outside world. More important was the cultural aspect of the process and this is best described in terms of secularization rather than peripheralization.

In the nineteenth century the Ottoman empire, like the Habsburg, was a state without a people: or, from a nationalist point of view, too many peoples. In the high days before 1800, the Ottoman state had ruled over a society of *millets* or religious communities, the Muslim millet being dominant and the Ottoman ruling institution exercising power within it. With the coming of modernization and mass politics, however, the *millets*, even reformed as they were in the Tanzimat era, ceased to be an adequate basis for the empire. The search was on for a more popular constituency. Of the various options canvassed: Ottomanism, Pan-Islamism, Pan-Turkism and Anatolianism; Ottomanism, a supra *millet* and supranational loyalty to the secular culture of Constantinople, meritocracy and a degree of modernization, was the most hopeful basis for the survival of the empire in its existing form. All the other options required the empire's radical reconstruction. Now the public debt administration was not only an Ottoman, but also an Ottomanist institution. In 1901 its staff consisted of 4853 persons. Of these 15 were Europeans, 4471 were Muslims, but 317 were Oriental Christians: Greeks and Armenians, the very people Ottomanism needed to attract into imperial service.[34] The administration's headquarters were in Constantinople, part of the world of Pera and Galata. Its basic aim was the introduction of meritocratic administrative methods and the elimination of time-honoured 'corruption' in favour of modern salaries, expense accounts and pensions. No wonder that Cavit, the most Ottomanist of the leaders of the Committee of Union and Progress, was a strong supporter of the Ottoman public debt administration and wanted to extend its role in the state.

THE SALT ADMINISTRATION IN THE OTTOMAN STATE

Salt was the most important of the revenues directly administered by the Ottoman public debt administration. Through that protean institution, it served the state not only in regular finance and diplomacy, but also in the civil and military emergencies which eventually overwhelmed the Ottoman empire, but might have rejuvenated it.

Regular Finance

As in the Habsburg empire, salt did not provide a large percentage of the revenue of the Ottoman state. Indeed, the similarity of the figures in the two empires is further evidence that the *Salzmonopol* was the proto-type behind the monopoly of 1861. In 1881 the salt monopoly produced a revenue of £600 000 out of a total Ottoman revenue of £16 million, a little over 3 per cent. In 1911–12, the salt monopoly, in the best year it ever recorded, produced a revenue of nearly £1 200 000 out of a total Ottoman revenue of £25 million still not yet 5 per cent.

Yet the importance of the salt revenues was greater than these figures might suggest. First, salt was the showpiece of the Ottoman public debt administration. Since 1881 it had overtaken tobacco as a source of revenue and was thus a good advertisement for direct administration. It might be outclassed by the so-called new revenues, those assigned since the decree of Muharrem, taken together, but most of these were farmed out, in particular the *öşür* or tithe, and were less at the disposition of the government and in the case of the *öşür* more liable to harvest fluctu-ations. The credit of the administration was thus closely bound up with its salt revenues. Second, the financial importance of the Ottoman public debt administration had grown considerably since 1881. In 1882–3, its revenue of £1 873 895 amounted to 10 per cent of total Ottoman revenue of £18 million. In 1913–14, its revenue of £5 382 472 amounted to 20 per cent of total Ottoman revenue of £25 million, and in some years it ran as high as 25 per cent or even 33 per cent. Salt was the showpiece of an institution which controlled an increasingly large share of Ottoman revenue. It was the part by which, because it was central and directly administered, the performance of the whole might be judged. In his reports therefore Sir Adam Block laid particular stress on the achieve-ments of his salt administration.

Besides its direct contribution to the budget and to fiscal health, salt through the Ottoman public debt administration performed two services to Ottoman finance.

First, it served as part security for new loans. Though the helter skelter borrowing of the Tanzimat era ceased with Abdulhamit's reorganization of 1881, state expenditure, as in most modernizing countries, continued to outrun state revenue. The Ottoman empire still needed to borrow. Between 1881 when the Ottoman debt was scaled down to £124 million and 1904–5, the empire borrowed a total of £33 million, of which nearly £23 million were raised through the Ottoman public debt administration. Yet it was now done in an orderly fashion without financial strain. Loans were amortized instead of being simply accumulated. In 1909, despite the further borrowing the external debt stood at about £80 million and the annual debt service at £3 500 000, a far cry from the situation of 1878. No doubt international banking has learnt much since 1914 about the management of large scale state debt, but it has few more successful examples than that of the Ottoman public debt administration.

Second, the Ottoman public debt administration, and in particular its directly administered salt department, set an example of efficient, 'uncorrupt' administration, which to some extent rubbed off on to other branches of the bureaucracy. The standards set by synarchy were catching and as Bulwer had predicted in 1860, 'honesty and regularity thus established in one branch of the Administration would introduce, eventually, a change in the others'.[35] Blaisdell underlines this function of the Ottoman public debt administration. First, he emphasizes the incorruptibility of its staff: 'regular payment of adequate salaries practically wiped out bribery and graft within their ranks'.[36] Next, he notes the effects:

> The policy of regular payment of sufficient salaries practically wiped out within the Administration's ranks the abuses of *baksheesh* (bribery) and of retention of collected receipts by local revenue agents, two vices which had sorely troubled the Imperial Government in attempts to reform its financial administration.[37]

Speaking of the increase of the revenues, he writes: 'In large measure this must be attributed to the honesty and efficiency of the Administration'.[38] Finally, he points to the demonstration effect: 'Thus, by the integrity and efficiency of its management, the council afforded to the government and to the population a striking example of the best features of European financial administration'.[39] This example was relayed to the Customs by Sir Richard Crawford, to the navy by Sir Arthur Limpus, to the army by Liman von Sanders, so that by 1914 Ottoman administration was much more modern than the outside world realized.

Diplomacy

For the most part Ottoman diplomacy served salt rather than salt Ottoman diplomacy. Particularly was this true of the main line of export, that of rock salt from Salif in the Yemen to India, which depended on British goodwill. After the First World War when the Yemen became independent, the trade fell off considerably. What Britain was prepared to concede to Ottoman diplomacy she was not prepared to concede to a small state on bad terms with both the colony of Aden and Britain's principal ally in the Arabian peninsula, King Ibn Saud.

Some diplomatic leverage, however, attached to Ottoman salt exports to the Balkans. Turkey set some store on continuing links with her former provinces and in 1905–6 Sir Adam Block complained of Tunisian and Italian competition in the Balkans. In 1907–8 the European provinces of the empire required 50 000 tons of salt a year of which 22 000 was produced locally and the rest came from Smyrna or Mitylene. One might have expected that if the economic links had been really strong, there would have been a big rise in exports following the territorial losses of 1912–13. In fact, as Table 10.5 shows, this did not happen, perhaps because Mitylene itself, with a production of 50 000 tons, was among the territories ceded. Included in the revenues assigned to the Ottoman public debt administration subsequent to the decree of Muharrem were the tributes from Montenegro, Serbia and Bulgaria, which preserved some vestigial Ottoman suzerainty in these areas. The sale of salt may have played some part in the payment of these, especially in the case of Eastern Rumelia, i.e. Southern Bulgaria. These vestigial rights were not entirely nugatory. Until the Balkan wars, there was still a substantial Muslim population in the former Ottoman territories and the empire might hope one day to reactivate its authority, as it did too in the case of Egypt and even Tunisia. We know that the empire never recovered its lost provinces, but that was not plain to contemporaries.

Emergencies

From 1881 to 1908 the Ottoman empire enjoyed relative tranquillity. Abdulhamit II, once surnamed the Damned, did not enjoy a good press from contemporaries or for many years afterwards, but he is increasingly recognized as 'one of the most eminent of all Ottoman sultans',[40] his reign the climax of the Tanzimat period and the basis for the Turkish renaissance of Ataturk. Certainly his final departure from the political scene in 1909 was followed by a series of emergencies: first, the externally inflicted emergencies of the Italian and Balkan wars; second, the self-inflicted emergency of participation in the First World War. In the first emergencies, the salt administration was a victim rather than an agent. Its sea trade was disrupted by first Italian and then Greek naval operations, the Italian being particularly deleterious in respect of Red Sea exports form Salif. In the second emergency, salt, via the Ottoman public debt administration, played a more active role.[41]

First, it was through the Ottoman public debt administration that the first Turkish banknotes were issued. This was due to Cavit who, even after he resigned from the ministry of finance in protest against the war policy, retained control from behind the scenes and wanted to drive the hardest possible bargain with the Germans. Like most countries, the Ottoman empire had to finance the war by inflation through the printing press. During the war, the Ottoman bank, despite its international connections, was virtually nationalized. The Germans wanted the bank to issue the notes: i.e., that the Turks take responsibility and pay for their own inflation. Cavit insisted that the notes be issued under the guarantee of the Ottoman public debt administration: i.e. that they be part of Turkey's international obligations. So that the administration could make the guarantee, the Germans must back the note issue with gold loans. To this the Germans, not wishing to quarrel with their ally and temporarily in charge of the administration because the Allied delegates had departed, decided to agree. Cavit thus used the gossamer threads of international finance to extract a gold loan from the Germans and to limit the inflationary effects of the note issue.

Second, Cavit also used the credit of the Ottoman public debt administration to raise ordinary war loans both abroad in Germany and Austria-Hungary and in 1918 at home in the Ottoman empire itself. This was the first publicly subscribed loan in Turkey as opposed to loans raised from the private Galata bankers. Such a loan will have done something to mop up excess money supply and limit wartime demand inflation. Cavit's preservation of the Ottoman public administration during the war allowed it to resume more normal activities at the end of it and to become the chief financial prop of the Constantinople regime between 1918 and 1922. Sir Adam Block returned to his post to issue three more lapidary reports as the Ottoman empire tottered to its end. Again, however, hindsight must be avoided. Mustafa Kemal's victory was not inevitable. The Greeks might have won, or the Constantinople regime rather than the Kemalists have put itself at the head of Turkish resurgence. Cavit, with his links in international finance, his pro-Allied record in the war, might have emerged as prime minister of a constitutional monarchist Turkey. What was in fact the deathbed of a state might have been its rebirth.

In conclusion, one should bear in mind the contribution of the Ottoman public debt administration to the First World War and Turkey's part in it. The First World War was disastrous to the Ottoman empire. Yet its war effort was disastrous to others too and played a significant part in shaping the postwar world. The failure of the Dardanelles campaign was fatal to Russia and nearly fatal to the career of Churchill, with all that might have entailed. To combat the Ottomans the Allies were led both to issue the Balfour declaration and to raise the Arab revolt. Neither Zionism nor the Arab awakening were creations of the war, but both were greatly strengthened by it. The Arab-Israeli conflict was in part a war of the Ottoman succession as was the Greek-Turkish conflict over Cyprus. The fall of the Ottoman sultan-caliphate, Sunni yet with Bektashi foundations, left the stark alternatives of Saudi Wahhabism and Shiite revivalism as poles of Islamic leadership. During the First World War the Allied leaders consistently underestimated Ottoman capacity. Kitchener in particular, the ex-colonial general, played a major part in wrecking the Dardanelles campaign by his refusal to regard the Turkish forces as more than a native army.[42] What he and others were underestimating was the degree of modernization accomplished under Abdulhamit II. In that degree of modernization, the Ottoman public debt administration and its salt revenues in particular had played a major role. The Ottoman salt administration was part of the European world order. It contributed to the modernization of its host, but this modernization, as it turned out, contributed to the weakening of that world order.

11 The Indian Salt Administration under the *Raj*

From the greatest Islamic state we pass to the greatest colonial empire. The Turkish salt administration under the Ottoman public debt administration was part of the synarchic dimension of the European-centred world order. It was therefore international, innovative and modernizing. The Indian salt administration under the *raj*, on the other hand, was part of the other side of the European-centred world order: direct colonialism by a single power. It was therefore national, conservative and stabilizing, though the stability provided scope for what has been called the modernity of tradition, India's special path of progress.

In comparison to institutions so far considered, the Indian salt administration under the *raj* was political. The Venetian salt administration was a business ancillary to other businesses. The *Gabelle* was the flagship of *finance*, part of the profitable interface between Bourbon state and Gallic society. The *Salzmonopol* was an aspect of *Landeshoheit*, an element in the estate management of the *Haus* Habsburg. The Ottoman salt administration after 1881 was part of a debt collecting agency, management put in by the creditors to avoid default, but then used by the borrowers to develop their own resources. The Indian salt administration under the *raj* was none of these things. It existed to serve the *raj* whose field was political, not economic, social or ideological. The *raj* began, it is true, in the commercial operations of the East India Company. Next, following the battle of Plassey, it became a gigantic system of jobbery, the ultimate in unreformed bureaucracies, though as H. Furber showed,[1] the pagoda tree which the nabobs shook was that of the English rather than the Indian taxpayer and result was redistribution within the English landed classes more than exploitation of India. Finally, following its reform prompted by Fox's attempt to annex Indian jobbery to English, the *raj* became a supplementary civil service, a spare army, a subsidy to some of the middle class, plus their denial to other countries: political ends in themselves so long as Britain wished and could afford to be an imperial power.

In its final political form, the *raj* reached its climax in the viceroyalty of Lord Curzon 1889–1905. During his administration, there was a serious conflict between the civil and military halves of the establishment, in which the military won a Pyrrhic victory. Moreover, the First World War subverted the basis of imperialism everywhere as Curzon himself was one of the first to see.[2] In 1919 the end of the *raj* was clearly envisaged in the Montagu–Chelmsford reforms, though not exactly in the form in which the end came. In 1919 too there occurred the Amritsar incident which lowered imperial prestige and produced another conflict between the civil and military halves of the establishment, in which the military now definitely lost. By the viceroyalty of Lord Irwin (the future Viscount and Earl of Halifax) 1925 to 1931, the *raj* was already on the decline, and Indian nationalism was pushing on a door which was only slow to open. In 1929 nationalist criticism of the salt administration, in particular its acceptance of large imports of foreign salt, led the government of India to instruct the Tariff Board to conduct an enquiry into the feasibility and desirability of making India self-supporting in salt. This enquiry, which produced a preliminary evidence volume in 1930 and two final evidence volumes later in that year, is a mine of information on the salt administration in the golden, but equinoctial, autumn of the *raj*.[3] It is therefore on this period of the *raj* that this chapter will focus, though with occasional glances both before and after.

Because it was primarily political did not mean that the salt administration under the *raj* was exclusively fiscal. What it did mean was that its non-fiscal welfare activities were conceived within a limited horizon. The populace must receive its salt, at a reasonable price, in the way it liked it, but there was no need to go beyond this. Unless there were strong reasons to the contrary, the producer, the distributor and the consumer should not be disturbed, lest they create political problems. There was a presumption in favour of the status quo and the administration should mind its own business. In this sense, the salt administration, like the *raj* as a whole, was superficial. It did not seek to reconstruct the body of society, though it left that body free to reconstruct itself. The salt administration was a comparatively humble and unprestigious part of the *raj*, but the *raj's* high political theme ran through all its variations: the state in the salt administration, the state's taxes, the people's livelihood, and the salt administration in the state; even as this theme had as its counterpoint the principle of *quieta non movere*.

THE STATE IN THE INDIAN SALT ADMINISTRATION UNDER THE *RAJ*

Unlike the Ottoman empire, premodern India, even under Muslim dynasties, had a tradition of salt administration. Pliny tells us that the rulers of northwest India obtained a greater revenue from their salt mines than from gold and pearls. The *durbar* of Dhrangadhra claimed that its interest in the subsoil solar salines of the Rann of Kutch went back to the twelfth century. The government of Akbar and his successors worked the Sambhar salt lake until in the eighteenth century it passed into the hands of the Rajput rulers of Jaipur and Jodhpur. In the twentieth century, the new Okha salt works on the gulf of Kutch received encouragement from the Gaekwar of Baroda, while the Maharaja of Nawanagar spoke to the Viceroy personally on behalf of the Kathiawar salt industry in Simla in May 1927. Unlike the Chinese, however, the Indian tradition was unsystematized: a bundle of miscellaneous regalian rights inscribed in the wider Indian tradition of heavy taxation.

These rights were gradually acquired by the *raj*. In 1765 the East India Company received the *diwan* or tax farm of Bengal, Bihar and Orissa from the Great Moghul. This included regalian rights over salt. In 1772 these rights were formalized as a monopoly of a kind which in China would have been called *shang-chih, kuan-shou, shang-yün, min-hsiao*: merchants manufacture, officials receive, merchants transport, people distribute. S. C. Nandy in his biography of Kanta Babu, the millionaire who was first a salt producer and then a transport merchant, describes the system:

> All salt pans from October 1772 were taken over by the Company who would sell the right to make salt for 5 years to the highest bidder. The Farmer of the salt pans (*khallaries*) would deliver his salt to the Company who would auction it to the salt dealers.[4]

The salt dealers then transported the salt, by boat mainly, to the local wholesalers and retailers. This system, complicated by rivalries between the company's servants and competing groups of Indian merchants, lasted in the Bengal presidency until 1863. In that year, at the instance of the Secretary of State, Sir Charles Wood, the monopoly was abolished and imports were permitted with the result that the local industry, which had been based on boiling,[5] was virtually destroyed and the salt administration in Bengal contracted to the collection of an import duty.

In Northern India, in the Rajputana, the British government took a mortgage on the Sambhar salt lake from the rulers of Jaipur and Jodhpur in 1844 and acquired a permanent lease in 1870,

> for an annual payment of Rs 700 000 (equivalent to about £47 000), on the condition that if the sales of salt exceeded 1 723 000 maunds (equivalent to about 64 000 tons) in any year, forty per cent of the sale price of such excess would be paid to the states as royalty.[6]

Similarly in 1878, the British government acquired a lease of the Pachbadra salt springs and of the Didwana salt wells from the government of Jodhpur. In the Salt Range, the Khewra mines came under British control with the occupation of the Punjab in 1849 and from 1872 mining was reorganized under the auspices of the Geological Survey of India. In Madras, a monopoly of acquisition from the producers was exercised from 1805, together with price fixing and state supervision of distribution: *kuan-shou* and *kuan-hsiao* in Chinese terms. For the remainder of the *raj*, Madras continued to be the area where state intervention was most extensive, in marked contrast to Bengal. In Bombay, the *raj* mostly contented itself with a simple excise, but from 1872 there was a large government salt works at Kharaghoda on the Lesser Rann of Kutch. Moreover, there was a policy of compulsory closure of minor salt works near Surat and south of Bombay and in the princely states of Gujerat, to facilitate control. Large salines were encouraged. In the vicinity of Bombay itself, 'certain capitalists in the Thana and Kolaba Districts were induced to lay out and develop such salt works in the areas selected by Government'.[7]

Until 1877 the salt administration of the *raj* did not form a unified whole. Tax was levied at various rates in the three presidencies of Bengal, Bombay and Madras and as a result there had to be a formidable internal customs barrier reminiscent of the *Gabelle* at its worst. Sir John Strachey, financial member under Lord Lytton, described it in his budget speech of March 1887:

> Along the greater part of this enormous system of internal customs lines . . . a physical barrier has been created comparable to nothing I can think of except the Great Wall of China. It consists principally of an impenetrable hedge of thorny trees and bushes, supplemented by stone walls and ditches across which no human being or beast of burden can pass without being subjected to detention and search.[8]

In 1878, Strachey unified the rates of tax, collected it as far as possible at source, and left tax paid salt free to find its own market anywhere in India. It was the system known in China as *chiu-ch'ang cheng-shui jen ch'i so chih*, taxation at source and minimal interference thereafter. From 1878 then there was a single salt administration in India, but because of different technical contexts, historical backgrounds and local conditions, it operated variously in its four divisions of Northern India, Bengal, Bombay and Madras.

Northern India

In 1928 the Northern India division handled 12 million maunds (480 000 tons) of salt a year. The principal sources were the Sambhar salt lake, 6 million maunds, and the Khewra mine, 3 million maunds. At both, production at the time of the enquiry was organized directly by the government. At an earlier period, part of the production at Sambhar had been subcontracted to some 400–500 operators who each managed 10–12 small salt fields of 100×50 ft. In 1930, however, most production came from 11 large, government constructed, salt fields called *kyars*. The *kyars* in turn were subdivided into between 20 and 60 evaporation basins, from 3–7 acres apiece which were arranged to form a series of catchment, condensers and crystallizers. Production was under the direction of a general manager subordinate to the Commissioner, Northern India Salt Revenue. At Khewra, too, the mine was a single government operated unit. At both the work-force were government employees: at Sambhar at the height of the season, between 2000 and 2500, skilled and unskilled; at Khewra, between 750 and 900.

In technology the two places were different. Sambhar was similar to the An-i *hsien* salt lake of Ho-tung in Shansi. The lake was the periodic creation of a brief summer monsoon. Each year an average of 20 inches fell on the silt, the salt content of whose first ten feet alone was estimated at 55 million tons. At its greatest extent at the end of September, the lake covered an area of 90 square miles with a maximum depth of 2 feet. It contained 700 million cubic feet of 3 per cent brine, which under the intense evaporation of the sun and wind after the monsoon rapidly reached 7 per cent brine. The brine was then pumped into the *kyars*, where by November or December it had reached 25 per cent and salt began to be precipitated in the crystallizers. When a density of 29 per cent was reached, say in January or February, more brine was brought in from the main lake. When the mixture had reached 30 per cent at the end of March or April, the salt began to be extracted. The average annual production of 6 million maunds was reckoned to be the equivalent of 500 million cubic feet of 3 per cent brine (or 50 million cubic feet of 30 per cent brine), so that a high percentage of the lake's annual brine formation was used in salt production.[9] By midyear, the lake might have dried up altogether leaving a crust of earth salt over its whole area. It was now ready for the summer monsoon to begin the cycle again. The technology as outlined was always successive basin solar evaporation, but in the early 1920s the lake had been improved for this purpose. In a major engineering project sponsored by the salt administration, a dam was built across the lake from north to south. The dam converted the western half, where there were no *kyars*, into a reservoir for the areas outside the *kyars* in the eastern half. These areas then acted as secondary reservoirs for the tertiary reservoirs inside the *kyars*, which supplied their condensers and crystallizers. The aim was to conserve the brine and to prevent its premature evaporation before it reached the crystallizers. The officials concerned claimed that the dam increased production by 2 million maunds.[10]

Khewra, on the other hand, was a mine. It did not follow these cyclical patterns of production, though the miners conventionally took a vacation in August and September. The mine was based on rock salt deposits of exceptional purity – 98.3 per cent in one sample, 94.97 per cent in another – which amounted to 10 cubic miles in the immediate vicinity of Khewra and 20 cubic miles in the Salt Range as a whole.[11] Excavation was by blasting, by compressed air drills, and by hand tools. Unlike Sambhar where production had reached its peak given the volume of brine, the authorities estimated that the annual production of 3 million maunds could easily be increased 100 per cent, and with improved electrical drills, even 400 per cent if there was sufficient effective demand.

The activities of the officials in Northern India did not cease with production. They also played a significant role in transportation, so that in Chinese terms the system might be described as *kuan-chih, kuan-yün, shang-hsiao* (officials produce, officials transport, merchants distribute). The railways, though mainly owned by private enterprise, were under considerable government influence in the Railway Board which held them already in a semi-nationalized position.

Ashton stressed the role of the railways at Sambhar in 1907. Having described the Banjaras and their bullocks in the past, he continued:

> The extension of railways and the more settled and peaceful condition of all parts of the country has affected this description of trade. . . . There are now great facilities for the removal of salt by railway from the lake direct to areas of consumption. . . . All of the storage platforms of the Kyars in the bed of the lake, and the storage grounds on its edge, are connected with the main line of railway by siding; the aggregate length of these latter is about fifteen miles and bags filled from the heaps of salt can at once be placed in railway waggons standing within easy distance.[12]

He then outlined the procedure of transportation:

> The salt is sold at nine shillings a ton, and for a further payment of sevenpence a ton, the British Officers at the lake undertake to clear the salt by railway to any destination. This convenience is largely availed of. Traders resident in areas of consumption many hundreds of miles distant, pay the price and the small fee for clearance into the nearest Government treasury or post office and send the necessary empty bag to the lake, whence their salt is sent to them expeditiously by railway. In Central India, the Indian Midland Railway, also receives salt revenue in this manner at different railway stations, and the system conduces to the cheap distribution of salt, by which the consumer benefits.[13]

At Sambhar, therefore, there were no transport merchants in the Chinese sense. The officials acted in their stead through a system of indents for salt sent in by major distributors. A similar system seems to have operated at Khewra.

The sales areas for different sources of supply was largely determined by the availability and cost of rail transport. The Commissioner described the position for Sambhar in 1930:

> The Rajputana sources are on the whole not inconveniently situated for the markets which they serve, these being in the United Provinces, the Central Provinces, Rajputana, Central India and portions of the Punjab. A small proportion of the salt goes to Bihar, but here the railway freights are against it and it has largely been driven out by cheap foreign salt.[14]

He cited the case of Buxar near Patna in Bihar:

> Aden salt imported by sea to Calcutta (sea freight Rs 8 per ton) and thence railed to Buxar (railway freight Rs 12–4 per ton) costs Rs 20–4 in total freight. Sambhar salt railed to Buxar from Sambhar costs Rs 22–5–9 per ton in freight. . . . Buxar is 619 miles from Sambhar but only 430 miles from Calcutta. It follows therefore that in respect of markets between Buxar and Calcutta imported salt has the advantage.[15]

Khewra was even more restricted. The Commissioner commented: 'The Salt Range is conveniently situated for supplying the Punjab, but the high railway freights have restricted the sale of Salt Range salt in the United Provinces, especially the eastern parts, in Bihar and in Bengal'.[16] Since Khewra, unlike Sambhar, had surplus capacity, this was particularly serious, but for both places, 'the chief difficulty in competition with foreign salt is railway freights'.[17] Nevertheless the administration was not without influence over freight rates. Talking about Khewra the Commissioner reported:

> These rates have recently been the subject of negotiations between the Central Board of Revenue and the Railway Companies concerned, and though I have not yet been officially informed of the result, it is understood that very substantial concessions have been obtained. An increased demand for Khewra salt may now be anticipated with some degree of confidence.[18]

Although there were no *yün-shang* in Northern India, at the end of the railway lines, there was a powerful ring of merchants who exercised a *de facto* monopoly over distribution: in Chinese terms, *an-shang*. Information about these people is contained in a letter sent to the enquiry by Messrs Diwan Chand and company of Delhi, a member of the Punjab chamber of commerce, an outsider, and an opponent of the ring.

Diwan Chand entered the salt business in 1920 with a plan to reduce costs to himself and thereby prices to the consumer.

> I studied the causes of the high market rate and came to the conclusion that as the whole salt business in Northern India was being done on the basis of cash system and traders' interest on the cash deposited in Treasuries amounted to about 10 per cent . . . and they also desired to earn about 10 per cent profit at the least, so the market rate was 20 per cent more than the issue price.[19]

The remedy was credit: 'I submitted the manifold advantages of credit system to the Salt Commissioner and convinced him that the traders would thereby save interest of their capital and other incidental charges. The Salt Department very kindly acceded to my request and allowed traders to work on the credit system'.[20]

Using credit, Diwan Chand undercut his competitors: 'Since the very introduction of the credit system I made up my mind to carry on salt business in full force. I began to sell Khewra salt wagons at 1 per cent more than the issue price and this step of mine astonished several persons as to how I was working on such a meagre profit'.[21] From Khewra he extended his operations to Sambhar. Here he encountered the ring:

> 'All the Sambhar traders except myself form a separate class by themselves and can very easily combine because they have been working together for the last 100 years. Sambhar traders were habituated to earn very high profits and thus became jealous of me. These people also made certain arrangements with banks and started competition with me.'[22]

Rivalry became fierce.

> I came to know from some source that Sambhar traders were secretly conspiring to oust me from the market by making a combine and were arranging to put in large indents . . . they grew furious and blamed me for the action which they themselves had conspired to take against me. . . . They alleged that I wanted to monopolize the market which idea never came to my mind.[23]

The outcome was first a draw and then a compromise. 'Though the Sambhar traders did not gain their object as completely as they desired yet their purpose was served to some extent'.[24] The credit system continued: 'Gradually other traders also came to know of the advantages of credit system and they also started business on credit system. In the meantime I had established a firm footing in the market'.[25] By 1929 Diwan Chand had become a monopolitan himself: 'I submit that 60 per cent of the business of Sambhar, Khewra and Warcha [another mine in the Salt Range] is already in my hands'.[26]

As in so many salt divisions in China, the salt administration under the *raj* in Northern India, ended in merchant monopoly, *shang-hsiao*. As a colonial regime, the *raj* lacked the strength, and perhaps the will, to create free enterprise by imposing capitalism on capitalists. Only at the retail level, *min-mai*, was there genuine free trade and that more by default than design.

Bengal

In Bengal presidency which included Bihar, Orissa and Assam and with which Burma was associated, the character of the salt administration differed from what it was in Northern India. It was direct but restricted, so that officials confined themselves to administering a customs barrier which collected an excise duty in 1930 of Rs 35 a ton or Rs 1.25 a maund on essentially imported salt. Bengal was a big consumer, over 15 million maunds a year on average, but of this only 500 000 was Indian and this came from Bombay. It was against this state of affairs, unprecedented in China except on the Mongolian border, that Indian nationalist opinion was beginning to protest and into which the Tariff Board was instructed to make its enquiry.

Question 71 of the salt enquiry asked: 'Do you consider it desirable in the national interests to encourage the production in India of salt suitable for consumption in those markets which are at present largely supplied from abroad?'[27] The Commissioner, Northern India Salt Revenue, A. L. Hoyle, contented himself with saying: 'This is a question of policy which seems to affect rather the government of India and for private manufacturers than for this department'.[28] The Collector of Salt Revenue, Madras, C. H. Masterman was unenthusiastic in so far as the proposal concerned his division:

If Indian salt is to take the place of imported salt in Bengal . . . the quality of the salt must be similar to that of the imported salt now sold in Bengal and the price at which it can be put on the market in Bengal should not exceed the existing price of salt in Bengal; otherwise the Bengal consumer is being unfairly treated. The quality of salt now

Table 11.1 Imports into Bengal, 1924–5 (tons)

Country of origin	Quantity	Percentage
UK	107 045	17.38
Germany	34 315	5.57
Spain	28 971	4.70
Aden	203 995	33.13
Egypt	166 884	27.10
Italian East Africa	47 638	7.73
British and French Somaliland	21 253	3.45
Tunis	5 608	0.91
Total	614 673	100.00

being produced in Madras can be manufactured cheaply but is not suitable for the Bengal market.[29]

Bengal had come to prefer European style white salt: Madras salt was black. The Collector of Salt Revenue, Bombay, H. T. Sorley, went furthest, though his division contained the most hopeful and modern Indian producers of white salt:

I see no necessity for nor desirability of encouraging the production in India of salt suitable for consumption in these markets which are at present largely supplied from abroad. The question raises the free trade and protection issue in an extremely crude form and would necessitate a consideration of the competing claims of a large number of conflicting interests. In practice it means chiefly forcing the inhabitants of Bengal to eat salt they do not like unless it is practicable to produce in India salt equally acceptable at an equally low price. This has still to be proved possible.[30]

The salt officials' superiors shared their point of view. At an earlier stage of the argument in 1926, the Central Board of Revenue, advised by D. N. Strathie 'an officer who had had considerable experience of salt administration in Madras' had come to three conclusions.[31]

First, The problem of making the mainland of India (as distinguished from Burma) self-supporting in the matter of salt supply resolves itself into that of capturing for Indian salt the market for white crushed salt in Bengal, since no attempt could reasonably be made to compel the consumer in Bengal to take the ordinary Madras or Bombay salt.
    Second, The cost of transporting salt to Bengal from those places in India at which salt suitable for that market could be produced, and the

extent to which such transport could be made available were factors of the greatest importance.

Third, The probable limitations upon the output of sources in India which could produce the required quality of salt were such that, on the evidence available, a reasonable probability that India could be made self-supporting in this respect could not be regarded as established.

Mr Strathie was against tariffs, except possibly in the case of Burma, but here too the Central Board of Revenue felt that 'the adoption of different rates of customs duty for goods imported into different ports of India would be a violation of important principles governing tariff policy'. It was only political pressure from the legislative Assembly and the financial member Sir George Schuster that forced the Central Board of Revenue to reopen the question and refer it to the Tariff Board for enquiry.

From these expressions of opinion it may be concluded first, that the salt administration under the *raj* and its superiors were a priori sympathetic to free trade; second, that, consonant with this, it put the interests of the Bengali consumer ahead of the interests of producers in other parts of India; and third, that it was doubtful, given the state of the industry and comparative freights, whether the Indian producer, even protected, could supply the Bengal market with what it wanted at reasonable cost. This third point, of course, was disputed by the protectionists and in particular by the new salt companies: Grax, Eduljee Dinshaw and Luxmi at Karachi, and largest of all, Okha on the gulf of Kutch in Baroda, which had commenced operations in 1926 using the most advanced techniques of successive basin solar evaporation. Okha believed it could, within two years, produce 12 million maunds of white crushed salt 'which is conceived to be roughly the whole of present imports into Bengal of foreign salt, excluding Aden'.[32] A fourth point, which was probably at the backs of the minds of the salt administrators but which they chose to leave unvoiced, was that canalization of the trade by import through Calcutta facilitated its control and taxation by the authorities.

Canalization at Calcutta, however, was one of the things objected to by the new Indian companies. From their objections, and the reply they prompted, can be perceived another feature of the salt administration in Bengal: the existence there of a powerful merchant ring similar to that revealed by Messrs Diwan Chand in the import from Sambhar. Government retreat was accompanied by the advance of a cartel.

Objections were most loudly voiced by Grax, a company with some Indian capital but all four directors English, which began to manufacture salt at Karachi in November 1927. Grax complained:

The Calcutta Market is entirely under the domination of a combine which is extremely wealthy and has in the past manipulated prices so as to suppress any competitor who introduces independent competition into the Market or so as to force him to join the combine under terms dictated by it as to the quantity of salt he may sell and the price at which he may operate.

Grax then gave a number of examples of the combine at work, for instance its opposition to the entry of Spanish salt in 1909–10, and provided some information about its *modus operandi*:

The power of the combine was at one time exercised by cornering the golas [official warehouses] which they retained by keeping small quantities of salt in them so as to prevent others from using the golas; Government was forced to take action to prevent this. The combine however still operates through tied buyers who are unable to take up salt except that of the combine. It still gives orders as to whether salt is to be taken *ex*-ship or *ex*-gola, and we believe that there is a system of secret commissions by which the quoted prices of salt are rendered unreliable.

Grax concluded:

If we are to obtain a footing in Calcutta for Karachi Salt and secure for it the important place which it can undoubtedly acquire there we submit that we must be protected against the tactics of the combine. If this is allowed to retain freedom to act as it has done in the past and by an arbitrary reduction in prices to force us out of the market or compel us to join it, our industry would be destroyed or crippled, for if we join the combine it would control our operations by assigning a percentage of the salt sold in Calcutta to which we would be bound to limit our trade. It would then be impossible for us to work up to the maximum expansion of which salt production in Karachi is capable and this would frustrate all hope of making India self supporting in the matter of Salt.[33]

Okha, 85 per cent of whose capital was Indian and only one of whose directors was European, voiced similar complaints: 'The foreign salt Makers' Conference has put up a united front against the entry of new comers into the Calcutta market, and it would appear, particularly against our Company'. One technique was price manipulation: 'Our second shipment was, therefore, very keenly awaited at Calcutta, and during the week of its arrival, a combined effort was made by the

Conference of foreign manufacturers to shut us out, as was anticipated in Mr. Strathie's Report, by lowering the rates by about 33 per cent'. But there were other weapons too:

> The older importers having an established market are in a better position to effect sales *ex*-ship than the new comers. Till last year, the Conference had maintained a difference of Rs 6 to Rs 8 between *ex*-ship and *ex*-golah rates. The difference represented the actual cost of conveyance and storage of salt into golahs; since the entry of the new comers this difference in the quotations has been reduced by the Conference to a nominal difference of Rs 2 to Rs 3. The buyers, therefore, particularly of the indigenous product prefer to buy their requirements *ex*-golah. Thus the newcomer is forced to suffer a heavy loss in the shape of golah charges.

Like Grax, Okha concluded: 'Indian manufacturers obviously need to be protected from the operation of such powerful foreign combinations. Indians should have freedom to develop their industry without being thus strangled by foreign interests'.[34]

The Salt Importers' Association of Bengal, of course, had its answers to these criticisms:

> In the opinion of members of this association such statements are calculated to give an entirely wrong impression on the objects of this Association and in this connection I am to point out that the aim of this Association is to prevent violent fluctuation in prices which in the past have led to speculation by middlemen with no benefit to the consumer, and to regulate the supply of salt in accordance with the demand. It has hitherto not been the policy of the Association to fight Indian made salts as it is recognized that such salts should have every opportunity of competing in the Calcutta market.[35]

The Association was not very forthcoming in its replies to the enquiry, but it did provide a certain amount of incidental information about itself. It consisted of the Calcutta agents of the Salt Union of Liverpool, the Union Salinera de Espana of Barcelona, the Societa Italiana per Saline Eritree of Rome, Hamburg salt interests, the Port Said salt association, Agostino Burgarella of Aden, and the Indo-Aden salt interests, i.e. the three companies at Aden besides Burgarella, all of which were owned by Indians. The Association had offices in the building of the Bengal Chamber of Commerce and the agents met once a week, 'to review the positions of the different members in regard to their cargoes in port and to arrive, as well as stocks in bond, with a view to regulating imports to meet market demands'. As a result of these meetings, 'an allotment is made to satisfy the estimated market requirements, and each member has a certain percentage of that allotment according to the agreement. Their shares are either reduced or increased according to the extent to which members oversold or undersold at the time of each meeting'.[36] At the time of writing the quotas were Liverpool 15.5 per cent, Hamburg 6 per cent, Spain 12 per cent, Port Said 18.5 per cent, Massowah 10 per cent, Aden 24 per cent, Indo-Aden 14 per cent.

In conclusion, the Association was insistent on its broad, constructive function:

> Members are of opinion that salt cargoes are very useful to Indian liners for ballast freights for the inward voyage and tend to enable freight rates for Indian exports to be kept at a low level. Should the Shipping Companies be deprived of these cargoes it follows that freight rates for Indian exports might have to be increased.[37]

The Association clearly felt that the Tariff Board and perhaps the salt administration were unsympathetic to it. It may have been wrong about this, as the administration must have been aware of its existence yet the first reaction of the Central Board of Revenue as advised by Mr Strathie was adverse to its critics. But the existence of the Association was a limitation to the application of the free trade principles which the salt administration genuinely espoused. Once again, in colonial circumstances, the absence of state control meant not privatization but monopoly. Bengal would have been regarded by the Chinese as a case of *shang-shou*, acquisition by privileged merchants.

Bombay

The salt administration in Bombay Presidency stood midway between Northern India and Bengal in terms of organization. Whereas in Northern India almost all salt was produced in government salines and in Bengal virtually none, in Bombay some salt was produced by the state, though the greater part came from private salines. Again, whereas in Northern India the salt administration played some part in transportation and in Bengal virtually none, in Bombay, a small part was played by officials in the movement of salt. Like Bengal, the salt administration in Bombay was basically an excise collecting agency; like Northern India, what it collected it from was Indian salt. Moreover the total quantity produced in Bombay was about the same as in Northern India: 12.5 million maunds or 500 000 tons.

The salines of the west coast of India fell into two groups: a group of larger salines north of Bombay, principally in Sind and Gujerat; and a group of smaller salines, around Bombay itself and south of it. In these two groups, three kinds of technology were practised. First, at the government works at Maurypur near Karachi and at both state and princely works in the Lesser Rann of Kutch, there was practised single basin evaporation. Rich subsoil brine from wells was allowed to evaporate in crystallizers, without much thought for the calcium or magnesium compounds. Second, in Bombay city itself and points south, in around 200 small works there was practised normal successive basin solar evaporation with a traditional catchment-condensers : crystallizers ratio of about 5:1. This industry, relatively new, as was Bombay itself, was probably derived from Sambhar and Bharatpur via earlier works at Surat. Third, in new private works at Karachi and on both sides of the Gulf of Kutch, in new modern salines, there was practised improved successive basin solar evaporation with an advanced Mediterranean catchment-condensers : crystallizers ratio of 8:1 or 10:1. In the period following the *raj* these Gujerat salines were to become the leading centres of the Indian salt industry.

In the northern group the presence of the salt administration expressed itself in government salt works: a small one at Maurypur 8.5 miles west of Karachi and a larger one at Kharaghoda on the Lesser Rann of Kutch.

The Maurypur works was established in 1878. It was really only a partial takeover of previously existing private works which gave the government the right of compulsory purchase, though this right was not always exercised. The Superintendent of Salt, Karachi, described the position in 1930:

> Until 1928 all salt manufactured by the Lunaris (hereditary salt manufacturers) was bought by the Government and issued to the public on payment of duty and cost of manufacture. Since 1928, practically the whole of the salt manufactured by the Lunaris has been disposed of by them direct to the public; although on paper they still manufacture for Government who sells to the Moon Company. The Moon Company's constituents are the lunaries themselves who formed themselves into an Association for the purpose of supplying the local market.[38]

The Lunaries (according to Ashton, *lun* is an Indian word which means salt),[39] however, were not happy with the situation, particularly in view of the opening of the three new successive basin solar evaporation works – Grax, Eduljee Dinshaw and Luxmi – at Karachi. The Moon salt company made representation direct to the enquiry and asked for full privatization:

> Under the circumstances, we place our case at your mercy. *We pray that the pans in which we are manufacturing salt may be permanently granted*

to our Company and we may enjoy the right like above three companies, thereby our interests will be safeguarded. And for this act of kindness, we shall ever remain grateful.[40]

The productive capacity of the government works at Maurypur was not large: 360 000 maunds or 288 000 cwt. Production was by single basin solar evaporation. Brine, already concentrated to 16–20 per cent salt content, was lifted from pits sunk near the seashore direct to crystallization basins. The quality was not good, but it found a ready market in Karachi, Hyderabad, and 'other large towns in Sind'.[41] Neither the Superintendent nor the lunaries saw much prospect of its sale in fastidious Bengal.

The government salt works at Kharaghoda was a larger and more significant institution. It was opened in 1872 when the administration established five sidings, or evaporation units linked to the railway, at Kharaghoda new village. In 1880–81 the associated Udu salt works were opened 6 miles from Kharaghoda; in 1913–14 a sixth siding was opened at Kharaghoda; and in 1918 a seventh between Kharaghoda and Udu. In 1930 the productive capacity of the whole complex was 3 million maunds (120 000 tons) and actual production had risen from 1 451 181 maunds in 1924–5 to 2 755 298 maunds in 1928–9. There were no lunaries as at Maurypur and the entire labour force of 3700 were government employees.

The method of production at Kharaghoda was basically the same as that of Maurypur: one crop a year being produced by single basin solar evaporation of naturally reinforced brine; but the scale and sophistication were greater.[42] First, 'The brine is obtained from circular wells about 9' in diameter which are sunk to a depth of 18 to 30 feet until the brine bearing stratum is struck'. These wells were situated on the edge of the Rann and had to be shifted from time to time as salinity changed. Next,

A small reservoir is provided for the reception of the brine before it passes into the pan. Much time and trouble are devoted to the preparation of the pans at the beginning of the season. Each pan is about 250 ft long by 60 ft wide and is also placed so that the length of the pan is exposed to the prevailing wind, so that the surface of the brine may be broken into long waves and the evaporation area be increased. The bottom of the pan which is formed of hard clay, is carefully levelled until it becomes comparatively water tight.

Altogether there were 614 of these pans, each with an average yield of 4300 maunds per annum. Third,

The pan is then flooded with brine to the depth of 4 to 5 inches and in a week's time a crust of salt about 0.75 inches thick forms at the bottom of the pan. The accretion system of manufacture is adopted, *i.e.* this salt is not scraped but is broken up by a man entering the pan . . . fresh brine is then admitted into the pan and the process is repeated until the crop is ready for removal, which is generally five months after the manufacture has commenced.

Finally, 'The mother liquor is removed from the pans once or twice during the manufacturing season to prevent the formation of deposits of magnesium which renders the salt highly hydroscopic'.

The large grained, coarse salt so produced was known as Baragra. It was not much better in quality than that produced at Maurypur:

No white salt is manufactured at Kharaghoda. The salt acquires a dull brown colour, under the present accretion process of manufacture under which salt is not removed from the pans for about five months from the date it begins to form in the pans.[43]

Nevertheless it found a wide circulation, first in Gujerat up to Baroda and then in parts of the Central Provinces, the United Provinces, Central India, Malwa and Rajputana, being distributed thereto by rail, particularly via Ahmedabad. Here an Indian firm acted as government salt agents:

In Gujarat Messrs Nowroji Pestonji and Co. of Ahmedabad are advanced Baragra salt from Kharaghoda on the strength of their adequate Government securities, for being stored at the depots opened by them. . . . They do not however hold a monopoly and any trader of a locality where there is a depot is free to indent for salt direct from Kharaghoda. The existence of the Government Salt Agents tends to keep the retail selling prices of salt at a minimum and safeguards against profiteering in case of a shortage of salt.[44]

The Ahmedabad firm might not hold a formal monopoly, but its function was not dissimilar from the Sambhar ring, Diwan Chand or the Association at Calcutta. In all three cases the Chinese would have spoken of *shang-hsiao* or distribution by privileged merchants.

Around Bombay itself and in the south of the presidency, the presence of the salt administration expressed itself, not in government salt works, but in closure and concentration to facilitate assessment. In their reply to the enquiry, 'certain leading owners in Kolaba and Thana districts' near Bombay sketched the past history and present situation of their industry:

The history of the Bombay sea salt works dates back to centuries. Originally salt works existed along the whole sea-board of this Presidency and supplied local as well as upcountry markets, so far as transport facilities permitted . . . and up to 1872 there were no restrictions on the manufacture of salt, wherever this was feasible. No doubt a license was needed, but such licenses were freely granted.

The *raj* in effect confined itself to collecting tax and could not always do that. After 1872 things changed:

It was in the early seventies of the last century that government discovered the loss in excise duty, which they suffered in consequence of the difficulty of effectively guarding such numerous and widely scattered salt works. They therefore adopted the policy of concentrating manufacture in central places whence salt could be cheaply transported by sea or rail to different centres and accordingly closed all the salt works in the Surat, Ratnagiri and Kanara Districts with the exception of those at Dharasna, Shiroda and Sanikatta and decided to open up instead through private agency larger ones in the Thana and Kolaba Districts within compact areas.[45]

This policy was put into effect and the authors of the submission were the beneficiaries:

In furtherance of this policy certain capitalists in the Thana and Kolaba Districts were induced to lay out and develop such salt works in the areas selected by Government during the 2 decades – 1870–1890 – and salt was accordingly produced sufficient for the requirements not only of the Bombay presidency (excluding Sind and Gujerat) but also of the Central Provinces and portions of the Nizam's territory, the Mysore state, a large portion of the Madras presidency and those areas of Bengal which consumed salt of the quality produced by the Bombay salt works.[46]

In fact, the export by Bombay of its rather low grade salt was not large: only 0.5 million maunds a year, but the Bombay merchants hoped to increase it given certain procedural changes, but the production of Bombay exclusive of Gujerat was large – nearly 10 million maunds – and some of the private salines quite substantial. For example, three companies controlled by Sir Vasantrao Anandrao Dabholkar and Hormasji Manelji Bhinwandiwalla and Co. of Bombay contained 832, 2100 and 6136 pans with a productive capacity respectively of 48 000, 120 000 and 900 000 maunds.

Among the procedures objected to by the Bombay merchants was one which indicates a considerable degree of control by the salt administration over the works. In contradistinction to works in Sind, Gujerat and Madras, the works in Bombay, it was claimed, were subject to a double supervision of weighment and issue:

At the Bombay Salt Works every maund of salt is weighed and then filled into the bags. Then the consignment is taken to a Preventive Station outside the limits of the salt works and 15 percent bags are retested before the consignment is taken to the steamer. This double handling entails greater expenses in regard to Bombay salt.[47]

A similar indication comes from the complaints of the 120 salt producers of Sanikatta in southern Bombay presidency, a small but ancient group of salt fields with a productive capacity of 300 000 maunds, against the privileges enjoyed by Goa. To secure Goa salt for its line, the railway company, they said, 'has undertaken to pay the salt duty at Castle rock on behalf of the purchaser and recover the same from him at destination before delivering the consignment'.[48] Sanikatta salt, on the other hand, had to pay tax as it left the salt field, so more capital was required for longer by the purchaser.

Less active than Northern India, more active than Bengal, the salt administration in Bombay under the *raj* performed a number of activities beyond the merely fiscal: production, decision as to sites, encouragement of private enterprise, organization of depots. It was an agenda with a distinct political component.

Madras

The salt administration in Madras Presidency, which had been established as early as 1805, was unusual in three respects. First, it was unusually extended, sometimes all the way from production to retail, though by 1930 this had been much attenuated. Ratton, writing in 1877, had contrasted the systems of Bengal and Madras and argued that of Madras was preferable. Second, Madras had its own peculiar form of successive basin solar evaporation, sufficiently different from those of Bombay to be considered almost a different system. It was one conducted on a fairly small scale, as on the French Atlantic coast, based on the *ryotwari* system. Third, Madras was an unusually large consumer of salt: 20–21 lb per head compared with 10–13 lb per head for India as a whole. Consequently Madras was a large producer of salt: around 13.5 million maunds, over 0.5 million tons. Most of it was consumed locally. Indeed, Madras imported salt from Bombay, though formerly it had exported it to Bengal.

The Madras salt administration was an example of what the Chinese salt reformer Ching Pen-po called *kuan-shou*, 'official acquisition'. This meant the interposition of an official stage between production and distribution with a view to influencing both but not operating either, in the interests essentially of social policy. Ching believed it was the best system and so did some officials of the *raj*.

Madras was not an easy area to administer. The Collector described the position in 1930:

> The Madras Presidency is long and narrow and for this reason the Madras factories are admirably situated at frequent intervals along the East Coast to supply the sea coast districts and a narrow hinterland. Nearly the whole of the Madras Presidency is thus supplied with cheap salt because the lead from the factories is not long and transport consequently not expensive. Only the very much shorter coast line on the West Coast of the Madras Presidency is inconveniently situated for supply from Madras salt sources and these are conveniently supplied by sea from the Bombay salt sources.[49]

Production was by a special form of successive basin solar evaporation. Again we may quote the Collector:

> Under this system the holding is divided into reservoirs, condensers and crystallizing beds and the area of the crystallizer in relation to the reservoir and condenser is generally as 1:2. Brine is baled into the reservoirs from channels and allowed to remain there till it attains a density of 7°. It is then let into the condensers and when it has attained a density of 17° it is led into the crystallizing beds to a depth of about one inch. The crystallizing process generally takes about 4 days and salt is then scraped and allowed to dry on the ridges prior to transport to the platforms.[50]

What is striking about this description is the change in the catchment-condensers : crystallizers ratio from the traditional 5:1, still followed broadly in the less than modern salines of Bombay, to a surprising 2:1. Indeed, the Inspector of Salt, Tuticorin circle, told the enquiry that there the condensers were either the same size as the crystallizers or smaller, so that the ratio could be as low as 1:10, i.e. the crystallizers were much bigger than the combined catchment-condensers.

The rationale for this change of the traditional ratio was probably sociological rather than technological. For everyone agreed that Madras salt was of poor quality judged by the usual criteria of purity, colour and crystallinity. Salt in Madras was produced by smallholders who needed to avoid the necessity of outside labour. Because it could be done by the family, they therefore practised the single irrigation, multiple harvest system, rather than the accretion, or multiple irrigation, single harvest system, which was prevalent in Bombay. In addition, they needed to desynchronize their work in the saltfields with their agricultural work. Hence speedy evaporation of sub-saturated brine, without much regard for calcium or magnesium compounds, was probably best for the salt-maker, given the state of consumer preference or absence of it. The Collector noted:

> The whitest salt manufactured in Madras is not of the same quality or appearance as the imported salt. . . . Certain consumers in certain areas prefer a salt which is red in colour and others a salt which is dark in colour. . . . The preference is probably not rational but due to custom.[51]

Aggarwal, in his discussion of the poor quality of salt in Madras which 'varies widely in colour from white and grey-white to a muddy dark brown', suggests that 'The chief factor responsible . . . is the prevailing practice of sale of salt by measure. . . . This has led to the manufacture of lighter varieties. . . . It yields a comparatively large bulk for weight'; but he continues, 'Another factor which is also responsible for the impure quality of salt is the mistaken notion that a large yield could be obtained by increasing the areas under crystallizers'.[52] One wonders whether from the smallholder's point of view, given his priorities, the notion really was mistaken. As Ratton suggested in his book in 1877, it looks more like a piece of peasant rationality. At any rate, despite continual disapproval from both the British and their successors, the Madras variant of successive basin solar evaporation has continued down to the present. Certainly, it conditioned the operation of the salt administration.

In 1930 the Madras salt works were administered under one of three systems. There were government factories where the salt administration bought all salt from the licensees; modified excise factories where the administration had an option to buy; and excise factories where it had no right of purchase, but only a right to subject to excise. By 1930, it seems, most factories operated under the modified excise system. The Collector defined this as follows: 'Under the modified excise system the Government have the right if they wish to do so to compel the licensees to store a certain proportion of their produce on Government account'.[53] This proportion was known as a *dittam*. Earlier many more factories had been government factories and the administration was in the process of divesting itself to modified excise. As the Southern India Chamber of Commerce at Madras put it, 'The Government is shaking off bit by bit the role of manufacturer'.[54] In 1930, however, all three systems co-existed and corresponded roughly to the size of the works: large, medium and small.

There were three sets of government factories. Two were small: Karambalam which supplied Pondicherry and Palavaram in Vizagapatam in northeast Madras which had a productive capacity of 200 000 maunds. Ennore, however, eleven miles south of Madras in Chingleput district, was large. It consisted of five factories of which one was founded in 1864 and the others at some undetermined date before 1855, the capital cost in all cases having come from the government. Production, however, was subcontracted: 'So far as the Government is concerned, the monopoly licensees are bound to manufacture and deliver the quantity fixed for each licensee during the season and it is these licensees who employ the labour'.[55] In Madras, therefore, the government salt factories were so in a different sense from Khewra, Sambhar, or Kharaghoda.

The salt then passed into a government depot: 'Salt is manufactured at the Ennore factories rather as a reserve and for supply to certain specific localities than in competition with Indian manufacturers at neighbouring factories'.[56] The specific localities were named as follows:

The Ennore factories are the chief source of supply of salt to the Madras City. Parts of the Chingleput, North Arcot, Chittoor and Salem districts and to a small extent the Mysore state also derive their supply of salt from the Ennore factories and as the Madras Salt Depot in which the salt of the Ennore factories is stored, has been provided with railway sidings, facilities exist for marketing the salt in the above Districts.[57]

Essentially the government factories performed the function, always difficult for a salt administration, of supplying and taxing salt used in a rich urbanized area close to extensive salines, which in this case contained the two great cities of Madras and Bangalore.

After Ennore the most important centre of production in Madras was Tuticorin in the far south which, thanks to climatic factors, had a longer productive season than Ennore. Here the more important factories were operated by licensees under the modified excise system: T. S. Shanumga Moopanar, 342 568 maunds; A. M. Veerappa Nadar and M. R. M. Rama Pillai, 80 580 maunds; S. V. Uallapernmal Pillai, 98 400 maunds; Machado, 282 400 maunds; Mannar Ayyah, 356 024 maunds; Mittadar Sundaram Ayyar, 295 640 maunds. In these factories, the government in some cases contributed running costs and capital outlay. Many of them had probably been at one time government factories. Other fair sized modified excise factories existed at Ganjam in the far northeast and at Sumadi further south. A.M.T.C. Hariram produced 290 512 maunds at the first and 157 200 maunds at the second. Negapatam was another area of considerable salt production, though the administration was trying to close some of the black salt factories.

Finally, at a humbler level, there were cooperatives of smaller producers, mostly operating on simple excise licences, whose aggregate production could still be quite considerable. Thus the Covelong Nithya-kalyanasami Salt Licensees' Cooperative in Chingleput produced 700 000 maunds of salt a year and could produce a million. It consisted of 200 members who manufactured salt in 700 acres: probably 200 acres of crystallizing basins to 500 acres of catchment and condensers. Each acre of crystallization field contained 80 basins. The salines were ancient: 'The manufacture of salt has been going on at Covelong for over 400 years'.[58] A similar group who put in a submission to the enquiry were the licensees of the Arasady salt factory 3 miles north of Tuticorin, 'one of oldest and largest in South India with an annual production of over 2.5 lakhs of maunds of the best salt'.[59] The licensees were part-timers, who manufactured salt for only 4–5 months of the potential 9 month year, and for the most part did not act as traders as well as manufacturers. Their chief complaint was the absence of the railway: 'The chief and perhaps the only way of ameliorating the condition of your Memorialists in to connect immediately our Arasady Factory with Tuticorin by Railway'.[60] Three miles could make such a difference! Here the salt administration touched an India which was not of its making, and over which it had, as a colonial regime, little influence: the world of the peasant.

THE STATE'S TAXES IN THE INDIAN SALT ADMINISTRATION UNDER THE *RAJ*

Sir Richard Dane, Commissioner of Salt Revenue, Northern India 1898–1907, Inspector-General of Excise and Salt 1907–9, and later Foreign Chief Inspector in China 1913–19, argued: 'the efficiency of a salt Administration is determined by two tests: (1) the amount of revenue obtained by the government, and (2) the cost of salt to the people'.[61] This principle was tantamount to the Chinese *kuo-chi min-sheng*, 'state's taxes and people's livelihood'. The next stage in his argument was less Chinese: 'In a properly organized salt administration the interests of the Government and of the people are identical'[62] The explanation was purely European and derived from Adam Smith: 'The cheaper salt is the more people will use, and the more salt is used, the larger will be the revenue'.[63] This philosophy of salt administration, which Dane was to apply so successfully in China, was derived from that of the Indian salt administration under the raj, which Dane himself had helped to form. It underlay the salt administration's primary operations of assessment, collection and receipt.

Assessment

From 1878 there was a single uniform assessment of salt to tax. The course of the rate of tax per maund was generally downward: in 1883 Rs 2; in 1888 Rs 2.5; in 1902 Rs 2; in 1905 Rs 1.5; in 1907 Rs 1; in 1930 Rs 1.25,[64] the major reductions of 1902 and 1905 being by Lord Curzon. Yet revenue was well maintained: Rs 76 million in 1904. Rs 100 million in 1947. Gandhi even made it a count against the salt administration that since consumption rose as rates of tax fell, the poor must be paying a higher percentage of the total tax![65] Moreover, the assessment was as near as possible comprehensive. The salt administration under the *raj* presents a case, remarkable to a French or Chinese administrator, of *Gabelle* without *faux saunage*, salt laws without 'owls'. The explanation lay in organization: a modern, incorrupt and determined officialdom, concentration of sources, modern transport which canalized trade, and, where these conditions did not prevail, closure against compensation.

Northern India was supplied essentially by the Sambhar salt lake and the Salt Range mines. Both were large, concentrated sources of salt in isolated areas and so easily subject to official control. Other sources of salt existed, especially in Rajputana. Diwan Chand, for example would have liked to have developed Darwari on the Jodhpur line. But most of them suffered from the same disadvantage from the smuggler's point of view, i.e. ease of control. Bengal was supplied largely from overseas through the single funnel of Calcutta. As we have seen, one of the reasons for the salt administration acceptance of massive imports and the *de facto* monopoly of the importer's association, was facilitation of control and assessment. In two out of the four Indian salt divisions assessment at source presented no problems.

In Bombay it was another matter. Salt could be produced virtually anywhere along the west coast of India. As we have seen, the salt administration dealt with this problem negatively by compulsory closure under the Bombay salt act which provided for suppression 'for failure to produce the minimal annual average of 5000 maunds during the last 3 years',[66] and positively by encouraging the opening of large, more modern salines in the vicinity of Bombay itself. It is significant that Gandhi aimed his salt *satyagraha* campaign in 1930 at the Surat region where such suppressions had earlier taken place. But it is equally significant that Gandhi entirely failed to swamp the salt administration with unlicensed and untaxed salt, so that his arrest on 5 May saved him from an embarrassing stance which might have discredited him altogether. The fact was that the manufacture of salt by solar evaporation is a more sophisticated technique and the Indian consumer more discriminating in his preferences than Gandhi supposed. Problems of control and assessment therefore could be mastered in Bombay and largely were.

Madras was even less promising territory for the salt administration than Bombay. Not only *could* salt be produced most of the way from Orissa to Cape Comorin, but it actually *was*: there were theoretically 60 factories or producing points under the jurisdiction of the Collector. Here again, however, the problem was largely dealt with: by suppression, as at Negapatam, so that only 40-odd out of the 60 factories were significant producers; by concentration, as in the co-operatives at Covelong and Tuticorin; and by control of the often single trade routes, generally railways, which ran from the factories to the backcountry. Even Madras therefore was not a great smuggling area.

Collection

When he was in China, Sir Richard Dane enunciated the axiom: 'The cardinal principle of successful salt administration is that the full duty . . . shall be levied before the salt leaves the works'.[67] This principle of a single deduction at source, known to the Chinese as *chiu-ch'ang cheng-shui* (lit., 'At the works levy the duty'), was the philosophy of the salt administration under the *raj* in Dane's time, but by 1930 it had been attenuated by political pressures. In theory, collection operated by *hsien-k'o hou-yen* ('first tax, then salt'): in practice, the administration often permitted *hsien-yen hou-li* ('first salt then toll'). This may be regarded as a sign of the decline of the *raj* following the Montagu–Chelmsford reforms: a growing inability to live up to its own principles.

The Sambhar salt lake and the Salt Range mines were well suited to a system of single collection at source. Indeed, for Sir Richard Dane, who had been Commissioner of Salt Revenue, Northern India from 1898 to 1907, they were probably the paradigm for the 'cardinal principle'. Tax, whether paid at the lake, the mine, a local treasury or a provincial railway station, came first: salt came second. Yet as we have seen, from 1920 this principle was subverted first by Diwan Chand and then by the Sambhar ring as a whole, who were able to persuade the administration to accept credit rather than cash for salt, in the interests supposedly of the consumers. In effect, tax was not collected until the salt passed into the hands certainly of the wholesalers and retailers, perhaps of the consumers, and then only at the discretion of Diwan Chand and his like. It was the same in Bombay with the Ahmedabad ring: 'In Gujerat Messrs Nowraji Pestonji and Co. of Ahmedabad are advanced Baragra salt from Kharaghoda on the strength of their adequate Government securities. . . . They recover from the consumers actual cost price of salt delivered at the depots (including duty), plus a sale commission of 9 pies per maund'.[68] In Bengal, imported salt was taxed on arrival at Calcutta, but according to Dane's principle, Aden salt at least, which was under the jurisdiction of the government of India, should have been taxed there rather than on arrival.

It was only in Madras that collection at source was enforced. A correspondent of the enquiry, Mr V. K. Appa Rao of Vikroli, Bombay, felt that this was an obstacle to Madras competing with non-Indian salt on the Bengal market and called for change:

> That transport of salt from the Coromandel Coast factories may be allowed to be effected within India and Burma without insisting upon duty being paid from the port of export, but at the time of actual sale of the commodity in Bengal and Burma and in the meanwhile have the stock held under Government contract under bond as is being done in regard to foreign salt.[69]

The Southern India Chamber of Commerce at Madras made the same point about internal trade: 'The absence of inland bonded warehouses for indigenous salt adds to the difficulties of marketing it, as it entails the early payment of duty which means the locking up of five times the cost of the article for an indefinite period'.[70] It is paradoxical that Madras, least suited to deduction at source because of its numerous salines in thickly populated areas, preserved it best. But the paradox is resolved when one remembers that the Madras producers and distributors, more artisanal in character, had less political influence than those of Northern India, Bengal and Bombay. Post-payment of tax was a privilege gained by pressure. It is significant that Madras interests had to be championed by a man from Bombay.

Receipt

The history of Indian finance, as it is usually presented, is one of decentralization rather than centralization. 'Before Mayo's viceroyalty', we are told, 'all the revenues of British India went into one purse, and the provinces were allotted for their annual expenditure only those sums which the Government of India thought fit, or which it could be persuaded to grant'.[71] However, given the 'corrupt' character of the *raj* administration before 1800 and the considerable autonomy of the presidencies after it, it may be doubted if consolidation of receipt was really as complete as this before the Mutiny. In 1870 Lord Mayo devolved certain functions to the provinces and introduced a system of block grants: 'The administration of departments such as education, police and medical were transferred to the provincial governments, which were given a fixed annual grant for this purpose, and the provincial authorities were allowed to impose certain local taxes'.[72] The Montagu–Chelmsford reforms went much further in the direction of decentralization. From 1921–2 several major sources of revenue, including the land tax and excises other than those on salt and opium, in particular those on liquor and *bhang*, were transferred to provincial control. Three-fifths of India's revenue became provincial rather than central. Salt and opium, however, remained to the central government, as did customs, state railway profits and the increasingly important income tax introduced in 1860 and extended in 1886. Until 1921 India did not possess a central bank when the Imperial Bank of India, advised by Keynes in 1913, was formed through the amalgamation of the presidency banks of Bengal, Bombay and Madras. But the absence had not prevented fiscal centralization and the presidency banks had sufficed at least for a consolidated salt account. From the consolidation of the rates of tax in 1878, the salt administration was an all-India body.

THE PEOPLE'S LIVELIHOOD IN THE INDIAN SALT ADMINISTRATION UNDER THE *RAJ*

Indian salt administrators, Sir Richard Dane among them, sometimes spoke as if the sole purpose of their institution was fiscal: or at least, that their duty to the public was discharged with low rates of tax, elimination of secondary taxation *en route* from producer to consumer, suppression of monopolies and other restrictions to trade. In fact, the functions of the salt administration under the *raj* were not limited to these activities. Political before it was fiscal, it concerned itself also with the work condition of salt workers, economic promotion and social policy. Part of the *raj*, it shared in the paternalism of the *raj*'s politics.

Work Conditions

The salt administration provided minimum welfare facilities at government salt works. In Northern India, at Sambhar,

> Government provides grass huts during the extraction season for workers from the more distant villages, and has also erected two model barracks at Jhapog and Gudha (two of the manufacturing centres on the Lake), each consisting of a number of rooms 12'×12' with a common verandah. . . . At Gudha and Nawa water is supplied by pipe line from a well. At Jhapog and Sambhar water is supplied free by a contractor, which is carried on pack animals or by the salt ballast trains to the works. The department maintains dispensaries at

Sambhar and Pachbadra. Latrines are not provided, but sweepers are employed for the removal of night soil.[73]

Similarly,

In the Salt Range, the workshop, loading and unloading labour are housed by Government in quarters approximating to the Public Works Department standard for the housing of labour. The miners build their own houses on land owned by the Salt Department and leased to the miners rent-free. At Khewra each miner owns two houses, one in the village and another on the heights of the Salt Range for the annual vacation. Government has provided a free supply of drinking water in the villages of Khewra and Warcha and employs four sweepers for conservancy at Khewra. The Department maintains dispensaries at Khewra and Warcha.[74]

In Bombay, at the small government salt works at Maurypur, Karachi,

A piece of land has been reserved . . . from which plots are granted to the labourers free of cost. They erect their own huts. The sanitation is looked after by the officer in charge of the works. Three sweepers are employed for the purpose. A hospital and dispensary were provided in 1926 at which medical treatment is given free of charge.[75]

At the large government salt works at Kharaghoda, the Collector reported five welfare measures for the 1234 *agarias* or skilled workers on the 614 pans.[76] First, low rent accommodation was provided at the works. Second, 'a piped water supply has been extended to the salt works'. Third, 'Government arable lands at Kharaghoda are leased to some of the old agarias'. Fourth, 'There is a Departmental dispensary at Kharaghoda of which the agarias take benefit'. Fifth, 'A departmental elementary school has been established mainly for the agarias children'.

In Madras, on the other hand, always more primitive, no such welfare arrangements seem to have been made by the authorities at the government salt factories at Ennore, Palavaram and Karambalam. Their control was indirect and manufacture was conducted by the licensees and not directly by the officials: 'As the labour is employed by the monopoly licensee who is responsible to Government for manufacturing the quality fixed, no arrangements are made by the department for housing the labour employed'.[77]

The salt administration's minimum standards rubbed off on to the private sector. The Bombay traditional producers reported that 'The labourers are properly housed during the season in temporary sheds and medical relief is provided for them. Skilled labour is also provided with food.'[78] The new modern companies went further. From Karachi Grax stated:

> As soon as arrangements can be made for a site we intend to build labour Quarters and we have our plans ready. Indeed we have marked off a site selected by us [for] our proposals for Houses, Shops and Public Institutions such as Schools, Hospitals, Mosques, Temples and Entertainment Rooms. We have a welfare Fund which makes loans and advances for Weddings, Deaths, Births, Sickness and other contingencies. We also pay for Medical relief for our labourers and their families. We have a Provident Fund for certain of our Lunaris who work for us under special conditions and we intend to establish a General Provident fund.[79]

By the standards of the day, at least, the salt industry under the *raj*, both public and private, was a good employer.

Economic Promotion

The salt administration under the *raj* was not actively engaged in economic promotion in the way the Ottoman public debt administration was in railway construction. Except perhaps in the traditional field of hydraulics, the *raj* did not see itself in those terms: its business was to govern. But both within the salt industry and beyond, the salt administration was not without its economic promotive aspects.

Within the salt industry, mention has already been made of the considerable improvements carried out at the Sambhar salt lake between 1920 and 1924. According to the evidence presented to the enquiry, these improvements, which involved impounding the water of the 60 square mile lake in a restricted primary reservoir of 8 square miles by means of a dam, were first conceived in 1918 or 1919 by Mr Fergusson, the then Commissioner, Northern India, Salt Revenue. They were then effected by Mr S. A. Bunting of the United Provinces' public works department. During the enquiry, the president criticized the improvements as amateurish and insufficiently radical, but the then salt officials defended them and production at Sambhar had certainly increased.[80] Mr Fergusson also encouraged the increasing use of the accretion, or multiple irrigation, single harvest, system at the Sambhar *kyars*. This produced a pure, large grained and only slightly discoloured salt, which was what the market seemed to prefer.[81] Another piece of at least attempted improvement was the experimental pans and model saltern in Voyalpur in Madras. Here, between about 1910 and 1922, experiments were made with what was called the Italian system: i.e., a catchment-condensers : crystallizers ratio of 8 : 1, attention to the removal of calcium and magnesium compounds, especially with regard to the latter, by not continuing evaporation after the brine had reached a density of 30 per cent. The experiment was successful in that a salt was produced of a higher degree of purity than that of the local product, but unsuccessful in that the cost was prohibitive.

> The result of the experiments made indicated that good white clean salt could be made in Madras which if crushed would probably be suitable for the Calcutta market in competition with the best imported salt, but only at a cost which was considered to be prohibitive from a commercial point of view.[82]

In other words, in Madras circumstances the peasant was right.

Beyond the salt industry too, the attitude of the salt administration was significant in one major field of Indian economic development.

Most of the salt producers on the Indian mainland when advancing claims to the enquiry for protection argued that the primary advantage of foreign salt in the Bengal market lay in its access to cheap ballast freight. Thus the Star Salt Manufacturing company of Karachi stated in oral evidence: 'The whole difficulty is shipping facilities. . . . Even to-day in Karachi one case of anything from London is cheaper than I can send it from here to Bombay' – let alone Calcutta, one should understand.[83] Again, the Tuticorin representatives expressed the common view when they declared: 'cheap freight from foreign countries and at times at ballast rates combined with cheap cost of production by machinery enable the foreign salt to be sold cheap, but with a high rate of profits and control the market by all sorts of unfair competition'.[84] Few of the petitioners, however, explored the economic background of the ballast rates and what their consequences were. Thus the Bombay merchants were unusual when they drew attention to the relations between salt and jute: 'Foreign salt is almost exclusively imported into Calcutta where owing to large exports of jute a very large number of steamers specially come bringing foreign salt in ballast'.[85]

Now if foreign salt was subsidized by Bengal jute, along with Patna rice and Indian coal, salt was also subsidizing jute along with these other commodities. There was a symbiosis between the movements of trade in the two directions, as there had been in the Venetian network between timber, metal goods and glass going east and salt, alum and soda coming west. This symbiosis was recognized by the managing director of the Port Said Salt Association, Mr G. L. Savon, when he said to the enquiry: 'We are keeping a certain number of shipping companies alive by shipping this salt to India' and it was invoked by the Association's representative on the Salt Importers Association of Bengal at Calcutta, Mr M. Grezoux, when he reminded the enquiry: 'The more ships come with salt, the more ships there are which are free to take back cargo from

Calcutta and allow reduced freight'.[86] How Venetian it all sounds! So when the salt administration accepted the massive import of foreign salt into India, they were influenced no doubt not only by abstract free trade principles, not simply by the ease of assessment it afforded, but also by the stimulus it gave to Indian exports, and in particular to the great jute industry of Bengal.

Social Policy

In his account of the government salt works at Kharaghoda, the Collector, Bombay stated: 'The settled policy of government being to supply the consumers with salt at the lowest possible price, Government salt is being sold at cost price'[88] – no doubt with duty added. At first sight the reason for this policy might be purely fiscal. As Dane said, the cheaper salt was the more would it be consumed and the greater would be the revenue received. However, the Collector's next sentence suggests a wider, social perspective: 'Consequently the prices of privately manufactured salt are automatically kept within a reasonable margin of profit'. This second, social objective was not consistently pursued by the salt administration. As one sees from the cases of the monopolists at Sambhar, Calcutta and Ahmedabad, discretion was often the better part of valour. In Madras, however, social policy was something more than intermittent paternalism.

Desire to influence prices for social as well as fiscal reasons was the rationale of the mixed system in Madras of government, excise and modified excise factories. Each element had a distinct role to play.

First, the government factories. The Collector defined their function as follows.

> government salt in Madras is manufactured and sold purely as a method of controlling prices in the interests of the consumer and no encouragement of larger production of Government salt is necessary in Madras nor in my opinion desirable, since Government should not, and is not in Madras, attempting to make a profit out of the sale of salt or run its factories as business concerns.[88]

Government salt however by itself could not determine price levels.

This was the sphere of the excise factories. The Collector explained: 'because the amount of Government salt is very small indeed as compared with the amount sold in the presidency by Excise licensees . . . consequently the price depends on the prices at which the licensees are selling their salt, which again depends primarily on supply and demand'.[89] After some discussion of the figures of costs he was submitting, he continued:

It is not, of course, possible for Government to control retail prices directly nor is this attempted. All that can be done is to exercise a general control over wholesale prices upon which owing to the force of competition among wholesale and retail merchants the retail price largely depends.[90]

How was this to be done? Here the modified excise factories played their part. The Collector explained:

If, for instance, it is noticed that in a particular bazaar the retail price has risen on a particular day, it is clearly impossible and useless to put some Government salt on the wholesale market at a low price. All that can be done is for Government to decide generally where owing to shortage of stocks prices are likely to rise and to form some Government reserves at those places which can be bought and sold, if necessary, during the year. This can only be done at modified excise factories and this is the only real difference between an excise and a modified excise factory. In the latter the Government have the right to reserve and buy a dittam [quota], in the former they have not.[91]

In other words, the Madras salt administration acted as a price stabilization agency, what in China would be called a *ch'ang-p'ing tsang* or ever normal granary. It used salt from the government factories, or compulsorily acquired from the modified excise factories, to moderate the price levels set by the excise factories. The Collector summed up the role of the salt administration in Madras as follows:

salt is manufactured at the Ennore factories rather as a reserve and for supply to certain specific localities than in competition with Indian manufacturers at neighbouring factories. It is sold at the market price and there is no intention to make a profit. Prices are controlled now by the modified excise system throughout the Presidency except at Ennore where the Government monopoly is kept as a general reserve at a convenient centre to control prices.[92]

It seems evident that the control of prices, from being a fiscal means, had, in Madras at least, become a social end.

THE SALT ADMINISTRATION IN THE INDIAN STATE UNDER THE *RAJ*

Whatever its social perspectives in Madras, the main orientation of the Indian salt administration under the *raj* remained political: to provide

316 *Salt and the State*

services to the state, mainly fiscal, of course, in regular finance, but also, like other salt administrations, in diplomacy and in emergencies. What was most distinctive here was the role of the salt administration in imperial strategic preparations.

Regular Finance

The salt administration under the *raj* followed the usual pattern of being more significant in the adolescence than in the maturity of the state. Until the unification of rates in 1878, salt was taxed very unevenly in the three presidencies. In the early 1850s, Bengal raised 14 million rupees from salt, Madras 4 million and Bombay 2 million, despite the fact that their consumptions were about the same. In Bengal, salt revenue was of some importance, at one time possible 25 per cent of the total, while in Bombay it was only 'one of the many small miscellaneous items of state income',[93] as it was in Madras. On balance it had been estimated that, 'The income derived from this source thus represented nearly 10 per cent of the total revenue of the country at the close of the Company's administration'.[94] The Mutiny and its aftermath produced a dip in the salt proportion, but it increased steadily thereafter: from 7.2 per cent in 1858/9, to 10.9 per cent in 1865/6 and to 11.9 per cent in 1870/71. This was before Sir John Strachey's reorganization of 1878. In 1882/3 the salt tax produced £6 per cent million out of a total revenue of £36 million, a proportion of over 16 per cent.

As the *raj* entered its high noon, however, the proportion of salt revenue was reduced, as other sources, such as customs and railway receipts expanded. Moreover, between 1888 and 1907, the rate of salt tax was more than halved, so that its receipts fell from £6 million (90 million rupees) to £3 million, and its percentage to less than 8 per cent. In 1920/21 salt provided only 2.5 per cent of total Indian revenue. In the 1920s the rate was increased again from Rs 1 a maund to Rs 1.25 a maund, but this made little difference. In 1926/7 the yield from the salt tax was 70 million rupees and there it stayed until wartime surcharges raised it to 100 million. In 1926/7 Central Government revenues amounted to 1300 million rupees and provincial government to 700 million, so that the salt proportion of the total stabilized at around 3.5 per cent.[95] In March 1947, the government of India contemplated the abolition of the salt tax, and while the revenue could not be spared at that time, the post-independence government did abolish it: an act of filial piety to salt *satyagraha* no doubt, but also no fiscal hardship. In this, as in much else, Congress was the heir of Curzon.

Diplomacy

The salt administration figured in both the internal and external diplomacy of the *raj*.

The internal diplomacy of the *raj* concerned the relations of British India with Princely India. One of the privileges of membership of British India was access to its market for salt, while exclusion was one of the costs of membership of Princely India. Thus the leading owners of salt works in Kolaba and Thana districts in Bombay declared:

> Another and new source of menace to our industry is the salt produced in the Indian States during the last 3 or 4 years. So long as this salt is produced and shipped to Calcutta we have nothing very serious to complain about but if it is allowed gradually to enter the market served by us our fate will be sealed. The Indian States have no right whatever to export their salt to British India. . . . The Salt Market in British India therefore has been created by artificial conditions and since British Indian subjects are not allowed to manufacture and market salt, except under grievous handicaps necessitated by the fiscal interests of Government, it is not fair and equitable that their salt should be burdened with the further handicap of competition from Indian States salt produced without any fiscal handicaps whatever and therefore at an appreciably lower cost than the salt produced by us.[96]

No doubt in this outburst the Bombay merchants had in mind the new Okha salt works patronized by the Gaekwar of Baroda. Other princes too were interested in acquiring salt privileges. We have already seen the Maharaja of Nawanagar speaking personally to the viceroy on the subject in May 1927. The Maharaja of Dhrangadhra, also in Gujerat, was another potential salt patron who was interested in a wider market. His government wrote to the enquiry on 20 September 1929:

> I have the honour to inform you that Dhrangadhra State is a large scale producer of a very superior quality of salt, and is, under the existing treaties with the Government of India, entitled to send its salt to the Bengal and Burma markets. . . . The Durbar are then vitally interested in the inquiry before the Tariff Board and wish they should have an equal opportunity of representing their views before the Board with similar other interests in India.[97]

Subsequently Dhrangadhra sent in a memorandum asking for freedom of trade in salt on an all India basis. This was refused, except for a limited outlet to Nepal and certain districts of Bihar and Orissa. Later again, thanks to association with chemical works and wartime shortages of alimentary salt, Dhrangadhra became a major producer with a capacity of 100 000 tons, overtaking the government works of Kharaghoda which fell into decline.[98]

Baroda, Nawanagar and Dhrangadhra were all considerable princely states. But even the small state of Wao on the Rann of Kutch which possessed a few *sebkhas* thought it worthwhile to write for a copy of the questionnaire and to set out its position:

> This State has on its Western boundary tolerable large plots of land producing natural salt in great quantities; up till now it has not been exported anywhere on account of the following reasons: (1) want and difficulty of transport (2) Imperial Salt policy. . . . If systematic arrangements can be made for the collection of salt from these plots, they would yield very great quantity; this has not been done here as there was no proper market for it; now that the market will be open, these plots will play very important part.[99]

Wao was hopeful, but its hopes, like the more realistic ones of Baroda, show that salt administration served an internal diplomatic function. It could serve in adjusting the relations of British India and Princely India which was so important a part of the agenda of the *raj* at this time. For Princely India, like the Anglo-Indian community, might have held a casting vote between the British and Congress.

The external diplomacy of the *raj* concerned the relation of India as a whole with the outside world. Here the salt administration played a part in India's strategic preparations by its acceptance, indeed encouragement, of imports of salt from Aden. A link on India's strategic lifeline to Suez and the west, Aden was also a coaling station. Indeed until the development of the salt industry, it was not much more. Most of the correspondents of the enquiry stressed the benefit of coal to salt, but, just as in the parallel economic case of salt and jute at Calcutta, so in the strategic case of Aden, salt was of benefit to coal. By opening Bengal to Aden the salt administration was giving a freight subsidy to the Admiralty. Again one is reminded of Venice.

Aden was annexed to British India in 1839. It became a coaling station soon afterwards, but of course it did not become part of India's lifeline till after the opening of the Suez Canal in 1869. The first concession for the production of salt was granted to Agostino Burgarella of Trapani in 1886 and on his proving the great potential for production, this was followed by concessions to the Indo-Aden salt works from Bombay in 1907, and to Hajeebhoy Aden and Little Aden, both of Indian origin, in 1923. In their joint submission to the enquiry, the four Aden companies pointed out that the local taxes they paid amounted to nearly half of the colony's revenue. In his covering letter, the Resident and commander-in-chief wrote: 'I can endorse their statement of the importance of this – the only considerable local – industry to the Aden Settlement'.[100]

In its individual submission[101] the Indo-Aden salt works showed that of the 12 ships in which it had exported 74 000 tons of salt to Bengal over the preceding twelve months, four had come to Aden exclusively carrying coal. It mentioned that it had 'built a coal pier for coaling the steamers coming into the harbour of Aden'. It noted too that it was 'prohibited from marketing our salt in the Arabian Littoral' so that its trade could only be with India. It pointed out that 'If salt shipments from Aden were reduced and consequently return freight was not available there could be no doubt that . . . the cost of shipment from Bengal, Assam and Burma of rice, coal etc would be somewhat dearer for the purchasers of Aden.' It was on this basis that Aden on the one hand defended its access to the Indian market and on the other asked for protection against foreign competitors, especially the new Italian salt works being developed in Eritrea and Italian Somaliland. The Little Aden Company summed up the argument:

> In addition to the income to Government, revenue accruing to the local authorities from these Salt Works under various heads forms the main stay on which Aden depends for her life, and so long as Aden is a political necessity to and part of India, Aden salt should be protected.[102]

Unfortunately for Aden, coaling stations were going out of fashion with the Royal Navy, its parents in India no longer wanted to know about it, and in 1937 it was passed from the India Office to the Colonial Office, part once more of the alien world of Arabia and East Africa.

Emergencies

India's salt supply, as it developed before the First World War, was highly dependent, not only on foreign sources, but also on availability of shipping. The war therefore produced an emergency to which the Maharashtra chamber of commerce referred when they gave as a reason for protection

> 'the serious situation created in the market of imported salt into India during the time of the great European war (1914–1919) as a consequence of the activity of the German cruiser "Emden" which was at large and baffled the attempts at capture by the British navy for a long time'.[103]

The *Emden* was disposed of in November 1914 but shipping problems continued and were particularly bad in 1917. The salt administration accordingly embarked on a crash programme of development. It encouraged private producers to open new salines in the Bombay area by granting favourable leases of marshy land. There were similar developments in Madras. The Tuticorin salt merchants syndicate stated: 'In 1917–18 extensive new salt extensions were formed throughout the salt producing centres in the Presidency to meet the urgent demands of the Bengal Government for salt. At Tuticorin alone about 600 acres have been newly brought under cultivation.[104] It was a remarkable achievement, but it stored up trouble for the future. With the end of the war and the return of foreign and Aden competition, there was surplus capacity, the Indian producers felt betrayed, and this became one of the roots of the pressure for protection. In the Second World War, there was similar shortage and similar expansion, especially in Gujarat on both sides of the Gulf of Kutch, but this time the expansion proved permanent. Gujerat and Madras captured the Bengal market.[105]

Finally, by this and in other ways, the salt administration, like other institutions of the *raj*, made a long-term contribution to the Indian state of the greatest importance: the politicization of Indians in an English mode. It is impossible to read the submissions to the salt enquiry, which we have done so often in this chapter, without being struck by the profound Anglicization politically of all classes of Indians. One is struck by the royal commission form of the enquiry; the presumption of rationality and fair play on the part of the government; the appeal to public opinion; the assumption of the legitimacy of the promotion of one's own interests for the general good within the framework of the law; a tradition of argument about free trade and tariff reform; an instinct for lobbying; and an understanding that compromise is the principle of combination. All these are themes of English nineteenth-century political history. The Indian salt administration under the *raj*, like the *raj* itself, was profoundly political. In accordance with English political principles, not the least of its achievements was to have created a loyal opposition in its own image. Part of the European-centred world order in its colonial form, it expressed that order's in-built tendency to decolonization.

12 The Chinese Salt Administration under the Late Empire and Early Republic

In the preceding chapters of Part II five salt administrations have been analysed with the conceptual tools developed by Chinese salt administrators. In conclusion we turn to China itself. Salt administration began in China. It had there a longer continuous history as a major institution of state than anywhere else. Only Venice could rival it in institutional elaboration. In intellectual sophistication, with its administrative handbooks, technical language and tradition of expert argument, it had no rival. It is for these reasons that China has provided us with our tools of analysis. For the same reasons, it is appropriate to conclude this part by an examination of the Chinese salt administration under the late empire and the early republic. For it was then, just before its eclipse under the People's Republic, that the salt administration in China reached its greatest institutional elaboration, intellectual sophistication and overall historical significance.

In comparison with the special features of other salt administrations: the economism of Venice, the *finance* of France, the estate management of the Habsburgs, the modernization of the Ottoman public debt administration, the politicism of the *raj*; the outlook of the Chinese salt administration under the late empire and early republic may be termed departmentalist. It was a specialized agency within a largely unspecialized bureaucracy, but a specialism with a variable content. Salt must be administered but how was open to argument, especially departmental argument.

Most Chinese government was unspecialized. Mainline civil officials from district magistrates to regional viceroys were maids of all work, theoretically omnicompetent. Contrapuntally, however, Chinese government did include a number of specialized agencies. The most important of these specialized agencies, were for salt (*yen-cheng*), grain (*ts'ao-yün*), water (*shui-li*), copper (*t'ung-cheng*), coinage (*ch'ien-cheng*), wood (*mu-cheng*), horses (*ma-cheng*), tea (*ch'a-cheng*), and, more discontinuously, famine relief (*huang-cheng*). In these agencies, the officials were, like all Chinese officials, generalists, who might at any time be appointed to the mainline or be switched to another agency. But many, by long service in one post or in a succession of similar posts, became *de facto* specialists. It was these people who created the tradition of departmentalism in the salt administration and other agencies. This departmentalism was enhanced by the coming of synarchy – foreign participation in Chinese administration – in the maritime customs, the post office and from 1913 the salt administration. The foreigner brought a new expertise, he remained distinct from the mainline bureaucracy, and he generally served his career in a single institution. He was a professional who reinforced professionalism.

If, by the late empire, the salt administration was an institutional constant, its administrative content was a variable. On one axis, administration might be limited to tax or extended to wholesale or even retail. On another, it might be conducted directly by officials or managed indirectly through merchants who might be few, many or without restriction. Though taxation figured in all the variables, the object and heads of assessment, the number and occasions of collection, and the places of receipt might differ considerably. Few salt divisions in China were ever completely uniform in their administration and there were fashions in salt administration philosophy. Such differences were particularly evident in the late empire and early republic as first domestic reform and then foreign participation brought an increased awareness of the options open to a salt administration. In particular, seven lines of thought succeeded one another, conflicted and blended to make the period 1800 to 1950 a great age of salt departmentalism.

First, in the reign of Tao-kuang, there was T'ao Chu's quasi-liberalism: the *p'iao* system in Huai-pei which opened trade if not to any at least to more merchants, small operators as well as big.[1] Second, following the Taiping rebellion, there was the neo-traditionalism of Tseng Kuo-fan: a return to merchant monopoly as in the past, but to one less narrow with greater freedom of trade and more independence of the authorities; a rule of capitalists if not of capitalism. Third, in delayed reaction to T'ao Chu, there was Ting Pao-chen's quasi-etatisme: the *kuan-yün* movement of official instead of merchant conduct of distribution, which was first introduced successfully on a large scale in Szechwan from 1877. It was the inspiration of the group of reformers associated with Ching Pen-po and the *Yen-cheng t'ao-lun hui* (salt administration discussion society), which he founded in 1912. Fourth, in opposition to Tseng Kuo-fan and ruling orthodoxy and so often in paradoxical alliance with Ching Pen-po's other opposition, there was the full liberalism of Chang Chien: the policy of *chiu-ch'ang cheng-shui, jen ch'i so chih* (taxation at source and minimal interference thereafter), which was based less on Adam Smith as on the supposed practice of Liu Yen of the T'ang and the theories of Li Wen and Ku Yen-wu in the early Ch'ing.[2] Fifth, with the appearance of the Sino-foreign inspectorate in 1913, there was Sir Richard Dane's positive *laissez-faire*: a liberalism of affirmative action, which not merely removed restrictions, but also established institutions to encourage enterprise, while intensifying official control for purely fiscal purposes.

Sixth, there was the negative *laissez-faire* of Frederick A. Cleveland and Oliver C. Lockhart: a more doctrinaire application of Western principles in non-Western circumstances at a time when those principles, rightly or wrongly, were under attack in the West. Seventh, between 1937 and 1945, there was the neo-etatisme of H. H. Kung and T. C. Chu: a mixture of wartime experience, Chinese tradition and Kuomintang socialism, which was applied and then only partially in Szechwan and Chekiang.

THE STATE IN THE CHINESE SALT ADMINISTRATION UNDER THE LATE EMPIRE AND EARLY REPUBLIC

Although the presence of the state in the salt administration in the late empire and early republic was not uniform either in space or across time, *kuan-tu shang-pan* 'officials supervise, merchants manage', a fairly extended monopoly operated for the most part indirectly through privileged merchants, remained the predominant form of organization, despite changes of preference and policy in departmental philosophy. This generalization, however, rests on a manifold of considerable complexity and to grasp this manifold we must look at the different parts of the salt administration.

Geographically the salt administration in the early twentieth century fell into four sections. First, there was a major east–west axis along the line of the Yangtze, still the heartland of China despite the changes introduced by the railways. Second, there was a minor north–south axis, stretching from the rivers of Manchuria, the Sungari and the Liao, via the Grand Canal or latterly the Peking to Hankow and Tientsin to Pukow railways, to the southbank tributaries of the Yangtze, the Hsiang and the Kan, and the waterways which converged on the Canton estuary. Third, between the arms of these axes on the seaward side, there were the eastern quadrants of coastal China. Fourth, between the arms of these axes on the landward side, there were the western quadrants of interior China.

Historically, there are two points of convenience for our analysis. First, there is 1911, the end of the Ch'ing, before the work of Sir Richard Dane and the Sino-foreign inspectorate, when the accumulated influence of T'ao Chu, Tseng Kuo-fan and Ting Pao-chen can be assessed. Second, there is 1919, after the partial modernization of the salt administration by Sir Richard Dane and his Chinese colleagues.

The Major East–West Axis

Here lay the two outstanding salt divisions of Huai-nan and Szechwan. In 1911 they contrasted markedly in their organization. Huai-nan reflected the quasi-liberalism of T'ao Chu as modified by Tseng Kuo-fan. Szechwan reflected the quasi-etatisme of Ting Pao-chen as extended by Ts'en Ch'un-hsüan and Chao Erh-hsün.

Huai-nan was the classic land of *kuan-tu shang-pan* 'officials supervise, merchants manage'. This meant a monopoly fairly extended in scope, but for the most part exercised indirectly through privileged merchants, though the Huai-nan monopoly was not as extended as some. In 1906 the Customs commissioner at Nanking estimated the total number of people employed in the salt business in Huai-nan and its smaller neighbour Huai-pei at 369 090. Of these, 24 090 were officials and underlings; 230 000 were salt workers; and 115 000 were merchants, their employees or junkmen. At least three quarters of all these people at each level would have been employed in Huai-nan. It was therefore a large organization.

The headquarters was at Yangchow on the Grand Canal and close to the northbank Yangtze port of Shih-erh-wei. Its core was the *Huai-nan tsung-chü* the office of the Liang-huai salt controller. He was a subordinate of the Liang-kiang governor-general, one of the leading political figures of the empire. The governor-general was always concurrently *tsung-li yen-cheng*, superintendant of the salt administration, but this was a supervisory rather than an executive position. Besides directing subordinate supply and distribution sections, the function of the *Huai-nan tsung-chü* was to assess, to collect and receive tax. It first took a 50 per cent prepayment of tax from the buyer, the *yün-shang* or transport merchant. He then went to Shih-erh-wei and made his bargain with the producer, the *ch'ang-shang* (lit., 'yard merchant, but in fact more of an export broker than a manufacturer). Next he returned to Yangchow which took the balance of the tax and issued him with a delivery permit (*fa-yen chao*), which allowed him to take and load his salt at Shih-erh-wei. Before sailing upriver, however, the *yün-shang* had to obtain a cargo certificate from the storehouse officials at Shih-erh-wei, an official communication from Yangchow to its provincial distribution section, and, most important, a passport (*hu-p'iao*) in triplicate, with the butt remaining at Yangchow, the middle portion travelling with the consignment and the left-hand portion (*tso-chao*) being forwarded to the provincial distribution section.

The supply section consisted of 20 *ch'ang-kuan* or yard magistracies, who each presided over one of the 20 *ch'ang* yards or factories, into which the centres of production in Huai-nan were divided. Production, which was by the brine reinforcement and boiling method, the brine being from marshes rather than directly from the sea, was in private hands. Nominally, it was in those of the *tsao-hu* or stove households, who were envisaged as independent yeomen. In fact it was in those of the *ch'ang-shang*, the yard merchants of Yangchow and Shih-erh-wei who, seeing to the export of salt, financed the *tsao-hu* and reduced them to a kind of debt peonage. The yard magistrate received daily reports from the *ch'ang-shang* about the production of his salines. It was through him that the *Huai-nan tsung-chü* issued requisition to the *ch'ang-shang* to send salt to the depots at Shih-erh-wei for sale to the *yün-shang*. The yard merchant first assembled his salt from his *tsao-hu* and then applied back to Yangchow for a transport permit (*ch'ung-yen chih-chao*) and to one of two branch offices (*fen-ssu*) at T'ung-chou or T'ai-chou for a cargo certificate (*ts'ang-tan*). Armed with these, he could move his salt to the depots and meet the *yün-shang*. In the supply section the *ch'ang-shang* was really a more important figure than the *ch'ang-kuan*.

In the distribution section, Huai-nan was divided into five subsections, in all of which the prime distribution was conducted by privileged merchants who had bought their privilege and could not easily be dispossessed. First, there were the *shih-an* (consuming ports), districts in Kiangsu with one exception and thus relatively close to the salines, where rates of tax were light and not much effort was made to see that the merchants did not transport more salt than they had paid tax for. In so far as the *shih-an* merchants were supervised, it was directly by the *Huai-nan tsung chü* at Yangchow. Second, much more important in the yield of tax, there were the *kang-an* (consignment ports) in Anhwei, Kiangsi, Hupei and Hunan, better known in the twentieth century as the four Yangtze *an* (*Yang-tzu ssu-an*) and named, after the literary or abbreviated names of their provinces respectively as the Wan-an, Hsi-an, O-an and Hsiang-an. In each of the four Yangtze *an* there was a *tu-hsiao tsung-chü* or provincial sales office. The *tu-hsiao tsung-chü* upriver performed much the same functions as the *Huai-nan tsung-chü* at Yangchow. It checked the documentation it had received from Yangchow against that proffered by the *yün-shang*. It supervised the transfer of salt from the prime distributor the *yün-shang*, to provincial distributors: *p'u-fan* in the vicinity of the headquarters, *shui-fan* out of town. It collected tax from the proceeds and issued licences for the onward journey of the salt.

Sir Richard Dane did not essentially change the organization of Huai-nan. Although he objected in abstract to its principles, he saw its practical convenience: 'Sir Richard Dane, when he inspected Lianghuai was so impressed with the potentiality of the system, so far as the collection of revenue in the four Provinces was concerned, that he did not recommend any material change in it'.[3] In particular, although a free trader in principle, in the circumstances and in practice he accepted merchant monopoly:

It is also only fair to the Yangtze Yin merchants to say that, although they make large profits, they do render to Government some service in return, as they bear the whole cost of the purchase and transportation of salt for sale under the Government monopoly. In this respect the Yin rights in the Yangtze differ materially from the similar rights in Huaipei and in the Changlu area[4]

where merchants commonly sublet their rights. Dane was in a long line of Chinese reformers who decided to leave well alone in Huai-nan. If Huai-nan already satisfied his revenue criterion of what a salt administration should be, Dane also wanted it to satisfy his other criterion of cheapness and quality to the public. Here, taking a leaf out of T'ao Chu's book, Dane allowed a steady increase in the flow of solar evaporated Huai-pei salt, especially from the new Chi-nan works founded in 1910 specifically for that purpose, into the Huai-nan sales area. In 1922 of the 4 763 382 cwt of salt issued at Shih-erh-wei for consumption in Huai-nan, only 334 235 originated in the division: all the rest was Huai-pei salt. Thus Dane combined Tseng Kuo-fan's neo-traditionalism of structure with T'ao Chu's quasi-liberalism of supply.

Szechwan, by contrast, was the classic land of *kuan-yün* 'official transport', even *kuan-hsiao*, 'official distribution', which meant a monopoly both extended and conducted directly by officials. This situation was the product of a series of extensions of offical intervention in the late empire.

First, in 1877 Ting Pao-chen instituted the *pien-an kuan-yün* on Szechwan salt transported to Kweichow, Yunnan and 33 districts of Szechwan itself south of the Yangtze. *Kuan-yün* was a known if rusty instrument of salt administration. It had been used, for example, in Kwangsi and Yunnan in the eighteenth century and in parts of Ho-tung after the Taiping rebellion. But this was the first time it had been used in a large part of a major salt division. Ting himself was no doctrinaire. In parts of Szechwan other than the *pien-an* he was quite prepared to use merchant monopoly or private enterprise. His aim was to raise funds for the subsidies assigned to his province for Tso Tsung-t'ang's reconquest of Central Asia. After initial difficulties, the *pien-an kuan-yün* was a huge success and introduced a new fashion in salt administration.

Next, in 1903 Governor-general Ts'en Ch'un-hsüan extended the principle of official transport to central Szechwan when he established the *chi-an kuan-yün* on salt supplied by water to 38 districts which included some of the richest areas of Szechwan: the Chengtu plain irrigated by the Kuan-hsien barrage, the tea country around Ya-chou, and the opium region of the Ch'ü-chiang or Sui-ting river. The *chi-an kuan-yün* also brought in a large profit to the government, at any rate on paper, to finance its various modernization projects. *Kuan-yün* became even more fashionable.

Finally, in 1909, confronted with rising expenses in the Sino-Tibetan borderlands and loss or revenue from opium through the current suppression campaign, Governor-general Chao Erh-hsün proposed to establish a *p'iao-an kuan-yün*. He planned to extend *kuan-yün* to landborne salt, the so-called *p'iao* trade, both in the 38 districts of central Szechwan and in the 68 districts of northern Szechwan where hitherto salt had been virtually untaxed. At the same time, Chao, or rather one of his agents because it was a radical suggestion, proposed a big increase in the sales area of Szechwan salt in Hupei and Hunan, the so-called *chi-ch'u*. Forty-five per cent of this trade too was already handled by nominal offical transport, the *chi-ch'u kuan-yün*, and the logic of Chao's policy was that all of it should be in fact. Chao's plans, were not fully implemented by the time the revolution of 1911 overtook the viceroyalty, but they amounted to a generalization of *kuan-yün* in what was becoming the biggest salt division in China.

Whatever its advantages to the exchequer, *kuan-yün* in its generalized form was not popular in Szechwan and was swept away by the revolution of 1911 in both the province and its salt dependencies. Dane therefore found Szechwan the largest free trade area in China and had only to defend it from attempts both by the central government and from within the province to restore, not *kuan-yün*, but what had existed before Ting Pao-chen's reforms, *shang-yün*, merchant monopoly. Dane himself was successful in this. This was a strong body of opinion, especially among newer producers at Tzu-liu-ching, against any form of monopoly. With his establishment of *kuan-yuan* or official depots, Dane was able to prevent the marketing of land carried *piao* salt, in which newer and smaller manufacturers were particularly involved, from being monopolized by a few big producers.

The Minor North–South Axis

Here lay the three major salt divisions of Manchuria, Ch'ang-lu and Kwangtung. These again contrasted in organization. Manchuria reflected the ongoing influence of Ting Pao-chen and the late imperial fashion for *kuan-yün*. Ch'ang-lu reflected the traditions of the salt administration before the reforms of T'ao Chu to which Tseng Kuo-fan made partial return as did his successor Li Hung-chang. Kwangtung, at the end of the empire, represented a system that had no official backer but was more widespread than many officials cared to admit, that of tax farming, *pao-shang*, 'merchants who guaranteed'.

Manchuria, administered in two out of its three provinces under a system both extended and direct, was the last creation of the imperial salt administration. Prior to 1908 there had only been light tolls collected on salt leaving the successive basin solar evaporation works along the coast of the southern province of Fengtien or Liaotung. In 1908, as part of the establishment of the new viceroyalty of the northeast where hitherto there had only been three military governorships, a fully fledged salt administration was set up. The chief element was a government transportation office at Ch'ang-ch'un which supplied official depots in the two northern provinces of Kirin and Heilungkiang by a mixture of sea and rail transport from the south. The southern province of Fengtien was still governed in effect by the system of tolls, but a local reform movement advocated the extension of the northern system of *kuan-shou kuan-yün kuan-mai* and following the revolution this became government policy. Dane did not like extended direct monopolies, but though he maintained free trade in Fengtien only strengthening official control at the works, he allowed the Ki-hei government transportation office to continue since:

'The circumstances of the two Provinces are particularly favourable for the successful working of a monopoly. . . . Moreover, as the Provinces extend over an enormous area, the establishment of salt stores at suitable centres is well calculated to benefit the local population, provided that the prices charged for the salt are not unreasonable'.[5]

The inspectorate operated the government transportation office with considerable success down to 1931, so that it became the growth area of the division. It was a testimony to the men of 1908: Governor-general Hsü Shich-ch'ang, Hsiung Hsi-ling first salt controller and Lu Tsung-yu first head of the Kirin-Heilungkiang government transportation office.

If Manchuria was the most modern of the salt divisions, the land of *kuan-yün*, Ch'ang-lu was the most traditional, the land of *shang-yün*, merchant monopoly impervious to the notions of both T'ao Chu and Ting Pao Chen. The Lu-kang, or salt merchants ring of Tientsin, was typical of the narrow oligarchies through which the salt administration worked before the reforms of the nineteenth century. Officials and merchants formed in effect a consortium. Until the Taiping rebellion the merchants partnership had been with, successively, a Manchu banner clique under K'ang-hsi, a reforming group associated with Prince I under Yung-cheng, and with the imperial household department from Ch'ien-lung to the end of Tao-kuang. From the Taiping rebellion, Ch'ang-lu passed increasingly into the orbit of the Chihli governor-general, first Li Hung-chang, then Yüan Shih-k'ai, of whose entourage the salt controller was an important member. From Yüan's viceregal clientele, the salt merchants passed over into his presidential clientele and into those of his successors, especially Ts'ao K'un whose power base was in Tientsin. The oligarchy's power was protean. Dane described it at a moment in 1915:

In the course of these enquiries it came to light that a company, called the Chang Li Kung Ssu had been formed in July 1914, which merely purchased salt from the Lu Kang, or yin merchants association (which purchased salt from the salt makers), and re-sold it at a profit to other merchants for transportation. The registration of merchants for free trade had in fact been a farce. The Changli Kung Ssu included a number of very influential names, and acted as a species of industrial Bank on the German model, making advances of funds to the transporting merchants and, without taking any part itself in the transportation of salt, securing a very large profit on the transactions.[6]

Down to the very late empire and earliest republic the organization of Ch'ang-lu, except in its seven most northerly districts of Yung-p'ing fu where old style *kuan-yün* was in force, was *shang-yün shang-hsiao*. The monopoly was extended but indirect; the officials confined their activities to levying tax at Tientsin, while the Lu-kang had sales monopolies down to retail for every district. In 1911, despite these privileges, merchants in 61 districts mostly in Honan became bankrupt and the salt controller was forced to intervene. In 1913 this intervention was formalized into a government transportation office directly under the ministry of finance to whose care it was proposed to consign 14 other Honan districts formally part of Huai-pei, but now conveniently supplied by Ch'ang-lu via the Peking–Hankow railway. Dane would have liked to have introduced free trade throughout Ch'ang-lu, but the influence of the salt merchants with the government was too strong for him. He secured the abolition of the Yung-ping fu government transportation office on 31 December 1914 and that in Honan in the course of 1914, but in Honan 'the right to transport and sell salt in the 61 districts was made over to the whole body of the Yin merchants, under the name of the Lu Kang Kung Yun'.[7] And in the rest of the division, as Dane said, free trade was a farce. Dane effected many other important administrative changes in Ch'ang-lu, but in the matter of organization he was defeated.

Kwangtung, which included Kwangsi and the southern parts of Hunan, Kiangsi and Fukien, was neither traditional nor modern in north China terms. Rather it represented a tradition of its own with a number of modern features. Where monopoly in Manchuria was extended and direct, in Kwangtung it was extended and indirect, but while in Ch'ang-lu relations between officials and merchants were close, in Kwangtung they were distant. Moreover where the Ch'ang-lu guilds were exclusive, the Kwangtung guilds were inclusive.

In Chapter 5 we noted Sun Shih-i's failure to introduce the *kang-shang* system of an inner ring of supermerchants on the model of Ch'ang-lu or pre T'ao Chu and Tseng Kuo-fan Huai-nan. For the rest of the nineteenth century the salt administration rode Kwangtung on a loose rein. Tax was farmed out to merchant consortia *pao-shang*, in territorial units known as *fou*. Eventually these were grouped together in seven units known as *kuei*, in only one of which, that of Ch'ao-ch'iao in the east, was there much official control. In the three largest *kuei*: northern, central and western, roughly Hunan, central Kwangtung and Kwangsi, the merchants had sales monopolies over their districts, as in other parts of China. In the other four: P'ing-kuei, eastern, southern, Ch'ao-ch'iao; arrangements were less formalized, but merchant power was still considerable. In 1911, the entire revenue of the division, all seven *kuei*, was formed to a single consortium rather like the general farm in the *Gabelle*, though the Ch'ao-ch'iao area, which always stood somewhat apart from the rest of Kwangtung, was subsequently subcontracted.

In the course of the revolution of 1911 the general farm broke down. Moreover free trade was introduced in the central, northern and western *kuei*. Following the revolution, the republican authorities would have liked to revive the general farm, or alternatively to introduce a system of government transport as in Manchuria, and did re-establish merchant farms in Ch'ao-ch'iao and P'ing-kuei. Dane strongly opposed these moves. He secured the rescindment of the two new monopolies in 1916. Kwangtung became, after Szechwan, the largest free trade area in China. Free trade was more lasting than in Szechwan. When in 1921 the Kuomintang salt commissioner Tsou Lu attempted to reintroduce a monopoly system, 'the proposed scheme was frustrated in consequence of the strong opposition of the Provincial Assembly and the salt merchants'.[8]

The Eastern Quadrants

Here, to the northeast and southeast of the line of the Yangtze, were the minor but still significant salt divisions of Shantung, Huai-pei, Liang-che and Fukien. These consisted essentially of coastal strips of salines which supplied populated hinterlands by means of water routes.

Shantung, which besides the 107 districts of the province also included nine districts in Honan, five in Kiangsu and two in Anhwei, was similar in organization to Ch'ang-lu, to which until the early nineteenth century it had been conjoined. Official control was limited, but there was a powerful merchant oligarchy, the Tung-kang, at Tsinan, the sleepy provincial capital, also river port and later railway junction.[9] Many of them were immigrants and members of the Shansi-Shensi guild from Ho-tung, but the local element organized in four *pang* or subguilds, especially from Ch'i or coastal Shantung, was of growing importance as Kiaochow became more important than Tsinan.

In 1912 the 123 districts of Shantung were organized in three sections:

79 districts, especially the more lucrative ones in western Shantung in the Grand canal zone, were under *kuan-tu shang-hsiao* with the merchants exercising hereditary sales monopolies over particular districts; 26 marginal districts where the merchants had gone bankrupt were under *kuan-yün kuan-hsiao*, conducted not by a centralized, government transport office as in Szechwan and Kirin-Heilungkiang, but by the local magistrates; and 18 districts in the promontory, where there was virtually no official presence, were left to a free trade of neglect, *min-yün min-hsiao*. Dane did not change this situation in essentials. In 1913 official transport was ended, but its 26 districts simply reverted to the Tung-kang. Free trade was maintained in the promontory, though as we shall see its sense changed with improvements in assessment. The biggest change in the organization of Shantung was the rendition to China in 1922 of Kiaochow. This made it the biggest producer in the division and its merchants the dominant element in the oligarchy. The basic character of the monopoly as extended but largely indirect remained the same.

Huai-pei served two functions of which the second increasingly outweighed the first. On the one hand, it supplied its own districts in northern Kiangsu, northern Anhwei and eastern Honan. On the other hand, it supplied Huai-nan indirectly by canal and sea to Shih-erh-wei and directly by upriver steamer to the ports of the Yangtze. Huai-pei was where T'ao Chu introduced the quasi-liberalism of his *p'iao* system. By the late empire, little, except the name, remained of this system, which had either reverted to type or been overlaid by subsequent developments. In 1913 when Dane took command, the 44 districts of Huai-pei were administered under four systems. In the *Wu-an*, or five districts closest to the works, there was virtually no administration. In the *Liu-an*, or six districts in Kiangsu between the *Wu-an* and the Grand Canal port of Hsi-pa, there was *de facto* free trade. In the six districts of Anhwei between Hsi-pa and the Huai river port of Cheng-yang-kuan, the *p'iao-shang*, now a restricted ring with hereditary rights, held a monopoly. In 13 districts of Anhwei west of Cheng-yang-kuan and beyond those nominally, for in fact their trade had been captured by Ch'ang-lu, in 14 districts of Honan, a recently established government transportation office was in operation at Cheng-yang-kuan. Dane acted in the spirit of T'ao Chu, but with greater radicalism. He abolished the government transportation office in 1914, the rights of the *p'iao-shang* with greater difficulty in 1915 and confined his officials to the collection of tax on the coast. Huai-pei thus became a small, but near perfect, example of the restricted but direct monopoly which was Dane's ideal of salt administration.

Liang-che, which besides Chekiang included 33 districts of Kiangsu south of the Yangtze, eight districts in southern Anhwei and seven in eastern Kiangsi, in organization combined elements of Ch'ang-lu and Kwangtung. Liang-che was an ancient saline. Like Ch'ang-lu, its merchants stood in a close relation to the imperial authorities and in the eighteenth century figured on the benevolence list between Huai-nan and Lu-Tung. Liang-che was a southern saline. Like Kwangtung, its merchants enjoyed considerable latitude and in a number of coastal districts the taxes were actually farmed. In 1863 Tso Tsung-t'ang had replaced the narrow *kang* system with the broader *p'iao* system, but in 1869 it had been restored by his successor. In many ways Liang-che was the *ancien régime* of the *yen-cheng* at its worst. Dane was unimpressed: 'The Liangcheh Salt Administration was exceedingly complicated and also, it may be added, very inefficient'. 'The inefficiency,' he continued, 'appears to have been due partly to the difficulty of establishing any effective control over the transportation of salt, as there are no natural trade routes offering special facilities for transportation, and partly also to the scattered nature of the salt works and the lawless character of the population.'[10] In Chekiang there were too many salt works and too many salt routes. Organization was bound to be complicated.

In 1913 Liang-che was organized into five sections. In all of them there was much merchant monopoly, some element of tax farming and little official control. First, there was the *kang-ti*, 33 districts in western Chekiang plus seven each in Anhwei and Kiangsi. Based on Hangchow, though mainly operated by immigrant merchants from Jui-chou, this was the heartland of the old pre-Taiping rebellion oligarchy and it was supplied with salt from the old boiling works at Hangchow and Shao-hsing. Second, there was the *yin-ti*, the 33 districts in Kiangsu south of the Yangtze generally known as the Su Wu-shu or five prefectures belonging to Soochow, plus one district in Anhwei. Dominated by merchants from Ningpo, it was a newer but more booming sales area, because of low taxes and the development of Shanghai and other places in the delta. Furthermore, because it was supplied by sea from the new *pan-shai* works at Yu-yao and in the Chusan archipelago, its procedures were less formalized. Third, there were the *chien-ti* and *chu-ti* six districts near Hangchow and two near Yu-yao which were more or less handed over to the local merchant as the equivalent of the *shih-an* in Huai-nan. Fourth, there were formal tax farms in the Shanghai settlements, two districts of Shao-hsing, 4.5 districts of Ningpo, 3.5 districts of T'ai-chou and three districts of Chin-hua/Ch'u-chou. Finally, there was the *li-ti*, 31 districts in southeastern Chekiang, supplied supposedly from Wenchow, in fact by imports from Fukien, on whose salt the authorities could do no more than impose a likin or transit duty on import.

Dane did not like Liang-che, but he did not introduce any radical changes in its organization. Dane wrote:

The extraordinary complexity of the Liangcheh arrangements made it difficult to introduce reforms, and the District Inspectors were exceedingly cautious in recommending any changes. An enormous amount of investigation was necessary to ascertain the manner in which the administration was supposed to be conducted, and there was not (as was the case in other Provinces) any clearly indicated high road to reform.[11]

He had to content himself with preventing the establishment of a government transportation office at Sung-kiang in the Su Wu-shu, abolishing the tax farms and introducing free trade at Shao-hsing, Ningpo and T'ai-chou.

Fukien, more or less coterminous with the province, was, like most divisions south of the Yangtze, traditionally underadministered. Unlike Liang-che, however, it had not as a result developed powerful merchant rings. Fukien was unique among salt divisions in that, although it possessed a normal coast to hinterland route up the Min river, more important were sea routes: northward to Wenchow, the alum port, and southeast Chekiang; southward, to inland Fukien eventually it is true, but via the Kwangtung seaport of Swatow and the Han river as part of the Ch'ao-chiao *kuei*. Even the Min river route was supplied on its first lap by sea from salines to the south of Foochow. Consequently if any element dominated in Fukien it was the seagoing junk guilds of Amoy, Chang-chou and Ch'uan-chou, the two last of which were bitterly divided against each other over the exploitation of Taiwan. Toward the end of the empire, probably at the time of the establishment of the Ki-hei government transportation office, the government began to take a hand in the transportation of salt in Fukien and a number of districts up the Min valley were placed under joint merchant and official transport.

Following the revolution of 1911, the local Chinese salt reformers sought to carry this further. Under the leadership of Liu Hung-shou who in 1913 became salt commissioner, they established a completely government operated monopoly of transportation and sale within Fukien. In this instance, Dane, who conceded that Liu Hung-shou was 'a man of considerable capacity and energy', decided to let the government transportation office stand as an 'experiment in administration',[12] concentrating his efforts on controlling the export of salt. But he was not in favour of such institutions and from 1918 it was progressively dismantled. By 1921 the introduction of free trade in Fukien was theoretically complete. By this time also, however, Fukien was passing from the central government to its own special form of naval warlordism under the admirals at Foochow which brought back various forms of tax farming, *pao-shang* and government transport, *kuan-yün*.

The Western Quadrants

Here, to northwest and southwest of the line of the Yangtze, lay the
lesser salt divisions of Ho-tung, the Mongolian borderlands and Yunnan. These consisted essentially of points of production – lakes, wells,
mines – from which radiated mainly land routes. Official control tended
to be confined to those points, but because of the variety of possible
routes no powerful merchant monopolies developed beyond it. The
yen-cheng was direct but restricted in its organization as Dane preferred.

Ho-tung under the late empire comprised 51 districts in southern
Shansi, 35 districts in eastern Shensi, and 34 districts in western Honan.
Organizationally there was a double dualism: both *kuan-yün* and *shang-yün*
and two different kinds of *shang-yün*. In ten of the Shansi districts, 14 of the
Shensi and nine of the Honan, a government transportation office, which
went back to reconstruction after the Taiping rebellion, was in operation.
Dane commented:

> The ostensible reason for this government transportation was the
> necessity of maintaining an adequate supply of salt in districts which
> could not be adequately supplied by the merchants. As a fact many of
> the districts supplied by the Government Transportation office were
> those in which the business was most profitable, the Yuncheng
> district itself being one of those selected.[13]

In the other 31 Shansi, 21 Shensi and 25 Honan districts, merchant
transport prevailed, but in two forms. In Shansi, it was extended: 'the
privilege of selling salt wholesale in the districts, which were not under
official transportation, was assigned to privileged merchants in the
usual manner, and all shops for the sale of salt were under the control of
these merchants'.[14] In Shensi and Honan, for which most salt was
carried as far as the Yellow River by Yun-cheng merchants though
Shensi merchants also transported some, merchant monopoly was
restricted: 'The transportation and sale by Honan and Shensi merchants
of salt which had crossed the Huang Ho was practically uncontrolled'.[15]
In Honan in particular, there was virtual free trade and merchants could
choose between Ho-tung and Ch'ang-lu salt. Dane noted that 'The
comparative absence of restrictions in Honan and Shensi on the sale of
Hotung salt after it had crossed the Huang Ho was a good point in the
system'.[16]

Dane saw Ho-tung in terms of Sambhar. He wrote:

> The reform of the Hotung administration, by the adoption of the
> Indian system, was simplicity itself. All that was necessary was to

impose a single direct duty and to collect it at one Collecting Office at the Lake, and to see that no salt was transported from the Lake without payment of this direct duty.[17]

In practice, things were more complex:

Owing, however, to the mistaken ideas which prevailed as to the necessity for interference with the transportation of salt, and, owing to the unwillingness of the salt commissioner first appointed to permit the introduction of reforms, the Hotung District gave much trouble and led to much correspondence in the early days of the reorganisation.[18]

In April 1914 Dane secured the abolition of the government transportation office and succeeded in maintaining the degree of free trade which existed in Shensi and Honan, but he made no attempt to remove the powerful monopoly in Shansi itself.

The Mongolian borderlands, supplied mainly by spontaneously producing lakes, *sebkhas*, never formed a single salt division. Under the late empire, salt administration, though intensifying, was still embryonic. Under the early republic, the region was divided into the three collectorates of K'ou-pei, Chin-pei and Hua-ting with their respective headquarters at Dolon nor, Taiyuan and Lanchow.

In K'ou-pei, once ten of its districts were transferred to Ch'ang-lu, the remainder in southern Chahar and Jehol were mostly supplied by lakes in Mongolia, chiefly that of the Prince of West Uchumuchin in the Silinghol league. Shortly before the revolution attempts were made to impose likin on these imports and shortly after it government transportation offices were established in Kalgan and Ch'eng-te for Chahar and Jehol respectively. Dane secured the abolition of these in 1914, but maintained the likin as salt tax. Thereafter free trade was conducted by the Mongolian princes in association with Chinese partners.

In Chin-pei, 60 districts in northern and central Shansi, supply came both from the Chilantai lake in the Mongolian principality of Alashan to the west of the Yellow River in Ninghsia and from numerous local earth salt and brine boiling establishments in the area itself. In 1913, with the support of the prince, a government transportation office was established to bring Chilantai red salt down the Yellow River to eliminate, hopefully, the supposedly untaxable and hence technically illegal earth salt. Dane was only able to set up the Chin-pei collectorate in 1918, but his successor, the less forceful Sir Reginald Gamble, was able to secure the abolition of the *Chin-pei kuan-yün* from Chilantai in 1920. Mongolian imports continued, however, now organized by the prince and the

Tungan merchant ring at Ninghsia. As regards the earth salt, which
Dane legalized and subjected to tax, there was free trade, conducted by
k'o-fan, travelling salesmen.

In Hua-ting, the province of Kansu and the 55 districts of Shensi
which were not supplied from Ho-tung, supply came from four sources:
local earth salt deposits; Mongolian salt lakes in Alashan and Kokonor;
the Hua-ma lakes on the Chinese side of the border on the east bank of
the Yellow River opposite Ninghsia; and, for 20 Shensi and two Kansu
districts, northern Szechwan. Before the revolution there was little salt
administration in Hua-ting except for sporadic attempts to prevent
Hua-ma salt from encroaching too much on Ho-tung. Between 1913 and
1917 the revenue was farmed out to three monopoly companies of
pao-shang. In 1917 Dane established a collectorate and the tax farms were
either resigned or not renewed on expiry. Free trade was proclaimed in
Lanchow shortly afterwards. Thereafter trade was conducted by Muslim
groups based on Ninghsia, Sining and Ho-chou, protected by the
Tungan warlords of the northwest and acting in partnership with the
Mongolian princes on the one hand and the salt boilers of northern
Szechwan on the other.

Yunnan supplied its province with salt made by boiling brine or
dissolved rock salt obtained from wells, shafts or mines in three groups
of factories: Hei-ching near Kunming, Pai-ching in the Tali region, and
Mo-hei-ching in the south not far from Szemao. From the middle of the
K'ang-hsi period Yunnan was administered under *kuan-yün kuan-hsiao*.
As in Shantung, organization was not carried on by a central office but
by the local magistrates. At the beginning of the nineteenth century,
however, in the reign of Chia-ch'ing, under the growing economic
liberalism of Chinese officials, official transport was converted into free
trade, *min-yün min-hsiao*. This was the organization still in force at the
end of the empire and the beginning of the republic. Since tax was
collected at source and production was conducted by private enterprise,
this might seem to approximate already to the system Dane wished to
introduce everywhere in China. Dane, indeed, wrote: 'The salt revenue
administration in Yunnan was in many respects the most simple and
practical of all systems of administration in force in China'.[19]

In fact, as Dane soon discovered, this appearance was deceptive. At
the level of production, mining, well sinking and the supply of brine
were all under official control, and only boiling was conducted by
private enterprise. Even here officials sometimes advanced funds to the
boilers and marketing was under official supervision:

> the price of the salt [Hsinpen] was not paid direct to the salt boiler by
> the purchaser, but was collected by the Salt Works Officer from the
> purchaser, and was then distributed by him to the salt boiler or boilers

entitled to receive it. It is practically certain that under this system the whole of the price paid did not reach the manufacturer.[20]

Despite nominal free trade, distribution followed a similar pattern. In 1913 the inspectors wrote:

> Control of transporting was in the hands of the Sales officers, who advanced from the revenue the large sums required to meet the expense of transportation. The Administration thus had practically a monopoly of transportation and sales and there were therefore no licensed transportation companies or merchants. Retail merchants purchased salt from the official sale and branch sale offices.[21]

Moreover actual government transportation offices had been established for the districts of K'ai-hua, Kuang-nan and Teng-yueh, respectively on the borders of Indo-China, Kwangsi and Burma, and for the internal trade between Hei-ching and Kunming and between Pai-ching and Hsia-suan. The reality was almost the opposite of the appearance.

Because of the power of the warlord T'ang Chi-yao, Dane was able to do little in Yunnan except secure the abolition of the government transportation offices. In his report he wrote: 'A single direct duty has been imposed and this duty is collected by the District Inspectors and their subordinate staff, but the administration on other matters is conducted substantially along the former lines'.[22]

The organization of the Chinese salt administration under the late empire and early republic was thus marked by a kind of positive inertia. Fashions in salt administration came and went but *kuan-tu shang-pan* continued. The work of reformers, whether Chinese or non-Chinese, traditional or modern, was swallowed up by routine, vested interests and the logic of situations. Practice was more important than theory. Such inertia or instinct is characteristic of departmentalism: 'specialization paralyses, ultraspecialization kills';[23] but it is also part of the vitality of institutions, the conservatism of life.

THE STATE'S TAXES IN THE CHINESE SALT ADMINISTRATION UNDER THE LATE EMPIRE AND THE EARLY REPUBLIC

If departmentalism produced inertia in the organization of the salt administration, it was much more responsive to movements of reform in its three primary fiscal operations of assessment, collection and receipt. Here Sir Richard Dane and the Sino-foreign inspectorate were able to effect a real modernization. Arguably a failure in organization, Dane was unquestionably a success in fiscal operations.

Assessment

It had long been received wisdom in the *yen-cheng* that it was impossible to bring all salt under assessment. The attempt to do so would be counterproductive fiscally and even dangerous to the stability of the state. Herein the *yen-cheng* agreed with the *Gabelle*. The wisdom reflected itself in the actual assessment procedures of the late empire. These were heavily concentrated on salt travelling long distance by water, because this was easiest and least frictionful to tax. By contrast, salt travelling by land, or short distance by water, went relatively untaxed. Assessment was far from comprehensive. Consequently much potential revenue was lost. Some areas paid too much, others too little. Dane commented: 'The inequality of the taxation was in fact one of the greatest blots on the administration',[24] whether one looked at it from the point of view of the revenue or the taxpayer.

Dane both sympathized with the Chinese policy and thought he saw how to correct it: 'The salt administration in China was very defective, but the men, who framed the policy of the administration, were not far from the right road'.[25] The basic defect was that assessment was in accordance with inability to avoid rather than ability to pay:

> The founders of the Chinese policy grasped the supreme importance of the transportation by water. In areas which had to be supplied with salt by water, because the cost of transportation by land would have been absolutely prohibitive, the administration was highly organized and the taxation was very high. The duties imposed varied with the distance of districts from the sources, and the further the salt had to go the higher were the duties imposed upon it.[26]

The result was 'The people to whom salt was naturally dear owing to the distance at which they lived from the salt sources had to pay the highest taxes. The people, who could best afford to pay a salt tax, namely, those to whom salt was naturally cheap, escaped almost entirely scot free'.[27] The remedy was equalization of rates and universalization of assessment, but its precondition was control: 'To secure a large revenue, however, control of production at the source is, of course, also necessary'.[28]

It was this 'control of production at the source' whose possibility Chinese conventional wisdom denied. Taxation at source, *chiu-ch'ang cheng-shui* (lit., 'at the yards levy taxes') or *chiu-ch'ang shou-shui* (lit., 'at the yards receive taxes') was the system ascribed to the founder of the salt administration, Liu Yen of the T'ang, but although its readoption had been suggested from time to time, it had always been rejected as Utopian in the circumstances of a larger China and more salt producing areas.

It was not until the early twentieth century, when all received wisdom was being called in question, that proposals for universal taxation at source began once more to be made. Most Chinese reformers, it is true, still preferred the alternative policy of government acquisition, transport and marketing, *kuan-shou, kuan-yün, kuan-mai*. As Dane said, 'A Government monopoly was supposed by all Chinese experts to be the ideal system of administration',[29] but even a monopoly might assess at source. Dane's success was due in part to the fact that he was preaching to the half converted the doctrine he set out in his memorandum of 24 June 1913 that 'The cardinal principle of successful salt administration is that the full duty (land revenue not included), whatever it may be, shall be levied before the salt leaves the works, whether these works are Government factories or are the property of private persons'.[30]

Dane's achievement was to show that conventional wisdom was wrong. He showed that *chiu-ch'ang cheng-shui* was possible and that it produced results. In 1911, 26 867 936 cwt of salt were subjected to tax out of an estimated 33 800 000 cwt distributed, an assessment rate of 81 per cent. In 1922, when Dane's reforms were at the peak of their efficiency, 38 473 205 cwt of salt were subject to tax out of an estimated 40 million cwt distributed, an assessment rate of 96 per cent. Moreover, output and consumption had been increased by liberalization.

Dane's technique was simple. He intensified official control of production by concentrating his personnel in the salt works areas. In some places this meant moving the office. In Szechwan, for example, the district inspectors moved their headquarters from Lu-chou on the Yangtze, the location of the former *kuan-yün chü* to Tzu-liu-ching itself. In others it meant establishing new offices. Thus Dane created two new salt divisions: Ch'uan-pei to control the scattered salt wells and short-distance land routes of northern Szechwan, and Sung-kiang to control the salt imported into the Su Wu-shu by the short-distance water routes across Hangchow Bay from Yu-yao and the Chusan archipelago. In most it meant the establishment of assistant inspectorates at salt works some distance from the main offices. Here young and energetic members of the service could enforce the regulations for storage, weighment and issue. Altogether Dane established 16 assistant inspectorates. Those which had the biggest impact on assessment were Chefoo which policed the 18 *tung-an* districts of the Shantung promontory; T'ai-chou and Shih-erh-wei in Huai-nan from which Kiangsu and Nanking were supplied; Liu-ho in Sung-kiang where the salt junks from Chekiang transshipped cargoes for the inland waters of the delta; Ningpo in Liang-che near where those same junks loaded; Ch'ao-ch'iao (Swatow) and P'ing-nan-kuei (Pakhoi) in Kwangtung which policed the hitherto underguarded flanks of Canton.

These techniques eliminated the worst instances of underassessment. In the *shih-an* of Huai-nan, taxed salt rose from 381 360 cwt before the reform to 1 490 976 cwt in 1922. In the *p'iao-an* of Szechwan, it rose from 1 375 000 cwt to 2 655 377 in 1918. In the Su Wu-shu of Kiangsu south of the Yangtze which belonged to Liang-che, where the official quota was only 408 720 cwt despite a population of over 12 million, by 1922 over a million cwt was being subject to assessment. In the Ch'ao-ch'iao sub-district of Kwangtung, taxed salt rose from 650 398 cwt before the reform to 906 727 cwt in 1922. In P'ing-nan-kuei, it rose from 161 402 cwt to 800 000 in 1919 and over a million in 1924. Another area where salt was brought under tax almost for the first time was the *tung-an* of the Shantung promontory where assessments rose from a prereform 68 000 cwt to 1 482 100 cwt in 1922, though admittedly this was rather an exceptional year, due to exports to Korea and smuggling to other parts of China, and the average was around 450 000 cwt.

A secondary form of underassessment was present in the weighment of such salt as did pass under taxation. Dane noted:

> Practically no measures were, however, taken to prevent the favoured holders of the monopolies of transportation or their agents and servants from transporting by the recognised routes and from the recognised depots a larger quantity of salt than they had paid duty for, and than was officially authorised.[31]

Government transportation offices were just as bad:

> A mistaken idea appears to have prevailed that, by the introduction of official transportation, it would be possible to save the large wastage allowances, or in other words the large quantity of salt, which it was customary to issue to the merchants free of duty. As a matter of fact the wastage allowances fixed in the case of official transportation, notably in the cases of the Provinces of Kirin and Heilungkiang in Manchuria, were much more liberal than those granted to the merchants holding monopolies of transportation.[32]

It was these kinds of evasion and avoidance which caused the most loss of revenue in China rather than the small time smuggling which obsessed moralistic Confucian officials. Here again Dane acted effectively. Government transportation offices were abolished or better audited. Weighment and issue to merchants was placed under more supervision. Dane gave the example of Ch'ang-lu:

> The introduction of improved arrangements for the weighment and issue of salt under passes issued by the District Inspectors against payment of duty, and the appointment of one foreigner to assist in these arrangements, raised the Changlu revenue from an estimated

amount of $6 224 627 in 1913 to an actual collection of $12 650 250 in 1914, without any large increase of taxation and without any marked extension of the area supplied with salt from this source.[33]

Avoidance and evasion on the regular channel was thus checked.

Collection

Chinese administrators distinguished between prepayment of tax, *hsien-k'o hou-yen*, and postpayment of tax, *hsien-yen hou-li*. They distinguished too single and multiple points of collection. Before the middle of the nineteenth century, Chinese salt administrators, basing themselves on the tradition of Liu Yen showed a preference for prepayment, if not of a single head of assessment then of a single major one, levied at a single point of collection, if not at the source, then at least not too far from it. Thus in Huai-nan, the *yün-shang*, the transport merchant, had to pay tax at Yangchow before he took delivery of his salt at Shih-erh-wei. Similarly, in Ch'ang-lu, the merchant paid tax at Tientsin before obtaining his salt at Feng-ts'ai or Lu-t'ai. Again, in Ho-tung, the *yün-shang* paid tax to the salt controller at Yun-ch'eng before he obtained his salt at the lake. As early as 1730, however, the tax was already assessed under several heads: there was the *cheng-k'o*, the regular tax, and there were the *tsa-k'o* the miscellaneous taxes. The regular tax was much the more important: 141 306 taels levied on 354 987 *yin* or licences. The miscellaneous taxes, which numbered 19, raised it to 171 728 taels, but they were small, related to additional *yin* and minor office expenses, so that the principle of a single prepaid tax collected at a single point was not yet seriously breached.

From the middle of the nineteenth century, the system of collection changed. Chinese salt administrators increasingly showed a preference for postpayment of a number of taxes assessed under several heads and levied at multiple points of collection generally in the districts of consumption rather than at source. Thus in Huainan, the payments at the upriver ports became larger than those at Yangchow and Shih-erh-wei and they were paid in arrear after resale to the provincial distributors.

There were two reasons for this major change in collection. First, there was the profound shift in the political structure of China which took place from the middle of the nineteenth century. To defeat domestic rebellion and accommodate to the foreign presence, Chinese government had to assume new functions and raise new taxes to pay for them. Because the rebellions and the foreign incursions were localized and because the throne was reluctant to involve its prestige directly against either, this restructuration was done on a regional rather than a metropolitan basis. Old functions were not decentralized, but the new functions were organized and the new taxes levied less by the Peking boards than by the greater regional viceroyalties, which thus became the leading element in politics. Second, as taxes increased, as trade expanded, more capital was required to pay taxes in advance, and transport merchants were happy to throw the burden back on the provincial distributors or the public. As a result of these two factors, the regular salt tax, *yen-k'o*, prepaid at or near the source, was eclipsed by salt likin, *yen-li*, postpaid at or near the district of consumption. To ordinary likin was subsequently added additional likin, *chia-li*, imposed for local reasons at regional initiative. When a comprehensive, if not entirely accurate, budget of salt revenue was compiled in 1910, likin and additional likin produced over half the receipts and possibly more, since the figure for government transport profit was optimistic. Dane was only exaggerating when he said that 'The taxation of salt in China was generally based on the principle that the duty, at whatever rate it might be imposed, was payable on the salt in the districts or place of consumption'.[34]

Such a system, of course, was anathema to Dane. He wanted a single duty collected by prepayment at source from the transport merchant. After prolonged discussions in Peking during the autumn of 1913, Dane got what he wanted and in effect returned China to her pre-1850 collection structure. President Yüan Shih-k'ai sanctioned new regulations on 24 December: 'In these Regulations the principle of taxation at the source or in other words at the salt-producing districts by the imposition of a single direct duty was definitely adopted; rates of duty were prescribed; and a uniform unit of weight was fixed for the assessment of duty and for the weighment and issue of salt'.[35] It now became a question of enforcement. Here Dane was flexible:

> in determining the place or places in each Administration where the direct duty was to be collected, the natural facilities for the transportation of salt and the existing arrangements for transportation were carefully considered by both Chief Inspectors. In places where the payment of the whole of the duty in advance before removal of salt from the works . . . would have placed too great a burden upon the transporting merchants, the transportation was permitted under supervision but without payment of duty, to Depots in closer proximity to the districts in which the salt was to be sold.[36]

In Fengtien, Dane insisted on prepayment of tax before salt left the works, but from reputable merchants who provided deposits he was prepared to accept payment in three-month promissory notes. In Ch'ang-lu, he recommended strictly: 'The discontinuance of the transport of salt to Tientsin without payment of duty: and the collection of the duty before removal of salt from the Depots at the works'.[37] Moreover,

Table 12.1 Salt revenue in China, 1910 (taels)

Heads of assessment	Amount
Salt land	245 617
Regular salt tax	7 677 074
Likin	8 376 333
Additional likin	18 610 403
Miscellaneous local	2 271 802
Government transportation profit	5 158 509
Tax farms	2 637 388
Other	247 843
Total	48 224 969

an assistant inspectorate was established at T'ang-ku in the works area. In Shantung collection was pushed back from the Huang-t'ai-ch'iao depot outside Tsinan to Yang-chia-k'ou on the coast where an assistant inspectorate was established. In Ho-tung second collections on salt crossing the Yellow River to Shensi and Honan were eliminated. Similarly in Huai-pei, second and third collections at Hsi-pa and Cheng-yang-kuan were abolished.

Huai-nan, however, was the biggest test for Dane's system because there the discrepancy between initial and subsequent collections was greatest. After much discussion he achieved a compromise. Both collections were retained, but the percentage paid down river was increased to 33 per cent, that up river was reduced to 66 per cent. Merchants now paid $1.50 a cwt at Yangchow 'payable in advance in ready money before transportation of salt from Shiherhwei' and $3.00 a cwt at the Yangtze port 'to be collected and remitted from the Transportation Officers from the proceeds of the sales of salt'.[38] Even this degree of change was strongly opposed by the transport merchants because it 'necessitated also the payment in ready money before the transportation of the salt of considerably larger sums than had previously been payable'.[39] For a time they organized a kind of strike, or rather, the typically Chinese procedure of a cessation of business:

> The system of collecting duty on salt transported to the 4 Provinces had been radically altered, and while the Yunshang were considering the subject, they ceased to transport salt. No duty was therefore paid on salt for transportation to the four provinces in the three months from 11th October 1914 to 23rd January 1915.[40]

Dane, however, held firm and his system was eventually accepted.

In Liang-che, assessment was more of a problem than collection. In Fukien, Dane, as we have seen, was content at first to leave the new government transportation office in operation. In Kwangtung too the principal problem was that of subjecting the trade routes in Ch'ao-ch'iao and P'ing-nan-kuei to assessment. For the principal avenue of trade, Canton was already the main and obvious point of collection. On 31 March 1915, Dane commented:

> Kwangtung lends itself to the introduction of a good system. Most of the salt for the province of Kwangtung, nearly all the salt for Kuangsi and all the Kwangtung salt which enters Hunan, Kweichow and Yunnan, must come up the Canton river. With proper arrangements therefore for collection at Canton of a moderate direct duty . . . I am sure that a very large revenue can be collected at Canton.[41]

Such proved to be the case, but he was forced also to accept a second collection at Wuchow for the benefit of the warlord of Kwangsi Lu Jung-t'ing, almost the first of the breed.

In Szechwan, Dane's work was facilitated by the collapse of *kuan-yün* during the revolution. Whereas before, tax had been collected in arrear when the government transportation offices sold their salt to the *an-shang* in the districts of consumption, now it was collected in advance at the works from the transport merchants. This became the position as regards the *pien-an*, the *chi-an* and the *p'iao-an*. On the *chi-ch'u*, however, as on the Huai-nan trade to the four Yangtze *an*, Dane had to accept a compromise. Here he recommended:

> That a duty of $3.00 per picul should be imposed on Tzeliuching salt transported to Ichang, $1.00 to be collected at Tzeliuching and $2.00 at Ichang, and that to prevent fraud the transporting merchants should be required to make a deposit equal to the difference between the advance payment and the proper Szechuan rate of duty, which should be refunded on notice from Ichang of the arrival of the salt.[42]

The proper Szechwan rate of duty for all the other *an* was $2.00 payable at Tzuliuching and the $1.00 deposit was to discourage merchants from obtaining salt ostensibly for the *chi-ch'u* and then shipping it to, say, the *pien-an* in Kweichow. Even in the *chi-ch'u* then Dane had increased considerably the percentage levied in the first collection, from 9 per cent to 33 per cent. In Yunnan too it was not too difficult to establish collection by a single prepayment.

Receipt

Before 1900 receipt both in Chinese taxation generally and in the salt administration in particular was unconsolidated. This had not always been so. It was the product of the rise of viceregal government in the second half of the nineteenth century. Receipts fell into three categories each further subdivisible.

First, there was the reported revenue, the subject of an annual report by the provincial authorities to the board of revenue in Peking (*Hu-pu*) known as *tsou-hsiao ts'e*. The contents of these reports was highly formalized and covered only the older strata of taxation. In the case of salt, the reported revenue was generally given as Tls 13 million and a Chinese newspaper in 1901 broke this down as Tls 5 740 000 regular salt tax, Tls 5 020 000 salt likin and Tls 2 740 000 miscellaneous taxes, making Tls 13 490 000 total. Reported revenue was divided into *ts'un-liu* (withheld taxes) which were at the disposal of the province of origin and *ch'i-yün* (taxes to be delivered) which were at the disposal of the *Hu-pu* in Peking. The *ch'i-yün* were in turn subdivided into *ching-hsiang* (capital funds) actually sent to the vaults of the *Hu-pu* and *hsieh-hsiang* (subsidy funds) which were assigned by it to other provinces where there was a deficit or imperial expenditure. Similarly, the *ts'un-liu* might be retained by the governor-general or governor in his own territory or might be sent, under arrangements either bilateral or set up by the throne, to another territory. The exact proportions of these elements and subelements of the reported revenue were a variable rather than a constant. They depended on circumstance, what was happening and the political bargaining power of the parties. Roughly speaking, in 1900 the regular salt tax was *ch'i-yün*, salt likin and miscellaneous taxes was *ts'un-liu*: most *ch'i-yün* was *ching-hsiang* and most *ts'un-liu* remained and was spent in the territory of origin.

Second, there were the authorized surcharges. These included additional likin, profit from government transportation, and the receipt of tax farms: in terms of the budget of 1910 shown in Table 12.1 a total of Tls 26 406 40l. All these items would have been memorialized to the throne by the relevant governor-general or governor and approved by it for a specific purpose: imperial, interregional, regional and provincial. The additional likins in particular were the means whereby funds were channelled from one regional authority to another. In this way was created a hierarchy of spending and support viceroyalties which carried most of the burden of China's suppression of rebellion and limited modernization in the nineteenth century. The *Hu-pu* was well aware of the existence of the authorized surcharges, but because of their officially temporary and emergency character, they were not formally reported to it in an annual budget.

Third, there were the unauthorized surcharges. These were the 'miscellaneous local' and 'other' of the budget of 1910. They were not unauthorized in the sense of being illegal. Their existence would be known to the *Hu-pu*, but in a general rather than a specific way, and they would not have been memorialized to the throne. Essentially they were taxes at the discretion of the governor or governor-general for customary, local or ephemeral purposes – office expenses, charities, sudden emergencies. Some financed the administration. The traditional Chinese bureaucracy was paid as much by fees, commissions and sweeteners as by regular salary.

Between 1900 and 1913 a number of steps were taken in the direction of the consolidation of the salt receipts. First, on 19 December 1909, the post of controller-general of the salt administration (*tu-pan yen-cheng ta-ch'en*) was established to hold general jurisdiction over all salt affairs. Duke Tsai-tse, finance minister and a rising figure in the government was appointed to the position. Next, in 1910, budgets were drawn up like that recorded in Table 12.1, which brought together all available figures – reported, authorized, unauthorized – from centre, region and province. The figures often erred on the optimistic side, but they were a genuine attempt to get at the true position and obtain the information indispensable for action. Finally, in 1911, the general control was con-verted into a department of salt affairs (*yen-cheng yuan*) which should have its own hierarchy of officials locally as well as nationally. It is clear that the intention was to create a national salt administration. It is equally clear, however, that this intention was not carried out by the empire before 1911 nor by the republic before the establishment of the inspectorate in 1913.

It was left to Dane and the Sino-foreign inspectorate to achieve a genuine consolidation of the salt revenue receipts. Except in a few refractory areas like Kwangsi, he made the salt tax exclusively a central government revenue, all *ch'i-yün* in terms of the old system, most of it *ching-hsiang*. In 1917 the Sino-foreign inspectorate collected $70 627 249, roughly the dollar equivalent of what the budget of 1910 showed in taels. Of this amount, $7 496 942 was withdrawn locally, with or with-out the consent of the central government; $63 130 307 was paid into the central salt administration account, from which, after the payment of obligations charged on the salt and the retention of a reserve for future liabilities, $61 116 428 was released into the general account of the Chinese government.

Formally, consolidation was achieved by regulations agreed on 16 May 1914 and issued to the inspectors on 1 July. Dane summarized them as follows:

> The principle upon which the regulations are based is that the gross Salt Revenue Collection, irrespective of the mode of payment of kind of duty, *e.g.* full cash payment for full duty, advance payment of half duty, deposit of half duty in promissory notes, etc. etc, are to be paid into a Chinese Government Bank, and that the *net* Revenue Collec-

tions, *i.e.* gross collections less administration expenses and expenses of maintenance of Preventive Forces, etc. are to be lodged with the Group Banks for payment of the charges secured on the Salt Gabelle.[43]

Any surplus, and under Dane's administration it was large, would then be released by the Chief Inspectors for the general purposes of the Chinese government.

Instrumentally, consolidation was achieved primarily by the zeal of the modern minded, salaried Sino-foreign inspectorate which Dane recruited at short notice. Secondarily, it owed much to the existence embryonically at least of a nation-wide Chinese banking system, whose activities the salt administration did much to expand. Revenue collected was paid into the Chinese banks who remitted it to the consolidated salt account with the Group Banks, i.e. the participants in the Reorganization loan of 1913, at Shanghai. More remotely, Dane could count on the pressure of those Group Banks who were anxious to see their security in one place, the encouragement of the British legation which wanted the *Gabelle* to be as good an advertisement for British direction as the maritime customs; and the support of President Yüan Shih-k'ai, for whom salt was one of the two largest and certainly the least earmarked source of revenue. In this way Dane and the early republic were able to accomplish what Duke Tsai-tse and the late empire had only envisaged.

Dane's consolidation was remarkably permanent. The rise of warlordism certainly increased local withdrawals, but between 1913 and 1925 central releases never fell below $30 million, though admittedly in 1924 and 1925 they were less than the local withdrawals. Thanks to his policy of keeping the organization intact even if it meant losing the revenue, his successors under the Kuomintang were able to restore his consolidation to some if not the same extent. In 1931, after several increases in rates of tax, the Sino-foreign inspectorate collected $170 444 000. Kuomintang statistics are reticent about how much of this reached the Nanking government. Warlords, it is true, sometimes permitted the transfer of collected salt revenue as an insurance policy with what might yet become an all China regime. Nevertheless, it is difficult to believe that much revenue reached Nanking from Manchuria (19.45 per cent) or Szechwan (8.60 per cent), not to speak of Yunnan or Kwangsi. Probably one third local withdrawals and two thirds central releases would be a reasonable estimate for the performance of the later inspectorate. Not as good as Dane's best years, but still a considerable advance over the prereform figure of at most 20 per cent for genuinely consolidated revenue.

THE PEOPLE'S LIVELIHOOD IN THE CHINESE SALT
ADMINISTRATION UNDER THE LATE EMPIRE AND EARLY
REPUBLIC

All salt administrations assessed, collected and received, but few were purely fiscal institutions, and their non-fiscal activities are of special interest, because as Lord Dacre has said, 'Men get how they can; it is in their spending that they illustrate their philosophy'.[44] What was distinctive of the non-fiscal activities of the *yen-cheng* was its strong cultural orientation. This characteristic it shared with all Chinese bureaucracy. Chinese government was light and spread thin over the vast empire, so that the ideological component needed to be high. Correct gestures, the right language, the appropriate protocol were central to it. Officialdom was quasi-priestly and saw its operations as promoting virtue by virtue (*te*) and repressing vice by majesty (*wei*). In this perspective, the *yen-cheng* had affinities with the *Gabelle* with its affirmation of royal justice as both beneficent and terrifying.

This cultural orientation of the traditional Chinese salt administration expressed itself at many levels: in its officially proclaimed goals, in the language of its regulations, in the character of its spacious offices; but perhaps most conspicuously in its patronage of explicitly cultural institutions and especially in the buildings in which they were embodied. *Yen-fa-chih* generally contain sections on the temples or other public buildings with whose upkeep the *yen-cheng* was associated and at whose ceremonies its officials from time to time assisted. Chinese government was liturgical and the salt administration played its part in Chinese religion. In particular, it was closely associated with the sacralities and ritual of *feng-shui*, that synchronistic interaction of man and nature, so basic to the Chinese religious outlook, especially in its local manifestations.

As an illustration of these cultural activities, we may take the case of Ho-tung as revealed by the *yen-fa-chih* of 1730. Here we find the salt administration supporting institutions and buildings Confucian, Taoist and what may be termed Sinistic, the native religion of China uninfluenced by higher philosophy.

The Confucian institution under the protection of the Ho-tung salt administration was the *shu-yuan* or literary academy. Founded in 1299 under the Yüan by the salt commissioner Ao-t'un-mou, probably a Mongol, the *shu-yuan* was a matter of pride to the editors of the *yen-fa-chih*:

The empire has six transport offices for salt but only Ho-tung transport office has a special school. Under the aegis of the state, the superfluity of people's wealth is made to do good, so that the way of the Teacher is established; through the transforming influence of teaching righteousness and enlightenment become effective; and so manners are perfected. That Ho-tung has a special school of mercantile origins is certainly worthy matter for this treatise.[45]

Despite the reference to teaching, the *shu-yuan* was an administrative and ceremonial centre rather than an educational one. It administered the special examination quota which was assigned to the sons of salt merchants and provided space for ceremonies such as the periodic readings of the Sacred Edict: an imperial encyclical designed to keep alive the zeal and orthodoxy of Confucian graduates. The *shu-yuan* was less a college than a guildhall, of that special fraternity the Confucianized sons of salt merchants. Founded to Confucianize Mongol soldiers and Uighur merchants, the *shu-yuan* was continued to Confucianize Chinese, often Muslim, merchants.

Non-Confucian cults also received attention. The chief non-Confucian institution to which Ho-tung gave support was the lake temple, the *Ch'ih-miao*, also known as the spirit temple, *Shen-miao*, of the luminous, gracious, rich and plenteous salt lake. Like the *shu-yuan*, it figured among the plates in the *yen-fa-chih* and received a special section in the text. The *Ch'ih-miao* had two main altars: one to the Spirit of the Chung-t'iao mountains to the south, the dominant element in the local *feng-shui*; the other to the Spirit of the Wind Cave just to the north of the mountains whence, according to local belief, came the drying wind which along with the sun made the salt. Lesser altars were associated with Kuan-ti the patron of the Shansi-Shensi guild, a god of risk really, and to the antagonistic spirits of the sun and rain. The whole complex with its emphasis on the interdependence of Heaven, earth and man may not unfairly be called Taoist: not the Taoism of elixirs and alchemy, but an astro-meteorological variant of *feng-shui* rather than the more familiar geomantical kind.

In addition to the lake temple, the salt administration gave patronage in the shape of donations, organization of repairs and occasional presence of officials at ceremonies to a total of 28 other temples and shrines, 13 inside Yun-ch'eng and 14 in the fairly close vicinity. Most of these may be classified as Sinistic. There were sacralities of space, like the temple of the city guardian or the two temples dedicated to T'ai-shan the eastern peak; sacralities of time defined by the periodicity of their festivals, such as the Black Dragon temple 25 *li* to the east of the lake which the An-i *hsien* magistrate visited in the second month of each year; sacralities of social function like the temple to Yao Wang, the medicine king, associated with *pharmacopeia* and the medicinal herb trade. All these sacralities contributed to the basic paradigms of Chinese belief and behaviour of which Confucianism was the peak and Taoism the middle.

In supporting them the salt administration was contributing to *min-sheng*, people's livelihood.

In the late empire the non-fiscal activities of the salt administration acquired a more economic character. The *yen-cheng* became less French and more Venetian. In particular, the salt administration was called to contribute by that fever for railway building which gripped China in the first decade of the twentieth century.[46] Both the state and the upper levels of society saw railway construction as a means of participation in the growth of the Chinese economy and of stimulating that growth further. The problem was capital and an increase in the price of salt seemed a way of raising it or at least of servicing loans. Thus in Ch'ang-lu in 1909 a levy of 4 cash a catty was placed on salt sold in Chihli to provide for railway expenses. This impost produced 750 000 taels a year, nearly a quarter of the 5 per cent interest on the Tientsin to Pukow railway loans of 65 million taels. Again, the Hu-kuang railway loan of 1911 was specifically secured on the relevant provincial salt revenues. Altogether there are some twenty decrees and memorials in the *shih-lu* which deal with the use of salt revenue for railway construction. Eight railway projects were involved: Hankow–Canton, Hankow–Szechwan, Tientsin–Pukow, Chin-chou–Aigun, the Shensi and Lunghai railways, and lines in Kiangsi and Inner Mongolia. Typical of these memorials is one of 27 June 1908 from Hu-kuang governor-general Ch'en K'uei-lung:

> The requirements of the Yueh-Han railway are urgent and critical. Gentry and people have consulted together and according to the precedent of increasing the salt catty contribution for the Boxer indemnity, request an increased contribution of 4 cash a catty on all salt, Ch'uan, Huai or Yueh, sold within the boundaries of Hunan.[47]

Salt revenue was also significant in the opening up of Manchuria which had an economic as well as political dimension.

With the coming of the Sino-foreign inspectorate some of these projects fell into the background. As a fiscal technician of the *laissez-faire* school and coming from the *raj* whose orientation was political rather than economic, Dane was more concerned with curbing than extending the non-fiscal activities of the salt administration, particularly some of those envisaged in the Reorganization loan agreement. Nevertheless his belief in the identity of the interests of state and taxpayers in large sales of cheap salt led him to accept a responsibility toward the consumer. This expressed itself in an affirmative and not merely negative view of *laissez-faire*.

Dane's most interesting move in this direction was his introduction of *kuan-yuan* or official markets in the *p'iao* salt trade of central and northern

Szechwan. The *p'iao-an*, one of the major under-assessed areas of the unreformed *yen-cheng*, was of considerable interest to Dane. Chao Erh-hsün's scheme to introduce government transportation had been set aside in the revolution of 1911 and Dane was keen to see free trade maintained and made effective. Its genuineness, however, was cast in doubt by the development of the *p'iao* trade centres of *kung-yuan*, or public markets, as intermediaries between the producers and the public. These institutions were sanctioned, against Dane's wishes, by the salt commissioner in regulations dated 1 June 1915. Dane described their operation as follows:

> The underlying principle of the Regulations was that the purchase of Piao or land-borne salt by merchants and peddlers for transportation and sale to the public was to be restricted to the places at which Kung Yuan were established. The merchants controlling the Kung Yuan were to purchase salt from the manufacturers and sell it to the transporters, and the purchase by the transporting merchants or peddlers of salt direct from the pan owners was prohibited.[48]

The *kung-yuan* were in effect monopoly brokers and they used their power restrictively: 'The scheme placed the salt boilers entirely in the power of the Kung Yuan merchants, and created a number of objectionable monopolies. The revenue also was insufficiently guarded'.[49]

Until 1917 Dane was not in a position to do anything about the *kung-yuan*. In that year he opened discussions with the inspectors to introduce a new institution, the *kuan-yuan*, to counterbalance the *kung-yuan*. The inspectors reported:

> The question of the conversion of the Chuannan Kungyuan into Government store-houses for Piao salt and the abolition of the monopoly enjoyed by the Kungyuan merchants, thereby allowing all Piao salt producers to share equally in the trade and release them from the control exercised by the monopolists . . . was taken up early in the year under review and the proposals submitted to the Chief Inspectors were approved.[50]

Nothing, however, could be done that year as the salt commissioner who had to give his approval left the province in August. In 1918 there were further delays, but the Ch'uan-nan inspectors gave a clearer description of the new institution:

> These establishments will be operated in conjunction, and in competition, with the present merchants Kungyuan and will give all p'iao

producers who are not shareholders in the present Kungyuan an opportunity of disposing of their salt, while the new establishments should tend to reduce the price of p'iao salt.[51]

In 1919 eight *kuan-yuan*, sometimes known as government *kung-yuan* were actually opened in Tzu-liu-ching. The Chuan-nan inspectors described them:

> The Government establishments, while operating in competition with the merchants' Kungyuan, are really salt marts where those small producers of p'iao salt who were dissatisfied with the treatment they received at the hands of the merchants' Kung-yuan store their salt and themselves offer it for sale to peddlers.[52]

They noted that 'the introduction of these eight Government Kungyuan was immediately followed by a decrease in the price of p'iao salt to peddlers'.[53] In 1922 the Chuan-nan inspectors were able to say: 'The establishment of Kuanyuan, which were allowed to trade side by side with the Kungyuan, produced a greatly stimulating effect on the P'iao salt trade'.[54]

Thus in the *p'iao-an* Dane made bureaucracy serve free enterprise. He inverted Sun Yat-sen's programme and made socialism create capitalism. This too was a kind of people's livelihood.

THE CHINESE SALT ADMINISTRATION IN THE STATE UNDER THE LATE EMPIRE AND EARLY REPUBLIC

The Chinese state under the late empire and early republic was a bewildering mixture of senescence and adolescence. It is not surprising that taxes on salt, easy to operate with reduced power and less than complete territorial control, played a major part in its regular finance, diplomacy and emergencies. Seldom can a great power have been so dependent on a single source of revenue.

Regular Finance

Table 12.2 sets out total and salt revenues in China from the eve of the Taiping rebellion to the last years of the Kuomintang. The salt revenue is in all cases the gross collection. It is not the amount available to the central government. Total revenue, on the other hand, is in the case of the imperial figures, the gross collection but, in the case of the republican figures, the net collection available to the central government. The figures for 1947 are particularly conjectural because of inflation, but a

Table 12.2 Total and salt revenues in China, 1850–1950 (million taels)

Year	Total revenue	Salt revenue	Salt (%)
1850	100	10	10
1900	200	24	12
1911	300	50	17
1914	86	40	50
1922	117	57	49
1931	357	113	32
1935	423	123	29
1947	846	111	13

number of indications suggest that the Kuomintang about doubled its fiscal power over the period of the Pacific War, though one must remember that much of the increase was through expansion of money supply. Hopefully, Table 12.2 gives a fair fiscal profile of the Chinese state and the place of salt in its finances between 1850 and 1950.

Under the late empire, the salt tax was of increasing importance. Greater indeed than what Table 12.2 might suggest because while much of the increase in the total revenue was on paper or in someone else's hands, the increase in the salt revenue was concrete and in the hands if not of the central government, those of its greater governors-general. As the financial requirements of defeating rebellion, accommodating to the foreigner, and initiating modernization rose, the phrase 'my solution is an increase in the price of salt' became a frequent refrain in the memorials of harassed governors-general. Indeed China's remarkable achievements in all three directions between 1840 and 1911 would hardly have been possible without the quintupling of the salt tax between the outbreak of the Taiping rebellion and the onset of the revolutionary confusion. An illustration of how salt revenue was expanded and apportioned may be found in the development of Szechwan between 1840 and 1910 as set out in Table 12.3.

Before the Taiping rebellion, only the regular salt tax (*cheng-k'o*) was levied in Szechwan. Following the rebellion, likin was imposed in 1855 and extended in 1860 to meet the costs of suppression. From 900 000 taels in 1875 it was increased by Ting Pao-chen between 1876 and 1886 to finance Tso Tung-t'ang's reconquest of the northwest. Ting also added the profit from the *pien-an kuan-yün* which he introduced for the same purpose. In 1895 the old surcharge of 2 cash a catty was imposed by Governor-general Liu Ping-chang during the Sino-Japanese War for the navy. In 1899 the new surcharge of 2 cash a catty was added by Governor-general K'uei-chun to help service China's postwar indemnity war loans. In 1901 K'uei-chun, along with most heads of salt divisions,

Table 12.3 Salt revenue in Szechwan 1850–1910 (taels)

Source	1850	1875	1886	1900	1909
Salt tax	225 064	225 064	315 064	315 064	315 064
Salt likin	—	900 000	1 340 000	1 340 000	1 340 000
Old surcharge	—	—	—	666 667	666 667
New surcharge	—	—	—	666 666	666 666
Boxer surcharge	—	—	—	—	1 000 000
Army surcharge	—	—	—	—	666 666
Opium surcharge	—	—	—	—	1 000 000
Government profit	—	—	344 936	344 936	1 132 348
Total	225 064	1 125 004	2 000 000	3 333 333	6 788 431

had to impose a surcharge of 3 cash a catty as his contribution to the Boxer indemnity. In 1907, Governor-general Hsi-liang introduced a surcharge of 2 cash a catty for Yüan Shih-k'ai's new army programme. In 1909, Governor-general Chao Erh-hsün added the opium surcharge of 3 cash a catty to recompense Szechwan for the revenue lost through the government's opium suppression campaign, which hit Szechwan, the empire's premier producer and consumer, particularly hard. Finally, in 1909, through the extension of *kuan-yün* actually to the *chi-an* and prospectively to the *p'iao-an*, profit from government transportation offices could now be estimated at 1 132 348 taels. Thus Szechwan salt contributed to the suppression of rebellion, accommodation with the foreigner and the beginnings of modernization. In particular, as part of a support viceroyalty, it contributed to two of the most notable Chinese enterprises of the nineteenth century: Tso Tsung-t'ang's restabilization of the Inner Asian frontier and Li Hung-chang's stabilization of the maritime frontier. In the twentieth century it contributed to another notable Chinese enterprise, the Chao brother's restabilization of the Tibetan frontier. Salt helped preserve the territorial integrity of China from the empire to the republic.

In the early republic, the salt revenue became even more important to the state. From the revolution of 1911 until halfway through the Pacific War, salt along with the maritime customs was virtually the only source of regular income of the central government. The land tax, which though it had long been of declining importance, was still the largest single item of revenue in 1911, simply ceased to be collected or was appropriated by local regimes. New taxes were introduced: on liquor, tobacco, income even; and domestic loans were raised through the Chinese banking system; but until the wartime Kuomintang's imposition of a grain tax in Szechwan, these expedients produced little revenue. With the outbreak of the First World War, salt became a more reliable source of revenue than the customs. This was why it was of such crucial importance to the regime of Yüan Shih-k'ai, in many ways the strongest and most centralized which China experienced before the coming of the Communists. Dane in effect was Yüan's paymaster-general and because of this could get his advice accepted and enforced even when it ran counter to the prejudices and interests of senior members of the president's entourage. Consequently, the refusal of the Group Banks, under Japanese pressure, to release salt revenue to Yüan on Dane's instructions during a critical moment of the revolt against him in 1916 was a contributory factor in his defeat. As Dane remarked to Jordan at Yüan's funeral, the old man might still be with them if Dane's advice had been listened to.

Diplomacy

Salt was part of the life-blood of Chinese politics. At no time was this more true than during the warlord period between 1917 and 1928. Indeed then, and down to 1949, China is best regarded less as a single state than as a group of states, a *Chine des patries*: Peking, Nanking, the warlords, the Japanese satellites. Between these states there was a kind of diplomacy in which, because of its revenue potential, salt was a significant factor.

Dane first encountered warlordism in 1913 with the refusal of Lu Jung-t'ing, the post-revolutionary ruler of Kwangsi, to permit the operation of the Sino-foreign inspectorate on his territory. As Yüan Shih-k'ai was not strong enough to compel him to do so, Dane had to accept that Lu manage and withdraw the receipts of the important salt likin station at Wuchow on the West river where Kwangtung salt from Canton entered Kwangsi. In Yunnan, in 1914, where the post-revolutionary ruler T'ang Chi-yao also showed some reluctance to admit the inspectorate, Dane also had to compromise, but obtained better terms. In return for allowing the inspectorate to function, T'ang was permitted to withdraw half the revenue collected. With the extension of warlordism beyond its original reservoir in the southwest in the revolt against Yüan Shih-k'ai in 1916 and still more with the secessions from the Peking government which followed Tuan Ch'i-jui's restoration of the republic in 1917, the problem of warlordism became generalized. Dane's policy was to accept the warlord's demand for money, against compensation from the central government to keep the books straight, but to persuade him to allow the inspectorate to go on collecting in the usual way, the inducement being that he might obtain more like this than by running his own salt administration. In this way, though the central government had to agree to subsidize its enemies, a national fiscal agency was kept in being which might be reactivated when diplomatic circumstances were more favourable. It was better, Dane believed, that the pipelines ceased to flow than that they be broken altogether.

In the 1920s this policy wore thin. The Chinese diplomatic correspondence becomes full of foreign complaints against military interference with the salt administration. Some warlords were better placed to take advantage of Dane's system of temporary devolution than others. Thus the Changs in Manchuria could conveniently take over and operate Fengtien and the Ki-Hei government transportation office. Yen Hsi-shan in Shansi positively welcomed the single tax assessment and collection in Ho-tung because its appropriation would not involve his control in Shensi or Honan. Similarly, the more static warlords in Shantung and Yunnan did not need to disrupt the salt administration to profit by it. Even the much divided warlords of Szechwan could be apportioned different areas to protect and exploit. It was the more mobile warlords of central China who interfered most with the salt administration. Operating largely in consumer areas, they could not benefit from its deduction at source, but must increase second collections or set up para-administrations. In particular, the Chihli clique, always short of money because they did not control the Peking ministries, were serious disruptors of the salt administration: notably Wu P'ei-fu when he controlled Ichang and Hankow. In February 1922, the Japanese legation spoke of the 'grave danger of ultimately inducing the unfortunate destruction of the entire system of Salt Administration provided for by the Agreement'.[55] Feng Yü-hsiang was another serious disruptor, setting up his own tax office at Sian. Eventually even stationary warlords took to disruption and in 1926 there were protests against the situation in Tientsin and Shantung. Nevertheless, the salt administration survived, and the allocation of its surpluses, or at least the legitimation of their seizure, was one of the weapons of the Peking government in its skilful and not unsuccessful struggle to maintain some control of the warlord mêlée.[56]

Emergencies

The three typical emergencies of traditional China were famine, flood and barbarian incursion, and the salt administration is to be found rising to all of them. In 1726 the *ch'ang-shang* of the Liang-huai founded at Yangchow and at the three production control points of T'ung-chou, T'ai-chou and Huai-an the *Liang-huai yen i-tsang* or Liang-huai charitable granaries.[57] A capital of 300 000 taels was involved and in 1766 half a million hectolitres of grain was stored, which could be brought on to the market or distributed free, in accordance with the dictates of the *huang-cheng*, or famine relief administration, under the governor of Kiangsu.

Flood works were the particular concern of Ch'ang-lu through whose territory ran both the Yellow River and the Grand Canal. At the turn of the eighteenth and nineteenth centuries when hydraulic conditions worsened all over China, Ch'ang-lu was called upon to provided 10 000's for washouts at the salines; 100 000's for the recurrent expenses of the Yellow River; and several million for major works (*ta-kung*) on the Grand Canal in 1809 and on the high dyke at Jung-yang in Honan in 1825. On this last occasion, the Ch'ang-lu merchants could pay no more, so the imperial household department (*nei-wu fu*) lent them treasury funds (*t'ang-pen*), but at substantial rates of interest. There was a further increase in taxation, a levy of 2 cash a catty on salt sold in Honan known as *Ho-fang chia-chia*, river defence price increase. As regards barbarian incursions, Ch'ang-lu found itself paying a *chiu-an chia-chia* (old cases price increase) of 1 cash a catty from 1895 to finance the four power loans needed to finance the Japanese indemnity and a *hsin-an chia-chia* (new cases price increase) of 4 cash a catty from 1903 to meet the indemnity imposed by the Boxer protocol of 1901.

Under the early republic salt was the security for the Reorganization loan which enabled the virtually bankrupt Peking government to get started in its new form under Yüan Shih-k'ai. Thanks to it Yüan was able to pay off a large number of the troops which had been raised by all parties in the revolution. Yüan is often regarded as the father of the warlords, but in fact he did his best to strangle them at birth. The Reorganization loan tided him over demobilization and the crises of the so-called second revolution in July 1913 until Aglen and Dane could produce regular customs and salt revenue. Thereafter the part of the salt administration in emergencies was less conspicuous, except in so far as the whole early life of the republic could be considered as an emergency.

The salt administration, however, did provide most of the funds for one institution set up as a result of an emergency. This was the Chihli river commission which was established in March 1918 after disastrous floods in the Tientsin area which swamped 15 000 square miles, inundated 19 000 villages, left 6 million people homeless and partly blocked the Hai-ho, the exit from the port, with silt. The leading figure on the Chinese side in organizing the commission, which took the first steps in a major reconstruction of the Peking and Tientsin waterways later completed by the People's republic, was Hsiung Hsi-ling, former salt controller in Manchuria and subsequently minister of finance in the early days of the reform. He wrote in 1918:

as river conservancy directly concerns navigation and the commerce of Tientsin and indirectly concerns the production of salt in Changlu District, I firmly hold the opinion that a request from the Government to the Group Banks and to Sir Richard Dane for the release of the balance of the London deposit and of $2 000 000 from the Group Banks deposit cannot be considered unreasonable.[58]

Dane complied and down to the end of 1925 the commission had spent nearly $6 million and the grand scheme it projected envisaged the expenditure of a further $100 million. The reformed salt administration, therefore did provide funds for one important piece of traditional emergency spending, though with its additional modern perspectives it was also able to take a longer view and look beyond the immediate emergency.

As a period of Chinese history, the late empire and early republic have not had a good press. Yet from the perspective of the salt administration: its expertise, technical skill and articulation of principles; in other words its departmentalism; it was a high point. It was a period of fruitful cooperation between Chinese tradition, itself not monolithic or static, and foreign innovation, willing to learn as well as teach. The result was good service to state and society, and even, through the demonstration effect of a successful piece of modernization, to culture. As China invented salt administrations, so, with foreign assistance, she carried them to their highest point of development, and that in a bad season. When the Communists after 1949 dismantled the salt administration they destroyed one of the most striking examples of premodern China's genius for the creation of institutions.

Notes

1 Primitivity

1. For two examples of commodity history one large, the other small, see Robert Delort, *Le Commerce des Fourrures en Occident à la fin du Moyen Age (vers 1300–vers 1450)* (Ecole Française de Rome, Rome, 1978); F. M. L. Thompson, 'Nineteenth Century Horse Sense', *Economic History Review*, XXIX, No. 1 (February 1976) pp. 60–81.
2. Jacques Nenquin, *Salt A Study in Economic Prehistory* (de Tempol, Brugge, 1961); Bernard Edeine, 'Les Techniques de Fabrication du Sel dans les sauneries pré et protohistoriques ainsi que Gallo-Romaines', *Annales de Bretagne et des Pays de l'Ouest*, Vol. 82 (1975) pp. 11–18; Jean-Paul Bertraux, 'L'Archéologie du Sel en Lorraine: Le Briquetage de la Seille', Guy Cabourdin (ed.), *Le Sel et Son Histoire* (Université de Nancy II, Nancy, 1981) pp. 519–38.
3. Peter S. Wells, 'Iron-Age Central Europe', *Archaeology*, Vol. 33, No. 5 (September–October 1980) pp. 6–11.
4. Nenquin, p. 53.
5. Giraldus Cambrensis, *The Itinerary through Wales and the Description of Wales* (Dent, London, 1919) p. 176.
6. Anthony P. Andrews, 'The Salt Trade of the Maya', *Archaeology*, Vol. 33, No. 4 (July–August 1980) pp. 16–33.
7. Eric C. Thompson, *Thomas Gage's Travels in the New World* (University of Oklahoma Press, Norman, 1958) pp. 167, 204.
8. Ibid., p. 61.
9. Antonio Vazquez de Espinosa, *Description of the Indies (c. 1620)*, tr, Charles Upson Clark (Smithsonian Institute Press, Washington, 1968) para 467.
10. Miguel O. de Mendizabal, *Influencia de la Sol en la distribucion geographica de los grupos indigenas de Mexico* (Mexico, 1928).
11. Father Joseph de Acosta, *The Natural and Moral History of the Indies*, 2 vols (Hakluyt Society, London, 1880) p. 155.
12. Vazquez de Espinosa, para 1437. Marianne Cardale-Schrimpff, 'Prehistoric Salt Production in Columbia, South America' (Colchester Archaeological Group), *Salt, The Study of an Ancient Industry (Colchester, 1975)* p. 84.
13. Chantal Caillavet, 'Le Sel d'Otavalo (Equateur) Continuités Indigenes et Ruptures Coloniales', *Melanges de La Casa de Velazquez*, Tome XV (1979) pp. 329–63.
14. Vazquez de Espinosa, para 1006.
15. Claude Lévi-Strauss, *Mythologiques IV, L'Homme Nu* (Plon, Paris, 1971) p. 83.
16. Vazquez de Espinosa, para 1419.
17. Ibid., para 1954.
18. Alexander von Humboldt, *Personal Narrative of Travels to the Equinoctial Regions of America during the Years 1799–1804*, 3 vols (George Bell, London, 1881) II, p. 365.
19. Herbert Eugene Bolton, *Spanish Exploration in the Southwest* (Barnes and Noble, New York, 1959) p. 220.
20. Claude Lévi-Strauss, 'The Use of Wild Plants in Tropical South America', Julian H. Steward (ed.), *Handbook of South American Indians*, Vol. 6, *Physical*

Anthropology, Linguistics and Cultural Geography of South American Indians (Cooper Square, New York, 1963) p. 482.

21. Humboldt, I, p. 179.
22. Claude Lévi-Strauss, *Mythologiques II Du Miel aux Cendres* (Plon, Paris, 1966) p. 42; *Mythologiques III Les Origines des Manières de Table* (Plon, Paris, 1968) p. 470.
23. W. G. L. Randles, 'La Civilisation Bantou, son essor et son declin', *Annales, Économies, Sociétés, Civilisations*, 29:2 (March–April 1974) pp. 267–81; Thurston Shaw, *Nigeria Its Archaeology and Early History* (Thames & Hudson, London, 1978).
24. P. Gouletquer and D. Kleinmann, 'Structure Sociale et Commerce du Sel dans l'Economie Touarègue', *Revue de l'Occident Musulman et de la Méditerranée*, 21, 1976, pp. 131–9; Michal Tymowski, 'La Saline d'Idjil en Mauritanie', *Africana Bulletin*, 30 (1981) pp. 7–37.
25. Paul E. Lovejoy, 'The Borno Salt Industry', *The International Journal Of African Historical Studies*, Vol. II (1978) no. 4, pp. 629–68.
26. Ibid., p. 629.
27. Ibid.
28. Ibid.
29. J. Clauzel, *L'Exploitation des Salines de Taoudenni*, Institu de Recherches sahariennes (Université d'Alger, Alger, 1960).
30. J. E. G. Sutton and A. D. Roberts, 'Uvinza and its Salt Industry', *Anzania*, 3 (1969) pp. 45–86.
31. Henry M. Stanley, *Through the Dark Continent*, 2 vols (Sampson Low, London, 1878) I, 508.
32. Charles M. Good, 'Salt, Trade, and Disease: Aspects of Development in Africa's Northern Great Lakes Region', *International Journal of African Historical Studies*, Vol. 5 (1972) no. 4, pp. 543–86.
33. Duke Adolphus Frederick of Mecklenburg, *In the Heart of Africa* (Cassell, London, 1910) pp. 191–2.
34. Ibid., p. 192.
35. Ibid.
36. Ibid.
37. Paul Pascon, 'Le Commerce de la Maison d'Iligh d'après le registre comptable de Husayn b. Hachem (Tazerwolt, 1850–1875)', *Annales, Économies, Sociétés, Civilisations*, 35:3–4 (May–August 1980) pp. 700–729.
38. Richard Gray and David Birmingham (eds), *Pre-Colonial African Trade, Essays on Trade in Central and Eastern Africa before 1900* (Oxford University Press, Oxford, 1970) p. 34.
39. Michael G. Kenny, 'Salt Trading in Eastern Lake Victoria', *Azania*, Vol. IX (1974) pp. 225–8, p. 226.
40. Good, p. 557.
41. Ibid.
42. Tadeusz Lewicki, *West African Food in the Middle Ages* (Cambridge University Press, Cambridge, 1974).
43. Ibid., p. 79.
44. Ibid., p. 116.
45. Ibid., pp. 116–17.
46. Ibid., p. 121.
47. Ibid., p. 218.
48. For an exception to this generalization, see I. B. Sutton, 'The Volta River Salt Trade: The Survival of an Indigenous Industry', *Journal of African History*, 22 (1981) pp. 43–61.

49. Lévi-Strauss, *Mythologiques III*, p. 355.
50. Nancy Lee Swan, *Food and Money in Ancient China* (Princeton University Press, Princeton, 1950) p. 347, quoting *Han-shu* 24:24b.
51. Robert P. Multhauf, *Neptune's Gift, A History of Common Salt* (Johns Hopkins University Press, Baltimore and London, 1978) p. 4.
52. Derek Denton, *The Hunger for Salt, An Anthropological, Physiological and Medical Analysis* (Springer-Verlag, Berlin, Heidelberg, New York, 1982).
53. E. A. Wallis Budge, *Syrian Anatomy, Pathology and Therapeutics or 'The Book of Medicine'*, 2 vols (Oxford University Press, Oxford, 1913) I, 339.
51. *Charaka-Samhita*, Translated and published by Kaviraj Arinash Chandra Kaviratna, 5 vols, Calcutta, 1896–1912, I, 9.
55. Ibid., II, 452.
56. Ilza Veith, *Huang Ti Nei Ching Su Wen, The Yellow Emperor's Classic of Internal Medicine* (Williams and Wilkins, Baltimore, 1949) pp. 120, 23.
57. Wallis Budge, I, 506.
58. *Charaka-Samhita*, II, 529, 532, 535.
59. Ibid., II, 532.
60. Veith, p. 141.
61. James E. Latham, *The Religious Symbolism of Salt* (Editions Beauchesne, Paris, 1982) p. 161.
62. Latham, p. 163.
63. S. C. Aggarwal, *The Salt Industry in India* (Government of India Press, New Delhi, 1976) p. 6.
64. For such diseases in one particular area, see James L. Maxwell, *The Diseases of China* (ABC Press, Shanghai, 1929) pp. 137–203 on Protozoal and Metazoal parasites.
65. Mirko D. Grmek, *Les maladies à l'aube de la Civilisation Occidentale* (Payot, Paris, 1983).
66. Lévi-Strauss, *Mythologiques II*, pp. 406–7, *Mythologiques III*, p. 397.

2 Antiquity

1. Ronald P. Legon, *Megara The Political History of a Greek City-state to 330 BC* (Cornell University Press, Ithaca and London, 1980) p. 25.
2. Dio Chrysostom, *Orations*, The Thirty-Sixth, or Borysthenitic Discourse.
3. Pliny, *Naturalis Historia*, Book XXXI, 39.
4. David Magie, *Roman Rule in Asia Minor to the End of the Third Century after Christ*, 2 vols (Princeton University Press, Princeton, New Jersey, 1950) p. 1312; Speros Vryonis, *The Decline of Medieval Hellenism in Asia Minor and the Process of Islamization from the Eleventh through the Fifteenth Century* (University of California Press, Berkeley, 1971).
5. Strabo, *Geographia*, Book XVI, 3, 3.
6. Pliny, Book XXXI, 39.
7. Paul Veyne, *Le Pain et Le Cirque, Sociologie Historique d'un Pluralisme Politique* (Editions du Seuil, Paris, 1976).
8. Dio Cassius, *Romaika*, Book XLIX.
9. Livy, *Ab Urbe Condita Libri*, Book II, 9. 6.
10. Livy, Book XXIX, 37, 3.
11. Tenney Frank (ed.), *An Economic Survey of Ancient Rome*, 5 vols (Pageant, Paterson, New Jersey, 1959) I, pp. 140, 151.
12. L. Wickert (ed.), *Corpus Inscriptionum*, Latinatum, Vol. 14, Supplement (Gruyter, Berlin, 1938) p. 78, S 4285; Hermann Dessau, *Inscriptiones Latinae Selectae*, Vol. II, part 1 (Weidmann, Berlin, 1902) pp. 556–7, no. 6178.

13. Léon Homo, *Essai sur le Regne de l'Empereur Aurélien* (Bretschneider, Paris, 1904) p. 179.
14. Clyde Pharr, *The Theodosean Code* (Greenwood Press, New York, 1952) pp. 412, 312.
15. Oswyn Murray, 'The Greek Symposion in History', *Times Literary Supplement*, 6 November 1981, pp. 1307–8; Denis Roussel, *Tribu et Cité* (Université de Besançon, Paris, 1976).
16. P. Grimal and Th. Monod, 'Sur la véritable nature du garum', *Revue des Études Anciennes*, Vol. 54 (1952) pp. 27–38.
17. W. B. Fisher (ed.), *The Cambridge History of Iran*, Vol. I, *The Land of Iran* (Cambridge University Press, Cambridge, 1968) p. 139.
18. Ibid., p. 69.
19. Daniel Potts, 'On Salt and Salt Gathering in Ancient Mesopotamia', *Journal of the Economic and Social History of the Orient*, XXVII, 3 (October 1984) pp. 225–71.
20. Richard W. Bulliet, *The Camel and the Wheel* (Harvard University Press, Cambridge, Massachusetts, 1975).
21. Pliny, Book XXXI, 39.
22. Strabo, Book SV, 1, 30.
23. Hsuan-tsang, *Si-yu-ki, Buddhist Records of the Western World*, trn Samuel Beal, 2 vols (Paragon, New York, 1968).
24. *Charaka-Samhita*, II, 452; A. L. Basham, *The Wonder that was India* (Grove, New York, 1959) p. 498; F. Ashton, 'The Salt Industry of Rajputana', *The Journal of Indian Art and Industry*, Vol. 9 (1902) pp. 23–32, p. 30; Aggarwal, pp. 420–421.
25. Sir George Dunbar, *History of India from Earliest Times to 1939*, 2 vols (Nicholson and Watson, London, 1949) I, 76.
26. *Shu-ching*, Part III, Book I, part 1, ch. 4, vv 24–6.
27. *Shih-chi*, 32.
28. Ibid., 129.
29. *Ssu-ch'uan yen-fa-chih* (Treatise on the salt laws of Szechwan), Ting Pao-chen, comp., 40 *chuan*, Chengtu, 1882, *ch* 4, 39.
30. *Han-shu*, 91.
31. *Shih-chi*, 106.
32. Lewis Maverick (ed.), *Economic Dialogues in Ancient China, Selections from the Kuan-tzu* (Lewis A. Maverick, Carbondale, Illinois, 1954).
33. Ibid., p. 113.
34. Ibid., p. 149.
35. Ibid.
36. *Han-shu*, 24.
37. Ibid.
38. Ibid.
39. *Chin-shu*, 26; L. S. Yang, *Studies in Chinese Institutional History* (Harvard University Press, Cambridge, Mass., 1961) pp. 188–9.
40. *Shih-chi*, 129.
41. K. C. Chang (ed.), *Food in Chinese Culture, Anthropological and Historical Perspectives* (Yale University Press, New Haven and London, 1977).
42. L. S. Yang, 'Great Families of Eastern Han', E-tu Zen Sun and John de Francis (eds), *Chinese Social History* (American Council of Learned Societies, Washington DC, 1956) pp. 103–34, p. 106.
43. Maverick, p. 113.

3 **The Dark and Light Ages**

1. For the link between military and monastic institutions in Western Europe, see Alexander Murray, *Reason and Society in the Middle Ages* (Clarendon Press, Oxford, 1978).
2. For salt production on the Tuscan coast, see Rutilius Namatianus, *De Reditu Suo*, which describes a solar salt field. Since there is mention of 'many small ponds', *multifidosque lacus*, this passage has been taken to refer to successive basin evaporation. There is no suggestion, however, that the brine was moved from one pond to another, nor that sodium chloride was distinguished from calcium and magnesium compounds. It would seem most natural, therefore, to interpret what the poet saw as a battery of single basins like those at Katwe, or, most probably, those at the mouth of the Tiber.
3. *Ho-tung yen-fa chih* (Treatise on the Ho-tung salt laws), Yung-cheng edition, 2 vols (Taipei, 1966) p. 10.
4. *Chung-kuo Yen-cheng shih-lu* (Veritable records of the Chinese salt administration) (Taipei, 1954).
5. *Ho-tung yen-fa-chih*, Vol. I, p. 103; Vol. II, p. 973.
6. W. F. J. Jenner, *Memories of Loyang, Yang Hsuan-chi and the Lost Capital (493–534)* (Clarendon Press, Oxford, 1981).
7. William T. Graham, *The Lament for the South, Yü Hsin's Ai Chiang-nan Fu* (Cambridge University Press, Cambridge, 1980).
8. *Ho-tung yen-fa-chih*, I, pp. 82–9.
9. Ibid., II, p. 974.
10. D. C. Twitchett, *Financial Administration under the T'ang Dynasty* (Cambridge University Press, Cambridge, 1965) pp. 165–72.
11. Joseph Needham, *Science and Civilisation in China* (Cambridge University Press, Cambridge, 1954) Vol. I, pp. 220–23.
12. John Henry Newman, *An Essay in aid of A Grammar of Assent* (Burns, Oates, London, 1870) p. 425.
13. Muhammed Hanazir Ahsan, *Social Life under the Abbasids 170–289 A.H., 786–902 A.D.* (Longman, London and New York, 1979) p. 104.
14. E. Ashtor, 'Essai surl'alimentation des diverses classes sociales dans l'Orient médieval', *Annales, Économies, Sociétés, Civilisations*, 23:5 (September–October 1968) pp. 1017–53, p. 1028.
15. Charles M. Doughty, *Travels in Arabia Deserta*, 2 vols (Cape, London, 1936) I, pp. 267–8.
16. For the distinction Islam/Islamdom, see Daniel Pipes, *Slaves Soldiers and Islam. The Genesis of a Military System* (Yale University Press, New Haven and London, 1981).
17. J. Leo Africanus, *The History and Description of Africa* (Hakluyt Edition, London, 1896) Vol. II, p. 467.
18. R. Mantran, *Istanbul dans la seconde moitié du XVIIe siècle* (Maisonneuve, Paris, 1962) p. 181.
19. Ahsan, p. 104.
20. Doughty, II, p. 488.
21. Richard W. Bulliet, 'Botr et Beranes: Hypothèses sur L'Histoire des Berbères', *Annales, Économics, Sociétés, Civilisations*, 36:1 (January–February 1981) pp. 104–16, p. 109; Claudette Vanacker, 'Géographie économique de l'Afrique du Nord selon les auteurs avabe de IXe siècle au milieu du XIIe siecle', *Annales Économies Sociétés, Civilisations*, 28:3 (May–June 1973) pp. 659–80, p. 675.

22. Edmond Bernus, *Touaregs Nigeriens, Unité culturelle et Diversité regionale d'un people pasteur* (Editions de l'office de la Recherche Scientifique et Technique Outre Mer, Paris, 1981) pp. 233–5.
23. Philip K. Hitti, *History of the Arabs* (Macmillan, London, 1940) p. 343.
24. Doughty, I, p. 340.
25. Ibid.
26. Ibid., II, p. 88.
27. Ibid., pp. 419–420.
28. Ibid., II, p. 501.
29. H. St. J. Philby, *Arabia of the Wahhabi* (Cass, London, 1928) p. 154.
30. Pierre Lemonnier, *Paludiers de Guérande, Production du Sel et Histoire économique* (Institut d'Ethnologie, Paris, 1984) pp. 25–33; Aggarwal, pp. 155, 181–2, 199, 202, 44.
31. Constantine Porphyrogenitus, *De Administrando Imperio*, ed. and trans. G. Y. Moravsik and R. J. H. Jenkins, 2 vols (Budapest and London, 1949–1962) I, 137–8.
32. William Roscoe Thayer, *A Short History of Venice* (Macmillan, New York, 1905) pp. 9–10.
33. Latham, p. 116.
34. Dom Gregory Dix, *The Shape of the Liturgy* (Dacre, Westminster, 1954) p. 745; A. Vasiliev, 'Economic Relations between Byzantium and Old Russia', *Journal of Economic and Business History*, 4, Feb. 1932, pp. 314–34.
35. Marcus Nathan Adler (ed.), *The Itinerary of Benjamin of Tudela* (Philipp Feldheim, New York, 1907) p. 13.
36. Michel Mollat (ed.), *Le Rôle du Sel dans L'Histoire* (Presses Universitaires de France, Paris, 1968) p. 13.
37. See Bernard Edeine, pp. 1–4.
38. H. C. Darby, *The Domesday Geography of Eastern England* (Cambridge University Press, Cambridge, 1952) pp. 69–71, 246–8.
39. H. C. Darby and I. B. Terrett, *The Domesday Geography of Midland England* (Cambridge University Press, Cambridge, 1954) pp. 251–6.
40. H. C. Darby and I. S. Maxwell, (eds), *The Domesday Geography of Northern England* (Cambridge University Press, Cambridge, 1952) pp. 362–4.
41. Dorothy Whitclock, *The Beginnings of English Society* (Penguin, Harmondsworth, 1952) p. 115.
42. Marion Dechamps, *Portrait of Brittany* (Robert Hale, London, 1980) pp. 89–90.
43. Edeine, p. 6.
44. Gwyn Jones, *A History of the Vikings* (Oxford University Press, Oxford, 1969) p. 211.
45. Michel Parisse, 'Un Pays du Sel: Le Saulnois en Lorraine (XII–XII siècles)', in Guy Cabourdin (ed.), *Le Sel et Son Histoire* (Publications Nancy II, Nancy 1981) pp. 37–50.
46. Pierre Joubert, *Les Structures du Latium Médiéval* (Ecole Française de Rome, Rome 1973) pp. 641–51, 681–3, 966, 972.
47. A. Dupont, 'L'Exploitation du Sel sur les étangs de Languedoc (IXe–XIIIe siècle)', *Annales du Midi*, Tome 70, 1958, fasc. 1, pp. 7–25, p. 22.
48. Darby and Terrett, p. 285.
49. Whitelock, p. 116.

4 The Middle Ages

1. Ching Pen-po, *Yen-wu ko-ming shih* (A history of the revolution in the salt

administration) (Ching-yen tsung-hui yen-cheng tsa-che she, Nanking, 1929).
2. Marco Polo, *The Travels of Marco Polo* (Penguin, Harmondsworth, 1958) p. 209.
3. Ibid., p. 188.
4. Donald F. Lach, *Asia in the Making of Europe*, Volume I, *The Century of Discovery*, Book One (University of Chicago Press, Chicago and London, 1965) p. 144. See also M. A. P. Meilink-Roelofsz, *Asian Trade and European Influence* (Martinus Nijhoff, The Hague, 1962) p. 224 for an estimate of pepper sales in Europe in 1621.
5. K. C. Chang, p. 144.
6. *Yuan-shih*, 97, 19a.
7. For Yuan salt figures, see Herbert Franz Schurmann, *Economic Structure of the Yuan Dynasty* (Harvard University Press, Cambridge, Mass., 1956) pp. 175–92, which translates *Yuan-shih*, 94.
8. For the history of Ho-tung, see the *Ho-tung yen-fa chih*: also Esson M. Gale and Ch'en Sung-ch'iao, 'China's Salt Administration: Excerpts from Native Sources', *Journal of Asiatic Studies*, 2.11 (June 1959) 273–316, pp. 288–93.
9. Karl A. Wittfogel and Feng Chia-sheng, *History of Chinese Society, Liao (907–1125)* (The American Philosophical Society, Philadelphia, 1949) p. 340. The authors wrongly quantify the *shih* at 1 cwt instead of, at this date, 1/2 cwt.
10. Marco Polo, pp. 165–6.
11. Ibid., pp. 142–3.
12. China, Imperial Maritime Customs, *Salt: Production and Taxation*, V Office Series, Customs Papers, No. 81 (The Statistical Department of the Inspectorate General of Customs, Shanghai, 1906) p. 229.
13. Edmund H. Worthy, 'Regional Control in the Southern Sung Salt Administration', in John Winthrop Haeger (ed.), *Crisis and Prosperity in Sung China* (University of Arizona, Tucson, 1975) pp. 101–141, p. 115.
14. Marco Polo, pp. 180–81.
15. Ibid., p. 200.
16. Hubert van Zeller, *The Benedictine Idea* (Burns & Oates, London, 1959) p. 225.
17. Pierre Chaunu, *Le Temps des Réformes* (Fayard, Paris, 1975) p. 47.
18. For institutionalization in early medieval Europe, see Caroline Walker Bynum, *Jesus as Mother, Studies in the Spirituality of the High Middle Ages* (University of California Press, Berkeley, 1982); also Alexander Murray.
19. For the *ordines salis*, see particularly the works of Jean-Claude Hocquet: 'Métrologie du sel et histoire comparée en Mediterranée', *Annales, Économies, Sociétés, Civilisations*, 29:2 (March–April 1974) pp. 383–424; *Le Sel et La Fortune de Venise*, Vol. I, *Production et Monopole* (Université de Lille, Lille, 1978); 'Ibiza, carrefour du commerce maritime et témoin d'une conjoncture méditerranéenne (1250–1650 env.)', *Studi in Memoria di Federigo Melis* (Giannini, Naples, 1978); 'Capitalisme marchand et classe marchande à Venise au temps de la Renaissance', *Annales, Économies, Sociétés, Civilisations*, 34:2, (Feb.–March 1979) pp. 279–304; *Le Sel et La Fortune de Venise*, Vol. II, *Voiliers et Commerce en Mediterranée 1200–1650* (Université de Lille, Lille, 1979).
20. Jacques Heers, *Gênes au XVe siècle, activité économique et problèmes sociaux* (S.E.V.P.E.N., Paris, 1961) pp. 349–56.
21. Alberto Mori, *Le Saline della Sardegna, Memorie di Geografi Economica*, Anno II. Luglio–Decembre 1950, Vol. III, Napoli; Italy, Ministero delle Finanze, Azienda Dei Sal, Relazione e Bilancio Industriale, Rome, 1898–1919.
22. J. Vila Valenti, 'Ibiza y Formentera, islas de la Sal', *Estudios Geographicos*,

August 1953, pp. 363–408; Jacqueline Guiral, 'Le Sel D'Ibiza et de La Mata à la fin du Moyen Age', Cabourdin, pp. 93–108.
23. Vila Valenti, p. 365.
24. Hocquet, *Le Sel*, Vol. II, p. 12.
25. Ibid., pp. 489, 521.
26. Christiane Villain-Gandossi (ed.), *Comptes du Sel de Franceso di Marco Datini pour sa compagnie d'Avignon 1376–1379* (Bibliothèque Nationale, Paris, 1969). See also Christiane Villain-Gandossi, 'Le *tirage* du sel de Peccais à la fin du XIVᵉ siècle d'après des livres de comptes de Francesco Datini (1368–1379)', Mollat, pp. 173–81; and Edouard Baratier, 'Production et débouchés du sel de Provence au bas Moyen Age' Mollat pp. 133–71.
27. Yves Grava, 'La Fiscalité du sel: pouvoir et société en Provence au XIVᵉ siècle. La Gabelle de Berre', Cabourdin, pp. 229–42.
28. J-G Gigot, 'Notes sur le sel dans l'histoire du Roussillon', Mollat, pp. 199–202; Emmanuel Le Roy Ladurie, *Montaillou, village occitan de 1294 à 1324* (Gallimard, Paris, 1975) pp. 29–30.
29. Philippe Dollinger, *The German Hansa* (Macmillan, London, 1964). See also Delort, pp. 989–90, 1192.
30. Multhauf, pp. 41–8, 253–62; Jean-Francois Bergier, *Une Histoire du Sel* (Presses Universitaires de France, Fribourg, 1982) pp. 71–81. Otto Volk, *Salzproduktion und Salzhandel Mittelalterlicher Zisterzienser-klöster* (Thorbecke, Sigmaringen, 1984).
31. Hoquet, *Le Sel*, Vol. II, p. 182.
32. J. Steven Watson, *A History of the Salters' Company* (London, 1963); A. R. Bridbury, *England and the Salt Trade in the Later Middle Ages* (Clarendon Press, Oxford, 1955); Elizabeth K. Berry, 'The Borough of Droitwich and its Salt Industry, 1215–1700', *University of Birmingham Historical Journal*, 6:1 (1952) pp. 39–61. Professor Bridbury, p. 145, doubts whether the Salters were any more concerned with the salt trade than any other city company. The evidence provided by Steven Watson seems to me, however, to go against this view.
33. Henri Touchard, 'Le Sel Breton dans l'Atlantique et les Mers étroites au XVᵉ at XVIᵉ siècles', Mollat, pp. 39–45.
34. Bridbury, p. 106.
35. Claude-Isabelle Brelot and Réné Locatelli, *Les Salines de Salins, un Millénaire d'Exploitation du Sel en Franche Comté* (CRDP, Besançon, 1981); H. Dubois, 'Le Téméraire, Les Suisses et Le Sel', *Revue Historique*, 526 (April–June 1978) pp. 309–33; Diana Cooper-Richet, 'Les Mines de Sel de Wieliczka', *L'Histoire*, 16, 1979, pp. 82–4.
36. Henri Dubois, 'Du XIIIᵉ siècle aux portes de la modernité: une société pour l'exploitation du sel comtois', Cabourdin, pp. 67–91.
37. Multhauf, p. 40.
38. Schurmann, p. 190.

5 Late Tradition, Early Modernity

1. J. J. L. Ratton, *A Handbook of Common Salt* (Madras, 1877).
2. Emmanuel Le Roy Ladurie, *Les Paysans de Languedoc*, S.E.V. P.E.N., 2 vols (Paris, 1966) p. 139.
3. Jean-Louis Flandrin, 'Le Goût et la Nécessité: sur l'usage des graisses dans les cuisines d'Europe occidentale (XIV–XVIIIᵉ siècle)', *Annales, Économies, Sociétés, Civilisations*, 38:2 (March–April 1983) pp. 269–401.

4. Gérard Sivéry, 'Les profits de l'eleveur et du cultivateur dans le Hainaut à la fin du Moyen Age', *Annales, Économies, Sociétés, Civilisations*, 31:3 (May–June 1976) pp. 604–630; Marie-Jeanne Tits-Dieuaide, 'L'Evolution des techniques agricoles en Flandre et en Brabant, XIV–XVI siècle', *Annales, Économies, Sociétés, Civilisations*, 36:3 (May–June 1981) pp. 362–81; Paul Servais, 'Les structures agraires du Limbourg et des pays d'Outre-Meuse du XVIIe au XIXe siècle', *Annales, Économies, Sociétés, Civilisations*, 37:2, (March–April 1982) pp. 303–19; Marie-Jeanne Tits-Dieuaide, 'Les Campagnes Flamandes du XIIIe au XVKIII^e siècle ou les succes d'une agriculture traditionaelle', *Annales Économies, Sociétés, Civilisations*, 39:3 (May–June 1984) pp. 590–610.
5. See Chapter 4, note 19 and Bibliography.
6. H. G. Koenigsberger, *The Government of Sicily under Philip II of Spain* (Staples Press, London and New York, 1951).
7. Pierre Chaunu, *Séville et L'Atlantique*, Vol. VIII, part one, (S.E.V.P.E.N., Paris, 1959) p. 607.
8. H. van der Wee, *The Growth of the Antwerp Market and the European Economy*, 3 vols (Martinus Nijhoff, The Hague, 1963).
9. Fernand Braudel, *Civilisation matérielle, Économie et capitalisme, XVe–XVIIIe siècle*, 3 vols (Librairie Armand Colin, Paris, 1979) Vol. III, *Le Temps du Monde*, p. 118.
10. J. A. Goris, *Étude sur les Colonies Marchandes Meridionales (Portugais, Espagnols, Italiens) à Anvers de 1488 à 1567, Contribution à L'Histoire des Débuts du Capitalisme Hoderne*, (Librairie Universitaire, Louvain, 1925) pp. 465–77.
11. D. W. Davies, *A Primer of Dutch Seventeenth Century Overseas Trade* (Martinus Nijhoff, The Hague, 1961); Aksel E. Christensen, *Dutch Trade to the Baltic about 1600* (Einar Munksgaard and Martinus Nijhoff, Copenhagen and The Hague, 1941).
12. Chaunu, *Séville*, VIII, part one, p. 218.
13. Albert F. Calvert, *Salt in Cheshire* (Spon and Chamberlain, London and New York, 1915); Brian Didsbury, 'Cheshire Saltworkers', in Raphael Samuel (ed.), *Miners, Quarrymen and Saltworkers* (Routledge & Kegan Paul, London, 1977) pp. 138–203.
14. J. U. Nef, *The Rise of the British Coal Industry*, 2 vols (George Routledge, London, 1932); Joyce Ellis, 'The Decline and Fall of the Tyneside Salt Industry 1660–1790, A Reexamination', *The Economic History Review*, Second Series, Vol. XXXIII, No. 1 (February 1980) pp. 45–58.
15. Calvert, p. 431.
16. Otto Karmin, *La Question du Sel pendant La Révolution* (Paris, 1912).
17. Marcel Delafosse and Claude Laveau, *Le Commerce du Sel de Brouage aux XVIIe et XVIIIe siècles* (Librairie Armand Colin, Paris, 1960).
18. Marcel Blanchard, 'Sel et Diplomatie en Savoie et dans les Cantons Suisses au XVIIe; et XVIIIe siècles', *Annales, Économies, Sociéts, Civilisation*, 15:6 (November–December 1960) pp. 1076–92; Philippe Gern, 'La Vente du Sel franc-comtois et lorrain aux cantons suisses au XVIIe siècle', Cabourdin, pp. 391–403. Georges Livet, 'La Suisse, Carrefour diplomatique de sels européens', Cabourdin, pp. 405–33; Lucien Febvre, *Philippe II et la Franche Comté* (Flammarion, Paris) 1970.
19. Charles Hiegel, 'Vente du sel lorrain en Suisse du milieu du XVIe siècle à la guerre de Trente Ans', Cabourdin, pp. 327–46; Yves Le Moigns, 'Le sel lorrain et la diplomatie lorraine et francaise au XVIIIe siècle', Cabourdin, pp. 435–53, esp. p. 443 for the introduction of coal fuel.
20. Kuno Ulshöfer and Herta Beutter (eds), *Hall und das Salz, Beiträge zur*

hällischen Stadt und Salinengeschichte (Jan Thorbecke Verlag, Sigmaringen, 1983).
21. Multhauf, pp. 80–81.
22. Ibid., p. 91.
23. For early modern Wieliczka, see Diana Cooper-Richet, pp. 82–4; Multhauf, pp. 40–41, 74, 110–12, 118–19, 269–70; Bergier, p. 76; Antonina Keckova, 'Polish Salt-Mines as a State Enterprise (XVII–XVIII centuries)', *Journal of European Economic History*, 10(3) (1981) pp. 619–81.
24. John P. LeDonne, 'Indirect Taxes in Catherine's Russia; The Salt Code of 1781', *Jahrbücher für Geschichte Osteuropas*, 23:2, 1975, pp. 161–90; Mark Mancall, *Russia and China, Their Diplomatic Relations to 1728* (Harvard University Press, Cambridge, Massachusetts, 1971) pp. 165–7, 176, 347–8; R. E. F. Smith and David Christian, *Bread and Salt, A Social and Economic History of Food and Drink in Russia* (Cambridge University Press, 1984) pp. 27–73.
25. R. Mantran, Alexandre Bennigson etc., *Le Khanat de Crimée dans les Archives du Musée du Palais de Topkapi* (Mouton, Paris) 1978; Berger, pp. 8, 92–3.
26. Irfan Habib, *The Agrarian System of Mughal India (1556–1707)* (Aligarh Muslim University, Asia Publishing House, 1963); Ashton; Aggarwal, pp. 464, 488, 37.
27. Ashton, p. 26.
28. Gilbert Rozman, *Urban Networks in Ch'ing China and Tokugawa Japan* (Princeton University Press, 1973).
29. Francoise Sabban, 'Le système des cuissons dans la tradition culinaire chinoise', *Annales, Économies, Sociétés, Civilisations*, 38:2 (March–April 1983), pp. 341–68; K. C. Chang, pp. 261–375.
30. Louise Stallard, *The Szechuan and Hunan Cookbook* (Sterling, New York, 1981).
31. M. A. P. Meilink–Roelofsz; Sarasin Viraphol, *Tribute and Profit, Sino-Siamese Trade 1652–1853*, Council on East Asian Studies (Harvard University, Cambridge, Mass. and London, 1977).
32. China, *Salt: Production and Taxation*, p. 2.
33. Ibid., p. 194.
34. Britain, Parliamentary Papers, *China No. 5 (1904)*, 'Report by Consul-General Hosie on the Province of Ssuch'uan', pp. 13, 17.
35. S. A. M. Adshead, 'An Energy Crisis in Early Modern China', *Ch'ing-shih wen-t'i*, Vol. III, no. 2 (December 1974), pp. 20–28.
36. *Ssu-ch'uan t'ung-chih* (Szechwan provincial gazetteer), Chia'ch'ing 21 edition, Vol. 50, *chüan* 71; *Hsü-chou fu-chih* (Hsü-chou prefecturel gazetteer), Kuang-hsü 21 edition, *chüan* 19; *Lung-chiang ch'uan-ch'ang-chih* (Treatise on the Lung-Chiang Shipyard) (Nanking, 1553).
37. *Yueh-tso chi-shih* (Essentials of the Kwangtung salt administration) (Canton, 1927). I am grateful to Dr James Hayes for the gift of this valuable book and much other material and help in connection with the history of salt in Liang-kuang. See also *Liang-kuang yen-fa-chih* (Treatise on the salt laws of Liang-kuang) (Canton, 1884); S. Y. Lin, 'Salt Manufacture in Hong Kong', *Journal of the Hong Kong Branch of the Royal Asiatic Society*, 7 (1967) pp. 138–51.
38. Nankai University, Department of History, comp., *Ch'ing shih-lu Ching-chi tzu-liao chi-yao* (A compendium of economic materials on the *Ch'ing shih-lu*) (Chung-hua shu-chü, Peking, 1959) p. 804.
39. *Fu-chien yen-fa-chih* (Treatise on the salt laws of Fukien) (Foochow, 1830).
40. Tao-chang Chiang, 'The Production of Salt in China, 1644–1911', *Annals of the Association of American Geographers*, Vol. 66, no. 4 (December 1976) pp. 516–30, p. 526.

41. *Chung-kuo yen-cheng shih-lu* (Veritable records of the Chinese salt administration), 4 vols (Nanking, 1933) I, 327.
42. *Ch'ing-shih* (History of the Ch'ing dynasty), 8 vols (Taipei, 1961), *chuan* 124, 37233a; Chiang, '1644–1911', p. 526.
43. Gale and Ch'en, p. 290.
44. Ferdinand von Richthofen, *Baron Richthofen's Letters 1870–1872*, North China Herald office (Shanghai, 1903) p. 135.
45. S. A. M. Adshead, 'Compensatory Urbanism and Dominant Rurality: Hotung Salt Division under the Late Empire and Early Republic', *Proceedings of the Fourth International Symposium on Asian Studies, 1982* (Asian Research Service, Hong Kong, 1982) pp. 1–7.
46. S. A. M. Adshead, 'Ch'ang-lu Salt Division: Bureaucracy and Modernization', *Proceedings of the Fifth International Symposium on Asian Studies, 1983* (Asian Research Service, Hong Kong, 1983) pp. 9–15; *Yen-cheng tsa-chih* (Salt administration magazine), (Peking, 1912–1915) nos 16–19.
47. Pierre–Etienne Will, 'Un cycle hydraulique en Chine: la province de Hubei du XVIᵉ au XIXᵉ siècles', *Bulletin de l'Ecole Francaise d'Extreme Orient*, 68 (1980) pp. 261–87.
48. *Ta Ch'ing li-ch'ao shih-lu* (Veritable records of successive reigns of the Ch'ing dynasty) (T'ai-wan hua-wen shu-chü, Taipei, 1963), Tao-kuang, 462:7–9.
49. *Yen-cheng shih-lu*, Nanking, II, 1267.
50. Alexander Hosie, 'The Salt Production and Salt Revenue of China', *Nineteenth Century and After*, 447, May 1914, pp. 1119–43, p. 1121.
51. Thomas A. Metzger, 'The Organizational Capabilities of the Ch'ing State in the Field of Commerce: The Liang-huai Salt Monopoly, 1740–1840', in W. E. Willmott (ed.), *Economic Organization in Chinese Society* (Stanford University Press, Stanford, California, 1972) pp. 9–45, 417–19; Jonathan D. Spence, *Ts'ao Yin and the K'ang-hsi Emperor, Bondservant and Master* (Yale University Press, New Haven and London, 1966) Ch. 5, 'Liang-huai Salt Administration', pp. 166–212.
52. Nankai, *Ch'ing shih-lu*, p. 832.
53. Metzger, 'Organizational Capabilities', p. 33.
54. *Ch'ing-shih*, Chuan 126, 37224a.
55. Thomas A. Metzger, *The Internal Organization of Ch'ing Bureaucracy* (Harvard University Press, Cambridge Massachusetts, 1973); William T. Rowe, *Hankow, Commerce and Society in a Chinese City 1796–1889* (Stanford, 1984).
56. S. A. M. Adshead, 'The Border Salt Trade in Northwest China, 1900–1950', *Proceedings of the Third International Symposium on Asian Studies, 1981* (Asian Research Service, Hong Kong, 1981) pp. 1–8; 'Further Sources on the Otogh Salt Lakes', *Bulletin of the School of Oriental and African Studies*, University of London, Vol. XLVI, part 2 (1983) pp. 333–5.

6 Modernity

1. Maurice Lombard, 'Un problème cartographié: Le Bois dans la Méditerranée musulmane (VIIᵉ–XIᵉ siècles)', *Annales, Économies, Sociétés, Civilisations*, 14:2 (April–June 1959) pp. 234–54.
2. Multhauf, pp. 84–5, 90; Jean-Marie Augustin, 'Administration et Justice dans les salines De salins sous les Habsbourg' Cabourdin pp. 269–318, p. 306; Le Moigne, p. 443.
3. Bergier, pp. 232–5.
4. Multhauf, pp. 69, 99.

370 *Notes*

6. Claudia Wallis, 'Salt: A New Villain', *Time*, 15 March 1982, pp. 48–56.
7. For monosodium glutamate, see Sabban, pp. 351, 362.
8. The leading member of the Eurasian school was Petr Nikolaevich Savitsky. His chief contributions are to be found in the volume of essays he published in Moscow in 1921 in collaboration with Prince Nikolai Trubetskoy and others, *Iskhod k Vostoku* (Exodus to the East). The Eurasians, though anti-Bolshevik, were the Russian version of Haushofer's Geopolitics.
9. A. and N. L. Clow, *The Chemical Revolution* (Batchworth, London, 1952); 'The Chemical Industry: Interaction with the Industrial Revolution', in Charles Singer, E. J. Holyard, A. R. Hall, and Trevor Williams (eds), *A History of Technology*, 5 vols (Clarendon, Oxford, 1954–1958) IV, pp. 230–57; W. J. Reader, *Imperial Chemical Industries, A History*, 2 vols (Oxford University Press, London, 1970–1975); Kenneth Warren, *Chemical Foundations: The Alkali Industry in Britain to 1926* (Clarendon, Oxford, 1980).
10. Pierre Chaunu, *Eglise, Culture et Société* (S. E. D. E. S., Paris, 1981).
11. Didsbury in Samuel, p. 166.
12. Etienne Juillard, *L'Europe Rhénanc* (Armand Colin, Paris, 1968).
13. Jean Coudert, 'La Naissance et Le Dévelop[pement] de L'Industrie du Sel dans Le Bassin de la Meurthe (1843–1911), Cabourdin, pp. 157–87; Juillard, pp. 112, 115.
14. Mario Pinna, 'Il Giacimento di Salgemma del Volterrano, Studio di Geografia economica', *Contributi alla Geografia della Toscana* (Università di Pisa, Pisa, 1958–59).
15. *Great Soviet Encyclopaedia* (Sovietskaia Entsiklopediia Publishing House, Moscow, 1970), 2–3746, 3–57a.
16. Ella Lonn, *Salt as a Factor in the Confederacy* (University of Alabama Press, Alabama, 1965).
17. J. Sampaio Fernandes, *Industria do Sal* (Rio de Janeiro, 1939); Dioclecio D. Duarte, *A Industria extativa do Sal e a sua importancia na economia do Brasil* (Rio de Janeiro, 1941); George Hawrylyshy, 'Revamping of the Salt Industry Improves Future Prospects', *Brazilian Business*, 55(5), May 1975, pp. 28–30.
18. A. E. Wileman, 'Salt Manufacture in Japan', *Transactions of the Asiatic Society of Japan*, Vol. 17 (1889) pp. 1–66.
19. Donald F. Lach, pp. 664, 676–7, 687.
20. Bureau of Statistics, *Statistical Handbook of Japan* (Office of the Prime Minister, Tokyo, 1969) p. 56.
21. I. B. Sutton.
22. Richard Gray and David Birmingham (eds), *Pre-colonial African Trade, Essays on Trade in Central and Eastern Africa before 1900* (Oxford University Press, London, 1970) p. 75.
23. Edmond Bernus.
24. Sutton and Roberts.
25. Tymowski; Bergier, pp. 96–8.
26. Ottoman Public Debt Administration, Annual and Special Reports, 1904–5 to 1907–8, 1909–10 to 1913–14, 1919–20, 1922–3.
27. Indian Tariff Board, *Evidence Recorded during Enquiry on the Salt Industry*, 2 vols (Calcutta, 1930).
28. Sadananda Choudhury, *Economic History of Colonialism, A Study of British Salt Policy in Orissa* (Inter-India Publications, Delhi, 1979); Aggarwal, pp. 55–82.
29. Indian Tariff Board, II, 820.
30. Ibid., I, 35.
31. Ibid., 277.

32. Ibid., 572.
33. Ibid., II, 148.
34. Ibid., I, 589.
35. Ibid., II, 839.
36. Ibid., pp. 348–77.
37. Ashton, pp. 26–7.
38. Indian Tariff Board, I, 409.
39. Ibid., 433.
40. S. A. M. Adshead, 'Tzu-liu-ching, the Chinese Face of Industrialization–Evidence, Facts Explorations', *Proceedings of the Second International Symposium on Asian Studies, 1980* (Asian Research Service, Hong Kong, 1980) pp. 1–10.
41. Ferdinand von Richthofen, p. 171.
42. *Scientific American*, Supplement, 18 November 1916, quoted in Sir Richard Dane, Report on the Reorganization of the Salt Revenue Administration in China, 1913–1917. There is a copy of this report in the Library of Congress.
43. G. R. G. Worcester, *The Junks and Sampans of the Yangtze* (Naval Institute Press, Annapolis, Maryland, 1971) p. 147; G. R. G. Worcester, *Notes on the Crooked-bow and Crooked-stern Junks of Szechwan, China*, The Maritime Customs, III, Miscellaneous Series: No. 53 (Shanghai, 1941) p. 13.
44. Gale and Ch'en, p. 311.
45. *Ta Ch'ing shih-lu*, Hsuan-t'ung, 24:14–13.
46. Ibid., 23:44–5.
47. 'Chung-kuo yen-cheng yen-ko shih' (A history of the development of the Chinese salt administration), *Yen-cheng tsa-chih*, No. 19, Chuan-chien 2:1–16, August 1915.
48. Reports by the District Inspectors, Auditors and Collectors on the Reorganization of the Salt Revenue Administration in China, 1919–1921, pp. 20, 1101, 17; 1913–1917, p. 40.
49. Reports etc. 1913–1917, pp. 103, 276.
50. Reports etc. 1919–1921, p. 79.
51. Peter Fleming, *One's Company* (Cape, London, 1940) p. 79.
52. Reports etc., 1913–1917, p. 14.
53. Dane, p. 98.
54. Reports etc., 1913–1917, p. 14.
55. Reports etc., 1919–1921, p. 21.
56. *Yen-cheng tsa-chih*, No. 17, *tsa-lu*, 1, February 1915.
57. Sabban, p. 362.
58. Reader, I, 224–6.
59. Hou Teh-pang, 'The Yungli Company: Pioneer of Chemical Industry in China', *China Reconstructs* 4:3, March 1955, pp. 21–4.
60. 'Light Industry in Communist China', excerpts from *Chung-kuo ch'ing-kung-yeh*, 1955 (United States Joint Publication Research Service, New York, 1959).
61. *First Five-Year Plan from Development of the National Economy of the People; Republic of China in 1953–1957* (Foreign Languages Press, Peking, 1956) pp. 49–50, 91.
62. 'Light Industry', p. 21.
63. Ibid., p. 22.

7 The Venetian Salt Administration

1. Toubert, pp. 646, 974.
2. Hocquet, *Le Sel*, Vol. II, p. 613.

3. E-tu Zen Sun (ed.), *Ch'ing Administrative Terms*, (Harvard University Press, Cambridge, Mass., 1961) p. 168.

4. Pierre-Étienne Will, *Bureaucratie et Famine en Chine au 18ᵉ siècle* (Mouton, Paris, 1980) p. 178.

5. *Yen-cheng tsa-chih*, No. 18, *chuan-chien* 2, April 1915.

6. For Venice, see the works of Jean-Claude Hocquet cited above Chapter 4, note 19, especially *Le Sel*, Vol. II; also Marco Brazzale, *Il Mercato del Sale nella Repubblica Veneta nella seconda metà del XVI secolo*, (Università di Venezia, Venezia, 1971); Frederic C. Lane, *Venice A Maritime Republic* (Johns Hopkins University Press, Baltimore and London, 1973).

7. Hocquet, *Le Sel*, Vol. I, pp. 166–8.

8. Ibid., Vol. II, pp. 660–61.

9. Jean-Claude Hocquet, 'Venise et le marché du sel dans la seconde moitié du XVIᵉ siècle', *Annales Économies, Sociétés, Civilisations*, 34:3, pp. 619–624h, May–June 1979, p. 621.

10. Hocquet, *Le Sel*, Vol. II, pp. 217, 351, 426.

11. Ibid., p. 670.

12. Hocquet, *Le Sel*, Vol. I, pp. 123–4, 114–16.

13. Ibid., pp. 148–53.

14. Ibid., Vol. II, pp. 447–52, 480–81.

15. Ibid., pp. 128–32, 512–16, 122–3, 139, 142.

16. Ibid., Vol. I, p. 340.

17. Brazzale, pp. 27–8.

18. Hocquet, *Le Sel*, Vol. II, pp. 410–11.

19. Jean-Claude Hocquet, 'Le *burchio*, outil privilégié du transport du sel en Vénétie', Cabourdin, 117–38.

20. Metzger, *Internal Organization*, pp. 57, 78–9, 292–3.

21. China, *Salt: Production and Taxation*, pp. 218, 101, 106, 216–17.

22. Hocquet, *Le Sel*, Vol. II, pp. 412–13, 415–17, 419–21, 426, 430–31.

23. For *fedi* and delays in their payment, see Hocquet, *Le Sel*, Vol. II, pp. 372, 443, 458–9, 465–6.

24. Hocquet, *Le Sel*, Vol. II, p. 429.

25. Ibid., pp. 410–11.

26. Ibid., pp. 415, 430–31; for current interest rates, see p. 486.

27. Hocquet, *Le Sel*, Vol. II, pp. 420–21.

28. For an instance, see the loans of the Priuli, Hocquet, *Le Sel*, Vol. II, pp. 475–8.

29. Evelyne Patlagean, *Pauvreté Économique et Pauvreté Sociale à Byzance, 4ᵉ–7ᵉ siècles* (Mouton, Paris, 1977); Jean Baechler, *The Origins of Capitalism* (Blackwell, Oxford, 1975).

30. Hocquet, *Le Sel*, Vol. II, pp. 200–201.

31. Ibid., pp. 436–7.

32. Hocquet, 'Capitalisme marchand et classe marchande', p. 297.

33. Hocquet, *Le Sel*, Vol. II, p. 473.

34. Ibid., p. 486.

35. Ibid., p. 478.

36. Carlo Poni, 'Les moulins à soie dans les états Vénétiens en 16ᵉ–18ᵉ siècles', *Annales, Économies, Sociétés, Civilisations*, 27:6 (November–December 1972) pp. 1475–96.

37. Hugh Trevor-Roper, *The Rise of Christian Europe* (Thames & Hudson, London, 1970) p. 184.

38. Hocquet, 'Capitalisme marchand et classe marchande', pp. 287–8.

39. Hocquet, *Le Sel*, Vol. II, p. 196.

40. Lane, p. 237.
41. Hocquet, *Le Sel*, Vol. II, p. 388.
42. Jean-Noel Biraben, *Les Hommes et la Peste en France et dans les Pays européens et mediterranéens*, Tome II, *Les Hommes face à la Peste* (Mouton, Paris, 1976).
43. Ch. Carrière, M. Courdurié and F. Rebuffat, *Marseille, Ville Mort, La Peste de 1720* (Maurice Garon, Marseille, 1968).
44. Hocquet, *Le Sel*, Vol. II, pp. 390, 425, 309.
45. Ibid., pp. 390–92, 398.
46. Ibid., pp. 220–21.
47. Donald F. Lach, Vol. I, pp. 30–48.
48. Colin Renfrew, *The Emergence of Civilisation, The Cyclades and the Aegean in the Third Millennium BC* (Methuen, London, 1972).
49. For a summary of 'The Westward flow of techniques', see Joseph Needham, *Science and Civilisation in China*, Vol. I, pp. 240–43.
50. Joseph Needham, *Science and Civilisation in China*, Vol. IV, part 3 (1971) pp. 613–15.
51. Needham, Vol. I, p. 219. For John of Rupescissa, see especially E. F. Jacob, 'John of Roquetaillade', *Bulletin of the John Rylands Library*, 39, 19456–7, pp. 75–95. Since Jacob wrote, much has been learnt about Taoism in China, and the Taoist character of John's medical alchemy is much more evident.
52. Marco Polo, p. 177.
53. Ibid., p. 166.
54. Ibid., p. 176.
55. Ibid., p. 177.
56. Ibid., p. 200.
57. Hocquet, *Le Sel*, Vol. II, p. 433.

8 The French Salt Administration

1. D. Dessert and J-L Journot, 'Le Lobby Colbert', *Annales, Économies, Sociétés, Civilisations*, 30:6, pp. 1304–29, November–December 1975. Surprisingly the *Gabelle* has not yet attracted a large, sophisticated modern study. Of older books, I have relied on J. Pasquier, *L'Impôt des Gabelles en France aux XVIIe et XVIIIe siècles* (Paris, 1905; Slatkine Reprints, Geneva, 1978); Of newer books, M. Delafosse and Cl. Laveau, *Le Commerce de Sel de Brouage aux XVIIe et XVIIIe siècles* (Armand Colin, Paris, 1960), and articles in Cabourdin. Unfortunately, Jean-Claude Hocquet, *Le Sel et le Pouvoir, De l'An Mil à la Revolution francaise* (Albin Michel, Paris, 1985), reached me too late to affect the main lines of this study.
2. Schurmann, p. 4; Ata-Malik Juvaini, *The History of the World Conqueror*, trns John Andrew Boyle, 2 vols (Harvard University Press, Cambridge, Mass., 1958) I, 209–10, II, 599–600, 605–6; Parhs M. Coble, Jr., *The Shanghai Capitalists and the Nationalist Government 1927–1937* (Council on East Asian Studies, Harvard University, Cambridge, Mass., 1980).
3. R. J. Knecht, *Francis I* (Cambridge University Press, Cambridge, 1982) p. 385.
4. Pasquier, p. 2.
5. J. F. Bosher, *French Finances 1770–1795 from Business to Bureaucracy* (Cambridge University Press, Cambridge, 1970) p. 305.
6. George T. Matthews, *The Royal General Farms in Eighteenth Century France* (Columbia University Press, New York, 1958).
7. J. F. Bosher, 'French Administration and Public Finance in their European

setting', in A. Goodwin (ed.), *The New Cambridge Modern History Vol. VIII, The American and French Revolutions 1763–93*, (Cambridge University Press, Cambridge, 1965) pp. 565–91.

8. Louis Dermigny, *La Chine et L'Occident, Le Commerce à Canton au XVIIIe siècle 1719–1833*, 3 vols (S.E.V.P.E.N., Paris, 1964) I, 349–52.

9. Emmanuel Le Roy Ladurie, *Le Carnaval de Romans* (Gallimard, Paris, 1979) pp. 324–5.

10. Hiegel in Cabourdin, interventions of Mme Ros. and M. Livet, pp. 342–6.

11. Jean-Marie Augustin, 'Administration et Jutice dans les Salines de Salins sous les Habsbourg', Cabourdin, pp. 289–318, p. 307.

12. Francois Vion-Delphin, 'Salines et Forets au XVIIIe siècle: Le Cas des Salines de Montmarot', Cabourdin, pp. 347–62.

13. Knecht, pp. 385–9.

14. Emmanuel Le Roy Ladurie and Michel Morineau, *Histoire Economique et Sociale de la France*, Tome I, *De 1450 à 1660*, Vol. 2, *Paysannerie et Croissance* (P.U.F., Paris, 1977) pp. 824–35.

15. J. H. M. Salmon, *Society in Crisis, France in the Sixteenth Century* (Benn, London, 1975) pp. 35–7.

16. Henri Fréville, *L'Intendance de Bretagne 1689–1790*, 3 vols, (Plihon, Rennes, 1953) I, 26, II, 316–19, III, 148.

17. On the technology involved, see Edeine.

18. Madeleine Foisil, *La Révolte des Nu-pieds et les révoltes normandes de 1639* (Paris, 1970); Yves-Narie Bercé, *Croquants et Nu-Pieds* (Gallimard/Julliard, Paris, 1974).

19. Dermigny, II, pp. 654–5, 662–3, 667–8.

20. For Richelieu, see Ernest Lavisse, *Histoire de la France Illustrée, Tome VI, Deuxième Partie, J. H. Mariejol, Henri IV et Louis XIII (1598–1643* (Hachette, Paris, 1911) pp. 425–30 and Henri Hauser, *La Pensée et l'Action Économique du Cardinal de Richelieu* (P.U.F. Paris, 1944) p. 176. For Calonne, see Pasquier, pp. 144–7.

21. Pasquier, p. 6.

22. Pierre Racine, 'Le Sel dans la Plaine du Po: Salsomaggiore entre les Communes de Parme et Plaisance (XIIe–XIIIe siècles)' (Cabourdin) pp. 51–65, pp. 57–8, 62, 64; Hocquet, *Le Sel*, Vol. II, p. 414.

23. Edouard Perroy, *The Hundred Years War* (Eyre & Spottiswoode, London, 1951) p. 153.

24. Robert D. Harris, *Necker, Reform Statesman of the Ancien Regime* (University of California Press, Berkeley, 1979).

25. Jacques-Louis Ménetra, *Journal de ma Vie*, ed. Daniel Roche (Montalba, Paris, 1983).

26. G. Pagès, *La Monarchie d'Ancien Régime France* (Armand Colin, Paris, 1946) p. 215.

27. H. R. Trevor-Roper, *Historical Essays* (Macmillan, London, 1957) p. 48.

28. Jean Delumeau, *La Peur en Occident (XIVe–XVIIIe siècles) : Une Cité Assiégée* (Fayard, Paris, 1978).

29. Arthur Young, *Travels in France during the years 1787, 1788, 1789*, ed. M. Betham-Edwards (Bell, London, 1913) pp. 315–16.

30. Georges Clauss, 'La Contrebands du Sel en Argonne à la Fin de l'Ancien Régime', Cabourdin, 363–88, pp. 370, 383, 388.

31. *J. B. Colbert, Lettres, Instructions, Memoires*, Imprimerie Nationale, 8 vols (Paris, 1861–1882, Kraus Reprint, Nenideln, Liechtenstein, 1979).

32. Colbert, II, 736, 477, 630–31; II, 488–9; II, 531, 667, II, 606.

33. Colbert, IV, 311, 574.
34. Arthur Young, pp. 32, 56.
35. Bergier, pp. 225–31, Appendix by Albert Hahling.
36. Tihomir J. Markovitch, 'La Crossance industrielle sous L'Ancien Regime', *Annales, Économies, Sociétés, Civilisations*, 31:3 (May–June 1976) pp. 644–55.
37. Cabourdin, pp. 452–3 Intervention of M. Hocquet.
38. On salt diplomacy, see Philippe Gern, 'Le Vente du Sel franc-camtois et lorrain aux cantons suisses au XVIII* siècle', Cabourdin, pp. 391–403, and Livret and Le Moigne, Cabourdin, pp. 405–53.
39. Alain Dubois, 'Economie Alpine et Capitaux Urbains: Les investissements du Genevois Hippolyte Rigaud en Valais au début du XVII* siècle', *Schweizerische Zeitschrift für Geschichte*, 29:1 (1979) pp. 287–300.
40. Francoise-Thérése Charpentier, 'Art et Economie: Solvay et l'Ecole de Nancy'; Cabourdin, pp. 15–23.

9 The Habsburg Salt Administration

1. For this period of Habsburg history, we rely particularly on R. J. W. Evans, *The Making of the Habsburg Monarchy 1550–1700* (Clarendon Press, Oxford, 1979), and on Victor-L Tapié, *Monarchie et Peuples du Danube* (Librairie Arthème Fayard, Paris, 1969). For salt and salt administration my leading authority is Rudolf Palme, *Rechts-Wirtschafts und Sozial Geschichte der Inner alpinen Salzwerke bis zu deren Monopolisierung* (Verlag Peter Lang, Frankfurt and Berne, 1983).
2. William M. Johnston, *The Austrian Mind, An Intellectual and Social History 1848–1938* (University of California, Berkeley, 1972) p. 48.
3. Tapié, pp. 65, 95.
4. Österreich, Finanzministerium, *Statistische Mitteilung über das Österreichische Salzmonopol im Jahre 1907–1908, 1912, 1913*, Vienna, 1910 and 1914.
5. Chang Chien, *A Plan for the Reform of the National Salt Administration* (The National Review Office, Shanghai, 1913) pp. 35–36.
6. Jean Bérenger, *Finances et Absolutisme Autrichien dans La Seconde Moitié du XVII* siècle* (Sorbonne, Paris, 1973).
7. Eckart Schremmer, 'Saltmining and the Salt-trade: A State-Monopoly in the XVth–XVIIth centuries. A Case-study in Public Enterprise and Development in Austria and the South German States', *Journal of European Economic History*, Vol. 8, (1979) pp. 291–312, p. 293.
8. Evans, p. 376.
9. Royal Society, *Philosophical Transactions*, Vol. I, 1665, 'Of the Mundus Subterraneus of Athanasius Kircher', pp. 109–117, pp. 117, 111, 112.
10. Athanasius Kircher, *Mundus Subterraneus* (Amsterdam, 1665), Vol. I, p. 345, Vol. II, Proemium; also Vol. I, pp. 38, 298.
11. Evans, pp. 361–2; N. J. Girardot, *Myth and Meaning in Early Taoism, The Theme of Chaos (hun-tun)* (University of California Press, Berkeley, 1983).
12. Evans, pp. 363–4, 366–7, 371–2.
13. Schremmer, pp. 298–9.
14. Multhauf, p. 45.
15. Ibid., p. 139.
16. Evans, p. 360.
17. Schremmer, p. 298.
18. Keckova, p. 631.
19. Tapié, pp. 295, 319.

20. Hocquet, *Le Sel*, Vol. II, p. 674.
21. Ibid., pp. 327–8.
22. Janes M. Bak and Bela K. Kiraly (eds), *From Hunyadi to Rákóczi, War and Society in Late Medieval and Early Modern Hungary* (Brooklyn College Press, New York, 1982).
23. Bak and Kiraly, p. 303.
24. Ibid., p. 360.
25. Ibid., pp. 370–71.
26. Otto Karmin, *La Question du Sel pendant la Révolution* (Paris, 1912). The French government considered handing the *Pays de Salines* over to Beust.
27. Cabourdin, pp. 412, 414.
28. Hocquet, *Le Sel*, Vol. II, pp. 625, 633, 635; Cabourdin, p. 415.
29. E. Rambot-Stilmant, 'Une Tentative de monopole d'Etat: La Raffinerie d'Ostend, 1756–1770', *Contributions à L'Histoire économique et sociale*, Brussels, Vol. 5, 1970, pp. 25–86.
30. Le Moigne in Cabourdin, p. 446.
31. Joel Mokyr, *Industrialization in the Low Countries 1795–1850* (Yale University Press, New Haven and London, 1976).
32. Archibald Little, *The Far East* (Oxford, 1905) p. 69.
33. Anton Einstberger, *Hans de Witte, Finanzmann Wallensteins, Vierteljahrschrift fur Sozial- und Wirtschaftgeschichte*, Beiheft (Cologne, 1954).
34. Keckova, pp. 630–31.
35. Bérenger, pp. 365–73.
36. Evans, pp. 136, 220; Anton Gindely, *Gegenreformation in Böhmen* (Duncker and Humblott, Leipzig, 1894) pp. 307–26.
37. Renée Simon (ed.), *Le P. Antoine Gaubil S. J. Correspondence de Pékin 1722–1759* (Librairie Droz, Geneva, 1970) pp. 576, 696, 761.
38. Schremmer, p. 294.
39. Heinrich Ritler von Srbik, *Studien zur Geschichte des Osterreichischen Salzwesens* (Innsbruck, 1917).
40. Hermann Schreiber, *The History of Roads, From Amber Route to Motorway* (Barrie & Rockliff, London, 1951) p. 261.
41. Cabourdin, p. 400.
42. John Stoye, *The Siege of Vienna* (Collins, London, 1964) p. 115.

10   The Ottoman Salt Administration

1. For the Ottoman public debt administration, see Ottoman Public Debt, Annual and Special Reports, 1904–5 to 1907–8, 1909–10 to 1913–14, 1919–20, 1922–23; also Donald C. Blaisdell, *European Financial Control in the Ottoman Empire* (Columbia University Press, New York, 1929).
2. Immanuel Wallerstein, *The Modern World System* (Academic Press, New York, 1974).
3. Stanford J. Shaw and Ezel Kural Shaw, *History of the Ottoman Empire and Modern Turkey*, Vol. II, *Reform, Revolution and Republic: The Rise of Modern Turkey, 1808–1975* (Cambridge University Press, Cambridge 1977); Roderick H. Davison, *Reform in the Ottoman Empire 1886–1876* (Princeton University Press, Princeton, New Jersey, 1963).
4. For synarchy, see John King Fairbank, *Trade and Diplomacy on the China Coast, The Opening of the Treaty Ports 1842–1856*, 2 vols (Harvard University Press, Cambridge, Mass., 1953), notably I, p. 465.
5. Mantran, pp. 444, 162, 202.

6. Alexandre Bennigsen, etc., p. 5; Le Donne, p. 168.
7. Stanford J. Shaw, *The Financial and Administrative Organization and Development of Ottoman Egypt 1517–1798* (Princeton University Press, Princeton, New Jersey, 1962); Stanford J. Shaw, *Ottoman Egypt in the Eighteenth Century* (Harvard University Press, Cambridge, Mass., 1962); Stanford J. Shaw, *Ottoman Egypt in the Age of the French Revolution* (Harvard University Press, Cambridge, Mass., 1964); British Parliamentary Papers, Lord Cromer's Financial reports, Egypt No. 3 (1892), Egypt No. 3 (1893), Egypt No. (1894), Egypt No. 1 (1895), Egypt No. 2 (1895), Egypt No. (1896), Egypt No. 2 (1897), Egypt No. 1 (1898), Egypt No. 3 (1899), Egypt No. 1 (1900), Egypt No. 1 (1907).
8. C. Max Kortepeter, *Ottoman Imperialism during the Reformation: Europe and the Caucasus* (New York University Press, New York, 1972), p. 55.
9. Hocquet, *Le Sel*, Vol. II, pp. 685–6, 699, 200, 321, 314, 317.
10. Shaw and Shaw, pp. 104–5.
11. Ibid., p. 101.
12. Ibid., pp. 104–5.
13. Ibid., p. 223.
14. Ibid., p. 211.
15. British Parliamentary Papers, *Papers Relating to Administrative and Financial Reforms in Turkey, 1858–61*, Bulwer to Russell, 12 November 1860.
16. Annette Destrée, *Les Fonctionaires Belges au service de la Perse 1898–1915* (Brill, Leiden, 1976); W. Morgan Shuster, *The Strangling of Persia* (New York, 1912); Arthur C. Millspaugh, *Americans in Persia, A Clinic for the New Internationalism* (Washington, 1946); Persia, Quarterly Reports of the Administrator General of the Finances of Persia, 1923–1928.
17. Stanley F. Wright, *Hart and the Chinese Customs* (Mullan Belfast, 1950).
18. S. A. M. Adshead, *The Modernization of the Chinese Salt Administration 1900–1920* (Harvard University Press, Cambridge, Mass., 1970).
19. British Parliamentary Papers, *Papers Relating to Administrative and Financial Reforms in Turkey, 1858–61*, Bulwer to Russell, 16 November 1860.
20. British Parliamentary Papers, *Papers Relating to Administrative and Financial Reform in Turkey, 1858–61*, Bulwer to Russell, 12 November 1860.
21. Ottoman Public Debt, Special Report 1909–10, pp. 8–9.
22. Ibid., p. 30.
23. Shaw and Shaw, pp. 104–5.
24. Ottoman Public Debt, Special Report 1909–10, p. 9.
25. Ottoman Public Debt, Special Report 1905–6, p. 23.
26. Ottoman Public Debt, Special Report 1907–8, pp. 29–30.
27. Ibid., p. 30.
28. Ottoman Public Debt, Special Report 1909–10, p. 31.
29. Ottoman Public Debt, Special Report 1910–11, p. 32.
30. Blaisdell, p. 124.
31. Ibid., p. 128–9.
32. Ottoman Public Debt, Special Report, 1905–6, pp. 24, 25–6, 27, 30.
33. Ottoman Public Debt, Special Report 1907–8, pp. 29–30.
34. Blaisdell, p. 118.
35. British Parliamentary Papers, *Papers Relating to Administrative and Financial Reforms in Turkey 1858–61*, Bulwer to Russell, 12 November 1860.
36. Blaisdell, p. 118.
37. Ibid., p. 7.
38. Ibid., p. 118.

39. Ibid., p. 6.
40. 40 Shaw and Shaw, p.
41. Ulrich Trumpener, *Germany and the Ottoman Empire, 1914–1918* (Princeton University Press, Princeton, New Jersey, 1968).
42. Martin Gilbert, *Winston S. Churchill*, Vol. III, 1914–1916 (Heinemann, London, 1971) pp. 307–11.

11   The Indian Salt Administration under the Raj

1. H. Furber, *John Company at Work, A Study of European Expansion in India in the Late Eighteenth Century* (Harvard University Press, Cambridge, Mass., 1951).
2. See Curzon's remarks to the Japanese ambassador in July 1919, E. L. Woodward and Rohan Butler (eds), *Documents on British Foreign Policy*, Vol. VI, June 1919 to April 1920 (Her Majesty's Stationery Office, London, 1956) p. 614.
3. Indian Tariff Board, Salt Enquiry, Preliminary Evidence Volume, Calcutta 1930; Indian Tariff Board, I and II as above Note 27 to Chapter 6; see also Aggarwal whose first edition appeared in 1936.
4. Somendra Chandra Nandy, *Life and Times of Cantoo Baboo (Krishna Kanta Nandy) The Banian of Warren Hastings*, Vol. I, *The Early Career of Cantoo Baboo (1742–1772) and his Trade in Salt and Silk* (Allied Publishers, Bombay, 1978) p. 97.
5. A. M. Serajuddin, 'The Condition of the Salt Manufacturers of Bengal under the Rule of the East India Company', *Asiatic Society of Bangladesh (Dacca)*, 18:1 (1973) pp. 54–73.
6. Ashton, p. 24.
7. Salt Enquiry, p. 73.
8. Sir George Dunbar, *History of India from Earliest Times to 1939*, 2 vols (Nicholson and Watson, London, 1949) II, p. 556.
9. Salt Enquiry, pp. 260, 273.
10. Salt Enquiry, pp. 281–2; Indian Tariff Board, II, pp. 445–7, 472.
11. Salt Enquiry, p. 274.
12. Ashton, p. 26.
13. Ibid., pp. 26–27.
14. Salt Enquiry, p. 271.
15. Ibid., pp. 278–9.
16. Ibid., p. 271.
17. Ibid., p. 281.
18. Ibid., p. 261.
19. Ibid., p. 93.
20. Ibid.
21. Ibid.
22. Ibid.
23. Ibid.
24. Ibid., p. 94.
25. Ibid., p. 93.
26. Ibid., p. 98.
27. Ibid., p. 106.
28. Ibid., p. 283.
29. Ibid., p. 256.
30. Ibid., p. 223.

31. Ibid., p. 1–2.
32. Ibid., p. 66.
33. Ibid., pp. 136–7.
34. Ibid., pp. 66–7.
35. Ibid., p. 183.
36. Ibid., p. 186.
37. Ibid., p. 188.
38. Ibid., p. 235.
39. Ashton, p. 23.
40. Salt Enquiry, p. 216.
41. Ibid., p. 237.
42. Ibid., p. 218.
43. Ibid., p. 217.
44. Ibid., p. 223.
45. Ibid., p. 73.
46. Ibid.
47. Ibid., p. 75.
48. Ibid., p. 85.
49. Ibid., p. 256.
50. Ibid., p. 225; see also Indian Tariff Board, II, pp. 378–80.
51. Salt Enquiry, p. 253.
52. Aggarwal, p. 265.
53. Salt Enquiry, p. 240.
54. Ibid., p. 89.
55. Ibid., p. 254.
56. Ibid.
57. Ibid., p. 253.
58. Ibid., p. 80.
59. Ibid., p. 202.
60. Ibid., p. 203.
61. Sir Richard Dane, Report by Sir Richard Dane, KCIE, on the Reorganization of the Salt Revenue Administration in China, 1913–1917 (Chief Inspectorate of the Central Salt Administration, Peking, 1918) p. 77.
62. Ibid., p. 79.
63. Ibid., p. 150.
64. Sahyasachi Bhattacharyya, *Financial Foundations of the British Raj* (Indian Institute of Advanced Study, Simla, 1971) pp. 197–202, p. 290; Sir John Strachey, *India, Its Administration and Progress* (Macmillan, London 1911) pp. 175–83; W. W. Hunter, *The Indian Empire, Its People, History and Products* (Truebner, London, 1884) pp. 452–5, 622–3.
65. India, Government of India, Ministry of Information and Broadcasting. The Publication Division, *The Collected Works of Mahatma Gandhi*, XLIII (March–June 1930), Ahmedabad, 1971, p. 167.
66. Salt Enquiry, p. 74.
67. Dane, p. 38.
68. Salt Enquiry, p. 223.
69. Ibid., p. 210.
70. Ibid., p. 88.
71. Dunbar, II, p. 543.
72. Ibid.
73. Salt Enquiry, p. 276.
74. Ibid.

75. Ibid., p. 237.
76. Ibid., p. 219.
77. Ibid., p. 254.
78. Ibid., p. 205.
79. Ibid., p. 136.
80. Indian Tariff Board, II, pp. 445–7, 472; Aggarwal, pp. 360–66.
81. Indian Tariff Board, II, pp. 401–3.
82. Ibid., pp. 411–13.
83. Ibid., pp. 157–80.
84. Salt Enquiry, p. 86.
85. Ibid., p. 205.
86. Indian Tariff Board, II, pp. 836–7.
87. Salt Enquiry, pp. 220–21.
88. Ibid., p. 256.
89. Ibid., p. 239.
90. Ibid., p. 240.
91. Ibid.
92. Ibid., p. 254.
93. Pramathanath Bannerjee, *A History of Indian Taxation* (Macmillan, London) p. 271.
94. Ibid., pp. 275–6.
95. K. T. Shah, *Sixty years of Indian Finance* (King, London and Bombay) pp. 213, 240, 46.
96. Salt Enquiry, p. 74.
97. Ibid., p. 78.
98. Aggarwal, pp. 103–10, 115, 88.
99. Salt Enquiry, p. 77.
100. Ibid., p. 6.
101. Ibid., p. 11–29.
102. Ibid., p. 30.
103. Ibid., p. 91.
104. Ibid., p. 85.
105. Aggarwal, pp. 69–71.

12 Chinese Salt Administration under the Late Empire and Early Republic

1. Thomas A. Metzger, 'T'ao Chu's Reform of the Huaipei Salt Monopoly', *Harvard Papers on China*, 16 (1962) pp. 1–19; Metzger, *Internal Organization*.
2. Samuel C. Chu, *Reformer in Modern China, Chang Chien 1853–1926* (Columbia University Press, New York and London, 1965).
3. Dane, p. 101.
4. Ibid., p. 102.
5. Ibid., p. 70.
6. Ibid., p. 180.
7. Ibid., p. 200.
8. Reports etc., 1919–1921, p. 215.
9. David D. Buck, *Urban Change in China, Politics and Development in Tsinan, Shantung, 1890–1949* (University of Wisconsin, Madison, Wisconsin, 1978).
10. Dane, p. 116.
11. Ibid., p. 122.
12. Ibid., pp. 124–5.
13. Ibid., p. 91.

14. Ibid.
15. Ibid.
16. Ibid., p. 92.
17. Ibid.
18. Ibid., pp. 92–3.
19. Ibid., p. 152.
20. Ibid., p. 153.
21. Reports etc., 1913–1917, p. 34.
22. Dane, pp. 206–7.
23. Pierre Teilhard de Chardin, *The Phenomenon of Man* (Collins, London, 1966), p. 175.
24. Dane, p. 18.
25. Ibid., p. 17.
26. Ibid.
27. Ibid., p. 18.
28. Ibid., p. 17.
29. Ibid., p. 125.
30. Ibid., p. 38.
31. Ibid., p. 36.
32. Ibid., p. 35.
33. Ibid., p. 36.
34. ibid., p. 51.
35. Ibid. p. 39.
36. Ibid., p. 64.
37. Ibid., p. 77.
38. Ibid., p. 110.
39. Ibid., p. 111.
40. Ibid., p. 116.
41. Ibid., p. 215.
42. Ibid., p. 174.
43. Ibid., p. 60.
44. H. R. Trevor Roper, *Historical Essays* (Macmillan, London, 1957) p. 129.
45. *Ho-tung yen-fa-chih*, Vol. II, p. 715.
46. Ralph William Huenemann, *The Dragon and the Iron Horse, The Economics of Railroads in China 1876–1977* (The Council on East Asian Studies, Harvard University, Cambridge, Mass., 1984) 461.
47. *Ta Ch'ing li-ch'ao shih-lu* (Taipei 1963), Kuang-hsü, 592:9.
48. Dane, p. 179.
49. Ibid.
50. Reports, etc. 1913–1917, p. 253.
51. Reports, etc., 1918, p. 76.
52. Reports, etc., 1918–1921, p. 52.
53. Reports, etc., 1919–1921, p. 52.
54. Reports, etc., 1922, p. 65.
55. Taiwan Diplomatic Documents, Box h, *Min-kuo* 11.2, Japanese Legation, 9 February 1922.
56. Andrew J. Nathan, *Peking Politics, 1918–1923, Factionalism and the Failure of Constitutionalism* (University of California Press, Berkeley, 1976).
57. Piere-Étienne Will, *Bureaucratie et Famine en Chine au 18ᵉ siècle* (Mouton, Paris) p. 178.
58. Chihli River Commission, *Final Report and Grand Scheme 1918–1925* (Hua Pei Press, Tientsin, 1925) p. 6.

Select Bibliography

Acosta, Father Joseph de, *The Natural and Moral History of the Indies*, 2 vols (Hakluyt Society, London, 1880).

Adler, Marcus Nathan (ed.), *The Itinerary of Benjamin of Tudela* (Philipp Feldheim, New York, 1907).

Adshead, S. A. M., *The Modernization of the Chinese Salt Administration* (Harvard University Press, Cambridge, Mass., 1970).

Aggarwal, S. C., *The Salt Industry in India* (Government of India Press, New Delhi, 1976).

Ahsan, Muhammed Manazir, *Social Life under the Abbasids 170–289 A. H. 786–902 AD* (Longman, London and New York, 1979).

Andrew, Anthony P., 'The Salt Trade of the Maya', *Archaeology*, Vol. 33, No. 4 (July–August 1980) pp. 16–33.

Ashton, F., 'The Salt Industry of Rajputana', *The Journal of Indian Art and Industry*, Vol. 9, 1902, pp. 23–32.

Baechler, Jean, *The Origins of Capitalism* (Blackwell, Oxford, 1975).

Bennigsen, Alexandre, Peter Naili Baralar, Dilek Desasive and Chantal Lemercier-Quelquejay, *Le Khanat de Crimée dans les Archives du Musée du Palais de Topkapi* (Mouton, Paris, 1978).

Bercé, Yves-Marie, *Croquants et Nu-Pieds* (Gallimard-Julliard, Paris, 1974).

Bérenger, Jean, *Finances et Absolutisme Autrichien dans La Seconde Moitié du XVIIe siècle* (Sorbonne, Paris, 1975).

Bergier, Jean-Francois, *Une Histoire du Sel* (Presses Universitaires de France, Fribourg, 1982).

Bernus Edmond, *Touaregs Nigeriens, Unité culturelle et Diversité regionale d'un peuple pasteur* (Editions de l' Office de la Recherche Scientifique et Technique Outre Mer, Paris, 1981).

Berry, Elizabeth K., 'The Borough of Droitwich and its Salt Industry, 1215–1700', *University of Birmingham Historical Journal*, 6:1 (1952) pp. 39–61.

Bhattacharyya, Sahyasachi, *Financial Foundations of the British Raj* (Indian Institute of Advanced Study, Simla, 1971).

Blaisdell, Donald C., *European Financial Control in the Ottoman Empire* (Columbia University Press, New York, 1929).

Blanchard, Marcel, 'Sel et Diplomatie en Savoie et dans les Cantons Suisses au XVIIe et XVIIIe siècles', *Annales, Économies, Sociétés, Civilisations*, 15:6 (November–December 1960) pp. 1076–1092.

Bosher, J. F., *French Finances 1770–1795. From Business to Bureaucracy* (Cambridge University Press, Cambridge, 1970).

Braudel, Fernand, *Civilisation Matérielle, Économie et Capitalisme, XVe-XVIIIe siècle*, 3 vols (Librairie Armand Colin, Paris, 1979).

Brazzale, Marco, *Il Mercato del Sale nella Repubblica Veneta nella Seconda Metà del XVI secolo* (Università di Venezia, Venezia, 1971).

Brelot, Claude-Isabelle, Réné Locatelli, *Un Millénaire d' Exploitation du Sel en Franche-Comté: Contribution à l' Archéologie Industrielle des Salines de Salins (Jura)* (CRDP, Besançon, 1981).

Bridbury, A. R., *England and the Salt Trade in the Later Middle Ages* (Clarendon Press, Oxford, 1955).

British Parliamentary Papers, *Papers Relating to Administrative and Financial Reforms in Turkey, 1858–61.*

British Parliamentary Papers, *Lord Cromer's Financial Reports, Egypt 1892–1907.*

British Parliamentary Papers, *China No. 5 (1904)* 'Report by Consul-General Hosie on the Province of Ssuch'uan'.

Buck, David D., *Urban Change in China, Politics and Development in Tsinan, Shantung, 1890–1949* (University of Wisconsin, Madison, Wisconsin, 1978).

Bulliet, Richard W., *The Camel and the Wheel* (Harvard University Press, Cambridge, Mass., 1975).

Buschmann, J. and Ottokar, Freiherr von, *Das Salz, dessen Vorkommen und Verwertung in Sämptlichen Staaten der Erde*, 2 vols (Engelmann, Leipzig, 1909).

Cabourdin, Guy (Ed.), *Le Sel et son Histoire* (Publications Nancy II, Nancy, 1981).

Caillavet, Chantal, 'Le Sel d'Otavalo (Equateur) Continuités Indigènes et Ruptures Coloniales', *Melanges de la Casa de Velazquez*, Tome XV (1979) pp. 329–63.

Calvert, Albert F., *Salt in Cheshire*, (Spon and Chamberlain, London and New York, 1915).

Candida, Luigi, *Saline Adriatiche (Margherita di Savoia, Cervia e Commacchio)*, Memorie di Geografie Economica, Anno III, Luiglio–Dicembre 1951, Vol. V, 89 pp.

Cardale-Schrimpff, Marianne, 'Prehistoric Salt Production in Columbia, South America', Colchester Archaeological Group, *Salt, The Study of an Ancient Industry* (Colchester, 1975) p. 84.

Chang Chien, *A Plan for the Reform of the National Salt Administration* (The National Review Office, Shanghai, 1913).

Chang, K. C. (ed.) *Food in Chinese Culture, Anthropological and Historical Perspectives* (Yale University Press, New Haven and London, 1977).

Ch'ang-lu yen-fa chih (treatise on the Ch'ang-lu salt laws), Yung-cheng edition, 2 vols (Taipei, 1966).

Ch'ang-lu yen-fa chih (treatise on the Ch'ang-lu salt laws), Chia-ch'ing 10 edition, 24 ts'e, 20 chuan.

Charaka-Samhita, Translated and published by Kaviroj Arinash Chandra Kaviratna, 5 vols, Calcutta, 1896–1912.

Chaunu, Pierre, *Séville et L'Atlantique*, Vol. VIII, part one (S.E.V.P.E.N., Paris, 1959).

Ch'en Ch'un, *Ao-po-t'u* (illustrations of the Boiling of Seawater), 1334, edition of Min-kuo 24, 10 ts'e.

Chiang Tao-chang, 'The Production of Salt in China 1644–1911', *Annals of the Association of American Geographers*, Vol. 66, No. 4, December 1976, pp. 516–30.

Chihli River Commission, *Final Report and Grand Scheme 1918–1925* (Hua Pei Press, Tientsin, 1925).

Chin-shu (History of the Chin dynasty).

China, Imperial Maritime Customs, *Salt: Production and Taxation*, V Office Series, Customs Papers, No. 81 (The Statistical Department of the Inspectorate General Customs, Shanghai, 1906).

Ch'ing-shih (History of the Ch'ing dynasty), 8 vols (Taipei, 1961).

Ching Pen-po, *Yen-wu ko-ming shih* (A history of the revolution in the salt administration). Ching-yen tsung-hui yen-cheng tsa-che she (Nanking, 1929).

Choudhury, Sadananda, *Economic History of Colonialism: A Study of British Salt Policy in Orissa* (Inter-India Publications, Delhi, 1979).

Christensen, Aksel E., *Dutch Trade to the Baltic about 1600* (Einar Munksgaard and Martinus Nijhoff, Copenhagen and the Hague, 1941).

Chu, Samuel C., *Reformer in Modern China, Chang Chien 1853–1926* (Columbia University Press, New York and London, 1965).

Chung-kuo yen-cheng shih-lu (Veritable records of the Chinese salt administration), 4 vols, Nanking, 1933.

Chung-kuo yen-cheng shih-lu (Veritable records of the Chinese salt administration) (Taipei, 1954).

'*Chung-kuo yen-cheng yen-ko shih*' *(A history of the development of the Chinese salt administration), Yen-cheng tsa-chih,* No. 19, chuan-chien 2 : 1–16, August 1915.

Clauzel, J., *L'Exploitation des Salines de Taoudenni* (Institut de Recherches Sahariennes, Université d'Alger, Alger, 1960).

Clow, A. and N. L., *The Chemical Revolution* (Batchworth, London 1952).

Coble, Parks M., *The Shanghai Capitalists and the Nationalist Government 1927–1937* (Council on East Asian Studies, Harvard University, Cambridge, Mass., 1980).

Colbert, J. B., *Lettres, Instructions, Memoires,* Imprimerie Nationale, 8 vols, Paris, 1861–1882, Kraus Reprint (Nendeln, Liechtenstein, 1979).

Colchester Archaeological Group, *Salt, The Study of an Ancient Industry* (Colchester, 1975).

Constantine Porphyrogenitus, *De Administrando Imperio,* ed. and trans G. Y. Moravsik and R. J. H. Jenkins, 2 vols (Budapest and London, 1949–1962).

Cooper-Richet, Diana, 'Les Mines de Sel de Wieliczka', *L'Histoire,* 16 (1979) pp. 82–4.

Cuinet, Vital, *La Turquie d' Asie,* 4 vols (Paris, 1891–1895).

Dane, Sir Richard, Report by Sir Richard Dane, KCIE on the Reorganization of the Salt Revenue Administration in China, 1913–1917, Chief Inspectorate of the Central Salt Administration (Peking, 1918).

Darby, H. C., *The Domesday Geography of Eastern England* (Cambridge University Press, Cambridge, 1952).

Darby, H. C. and I. S. Maxwell, (eds), *The Domesday Geography of Northern England (Cambridge University Press, Cambridge, 1952).*

Darby, H. C. and I. B. Terrett, *The Domesday Geography of Midland England* (Cambridge University Press, Cambridge, 1954).

Davies, D. W., *A Primer of Dutch Seventeenth Century Overseas Trade* (Martinus Nijhoff, The Hague, 1961).

Davison, Roderick H., *Reform in the Ottoman Empire 1856–1876,* Princeton University Press, Princeton, New Jersey, 1963. Delafosse, Marcel, Claude Laveau, *Le Commerce du Sel de Brouage aux XVIIe et XVIIIe siècles* (Librairie Armond Colin, Paris, 1960).

Delort, Robert, *Le Commerc des Fourrures en Occident à la fin du Moyen Age (vers 1300–vers 1450)* (Ecole Francaise de Rome, Rome, 1978).

Denton, Derek, *The Hunger for Salt, An Anthropological Physiological and Medical Analysis* (Springer-Verlag, Berlin, Heidelberg, New York, 1982).

Dermigny, Louis, *La Chine et L'Occident, Le Commerce à Canton au XVIIIe siècle 1719–1833,* 3 vols (S.E.V.P.E.N., Paris, 1964).

Deschamps, Marion, *Portrait of Brittany* (Robert Hale, London, 1980).

Dessau, Hermann, *Inscriptiones Latinae Selectae,* Vol. II, part 1 (Weidmann, Berlin, 1902).

Dessert, Daniel, *Argent, Pouvoir et Société au Grand Siècle* (Fayard, Paris, 1984).

Destreée, Annette, *Les Fonctionaires Belge au service de la Perse 1898–1915* (Brill, Leiden, 1976).

Didsbury, Brian, 'Cheshire Saltworkers', in Raphael Samuel (ed.), *Miners, Quarrymen and Saltworkers,* (Routledge & Kegan Paul, London, 1977).

Dio Cassius, *Romaika.*

Dio Clhrysostom, *Orations.*

Dollinger, Philipps, *The German Hansa* (Macmillan, London, 1964).

Doughty, Charles M., *Travels in Arabia Deserta*, 2 vols (Cape, London, 1936).

Duarte, Dioclecio D., *A Industria extrativa do Sal e a sua importancia na economia do Brasil* (Rio de Janeiro, 1941).

Dubois, H., 'Le Téméraire, Les Suisses et Le Sel', *Revue Historique*, 526 (April–June 1978) pp. 309–33.

Dumarest, Jacques, *Les Monopoles de l'Opium et du Sel en Indochine* (Base, Lyon, 1938).

Dunbar, Sir George, *History of India from earliest times to 1939*, 2 vols (Nicholson and Watson, 1949).

Dupont, A., 'L'Exploitation du Sel sur les étangs de Languedoc (IXe–XIIIe siècle)', *Annales du Midi*, Tome 70, 1958, fasc. 1, pp. 7–25.

Edeine, Bernard, 'Les Techniques de Fabrication du Sel dans les sauneries pré et protohistoriques ainsi que Gallo-Romaines', *Annales de Bregagne et des Pays de l'Ouest*, Vol. 82 (1975) pp. 1–18.

Ellis, Joyce, 'The Decline and Fall of the Tyneside Salt industry 1660–1790, A Reexamination', *The Economic History Review*, Second series, Vol. XXXIII, No. 1 (February 1980) pp. 45–58.

Evans, R. J. W., *The Making of the Habsburg Monarchy 1550–1700* (Clarendon Press, Oxford, 1979).

Ewald, Ursula, *The Mexican Salt Industry 1560–1980* (Fischer, Stuttgart, 1985).

Fairbank, John King, *Trade and Diplomacy on the China Coast, The Opening of the Treaty Ports, 1842–1856*, 2 vols (Harvard University Press, Cambridge, Mass., 1953).

Febvre, Lucien, *Philippe II et La Franche Comté* (Flammarion, Paris, 1970).

Fernandes, J. Sampaio, *Industria do Sal* (Rio de Janeiro, 1939).

First Five-Year Plan for Development of the National Economy of the People's Republic of China in 1953–1957 (Foreign Languages Press, Peking, 1956).

Fisher, W. B. (ed.), *The Cambridge History of Iran*, Vol. I, *The Land of Iran* (Cambridge University Press, Cambridge 1968).

Flandrin, Jean-Louis, 'Le Goût et la Nécessité: sur l'usage des graisses dans les cuisines d'Europe occidentale (XIV–XVIIIe)', *Annales, Économies, Sociétés, Civilisations*, 38:2 (March–April 1983) pp. 369–401.

Foisil, Madeleine, *La Révolte des Nu-pieds et les révoltes Normandes de 1639* (Paris, 1970).

Frank, Tenney (ed.), *An Economic Survey of Ancient Rome*, 5 vols (Pageant, Peterson, New Jersey, 1959).

Fu-chien yen-fa chih (Treatise on the salt laws of Fukien) (Foochow, 1830).

Furber, H., *John Company at Work. A Study of European Expansion in India in the Late Eighteenth Century* (Harvard University Press, Cambridge, Mass., 1951).

Gale, Esson M., *Salt for the Dragon, A Personal History of China 1908–1945* (The Michigan State College Press, 1953).

Gale, Esson M. and Ch'en Sung-ch'iao, 'China's Salt Administration: Excerpts from Native Sources', *Journal of Asiatic Studies*, 2.1 (June 1959) pp. 273–316.

Gindely, Anton, *Gegenreformation in Böhmen* (Duncker and Humblott, Leipzig, 1894).

Giraldus Cambrensis, *The Itinerary through Wales and the Description of Wales* (Dent, London, 1919).

Good, Charles M., 'Salt, Trade and Disease: Aspects of Development in Africa's Northern Great Lakes Region', *International Journal of African Historical Studies*, Vol. 5 (1972) No. 4, pp. 543–86.

Goris, J. A., *Étude sur les Colonies Marchandes Meridionales (Portugais, Espagnols,*

Italiens) à Anvers de 1488 à 1567, Contribution à L'Histoire des Debuts du Capitalisme Moderne (Librairie Universitaire, Louvain, 1925) pp. 465–77.

Gouletquer, P. and Kleinmann, D. 'Structure Sociale et Commerce du Sel dans l'Economie Touarègue', *Revue de l'Occident Musulman et de la Mediterranée*, 21 (1976) pp. 131–9.

Graham, William J., *The Lament for the South, Yü Hsin's Ai Chiang-nan Fu* (Cambridge University Press, Cambridge, 1980).

Gray, Richard and Birmingham, David (eds), *Pre-Colonial African trade, Essays on Trade in Central and Eastern Africa before 1900* (Oxford University Press, Oxford, 1970).

Green, O. H., *The Foreigner in China* (Hutchinson, London, n.d. c. 1943).

Grimal, P. and Monod, Th. 'Sur la véritable nature du garum', *Revue des Études Anciennes*, Vol. 54 (1952) pp. 27–38.

Grmek, Mirko D., *Les maladies à l'aube de la Civilisation Occidentale* (Payot, Paris, 1983).

Gümpel, C. Godfrey, *Common Salt, Its use and necessity for the maintenance of health and the prevention of disease* (Swann Sonnenschein, London, 1989).

Habib, Irfan, *The Agrarian System of Mughal India (1556–1707)* (Aligarh Muslim University, Asia Publishing House, 1963).

Haeger, John Winthrop (ed.), *Crisis and Prosperity in Sung China*, (University of Arizona, Tucson, 1975).

Han-shu (History of the former Han dynasty).

Harris, Robert D., *Necker, Reform Statesman of the Ancien Regime* (University of California Press, Berkeley, 1979).

Hauser, Henri, *La Pensée et L'Action Économique du Cardinal de Richelieu* (P.U.F., Paris, 1944).

Hawrylyshyn, George, 'Revamping of the Salt Industry Improves Future Prospects', *Brazilian Business*, 55(5) (May 1975) pp. 28–30.

Heers, Jacques, *Gênes au XVᵉ siècle, activité économique et problèmes sociaux* (S.E.V. P.E.N., Paris, 1961).

Hocquet, Jean-Claude, *Le Sel et La Fortune de Venise*, Vol. I, *Production et Monopole* (Université de Lille, Lille, 1978).

Hocquet, Jean-Claude, *Le Sel et La Fortune de Venise*, Vol. II, *Voiliers et Commerce en Mediteranée 1200–1650* (Université de Lille, Lille, 1979).

Hocquet, Jean-Claude, *Le Sel et le Pouvoir, de l'An Mil à la Revolution francaise* (Albin Michel, Paris, 1985).

Hocquet, Jean-Claude (ed.), *Le Roi, Le Marchand et Le Sel* (Université de Lille, Lille, 1987).

Homo, Léon, *Essai sur Le Regne de l'Empereur Aurélian* (Bretscheider, Paris, 1904).

Hosie, Alexander, 'The Salt Production and Salt Revenue of China', *Nineteenth Century and After*, 447 (May 1914) pp. 1119–43.

Ho-tung yen-fa chih (Treatise on the Ho-tung salt laws), Yung-cheng edition, 2 vols (Taipei, 1966).

Hou Teh-pang, 'The Yungli Company: Pioneer of Chemical Industry in China', *China Reconstructs*, 4:3 (March 1955) pp. 21–4.

Hsuan-tsang, *Si-yu-ki, Buddhist Records of the Western World*, trn, Samuel Beal, 2 vols (Paragon, New York, 1968).

Hsü-chou fu-chih (Hsü-chou prefectural gazetteer), Kuang-hsü 21 edition.

Huenemann, Ralph William, *The Dragon and the Iron Horse, The Economics of Railroads in China 1876–1937* (The Council on East Asian Studies, Harvard University, Cambridge, Mass., 1984).

Humboldt, Alexander von, *Personal Narrative of Travels to the Equinoctial Regions of*

America during the Years 1799–1804, 3 vols (George Bell, London, 1881).
Indian Tariff Board, Salt Enquiry, Preliminary Evidence Volume (Calcutta, 1930).
Indian Tariff Board, *Evidence Recorded During Enquiry on the Salt Industry*, 2 vols (Calcutta, 1930).
Italy, Ministero delle Finanze, Azienda Dei Sali, Relazione e Bilanca Industriale, 1898/99–1918/19 (Rome, 1900–1922).
Jenner, W. F. J., *Memories of Loyang, Yang Hsüan-chih and the Lost Capital (493–534)* (Clarendon Press, Oxford, 1981).
Jones, Gwyn, *A History of the Vikings* (Oxford University Press, Oxford, 1969).
Juillard, Etienne, *L'Europe Rhénane* (Armand Colin, Paris, 1968).
Juvaini, Ata-Malik, *The History of the World Conqueror*, trns John Andrew Boyle, 2 vols (Harvard University Press, Cambridge, Mass., 1958).
Kansu yen-fa chih (Treatise on the salt laws of Kansu), 8 *ts'e*, 10 *chuan*, Min-kuo 19.
Karmin, Otto, *La Question du Sel pendant La Révolution* (Paris, 1912).
Keckova, Antonina, 'Polish Salt-Mines as a State Enterprise (XIII–XVIIIth centuries)', *Journal of European Economic History*, 10(3) (1981) pp. 619–631.
Kenny, Michael G., 'Salt Trading in Eastern Lake Victoria', *Azania*, Vol. IX, 1974, pp. 225–8.
Kircher, Athanasius, *Mundus Subterraneus* (Amsterdam, 1665).
Knecht, R. J., *Francis I* (Cambridge University Press, Cambridge, 1982).
Kortepeter, C. Max, *Ottoman Imperialism during the Reformation: Europe and the Caucasus* (New York University Press, New York, 1972).
Lach, Donald F., *Asia in the Making of Europe* (University of Chicago Press, Chicago and London, 1965).
Lane, Frederic C., *Venice A Maritime Republic* (Johns Hopkins University Press, Baltimore and London, 1973).
Latham, James E., *The Religious Symbolism of Salt* (Editions Beauchesne, Paris, 1982).
Le Donne, John P., 'Indirect Taxes in Catherine's Russia: The Salt Code of 1781', *Jahrbücher für Geschichte Osteuropas*, 23:2 (1975) pp. 161–90.
Legon, Ronald P., *Megara The Political History of a Greek City-state to 330 BC* (Cornell University Press, Ithaca and London, 1980).
Lemonnier, Pierre, *Paludiers de Guérande, Production du sel et Histoire économique* (Institut d'Ethnologie, Paris, 1984).
Leo Africanus, J., *The History and Description of Africa* (Hakluyt Edition, London, 1896).
Le Roy Ladurie, Emmanuel and Morineau, Michel *Histoire Économique et Sociale de la France*, Tome I, *De 1450 à 1660*, vol. 2, *Paysannerie et Croissance* (P.U.F., Paris, 1977).
Lévi-Strauss, Claude, 'The Use of Wild Plants in Tropical South America', Julian H. Steward (ed.), *Handbook of South American Indians*, Vol. 6, *Physical Anthropology, Linguistics and Cultural Geography of South American Indians* (Cooper Square, New York, 1963).
Lévi-Strauss, Claude, *Mythologiques II Du Miel aux Cendres* (Plon, Paris, 1966); *Mythologiques III Les Origines des Manières de Table* (Plon, Paris, 1968); *Mythologiques IV L'Homme Nu* (Plon, Paris, 1971).
Lévi-Strauss, Claude, *Tristes Tropiques* (Penguin, Harmondsworth, 1976).
Lewicki, Tadeusz, *West African Food in the Middle Ages* (Cambridge University Press, Cambridge, 1974).
Liang-che yen-fa chih (Treatise on the Chekiang salt laws), Chia-ch'ing 6 edition, 24 *ts'e*, 30 *chuan*.

Liang-huai yen-fa chih (Treatise on the Liang-huai salt laws), Kuang-hsü 30 edition, 160 *chuan*.

Liang-kuang yen-fa chih (Treatise on the Kwangtung salt laws), Kuang-hsü 10 edition, 23 *ts'e*, 55 *chuan*.

'Light industry in Communist China' excerpts from *Chung-kuo ch'ing-kung-yeh*, 1955 (United States Joint Publications Research Service, New York, 1959).

Lin, S. Y., 'Salt Manufacture in Hong Kong', *Journal of the Hong Kong Branch of the Royal Asiatic Society*, 7 (1967) pp. 138–51.

Lister, Martin, *A Journey to Paris in the Year 1698* (London, 1699).

Livy, *Ab Urbe Condita Libri*.

Lonn, Ella, *Salt as a Factor in the Confederacy* (University of Alabama Press, Alabama, 1965).

Lovejoy, Paul E., 'The Borno Salt Industry', *The International Journal of African Historical Studies*, Vol. 11 (1978) No. 4, pp. 629–68.

Lovejoy, Paul E., *Salt of the Desert Sun, A History of Salt Production and Trade in the Central Sudan* (Cambridge University Press, Cambridge, 1986).

Magie, David, *Roman Rule in Asia Minor to the End of the Third Century after Christ*, 2 vols (Princeton University Press, Princeton, New Jersey, 1950).

Mancall, Mark, *Russia and China, Their Diplomatic Relations to 1728*, (Harvard University Press, Cambridge, Mass., 1971).

Mantran, R., *Istanbul dans la seconde moitié du XVIIᵉ siècle*, (Maisonneuve, Paris, 1962).

Martin, Geoffrey, Smith, Stanley and Milson, F. *The Salt and Alkali Industry* (Crosby Lockwood, London, 1916).

Matthews, George T., *The Royal General Farms in Eighteenth Century France* (Columbia University Press, New York, 1958).

Maverick, Lewis (ed.), *Economic Dialogues in Ancient China, Selections from the Kuan-tzu* (Lewis A. Maverick, Carbondale, Illinois, 1954).

Maxwell, James L., *The Diseases of China* (ABC Press, Shanghai, 1929).

Mecklenburg, Duke Adolphus Frederick of, *In the Heart of Africa* (Cassell, London, 1910).

Meilink-Roelofsz, M. A. P., *Asian Trade and European Influence* (Martinus Nijhoff, The Hague, 1962).

Mendizabal, Miguel O. de, *Influencia de la Sal en la distribucion geographica de los grupos indigenos de Mexico* (Mexico, 1928).

Metzger, Thomas A., 'T'ao Chu's Reform of the Huaipei Salt Monopoly', *Harvard Papers on China*, 16 (1962) pp. 1–19.

Metzger, Thomas A., 'The Organizational Capabilities of the Ch'ing State in the Field of Commerce: The Liang-huai Salt Monopoly, 1740–1840', in W. E. Willmott (ed.), *Economic Organization in Chinese Society* (Stanford University Press, Stanford, California, 1972).

Metzger, Thomas A., *The Internal Organization of Ch'ing Bureaucracy* (Harvard University Press, Cambridge, Mass., 1973).

Millspaugh, Arthur C., *Americans in Persia, A Clinic for the New Internationalism* (Washington, 1946).

Mollat, Michel (ed.), *Le Rôle du Sel dans L'Histoire* (Presses Universitaires de France, Paris, 1968).

Mori, Alberto, *Le Saline della Sardegna, Memorie di Geografia Economica*, Anno II, Luglio–Decembre 1950, Vol. III, Napoli.

Multhauf, Robert P., *Neptune's Gift, A History of Common Salt* (Johns Hopkins University Press, Baltimore and London, 1978).

Nandy, Somendra Chandra, *Life and Times of Cantoo Baboo (Krishna Kanta Nandy)*

The Banian of Warren Hastings, Vol. I, *The Early Career of Cantoo Baboo (1742–1772) and his Trade in Salt and Silk* (Allied Publishers, Bombay, 1978).

Nankai University, Department of History, comp. *Ch'ing Shih-lu Ching-chi tzu-liao chi-yao* (A compendium of economic materials in the *Ch'ing shih-lu*) Chung-hua shu-chü (Peking, 1959).

Nathan, Andrew J., *Peking Politics 1918–1923 Factionalism and the Failure of Constitutionalism* (University of California Press, Berkeley, 1976).

Needham, Joseph, *Science and Civilisation in China*, Vol. I (Cambridge University Press, Cambridge, 1954); Vol. IV, part 3, 1971.

Nef, J. U., *The Rise of the British Coal Industry*, 2 vols (George Routledge, London, 1932).

Nenquin, Jacques, *Salt A Study in Economic Prehistory* (de Tempel, Bruge, 1961).

Österreich, Finanzministerium, *Staatische Mitteilung über das Österreichische Salzmonopol im Jahre 1907–1908, 1912, 1913* (Vienna, 1910–1914).

Ottoman Public Debt Administration, Annual and Special Reports, 1904–5 to 1907–8, 1909–10 to 1913–14, 1919–20, 1922–3.

Pagès, G., *La Monarchie d'Ancien Regime en France* (Armand Colin, Paris, 1946).

Palme, Rudolf, *Rechts-Wirtschafts und Sozial Geschichte der Inneralpinen Salzwerke bis zu deren Monopolisierung* (Verlag Peter Lang, Frankfurt and Berne, 1983).

Pasquier, J., *L'Impôt des Gabelles en France aux XVIIᵉ et XVIIIᵉ siècles* (Paris, 1905; Slatkine Reprints, Geneva, 1978).

Patlagean, Evelyne, *Pauvreté Economique et Pauvreté Sociale à Byzance, 4ᵉ–7ᵉ siècles* (Mouton, Paris, 1977).

Persia, Quarterly Reports of the Administrator General of the Finances of Persia, 1923–1928.

Pharr, Clyde, *The Theodesian Code* (Greenwood Press, New York, 1952).

Philby, H. St. J., *Arabia of the Wahhabi* (Cass, London, 1928).

Pinna, Mario, 'Il Giacimento di Salgemma del Volterrano, Studio di Geografia economica', *Contributi alle Geografia della Toscana* (Università di Pisa, Pisa, 1958–9).

Pipes, Daniel, *Slave Soldiers and Islam, The Genesis of a Military System* (Yale University Press, New Haven and London, 1981).

Pliny, *Naturalis Historia*.

Polo, Marco, *The Travels of Marco Polo* (Penguin, Harmondsworth, 1958).

Potts, Daniel, 'On Salt and Salt Gathering in Ancient Mesopotamia', *Journal of the Economic and Social History of the Orient*, XXVII, 3, October 1984, pp. 225–71.

Rambot-Stilmant, E., 'Une Tentative du monopole d'Etatl, La Raffinerie d'Ostend, 1754–1770', *Contributions à L'Histoire économique et sociale*, Brussels, Vol. 5 (1970) pp. 25–86.

Randles, W. G. L., 'La Civilisation Bantou, son essor et san declin', *Annales, Économies, Sociétés, Civilisations*, 29:2, March–April 1974, pp. 267–81.

Ratton, J. J. L., *A Handbook of Common Salt* (Madras, 1977).

Reader, W. J., *Imperial Chemical Industries, A History*, 2 vols (Oxford University Press, London, 1970–75).

Reid, Jensen, *Salt for New Zealand* (Dominion Salt Ltd, Grassmere, 1976).

Renfrew, Colin, *The Emergence of Civilisation, The Cyclades and the Aegean in the Third Millennium B.C.* (Methuen, London, 1972).

Reports by the District Inspectors, Auditors and Collectors on the Reorganisation of the Salt Revenue Administration in China, 1913–1917, 1918, 1919–1922, 1922.

Richthofen, Ferdinand von, *Baron Richthofen's Letters 1870–1872* (North China Herald Office, Shanghai, 1903).

Rowe, William T., *Hankow, Commerce and Society in a Chinese City 1796–1889* (Stanford University Press, Stanford, 1984).

Royal Society, *Philosophical Transactions*, Vol. I, 1665. 'Of the Mundus Subterraneus of Athanasius Kircher', pp. 109–17.

Rutilius Namatianus, *De Reditu Suo.*

Sabban, Francoise, 'Le système des cuissons dans la tradition culinaire Chinoise', *Annales, Economies, Sociétés, Civilisations*, 38:2 (March–April 1973) pp. 341–68.

Samuel, Raphael (ed.), *Miners, Quarrymen and Saltworkers* (Routledge & Kegan Paul, London, 1977).

Schreiber, Hermann, *The History of Roads, From Amber Route to Motorway* (Barrie & Rockliff, London, 1961).

Schremmer, Eckart, 'Saltmining and the Salt Trade: A State-Monopoly in the XVIth–XVIIth Centuries: A Case-Study in Public Enterprise and Development in Austria and the South German States', *Journal of European Economic History*, Vol. 8, 1979, pp. 291–312.

Schurmann, Herbert Franz, *Economic Structure of the Yuan Dynasty* (Harvard University Press, Cambridge, Mass., 1956).

Serajuddin, B. M., 'The Condition of the Salt Manufacturers of Bengal under the Rule of the East India Company', *Asiatic Society of Bangladesh (Dacca)*, 18:1 (1973) pp. 54–73.

Shan-tung yen-fa chih (Treatise on the Shantung salt laws), Chia-ch'ing 14 edition, 22 *chuan.*

Shaw, Stanford J., *The Financial and Administrative Organization and Development of Ottoman Egypt 1517–1798* (Princeton University Press, Princeton, New Jersey, 1962).

Shaw, Stanford J., *History of the Ottoman Empire and Modern Turkey*, Vol. II, *Reform, Revolution and Republic: The Rise of Modern Turkey, 1808–1975h* (Cambridge University Press, Cambridge, 1977).

Shaw, Thurstan, *Nigeria, Its Archaeology and Early History* (Thames & Hudson, London, 1978).

Shih-chi (Historical records) by Ssu-ma Ch'ien.

Shu-ching (Classic of History).

Shuster, W. Morgan, *The Strangling of Persia* (New York, 1912).

Smith, R. E. F., and David Christian, *Bread and Salt, A Social and Economic History of Food and Drink in Russia* (Cambridge University Press, Cambridge, 1984).

Spence, Jonathan D., *Ts'ao Yin and the K'ang-hsi Emperor, Bondservant and Master* (Yale University Press, New Haven and London, 1966).

Srbik, Heinrich, Ritter von, *Studien zur Geschichte des Osterreichischen Salzwesens* (Innsbruck, 1917).

Ssu-ch'uan t'ung-chih (Szechwan provincial gazetteer), Chia-Ching 16 edition.

Ssu-chuan yen-fa chih (Treatise on the salt laws of Szechwan), Ting Pao-chen comp., 40 *chuan,* Chengtu, 1882.

Stanley, Henry M., *Through the Dark Continent*, 2 vols (Sampson Low, London, 1978).

Steward, Julian H. (ed.), *Handbook of South American Indians*, Vol. 6, *Physical Anthropology, Linguistics and Cultural Geography of South American Indians* (Cooper Square, New York, 1963).

Strabo, *Geographia.*

Strachey, Sir John, *India: Its Administration and Progress* (Macmillan, London, 1911).

Sutton, I. B., 'The Volta River Salt Trade: The Survival of an Indigenous

Industry', *Journal of African History*, 22 (1981) pp. 43–61.

Sutton, J. E. G. and Roberts, A. D. 'Uvinza and its Salt Industry', *Anzania*, 3 (1969) pp. 45–86.

Swann, Nancy Lee, *Food and Money in Ancient China* (Princeton University Press, Princeton, 1950).

Ta Ch'ing li-ch'ao Shih-lu (Veritable records of successive reigns of the Ch'ing dynasty), T'ai-wan hua-wen shu-chü, Taipei, 1963.

Taiwan Diplomatic Documents (Academia Sinica, Taipei).

Tapié, Victor-L, *Monarchie et Peuples du Danube* (Librairie Arthème, Fayard, Paris, 1969).

Teilhard de Chardin, Pierre, *The Phenomenon of Man* (Collins, London, 1966).

Thayer, William Roscoe, *A Short History of Venice* (Macmillan, New York, 1905).

Thompson, Eric S., *Thomas Gage's Travels in the New World* (University of Oklahoma Press, Norman, 1958).

Thompson, F. M. L., 'Nineteenth Century Horse Sense', *Economic History Review*, XXIX, No. 1 (February 1976), pp. 60–81.

Toubert, Pierre, *Les Structures du Latium Médiéval* (École Française de Rome, Rome, 1973).

Trevor-Roper, H. R., *Historical Essays* (Macmillan, London, 1957).

Tseng Tang-feng, 'I Ting-en' (In memory of Dane). *Yen-yeh t'ung-hsün* (Salt Trade Bulletin), 77 (January 1958), pp. 10–11.

Tung san-sheng yen-fa hsin-chin (A new survey of the salt laws of Manchuria), Min-kuo 17, 20 ts'e, 40 *chuan*.

Twitchett, D. C., *Financial Administration under the T'ang Dynasty* (Cambridge University Press, Cambridge, 1965).

Tymowski, Michal, 'La Saline d'Idjil en Mauritanie', *Africana Bulletin*, 30, 1981, pp. 7–37.

Ulshöfer, Kuno and Beutter, Herta (eds), *Hall und das Salz, Beiträge zur hällischen Stadt und Salinengeschichte* (Jan Thorbecke Verlag, Sigmaringen, 1983).

Vasiliev, A., 'Economic Relations between Byzantium and Old Russia', *Journal of Economic and Business History*, 4, February 1932, pp. 314–34.

Vazques de Espinosa, Antonio, *Description of the Indies (c.1620)*, tr. Charles Upson Clark (Smithsonian Institute Press, Washington, 1968).

Veith, Ilza, *Huang Ti Nei Ching Su Wen, The Yellow Emperor's Classic of Internal Medicine* (Williams and Wilkins, Baltimore, 1949).

Veyne, Paul, *Le Pain et Le Cirque, Sociologie Historique d'un Pluralisme Politique* (Editions du Seuil, Paris, 1976).

Vila Valenti, J., 'Ibiza y Formentera, islas de la Sal', *Estudios Geographicos* (August 1953), pp. 363–408.

Viraphol, Sarasin, *Tribute and Profit, Sino-Siamese Trade 1652–1853* (Council on East Asian Studies, Harvard University, Cambridge, Mass. and London, 1977).

Vittorio, Antonio di (ed.), *Sale e Saline nell' Adriatico* (Giannini, Naples, 1981).

Volk, Otto, *Salzproduktion und Salzhandel mittelalterlicher Zisterzienser klöster* (Thorbecke, Sigmaringen, 1984).

Wallerstein, Immanuel, *The Modern World System* (Academic Press, New York, 1974).

Wallis, Claudia, 'Salt: A New Villain', *Time*, 15 March 1982, pp. 48–56.

Wallis, Budge, E. A., *Syrian Anatomy, Pathology and Therapeutics, or 'The Book of Medicines'*, 2 vols (Oxford University Press, Oxford, 1913).

Warren, Kenneth, *Chemical Foundations: The Alkali Industry in Britain to 1926* (Clarendon, Oxford, 1980).

Watson, J. Steven, *A History of the Salters' Company* (London, 1963).

Wee, H. van der, *The Growth of the Antwerp Market and the European Economy*, 3 vols (Martinus Nijhoff, The Hague, 1963).

Wells, Peter S., 'Iron-Age Central Europe', *Archaeology*, Vol. 33, No. 5, September–October 1980, pp. 6–11.

Whitelock, Dorothy, *The Beginnings of English Society* (Penguin, Harmondsworth, 1952).

Wickert, L., (ed.), *Corpus Inscriptionum Latinorum*, Vol. 14, Supplement (Gruyter, Berlin, 1930).

Wileman, A. E., 'Salt Manufacture in Japan', *Transactions of the Asiatic Society of Japan*, Vol. 17 (1889) pp. 1–66.

Will, Pierre-Étienne, 'Un cycle hydraulique en Chine: la province de Hubei du XVIe au XIXe siècles', *Bulletin de l'École Francaise d'Extreme Orient*, 68 (1980) pp. 261–87.

Will, Pierre-Étienne, *Bureaucratie et famine en Chine au 18e siècle* (Mouton, Paris, 1980).

Willmott, W. F. (ed.), *Economic Organization in Chinese Society* (Stanford University Press, Stanford, California, 1972).

Wittfogel, Karl A. and Feng Chia-sheng, *History of Chinese Society Liao (907–1175)* (The American Philosophical Society, Philadelphia) p. 340.

Worcester, G. R. G., *Notes on the Crooked-bow and Crooked-stern Junks of Szechwan*, China, The Maritime Customs, III, Miscellaneous Series: No. 53 (Shanghai, 1941).

Worcester, G. R. G., *The Junks and Sampans of the Yangtze* (Naval Institute Press, Annapolis, Maryland, 1971).

Worthy, Edmund H., 'Regional Control in the Southern Sung Salt Administration', John Winthrop Haeger (ed.), *Crisis and Prosperity in Sung China* (University of Arizona, Tucson, 1975).

Wright, Stanley, F., *Hart and the Chinese Customs* (Mullan, Belfast, 1950).

Yang, L. S., 'Great Families of Eastern Han', E-tu Zen Sun and John de Francis (eds), *Chinese Social History* (American Council of Learned Societies, Washington, DC, 1956).

Yang, L. S., *Studies in Chinese Institutional History* (Harvard University Press, Cambridge, Mass., 1961).

Yen-cheng tsa-chih (Salt administration miscellany) (Peking, 1912–1915).

Yen-yeh t'ung-hsün (Salt Trade Bulletin) (Taipei).

Young, Arthur, N., *China and the Helping Hand* (Harvard University Press, Cambridge, Mass., 1963).

Yuan-shih (The history of the Yuan dynasty).

Yueh-tso chi=shih (Essentials of the Kwangtung salt administration), (Canton, 1927).

Zelin, Madeleine, *The Magistrate's Teal* (University of California Press, Berkeley, 1984).

Zen Sun, E-tu and de Francis, John (eds), *Chinese Social History* (American Council of Learned Societies, Washington, DC, 1956).

Zen Sun, E-tu, *Ch'ing Administrative Terms* (Harvard University Press, Cambridge, Mass., 1961).

Index

272, 306, 308–10, 314, 322, 323,
     325–33, 335–40, 342–4, 346, 347,
     350–2, 355–8
Dantzig 94, 98
Danube river 150, 230, 237, 238,
     240, 253
Dardanelles 270, 283
Darfur 16, 17, 20, 60
Datini, Francesco di Marco 90, 91
Dauphiné 90
de Acosta, José 11
de Chardonnet, Count Hilaire
     Bernigaud 144
de Poitiers, Diane 208
de Witte, Hans 249
Dead sea 262
decree of Muharrem 157, 259, 265,
     274, 279, 281
Delhi 61, 115, 116, 291
Denmark 92, 223
Dermigny, Louis 210
Deutsche Brucke 92
Dharasna 301
Dhrangadhra 285, 317, 318
Diadora 64
Didwana 38, 49, 161
Dieppe 209
Dieuze 69, 108, 148, 211, 212, 216,
     225, 228
Dio Cassius 32
Dio Chrysostom 29, 64
Diocletian, Roman emperor 36
Ditchling beacon 7
Diwan Chand 291, 292, 294, 300,
     307, 308
Djavid Bey 267, 274
Djebaul 269
Djerba 61
Djibouti 159
Dnepropetrovsk 152
Dnieper, river 28, 29, 64, 65
Dodecanese, the 64
Dogana da Mar 184
Dolon nor 335
Dombasle 138, 148
Domesday book 67, 69, 70
Donauworth 238, 252
Donets 152
Dorgon 125
Dorpat 92
Dorset 5
Drake, Edwin L. 153

Drin river 91, 102
Drohobycz 111
Droitwich 67, 69, 70, 95, 105
Duisburg 138
Dunkirk 214
Durance 91
Durazzo 64, 269
Durham 67, 105
Durrnberg 4, 5, 149
Dwarka 160
Dyrrachium 64

Eastern Europe 6, 47, 231, 249, 252,
     258
Eastern Sanuki 155
Ebensee 110, 233, 234, 253
Eberhard II, Archbishop 238
Ebi-nor 60
Ebro river 62, 86, 91
Ecuador 113
Edeine, Bernard 4
Edirne 271
Edo 155
Eduljee Dinshaw salt works 160,
     294, 298
Edward III, king of England 229
Egypt 28, 57, 60, 61, 115, 142, 159,
     261, 262, 266, 270, 272, 281, 293
Emilia 185, 198
Engelszell 93
England 19, 67, 69, 94, 95–6, 99,
     104–6, 107, 114, 136, 138, 139,
     143, 145, 146, 147, 159, 170, 213,
     217, 226, 227, 245, 265
Ennin 56
Ennore 305, 311, 315
Ephesus 28
Epirus 28, 31, 271
Er-lien 55
Erasmus 222
Erhlien 173
Eritrea 16, 156, 319
Erzerum 157, 158, 270
Eskisehir 158, 271, 277
Essex 5, 6, 29, 67, 70
Esztergom 232
Eupatoria 152
European Economic
     Community 147
evaporation 4, 5, 10, 11, 17–19, 23,
     28–31, 35, 38–41, 44, 47–50, 52,
     60–3, 65, 67, 68, 70, 71, 72,

Phanar 115
Philip II, king of Spain 101, 103, 104, 108, 183, 245
Philip IV, king of Spain 108
Philip IV, king of France 205, 229
Phocea 115, 157, 158, 269, 271, 274, 275, 276, 278
Phoenicians 6
Phrygia 58
Piacenza 218
Pien-an 164, 165
Pien-chou 53
pimento 13–15
pineapples 22
Piran 89, 90, 102, 185, 186, 187, 199, 235, 240, 241
Pisa 86, 90
Pissard, M. Leon 267
Plate 102
Pliny 7, 30, 31, 34, 36, 37, 41, 177, 269, 285
Plutarch 8
Po river 102, 182, 198
Po-hai 39
Podlachia 240
Pohai Chemical Industries company 171
Poitou 94, 212, 214
Pola 185
Poland 150, 153, 199, 231, 239, 240, 241, 243, 245, 248, 250, 257, 258
Polanyi, Karl 12
Pomposa 89
Pondicherry 305
Pont-Saint-Esprit 91
poppy 118
pork 29, 33, 35, 47, 55, 57, 74, 100, 118, 141, 222
Port Hedland 155
Port Said 159, 160, 296, 297, 313
Port Said Salt Association 159
Porto 68
Portugal 29, 94, 208, 245
Posen 239
potatoes 12, 22, 117
Potosi 113, 142
Pozsony 250
Prague 250, 251, 255, 257
Priene 28
Provence 86, 90, 91, 107, 205, 209, 210, 248
Provveditori al Sal 183, 197, 184

Provveditori di Sanita 199, 200
Prussia 92, 110, 149, 245
Przemysl 239
Pu Yang 43
Public debt administration (Ottoman) 259, 262, 264, 266, 267, 268, 270, 271, 272, 273, 274, 276, 277, 278, 279, 280, 282, 283, 284, 312, 321
Puits à Muire 96, 211
Pukow 166, 168, 323, 350
Punjab 38, 61, 116, 161, 287, 290, 291
Punjab Salt Range 37, 177
Pydna 28
Pyrenees 91

Quarantia 183
Quart Bouillon 107, 154, 207, 214, 215, 216, 220
Questenburg, Caspar von 251
Quito 11, 13

Ragusa 64, 87, 102, 185
Railway Board 289
Rain, Johann Frieduich von 234
Raittenau, Wolf Dietrich von 237
Rajasthan 38, 49, 61, 62, 116
Rajput Pratiharas 37
Rajputana 116, 161, 286, 290, 300, 307
Rakoczi, Ferenc II 243
Rangoon 160
Rann of Kutch 38, 49, 160, 285, 287, 298
rape 118
Ras al-Makhbaz 31, 61, 87, 89, 186
Rastatt 245
Ratnagiri 301
Ravenna 30, 89, 182
Rawalpindi 37
Recife 113, 154
Red sea 15, 146, 151, 159, 160, 161, 272, 282
Reichenbach, Georg von 110, 140
Reichenhall 93, 109, 110, 140, 149, 228, 236, 237, 238, 239, 253, 256, 257
Reiffenstuhl, Hans 110, 140, 237, 238
Restitutianus Cornelianus 33
Reval 92, 94

Index